LIBRARY
UNIVERSITY OF NEW BRUNSWICK
IN SAINT JOHN

DA
30
O54
v. 8
1948

A History of England in Eight Volumes

Founder Editor, Sir Charles Oman

Volume VIII
MODERN ENGLAND

Please return or renew by
latest date below

MAR. 20. 1968

APR. 14 1977

MAY 04 1978

OCT 30 1980

A History of England in Eight Volumes

I
ENGLAND BEFORE THE NORMAN CONQUEST
by Sir Charles Oman

II
ENGLAND UNDER THE NORMANS AND ANGEVINS
by H. W. C. Davis

III
ENGLAND IN THE LATER MIDDLE AGES
by Kenneth H. Vickers

IV
ENGLAND UNDER THE TUDORS
by G. R. Elton

V
ENGLAND UNDER THE STUARTS
by G. M. Trevelyan

VI
ENGLAND UNDER THE HANOVERIANS
by Sir Charles Grant Robertson

VII
ENGLAND SINCE WATERLOO
by Sir J. A. R. Marriott

VIII
MODERN ENGLAND 1885–1945
by Sir J. A. R. Marriott

MODERN ENGLAND
1885-1945
A HISTORY OF MY OWN TIMES

—

Sir J. A. R. Marriott

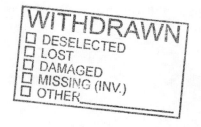

WITHDRAWN
☐ DESELECTED
☐ LOST
☐ DAMAGED
☐ MISSING (INV.)
☐ OTHER

LONDON: METHUEN & CO LTD
NEW YORK: BARNES & NOBLE INC

First published August 16th 1934
Second edition July 1942
Third edition, revised and enlarged, October 1946
Fourth edition 1948
Reprinted twice
Reprinted 1963
Printed in Great Britain by
Butler & Tanner Ltd, Frome

CATALOGUE NO 2/3378/10 (METHUEN)

4.4

DA
30
O54
v.8
1948

LIBRARY
UNIVERSITY OF NEW BRUNSWICK
IN SAINT JOHN

PREFACE

THIS book has been written as a sequel to my *England since Waterloo* (Methuen & Co., 1st ed. 1913, 10th ed. 1932), and forms the eighth and concluding volume of Sir Charles Oman's *History of England* (Methuen). The previous volume brought the story down to the passing of the Parliamentary Reform Bills, 1884–5. Taking up the story at that point the present work brings it down to 1932.

The sub-title recalls the fact that the period under review synchronizes with my own public life, and may serve to remind readers in time to come that this volume is the work of a contemporary, that it has been written partly from personal recollection of political events, and that many of the portraits it contains have been drawn from life. That this fact renders more difficult the task of the historian who desires to write *sine ira et studio*, is obvious; but I hope that it may have rendered the narrative more vivid, and the portraits less wooden. Very occasionally I have added a footnote to indicate personal knowledge of the facts. Of other footnotes I have tried to reduce the number to a minimum, but the contemporary historian, even more than others, is bound to give his readers the opportunity of checking his statements. For the rest the reader is referred to the Bibliography.

That Bibliography illustrates one of the difficulties confronting the historian of this period—the avalanche of materials, primary and secondary, with which he must needs grapple. With many of those materials I made acquaintance, as a reviewer, on their first appearance, and that acquaintance (in the case of important items) I have sedulously improved. The nature and measure of the task is, however, very partially revealed by the Bibliography. I have tried to make it of practical use to students, but it is not, of course, exhaustive, nor even co-extensive with my own studies. In making my selection of 'Authorities', primary and secondary, I have not, I confess, gone much beyond the shelves of my own Library, which groan beneath loads of Blue Books, Parliamentary Papers, etc., besides a large collection of books bearing on this period. It seemed to me that I could best help other students by referring them to authorities which have become (for the most part) my own most intimate friends. But even so the list is merely selective, though it is, I trust, fairly representative of *political* history. To that field the book is restricted : it does not touch literature or art nor science except in so far as science reacts on politics.

I have also relied on MS. memoranda, pamphlets, newspaper cuttings and the like, laboriously accumulated during the last half-century. Only a fraction of these materials have I been able, in the present work, to utilize to the full ; and I am considering how I may make them available for those who in the future will dig deep into ground of which I have only scratched the surface.

Any historian who has been set the task of writing the history of a crowded period in relatively few pages will, I am confident, judge leniently any omissions he may detect, or compressed statements he may deplore. No one can be so conscious of them as the author. It had been far easier for me to write this work in three volumes instead of one. But I have had to conform to the general plan of the work of which this volume forms the conclusion. This being so, I have aimed primarily at lucidity, at the preservation of perspective and proportion. How far I have succeeded it is for my readers to judge.

It is, perhaps, proper to add that where the present

narrative overlaps previous works of my own [1] I have not hesitated to borrow from them, and have ventured to refer to them for fuller information on the subjects under treatment. I have also utilized the articles—some two hundred in number—contributed by me, during the last thirty-five years, to *The Quarterly, The Edinburgh, The Fortnightly, The Nineteenth Century and After,* and other Reviews.

Readers will observe that, though the general sequence of *chapters* is roughly chronological, the treatment of topics frequently departs from strict chronology. I am well aware of the danger of this method which involves infinitely greater labour and anxiety to the writer. But the alternative method has always seemed to me to be—except in the hands of a great master—arid in the extreme, and to issue in the writing not of scientific *History,* but of mere *Annals*—a bare chronicle of events. I have tried to minimize the dangers inherent in the method adopted by the regular inclusion of dates.

It remains only to acknowledge a heavy debt to previous writers who have covered parts of the same ground—I am not aware of any one who has covered the whole of it— and to express my gratitude to an old friend and (in two spheres) colleague, Sir Charles Oman, K.B.E., M.P., for the careful revision, in proof, of the whole book. I am grateful also to Mr. Rudyard Kipling for permission to quote from two of his poems, and to the Marquess of Salisbury, Mr. Lloyd George, Lord Carson and Sir Austen Chamberlain, who have been kind enough to help my personal recollections by answering questions addressed to them. In no case, however, are they responsible for the use I have made of their answers.

J. A. R. MARRIOTT

June 12, 1934

[1] Notably : *A History of Europe, 1815–1937* (Methuen, 1938) ; *Europe and Beyond* (Methuen, 1933) ; *The Mechanism of the Modern State* (Clarendon Press, 1927) ; *The English in India* (Clar. Press, 1932) ; *Second Chambers* (Clar. Press, 1927) ; *The Eastern Question* (Clar. Press, 1940) ; and *Queen Victoria and Her Ministers* (Murray, 1933).

NOTE TO THIRD EDITION

THIS book has again been thoroughly revised, the concluding chapters have been largely rewritten, and two new chapters have been added in an endeavour—perhaps vain and of doubtful expediency—to bring the narrative up to date. It is the penalty—no light one—of writing contemporary history, and in the present case has been increased by my enforced exile, which has cut me off from all great libraries and even from my own. All the greater, however, is my gratitude to correspondents, and in particular to an old pupil, Sir Henry Badeley, K.C.B., C.B.E., Clerk of the Parliaments, whose help would constitute an obligation had it not been so readily and gracefully tendered.

J. A. R. MARRIOTT

January, 1945

PUBLISHER'S NOTE

SIR JOHN MARRIOTT delivered the new matter to be embodied in the third edition of this book in January, 1945. He died in June of the same year, before proofs could be submitted to him.

January, 1946.

INTRODUCTORY NOTE

BY THE GENERAL EDITOR

EVEN in these most troublous days it is necessary that the record of History should be from time to time revised, as new information keeps coming to hand.

In England, as in France and Germany, the main characteristic of the last fifty years, from the point of view of the student of history, has been that new material has been accumulating much faster than it can be assimilated or absorbed. The standard works of the nineteenth-century historians need to be revised, or even to be put aside as obsolete, in the light of the new information that is coming in so rapidly and in such vast bulk.

The series of which this volume forms a part is intended to do something towards meeting the demand for information brought up to date. Individual historians will not sit down, as once they were wont, to write twenty-volume works in the style of Hume or Lingard, embracing a dozen centuries of annals. It is not to be desired that they should—the writer who is most satisfactory in dealing with Anglo-Saxon antiquities is not likely to be the one who will best discuss the antecedents of the Reformation, or the constitutional history of the Stuart period. But something can be done by judicious co-operation. In the thirty-seven years since the first volume of this series appeared in 1904, it would seem that the idea has justified itself, as the various sections have passed through many editions and revisions varying from six to eighteen.

Each is intended to give something more than a mere outline of one period of our national annals, but they have little space for controversy or the discussion of sources. There is, however, a bibliography annexed to most of the series, which will show the inquirer where information of the more special kind is to be sought. Moreover, a number of maps are to be found at the end of each volume which, as it is hoped, will make it unnecessary for the reader to be continually referring to large historical atlases—tomes which (as we must confess with regret) are not to be discovered in every private library.

The general editor and his collaborators have been touched lightly by the hand of time. All regret the too early decease of our colleague Henry Carless Davis, sometime Regius Professor of Modern History in this University, who wrote the second of the eight volumes of the series. He had several times revised his contribution. Most of us survivors continue to do the same from time to time, as the pen (or sometimes the spade) produces new sources of information. Naturally the spade is particularly active for the purveying of fresh material for the first of our volumes, and the pen (or the press) for the two last. Information must be kept up to date, whatever the epoch concerned, even though it is known that much undiscovered evidence may yet be forthcoming in the near future. For the volumes dealing with the latest periods, of which this is one, new light is continually cropping up from newly-published memoirs, or state papers long kept unpublished. It leads from time to time to alterations of a necessary sort.

C. OMAN

OXFORD,
May 1st, 1941

CONTENTS

BOOK I

LIST OF MAPS

BOOK I

CHAPTER I

PROLOGUE

THE half-century surveyed in this volume marks a distinct epoch in the history of England, of the British Empire, and of the World. The apex of the period is reached in the Great War of 1914–18. Involved in the War as a unit, the British Empire played in it a decisive part, and on the shoulders of that weary Titan has been imposed a large share of responsibility for saving the World from the chaos and bankruptcy, material and moral, resulting therefrom. With these matters the last Book (III) of this volume will be largely concerned. Of the two preceding Books, the first deals with the last years of the Victorian Era ; the second, covering the whole of King Edward's and the first four years of King George's reign, deals with the period of the ' Armed Peace '.

Regarding the period as a whole it will be seen to possess certain outstanding features which it may be convenient, at the outset, to distinguish.

The first is the reaction of Science upon Politics and industry. Science was responsible for the shrinkage of the globe : the shortening of distances, and the improvement of communications between continent and continent, between country and country, differentiated this era from all those which preceded it. This phenomenon must be attributed, primarily, to a series of remarkable mechanical inventions. It was in 1856 that (Sir) Henry Bessemer first announced at a meeting of the British Association the invention of a process for the production of cheap steel. The most important practical outcome of Bessemer's invention was the substitution of steel for iron rails. This invention entitles Bessemer to be numbered among the greatest of our Empire builders, for, as we shall see in Chapter VII, the economic development of the British Empire—alike Dependent and Self-Governing—has been in large measure due to the contribution made by railways to the cheapening of land transport. Not, however, until the period now under review was Bessemer's great invention, on a large scale, commercially utilized. About the same time steel began to be increasingly used in shipbuilding. As a result, steel being both lighter and more durable than iron, the cost of ocean transport was substantially diminished.

Two other inventions, brought into common use after 1870, contributed to the same result. We are apt to forget that until the 'eighties of the nineteenth century the great bulk of the world's trade was still carried in sailing ships. When Queen Victoria came to the throne the voyage from England to Australia, now accomplished in about forty days, occupied from six to eight months. Steamships had indeed made their appearance early in the century; they came into general use for river and cross-Channel purposes in the 'twenties; in another ten years they began to feel their way over the Atlantic; but the engines of those days consumed large quantities of coal, the voyages of steamships were, therefore, conditioned by the availability of coaling stations. Moreover, ocean-going ships had to provide large storage space for fresh water; sea water could not be used for the boilers, which were quickly ruined by salt; fresh water could not be used more than once owing to evaporation. Consequently, for long voyages steamers were not generally used except for the conveyance of first-class passengers and mails. There was little room on them for cargo, except for such things as gold bullion, the value of which was great and the bulk small.

Ocean transport   Two inventions then came to revolutionize ocean transport. The first was that of the compound engine which from 1860 onwards greatly economized the use of coal. Ten years later the perfecting of the surface condenser made it possible to pass the same water through the boilers as often as might be needed. These inventions not only liberated space for cargo but also made for a great reduction in working costs. By this time sailing ships had been improved out of recognition, but even so they could not

hold their own against the compound engine and the surface
condenser, not to mention the Suez Canal which shortened the
voyage, but only for steamers, from London to Bombay by over
40 per cent. of nautical miles, and to Hong Kong by 25 per
cent.[1]

Ancillary to the development of transport facilities has been Communica-
the improvement in means of communication by the telegraph tions
and telephone. The first submarine cable was laid under the
Straits of Dover in 1851, and in 1865, after various vain attempts,
a cable connecting England and America was successfully laid.
Thereafter, progress was steady, and by 1887 over 100,000 nautical miles of cable had been laid, almost entirely at the expense
of private capitalists in this country. The nautical mileage now
(1933) exceeds 300,000 ; but cable telegraphy has since the
'nineties encountered serious rivals in the development of long-
distance telephony and in the wireless telegraphy which Signor
Marconi was the first to bring into commercial use. To insist
on the extent to which such inventions have consolidated the
Empire, and promoted Empire trade, would be to labour the
obvious.

No single invention has done more to bring the products of Refriger-
the outer Empire into common use in English homes than that ation
of refrigeration and cold storage. Refrigeration for industrial
and transport purposes dates only from the early 'eighties. The
Refrigerator Car first made its appearance in the United States
in 1868, and in 1882 the system was adopted by the New Zealand Shipping Company. Since that date the export of mutton
and lamb from that Dominion to the United Kingdom has steadily
increased, and is now about 3,000,000 cwt. annually. New Zealand, Australia, Canada, South Africa and the West Indies all
send to this country fresh fruit in increasing quantities and of
constantly improving quality ; butter and eggs arrive in perfect
condition from the Antipodes ; bacon and beans from Canada.
Of chilled beef only a negligible quantity is imported from Australasia, as beef in the chilled state remains in good condition
only for about thirty days. South America, consequently, has

[1] Cf. L. C. A. Knowles, *The Economic Development of the British Overseas
Empire*, I, pp. 17–18. 3 vols., London, 1924 and 1930. To this admirable
work these paragraphs owe much.

almost a monopoly of the supply of this commodity, but there is confident hope in the Australasian Dominions that before long patient research, which has already done so much for their products, will enable them to compete successfully in the British market with South America.

The bearing of these inventions upon the political unity of the Sea Empire and upon the development of inter-imperial trade calls for no elaborate demonstration.

Welt-Politik

Within the sphere of the British Empire the reflex action of Science upon Politics, of Politics upon Science, was harmonious and complementary. Beyond that sphere, it was contradictory. Under the influence of Science the globe was shrinking; under the impulse of Politics and the stress of Economics Europe was expanding. The 'seventies had witnessed the attainment of national unity in Germany and Italy. In both countries political unification was the starting-point of economic development and commercial expansion. Both began to pass under the dominion of forces which had long ago revolutionized the social and economic condition of Great Britain. Though more slowly and less completely than Great Britain, Germany and Italy were industrialized and urbanized. Population, increasing rapidly, tended to congregate in cities and to work in factories. Industrialization increased the demand for raw materials, many of which could be obtained only from tropical countries. Large-scale production revealed the necessity for oversea markets wherein to dispose of surplus products. Hence the keen competition for colonial possessions—notably in Africa.

Thus the economic expansion of Europe led of necessity to the development of *Welt-Politik*. Diplomacy began to concern itself no longer with Europe only, but with all the continents of the world. The European Chancelleries were occupied as much with the problem of the Far East as with that of the Near East, with the Pacific as much as with the Mediterranean, with Africa even more than with Europe. Early in the 'seventies Japan emerged with amazing rapidity from the isolation which she had for centuries successfully preserved. Not even the United States could maintain the attitude of aloofness enjoined by Washington and Jefferson, and emphasized by President Monroe. Truly the globe was shrinking, and its shrinkage was of special significance to the Power whose possessions were most widely distributed. Every part of the British Empire became conscious of the presence of European neighbours, and increasingly sensitive to European competition. It is, then, against the background of world-history that the events of English History must in this period be reviewed.

Passing from external to domestic affairs, we must note the completion of the process by which political power has been transferred from the few to the many, from an aristocracy to the democracy. The earlier stages of that movement were described in the preceding volume of this work.[1] The process was resumed by the enactment of the Parliamentary Reform Acts of 1884 and 1885. With the passing of those Acts the present volume opens. The series was completed by the Act of 1928 which conferred the parliamentary franchise on all adult citizens of both sexes. *Democracy*

The culmination of Parliamentary Democracy as the principle of the Central Government had its counterpart in the democratization of Local Government. The Act of 1888 established elective County Councils; the Act of 1894 extended the same principle to District and Parish Councils.

Political machinery is not, however, an end but a means. The newly enfranchised electors were quick to use the new weapon placed in their hands. They looked to Parliament for legislation designed to ameliorate the social and economic condition of the people at large. Nor did they look in vain. Conservatives and Liberals vied with each other in the promotion of social reform. *Social Reform*

The political field was not, in fact, left to these historic Parties. The period under revision is remarkable for the organization, political and industrial, of the wage-earners. Combination among the manual workers was, indeed, no new thing. Trade Unionism and Co-operation had made considerable progress before 1885. But up till that time the activities of both these working-class movements were exclusively economic. The former aimed at obtaining for the wage-earners better conditions of employment, higher wages, shorter hours and so forth, as well as at succouring them in sickness and in periods of unemployment. The object of the Co-operative Movement was to enable the working classes *Labour*

[1] Marriott, *England since Waterloo* (13th ed., 1945).

to lay out their wages to better advantage and to encourage saving. Neither Trade Unionism nor Co-operation was in its inception political. But the enfranchisement of the wage-earners awakened the political ambition of their industrial associations. The Trade Unions supplied from the first the nucleus, and still form the backbone, of the Labour-Socialist Party and with this Party the Co-operative Movement also is now closely associated. To these and parallel developments Chapters III, XIII and XIX will be largely devoted.

Education

Too tardily did England heed the sagacious advice of Robert Lowe and proceed to educate her new masters. But the development of a national system of education—primary, secondary, technical and University—is another characteristic product of this period. Logically, educational reform ought to have preceded political enfranchisement. In the case of women it did, as Chapter XVIII will show. But the State was not moved to educate its male citizens until after it had endowed them with political power.

Ireland

Political enfranchisement did not stop short at the shores of Great Britain, and the effect of the legislation of 1884–5 was demonstrated in Ireland even more quickly than in England. Consequently Irish affairs must needs occupy a considerable space in this volume. From the Home Rule struggle of 1885–92 down to the Rebellion of 1916 and the Treaty of 1921 Ireland played a conspicuous and even dominating part in the politics of the United Kingdom. 'It was an evil day,' wrote Thomas Carlyle, ' when Strigul first meddled with that people.'[1] Readers who are at pains to ponder the contents of Chapters IV, XVII, XIX and XXVII may well be disposed to assent to this aphorism. It is already painfully clear that the problem initiated by the half-completed conquest of Henry II was not solved by the ' Treaty ' of 1921. The sore which for eight centuries has been festering yet remains open. Ireland is still to Great Britain as the heel of Achilles.

The Overseas Empire

In sharp and pleasing contrast with the depression engendered by contemplation of the Irish problem is the buoyant hope inspired by the progress of the Overseas Empire. Of all developments to which this volume must draw attention, perhaps the

---

[1] Essay on Chartism, *Works*, vi. 127.

most distinctive is the growth of a new spirit in the relations between the Motherland on the one hand and the Dominions and Dependencies on the other. From the days of Adam Smith to those of Richard Cobden English colonial policy was dominated by the *laisser-faire* doctrines of the 'Manchester School'. Chapter VII will disclose the reaction which the 'eighties initiated. The Imperial sentiment demonstrated at the first Jubilee (1887) deepened and widened down to the close of the Great War. If since the Peace Conference centrifugal forces have, in the political sphere, predominated, they have been counteracted by economic forces making for integration. Both processes will demand attention in the pages that follow.

The centripetal tendencies revealed at the Ottawa Conference of 1932 cannot indeed be dissociated from the general reaction against *laisser-faire*. The fiscal policy to which from 1846 to 1932 England adhered represented only one manifestation of the philosophy of the Manchester School. The strength of Benthamite Liberalism was its doctrinal coherence. The State was to stand aside and allow free play to the activities of the individual citizen. The greatest good of the greatest number would, it was held, be most effectually promoted by a minimum of State interference. Free Trade was only one illustration of a principle extending to the whole sphere of government. But the strength of the Benthamite School was not without a corresponding weakness. The disciples of Cobden and Bright adhered to a *laisser-faire* policy in relation to foreign trade long after their doctrines had ceased to dominate domestic legislation. State control of industry cannot coexist with fiscal *laisser-faire*. Trade Unionism is philosophically inconsistent with Free Trade. 'A nation cannot,' said Abraham Lincoln, 'exist half-slave and half-free.' The aphorism has a wider application. The State cannot protect labour and refuse to protect trade. If the State compels the industrialist and the farmer to shorten hours or raise wages, it cannot leave their products unprotected from the competition of commodities produced under conditions less favourable to labour, more advantageous to those who employ it.

Considerations, stated thus crudely, have profoundly, if not consciously, influenced legislation in this latest period of English History.

Economics and Politics

The change in the spirit of legislation has involved changes, even more radical, in the machinery of administration.

Bureau-cracy
The term *Bureaucracy* has only recently been naturalized in England. The Government ' official ' was not wont in former times to obtrude himself upon the attention of the individual citizen. To-day the Government inspector is everywhere : in the shop and the factory ; in the farmyard, the schoolroom, and the market. From the cradle to the grave the citizen is dogged by the duty of registration; his life is largely occupied by filling in official forms and making returns to Government. That all this has contributed to the general well-being : to a marked improvement in public health ; to the protection of the weak and the restraint of the strong ; to the abolition of abuses and the provision of amenities, is undeniable. But all this positive good has been purchased at a price. The Government inspector is but a symptom of the growth of bureaucracy. Official forms are merely the outward and visible signs of the extension of the functions of the State and the multiplication of public Departments. So gravely is this development viewed in some responsible quarters that a latter-day Coke has recently descended from the forum into the market-place. Lord Hewart, the Lord Chief Justice of England, has thought it incumbent on him to issue *urbi* if not *orbi* a warning against the encroachments of the Executive upon the functions of the Legislature and of the Judicature.[1] Lord Hewart's misgivings, though shared by many of his brethren, are by some derided as ' Victorian '. Nor were they entirely dissipated by the Report of a Committee appointed by the Lord Chancellor (Lord Sankey) to consider the powers exercised by, or under the direction of, Ministers of the Crown by way of delegated legislation and judicial or quasi-judicial decisions.[2] Detailed discussion of this important problem is obviously beyond the scope of an introductory chapter. There can, however, be no doubt that the increase in the powers and functions of the Executive, whether it be innocent or noxious, whether it can or cannot be restrained, represents one of the most significant tendencies in the sphere of government during the years now under review.

And it is with the sphere of government, with the relations between the State and its citizen, with political events and ten-

---

[1] *The New Despotism.* London, 1929. [2] Cmd. 4060.

dencies, that this book is concerned.   It will not, however, escape notice that Politics (in the narrower sense), is increasingly merged in Economics.   Constitutional questions which loomed so large in parliamentary debates during the first three-quarters of Queen Victoria's reign have in recent days fallen into the background. The work of Parliament and the interest of the electorate are now almost exclusively concentrated on economic questions and international affairs.   The term ' Politics ' must, then, be broadly interpreted.   So interpreted it supplies the central theme of the chapters that follow.

Of the forces that operate in Politics, one of the most powerful is, if paradox be permitted, the *vis inertiae*.   The stream of commerce is not readily diverted under normal circumstances from the channels in which it is accustomed to flow.   A series of momentous discoveries such as those which distinguished the last years of the eighteenth century may, indeed, bring about a sudden revolution.   The inventions of Hargreaves and Arkwright, of Watt and Stephenson, of Telford and Macadam, revolutionized industry and transport, and gave to Great Britain a place in world-economy such as she had never known before.   That preeminent place she retained down to the close of the Queen Victoria's reign.   Her remarkable success in the field of industry gave her also political pre-eminence.   All the progressive nations of the world (with the notable exception of the United States), envious of her economic prosperity, took to copying her Parliamentary Constitution.   Imitation was their undoing ; political institutions do not bear transportation.   One country's food is another country's poison.   Parliamentary Democracy is, of all forms of government, the most delicately poised.   It calls for the most precise adjustment to political conditions.   Those conditions existed in the England of the nineteenth century ; the forces which make for the success of Parliamentary government were, under Queen Victoria, perfectly balanced.   Nowhere else did the essential conditions exist ; other peoples had not passed through the same indispensable apprenticeship.   Consequently, nowhere did a copy reproduce the success of the original.   In many cases the experiment has now been abandoned.

Thus England no longer leads the world politically ; her easy supremacy in commerce and industry has passed away.   Still

The Vis Inertiae

more serious for an insular State, the centre of a Sea Empire, is the loss of her ascendancy in shipping. It becomes, therefore, a grave question whether Great Britain can continue to sustain a teeming population which has come into being under conditions no longer fulfilled. Thus far, the surplus population has been maintained by taxing the accumulated resources of the wealthier classes. Nor has there been any deterioration in the physique or in the general well-being of the population. On the contrary, the people as a whole are better housed, better clothed and better fed than they were in the noontide of national prosperity.[1]

The economic momentum derived from Victorian days has not yet exhausted itself. Any decline that may be discerned is merely relative to other nations; of absolute decline there is no evidence.

Nevertheless, the doubt persists how long the momentum can last. Adversity has undoubtedly taught some salutary lessons : the leaders of industry have learnt that they cannot expect the favours of Providence to be poured into their laps without effort, that changing conditions demand new methods ; traders have learnt that even British goods will not sell themselves ; wage-earners have learnt that no concern can permanently pay out in wages more than it receives from the sale of its products ; politicians have learnt that in the midst of a world fiscally armed to the teeth this country cannot remain wholly unprotected ; they have learnt that continued neglect of agriculture has brought on them the inevitable, if dilatory, nemesis ; above all they have learnt that a nation, no more than an individual, can live beyond its means without incurring the penalty of bankruptcy.

The post-War years have been years of difficulty, culminating at times in crises. Yet, despite the hardness of the times, despite the crushing burden of taxation the nation has had to carry, the stream of charity has never failed, no appeal from any people in any quarter of the world has ever remained unanswered, while the public ' social services ' have been maintained on a scale of generosity such as no other country in the world has even attempted to emulate.

But the most generous purses, public or private, are not bottomless. By behaving as though they were, this country was brought

[1] *A Survey of London* (1934).

in 1931 to the brink of bankruptcy. It was forced off the gold exchange standard, but by a supreme effort of the national will bankruptcy was averted. At the critical moment the King intervened, and once again demonstrated the immense value of an hereditary monarchy, standing serenely above all party issues, and assuming direct responsibility only when that assumption was essential to the safety of the State.

The King staved off disaster. Only the nation could save itself. To the call for sacrifice it responded nobly. For the third time in the last two decades, the people of this land proved themselves to be of the breed of giants. The whole world looked on with wonder and admiration. As in 1914, as in 1926, so again in 1931–2, Britons proved that the national fibre is still sound, that in real stamina, moral or physical, there has in fact been no decay : they remain

> A nation yet, the rulers and the ruled.
> Some sense of duty, something of a faith,
> Some reverence for the laws ourselves have made,
> Some patient force to change them when we will,
> Some civic manhood, firm against the crowd.

With the grim fight against imminent disaster ; with the gaining, inch by inch, of ground that should lead to the haven of national security, if it may be of national prosperity, this work will close.[1]

---

[1] To the later editions an epilogue has been added, bringing the narrative as far as possible up to date.

CHAPTER II

THE ADVENT OF DEMOCRACY—ENGLISH PARTIES AND IRISH HOPES

Parlia-
mentary
Reform

THE Reform Acts of 1884–5 announced the advent of Democracy. All classes of the community were at last represented in the Imperial Parliament at Westminster. That fact governs the domestic politics of Great Britain and Ireland during the period surveyed in this book. Down to the Revolution of 1688, the English monarch not only reigned but ruled. As was the monarch, such was the condition of the people ; such was the place of England among the nations. A strong and wise king meant strong and wise government ; under a weak king the people suffered and the country was abased. After the Revolution of 1688, more particularly after the accession of the Hanoverian Sovereigns in 1714, the Royal Power, never quite absolute, was more and more limited by Parliament and by Ministers responsible thereto. But until 1832 both Houses of Parliament were dominated by a group of great families, the heads of which not only composed the House of Lords, but to a large extent controlled elections to the House of Commons.

The Reform Act of 1832 dethroned this territorial oligarchy ; the balance of political power passed to the middle classes, of whom the new electorate was mainly composed. But though the middle classes controlled the House of Commons, executive power still rested with the older aristocracy. A Peel or a Gladstone, representatives of the new aristocracy of commerce, might reach the highest place in the political hierarchy, but they formed the exception. Every Prime Minister between 1832 and 1867 belonged to a noble family, as did most of his Cabinet colleagues.[1]

[1] Except Peel.

The Reform Bill of 1867 admitted to the parliamentary fran- The County
chise some 1,000,000 new electors, mostly urban artisans. It was Fran-
based on the principle of 'household suffrage'. It was not long, chise,
however, before there was a demand championed by Mr. (after- 1884
wards Sir George) Trevelyan for the assimilation of the county
to the borough franchise and the consequent admission to electoral power of the great mass of the agricultural labourers. The
Bill of 1884 conceded this demand, and, as ultimately passed,
added some 2,000,000 voters to the electorate. But the Franchise Bill was to be followed by a Bill for the redistribution of
seats, and the House of Lords, on the motion of Lord Cairns,
declined to assent to a 'fundamental change in the electoral
body' until the Government produced its scheme for the readjustment of the constituencies.

The action of the Lords, though eminently reasonable, evoked Redistri-
a furious agitation in the country, and a serious conflict between bution
the two Houses, or, as others put it, between 'the Peers and the 1885
People', was averted only by the intervention of Queen Victoria.
She exerted herself strenuously to bring the parties together, and
with such success that the Lords accepted the Franchise Bill,
and the Redistribution of Seats Bill was passed virtually without
opposition. Not for the first time in his ministerial career, Mr.
Gladstone had good reason to 'tender his grateful thanks' to
the Queen 'for the wise, gracious and steady influence on Her
Majesty's part' which had 'so powerfully contributed to . . .
avert a serious crisis of affairs'. Under the new *Act* all boroughs
with less than 15,000 inhabitants were deprived of separate
representation and were merged in the counties to which they
belonged; boroughs with less than 50,000 inhabitants lost one
member. For the rest, with the exception of twenty-two middle-
sized boroughs, such as Preston, Brighton, and Stockport, and
certain Universities, the whole country was divided into single-
member constituencies, thus approximating to the idea of equal
electoral areas. In order to facilitate this change twelve additional members were added to the House, bringing its numbers
up to 670.

Even so the principle of equal representation, one vote one
value, was most inadequately realized. Two votes in Ireland,
for example, were of equal electoral value to three in England,

while in England itself the growth, and still more the shifting, of population quickly reduced the idea of equal distribution to a grotesque absurdity. Nor did the system of single-member constituencies secure, as was hoped, the adequate representation of minorities, or help men of independent opinions to obtain seats in Parliament. On the contrary, it tended to accentuate the over-representation of majorities, and to increase the rigidity of party organization—both central and local. Yet no alternative has yet commended itself to any one of the fourteen Parliaments elected since 1885.

Resignation of Mr. Gladstone

The new system was soon put to the test. Hardly were the Reform Bills on the Statute-book when Mr. Gladstone's ministry was defeated in the House of Commons (June 8). The occasion of their defeat was a clause in the Finance Bill of the year. The cause is to be found in a rapidly accumulating burden of unpopularity, evoked mainly by the disastrous policy pursued by the Government in Egypt, partly also by the failure of their successive and contradictory policies in Ireland. Alternate doses of coercion and conciliation excited mingled hatred and contempt in Ireland, and led English people to despair of finding any solution of an immemorial problem. Though the majority against him was only twelve, and though the reverse might have been retrieved, Mr. Gladstone insisted on resignation. His insistence bespoke the shrewd tactician. Now as always the Queen resented the intrusion of party tactics, but after a vain protest sent for Lord Salisbury, the leader of the Conservative Party in the Lords, rightly judging that he was better equipped for the post of Prime Minister than Sir Stafford Northcote who led a somewhat undisciplined party in the Commons.

Lord Salisbury, agreeing with the Queen that Gladstone's resignation was uncalled for, was unwilling to take office. Moreover, he was in a dilemma. Under ordinary circumstances he could have taken office and then immediately have asked for a dissolution of Parliament. But the Reform Acts interposed inevitable delay.[1] No election could take place before November, and Lord Salisbury, accordingly, declined to take office in a minority unless Gladstone would undertake to help the Conservatives to obtain the necessary supplies and carry on the routine

[1] Involving a new register of electors.

business of State. Gladstone would give no pledges ; a tense situation was protracted for nearly a fortnight, and was then relieved only by the strenuous exertions of the Queen. She pressed an Earldom on Gladstone in a letter which, as he wrote to Lord Granville, ' moves and almost upsets me. It must have cost her much to write and is really a pearl of great price.' The peerage was declined, but the rival leaders at length arrived at an understanding and Lord Salisbury kissed hands as Prime Minister.

In forming his ministry Lord Salisbury was confronted by a *The first Salisbury Ministry* difficulty. Some of the younger and more energetic Conservatives in the House of Commons had long chafed under the leadership of Northcote. The rebel leader, Lord Randolph Churchill, now refused to take office unless Northcote was translated to the Lords. Salisbury demurred to this ultimatum ; he had a real affection and respect—shared by all who knew him—for North-cote, and was unwilling to put this gross affront upon a man, already disappointed of the fulfilment of his legitimate ambitions. Lord Randolph, however, was adamant. Sir Michael Hicks Beach, who stood next to Northcote in the official hierarchy, supported Churchill, and Salisbury gave way. He had no alternative. Northcote became Earl of Iddesleigh and First Lord of the Treasury. Salisbury himself took the Foreign Office, the best of all possible arrangements had that office not been combined with the Premiership. Hicks Beach became Chancellor of the Exchequer with the lead of the House of Commons ; Lord Randolph went to the India Office, where he quickly won golden opinions from the permanent officials ; Mr. R. A. Cross, to the Queen's satisfaction, returned to the Home Office ; Mr. W. H. Smith went to the War Office and Lord George Hamilton to the Admiralty ; Mr. A. J. Balfour, a nephew of the Prime Minister, and one of Lord Randolph's lieutenants, became President of the Local Government Board, but without Cabinet rank ; another rebel, Sir John Gorst, became, not too appropriately, Solicitor-General. But the Irish offices furnished the key positions. Mr. Gibson, an Irish lawyer, who for some years had done yeoman service on party platforms, became Lord Chancellor of Ireland with a peerage (Lord Ashbourne) and a seat in the Cabinet. Most significant of all the appointments, however, was that of Lord Carnarvon.

The Irish situation was of the utmost complexity.[1] At the election of 1880 Lord Beaconsfield had attempted to concentrate the attention of the English electorate upon it. He warned them that Ireland would attempt ' to sever the constitutional tie which unites it to Great Britain '. Nobody at the time believed that his warning was other than an electoral device to divert attention from a tarnished record in foreign policy. The next five years were to prove the accuracy of his forecast. During those years the condition of Ireland went from bad to worse. Land Acts had failed to conciliate ; coercion failed to restore order. Was there a *sors tertia* open to Lord Carnarvon and his Conservative colleagues ?

Lord Carnarvon and Ireland

Lord Carnarvon was a close friend of the new Prime Minister, and like him had resigned from Disraeli's first ministry, rather than accept the Reform Bill of 1867. Admitted to Disraeli's second ministry in 1874 he had again seceded—this time on the Eastern Question. Carnarvon's mind was of too fine a texture, his conscientiousness too great for the day-to-day work of administration. He was a scholar-philosopher who, under a high sense of public duty, had descended into the dusty arena of politics. He had presided with conspicuous success over the concluding stages of the great measure for Canadian confederation. He had been anxious to apply the federal principle in South Africa, and his mind was turning towards some form of devolution in Ireland when in June 1885 he accepted the Viceroyalty and as a Cabinet Minister became primarily responsible for the Irish policy of the new Government.

Only with reluctance did he yield to the pressure of his old friend and colleague. Nor was Lord Salisbury unaware of the risk the appointment involved. ' Our best and almost only hope is to come to some fair and reasonable arrangement for Home Rule ' with safeguards. So Carnarvon had written to Salisbury in February. Lord Salisbury was not hopeful of the suggested solution, but nevertheless pressed Carnarvon to go to Ireland. He ultimately accepted the post as ' a special mission limited to the period indicated (i.e. until after the General Election or the meeting of the new Parliament) and knowing,' as he wrote on

---

[1] It is analysed in detail in the preceding volume of this work. Cf. Marriott : *England since Waterloo*, pp. 482–5, 492–8.

June 16, ' that I may implicitly count upon the fullest support of yourself and my colleagues at home.'

Other Conservative leaders were moving, if not towards Home Rule at least away from ' Coercion '. On May 7, 1885, Hicks Beach had written to Salisbury after ' a long talk with Churchill ' expressing his opinion that the Tories ought not to turn Gladstone out ' unless we feel that we, if in office, could do without a renewal of the Irish Coercion Bill ' ; and he added, ' I do not like Spencer's system, and do not believe in its necessity.' [1] The Tories and the National-ists

Churchill was, at that time, in communication with Parnell, the leader of the Irish Nationalists. Speaking at St. Stephen's Club to his Conservative friends on May 20, he concluded with these grave words : ' I believe most firmly that this ought to be the attitude of the Tory party—that while they are ready and willing to grant to any Government of the Queen whatever powers may be necessary, on evidence adduced, for the preservation of law and order, they ought . . . not to be committed to any act or policy which should unnecessarily wound and injure the feelings and sentiments of our brothers on the other side of the channel of St. George.' [2] Not that Lord Randolph ever wavered for an instant in his attachment to the Legislative Union. ' On that issue he was immovable. I never heard him use but one language with regard to it—that it was impossible.' That is the testimony of his intimate friend, Lord Rosebery ; and it is conclusive.[3] But short of Home Rule, there was no concession which he was not prepared and anxious to make ; particularly if he might thereby satisfy the Irish Catholics in the matter of religion.

The attitude of the Tories reacted not only on the Parnellites, but also on the Radical wing of the Liberal Party, already in semi-revolt against Gladstone and the Whigs, and far from dismayed by the downfall of his Government. Among these Radicals two stood out prominent. The Radicals

One was Sir Charles Dilke, who had been admitted to Gladstone's Cabinet as President of the Local Government Board in 1882, had served as Chairman of the Royal Commission on the Dilke and Cham-berlain

---

[1] Hicks Beach, *Life*, i. 230.

[2] Winston Churchill, *Life of Lord Randolph Churchill*, i. 291.

[3] Rosebery, *Lord R. C.*, p. 22.

housing of the working classes in 1884, and had displayed conspicuous parliamentary ability in piloting the Redistribution Bill
through the House of Commons.   Down to 1885 Dilke was regarded as the predestined successor to Gladstone in the leadership of the Liberal Party ; but in that year he became involved
in divorce proceedings, and, though not adjudged guilty of the
more scandalous charges alleged against him, his political career,
at that time full of brilliant promise, was prematurely ended.

Closely connected with Dilke in ties of personal and political
friendship was Joseph Chamberlain.   During the period immediately under review Chamberlain was, of all English statesmen,
the most representative and one of the most influential.   Firmly
convinced of the merits of parliamentary democracy, an ardent
social reformer though opposed to social revolution, above all a
whole-hearted believer in the Imperial mission of the British race,
Chamberlain pre-eminently embodied the most vital and the most
characteristic ideas of that epoch.   Born in 1836 of middle-class
stock, with strong Nonconformist traditions, Joseph Chamberlain, though a Londoner by birth, was from the age of eighteen
continuously associated with Birmingham.   Entering the business of his uncle, Mr. Nettlefold, a screw manufacturer, in 1854,
he was so successful that within twenty years he was able to
retire from active business with a considerable fortune.   Meanwhile, he had already exhibited his keen interest in public affairs.
He became Chairman of the National Education League in Birmingham in 1868, was elected to the City Council in 1869, to the
first Birmingham School Board in 1870, and served as Mayor of
Birmingham in 1873, 1874 and 1875.   A strong advocate of
municipal enterprise, he stimulated the Corporation to purchase
the gas-works, the water-works, the sewage farm, and, by an
extensive scheme of slum clearance and rehousing, he transformed
the outward aspect of the city of his adoption.   He keenly supported the movement for the provision of Art Galleries and Free
Libraries, and by every means within the reach of individuals
and of Local Authorities he sought to promote the material and
moral well-being of the whole community.

But there were reforms, on which he had set his heart, outside
the competence of Local Authorities.   To achieve them he sought
a seat in Parliament.   Defeated at Sheffield in the General

Election of 1874, he was returned for Birmingham at a by-election in 1876, and promptly set to work to reorganize the local Liberal Associations on a representative basis. He thus became with Mr. Schnadhorst the reputed father of the ' Caucus '. The fruit of his labours was reaped in the Liberal victory of 1880.

Some personal reward could hardly have been withheld ; but Chamberlain and Dilke had mutually agreed to swim or sink together. Mr. Gladstone and his Sovereign were more than willing that both should sink. Their co-operation was, however, essential to the success of the new Government. Chamberlain was accordingly admitted to the Cabinet as President of the Board of Trade. Dilke represented the Foreign Office in the House of Commons, and two years later was promoted to Cabinet rank. Gladstone had recommended Chamberlain to the Queen on the ground that ' he was very pleasing and refined in feelings and manner ' that ' he had never spoken against [the Queen] or the Royal Family, or had expressed Republican views '. The Queen, however, found him ' most dangerous ' and frequently complained to the Prime Minister about his impetuous colleague's speeches. They were, indeed, hardly less distasteful to Gladstone than to the Queen : but Gladstone had the fortunes of the Party to consider ; the Queen had no thought but for the country. From the Party point of view Chamberlain's support became increasingly indispensable. But it was rendered with increasing reluctance. Chamberlain liked coercion no more than did Churchill, and long before Gladstone's conversion to Home Rule propounded a large scheme for the reorganization of local government, on an elective basis, with a representative Central Board for the whole of Ireland, to be charged with such matters as primary education, public works and poor relief, but not to be in any sense a parliament with an executive responsible thereto. His scheme was turned down by the Cabinet, but from the principle which underlay it he never swerved.

Responsibility for the government of Ireland had, however, Tory policy in Ireland passed into other hands. The policy of the Salisbury Ministry was announced by Lord Carnarvon in the House of Lords, on July 6,[1] and his statement was briefly endorsed, a day later, by

---

[1] Cf. Carnarvon, *Life*, III, 165–7 ; Hansard, 6. vii. '85.

Hicks Beach in the Commons. The Government had decided not to renew the Coercion Act or any part of it, but to make an earnest attempt to rule Ireland by a 'vigorous and vigilant administration of the ordinary law '.

Ten days later Parnell demanded a public inquiry into the justice of the sentences passed on various persons convicted of murder in the Maamtrasna and other recent cases. The sentences had been confirmed by Lord Spencer; Carnarvon was opposed to the reopening of the question, and the Cabinet supported his decision. Hicks Beach, however, was uneasy about the matter and induced the Viceroy to promise a full inquiry into the matter. The inquiry was held and as a result Carnarvon confirmed the decisions of Lord Spencer.

On August 1, however, Lord Carnarvon met Parnell with every circumstance of secrecy in an empty house in Hill Street. Salisbury was informed of the proposed meeting beforehand, and received from Carnarvon both a verbal and a written report of the conversation immediately after the interview.[1] He had urged the Viceroy to be ' extremely cautious ' in all that he might say, and was dismayed to learn that Carnarvon had neglected the precaution of having Lord Ashbourne present as a third party. Carnarvon desired that the Queen but not the Cabinet should be informed about the interview; Lord Salisbury demurred, and neither the Queen nor the Cabinet [2] heard anything about it until in June 1886 it became public property.

On the night of June 7-8, 1886, two hours before the fateful division on the Home Rule Bill, Parnell created a great sensation by stating that he ' had every reason to know that the Conservative Party, if they should be successful at the polls, would have offered Ireland a Statutory Legislature with a right to protect her own industries, and that this would have been coupled with the settlement of the Irish Land Question, on the basis of purchase, on a larger scale than that now proposed by ' Mr. Gladstone.[3] Sir M. H. Beach emphatically contradicted the statement of Parnell, who then rose and stated positively that he spoke on the authority of one who was then a Minister of the Crown. Challenged to name the individual he stated that he

---

[1] Printed in Carnarvon's *Life*, III, 178-81.
[2] Except Lord Ashbourne.　　　　　[3] Hansard, 7. vi. p. 1181.

would do it when he received permission from him to do so.[1]
Hicks Beach spoke of course in perfect good faith; he was evidently believed; the incident had little if any effect on the division.

The Press immediately identified Carnarvon as the Minister indicated by Parnell, and on June 10 the ex-Viceroy [2] made a brief statement in the Lords. 'He did not,' Lord Kimberley reported to the Queen, 'give any information as to the nature of these communications [with Parnell] except that they were made without the cognizance of any of his colleagues, and conveyed no promises. . . .' The pertinent passage in Carnarvon's speech ran as follows : 'Let me endeavour to say in the plainest language I can command that I was not acting for the Cabinet nor authorized by them. . . . I never communicated to them even that which I had done. Therefore, the responsibility was simply and solely mine; they were not cognizant of my action.' As to bargain with Parnell there was none. 'We both left the room as free as when we entered it.' [3] In assuming ' sole responsibility ' Lord Carnarvon repudiated in greater detail the account of the interview which in the interval Parnell had given. Carnarvon was more generous towards his chief than his chief towards him. To the Queen, who was greatly annoyed at having been kept in the dark, Salisbury wrote (June 14) that Lord Carnarvon ' acted impulsively and with little foresight ' and took singularly little precaution to protect either himself or his colleagues from misunderstanding. That was undeniable.

In order to complete the story of a curious incident the sequence of events has been anticipated. To return. Carnarvon was not alone among the Conservative leaders in his anxiety to make terms with Parnell. 'There was no compact or bargain of any kind,' said Churchill to an intimate friend; 'but I told Parnell when he sat on that sofa [in Churchill's study] that if the Tories took office and I was a member of their Government, I would not consent to renew the Crimes Act. Parnell replied, " In that case you will have the Irish vote at the elections." ' [4]

---

[1] Mr. Gladstone to the Queen (*Q.V.L.*, 3rd Series, 1, 142). Two years later (May 1888).
[2] Carnarvon had resigned in January 1886.
[3] Hansard, 10. vi. pp. 1256-9.   [4] R. C., *Life*, 1. 395.

The Crimes Act was not renewed, and during the brief remnant of the session a Land Bill known as the *Ashbourne Act*, was passed. That Act laid the foundations of the gradual process which, by the use of English credit, converted the tenant-cultivators into the proprietors of the soil. Under this Act, a tenant could, by voluntary agreement with his landlord, purchase his farm, borrowing the whole amount of the purchase money from the State at 4 per cent. Not only did he thus secure an immediate reduction of rent (generally reckoned at about 20 per cent. as compared with the ' judicial ' rent of 1881), but at the end of forty-nine years he became automatically the owner of his farm. The total sum to be advanced by the State (out of the Irish Church surplus) was limited to £5,000,000. But the experiment, though on a modest scale, formed the basis of all subsequent land-purchase legislation down to the great measure passed by Mr. George Wyndham in 1903.

The General Election of 1885

The Parliament elected in 1880 had now run its course. Its successor would reflect the judgement of a greatly enlarged electorate. To the enlightenment and stimulation of that electorate the autumn was devoted by all parties. Interest, however, was largely concentrated on the speeches of Mr. Chamberlain. In July the blow, almost as terrible to him as to his friend, had fallen on Dilke. The campaign planned by them in common had to be fought by Chamberlain alone, and with an added sense of responsibility. For if Dilke were driven out of public life, on whom could Gladstone's mantle fall but on Chamberlain himself ? Gladstone had in fact no intention of retiring, and, not without subtlety, obtained from both wings of his party a written assurance that they wished him to retain the leadership. Nevertheless, Chamberlain launched his ' unauthorized programme ' and in a series of masterly speeches delivered in all parts of the country expounded its details.

The ' Unauthorized Programme '

Chamberlain was at that time regarded by all Conservatives and many Liberals as a dangerous agitator, a modern ' Jack Cade '.[1] Be that as it may, he had gauged more accurately than any one else the significance of the Reform Acts of 1884–5. ' I am confident that the inclusion of the whole people in the work of

---

[1] To this the writer, who took an active part in the political campaign, can personally testify.

Government will compel a larger measure of attention to those
social questions which as they concern the greatest happiness
of the greatest number ought to be the first object of Liberal
policy.'

Those words were in the forefront of his election address to
the electors of West Birmingham. His numerous speeches supplied a powerful and incisive commentary on that text. The
' programme ' as summarized by his biographer contained seven
principal propositions : (1) Free Primary Education ; (2) Reorganization of local government, on an elective basis, for rural
areas ; (3) Financial reform, partly by graduated taxation moder-
ately applied, through death duties and house-duties, not income
tax, partly by a levy on ' unearned increment ' (the doctrine
of ' ransom ' on which opponents fixed), with the object of
lightening indirect taxation and paying for social reforms—
particularly for slum clearance ; (4) Land Reform, especially
designed to give the labourer a stake in the soil, and re-create a
race of smallholders and yeomen, by the action of local authorities
equipped with compulsory powers for the acquisition of land at
an equitable price ; (5) Disestablishment of State Churches in
England, Scotland and Wales ; (6) Manhood suffrage and payment of members. It is noticeable that every one of these items,
with the partial exception of (3) and (5) have since been conceded.
Finally : as regards Ireland. On that, as on all other matters,
the Radical leader spoke without ambiguity or periphrasis.
Speaking at Dublin on August 24, Parnell had put forward his
demand for a separate and independent Parliament for Ireland,
and declared that its first object would be to impose a protective
duty on all English manufacturers. To that speech Chamberlain
replied in his historic speech at Warrington (September 8). ' If
these, and these alone, are the terms on which Mr. Parnell's support
is to be obtained I will not enter into competition for it.' Nor
did he. He had already demonstrated his sympathy with the
Irish people ; he had declared for ' Home-Rule-All-Round '—on
equal terms for the different parts of the United Kingdom, but
preserving its unity, and leaving the Imperial Parliament, unimpaired in composition and authority, as the supreme legislature of
a common realm.[1] To the idea of an independent Parliament, based

---

[1] Garvin, *Joseph Chamberlain*, II, 75.

General
Election
of 1885.

on the recognition of Ireland as a separate nation, Chamberlain would never listen.

The momentous election opened towards the end of November. The earlier returns from English boroughs seemed to portend a sweeping Tory majority, and they did finally return 116 Tories against 106 Liberals. Liverpool returned 8 Tories and 1 Home Ruler; Manchester 6 Tories and 1 Liberal; London 36 against 26. But the balance was redressed by the English counties, which returned 184 Liberals against 108 Tories, and by Scotland and Wales where Tories were hard put to it to find any seats at all. Thus the final result was 335 Liberals; 249 Tories (of whom 18 came from Ireland); and 86 Nationalists. Parnell held the balance. His astute calculations had been precisely realized. If he united with the Tories he could reduce the Liberals to impotence. In conjunction with a united Liberal Party he could dictate to the House of Commons.

But were the Liberals likely as a united Party to form an alliance with Parnell?

To Mr. Gladstone Parnell's victory in Ireland appeared conclusive. The new Irish electorate, increased by Gladstone's Bill from 200,000 to 700,000, had spoken. On December 17 his 'conversion' to the principle of Home Rule was publicly announced by the 'mischievous machinations' (the phrase is John Morley's) of his son Herbert. Labouchere, a Radical free-lance, not without influence, ascribed Gladstone's conversion to the 'senile passion of an old man' for power. Labouchere was not only cynical, but unjust.[1] Gladstone would gladly have seen the Irish question settled by the Tories, and actually suggested that solution to Mr. Balfour, who duly reported it to his uncle, Lord Salisbury. The latter was, however, adamant against Home Rule. So was Churchill, who admitted that the Tories had been badly advised in their Irish policy and by dropping Coercion and flirting with Parnell had largely contributed to Gladstone's 'conversion'. But there was to be no further surrender. Lord Carnarvon's attempt to govern by the ordinary law had lamentably

---

[1] Injustice did not, however, blunt the edge of his wit. 'To get into power I really believe,' wrote Labouchere (December 23), 'that he would not only give up Ireland but Mrs. Gladstone and Herbert.' Lord Salisbury was of the same opinion: 'Gladstone is mad to take office,' he wrote on December 11.

failed. ' Almost immediately after the lapse of the Crimes Act
boycotting increased fourfold.' Those were Gladstone's own
words (April 8, 1886). The National League had trebled the
number of its branches ; magistrates and juries were intimidated,
and in many parts of Ireland the law was openly defied.

Such was the situation when on January 12th the new Par- The New
liament met. A few days later Lord Carnarvon and his Chief Parlia-
Secretary, Sir W. Hart Dyke, resigned,[1] and Mr. W. H. Smith ment
became Chief Secretary and primarily responsible for the government of Ireland.

The Queen's Speech hinted haltingly at a renewal of Coercion,
and on January 26 Hicks Beach gave notice of a motion to suspend all other business, in order to pass a measure for the suppression of the National League. At long last the Cabinet had
decided on resolute action. The die was cast. On the same
night the Government was defeated by 331 to 252 on an amendment to the address moved by Chamberlain's lieutenant, Mr.
Jesse Collings. The amendment regretted the omission from the
Queen's Speech of any measure about allotments for labourers.
' Three Acres and a Cow ' was thus made to play an historic part.
But Ireland was the real point at issue. Chamberlain's brilliant
campaign was crowned with the imprimatur of Parliament ; but
Parnell dominated the situation. Of the majority of 79, 74 were
Parnellites.

Lord Salisbury immediately resigned ; and the Queen, who
for some weeks had been in correspondence with Mr. Goschen,
summoned him to Osborne.

Goschen, standing aloof from all the recognized parties, held Mr.
a unique position among the statesmen of that day. He had Goschen
entered the Cabinet under the premiership of Lord Russell in
1866, and served under Gladstone from 1868 to 1874. He was
out of sympathy, however, with Gladstone both on foreign and
domestic questions, and declined to rejoin him in 1880. His
reputation for sanity and moderation, combined with ardent
patriotism, was an exceptional one, and he might had he chosen
have been Viceroy of India or Speaker of the House of Commons.
The Queen relied greatly on his judgement and almost pathetically

---

[1] For letters interchanged with Lord Salisbury, see Carnarvon's *Life*, III,
211, and for his memorandum for the Cabinet, ibid., 256 f.

turned to him for counsel in her anxiety and perplexity. 'I hope and think Mr. Gladstone could not form a Government.' So she wrote to him on January 27. Lord Salisbury shared her belief. Mr. Goschen did not; and begged to be excused from going to Osborne on the ground that to do so would expose the Queen 'to much misconstruction and misinterpretation and might further compromise the present most critical situation.' He strongly advised the Queen to send, without delay, for Gladstone. Gladstone was accordingly sent for, unhesitatingly accepted office, and formed his third Ministry.

The Third Gladstone Ministry

The new Government differed greatly in personnel from that which had resigned six months earlier. Hartington, Goschen, Derby and Bright all refused to join it. So did Lord Selborne, the great lawyer who occupied the Woolsack in 1880, and Sir Henry James who might have had it in 1886. The Queen refused to allow Lord Granville to return to the Foreign Office, which was given to Lord Rosebery; but the most significant appointment to the new Cabinet was that of Mr. John Morley, an eminent journalist and man of letters, who had entered Parliament in 1883 and now took office for the first time as Chief Secretary for Ireland. Mr. Chamberlain and Sir George Trevelyan joined the ministry on the understanding that they were committed thereby only to 'inquiry'; and when the inquiry led to a conclusion repugnant to them they resigned (March).

It was hinted that had Gladstone handled Chamberlain more tactfully, had he gratified his wish for the Colonial Office, the breach might have been, if not averted, postponed. It is unlikely; for Chamberlain, from first to last, never swerved from the principles on which his own policy was based. 'Sooner than consent to what I fear Mr. G. is contemplating I would go out of politics altogether.' So he had written to Morley on December 28.

Chamberlain and Ireland

On four points Chamberlain was adamant. (1) The scheme of 'Home Rule' must be *federal*, not separatist, consequently Ireland must continue to be represented at Westminster; (2) the taxative powers of the Irish Central Council must be severely restricted; (3) the appointment of judges and magistrates must be retained by the Imperial Government; (4) the 'residual' powers of legislation must be vested in the Imperial Parliament;

the Irish Legislature must exercise only such powers as were delegated to it. In short, Ireland might have a *Provincial* Parliament on terms similar to Ontario, not a *Dominion* Parliament on
the lines of Canada.

On April 8, Gladstone, in a speech of great power, introduced The First
the Home Rule Bill. There was to be a Legislative Body in Dublin to deal with Irish affairs in strict subordination to the Imperial
Parliament. In the Legislature there were to be two ' Orders ' :
one consisting of the 28 Representative Peers of Ireland and 75
members elected by select constituencies ; the other consisting
of 206 members elected by the existing constituencies. The two
' Orders ' were to sit together, though either might demand a
separate vote, and thus exercise a suspensive veto upon the other.
The Irish Legislature was forbidden to make laws relating to the
Crown, the Army, Navy, or defences, treaties, peace or war,
trade and navigation, coinage, customs, excise, and various other
matters ; nor was it to establish or endow any particular Church.
Irish members were no longer to sit in the Imperial Parliament.
As to the Executive, the Lord-Lieutenant was to be converted
into a Constitutional ruler, assisted by a Privy Council, but acting,
ordinarily, on the advice of Ministers responsible to the local
Legislature. This Executive was ultimately to control the Police,
and to appoint the Judges. A week later the Prime Minister
explained the details of his Land Bill : Irish landlords were to
have the option of selling their estates, normally at the price of
twenty years' purchase of the net rental, to the State. The freehold of the farms was then, at their option, to be vested in the
tenants, who were to purchase outright or by a series of annuities
spread over forty-nine years. This scheme was very severely
criticized from more than one quarter, and its unpopularity
reacted unfavourably on the prospects of the Home Rule Bill
with which it was said to be inseparably linked.

Not that the latter had much chance of success. Against
Gadstone was arrayed not only the whole Conservative Opposition, now firmly united, but the flower of the Liberal Party in
both Houses of Parliament, and outside Parliament almost the
whole aristocracy of birth, of intellect and of commerce. Gladstone himself was under no illusions. In a manifesto issued to
his constituents on May 1 he wrote : ' On the side adverse tc the

Government are found, as I sorrowfully admit, in profuse abundance, station, title, wealth, social influence, the professions, or the large majority of them—in a word, the spirit and power of class.' 'He put his faith not in the classes which on many great issues in the past had fought uniformly on the wrong side.' But they had ' uniformly been beaten by a power more difficult to marshal but resistless when marshalled—by the upright sense of the nation.' ' The classes versus the masses.' That was the appeal of the demagogue : and the response of the masses, so lately enfranchised by Gladstone himself, was unequivocal.

Lord Hartington

In the House of Commons Lord Hartington led the opposition to the Bill and was powerfully supported by Goschen and Chamberlain, as well as by Churchill, Hicks Beach and the Tories. Great efforts were made before the Second Reading debate to detach Chamberlain from his new allies, mainly through Labouchere as intermediary ; but in vain. He had taken up his position, after mature deliberation, and nothing would move him from it. Schnadhorst went over to the enemy and tried to carry the Birmingham organization with him. But after a stiff fight Chamberlain emerged triumphant.

Lord Salisbury's Alternative Recipe

On May 15 Lord Salisbury issued a counter-manifesto to Gladstone's in which he set forth the alternative policy on which his Party subsequently fought : ' My alternative policy is that Parliament should enable the Government of England to govern Ireland : apply that recipe honestly, consistently, and resolutely for twenty years, and at the end of that time you will find that Ireland will be fit to accept any gifts in the way of local government or repeal of coercion laws that you may wish to give her. What she wants is government—government that does not flinch, that does not vary ; government that she cannot hope to beat down by agitations at Westminster ; government that is not altered in its resolutions or its temperature by the party changes which take place at Westminster.'

The Second Reading of the Bill was moved on May 10th, but not until June 8 did the division take place, when it was defeated by 343 votes against 313. In the majority were no fewer than 93 Liberals, of whom 46 were reckoned to belong to the Chamberlain wing of a Party now definitely organized as ' Liberal Unionists '.

Gladstone promptly appealed to the constituencies. Parlia- ment was dissolved at the end of June; a terrific fight ensued; but the verdict declared in July was decisive. The Gladstonian Liberals returned less than 200 strong, and but for the staunch adherence of Scotland and Wales to Radicalism would have been still weaker. The English boroughs returned 169 Unionists against 67 Gladstonians, while the counties which had given the Liberals a majority of 50 in December returned in July 172 Unionists against 81 Gladstonians. In all, the Unionists in the new Parliament numbered close on 400, of whom 318 were Tories. The old Liberal Party was shattered; and for twenty years, with one insignificant interlude, the Unionists retained both office and power.

CHAPTER III

THE SALISBURY GOVERNMENT (1886–1892)—DOMESTIC REFORMS

Lord
Salis-
bury's
Second
Ministry

ACCEPTING the verdict of the constituencies, Mr. Gladstone resigned office without awaiting a vote in Parliament.
The Queen at once appealed to Lord Salisbury ' to undertake to
form a Government and *as strong a one as* he *possibly can form* '.
' It seems to her,' she proceeded, ' to be a *time* when every nerve
should be strained, every personal and party feeling should be
set aside, for the *public good* ; and it would be a *great* thing, and
what the *country earnestly wishes* for and *expects*, if he could secure
the assistance of some of the Liberal Unionists.' [1]
    Lord Salisbury's wishes coincided with the Queen's. He
appealed to Lord Hartington to form a Government and offered
to serve under him, conscious that he was better fitted for the
Foreign Office than for the Premiership. Lord Hartington, however, refused.[2] Lord Salisbury proceeded to form a purely Conservative Ministry. The Foreign Office was the main difficulty.
Various names were suggested, notably that of Lord Lyons, the
most distinguished of British diplomatists and still at the Paris
Embassy. Ultimately the office was given as a tardy reparation
to Lord Iddesleigh. The Queen, greatly as she was attached to
that statesman, had her misgivings about his fitness for that
particular post. Six months' tenure of it unfortunately justified
them. Hicks Beach insisted that Churchill should lead the House
as Chancellor of the Exchequer. The Queen objected : ' He is
so mad and odd and has also bad health.' But Hicks Beach prevailed, choosing for himself, with characteristic modesty, courage
and patriotism, the post of greatest difficulty and danger—the
Irish Office. Cross, to the Queen's annoyance, was sent to join

---

[1] *Q.V.L.* (3rd), 1, 164.
[2] For his reasons, cf. Holland, *Devonshire*, II. 169.

Lord Iddesleigh in the Lords, but solaced with the India Office. Churchill insisted that Cross's place at the Home Office should be given to Mr. Henry Matthews, a clever lawyer, who had won a Birmingham seat, but had little Parliamentary experience.[1]

It was believed that Matthews would bring great strength to the Treasury Bench, in ' oratorical power, in which ' (in Salisbury's view) it was ' lamentably weak ' ; and that being a Roman Catholic his appointment would ' favourably influence the moderate Roman Catholics in Ireland '. In neither respect were anticipations fulfilled. In 1895 Matthews went to the House of Lords as Viscount Llandaff. For the rest, the team was composed of much the same men as in 1885, though there was the usual shifting of places.

Strongly entrenched in the House of Commons (so long as Unionist the Liberal Unionists did not oppose them) the Salisbury Government had no easy task before them. Twice within the last twelve months had the enfranchised Celts of Ireland declared, with virtual unanimity, in favour of Home Rule. Their cause had now been espoused with enthusiasm by the most conspicuous statesman of the day. For a moment it had seemed not impossible that his genius and vigour might prevail. Once again, as in the days of Lord Fitzwilliam, Irish hopes had been raised only to be dashed to the ground. How were the Unionists going to tackle the situation ?

Lord Salisbury had declared that what Ireland needed was twenty years of consistently strong and resolute government. The restoration of social order was, therefore, the first plank in the Unionist platform. Sir Redvers Buller, a distinguished soldier, was sent into the West of Ireland to suppress outrages and crimes, whereupon Mr. Parnell produced, in his *Tenants' Relief Bill*, an alternative prescription. In Ireland, as in England, there was genuine distress among agriculturists, but whereas in England the landlords behaved with extraordinary consideration towards their tenants, in Ireland there were some landlords who were disposed to press their legal rights to the uttermost. Parnell, therefore, proposed that rents fixed before 1885 should be

[1] He had sat as a Conservative Home Ruler for Dungarvan (1868–74), where his success was due, by his own account, to a combination of Nationalist and Tory votes gained at the cost of ' 800 bottles of whisky '.

reduced by the Land Court, that leaseholders should be brought under the Act of 1881, and that no tenant should be evicted who paid up his arrears and half his rent. The Bill was rejected by a majority of nearly 100.

The 'Plan of Campaign'

Prompt came the response from Ireland in the ' Plan of Campaign '. This new strategical device was invented by John Dillon and William O'Brien, and was frowned upon by their leader. The device was simplicity itself. The tenants of any given estate were to agree on a ' fair ' rent ; should their offer be declined, the money was to be paid into a war chest and spent on organized resistance to evictions. The ' plan ' was inaugurated in the autumn of 1886, and throughout 1887 the campaign was vigorously sustained. It was a direct challenge to the elementary principles of law, and no Government worthy of the name could have refused to take it up. Consequently, the first business of the new Session (1887) was a Bill to amend the Criminal Law in Ireland. Before this Bill was introduced the personnel of the Ministry had already undergone considerable modification.

Resignation of Lord Randolph Churchill

On the eve of Christmas (1886) the world was startled by the announcement that Lord Salisbury's principal lieutenant had resigned. Lord Randolph Churchill's ministerial career had scarcely begun. By a few months' tenure of the India Office he had established a reputation as a first-rate administrator ; a few weeks' leadership of the House of Commons had convinced friends and foes alike that he would take rank among the great Parliamentarians of the Victorian era ; he had earned the approbation of the Sovereign, and in the Party his supremacy was unquestioned. Well might he regard himself as not only omnipotent but indispensable. Some of his opinions may have sat lightly upon him ; in regard to national economy he had genuine convictions. He believed, with Mr. Gladstone, that so far from being incompatible with efficiency, economy is the complement and test of it.[1] He was determined, moreover, to enforce his views upon his colleagues. Neither Mr. W. H. Smith at the War Office, nor Lord George Hamilton at the Admiralty, would abate materially demands already reduced to a minimum ; the Prime Minister supported them, and Lord Randolph resigned. That he expected

[1] Cf. e.g. Speech at Blackpool, January 24th, 1884, *Speeches*, p. 37.

to be recalled on his own terms is indubitable ; but he had made one grave miscalculation. He afterwards confessed to having ' forgotten Goschen '. His lapse of memory was fatal; his resignation virtually ended a brief but brilliant political career. This narrative may, therefore, regretfully take leave of this ' wayward and spoilt child ' of fortune. Lord Rosebery, who supplied these epithets, held that Lord Randolph could never have continued to co-operate with Lord Salisbury, since the differences between them were fundamental. Mr. Winston Churchill concurs in that view. But it is not easy to understand why the policy which secured the adhesion of a Chamberlain should have alienated a Churchill. The latter was his own worst enemy, or rather was the hapless victim of congenital disease. Consequently the period which elapsed between his resignation and his death (1894) was one of deepening tragedy, and the historian may pass it over in silence, though the biographer may not. The estimate of two friends may, however, be quoted. ' He rarely,' said Mr. Balfour, ' took advice. Even more rarely did he take good advice. Though admirable with subordinates, with equals he was difficult and sometimes impossible.'

A truer judgement was never passed. But equally true was Lord Rosebery's appreciation. ' Randolph's was a generous nature in the largest and strictest sense of the word. . . . His lack of jealousy and personal charm arose from the same quality —that there was no perfection or claim of perfection about him. He was human, eminently human ; full of faults as he himself well knew ; but not base or unpardonable faults ; pugnacious, outrageous, fitful, petulant, but eminently lovable and winning.' Let those words stand as his epitaph ; let his memory rest in peace.

In face of Churchill's resignation Hicks Beach took the view that, failing a coalition with the Liberal Unionists, the Government should resign. Lord Salisbury lost no time in renewing to Lord Hartington the offer declined in July. The latter adhered to his decision, but was willing that Goschen, who had held no office since 1874,[1] should enter the Conservative Government. Goschen, therefore, succeeded Lord Randolph at the Exchequer and proved a tower of strength to the Party with which he was

[1] On account of his opposition to an extension of the franchise.

henceforth associated. W. H. Smith resigned the War Office to Edward Stanhope, and himself became First Lord of the Treasury and Leader of the House of Commons. These changes involved others. Lord Iddesleigh, with characteristic unselfishness, had placed his seat in the Cabinet at the Premier's disposal, in order to facilitate negotiations with the Liberal Unionists. It was, however, from the newspapers that he first learnt that his offer had been accepted and that Lord Salisbury had himself taken over the Foreign Office (Jan. 4th, 1887). He declined the Presidency of the Council, and on January 12th the country was shocked to learn that he had died suddenly in the ante-room of the Premier's official residence at 10 Downing Street. Thus closed, amid circumstances almost tragic, a life of high utility and complete blamelessness. Three months later Sir M. Hicks Beach was compelled, by temporary ill-health, to resign the Irish Office in which he was succeeded by Mr. A. J. Balfour.

Mr. Balfour's rule opens a new chapter in Anglo-Irish relations ; but although Ireland continued, for the next ten years, to hold the centre of the political stage, the story must, for the sake of lucidity, be postponed.

The record of the Salisbury Government in purely domestic affairs was far from insignificant, and may, first, engage attention.

Parliamentary Procedure

The Irish Nationalists threatened to make governments impossible not only in Ireland but at Westminster. Mr. Smith's first task, therefore, was to restore some measure of efficiency and decorum to the House which he was appointed to lead. The new rules of procedure adopted on Gladstone's motion in 1882 had proved insufficient for the purpose, and in March 1887 the House resolved that a debate might be closured by a bare majority, on the motion of any member, provided the Chair accepted the motion and was supported by at least 200 members. A year later the minimum number of supporters was reduced to 100, and the hours of business were rearranged with a view to greater efficiency and dispatch. Mr. Chamberlain, returning to the House, after some months' absence, in March 1888, found the change ' marvellous '. ' The new rules,' he wrote, ' work well and the House has resumed the orderly and dignified conduct of public business. . . . I always felt confident that sooner or later we should shake off the incubus of obstruction, but the

reformation has come and is more complete than I expected.'
The ' reformation ' extended to the writer.   He had just returned
from a sojourn in the United States where, as head of a British
mission, he had succeeded in negotiating terms for the settlement of the long-standing dispute about Fisheries between the
States and Canada.   The Chief Commissioner won golden opinions
on all sides.   He also won, in the person of Miss Mary Endicott,
a very charming bride whom in November 1888 he married as
his third wife.   No wonder that the dual success made him, as
his biographer says, a ' new man ', and that he found the House
' marvellously ' changed for the better.[1]

But the Salisbury Government had not yet sailed into smooth *Depres-*
waters.   Loyally as Lord Hartington supported it, the *entente* *sion of*
between the two wings of the Unionist Party was still far short *Trade*
of an alliance, and the parliamentary position was consequently *and Agri-*
precarious.   Moreover, quite apart from Ireland, apart also from *culture*
the European situation which threatened to issue at any moment
in war,[2] times were difficult.   The agricultural depression which
began in 1879 had become steadily worse ; prices, not only of
agricultural produce, were so low as to discourage enterprise ;
trade was shifty ; employment precarious ; industrial disputes
alarmingly frequent.   A Royal Commission which had been
appointed to inquire into the causes of trade depression reported
in January 1887.   A small minority of four commissioners favoured
a return to Protection under the name of ' Fair Trade ', but a
large majority preferred to recommend less controversial and
less drastic expedients such as cheapening the cost of production,
an improvement of transport facilities, and of technical education
and so on.   They insisted that wages were too high in relation
to prices which were affected not only by foreign competition
but by a scarcity of gold.   The Report served to damp down
the Protectionist agitation, but produced little effect on the
general situation.

Least of all could it be expected to appease the discontent *The un-*
among the unemployed, or to arrest the activities of the agitators *employed*
who menaced social order in London and other great towns.   In
February 1886 a small army organized by the Social Democratic
Federation and headed by John Burns, a working engineer, and

[1] Garvin, II. c. xxxvii.   [2] See *infra*, p. 82 f.

H. M. Hyndman, an ex-Cambridge cricketer, invaded a Fair Trade demonstration in Trafalgar Square, and having dispossessed the demonstration, marched through Clubland, and many of the chief shopping centres of the West End, smashing windows, over-turning carriages and otherwise striking terror into the hearts of law-abiding citizens. For two hours or more, Central London was at the mercy of the mob, though the damage to persons and property was inconsiderable. No arrests were made at the time, but four Socialist leaders, Burns, Hyndman, H. H. Champion (an ex-officer of the R.A.) and Williams, were subsequently prose-cuted for seditious speeches, and after a long trial, in which they conducted with conspicuous ability their own defence, were acquitted, though the jury condemned the language of Burns and Champion as inflammatory.

There was a renewal of ' demonstrations ' in London in the autumn, and again in November 1887, when a serious conflict occurred between the police and a large mob in Trafalgar Square. Meetings in the Square had been prohibited on the technical ground that it was Crown property : but the agitators contested the prohibition. So menacing did the attitude of the mob become that a battalion of Foot Guards and two squadrons of the Life Guards were summoned to the assistance of the police. Nor were the disturbances confined to the metropolis. Riots occurred in 1886–7, in Manchester, Liverpool, Sheffield, Notting-ham, Cardiff and other towns. The exciting causes varied from place to place, and from time to time ; but the great mass of law-abiding citizens could not fail to be perturbed by outward demonstrations of a discontented if not revolutionary spirit. The discontent might arise from legitimate impatience with social and economic conditions. It might, on the other hand, be fomented by those who, from honest conviction or mere malice, desired the overthrow of the existing order. Anyhow, the symp-toms were disquieting : the public was alarmed and perplexed.

Capital and Labour

Even more disquieting than the riotous demonstrations were the recurring conflicts between employers and their workmen, misdescribed as disputes between ' capital and labour '. For no one could pretend that the remuneration of mere capital was, on the average, excessive, or that the ' employer ' was any longer synonymous with the ' capitalist '. The day of the capitalist-employer, of the one man- or family-business, was rapidly passing. Thanks to the *Limited Liability Act* of 1855, capital, instead of being concentrated in relatively few hands, was now very widely diffused. The capital of a single firm was frequently subscribed by thousands of ' shareholders '. This change, destined to work nothing less than a revolution, was, however, hardly realized in the 'eighties, and its economic and social significance was very imperfectly apprehended. Consequently ' labour ' found itself arrayed against ' capital ', provided, in some cases (notably in the cotton mills of Lancashire), by the wage-earners themselves, and in many more by innumerable thrifty folk drawn from all classes.

Nevertheless, despite the diffusion of industrial capital there was a real conflict of economic interests between the different parties among which the total product of an industry or business was distributed, though it was to the common interest of all that the product should be as profitable and large as possible.

Strikes were consequently frequent and in some cases prolonged. In the year 1888 there were over 500 strikes, most of which were settled by arbitration. Among them a strike of the girls employed in match-making by Messrs. Bryant & May attracted special attention. Early in that year the public conscience had been stirred by the publication of a Board of Trade Report on sweated labour. The match-girls afforded a striking illustration of the main thesis of the Report. They were wholly unorganized, but encouraged by the outcry against ' sweating ' they struck work, and the directors, in due course, conceded their demand, more in deference to the pressure of public opinion than to that of their match-girls whose services could easily have been replaced. *Strikes*

Of far wider significance was the strike of the unskilled dock labourers in 1889. The more skilled workers had already combined in their Stevedores' Union ; but the great mass of labourers at the London Docks were unskilled and unorganized, and their employment was casual and intermittent. Many of them had, however, been listening of late to the orators in Trafalgar Square and at dozens of street-corners. Accordingly, when Ben Tillett, a fiery orator, engaged in a tea-warehouse near London Bridge, urged them to form a Union a few of them agreed to do so. They *The Dockers' Strike*

persuaded the dock labourers to demand a uniform rate of pay
of sixpence an hour, for a minimum of four hours. Even thus
the lucky ones might not earn more than 8s. to 10s. a week, since
employment was entirely casual, and the supply of labour greatly
exceeded, except at times of pressure, the demand. The Dock
Companies refused the men's demands ; on 12 August 2,500 men
struck work. John Burns and Tom Mann promptly went to
the assistance of Tillett ; and within a week the strike had
extended to all the London docks. The dockers of Liverpool,
Hull, Grimsby and Glasgow promised to support their brethren
in London, if ships were transferred from London to other ports ;
subscriptions, amounting in all to nearly £50,000, poured in from
sympathizers in all classes ; Cardinal Manning, Canon Liddon,
and Mr. Sydney Buxton, then M.P. for Poplar, laboured hard to
arrange terms of peace ; and the Dock Companies, finding themselves in conflict not only with the labourers but with the ship-
owners and with public opinion in general, after a month's contest gave way. The dockers got their ' tanner ', and what was
even more important a strong Union. On the whole the strike,
thanks in large measure to the influence of John Burns, had been
conducted without disorder ; it had, however, for the time being,
paralysed not only the shipping industry but the wholesale trade
of London, in particular Mincing Lane, and the Corn and Coal
Exchanges. One significant result of the Dockers' Strike was
that the London County Council followed the example already
set by the London School Board and in all its contracts inserted
a ' Fair-wages '-clause. Another was seen in the immense impetus given to Trade Unionism. In a very short time the Dock,
Wharf and Riverside Labourers' Union had, with the energetic
help of Tom Mann as General Secretary, enrolled 40,000 members.
During the last few months of 1889 the Sailors and Firemen's
Union enrolled some 50,000 new members ; Joseph Arch's Agricultural Labourers' Union, which had languished since 1874, suddenly increased its membership from 3,000 to 17,000 ; the Miners'
Federation from 36,000 (1888) to 147,000 (1891) ; the Bricklayers
from 7,000 to 17,000 ; and so on.

But the triumph of the Dockers was not reflected only in a
vast increase in Trade Union membership. It meant, for better
or worse, a revolution in the spirit and aims of Trade Unionism.

Hitherto the Unions had aimed at securing better conditions for wage-earners within the limits of the existing organization of Industry. Henceforward, the 'new' Trade Unionists began to aim at a fundamental reconstruction of the existing order of Society, beginning with the Industrial system on which that order rested. This revolution was to be effected not by force and bloodshed, but by the ballot box and the capture of the parliamentary machine. The Dockers' Strike, then, gave birth, in due course, to the Parliamentary Labour Party. But that is to anticipate events. In the meantime, the strike of the Dockers was followed by many others, among which that among the employés of the South Metropolitan Gas Works was of special significance. It originated in a demand not for higher wages but for improved 'status', and in particular for a voice in the control of workshop conditions, for the regulation of piece-work and the abolition of overtime. The Directors wisely responded by the offer of a profit-sharing scheme. The Union discerned in this offer a subtle attempt to undermine their authority and divert the allegiance of the men. The strike was accordingly prolonged and did not end until February 1890, when the Company's terms were accepted. The profit-sharing principle was adopted : the men were to receive one per cent. increase in wages for every penny by which the price fell below 2s. 8d. per thousand cubic feet. Since every increase in profits is accompanied by a decrease in price, the wage-earners would share in any increment of profit accruing to shareholders. Moreover, the wage-earners were obliged to capitalize at least 50 per cent. of their bonus on wages, thus becoming shareholders in the Company, and were entitled to elect their own representatives on to the Board of Directors, in proportion to the amount of wage-earners' capital. Profit sharing would, at first sight, appear to offer an ideally just solution of the industrial problem. But the Trade Unions, for reasons obvious if not always avowed, have consistently opposed it, while the material advantage to the employés has been, as a rule, insignificant as compared with the substantial increment in wage-rates secured (as they believed) by Trade Union activities. Consequently (except in statutory undertakings such as Gas Companies where profits are regulated by law), the success achieved by Profit-sharing Schemes has been disappointingly meagre and intermittent. At present (1933) there are in operation less than 500 such schemes ; only about 260,000 wage-earners are sharing in profits, and the average bonus is only £9 10s. 2d. per annum, or 4·8 per cent. on earnings.

The Status of Labour To attribute the manifestations of industrial unrest to electoral reform would be fantastic, but the Reform Acts of 1867 and 1884 did undoubtedly tend to inspire the classes then admitted to citizenship with an unwonted sense of their important place in the national economy. The younger wage-earners were, moreover, the product of the new primary schools ; there they had learnt to read ; but only in a few cases had they as yet been taught to think. With a smattering of education and suddenly entrusted with supreme political power, it was small wonder if many of the younger workmen listened eagerly to prophets who prophesied less truthfully than smoothly.

Reform of Local Government Nor did reform stop at Parliament. It extended to the reform of local government in the rural districts. Half a century had elapsed since the abolition of the urban oligarchies, and the time for the application of the democratic principle to rural areas was overdue. The State was anxious to delegate some of its rapidly multiplying responsibilities to local bodies, but most of these involved finance, and it was contrary to fashionable principles to entrust fiscal responsibility to non-elected bodies.

There was an even more urgent reason for reform. During the last half-century local government had been sinking deeper and deeper into chaos. It was, said Mr. Goschen, a ' chaos of authorities, a chaos of jurisdictions, a chaos of rates, a chaos of franchises, a chaos worst of all of areas '. In 1888 there were no fewer than 27,069 independent local authorities taxing the English ratepayer, and taxing him by eighteen different kinds of rates. Among the ' authorities ' were Counties (52), Municipal Boroughs (239), Improvement Act Districts (70), Urban Sanitary Districts (1,006), Port Sanitary Authorities (41), Rural Sanitary Districts (577), School Board Districts (2,051), Highway Districts (424), Burial Board Districts (853), Unions (649), Lighting and Watching Districts (194), Poor Law Parishes (14,946), Highway Parishes not included in urban or highway districts (5,064), Ecclesiastical Parishes (about 1,300).

How had this ' jungle of jurisdictions ' arisen ? For the last half-century Parliament had been busily at work attempting to adapt the existing framework of the administrative system to rapidly changing conditions. And this had been done, perhaps inevitably, by a long course of tinkering, piecemeal legislation. No attempt was made to fit in the new with the old. Act was piled upon Act; each involving new administrative functions and each creating a new authority to perform them. The result was an appalling mass of overlapping, intersecting, and conflicting jurisdictions, authorities, and areas, bewildering to the student and fatal to orderly administration.

Reform, then, was imperatively demanded in two directions: first, the concentration of authorities; and, secondly, the re-adjustment and simplification of areas.

These may be regarded as the guiding principles of the Local Government Acts of 1888 and 1894. The former, popularly known as the County Councils Act, provided for the creation of sixty-two 'Administrative Counties', some of them coterminous with the fifty-two historic shires, but some representing sub-divisions of the same, and sixty or more [1] 'county boroughs'— towns with more than 50,000 inhabitants. It set up in each county or county borough a council consisting of (a) councillors elected for a term of three years by the ratepayers, (b) co-opted aldermen, who were not to exceed in number one-third of the elected councillors. It transferred to these councils the *administrative* functions of *Quarter Sessions*, such as the control of pauper lunatic asylums, of reformatory and industrial schools, local finance, the care of roads and bridges, the appointment of certain county officials, &c.; but while leaving to the *Justices of the Peace* all their *judicial* and licensing functions, it committed to a *Joint Committee* of Justices and County Councillors the control of the county police force. To the above important functions of the County Councils, subsequent Acts (1889 and 1902) added that of the control of education, higher, secondary, and elementary.

A Local Government Act for Scotland, framed on similar lines, was passed in 1889. Meanwhile two spectacular features of the English Bill of 1888 demand further notice. As originally intro-duced the Bill dealt with the thorny question of 'Licensing'. The new County Councils were empowered to extinguish public-

[1] There are now (1945) 83 County Boroughs.

house licences to sell alcoholic liquors, on payment of compensation. But these provisions were so bitterly attacked from both flanks, both by the liquor interest and the temperance reformers, that the Government wisely dropped them, and so lightened the ship.

The reconstruction of London government, also a question bristling with difficulties, constituted, however, an integral part of the scheme, and the Government successfully defended their proposals. The square mile of ' City ' over which the Lord Mayor and Corporation exercised their ancient jurisdiction was prudently left intact. But the rest of London, or more precisely the vast area which since 1856 had come under the Metropolitan Board of Works, was formed into an ' Administrative County ' to be governed, like other counties, by a body directly elected by the ratepayers. The Council consists of 144 members, of whom twenty are Aldermen elected by the Councillors. Each parliamentary division except the City, elects two Councillors ; the City elects four.

The first elections to the new Councils took place in March 1889 and, especially in London, evoked considerable excitement. The new government for London started under the happiest auspices, with Lord Rosebery as the first Chairman of a Council which also included men of great eminence in all walks of life.

The structure of London government was completed by an Act passed in 1899. The Act swept away all the old Vestries and Local Boards, and in their place established twenty-eight Borough Councils composed like other Municipal Councils and endowed with powers similar to, though more restricted than, theirs.

Taken as a whole, the Act of 1888, at once radical in scope and conservative in temper, more than fulfilled the anticipations of its authors. The county magistrates, instead of sulking at their partial dethronement, came forward with public spirit to assume a new rôle and new duties. To their experienced guidance it was due that a profound transition was effected without friction and without breach of continuity.

The reorganization of local government begun by one Conservative Government in 1888, was completed as we have seen by another in 1899. Meanwhile, an important addition to the structure was contributed by the Rosebery Government in 1894. Under the *District and Parish Councils Act* of that year every county was divided into *Districts*, urban and rural, and every district into *Parishes*. In every district and in every rural parish (with more than three hundred inhabitants) there was to be an elected council; in the smallest parishes a primary meeting of all persons on the local government and parliamentary register.[1] To the parish council or meeting the Act transferred all the civil functions of the Vestries, with the control of parish properties, charities, footpaths, &c. To ambitious parish councils was also given power to 'adopt' certain permissive Acts for providing the parish with libraries, baths, light, recreation grounds, &c. The Vestry still retained control over purely ecclesiastical matters —including ecclesiastical charities.

To the intermediate or district council, whether urban or rural, were transferred the control of sanitary affairs and highways. Councillors for rural districts were also to act as Poor Law Guardians. An urban district was virtually a municipality with something less of dignity and less coherence, but with equal powers. The largest districts tend naturally to apply for and obtain 'incorporation' as 'boroughs'.

The Acts of 1888 and 1894 did much to bring order out of the chaos which had existed in local government for the previous half-century, and more recent legislation, notably the Education Act of 1902, illustrated the increasing tendency to simplify areas and consolidate authorities.

Though undeniably efficient, the new scheme of local administration did not make for economy in expenditure. Local taxation and local indebtedness increased indeed with appalling rapidity. The debt liability of Local Authorities in England and Wales which in 1875 stood at about £92,000,000 had increased by 1905 to £483,000,000, and by 1936 to about £1,500,000,000.

In this respect, it is fair to add, Local Authorities did but imitate the extravagance of the Imperial Government. Sir Robert Peel's last budget (1846) provided for an expenditure of £55,000,000. By 1898 it had reached £102,000,000, a figure which

---

[1] This includes women and lodgers. Parishes of less than 300 inhabitants *might* have councils, if they desired it. The smallest Parishes (under 100 inhabitants) were required to obtain the consent of the County Council.

in comparison with an expenditure of £943,649,000 (1938-9) seems almost paltry, but was then regarded as alarming.

During the period under review (1886-92) national finance was in the highly competent hands of Mr. Goschen, but in connexion therewith only two points call for particular notice. In 1888 Goschen carried through a scheme for the conversion of the greater part of the funded debt of the country. The fact that ' Consols ' bearing interest at 3 per cent. stood at that time well above par facilitated an immediate reduction of interest to $2\frac{3}{4}$ per cent., and a further reduction, after 1903, to $2\frac{1}{2}$. The policy did not lack critics, but Goschen's ' City ' experience and connexions stood him in good stead. The hook was craftily baited and greedily swallowed. Nor did the transaction lack the justification of success. Thanks to a long spell of cheap money (due largely to falling trade) ' Goschens ' in 1897 touched $113\frac{7}{8}$. In 1890 Goschen effected important changes in the relations between Imperial and Local Finance. An additional tax was imposed on spirits, and the proceeds of this and part of the existing tax on beer were earmarked to provide compensation for the extinction of publicans' licences. Parliament refused to sanction this appropriation, and eventually the greater part of the money amounting to over £500,000 a year was placed at the disposal of the Local Authorities with a strong hint that they should apply it to technical education.

The State had hitherto been far from lavish in expenditure on education. Not until 1833 did it make any contribution at all; in 1839 the grant was increased to £30,000 a year and in 1846 to £100,000. Only, however, with the passing of the Act of 1870 were Local Authorities empowered to levy a compulsory rate to supplement voluntary efforts for providing elementary education. The Acts of 1876 and 1880 made attendance compulsory. Further steps were taken by Sir William Hart Dyke, who as Vice-President of the Council, was responsible for education from 1886 to 1892. The *Code* of 1890 made it possible to maintain evening continuation schools ; payment on the results of individual examinations—the system initiated by Robert Lowe in 1861—was abolished, and for it a ' block ' grant reckoned on the basis of average attendance was substituted. In 1891 a still more important change was effected. The fees paid by parents were abolished and the State undertook to make good to the Local Authorities the deficiency, then estimated at £2,000,000 a year. Thus elementary education became not merely compulsory but gratuitous. Certain fee-paying schools were, to the satisfaction of not a few parents, permitted to survive, but were sacrificed in 1918 to the doctrinaire passion for uniformity and the democratic jealousy of 'inequality '.

Meanwhile, the State was beginning to take thought about secondary education, conscious, perhaps, of the truth enunciated by Sir Richard Jebb that ' elementary instruction, unless crowned by something higher, is not only barren but may even be dangerous '. Not, however, until the establishment of the new County Councils was any effective step taken towards evolving a coherent system of secondary education for the nation at large. The *Technical Instruction Act* of 1889 empowered the Councils of counties and boroughs to provide technical instruction and for this purpose to levy a rate not exceeding one penny in the £. In 1890 came the windfall mentioned above ; the term ' technical ' was generously interpreted, and thus the ' whisky money ' facilitated a real advance in the national system of education.[1]

Nor did the reforms already enumerated stand alone. An Act of 1888 extended, in the workman's favour, the principle of the Act of 1880, which had established the liability of employers for accidents occurring in the course of their employment to workmen. It also made the Act applicable to seamen—thus achieving an object at which Chamberlain had long aimed. Equally congenial to Chamberlain was the Act of 1887 which made a beginning, if a meagre one, with the provision of allotments for farm labourers. Another Act passed in 1887 conceded the claim persistently urged by the colliers that the majority of the men employed in any coal pit should be entitled to appoint, at the owner's expense, a check-weigher to keep an independent record of each miner's output. The same year witnessed the passing of a Merchandise Marks Act designed to deal with the practice of importing foreign goods and selling them as English. That Act also was the parent of a numerous progeny.

To the two outstanding events of that year, the first meeting of a Colonial Conference and the celebration of the Fiftieth

Social Reform

---

[1] See *infra.* c. xi.

Anniversary of Queen Victoria's accession to the Throne, more detailed reference must be made in a later chapter. Here it must only be added that the record of useful legislation begun in 1887 was maintained until the Parliament elected in 1886 reached its end in the dissolution of 1892. A few examples typical of the legislation of this period may be cited.

An Act passed in 1890 gave effect to many of the recommendations of the Royal Commission on the Housing of the Poor and carried several stages further the provision of Artisans' Dwellings begun by the Disraeli Government in 1875. Provision was made for the ' clearing of insanitary areas, the removal of unhealthy or obstructive buildings, the rehousing of persons displaced, and the erection of dwellings for persons of the working classes '. Complaint was subsequently made that the Act was inadequate, but there were some among the supporters of the Government who in 1890 thought the Act too drastic, and subsequent criticism is difficult to reconcile with the Census Report of 1901. That Report showed a notable decline during the intervening decade in overcrowding, all over the country. Much remained to be done : but to say that is not to depreciate the value and volume of results achieved under the Act of 1890.

A *Tithe Rent Recovery Bill* was introduced in December 1890 and passed into law, despite some factious opposition from certain Welsh members, in 1891. By transferring the responsibility for the payment of Tithes from the occupier to the owner it put a stop for thirty years to an agitation which was provoking strife between clerical tithe owners and their parishioners, and eased the burdens of agricultural tenants as a class at the expense of their landlords. After the extensive purchase of farms by occupying tenants in post-War years the alleged grievance reemerged, but has been finally extinguished by the *Tithe Redemption Act* of 1936.

Earlier legislation was in several important respects amended and enlarged by the *Factory Act* of 1890. Power was given to local authorities to enforce sanitary conditions in factories, and the Home Secretary was empowered to act, should the local authorities prove negligent. He was also empowered to certify dangerous and unhealthy trades, and to insist that every occupier of a workshop and contractor for work should keep a list of his outworkers.

The last days of the Salisbury Government were devoted to two useful measures. A *Shop Hours Act* (1892) prohibited the employment of young persons under eighteen years of age for more than seventy-four hours in a week, including meal-times ; while in 1892 Mr. Henry Chaplin signalized the close of his reign at the Board of Agriculture, which at long last had come into being in 1889, by placing on the Statute book his *Small Agricultural Holdings Bill.* This Act enabled the County Councils to acquire, by voluntary agreement, land suitable for reselling in lots of from one to fifty acres to purchasers prepared to cultivate it, ' to deposit one-fifth of the purchase money and undertake to pay the interest and the remainder of the capital money over a period of fifty years '. Lots not exceeding ten acres might be let on certain conditions instead of sold. The Act failed to achieve its purpose. By 1895 only eight County Councils had put the Act in operation, and the total amount of land purchased in Great Britain aggregated only 483 acres. An amending Act of 1907 met no better fate. The truth is that the multiplication of small-holdings is a panacea chiefly though vociferously advocated by doctrinaires, who have little experience of farming conditions, and are only superficially acquainted with the idiosyncrasies of the English agricultural population. Nor have these folk learnt wisdom from the expensive experiments in land settlement tried in post-War days. The reasons for the failure of much experimental legislation since 1892 are to be found, indeed, as much in psychology as in economic and climatic conditions, or in fiscal policy.

The foregoing summary, though hardly more than catalogic, should suffice to show that the legislative output of the Salisbury Parliament, despite the unavoidable preoccupation of the Premier with Foreign Affairs, and of the Government as a whole with Ireland, compares favourably with that of any similar period. As regards social reform there had, indeed, been nothing comparable with it except the Disraeli Parliament of 1874–80. That the results of this legislative activity were disappointing may frankly be conceded. Legislation rarely achieves the anticipated results ; and for an obvious reason. It generally touches only the surface of things ; it deals not with causes but with symptoms. This is inevitable :

> How small of all that human hearts endure
> The part which laws or kings can cause or cure.

Dr. Johnson penetrated to the heart of the problem. The laws, as Burke said, reach but a very little way. But they do reach some way ; as Ireland in these years demonstrated. The amazing improvement in the state of Ireland was, indeed, due not to laws, new or old, but, as the next chapter will disclose, to the skilful, strong and sympathetic administration of Mr. Balfour. By 1891 he had so far accomplished the work he had set out to do that he felt justified in handing over the reins to another Whip. On the same day that Parnell died at Brighton (October 6) there passed away full of years and honour W. H. Smith, who since 1887 had led the House of Commons with conspicuous ability and success. W. H. Smith was a fine type of the middle-class Englishman. Endowed with great business acumen he had made a large fortune, and in making it had done nothing but good to his fellow citizens. As a member of the first London School Board (1871), as the representative of Westminster in the House of Commons from 1868 until the day of his death, at the Treasury, at the Admiralty, and at the War Office, he had served well his generation. Utterly devoid of vanity and selfishness he had sought no reward but that of honourable service. Disarmingly simple, transparently honest, invariably courteous, ' Old Morality ' won the respect of his opponents while retaining the affection of his friends. He died, a victim to the overwork necessitated by the great position he had never sought, by all parties sincerely mourned. By the universal acclaim of his Party the man who had achieved brilliant success as Chief Secretary for Ireland was called to fill the vacant place. But his uncle and leader was not without misgivings. ' There is no help for it,—Arthur must take it. Beach was possible : Goschen is not. But I think it is bad for Arthur, and I do not feel certain how the experiment will end.' So the Prime Minister wrote to Lady Salisbury on October 14, 1891. His misgivings, shared by Mr. Balfour himself, were not wholly without foundation.

Death of
W. H.
Smith

CHAPTER IV

ENGLISH PARTIES AND IRISH HOPES

GOOD as was its record in domestic legislation, and brilliantly Mr. Balfour's
rule in
Ireland as Lord Salisbury had directed the work of the Foreign Office, it is by its administration of Ireland that his Government will, at the bar of History, be judged.

That administration was primarily the work of one man.

Arthur Balfour's rise to fame was rapid. A Scottish laird, nephew of Lord Salisbury, a distinguished *alumnus* of Trinity College, Cambridge, he entered the House of Commons in 1875 as a man of twenty-seven under his uncle's auspices as member for the borough of Hertford. In the 1880 Parliament he was a somewhat detached member of the *Fourth Party*, which under the intrepid leadership of Lord Randolph Churchill gave some trouble to Mr. Gladstone and much more to Sir Stafford Northcote. 'As he sprawled' (to quote 'Toby, M.P.', Punch's brilliant diarist) 'on the bench below the gangway he was taken at best for a Parliamentary *flaneur*, a trifler with debate, anxious chiefly in some leisure moments to practise the paces learned in the hall of the Union at Cambridge. He was not sufficiently in earnest or adequately industrious to take his full share in the labours of the Fourth Party. . . . The fair-faced, languid youth, too indolent to stand bolt upright, was the very last person likely to develop into a civil Cromwell, the most unbending thorough administrator of iron rule Ireland has known since '98.'

But little as its presence was suspected there was under the silken glove the mailed hand.

A man of high courage, perfect temper, and winning personality Arthur Balfour was admirably qualified for his difficult task. Neither lawlessness in Ireland nor abuse at Westminster disturbed his serenity, or deflected his course of action. Having armed himself with a new and effective weapon he pursued the policy marked out for him without haste, without acerbity, and with unfaltering determination and consistency. The new weapon was the Criminal Law Amendment Act (Ireland) of 1887. This Act differed from previous Coercion Acts in that its provisions were permanent. The Lord-Lieutenant was authorized to declare an association to be 'unlawful', and to proclaim a district as

Parnell-ism and Crime

'disturbed'. The powers of the Resident Magistrates—'Balfour's removables' as they were nicknamed—were greatly enlarged; in particular they were empowered to try summarily cases of conspiracy. The passing of this Crimes Act was facilitated, on the one hand by the new rules of procedure which, as mentioned before, were adroitly carried through the House by Mr. Smith, on the other by the publication in *The Times* of a series of articles on *Parnellism and Crime*. The object of the articles was to establish the complicity of the Nationalist leaders in recent agrarian crime. On April 18th, 1887—the date appointed for the Second Reading of the Crimes Bill—*The Times* printed in facsimile what purported to be a letter from Mr. Parnell to an anonymous correspondent, apologizing for having had to denounce the murder of Mr. Burke in Phoenix Park.

The letter dated ' 15.v. 82 ', nine days after the Phoenix Park murders, ran as follows :—

' DEAR SIR,—

I am not surprised at your friend's anger, but he and you should know that to denounce the murders was the only course open to us. To do that promptly was plainly our best policy. But you can tell him and all others concerned that, though I regret the accident of Lord F. Cavendish's death, I cannot refuse to admit that Burke got no more than his deserts. You are at liberty to show him this, and others whom you can trust also, but let not my address be known. He can write to House of Commons.

Yours very truly
CHA.ˢ S PARNELL.'

C. S. Parnell

The letter created an immense sensation. At the time when it appeared Parnell had attained a position unique in the history of Irish politics. By descent an English aristocrat, in religion a

Protestant Episcopalian, he had inherited from his father a fine estate in Ireland and from his mother a bitter hatred of England. Entering the House of Commons in the same year as Mr. Balfour (1875), he found some fifty Irish Repealers led by Isaac Butt, a moderate Home Ruler, but successfully incited to obstructive tactics by Joseph Biggar. Biggar was a man of some business ability—he had made a large fortune out of pork in Belfast—but a poor speaker, hideous in aspect, of indifferent character but unbounded impudence. He had no endowments of body or mind wherewith to impress Parliament, but he determined, if not to dominate, to debase it, and bring it into contempt. In striking contrast to this satyr was the young member for Co. Meath. His morals were not perhaps much better than Biggar's, but he was of gentle birth, fine presence and fastidious tastes. He was no orator in the Irish sense ; if he was inspired by enthusiasm he rarely displayed it, nor was he at any pains to conceal his contempt for the men whom he had to call colleagues. He dominated them by sheer force of intellect and will, as a fearless rider masters a restive horse. Though he had been at Cambridge for a time he had little or no book learning, he was grossly superstitious, and could not bear the thought of death or the sight of blood.

On Isaac Butt's death in 1879, Parnell, who had ousted him from the Presidency of the Home Rule Confederation of Great Britain in 1877, was elected Chairman of the Irish Parliamentary Party. Crime, especially if it involved cruelty to man or beast, repelled this sensitive man. But in the Land League founded by Michael Davitt in 1879 he perceived a serviceable weapon wherewith to attack the landlord garrison in Ireland and so achieve his own purely political end, the destruction of English ascendancy. He could not, therefore, repudiate or repress the agrarian agitation, and his public association with it led in October 1881 to his imprisonment in Kilmainham. Thence issued the famous ' No Rent ' manifesto. Parnell's release (May 8) was immediately followed by the Phoenix Park murders, the news of which so completely unnerved him that he offered his resignation to Mr. Gladstone.

Like Chamberlain and Churchill, Parnell was quick to perceive the significance of the Reform Bill which raised the Irish electorate from 200,000 to 700,000. Speaking at Cork in 1885 he made an historic declaration : ' No man has a right to fix a boundary to the march of a nation. . . . We have never attempted to fix the *ne plus ultra* to the progress of Ireland's nationhood and we never shall.' Chamberlain denied the nationhood ; Gladstone, like the British signatories of the Treaty of 1921, fondly imagined that, while recognizing it, he could fix a boundary to it.

The Crimes Act and the Parnell Letter

The ' Parnell letter ' appeared on April 18, 1887. On that evening the *Crimes Bill* passed its second reading in the House of Commons by a majority of 101 (370 to 269). Immediately before the division Parnell rose, and passionately disclaimed all knowledge of the ' villainous and barefaced forgery,' this ' unblushing fabrication '. ' I certainly never heard of the letter,' he declared, ' I never directed such a letter to be written. I never saw such a letter before I saw it in *The Times* this morning. . . .'

Parnell, as we now know, spoke the truth ; but though Gladstone and his colleagues accepted his disclaimer, the public at large was more sceptical. Scepticism deepened when Parnell refused the offer of the Government to pay the expenses of a libel action against *The Times*. Gladstone proposed the appointment of a Select Committee, but that was negatived and for twelve months the matter dropped.

Meanwhile, the *Crimes Act* was passed, together with a *Land Act*, which gave power to the Land Court to revise the rents judicially fixed under the Act of 1881, and admitted leaseholders to the benefits of that Act.

The state of Ireland

In Ireland, however, things went from bad to worse.

Lawlessness probably reached its acme in the autumn of 1887. Balfour and his Crimes Act were defied by the Nationalist leaders ; but in July eighteen counties were proclaimed under the Act, and on August 19th the National League was proclaimed as an unlawful association. On September 9th a meeting attended by 8,000 persons was held in the market-place of Michelstown, Co. Cork. The police, while attempting to protect the Government reporter, were attacked with stones and blackthorns and compelled to retreat to barracks, whence they fired, with fatal effect, on the crowd. ' Remember Michelstown ' was immediately adopted as a slogan by the Nationalists. Before the close of the year Mr. William O'Brien, M.P. for Co. Cork, and several other members of Parliament, Mr. T. D. Sullivan, Lord Mayor of Dublin, and Mr. Wilfrid Scawen Blunt, an English sympathizer, who had mixed himself up in Irish eviction affrays, were convicted under the Crimes Act and imprisoned. It was a struggle *à outrance* between the forces of order and disorder, but the law, thanks to the steady persistence of Mr. Balfour, slowly but surely won.

In the summer of 1888 the controversy aroused by *Parnellism and Crime* was revived by an action for libel entered against *The Times* by one F. H. O'Donnell, a former member of the Irish Parliamentary Party. The Attorney-General, Sir Richard Webster, counsel for *The Times*, practically converted his defence of his clients into an indictment of Parnell, and stated his intention of proving that not only the letter published in April but others of a like nature were actually written by Parnell. O'Donnell declined to go into the witness-box, and the case terminated somewhat abruptly in a verdict for *The Times* (July 5).

On the following day Parnell rose from his place in the House to contradict the charges made against him by the Attorney-General. In a level unimpassioned tone he read out the incriminating letters, one after another, seven in all, and simply denied all knowledge of them. 'I will only say,' he concluded, ' that the absurdity of the whole series of letters, with one or two trifling exceptions which I have pointed out, must be palpable on the face of them to every fair-minded man.' [1]

The Times retorted that they were prepared with legal proof of the authenticity of the letters ; Parnell then asked for a Select Committee which the Government refused to grant. In its stead they introduced, and after long debate, Parliament passed, a Bill setting up a Special Commission to investigate the charges.

The Parnell Commission

[1] I happened to be at the House, as a visitor, during this statement and prejudiced as I was against Parnell, was impressed by his apparent sincerity. Three months later I was dining with a friend in Dublin, who asked me my opinion about the ' Parnell Letters '. I replied, rather carelessly, ' I suppose Parnell wrote them.' ' He did not,' retorted my host, ' and I will tell you who did—Richard Pigott.' It was in September 1888, a month before the Commission began its hearing, and five months before Pigott was put into the box that a casual visitor to Dublin learned (in confidence) the name of the forger of the famous letter.

Three distinguished Judges, Sir James Hannen, Sir John Day, and Sir A. L. Smith, consented to serve on the Commission which was in effect, if not in form, a State trial of high significance. The Attorney-General was the principal counsel for *The Times*, Sir Charles Russell, afterwards Lord Russell of Killowen and Lord Chief Justice of England, for the defendants. The Commission sat for 128 days,[1] and examined more than 450 witnesses. Only at one moment during this protracted period was the dramatic interest really tense. That was when, towards the end of February, an old and broken man was put into the witness-box, and subjected to a scathing cross-examination by Sir Charles Russell. The man was Richard Pigott, a needy journalist, and now revealed to the world as the forger of the famous letter. After enduring torture in the witness-box for two days the miserable man fled the country, leaving a full confession behind him. Before the police could execute a warrant for his arrest he shot himself in Madrid (March 1st). Meanwhile Parnell had gone into the box, and had denied on oath the authenticity of the letters, whereupon *The Times* offered an apology and withdrew the forged documents. With this withdrawal much of the popular interest in the case evaporated, but by no means all its significance.

The Liberals naturally made all the party-capital they could out of the incident. Parnell was the hero of the hour. He was entertained by Liberal Clubs, received the freedom of Edinburgh, stayed with Mr. Gladstone at Hawarden, and accepted a gift of £3,000, publicly subscribed, towards his expenses in connexion with the Special Commission.

Report of the Commission   On February 13th, 1890, the Commissioners presented their Report. They found, of course, that the facsimile letter was a forgery, and they acquitted Mr. Parnell and his colleagues of the charge of insincerity in their denunciation of the Phoenix Park murders. They found that the respondents collectively were not members of a conspiracy having for its object the absolute independence of Ireland, ' but that some of them had established the Land League ' with the intention by its means to bring about the absolute independence of Ireland, and that they had conspired, by means of an agrarian agitation, to ' impoverish and expel from the country ' the Irish landlords who were styled the ' English

[1] Until November 1889.

Garrison'; that they had incited to the intimidation that produced crime, and had promoted the defence of agrarian crime.

What was to be done with the Report? The Government moved that the House thank the Commissioners for their just and impartial conduct, adopt the Report and enter it upon the Journals. Mr. Gladstone tried to persuade the House to record 'its reprobation of the false charges of the gravest and most odious description, based on calumny and on forgery that had been brought against members of the House'. It was clear that the terms of Gladstone's amendment went, in exculpation, far beyond the findings of the Commission; it was rejected by a substantial majority, and the Government had its way.

No impartial person could interpret the findings of the Commission as a general acquittal for the Parnellites. Nevertheless, it was inevitable that the revelation of the carelessness and blunders of *The Times*, and the exposure of Pigott's forgery, should have caused some revulsion of popular feeling. Mr. Gladstone and his Party were immensely elated by the issue, and the Unionists correspondingly chagrined. But the elation was short-lived. Mr. Parnell had entered an action for libel against *The Times* in 1888; in February 1890 the case was compromised by the payment of £5,000 damages. Before the compromise was reached Parnell was already involved in litigation of another kind.

He was cited as co-respondent in a suit brought by Captain O'Shea for divorce from his wife. O'Shea was an Irish Roman Catholic who had held a commission in the 18th Hussars and in 1880 entered Parliament as member for Co. Clare. Mrs. O'Shea (née Page Wood), the daughter of a parson and niece of a Lord Chancellor, met Parnell for the first time in 1880, and from then until his death in 1891 Parnell was her lover. Both O'Shea and his wife acted for many years as intermediaries between the Radicals and the Irish Nationalists; but in 1886 O'Shea retired from politics, and in November 1890 filed a petition against his wife and Parnell. There was no defence; and as soon as the decree *nisi* was made absolute Parnell and Kitty O'Shea were married (June 25, 1891).

In the meantime much had happened of high consequence to the Irish Nationalists and their English allies.

Glad-
stone and
Parnell

Parnell had affected to believe that the divorce suit was a matter of merely personal interest and on the pronouncement of the decree *nisi* (November 15, 1890) the Irish National League, at the instigation of John Redmond, resolved to stand by him. Gladstone held that ' abstractedly ' the Irish had a right to decide the question ; but it was not the abstract aspect of the matter that interested his followers. Their concern was with the concrete effect of the scandal upon the fortunes of the Liberal Party. Much of the strength of that Party was derived from Scotland. ' Whether they are right or wrong my belief is that the Scotch will not tolerate P. in his position of quasi-partnership with the Liberal leaders.' So Sir Henry Campbell-Bannerman wrote (November 20) to Harcourt. On the next day the National Liberal Federation met at Sheffield. With the greatest difficulty Harcourt and Morley averted a formal pronouncement in the sense indicated by Campbell-Bannerman, and on the 22nd Harcourt reported to Gladstone that ' the opinion was *absolutely unanimous and extremely strong* that, if Parnell is allowed to remain as the leader of the Irish Party, all further co-operation between them and the English Liberals must be at an end. You know that the Nonconformists are the backbone of our Party, and their judgement on this matter is unhesitating and decisive '. Mr. Gladstone at once accepted that judgement and on November 24 in a letter to Morley to be communicated to Parnell Gladstone expressed his view that Parnell's ' continuance in the leadership would be productive of consequences disastrous in the highest degree to the cause of Ireland '.

The same evening Gladstone sent for Mr. Justin McCarthy [1] and gave him an identical message. As far as is known it never reached Parnell. On November 25 Parliament met. The Irish Party met as usual to elect their Chairman. Parnell entered the Committee Room ' looking as if we had committed adultery with his wife '. With great enthusiasm he was unanimously re-elected Chairman. Only after the meeting did Morley run Parnell to earth and read to him Gladstone's letter. He was perfectly unconcerned, and perfectly obdurate. ' Of course,' he said, ' Mr. Gladstone will have to attack me. I shall expect that. He will have a right to do that.' No more.

[1] A distinguished journalist and highly respected member of the Irish Party.

To Mr. Gladstone only one course was open. He immediately published his letter. The thundercloud burst. For some weeks confusion prevailed in the Home Rule camp. Dillon and O'Brien, then in the United States, called upon Parnell to resign ; Healy vehemently urged the same conclusion upon his colleagues in Committee Room No. 15 ; the Roman Catholic Bishops issued a pronouncement of similar purport. But Parnell held grimly on. He would neither abdicate, nor submit to deposition. At length (December 6th) a majority of his colleagues, forty-four in number, withdrew their allegiance, and elected Mr. Justin McCarthy as their leader. Twenty-six remained faithful to the old Chief. For nine months Parnell made frantic efforts to maintain his position in Ireland. His pluck was superb, but all the cards were against him, and on October 6th, 1891, the painful struggle was terminated by his premature death. Thus was removed from the political stage one of the most remarkable personalities of the century. ' On the list of Irish patriots ' Mr. Gladstone placed him ' with or next to Daniel O'Connell ', deeming him to be ' of more masculine and stronger character than Grattan '. That he loved Ireland is certain ; whether his love for Ireland was as intense as his hatred of England is doubtful. His family history suggests that there was madness in his blood ; his own behaviour confirms the suspicion. Yet no statesman of the time was more clear as to his objective, or more resolute in pursuit of it. That his objective was an independent Irish Republic there can be little doubt ; still less that had he lived to become its President his rule in Ireland would have been as dictatorial as it was in Committee Room No. 15. He required of his followers unquestioning obedience : it was given. He sought not their love ; nor did he obtain it. Healy's venomous description of his Chief as ' a cold-blooded sensualist ' was as unjust as it was inapt. Not for him was the promiscuous dalliance characteristic of some of his colleagues. His affections were fixed on one woman ; that she was the wife of a friend was grievously unfortunate : that he was as passionately devoted to her as she to him is certain. ' Tragedy ' is a term now applied to every sordid crime or violent death, but if there ever was in politics a truly tragic career—pure drama from start to finish—it was that of Charles Stewart Parnell.

Death of Parnell

Parnell's death was followed almost immediately by the transference of Mr. Balfour from the Irish Office to the Treasury, and his succession to the leadership of the House of Commons. He had accomplished the task to which he had set his hand in Ireland. He had shown himself sympathetic towards undeserved suffering, quick to devise healing remedies, but, above all, inflexibly firm in the vindication of law. He had greatly extended the operation of the Ashbourne Act, and had set up a Commission for dealing with congested districts. He proposed, in 1892, to crown his work by a large measure of Local Government, but the scheme was coldly received, and early in June it was abandoned. A few weeks later Parliament was dissolved.

General Election of 1892

The General Election which ensued grievously disappointed the hopes of Mr. Gladstone. Instead of the majority of at least 100 on which he had confidently counted, the country gave him one of 40, and that highly precarious in composition. England was still staunchly Unionist, but was overborne by the ' Celtic fringe '. In the new Parliament the Unionists numbered 315, of whom 269 were Conservatives, the Gladstonian Liberals 269, and the Irish Home Rulers 81. Of the latter 9 counted as Parnellites. Mr. Gladstone's own majority at Midlothian dropped from 4,000 to 690. In view of the composite majority opposed to him Lord Salisbury decided to meet Parliament, but, on an amendment to the Address, he was beaten by a majority of 40,

Mr. Gladstone's Fourth Ministry

and in August he gave way to Mr. Gladstone, who, at the age of 83, took office for the fourth time. The Cabinet of 1892 differed little in personnel from that of 1886, but was reinforced by Mr. H. H. Asquith, a young Oxonian who had quickly established a reputation at the Bar and in Parliament, and now became Home Secretary, by Mr. Bryce, a great jurist, by Mr. H. H. Fowler, a shrewd provincial solicitor, who did admirable work at the Local Government Board, and by Mr. A. H. D. Acland, a zealot for education. The new Ministry at once (September 1892) suspended by proclamation the operation of the Crimes Act in Ireland, and thus cleared the decks for the great measure of 1893.

The second edition of Home Rule, 1893

The second edition of Home Rule was disclosed to the House by the Prime Minister on February 13th, 1893. In several important particulars it differed from the first. The single-chamber device with its two ' Orders ' was dropped, and the bicameral system was frankly adopted.   The Legislative Council of forty-eight members was to be elected for eight years by persons who owned or occupied land of the rateable value of £20 per annum. The Legislative Assembly was to consist of 103 members, elected by the existing constituencies, except Trinity College.   Should the two Chambers disagree, the question was to be decided, but only after the lapse of two years, in joint session by a majority. In the original draft Irish members, to the number of eighty, were to be retained at Westminster, but not to vote on questions affecting Great Britain exclusively.   This ' in and out ' clause was subsequently dropped, and the Irish members were retained for all purposes.

The Second Reading of the Bill proposed on April 6 was carried, after a debate extending over twelve days, by a majority of 43.   Protracted as it was, the debate was sustained at a high level by Gladstone, Asquith and Morley on the one side, and Balfour, Chamberlain, Goschen, Hicks Beach, Carson and David Plunket on the other.   The Committee stage of the Bill occupied sixty-three sittings and the whole proceedings eighty-two.   Not until September 1 was the Third Reading at last carried by 301 votes against 267.   The driving power of the octogenarian who had literally pushed the Bill through was nothing short of amazing, and extorted the admiration of foes no less than friends. ' Talma, Keen, Kemble,' wrote Morley, ' might have envied his magical transitions . . . in spite of party passion the whole House watched him with wonder and delight as children watch a wizard.' [1]   But ' magic ' had some drawbacks, as Morley admitted, when the Bill was in Committee.   Gladstone's ' discursive treatment exposed an enormous surface.   His abundance of illustration multiplied points for debate '.   He ' always supposed that a great theme needs to be copiously handled, which is perhaps doubtful, and indeed is often an exact inversion of the true state of things '.   The protraction of the debate was not, then, wholly due, as was commonly alleged, to the obstructive tactics of the Unionist Opposition.

The Lords made short work of the Bill which, after four nights of brilliant debate, they rejected by 419 votes to 41 (September 8).   Not, however, until March 5, 1894, was this Session,

---

[1] *Recollections*, i. 358.

the most protracted in the history of Parliament, brought to a close.

Ought Mr. Gladstone, on the rejection of the Bill by the House of Lords, to have appealed to the country ? On the tactical question there was some division of opinion. Gladstone strongly favoured a dissolution, and an appeal to the electorate on the single issue of Commons *v.* Lords. But to his lasting regret he was overborne by his colleagues. The country might have given him the mandate he wanted ; or it might not. Denied the opportunity of bringing the matter to an issue, Mr. Gladstone decided that his part in the great drama was played. Moreover, between him and some of his most important colleagues there was on the Estimates for the Navy what Gladstone himself described as ' profound disagreement '.

Resignation of Gladstone

Accordingly, on his return from Biarritz (February 1894), weighed down by increasing infirmity of sight and hearing, and sincerely desiring a quiet interval between the turmoil of politics and the grave, he resigned office. He held his last Cabinet on March 1, and on the same day made his last speech in the House of Commons. The speech, made on the Lords' Amendments to the *District and Parish Councils Bill,* was a call to battle against the hereditary Chamber. Those Amendments, though in themselves of slight importance, seemed to him to raise a ' question enormously large, a question which has become profoundly acute, which will demand a settlement and must receive at an early date that settlement from the highest authority '—the electorate. That was Mr. Gladstone's farewell to a Chamber which he had first entered sixty-one years before.

Death of Gladstone

The interval he had desired between Parliament and the grave lasted for four years. He emerged from his retirement to plead the cause of the Armenian Christians in 1896 ; on May 19th, 1898, after some months of suffering, he passed away.

In both Houses of Parliament and by the Press of the whole world, noble tributes were paid to Gladstone's memory ; Lord Salisbury emphasized ' the universal consent of all persons, of all classes and of all schools of thought in doing honour to a man who has been more mixed up in political conflict than probably any man that our history records '. The reason for this unanimity he characteristically found in Mr. Gladstone's pursuit of a ' high moral ideal '. ' What he sought was the achievement of great ideals, and whether they were based upon sound convictions or not they could have issued from nothing but the purest moral aspirations. . . . He will leave behind him . . . the memory of a great Christian statesman.' Lord Rosebery sounded the same note. Mr. Balfour spoke of him as ' the greatest member of the greatest deliberative assembly which so far the world has seen '. ' He brought to our debates,' he added, ' a genius which raised in the general estimation the whole level of our proceedings.' Sir William Harcourt spoke with great affection of his old Chief, of his patience, his modesty, his tolerance, while a tribute not less sincere or eloquent was paid on behalf of Ireland by John Dillon.

To Gladstone's charm, as a man, to his courtesy, to his eager pursuit of knowledge, his modest anxiety to learn of all who could teach him, his marvellous versatility and mental energy even to extreme old age innumerable tributes have been paid, but none more striking than those of two unbending Tories, who as young men were brought into contact with Mr. Gladstone, when as an old man he revisited Oxford and stayed in College rooms at All Souls. [1]

For a final appreciation of a statesman who played so large and so controversial a part in public affairs, who excited in unusual measure alike admiration and detestation, the time has not, perhaps, arrived. But this much may be said. Though lacking the simplicity and directness characteristic of Bright, he was a consummate orator. Endowed by nature with a commanding presence and a sonorous voice, he acquired by art an extraordinary command of language and uncommon felicity of illustration. As a debater he was not equal to Disraeli, lacking his imperturbable temper and his sense of humour ; and although he could rouse intense enthusiasm among his followers, he cannot be said, like Peel, to have ' played on the House like an old fiddle '. Great as an orator he was still greater as a man ; marvellous in the versatility of his interests, and touching life on many sides ; a genuine scholar of the old Oxford School, and a devoted son of the Anglican Church. As a statesman his greatest strength

[1] C. R. L. Fletcher, *Mr. Gladstone at All Souls* (1908) ; Sir C. Oman, *Things I Have Seen* (1933).

lay in finance. He had been admirably trained in the school of Peel, and he was, throughout his career, a jealous guardian of the public purse. Perhaps he spent too much of his ministerial life at the Treasury ; undoubtedly he spent too much of his public life in the House of Commons. Consequently his statesmanship was of the strictly parliamentary type ; his gaze was too closely concentrated upon tactics, sometimes, as in 1884–5, with disastrous results. To say that his outlook was insular would be untrue ; no man had a more vivid sympathy with oppressed nationalities, or a more touching faith in the universal efficacy of parliamentary institutions. But although he was frequently aroused to vehement speech by tales of oppression and occasionally to prompt action, as, for example, by the bad faith of Russia in regard to the Penjdeh incident, yet his interest in external affairs was intermittent, and his temper, in such matters only, was apt to be procrastinating. Nevertheless, no one could look upon him without a sense that here was a man cast in an heroic mould, and that whether right on a given question or wrong, in nothing was he less than great.

CHAPTER V

LIBERALISM IN FETTERS

AFTER Gladstone's resignation his Party fell on evil days. Some held that Liberalism had done its essential work; certain it was that the era of liberating reform was closed. As a prevalent philosophy *laisser-faire*, if not actually dead, was passing to a grave less honoured than it should be. Even if it be true that its influence lingered too long, it will hardly be denied that under the inspiration of its leading doctrine legislation had aimed at securing the greatest happiness of the greatest number, and considerable practical results had been achieved. But towards the close of the century political interest began to shift from questions of administrative and constitutional reform on the one hand to economic and social problems, the solution of which appeared to involve the interference of the State; on the other to problems Imperial and International.

Gladstone was a typical representative of the Manchester School in relation alike to domestic and external affairs.

To whatever school his successor belonged it was not that. The Who that successor would be was a question eagerly canvassed Rosebery Ministry before Gladstone's retirement. It was decided by the Queen. Had Gladstone been consulted he would have named not (as was generally supposed) Sir William Harcourt, who ' he was told was not popular ', but Lord Spencer. The Queen sent for Lord Rosebery, who after much hesitation accepted the commission to form a Government. Harcourt agreed to remain Chancellor of the Exchequer with the leadership of the House of Commons, on condition that he saw all the Foreign Office papers, had some control over patronage, and was free to act, on occasion, without consulting the Prime Minister. Rosebery was, in fact, as ' strongly averse to serving " over " Harcourt ', as Harcourt was to serving under Rosebery; but the Cabinet was almost unanimously opposed to Harcourt's succession. John Morley was determined not to serve under Harcourt; he was even doubtful whether he could serve with him. He coveted the Foreign Office and was angry with Rosebery for preferring Lord Kimberley.

Lord Rosebery's position was, from the first, almost impossible. As he himself expressed it, his was 'the most uneasy throne in Europe since that of Poland'. Yet to this spoiled child of fortune the Premiership had been an object of lifelong ambition, and he attained it at the age of 47. Unfortunately he had been deprived by his early succession to the peerage of the disciplining effect of service in the House of Commons; nor had his official apprenticeship been arduous or prolonged. Born in 1847 he had first come into public notice as Gladstone's host during the Midlothian campaign of 1879–80. He served under Harcourt, as Under-Secretary at the Home Office, 1881–3, entered the Cabinet as Lord Privy Seal and First Commissioner for Public Works in 1885, was designated by Gladstone, in 1885, as 'the man of the future', and in the brief Liberal Ministry of 1886 served as Foreign Secretary, an office which in 1892 he resumed. The Queen would have liked him to retain it together with the Premiership in 1894. But always mistrustful of his own powers, and anxious, not groundlessly, about his physical powers of endurance he declined.

Rosebery and Harcourt   Even as it was the task proved too heavy for a man of his self-tormenting temperament. Difficult at any time it was, under the actual circumstances, unendurable. With a Cabinet divided both on personal and political issues; with a small and precarious majority in the House of Commons and in a hopeless minority in the Lords, a Peer-Premier who was (literally) not on speaking terms with the leader of the House of Commons had no chance of winning distinction for himself, or of doing good service for the country.

The Newcastle Programme   The Liberal Party, anticipating an appeal to the country and their own restoration to power, had, at a meeting held at Newcastle (October 1891), formulated a 'programme'. Retaining Home Rule for Ireland in the forefront of the programme the Party Organization had also committed itself to the Disestablishment of the Church in Wales; the establishment of elective

councils in Districts and Parishes; the reform of the land laws
and the taxation of land values and ground rents; the direct
popular veto on the Liquor Traffic; the payment of Members
of Parliament and the reform of registration and electoral laws;
the ' mending or ending ' of the House of Lords, and other drastic
reforms.

The unwisdom of loading the parliamentary ship with such a
top-heavy cargo was conclusively illustrated during the next few
years. The ' Newcastle Programme ', as it was quickly nicknamed, not merely evoked against the Party which adopted it
the opposition of many powerful interests, but seriously weakened
internally a Party which could ill-afford a further loss of blood.

The Liberal Government of 1892 was triply fettered: by 'Filling
dependence on the Irish vote in the House of Commons, by a up the
solid and unyielding majority opposed to it in the House of Lords, Cup'
and by the supremacy of the Caucus which had dictated the preposterous programme at Newcastle. As a consequence the three
years of its uneasy existence were largely spent in ' ploughing
the sands ' or ' filling up the cup ', as the process of passing Bills
through the Commons, with the prospect of their drastic amendment or rejection in the Lords, was alternatively described by
foes and friends. Of the victims thus adorned for sacrifice the
two which, apart from the Home Rule Bill, encountered the
bitterest hostility were Welsh Disestablishment and the Local
Veto.

To prepare the way for the former, Asquith, the new Home The
Secretary, introduced (February 23, 1893) a Suspensory Bill, pro- Welsh
viding that ' a person appointed after the passing of this Act to Church
any bishopric, ecclesiastical dignity or preferment in Wales or
Monmouthshire or to any lay office in connexion therewith, shall
hold the emoluments of his office subject to the pleasure of Parliament '. The Act was to operate until August 1, 1894, or if
Parliament were sitting, then to the end of the current session.
The substantive measure was introduced in April 1894. It was
based upon a distinction between ancient and relatively modern
endowments. All ecclesiastical property in Wales and Monmouthshire, except private benefactions made since 1703, was to
vest in three commissioners. All ecclesiastical corporations were
to be dissolved, and a Representative Church Body to be formed.

To this Body the Churches and parsonages were to be handed over ; the Cathedrals to the Commissioners. Glebe lands were to be vested in the local Councils, Borough, Urban District or Parish ; the tithes to the County Councils. Incumbents and other holders of freehold offices were to continue to hold them for life, with the emoluments attached thereto, but might exchange them for annuities. The Bill encountered the most determined opposition both inside and outside Parliament. Gladstone had defended it on the ground that it was demanded by twenty-eight out of thirty members returned for Welsh constituencies, and (in reply to the protests of the Queen) disclaimed the suggestion that it was ' a first step towards the disestablishment or disendowment of the Church of England '. That the Bill was so regarded by the great bulk of English Churchmen was not less certain than that it was desired by the bulk of the Welsh people.

Mr. Asquith who, both as Home Secretary and a born Nonconformist, was appropriately put in charge of the Bill, piloted it through the House of Commons with marked ability, defending it against the assaults of Churchmen who regarded it as ' sacrilege ' and of those Welsh Nonconformists who like Mr. Lloyd George, a young Welsh Baptist who had entered the House in 1890, attacked its provisions as too tender towards the Church they wished to despoil. The Bill was read a second time on April 1, 1895, by 304 to 260, but had not emerged from the ordeal of Committee when the Government fell. No more was heard until 1912 when Asquith, as Prime Minister, passed it, with the aid of the Irish Roman Catholics, through the Commons, only to meet inevitable rejection in the House of Lords. Its subsequent fate will demand attention later.

Local
Veto

Four days after Asquith had introduced the Welsh Church Suspensory Bill came the third instalment of the Newcastle Programme. The apostles of total abstinence and other more moderate advocates of restrictions on the sale of alcoholic liquors had, of late years, been making great headway in all parts of Great Britain. They were especially strong in the various Nonconformist Bodies, and by the 'eighties had become so important an element in the electoral strength of the Liberal Party that their demands could no longer be ignored. As to the best means of dealing with the vice of drunkenness, and with the trade which was held to foster it, opinions differed.   Many schemes were put forward, but the device most favoured in the 'nineties was that of a local veto upon the grant of licences for the sale of intoxicating liquors.   The Conservatives had so far conceded the principle as to include in the County Councils Bill, as originally introduced, clauses dealing with liquor licences.   The elected Councils were to be empowered to refuse the renewal of licences to public-houses on payment of compensation to licensees.   The proposal found few friends.   The brewers and publicans were alarmed at the prospect of being placed under the control of popularly elected Councils.   Temperance reformers jibbed at the principle of recognizing by compensation a vested interest in vice. Persons who had practical knowledge of a difficult problem found in the Bill no guidance as to the basis on which compensation was to be computed.   The proposals had evidently been insufficiently considered, and in face of an outcry from many quarters were withdrawn.

The Liberals, however, on returning to office in 1892 attempted a solution of the problem.   Harcourt's Bill of 1893 was framed with singular unwisdom.   A Liberal politician and historian has justly described it as 'perhaps the most unpopular measure ever introduced into the House of Commons '.[1]   It proposed that on the demand of one-tenth of County Council electors, in any ward of a borough or any parish, a poll might be taken on the question of the total closing of all public-houses in the area.   If supported by a two-thirds majority of the votes polled, no licence should be granted or renewed for the sale of intoxicating liquor within the area, save in hotels, refreshment rooms or eating houses.

To the brewers and publicans this appeared to spell confiscation ; the working man who liked his glass of beer regarded it quite reasonably as class legislation.   Thoughtful temperance reformers complained that Harcourt, as Chamberlain remarked, appeared ' more anxious to punish the publican than to reclaim the drunkard'.   Chamberlain himself contended that the only constructive solution of a difficult problem was, having compensated the licensee, to substitute public ownership and disinterested management for private control, and to provide facilities for alcoholic

---

[1] H. Paul, *Modern England*, v. 263.

refreshment under decent conditions.   Harcourt's Bill was immediately damned and soon dead.   Partial experiments have in
recent years been made on the lines advocated by Chamberlain,
but a marked diminution of drunkenness in England has combined with the spectacular failure of ' prohibition ' in the United
States to take Local Veto out of the category of urgent reforms.

A happier fate attended, as we have already seen, the Bill
for the establishment of District and Parish Councils.   Introduced in March 1893 it became law a year later.[1]

Em-
ployers'
Liability

Mr. Asquith, already in charge of the Welsh Disestablishment
Bill, was also deputed to introduce an Employers' Liability Bill.
The Bill abolished the last remnant of the Common Law doctrine
of ' common employment ', and made the employer liable for an
accident due to the negligence of a servant, even though that
servant and the injured person were alike in his employment.   It
also included various classes of workpeople hitherto excluded,
such as domestic servants and seamen ; and forbade ' contracting
out '.   The latter provision was hotly contested in the Commons,
and deleted in the Lords, whereupon the Government refused to
proceed with a measure so shamefully ' mangled '.   It served
none the less to ' fill up the cup '.

Hours of
Labour

The Government did, however, succeed in passing a modest
measure for limiting the hours of railway servants, but although
in some other occupations the Trade Unions were agitating for
an ' eight-hours day ', the railway servants were far from unanimous in their welcome to this extension of State interference.
One of the last acts of the Gladstone Government was, however, to introduce the eight-hours day for workmen in the
ordnance factories under the War Office, and the Rosebery
Government applied the same rule to workmen in the Royal
Dockyards.

Asquith
at the
Home
Office

Mr. Acland, more fortunate than most of his colleagues,
earned credit for a new Code for Evening Continuation Schools
issued in 1893, and for the passage of two Acts, one of which raised
the compulsory limit of age for school attendance to 11, and the
other made better provision for the education of blind and deaf
children.   Mr. Asquith also, though doomed to disappointment
as regards the ambitious legislative projects committed to his

[1] See *supra*, p. 40 f.

charge, acquired a high reputation as an administrator. As Home Secretary he was confronted with several difficult problems. The first was the use and abuse of Trafalgar Square for demonstrations. The Square is Crown property but it would seem that the public has by long use acquired a right of way through the Square, though not the right to use it for public meetings. The increasing abuse of the Square for demonstrations of various sorts had, as already noted, led the previous Government to forbid the use of it for that purpose. But at the election of 1892 Mr. John Burns, whom Asquith had unsuccessfully defended in 1887, had in 1889 become Lord Rosebery's colleague on the London County Council, and in 1892 had been returned to Parliament as member for Battersea. At the same election Mr. Keir Hardie, a Scottish collier who had espoused with zeal the Socialist creed, had been returned for South-West Ham, and had arrived at Westminster, in the cloth cap of a miner and to the blatant accompaniment if not of a brass band, at least of a cornet. The advent of these men announced the opening of a new chapter in English politics. The Liberal Government would ignore its significance at their peril.

Trafalgar Square

Hardly was Asquith installed at the Home Office before he was called upon (October 1892) to receive a deputation from the Metropolitan Radical Federation on the subject of Trafalgar Square. He announced his decision with characteristic courtesy and clearness. The use of the Square for meetings was a favour, not a right, but meetings would be permitted, during daylight hours, on Sundays and Saturday afternoons (when shops were shut and traffic at its lightest), and subject to arrangements made with and by the First Commissioner of Works (representing the Crown) and the Commissioner of Metropolitan Police. All British parties were satisfied with this reasonable compromise.

Not so the Irish Nationalists, who, conscious of their parliamentary power, demanded (January 1893) the release of the prisoners still serving their sentences for their part in the dynamite outrages of the early 'eighties. On this question Asquith was quite uncompromising. No dynamiter, however ' political ' the motives which inspired his crime, need expect more favourable treatment from him than any other convicted criminal. The Nationalists were bitterly chagrined ; but supported on an issue such as this by the Unionists, the Ministry could and did defy them.

A third question of law and order arose in connexion with the great coal dispute which broke out in the summer of 1893. In that act of the political drama Lord Rosebery ultimately played the part of the hero ; Asquith was most inappropriately cast for that of villain.

Great depression in the coal trade had necessitated a reduction of wages. The demand of the owners was not seriously resisted in South Wales, and the colliers in the Northumberland and Durham coal-field never joined the strike. But it spread with such rapidity in Yorkshire, Lancashire and the Midlands that 250,000 men were involved. The dispute had already lasted about two months when a regrettable incident occurred at Featherstone Colliery near Pontefract. The Doncaster races were in progress ; large bodies of the local police forces had, as usual, been drafted to Doncaster, and the strikers seized the opportunity to attack the collieries of Lord Masham who had imported nonunionists from other districts to work his pits. The weakened police force was overpowered ; a small body of troops summoned from York were compelled to open fire and two colliers were unfortunately killed. Mr. Asquith, as Home Secretary, was bitterly attacked in Parliament and for years afterwards his appearance on public platforms was frequently greeted by murmurs of ' Featherstone ' and ' murderer '. In face of those unfair attacks he comported himself with dignity. On one occasion, when a voice cried, ' That was when you murdered the miners at Featherstone in 1892 ', his only retort was ' In 1893 '. The Featherstone riots raised, however, important questions both of law and fact. A small Commission under the chairmanship of Lord Bowen, a judge of the highest distinction, found that the soldiers who fired and the officer who commanded them to do so had ' done nothing except what was (their) strict legal duty '.[1]

The strike was not interrupted by ' Featherstone '. Not until after it had lasted for fifteen weeks, had inflicted great hardship on the poor, and caused loss and inconvenience on all classes, did the Government intervene. Fourteen owners and fourteen miners were then brought into conference at the Foreign Office under

[1] Parliamentary Papers, Cd. 7234, Dec. 6, 1893.

the chairmanship of Lord Rosebery. After six hours of nerve-wracking negotiation, the chairman succeeded in arranging terms of peace. His diary for the day reads : ' One of the most anxious and happiest days of my life. . . . Dined alone, very tired. But it would have been a good day to die on.'

The owners agreed to take the miners back to work at the old rates until February 1, 1894 ; after that date the rate of wages was to be fixed by a Conciliation Board of fourteen a side, under an impartial chairman, with a casting vote.

Lord Rosebery had good reason to be satisfied with his day's work. It immensely enhanced his reputation in the country, and might have eased his position as Prime Minister, even though it did not conduce to his appointment. His selection was, in fact, due to other reasons. The Queen had noted with satisfaction his conduct of Foreign affairs, and thought that in contrast with those who had been associated for a longer period with Mr. Gladstone, he could be trusted to maintain the honour of the country. For that was the real cause of the growing estrangement between Queen Victoria and the outgoing Minister. In the monarchy as an institution Gladstone had a deep-rooted belief ; for the Queen herself a profound respect. The Queen, on her part, always gratefully remembered Mr. Gladstone's ' devotion and zeal in all that concerned [her] personal welfare and that of [her family] ', but she held that he had lowered the place of his country among the nations of the world. She hoped that Lord Rosebery would not only exercise a moderating influence upon his colleagues in domestic affairs, but carry on the Foreign policy inherited from Lord Salisbury.

Queen Victoria and Lord Rosebery

Lord Rosebery disappointed her expectations. On social questions his views were, indeed, more ' advanced ' than those of his older colleagues, and as regards the House of Lords his tone was decidedly more aggressive. With a speech made on the latter question by the Prime Minister at Bradford (October 27) the Queen was so seriously displeased that she contemplated the possibility of dissolving Parliament—a course from which she was dissuaded by the Unionist leaders. Accordingly, she contented herself with administering a sharp rebuke to her Minister.[1]

In disgrace with the Queen, the Prime Minister had also evoked

[1] *Q.V.L.* (3rd), II. 431 f.

the displeasure of his colleagues, and still more of their masters in the House of Commons.   In his first speech as Prime Minister (March 12, 1894) he made an admission which greatly perturbed the Irish Nationalists.   ' Before Irish Home Rule is conceded,' he said, ' by the Imperial Parliament, England as the predominant member in the partnership of the three kingdoms will have to be convinced of its justice.'   The statement was, as he subsequently explained, electorally truistic ; but the ' predominant partner ' speech was never forgotten, nor in some quarters forgiven.   It was instantly repudiated by the Radicals and Nationalists who, on the very next day, under the leadership of Mr. Labouchere, carried against the Government an amendment to the Address. The majority was only two : but it was a bad start for the Rose-bery Government.

Har-court's Budget, 1894

The only parliamentary success achieved by that unhappy ministry fell to Sir William Harcourt.   The Budget of 1894, piloted through the House by him with consummate adroitness, made financial history.   Faced with an estimated deficit of about £4,000,000 Harcourt was compelled to impose fresh taxation. He put an extra 1d. on the income tax and an extra 6d. per gallon on spirits and 6d. per barrel on beer.   But the outstanding feature of the Budget was a revolution in the Death Duties.   The new scheme of Duties was based on two main principles : first, that land (' realty ') should be put for the first time on the same foot-ing as other kinds of property (' personalty ') ; secondly, that the rate of duty should be graduated according to the aggregate value of the property passing on the death of the deceased person.

For the smaller folk the pill of the extra 1d. on income tax was sugared by raising the limit of total exemption from £150 to £160, and by an abatement of £160 on all incomes up to £400 and of £100 on those between £400 and £500.   There was also a sop for landlords.   In the assessment of real estate under Schedule A a step was taken towards the substitution of *net* for *gross* income, by an allowance of one-tenth (afterwards one-eighth) in respect of land and one-sixth in respect of houses. But this was small compensation to landowners for the terrible burden imposed on land.

Death Duties

Harcourt's proposals were bitterly attacked and resisted.   It was contended, and justly, that the duty ought to be graduated

according to the amount received by individuals, not according
to the aggregate amount left by a testator. Otherwise a bene-
ficiary was cruelly penalized, however small the benefit received,
if his portion happened to come out of a large pool. Lord Randolph Churchill's stillborn Budget of 1887 would, we now know,
have contained proposals hardly less drastic than those of 1894,
but he definitely rejected the principle of graduation based on
the aggregate estate, in favour of one based on the individual
succession. 'My instinct,' he said, after a long discussion of the
question at Somerset House, ' tells me that it is wrong.'

Nevertheless, bitterly as Harcourt's Budget was assailed, no
subsequent Chancellor of the Exchequer, Conservative or Radical,
ever dreamt of financial disarmament, of foregoing the employment of the terribly effective weapon which Harcourt forged.
Harcourt anticipated a revenue of £14,000,000 from his Death
Duties. A Conservative successor collected £80,000,000. The
convenience of this method of raising revenue is unquestionable ;
but it involves a levy on capital, and the revenue so raised ought
not, in the view of financial purists, to be devoted to any purpose
save the reduction of capital liabilities, in short to the reduction
of debt.

The Lords, though they detested Harcourt's proposals, did not
venture to reject them : but almost every other proposal emanating from the Rosebery Government they either rejected outright,
or ' maimed and mauled ' so drastically that the ministerial
parents could not recognize their own progeny, and allowed them
to perish.

Rosebery himself would have preferred to deal with causes,
rather than effects, by a drastic reform of the Second Chamber.
His colleagues thought they saw more electoral advantage in
' filling up the cup '. A number of highly controversial measures,
including the Welsh Church and the Local Veto Bills, were,
accordingly, introduced or reintroduced in the Commons, with
small prospect of their reaching, and none of their passing, the
Upper Chamber. This futile performance was, however, brought
to an abrupt conclusion when the Government were defeated on
their Army Estimates (June 21) and sought escape from a humiliating situation by immediate resignation. Mr. Campbell-Bannerman, Secretary of State for War, had but a few hours before the

fatal Division made the important announcement that, in order
to facilitate certain changes in Army organization, the Duke of
Cambridge was about to retire from the post of Commander-in-
Chief. The Duke was first cousin to Queen Victoria; he was
exceedingly popular with the Army and had held his post, with
devotion if not distinction, for close on forty years. A Royal
Commission presided over by Lord Hartington had recommended
(1890) the abolition of the post. The Duke, though 76,[1] was
reluctant to retire. The Queen shared his reluctance, the more
so when it was made plain to her that the Duke of Connaught
would not be appointed to succeed him. The Duke of Cambridge,
handled with kindly tact by Campbell-Bannerman, ultimately
placed himself in the Queen's hands, and she decided, ' though
with *much* pain ', to accept his resignation, but only on condition
that the office should be retained, and that her son should not
be debarred from appointment to it in due course. The Duke of
Connaught, though ' a little disappointed ', was according to
Colonel Bigge ' very dignified and sensible ' about the matter.
The same could not be said of the Duke of Cambridge, whose
annoyance at his compulsory retirement was aggravated by the
refusal of an additional pension.

Meanwhile, the Government had fallen. The Queen took
leave of Lord Rosebery in gracious terms, but she added a ' few
words of kindly advice towards one in whom she will always take
a sincere interest. It is that he should in his public speeches be
very careful not to hamper himself by strong expressions which
would hamper him hereafter.' The advice was sound; but for
Lord Rosebery there was no political ' hereafter '. The breach
between him and Harcourt reached a climax in August 1895, and
in October 1896 he resigned the leadership of the Liberal Party.
For many years to come he brilliantly fulfilled the function of
the ' Public Orator of the Empire '; he became Chancellor of
two Universities; he did fine literary work; but he repeatedly
repelled the advances of Liberal Imperialists who would gladly
have accepted his leadership and in the event he never again
played any official part in public affairs. Reading of himself as
a ' failure ' he half admitted, and half repudiated, the impeach-

---

[1] Exactly the same age as and not less vigorous than the Queen herself,
whom he outlived by three years.

ment ; yet as he himself wrote of Lord Randolph Churchill, ' his career was not a complete success . . . his achievement came infinitely short of anticipation '. ' The secret of my life ', he wrote, ' is that I always detested politics.' It was not politics he detested ; politics was the breath of his nostrils ; but the sordid concomitants of party warfare. Shy, fastidious and tortured by self-consciousness, he could not endure the rough and tumble of political life under the conditions imposed by Representative Democracy. So Lord Rosebery, like Lord Randolph Churchill (though for reasons widely different), goes down to history as a man of promise unfulfilled.

On Lord Rosebery's resignation the Queen immediately sent for Lord Salisbury, who kissed hands as Prime Minister on June 25, 1895. Three years in opposition had cemented the alliance between the two wings of the Unionist Party, and Lord Salisbury had no difficulty in persuading the Liberal Unionist leaders to join his Ministry : the Duke of Devonshire as President of the Council, Goschen (Admiralty), Lord Lansdowne (War) and Lord James of Hereford as Chancellor of the Duchy of Lancaster. Mr. Chamberlain selected the Colonial Office. Mr. Balfour led the House of Commons, Hicks Beach became Chancellor of the Exchequer, and Lord Salisbury himself took the Foreign Office in conjunction with the Premiership. The Queen insisted that Lord Cross should be retained in the Cabinet, with the sinecure office of Privy Seal, while other Conservatives included in a Cabinet of nineteen were Lord Halsbury (Lord Chancellor), Sir M. White Ridley (Home Office), Lord George Hamilton (India), Lord Balfour of Burleigh (Scottish Secretary), Lord Cadogan (Lord-Lieutenant) and Lord Ashbourne (Lord Chancellor of Ireland) ; Mr. C. T. Ritchie (Board of Trade), Mr. Chaplin (Local Government), Mr. W. H. Long (Agriculture) and Mr. Akers Douglas (Commissioner of Works). *Third Salisbury Ministry*

Parliament was dissolved on July 8, and at the ensuing General Election the Liberal Party was routed. The Unionists obtained a majority of 152 over all other parties combined, 411 Unionists, of whom 71 were Liberals, being returned against 177 Liberals and 82 Nationalists. But for the staunch support of the ' Celtic Fringe ' the Liberal Party would have been almost annihilated. *General Election of 1895*

As it was its plight was pitiable ; rent by internal dissensions, repudiated by the ' predominant partner ', it remained for a full decade in political eclipse. For the first time for over sixty years Mr. Gladstone did not offer himself as a candidate. Harcourt failed to secure re-election at Derby, and John Morley at Newcastle. Labour fared as badly as Liberalism, Keir Hardie and most of the other Socialist candidates being defeated.

The electorate emphatically endorsed the action of the House of Lords in rejecting the Home Rule Bill. For the rest, it was evidently determined to put into power a Government which could govern. The final fusion of the Liberal Unionist and Conservative Parties gave promise of strength ; how far that promise was redeemed subsequent chapters will disclose.

CHAPTER VI

ENGLAND AND HER NEIGHBOURS, 1885–99

FROM preceding chapters all reference to Foreign Affairs has been excluded. The omission must now be repaired. During the last fifteen years of the century the conduct of Foreign policy was in the hands of only two statesmen. There were, indeed, two brief interludes when Lord Iddesleigh and Lord Kimberley respectively held the office of Foreign Secretary, but in the one case Lord Salisbury, in the other Lord Rosebery, was at hand in Downing Street, and it is a convention of the Cabinet system that the Prime Minister should be in close touch with the Foreign Minister. From 1885, then, until 1901 Salisbury and Rosebery were in continuous control.

As domestic affairs were conducted throughout this period against the background of Ireland, so Egypt dominated the European situation. *The Egyptian Problem*

To the importance of the Egyptian problem England had but tardily awakened. Even Napoleon's broad hint had been lost upon her. ' Really to ruin England we must make ourselves masters of Egypt.' So General Buonaparte had written in August 1797. Egypt was in his view, even then, the nerve-centre of the British Empire. The Czar Nicholas I of Russia was of the same opinion. Twice he proposed to England that she should take Egypt as her share in the imminent partition of the Ottoman Empire. But neither in 1844 nor in 1853 were British statesmen disposed to listen to the voice of the tempter. Until the cutting of the Suez Canal, Cape Colony was regarded, naturally enough, as more important to the Sea Empire than Egypt.

To the construction of the Canal English statesmen were, moreover, stoutly opposed, and not one penny of the capital raised by M. de Lesseps was subscribed in England. Yet from

M.E.—4

SCALE 0 100 200 300 400 Eng. Miles

EGYPT AND THE SOUDAN.

78

the day it was opened (1869) Great Britain contributed 75 to 80 per cent. of the traffic, and more than that proportion of the revenue. Not, however, until 1874 did there come into power in England a statesman who realized that new conditions of world-politics had arisen, that there were ' vast and novel elements in the distribution of power '.

In 1875 an opportunity arose whereby England might, if she The Suez could act promptly and boldly, redeem the errors of the past. Shares Out of 400,000 shares in the Suez Canal Company Ismail, the Khedive of Egypt, held 176,602. Brought to the verge of bankruptcy by an orgy of extravagance, he decided in 1875 to sell them. Disraeli, with the help of the Rothschilds, bought them for Great Britain.[1] Both on financial and political grounds the investment was brilliantly justified. It opened a new era in the history of the Egyptian problem and of English Foreign Policy.

The sale of the shares did not solve Ismail's difficulties. The debt, which at his accession stood at £3,293,000, had mounted by 1876 to £94,000,000—a crushing burden for a country which was small and poor. The Khedive's creditors, particularly in France and England, became alarmed about their security, and in 1875 the British Government at the ' request '—perhaps gently prompted —of the Khedive, sent out Mr. (afterwards Sir) Stephen Cave, a distinguished Member of Parliament, to investigate and report upon the financial situation of the country.

The French Government, alarmed by the growth of British influence in Egypt, proposed the creation of a joint Commission for the control of Egyptian finance, but Lord Derby was opposed to any measure that might entail ' interference with the independence of Egypt '. How ironically did events mock his cautious rectitude. They ensued in rapid sequence. In 1879 the Sultan was induced by the Powers to procure the abdication of his vassal Ismail. ' His abdication,' writes Lord Cromer, ' sounded the death knell of arbitrary personal rule in Egypt.' No doubt : but the situation was not thereby immediately improved. Tewfik, Ismail's son and successor, though well intentioned, was even less capable than Ismail. The condition of his subjects was deplorable and of the prevailing discontent Arabi Bey, a soldier of

---

[1] For details of this brilliant transaction cf. Marriott, *Europe since 1815,* pp. 313–18.

humble birth but great ambition, made himself the mouthpiece. In February 1882 Arabi became War Minister, and in June revolution broke out. Arabi's revolt represented a long-accumulating mass of discontent among all classes of the native population.

Rebellion of Arabi Though military in origin, it was nationalistic in purpose, being directed partly against the suzerainty of the Sultan, partly against Occidental intervention in Egyptian affairs. At the end of May 1882 British and French squadrons had been sent to Alexandria for the protection of the large foreign population. Not without reason. On June 11 the Arabs attacked the European population in Alexandria, massacred fifty or more of them, mostly Greeks, and looted the city. Order had to be restored; but how? Tewfik was powerless; his Suzerain could give him no help. France, though jealous of England, refused, when the moment for action came, to participate. The French fleet sailed away. England was compelled to act alone. Sir Beauchamp Seymour, the Admiral in command, bombarded Alexandria. Arabi, having released the convicts, abandoned the city which was handed over to fire, pillage and massacre. The Admiral then landed a body of bluejackets and marines and order was tardily restored.

Troops were dispatched from England and India, and under the command of Sir Garnet Wolseley inflicted a crushing defeat on Arabi at Tel-el-Kebir (September 13th). On the 14th Cairo surrendered to a couple of squadrons of British cavalry. Arabi was captured, tried, and finally deported to Ceylon.[1] England was to all intents mistress of Egypt. France never forgave herself for a pusillanimous abdication.

The English Occupation England, however, had no desire to remain in permanent occupation of Egypt. Minister after minister reiterated the intention to retire as soon as ' the authority of the Khedive ' was completely restored and a regime of permanent stability established. But again events mocked their intentions. In 1883 the Soudanese, led by a religious fanatic who styled himself the ' Madhi ', revolted against their Egyptian taskmasters. General

---

[1] There he remained for some years, but was eventually allowed to return to Egypt, where he died in obscurity. Valentine Chirol (*Fifty Years*, pp. 32–4) says that Arabi was sincerely grateful to the British for the benefits they had conferred upon the *fellaheen* from whom he had himself sprung.

Hicks, an English soldier, was dispatched to quell the rebellion. But the Egyptian force under his command was wholly inadequate and ill-disciplined, and the General, his European staff and his Egyptian soldiers were cut to pieces.

What was to be done ? The distracted Cabinet at home Gordon sought the advice of General Charles Gordon, who until 1879 and the had been Governor of the Soudan under Ismail. Acting on it, they dispatched Gordon himself to report on the situation. Appointed Governor-General of the Soudan by the Khedive, Gordon went to Khartum and quickly found himself besieged by the Mahdists (February 1884). Sir Evelyn Baring (Lord Cromer), who went to Egypt in 1883 as Consul-General, disapproved of Gordon's mission, but insisted that he must be rescued. At home the Queen was equally insistent. ' If not for humanity's sake, for the honour of the Government and the nation he must not be abandoned.' But the Cabinet still delayed. Month after month passed by. Nothing was done. Not until August did the Gladstone Cabinet decide to send out a relieving expedition under the command of Sir Garnet Wolseley. Wolseley made all possible haste ; but he was too late. On January 26, 1885, the Mahdi stormed Khartum. Gordon was killed. A Death of British force came in sight of the city two days after it had Gordon fallen.

The Cabinet decided that the power of the Mahdi must be crushed ; but in April 1885 reversed the decision ; Suakin, the port of the Soudan on the Red Sea, was retained, but the whole Nile Valley south of Wady Halfa was abandoned to the Mahdi.

Danger was threatening from another quarter.[1] The renewal England of Russian activity in Central Asia had, in the last few years, and been exciting serious alarm both in London and at Calcutta. in Central There were rumours in 1881 that Russia was preparing to occupy Asia Merv, a vital point in South Turkestan, now an important junction on the Trans-Caspian Railway. From Merv a short line runs south to the Afghan frontier in the neighbourhood of Herat. The Russian Government promptly disavowed the rumoured intention. That was in 1882. Early in 1884 Russia, encouraged doubtless by England's difficulties in the Soudan, occupied Merv

[1] For events leading up to the situation, see Marriott, *A History of Europe* (1815–1939), c. xix; and Marriott, *Anglo-Russian Relations*, c. xiv.

and Saraks, and thus came within 200 miles of Herat and the frontier of Afghanistan.

Despite this gross breach of faith the British Government assented to a proposal for the appointment of a joint Anglo-Russian Commission to delimit the northern frontier of Afghanistan. Sir Peter Lumsden, the British Commissioner, punctually arrived; his Russian colleague, General Zelenoi, tarried, and made excuse after excuse for the delay. The Russians usefully employed the interval by occupying various points in dispute, in order to present to the Commissioners a *fait accompli*.

The Penjdeh Incident

Matters reached a crisis when on March 30th, while Wolseley was still in the Soudan, Russia attacked Penjdeh, a village some hundred miles south of Merv, and drove out the Afghans with a loss of 500 lives. News of the incident aroused public excitement in England to the highest pitch. The Government acting with unusual promptitude called out the Reserves, and asked for a vote of credit for £11,000,000, of which £4,500,000 was for the Soudan expedition. The Vote was agreed to without a dissentient voice. Russia took the hint. The Ameer of Afghanistan, Abdur Rahman, happened at the moment to be the guest of the Viceroy, Lord Dufferin, at Rawal Pindi. The Viceroy exerted all his diplomatic skill to avert war, and persuaded Abdur Rahman that Penjdeh was of small importance as compared with the Zulfikar Pass. So Russia retained Penjdeh: the exclusive control of the Zulfikar Pass was secured to the Ameer.

Between Afghanistan and Russia the matter was satisfactorily adjusted. Between Russia and England negotiations dragged on until July 1887 when the frontier was settled up to the line of the Oxus and a definite check was put upon Russian advance towards Afghanistan. Meanwhile, the Quetta district, under the designation of British Baluchistan, was annexed to British India.

Salisbury's Policy

Such, in rough outline, was the position when in 1885 Lord Salisbury assumed the control of British policy. An ardent patriot, Lord Salisbury was also a genuine lover of peace. Determined to maintain the honour of his own country, he was scrupulous in respecting the rights and consulting the susceptibilities of its neighbours. From the first, therefore, he was anxious to determine the British occupation of Egypt, partly because our presence in Egypt meant an open sore in our relations with

France, and still more because it gave Bismarck the opportunity
of playing a diplomatic game precisely adapted to his peculiar
genius. In a letter (February 1887) to Sir Edward Malet, then
British Ambassador in Berlin, he expressed this view very strongly.

'He [Bismarck] is hard to please. Unless we take the chest- Salisbury
nuts out of the hottest part of the fire, he thinks we are shirking and Bismarck
our work. But we cannot go beyond a certain point to please
him . . . when he wants us—as he evidently does—to quarrel
with France downright over Egypt, I think he is driving too hard
a bargain. It is not worth our while. Our policy is not, if we
can help it, to allow France either to force us out of Egypt
altogether or to force us into a quarrel over Egypt. . . . Our
position in Egypt is . . . a disastrous inheritance, for it enables
[Bismarck] to demand rather unreasonable terms as the price,
not of his assistance, but of his refusal to join a coalition against
us.' (February 23, 1887.)

In similar strain he wrote on the same day to Sir Henry
Drummond Wolff :

'We are steering in very narrow channels, and we are in constant danger of running aground on one side or the other. On
the one hand English opinion is not prepared for an evacuation
of Egypt. . . . On the other hand, we must keep it diplomati-
cally in our power to satisfy France, on account of Bismarck's
attitude. . . . I heartily wish we had never gone into Egypt.
Had we not done, we could snap our fingers at the whole world.'

Egypt was, then, the 'heel of Achilles' for Great Britain in France
her foreign, as Ireland was in her domestic, relations. The occu- and Germany
pation of it complicated the European situation. But the immediate danger to European peace arose from the relations of France
and Germany.

The recovery of France after the disasters of 1870–1 was, in
an economic sense, astonishingly rapid. So rapid that Bismarck,
regretting that he had not 'bled France white', contemplated
a renewal of war, in 1875, in order to complete the process. The
crime contemplated by Bismarck was averted by the personal
intervention at Berlin of Queen Victoria and the Czar Alexander
of Russia. The threat was renewed in 1887. The arrest (April 20)
of M. Schnaebele, a French Police Commissioner, by German
agents on the Alsatian frontier led the Czar to suspect that

Bismarck was at his old game and wanted to provoke France to war.

France and Russia

Between France and Russia there had not hitherto been any real political friendship. It was one of the governing principles of Bismarck's diplomacy to prevent it. Thus far, despite the war-scare of 1875, despite also his quarrel with Gortschakoff at the Congress of Berlin, he had succeeded in ' keeping open the wires between Berlin and Petersburg '. But in February 1887 there appeared in *Le Nord*, the organ of the Russian Minister, de Giers, an article containing these significant words : ' Henceforth Russia will watch the events on the Rhine and will relegate the Eastern Question to the second place. . . . The Cabinet of Petersburg will in no case permit a further weakening of France.' Two months later, after the news of the Schnaebele incident had reached Petersburg, the Czar Alexander III wrote to the German Emperor formally announcing that he no longer regarded himself as under any obligation to maintain neutrality in the event of war between France and Germany. Schnaebele was promptly released.

England and France

A second crisis was averted. Relations between France and Germany remained, however, tense. They were hardly more satisfactory between France and England. Lord Salisbury, peace-lover that he was, could not understand the provocative attitude of France. ' She is an insupportable neighbour.' So he wrote to a friend on July 3, 1887. A few days later he wrote to the British Ambassador in Paris : ' Our relations with France are not pleasant at present. There are five or six different places where we are at odds :

1. She has destroyed the Convention at Constantinople.
2. She will allow no Press law to pass [Egypt].
3. She is trying to back out of the arrangement on the Somali coast.
4. She still occupies the New Hebrides.
5. She destroys our fishing tackle, etc. [in Newfoundland].
6. She is trying to elbow us out of at least two unpronounceable places on the West Coast of Africa.

Can you wonder that there is, to my eyes, a silver lining even to the great black cloud of a Franco-German War ? ' On August 10th we find him writing to Sir William White at Constantinople :

'For the present the enemy is France. Her conduct is hard to explain on any theory. She is trailing her coat to us almost as ostentatiously as she does it to Germany.'[1]

The childish and provocative behaviour of France did not, however, drive Lord Salisbury into the arms of Bismarck. Were they ready to receive him ? Despite the opening of archives, and the publication of countless diplomatic documents, it is still difficult to discern the exact relations between Germany and England during the last decades of the nineteenth century. But it is clear that on no fewer than six occasions between 1876 and 1903 Germany approached Great Britain with a view to the conclusion of an alliance. No alliance was, in fact, ever concluded ; but we were nearer to it perhaps in 1887 than at any time before or since.

England and Germany

In 1881 Bismarck, in order to keep France at loggerheads with Italy, had encouraged her to occupy Tunis. He was rewarded, in 1882, by the adhesion of Italy to the Austro-German alliance. The Triple Alliance formed the pivot of German policy down to the outbreak of the Great War. Concluded in the first instance for five years it was renewed in 1887 and again in 1891, 1902 and 1912.

From the first, however, Italy was anxious that it should be made clear that her alliance with Germany and Austria would not interrupt her friendship with England to whom, ever since the days of the *Risorgimento*, she had been bound by ties of gratitude and affection. Between Great Britain and Austria-Hungary also relations were consistently friendly, at any rate with a Conservative Government in power. Accordingly, in February 1887 Lord Salisbury concluded with Italy and Austria an agreement to maintain the *status quo* in the Orient (including the independence of Turkey), in the Mediterranean, the Adriatic, and the Black Sea. Italy agreed to support England in Egypt. Great Britain promised to support Italy 'at every other point whatsoever of the North African Coast districts, and in particular in Tripolitania and Cyrenaica'. This meant, in effect, as an Austrian Professor has pointed out, 'the co-operation of the British fleet against French advances in the Western Mediterranean and also against the Russian menace to Constantinople and the

England and Italy

[1] Salisbury's *Life*, iv. 48–50.

Dardanelles '. It is, however, erroneous to suggest that in these negotiations the initiative came from Lord Salisbury. On the contrary, from the latter's correspondence with the Queen, it is clear that the proposal came from Italy, that it was strongly supported both from Vienna and Berlin, and that the final result was a ' cautiously limited *entente* '. Cautious and limited it was; yet, writing to the Queen (February 10), Lord Salisbury used significant words : ' Short of a pledge upon this subject, it [the agreement with Italy] undoubtedly carries very far the " *relations plus intimes* " which have been urged upon us. It is as close an alliance as the parliamentary character of our institutions will permit.' On the difficulties to effective diplomacy presented by those institutions Lord Salisbury frequently insisted. Still more were they a stumbling-block to Bismarck, and neither he nor the Emperor William II nor Prince von Bülow ever again touched the high-water mark of ' *relations plus intimes* ' reached in 1887.

Dropping the Pilot So matters stood when William II came to the throne after his father's reign of 88 days. Two years later (1890) he ' dropped the pilot ' who had steered the ship of State into a safe harbour. The Iron Chancellor had not merely created a united Germany, but had with infinite patience and skill constructed a diplomatic edifice which seemed to stand four square to all the winds that blew. He had carefully cemented friendships, and had sedulously fomented the jealousies and rivalries of potential enemies. The old friendship with Russia, though weakening since 1878, had been re-cemented by the Reinsurance Treaty of 1884 ; Austria was closely allied with Germany ; Italy had been brought in as a third partner in the Triple Alliance. On the other hand, Italy was estranged (thanks to Tunis) from France ; France (thanks to Egypt) from England ; England, by rivalry in the Near and Middle East, from Russia.

Thus in 1890 Germany was surrounded by Powers at least as friendly to her as to each other. Within twenty years she was confronted by a *Triple Entente* equal in strength, and not inferior in cohesion, to the *Triple Alliance* so laboriously constructed by Bismarck.

What had wrought the diplomatic transformation ?

Historical criticism in Germany, based on a careful study of the published documents, has appealed to the *Weltgericht* for a verdict of acquittal on the charge of ' war-guilt '. But while Emperor
William
II repudiating the criminal charge, there has been no attempt to extenuate the clumsiness and stupidity of German diplomacy since the fall of Bismarck. How far responsibility must be fixed on the Emperor William II is a point still in dispute. Certain it is, however, that the Emperor was a man of many moods, of unstable character, and contradictory impulses. Consequently, throughout his reign, German diplomacy pursued a tortuous course.

As regards England, William II was torn by the conflicting The
Kaiser
and
England emotions of ' aversion, admiration and jealousy '.[1] When he came to the throne German feeling against England was peculiarly bitter. His mother, the Empress Frederick, Princess Royal of England, though a woman of strong character and great ability, was not conspicuous for tact. She had, moreover, incurred the hostility of Bismarck, who well understood that whenever his old master should pass away, the English Princess would become the ruler of Germany. Bismarck instilled his own misgivings into the mind of the young Prince William. Feelings were further embittered by the dispute between the German and the English doctors as to the exact nature of the illness which some two years before his father's death the Crown Prince Frederick developed. The absurd allegations against the Empress Frederick and Queen Victoria current in Germany in 1888 have now been conclusively disproved. But at the time they were widely believed and poisoned the mind of the young Emperor against his mother and the country whence she had come.[2]

Nevertheless, the Kaiser William's first inclinations were towards a good understanding with England; nor was Lord Salisbury, for reasons already indicated, disinclined to reciprocate them. During his first tenure of the Foreign Office Salisbury had written to our Ambassador at Berlin : ' Germany is clearly cut out to be our ally.' ' Even our ancient friend Austria ', he added, ' is not so completely free as Germany from any plans or interests which cross our own for the present.' (Jan. 14, 1880.)

---

[1] Ludwig, *Life*, p. 15.

[2] On the whole episode cf. Marriott, *Europe from 1815 to 1939*, pp. 374 f. As to contemporary feeling in Germany I can personally testify, as I was in Germany at the time.

During the eight years' interval events had tended to confirm that opinion. Germany, on her side, had every reason to be grateful to Great Britain for facilitating the realization of her colonial ambitions.

German
Colonies

Down to the year 1884 Germany did not own one foot of territory outside Europe. Only in recent years, and under the pressure of economic and social developments, had she begun to feel the need of oversea possessions. Thus the cry for a forward colonial policy became irresistible. But where were colonies to be found ? The first inclination was to look towards Brazil, where there was already a large and increasing German population ; but the entrance to South America was barred by the Monroe doctrine. Germany therefore turned to Africa.

Africa offered everything which Germany was seeking : untold wealth in raw material ; inexhaustible man-power, which, if brought under German discipline, might well be utilized for European warfare ; strategical points of immense significance—especially in relation to the eventual conflict with the British Empire to which the thoughts of far-seeing Germans were already beginning to turn.

The notorious unrest among the Dutch in South Africa seemed to offer a favourable opportunity for German activities. Paul Kruger had already visited Berlin to seek German intervention at the time of the first British annexation of the Transvaal. He visited it again in 1884, and was cordially welcomed both by the Emperor and his Chancellor. Meanwhile a resolute attempt had been made by Germany to secure a footing at Delagoa Bay, at St. Lucia Bay and in Pondoland, and it was subsequently stated by Sir Donald Currie, speaking with knowledge, that ' the German Government would have secured St. Lucia Bay, and the coastline between Natal and the possessions of Portugal, had not the British Government telegraphed instructions to dispatch a gunboat from Cape Town with orders to hoist the British Flag at St. Lucia Bay '.

German
Africa

The German effort in Africa did not go unrewarded. In the course of less than two years (1884–5), she leapt into the position of the third European Power in Africa. She established a Protectorate over Damaraland and Namaqualand, a district with an area of 332,450 square miles, which was afterwards known as

German South-West Africa. Two more German Colonies were established by the annexation of Togoland and the Cameroons. Most important of all, however, alike from the point of view of strategy, of man-power, and of raw materials, was the great province on the East Coast with an area of 384,180 square miles and a population of 7,645,770 persons, mostly belonging to strong fighting races. This province became known as German East Africa.

Coincident with these German annexations in Africa was the acquisition of German possessions in the Pacific. The northern coast of New Guinea, subsequently known as Kaiser Wilhelm's Land, and the group of islands collectively known as the Bismarck Archipelago were acquired in 1884. The German settlements in South Africa and in the Pacific were not effected without loud protests from Englishmen on the spot. But to these protests the Government at home refused to listen. ' If Germany is to become a great colonizing power, all I say is, God speed her. She becomes our ally and partner in the execution of the great purposes of Providence for the advantage of mankind.' So said Mr. Gladstone. Nor was Lord Salisbury more grudging towards German expansion. Meanwhile an International Conference had met at Berlin in November 1884 under the presidency of Prince Bismarck to discuss the whole African situation. The General Act of the Conference was approved by Great Britain, France, Germany, Belgium, Portugal, as well as other Powers. The Act laid down regulations as to the traffic in slaves; in regard to freedom of trade in the Congo Basin; to the neutrality of territories in the same region; to the navigation of the Congo and the Niger; and finally in regard to the treatment of the native populations.[1] The Congo State under King Leopold was recognized, and in 1908 was transferred to the Belgian Kingdom.

The entrance of Germany into the colonial field did not, however, arrest British progress in Africa. A Charter granted in 1888 to the British East Africa Company recovered for England that hold over the sources of the Upper Nile which were endangered by Lord Iddesleigh's agreement with Germany in 1886. In 1889 a Charter was granted to the British South Africa Com-

The Partition of Africa, 1890

---

[1] For text of the *General Act* cf. P. Albin, *Les Grands traités politiques*, pp. 368–406.

pany, and the preposterous claims put forward by Portugal to the upper reaches of the Zambesi were firmly repudiated, not indeed without friction, but happily without hostilities.

Agreement with Portugal was followed by agreements with France and Germany. Great Britain recognized the French Protectorate over Madagascar ; France recognized the British Protectorate over the islands held by the Sultan of Zanzibar. Germany did the same. She also acknowledged the claims of Great Britain to the northern half of the shores and waters of Lake Victoria Nyanza, to the valley of the Upper Nile, and to the coast of the Indian Ocean about Vitu, and thence north-wards to Kismayu. On the other hand, Great Britain recognized German claims to the land north of Lake Nyassa, and ceded to her the island of Heligoland, a strategic point only too valuable, as was proved in the Great War, to Germany, but one which would have been of little use to Great Britain.

The final partition of Africa left France in a territorial sense the largest of African Powers, but much of her territory was desert ; Great Britain emerged with an area of something less than 3,000,000 square miles ; Germany possessed nearly 1,000,000. Portugal, Italy, and Belgium also had their shares in the spoil. Though quantitatively inferior to that of France, Great Britain's position, controlling as she did three out of the four great arterial rivers of Africa, possessing in South Africa the only great con-solidated area adapted for white colonization, and holding all the most important strategic points on the East, South, and West Coasts, was incomparably the strongest. At the same time, the reasonable claims of other nations were satisfied, and a most difficult diplomatic corner was turned without a collision involv-ing loss of life. It was a great and a characteristic achievement. The success that Lord Salisbury achieved was not dramatic. He would have been greatly dismayed if it had been. He shunned the limelight. He cared nothing for popular applause. Intensely jealous for his country's honour, he was profoundly convinced that her true strength lay in, ' quietness and confidence '. ' *Im Herzen ein stolzer Patriot* ' was the discerning analysis of his char-acter arrived at by Wolff-Metternich, who as German Ambassador in London had good opportunities for studying it. But patriot though he was, he was no Chauvinist. ' Boastfulness or self-congratulation in diplomacy was to him,' as a kinsman justly observed, ' not only an offence against good manners, but the very way to make the worsted negotiator recognize and resent his defeat.'

Problems arising from the relations between the Western Powers in Africa, though of pre-eminent importance, did not monopolize during these years the attention of Downing Street. The Balkanic volcanoes are never long quiescent. The most eruptive of them was at this time the Bulgarian. _{England and the Near East}

The Treaty of Berlin (1878) had destroyed the Russian scheme of a Greater Bulgaria to be brought into being under Russian protection. But the division effected by Lord Beaconsfield endured for less than a decade. Bulgaria proper and Eastern Roumelia resolved (1885) on union, but under conditions wholly different from those of 1878. The Greater Bulgaria of 1878 would have come into being as a Russian province, establishing Russia within striking distance of Constantinople. The united Bulgaria of 1885 was, on the contrary, intensely Nationalist and it constituted an effective barrier against the advance of Russia towards Constantinople. ' If you can help to build up these peoples into a bulwark of independent States and thus screen the " sick man " from the fury of the northern blast, for God's sake do it.' Thus wrote Sir Robert Morier from Petersburg to Sir William White at Constantinople at the height of the Bulgarian crisis in December 1885. ' These newly emancipated races want to breathe free air,' wrote White, ' and not through Russian nostrils.' Lord Salisbury was in complete accord with the views of the two Ambassadors. ' A Bulgaria, friendly to the Porte, and jealous of foreign influence, would ', he said, ' be a far surer bulwark against foreign aggression than two Bulgarias severed in administration, but united in considering the Porte as the only obstacle to their national development.'

But the erection of the bulwark involved serious complications. The Porte did indeed recognize the union of the Bulgarias under Prince Alexander, but Bulgaria had to repel an attack from Serbia, and the Czar of Russia was infuriated by the independent attitude of his quondam protégé, the Prince of Bulgaria.

In August, 1886, Prince Alexander was kidnapped by military conspirators, compelled to abdicate, and carried off as a prisoner. No one was more gravely perturbed by the outrage than Queen Victoria. In July 1885 her youngest daughter, Princess Beatrice, had become the wife of Prince Alexander's youngest brother, Prince Henry of Battenberg. An elder brother, Prince Louis, a distinguished officer in the English Navy, had in 1884 married the Queen's granddaughter, Princess Victoria of Hesse, the eldest daughter of Princess Alice. Moreover, at the moment of Prince Alexander's abduction the Queen was interesting herself in a projected marriage between the Prince himself and another granddaughter, Princess Victoria of Prussia. This latter marriage was, however, frustrated by Bismarck, and the Prince married an opera singer. But before then he had ceased to be a reigning Prince. Though restored, after a ten days' detention, to his capital and his people, he weakly yielded to Russian pressure, resigned his throne, and retired into private life. He died in 1893. The Bulgarian Sobranje, rejecting a Russian nominee, had in 1887 elected as Alexander's successor, Prince Ferdinand of Saxe-Coburg-Gotha, who, strong in the support of the Emperor Francis Joseph, in whose army he had served, defied Russia, and played during the ensuing thirty years an increasingly important part, not only in Balkan but in European diplomacy.

Greeks and Turks

Great Britain was not less interested in Greece than in Bulgaria. Like the Bulgarians the Greeks had hoped much from the Congress of Berlin, but had returned from it empty-handed, and it was not until 1881 that Mr. Goschen, acting as a special Envoy at Constantinople, wrung from an unwilling Sultan, for our Greek friends, a large slice of Epirus and the greater part of Thessaly. Crete presented another problem. In February 1897 the Cretans proclaimed the union of their island with the Hellenic kingdom. The Powers, anxious to avert a general eruption in the Near East, intervened, and while reasserting the nominal suzerainty of the Porte assured to the Cretans practical autonomy under a European guarantee. The Greeks of the mainland were not satisfied with this arrangement, invaded Turkey and in the 'Thirty Days' War' were heavily defeated by the Turks.

For the Turks had found a new friend. Their spectacular victory over the Greeks was won by an army which had been reorganized under a German scholar-soldier—Baron von der Goltz.

The Emperor William II, departing from the policy of Bismarck who 'never even opened the dispatches from Constantinople', paid two State visits to the Sultan Abdul Hamid (1889 and 1898). He was quick to perceive that England and France had forfeited the favour of the Porte, and that there was consequently a diplomatic vacancy at Constantinople. He resolved to apply for it. Moreover, during the four years previous to the Kaiser's second visit (1898) Christendom had been resounding with the cries of the Armenian Christians butchered in their thousands to make a Sultan's holiday. Those cries had drawn Mr. Gladstone, an old man nearing 90, out of retirement in 1897. Lord Salisbury, then at the Foreign Office, was not less deeply moved than Gladstone by the tale of horror. By the Cyprus Convention of 1878 Great Britain had assumed a peculiar responsibility for the Christian subjects of the Sultan. The responsibility was not fulfilled ; perhaps it was impossible of fulfilment ; for the Sultan alleged provocation on the part of a restless population, and the truth was hard to come by. The Powers, led by England, sent out commissions of inquiry, but the massacres went on. In 1894–5 the victims in Armenia numbered at least 50,000 ; in 1896, on a single day, 6,000 Gregorian Armenians were butchered in Constantinople. These had undoubtedly offered provocation ; the hands of England and the other Powers were tied.

Kaiser and Sultan

Meanwhile, birthday presents continued to arrive from Berlin ; in 1898 came the Kaiser himself ; in 1889 the Ottoman Company of Anatolian Railways was promoted under the auspices of two German banks ; in 1902 the convention for the construction of a railway from Constantinople to Baghdad was concluded. That was only the last link of a long chain stretching from Hamburg, via Buda-Pesth, Belgrade and Nish to Constantinople. Some day it was hoped to carry it on from Baghdad to Basra.

In regard to all these developments England pursued, from 1885 to 1902, a consistent policy. When in 1886 and in 1892 Lord Rosebery took over the Foreign Office from Lord Salisbury, the Queen impressed on him most emphatically the importance of maintaining unbroken continuity. She was entitled to insist. Never for a moment in the course of fifty years had she ever relaxed her vigilant control of the conduct of Foreign affairs. She

The English in Egypt

had vast experience ; the young Minister had none ; and he was her personal selection in preference both to Lord Granville and to Lord Kimberley.   Nor had Lord Rosebery any inclination to deviate from the paths of wisdom trodden by Lord Salisbury.

The style of both those brilliant diplomatists was, however, cramped by the continued occupation of Egypt.   But it had been far easier to get into than to get out of it.   ' In the long and complicated Egyptian business', wrote Gladstone in 1888, ' we were for the most part, as I think, drawn on inevitably by a necessity of honour.'   That was the simple truth.   From the first it was announced and sincerely intended that the British occupation should be merely temporary.

' We shall not ', said Lord Granville in the House of Lords, ' keep our troops in Egypt any longer than is necessary ; but it would be an act of treachery to ourselves, to Egypt, and to Europe, if we withdrew them without having a certainty or . . . until there is reasonable expectation, of a stable, a permanent and a beneficial Government being established in Egypt.'   This policy was announced to the Great Powers in the dispatch of 3rd January, 1883, which further intimated that ' the position in which Her Majesty's Government is placed towards the Khedive imposes upon them the duty of giving advice, with the object of securing that the order of things to be established shall be of a satisfactory character, and possesses the elements of stability and progress.'   Giving advice is, as Lord Milner grimly observed, ' a charming euphemism of the best Granvillian brand ' ; but of the sincerity of the Government's intentions there could be no question.

But intentions are often overruled by circumstances.   The conditions precedent to evacuation remained for long years unfulfilled.   In the meantime, Lord Cromer (to give him by anticipation the name by which he will to all time be known) was doing a work in Egypt to which even the brilliant records of the British Empire furnish few parallels.

Cromer's Work

Lord Cromer took up his task in Egypt in September 1883. His official position was an ambiguous one.   He was merely ' British Agent and Consul-General with plenipotentiary diplomatic rank, the junior of the other similarly accredited representatives of the Powers ; but, as representative of the one Power occupying the country in force, he was *de facto* to impose the

British will'.[1]   The British 'will' meant the regeneration of Egypt.
That work was accomplished in the face of difficulties almost
incredible :   an empty treasury ;   the obstructive jealousy of
France and other Powers ;   a tangle of conflicting jurisdictions ;
a financial system which impoverished the people without enrich-
ing the State ;   vast extravagance on the part of the rulers ;   bitter
poverty the lot of the fellaheen—all these difficulties had to be
surmounted by a man whose position depended solely on personality.   ' I had not to govern Egypt,' he wrote, ' but to assist
in the government without the appearance of doing so, and without any legitimate authority over the agents with whom I had
to deal.'   Yet in less than twenty-five years the Herculean task
was accomplished.   The people were relieved from the burden
of taxation so long endured, yet the revenue rose from less than
£9,000,000 in 1883 to £13,000,000 in 1903 ;   large sums were in
the meantime expended out of revenue upon reproductive works ;
the fertility of the country was marvellously increased by a scientific system of irrigation ;   canals were cut ;   drainage improved ;
roads constructed, and the great Assouan Dam completed.   The
administration of justice was simplified and purified :   the Army,
thanks to the patient labours of General Grenfell and General
Kitchener, was completely reorganized.

By 1896 the Army was judged to be ready for the accom- Recon-
plishment of a task long contemplated.   In 1885 the British quest of
Government had, as we have seen, decided to withdraw from the Soudan
Soudan, and for ten years that unhappy province was a prey to
anarchy.   In 1896, however, the Government of the Khedive
determined to attempt its reconquest.   General Kitchener, in
command of the Nile expedition, patiently advanced towards
the completion of his great design.   Before the end of September
1896 he was in possession of Dongola ;   Abu Hamed was taken
in August 1897, and at the Atbara the Dervishes were scattered
(April 7, 1898).   On September 2 the power of Mahdiism was
finally annihilated by the great victory of Omdurman.   Two days
later the British and Egyptian forces were paraded before the
ruined palace of Khartum and the shattered tomb of the Mahdi,
and there, on the spot where Gordon had perished, a funeral
service was held in solemn memory of the dead knight-errant.

[1] D. G. Hogarth, *ap. D.N.B.*, s.v. Cromer.

Hardly had Kitchener reached Khartum when the diplomatic sky became suddenly overcast. The French Government had never forgiven themselves for their withdrawal from Egypt in 1882. For more than a decade they had impeded in every possible way the work of financial and political reconstruction undertaken by Great Britain in Egypt. That task, unwillingly assumed but patiently fulfilled, seemed now to be on the point of final consummation.

French adventurers had, meanwhile, been displaying remarkable activity in Central Africa. The Anglo-German Agreement of 1890 had been followed by a similar attempt to delimit the French and British spheres of influence in the neighbourhood of Lake Chad. In 1894 the British, operating from the east, established a Protectorate over Uganda, and in the same year the French, operating in West Africa, captured the city of Timbuktu. In May 1894 Great Britain had also concluded an Anglo-Congolese Convention, according to which England ceded to the Congo Free State the left bank of the Upper Nile in return for a recognition of the acquisition of the right bank by Great Britain. In deference to French susceptibilities, the Convention was annulled, and France in her turn secured from the Free State the recognition of her rights, with certain limitations, to the left bank of the Upper Nile. In March 1895, however, Sir Edward Grey declared that the dispatch of a French expedition to the Upper Nile would be regarded by Great Britain as ' an unfriendly act '. The situation was already delicate when in June 1896 Major Marchand left France to take command of the expeditionary force in the French Congo. In the course of two years and in the face of incredible difficulties this intrepid Frenchman pushed his way from the French Congo across Central Africa. Marchand in leading his expedition from the west was counting on a junction with another force led by French officers which was to make its way from the east coast by way of Abyssinia to the Upper Nile. With this force there was also a sprinkling of Russian officers under a well-known figure, Count Leountieff. Consequently, Marchand, on his arrival at Fashoda, found himself unsupported, face to face with General Kitchener and the British forces.

Kitchener denied Marchand's right to be at Fashoda as the

political representative of France; but though the victory of Omdurman was a potent argument, Marchand refused to yield to it. The quarrel was then referred to the diplomatists. Lord Salisbury claimed for the Khedive all the lands over which the Khalifa had borne sway, and made it clear to the French Government that the claim would be asserted by the whole force of Great Britain. In the autumn of 1898 the two nations were on the brink of war. France, however, gave way, recalled Marchand, and in March 1899 concluded with Great Britain a comprehensive agreement in regard to the Soudan. By this treaty the rights of Great Britain over the whole Nile Basin, from the source of that river to its mouth, were acknowledged; France was confirmed in possession of a great West African Empire, but the whole of the Egyptian Soudan was to be subject to the power which ruled at Cairo. Thus the way to the Cape was still open, unblocked by any other European Power. From that moment Anglo-French relations rapidly improved, until in 1904 the Anglo-French Agreement was concluded and France agreed to give Great Britain a free hand in Egypt.

Before that Agreement was concluded the 'last of the great Victorian statesmen', the man who had dealt so firmly but so tactfully with the Fashoda crisis, was dead. So also was the Queen he had faithfully served.

Apart from the matters already dealt with in this chapter Lord Salisbury, during his third tenure of the Foreign Secretaryship, had several diplomatic achievements to his credit; but summary mention of them must suffice. Perhaps the most important was his masterly handling of the Venezuela Boundary dispute in 1895. For many years past there had been some dispute as to the precise boundary between Venezuela and British Guiana. Lord Aberdeen had attempted to effect a settlement of the question as long ago as 1844, but his suggested delimitation was declined. Thirty years later Venezuela professed its willingness to accept the Aberdeen line, but Great Britain then refused to concede it. The dispute dragged on until, in July 1895, Mr. Olney, Secretary of State under President Cleveland, suddenly interfered and called upon the parties to accept arbitration. The demand itself was startling, the terms in which it was made were not far short of insolent.

The Venezuelan Question

The United States attempted to justify their interference by an appeal to the doctrine enunciated in 1823 in the famous message of President Monroe. That doctrine had been for seventy years the sheet-anchor of American diplomacy, but not until 1895 had it been invoked by the United States in a matter of serious importance. It was now asserted in the most extreme form in respect to a matter with which the concern of the United States was remote.

England and U.S.A.

' That distance and three thousand miles of intervening ocean make any permanent political union between a European and an American State unnatural and inexpedient will hardly be denied. . . . The States of America, south as well as north, by geographical proximity, by natural sympathy, by similarity of governmental constitutions, are friends and allies, commercially and politically, of the United States. . . . To-day the United States is practically sovereign on this continent, and its fiat is law upon the subjects to which it confines its interposition. . . . There is, then, a doctrine of American public law, well founded in principle, and abundantly sanctioned by precedent, which entitles and requires the United States to treat as an injury to itself the forcible assumption by a European Power of political control over an American State.' Such was the remarkable language of the Olney Dispatch.

That dispatch unquestionably gave a wide extension to the principle which was laid down by President Monroe, and was highly provocative in tone. Fortunately Lord Salisbury declined to be provoked. He did, indeed, refuse to accept unrestricted arbitration : he politely questioned the applicability of the Monroe doctrine to the particular dispute, and he insisted that the United States was not entitled to affirm ' with reference to a number of States for whose conduct it assumes no responsibility, that its interests are necessarily concerned in whatever may befall those States, simply because they are situated in the Western hemisphere '. At the same time, Lord Salisbury made it clear that he had no intention of allowing Great Britain to be drawn into a serious quarrel with the United States. Unfortunately the attitude of American statesmen rendered it none too easy to keep the peace. On December 17, 1895, President Cleveland sent a strongly worded message to Congress. Had the direction of

English policy been in less wise and experienced hands, his language might easily have led to war. As it was, the message
accentuated a difficult situation and feeling began to run high in
America. 'Fortunately for us,' wrote an American publicist,
'Lord Salisbury had a very good sense of humour and declined
to take the matter too seriously.'[1] Both Great Britain and
Venezuela agreed to submit the evidence for their conflicting
claims to a 'committee of investigation' appointed by the United
States; and the investigation issued in a Treaty of Arbitration,
concluded nominally between the immediate disputants, but in
reality between Great Britain and the United States. The result
of the arbitration was, on the whole, to substantiate the British
claim. A still more important result ensued. In January 1897
a General Arbitration Treaty between the two great English-
speaking nations was signed by Sir Julian Paunceforte and Secretary Olney. The Senate, however, refused its assent, and the
treaty was not actually concluded until November 1914.

In the meantime much had happened. The Venezuelan affair
really brought to an end the period of American isolation in world-
politics. 'Cleveland's policy', writes an American historian, 'as
to the Venezuelan boundary, announced to the world with seismic
suddenness and violence that the American democracy was of
age.'[2] From the position asserted by Cleveland and Olney in
1895, their countrymen could not well recede, and the position
involved important corollaries.

One corollary was the war which broke out between the United
States and Spain in 1898. The outstanding result of that war
was to bring the United States on to the international stage as
a World-Power, with special interests in the South Pacific. The
Philippine Islands fell to her as the result of her victory over
Spain; in the same year (1898) she annexed the Sandwich Islands
(Hawaii); and in 1899 the Samoan group of islands was partitioned between the United States and Germany. Five years later
the United States purchased from the Republic of Panama a
10-mile strip with the object of cutting a canal to connect the
Atlantic and the Pacific Oceans. After ten years' labour greatly
lightened, if not rendered possible, by the researches of Sir Ronald

Hispano-American War

---

[1] Bingham, *The Monroe Doctrine*, p. 12.
[2] W. A. Dunning, *The British Empire and the United States*, p. 368.

Ross and other English pioneers in tropical medicine, the Canal was completed and opened in 1914.

The point of immediate significance in relation to English Foreign Policy is that the ' expansion ' of the United States, their début on the international stage, was viewed with something more than benevolence by England. Other Powers regarded this development with more jealous eyes, and it may be that only English sea power averted in 1898 European intervention on behalf of Spain. From a policy of strict neutrality during that brief struggle Lord Salisbury never departed ; but it was made clear to other Powers that if Great Britain observed the limits of neutrality so also must they.

Of British benevolence the United States were not unmindful ; and the debt thus incurred was at least partially repaid during the South African War. For the outbreak of that war Lord Salisbury was not directly responsible. South African business came within the sphere of the Colonial Office. To the Foreign Secretary, however, it fell to repudiate the idea of foreign mediation in 1900 between Great Britain and the Boer Republics, though of the principle of international arbitration Lord Salisbury was a consistent advocate.

The First Hague Peace Conference, 1899

Truthfully it has been said of him that he above all the statesmen of his time possessed the ' international mind '. It was, therefore, appropriate that he should have been the Minister responsible for the participation of Great Britain in the First Hague Conference, which met in 1899 on the invitation of the Czar Nicholas II. Lord Salisbury had cordially responded to that invitation and had expressed the ' earnest desire ' of the British Government ' to promote, by all possible means, the principle of recourse to mediation and arbitration for the prevention of war '. Germany accepted the Czar's invitation in the hope that ' this Peace and Disarmament idea, which under its ideal outward form, makes a real danger of war, would be wrecked on England's objections, without Germany having to appear in the foreground '.[1]

The Hague Conference undoubtedly stimulated interest in the difficult problems of disarmament and arbitration ; it set up an Arbitral (Optional) Court ; it evoked from the Powers a

[1] G. P., xv. Nos. 4222 and 4217, and Spender, *Fifty Years*, p. 173.

platonic assent to general principles ; but beyond that achieved little.[1] It was, therefore, on a rather pessimistic note that, in the sphere of diplomacy, the nineteenth century closed.

That note was accentuated by a sinister coincidence. The Peace Conference at the Hague was immediately followed by the outbreak of war between Great Britain and the Boer Republics in South Africa.

[1] See F. W. Holls, *The Peace Conference at the Hague.* Macmillan, 1900.

CHAPTER VII

THE NEW IMPERIALISM—THE JUBILEES

A New
Era

THE last decades of the nineteenth century witnessed nothing less than a revolution in regard to the Overseas Empire. The revolution was at once material and spiritual : a change in conditions and a change of sentiment. Material conditions were revolutionized by a series of remarkable inventions and discoveries, and by their appropriation to the service of man. Distance and Time were annihilated ; medical research went far to conquer tropical diseases, and thus enabled the white man to exploit vast territories, to supply the industrialists of Europe with the raw materials they sorely needed, and in return to receive from Europe services and commodities which have transformed the life of more than one continent. Economically and commercially the whole world became one vast unit.

Significant as were these developments for all peoples of the old world and the new, they possessed peculiar significance for the greatest and most widely extended of World-Empires.

England had in the past fought a hard fight against her European neighbours for commercial and colonial ascendancy. She had emerged from the fight victorious. The contest with Spain was decided by the end of the sixteenth century ; with the Dutch by the end of the seventeenth ; with the French in 1815 if not in 1763. Between 1815 and 1884 we had had no real rival in the colonial field, and not many European neighbours.

In the last decades of the nineteenth century the position rapidly changed. New nations like Germany and Italy were driven, partly under the pressure of economic forces, partly by newly aroused national self-consciousness, into the colonial field. Our Australasian Colonies, who had long been acutely conscious

of the presence of the French in New Caledonia and the New
Hebrides, were further alarmed by the advent of the Germans
and the Americans into the Pacific. But the Home Government
had not the wish, even if they had the power, to prevent this
'intrusion'. Evidently the globe was shrinking; evidently
Europe was expanding.

To the process both of contraction and expansion nothing
contributed more than the construction of railways, the improvement of steamships and the development in the art of cold storage
and refrigeration.

Of the importance of these developments the British Posses- Africa
sions in Africa afford a signal illustration.

Africa has no great inland waterways: to inland transport
the river rapids and the 'ranges of terraced mountains are serious
barriers'; 'horse sickness periodically destroyed the horses',
the tsetse-fly, the rinderpest and coast fever took terrible toll of
the bullocks.[1] 'The development of the African continent',
wrote Lord Lugard, 'is impossible without railways, and has
awaited their advent. A railway reduces administration expenses
in the transport of stores and in the time of officials in reaching
their work: it saves the lives and health of officers; it reduces
the number and cost of troops required for policing the country
by increasing their mobility: it renders direct taxation possible,
by affording a market for produce and increasing the wealth of
the people [2]: it has opened up new markets for British trade:
it has killed the slave trade: it liberates labour engaged on
transport for productive work: and by proper methods of construction it forms the most valuable of educational agencies for
a free labour supply. It has been calculated that one railway
train of average capacity and engine power will do the work of
13,000 carriers at one-twentieth the cost.' [3]

Except in South Africa there was little or no railway develop- South
ment in Africa until the 'nineties. Even in the south it was not Africa
much earlier. When in 1872 the Cape Government took over
the railways of the Cape Colony the total length of lines was less

---

[1] Cf. Mrs. Knowles, *Overseas Empire*, I. 17, and supra, c. i.
[2] After the railway reached Karro (Nigeria) ground nuts which had been
sold at £3 10s. a ton fetched £40 to £45. Lugard, *Dual Mandate*, p. 298.
[3] Ibid., p. 463.

than 64 miles.   Before the close of the century unbroken railway connexion had been established between Cape Town, through the (then) Republics, to Delagoa Bay.   The mileage of the railways in the Union of South Africa, merged into a single State system in 1910, now (1933) exceeds 13,000.   As late as 1890, however, when the pioneer expedition of the Chartered Company into Mashonaland was organized, it took from May 6th to September 16th to get, ' under very favourable circumstances ', from Kimberley to Salisbury.   With the 'nineties railway development began in Rhodesia.   Cecil Rhodes constructed a line between these two points, and it was subsequently extended across the Zambesi into Northern Rhodesia and the Belgian Congo.   In 1895 the great Uganda railway was started, and reached Lake Victoria in 1903.   Unlike the Rhodesian railways, which have been constructed by private capital, the Uganda railway was built as an Imperial enterprise at the expense of the Imperial Government.   Most of the railways in East and West Africa have, however, been constructed by and at the expense of the local governments, and exceedingly costly, for obvious reasons, most of them have been.

Australia   The railway system of Australia, which now has a mileage of some 27,000 miles, is also a Government enterprise.   The several Colonial Governments which were responsible for it showed little foresight or prudence ;   the gauge adopted for the New South Wales lines differed from that in Victoria and South Australia, and the extravagant cost of construction has imposed additional burdens on the heavily burdened taxpayers.

Canada   Canada affords, however, the most conspicuous example of the political importance of a railway system.   Canada has indeed 2,700 miles of internal navigable waterways.   Ocean-going steamers can now sail without breaking bulk from the Great Lakes to the Atlantic, and in the year 1931 carried over 16,000,000 tons of freight.   Nevertheless, it is true to say that Federated Canada is the creation of the railway engineers.   *The British North America Act* was passed in 1867, yet ten years later Lord Dufferin, when as Governor-General he visited British Columbia, had to travel from Ottawa by way of Chicago to San Francisco over 2,000 miles of foreign railways, and from San Francisco make a sea voyage of 800 miles by H.M.S. *Amethyst* to Esquimault, in Vancouver Island. Little wonder that British Columbia refused to enter the Confederation, as it did in 1871, except on condition that it was within ten years to be connected by rail with the railway system of Canada. When Lord Dufferin visited Victoria one of the triumphal arches erected in his honour bore the legend 'Carnarvon terms or separation.' Very properly he refused to pass under it. None the less, the legend bore fruits.

The story of the great enterprise which ensured fruition is one of the great romances of Imperial history ; and it belongs to the period now under review. The Maritime Provinces had also stipulated that they should be linked up by rail with Ottawa, and that line was completed and opened in 1876. But a transcontinental link, running for 2,500 miles through lands mainly uninhabited, and crossing one of the great mountain ranges of the world, was a wholly different matter. A contract was, however, concluded in 1881 between Sir Charles Tupper on behalf of the Government and George Stephen (afterwards Lord Mount Stephen) and six others on behalf of the Company. The Government granted a cash subsidy of 25 million dollars, and a subsidy in land of 25 million acres.[1] Almost incredible were the difficulties encountered—difficulties physical, political and financial—but they were overcome, thanks largely to the skill, the perseverance and indomitable pluck of a small group of men, George Stephen, Donald Smith (Lord Strathcona), Sir William Van Horne. On November 7, 1885, the rail constructed from the east met the rail constructed from the west, and in the Eagle Pass in the heart of the Rockies the last spike was driven by Donald Smith. The line was completed six years ahead of the scheduled time.

Canada now (1933) possesses nearly 60,000 miles of railways. The commercial aspect of this development calls for no emphasis. The construction of the Canadian Pacific Railway opened up a vast wheat area, the product of which can be transported in a few weeks from the prairies to Southampton or Liverpool. Most of the grain is carried via Montreal or Halifax. Montreal, with its superb harbour, is now—despite its five months of ice-binding

[1] These subsidies were greatly increased and the total amount of public assistance was ultimately reckoned at $228,500,925. (Report of Drayton-Acworth Commission, 1917.)

winter—the greatest grain-exporting seaport in the world, and handles nearly one-third of the foreign trade of the whole Dominion. But the Canadian Pacific, as its name implies, looks west as well as east. Vancouver, whence forty-five steamer lines now radiate, is unquestionably destined to become the Liverpool of the Pacific. The Prairie Provinces, especially Alberta, have begun to look to Vancouver as a possible alternative to Montreal and Halifax. Regina is 1,312 miles nearer to Vancouver than to Halifax, and the cutting of the Panama Canal has reduced the distance by sea from British Columbia to England by some 6,000 miles. Whether we look eastwards or westwards the future of Vancouver, with its magnificent harbour, is then absolutely assured.

But the commercial aspect of Canadian railway development is not the only one. The Canadian Pacific and the Canadian National are great Imperial highways of immense political and strategical significance. Esquimault, the naval station on Vancouver Island, has a dry dock which will hold the biggest battleship afloat, and naval ratings, thanks to the great transcontinental railways, can now be reinforced from Portsmouth in a fortnight. What that means to the position of Great Britain as a Pacific Power, what it might mean at a crisis for Australia and New Zealand, need not be emphasized.

One other point demands attention. Since 1886 the Canadian railways have mostly run east and west, and have thus determined for all time the destiny of the Dominion. Before 1886 they ran mostly north and south, linking up with the lines to the south of the international border. Had that tendency persisted, Canada could hardly have resisted commercial if not political absorption into the United States. True of Canada as a whole, that was particularly true of the then distant and isolated Province of British Columbia. 'Under the existing circumstances', said Sir Charles Tupper, 'it had no means of advancement except by throwing in its lot with the great nation to the south, with which it had constant communication both by land and sea.' The Canadian Pacific saved Canada for the Empire.

Ocean Communications The improvement of ocean communication was, in the period under review, hardly less important than railways as a factor making for the integrity of the Empire. Colonial enterprise was

from the earliest days conditioned by the skill and hardihood of
English mariners and the ingenuity of English shipbuilders.   ' We
shall rear merchant ship both fair and tall ', said one, ' so that
nothing that swimmeth shall make them vail nor stoop, which
shall make this little northern corner of the world the richest
storehouse for merchandize in all Christendom.' [1]

To the same high qualities of skill and courage the British
Empire and Imperial Commerce owe the acquisition of those
military, naval and coaling stations, by which unbroken communication is maintained between the far-flung units of the
great Sea Empire.   Each of the main ocean-routes is safeguarded
by one or more of these outposts, sometimes no more than coaling
stations, sometimes great naval stations.   Bermuda guards the
route from England to Canada.   On the way to India viâ the
Suez Canal we have Gibraltar and Malta.   On the latter the
Mediterranean fleet is based, as Valetta possesses not only a first-
rate fortified harbour but an aircraft station and a high-power
wireless installation.   Cyprus, acquired in 1878 and formally
annexed in 1914, has no good harbour, but east of Suez we have
Aden, a naval and coaling station acquired in 1837, Perim (1859) on
the Straits of Bab el Mandeb, Sokotra (occupied by the East India
Company in 1839 and formally declared a British Protectorate
in 1886), and Zanzibar (1890).   The Cape route to India is some
4,500 miles longer than by the Canal ; to Melbourne, on the
other hand, it is only about 500 miles longer ; but in the former
hardly less than in the latter case it might become once again
supremely useful.   Its safeguarding is, consequently, a matter of
high Imperial significance.   With coaling stations at Freetown,
Ascension and St. Helena, with the harbour of Table Bay, with
the Mauritius and Seychelles in the Indian Ocean, and with
Colombo, it is admirably provided with ' stepping-stones ' to
India.   Proceeding southwards towards Australasia, we have
Singapore, acquired for the East India Company by Sir Stamford
Raffles in 1819, and since developed into a magnificent port.
Sarawak was acquired by Rajah Brooke in 1842, and his successor
placed its foreign policy under the control of Great Britain in
1888.   The British Government took over Labuan, as a base for
the suppression of piracy, in 1846 and British North Borneo in

Links of
Empire

---

[1] Quoted by Knowles, op. cit., i. 68.

1881. Fiji, as already mentioned, was taken in 1874, and British New Guinea in 1884. Most of the rampart of islands (south of the Equator) which guard Australasia are (since 1919) administered under mandates by the Commonwealth of Australia or New Zealand. Hong Kong, acquired from China in 1841, similarly acts as sentinel in the China Seas. The ocean highways are thus well guarded.

Joint
Stock
Capital

Before passing from the material background of the new Imperialism one other point demands notice. Railways, steamships, submarine cables—the annihilation of space and time— all testify to the patience and skill of the engineers and other workers and to their assiduity in the application of Science to industry. Yet their labours could never have been brought to fruition except with the aid of a multitude of men and women who by thrift and self-denial accumulated in the aggregate great reserves of capital, and thus made possible the victory of man over nature. In this connexion the Limited Liability Act of 1855 is of capital importance. Its enactment marked the beginning of a new epoch in the industrial organization of this country, indeed of the civilized world. The Act legalized the principle that the shareholder in a Limited Liability Company is responsible for the debts of the Company only to the extent of his share in its capital. Until then the capital was provided by the ' employer '. The terms capitalist and employer were, in fact, interchangeable. After 1855 the ' Company ' tended to supersede the private or family ' firm '. The capital was subscribed on the joint stock and limited liability principles by a number of shareholders. By the early 'eighties 10,000 such companies had been registered in Great Britain. Half a century later (1930) there were 113,327 Joint Stock Companies, with a paid-up capital of over £5,500,000,000. Many of the individual holdings are small. Thus the five great Joint Stock Banks have between them more than 275,000 shareholders; a single Steamship Company (the Cunard) has over 27,000 shareholders, the railway companies have 800,000. This development has a twofold significance : it means, first, that people of small means have a new inducement to save, and a much wider field for the investment of small sums than ever before, and, secondly, that the accumulated wealth of the country is widely distributed. To the small capitalists of the Motherland colonial development owes no small debt.

Material development has thus been phenomenal.   Even more significant has been the revolution in mental and spiritual outlook. During the first half of the Victorian era the 'Manchester School' dominated both politics and philosophy.   The core of their creed was derived from the French *Philosophes* or *Physiocrats* of the eighteenth century.   *Laisser-faire—laisser-aller*.   Governments should stand aside and let nature work.   It was an era of emancipation :   everybody and everything was to be free : Thought, Trade, Colonies.   The first Empire had ended in disintegration :   the American Colonies had won their 'freedom'; the Second Empire would follow a like course.   Had not Turgot taught that ' colonies are like fruits : they cling to the tree only till they ripen ' ?   Such is the power of analogies in politics that men of all parties began to look forward to the ' ripening ' of the Colonies and their eventual ' emancipation '.   Cobden was naturally an unqualified separatist :   ' The Colonial system ', he declared, ' with all its dazzling appeals to the passions of the people, can never be got rid of except by the indirect process of Free Trade, which will gradually and imperceptibly loose the bands which unite our Colonies to us by a mistaken notion of self-interest.'[1]   The appeal, dazzling or dull, was at that time non-existent, but the passage is significant alike for the end desired and for the forecasting of the means by which it would be achieved.   More considered and more authoritative is the following passage from Sir George Cornewall Lewis's *Government of Dependencies* (1841), the most representative work of that period.

' If a dominant country understood the true nature of the advantages arising from the supremacy and dependence of the related communities, it would voluntarily recognize the legal independence of each of its own dependencies as were fit for independence ;   it would, by its political arrangements, study to prepare for independence those which were still unable to stand alone ; and it would seek to promote colonization for the purpose of extending its trade rather than its empire, and without intending

Colonial Policy : The Manchester School

[1] Morley, *Cobden*, i. 230.

to maintain the dependence of its colonies beyond the time when they need its protection.' [1]

Mr. Arthur Mills undoubtedly expressed the prevailing view when in his *Colonial Constitutions* (1856) he wrote : " To ripen these communities (the Colonies) to the earliest possible maturity social, political, commercial, to qualify them by all the appliances within the reach of the parent State for present self-government and eventual independence is now the universally admitted aim of our Colonial policy.' [2]   ' As to our American possessions I have long held and often expressed the opinion that they are a sort of *damnosa haereditas*.'   So Sir Henry Taylor, an official at the Colonial Office, wrote to his chief, the Duke of Newcastle (February 26, 1864).   Little wonder that Sir Alexander Galt, the eminent Canadian statesman, wrote home from London in 1867 : ' I am more than ever disappointed at the tone of feeling here as to the colonies.   I cannot shut my eyes to the fact that they want to get rid of us.   They have a servile fear of the United States and would rather give us up than defend us, or incur the risk of war with that country.'   It was true.   So late, indeed, as 1872, Tennyson was constrained to repudiate the suggestion of *The Times* that the Canadians should ' take up their freedom as the days of their apprenticeship were over ' :

> And that true North whereof we lately heard
> A strain to shame us, keep you to yourselves,
> So loyal is too costly ! Friends, your love
> Is but a burden : loose the bond and go !
> Is this the tone of Empire ?

The tone of Empire it was not : but Tennyson's words struck a note which was re-echoed throughout the Empire.   On behalf of Canada, Lord Dufferin, the Governor-General, wrote to thank the Poet Laureate for the ' spirited denunciation ' with which he had ' branded those who are seeking to dissolve the Empire and to alienate and to disgust the inhabitants of this most powerful and prosperous colony '.   ' Your noble words ', he added, ' have struck responsive fire through every heart ; . . . and have been completely effectual to heal the wounds occasioned by the senseless language of *The Times*.'

Imperial-   The turn of the tide was, however, already perceptible.   The
ism

[1] p. 324 (ed. 1891).   [2] p. lxix.

Separatist force had spent itself. The dream of the Manchester
School was fading. *Laisser-faire* as an economic prescription was
rapidly losing its popularity and efficacy. The worship of the
State was supplanting adoration of the deity of ' freedom '.

Among party leaders in England Disraeli was the first to *Disraeli*
preach the gospel of the new Imperialism, and to repudiate the
dogmas accepted by him in his political youth. In 1852 he had
predicted that ' these wretched Colonies will all be independent
in a few years and are a millstone round our necks '.[1] Very different was his tone when, as leader of the Conservative Party,
he addressed a great meeting at the Crystal Palace in 1872—on
the eve of his greatest electoral triumph. To the principle of
Colonial self-government he remained faithful, but he added :

' Self-government, in my opinion, when it was conceded ought
to have been conceded as part of a great policy of imperial consolidation. It ought to have been accompanied with an imperial
tariff, by securities for the people of England for the enjoyment
of the unappropriated lands which belonged to the Sovereign as
their trustee, and by a military code which should have precisely
defined the means and the responsibilities by which the colonies
should be defended, and by which, if necessary, this country
should call for aid from the colonies themselves. It ought,
further, to have been accompanied by some representative council
in the metropolis, which would have brought the colonies into
constant and continuous relations with the home Government.
All this, however, was omitted, because those who advised that
policy—and I believe their convictions were sincere—looked upon
the colonies of England, looked even upon our connexion with
India, as a burden on this country, viewing everything in a
financial aspect, and totally passing by those moral and political
considerations which make nations great and by the influence of
which alone men are distinguished from animals.' [2]

During the next twenty years the reaction against Separatism *The Ex-*
made rapid headway. From the middle 'seventies onwards there *pansion*
was an immense output of books, pamphlets and articles advo- *England*
cating closer union between the Mother Country and the daughter
lands. The material obstacles, as we have seen, were being rapidly
overcome : new spiritual links were rapidly forged. Among

---

[1] *Life*, iii. 385. [2] *Speeches* (ed. Kebbel), II. 530–1.

those who contributed industriously to the change of outlook were Lord John Russell,[1] Edward Jenkin,[2], F. P. de Labillière,[3] F. Young,[4] J. Stanley Little,[5] G. R. Parkin,[6] and others too numerous to mention. But it was the publication in 1883 of Sir John Seeley's remarkable volume, *The Expansion of England*, which for the first time concentrated public attention on the Imperial problem. Seeley gave to the political history of England during the two previous centuries a new interpretation. The loss of the first Colonial Empire was not a ' blessing in disguise '. We lost it by the adoption of a false theory of colonial relations. The second Empire may be preserved by the promulgation of a sound theory. England may still ' prove able to do what the United States does so easily, that is hold together in a federal union counties very remote from each other '. ' Here, too, is a great homogeneous people, one in blood, language, religion and laws, but dispersed over a boundless space. . . . If we are disposed to doubt whether any system can be devised capable of holding together communities so distant from each other, then is the time to recollect the history of the United States of America. They have solved this problem, why should not England also solve it ? '

Imperial Federation League

As a practical answer to this question the Imperial Federation League came into being in 1884 under the auspices of statesmen like W. E. Forster, Lord Rosebery, Edward Stanhope, W. H. Smith, Sir Charles Tupper of Canada, and Sir Charles Gavan Duffy and Sir Henry Parkes of Australia. It attracted also the adhesion of eminent historians like Seeley, J. A. Froude and James (Viscount) Bryce. The League was not committed to any particular form of Federation, but while respecting the complete autonomy of the several units of the Empire as regards local affairs, it was pledged to work for the permanent unity of the Empire, and to devise some organization for common defence and co-operation in foreign policy. ' The Federation we aim at ', said Lord Rosebery in 1888, ' is the closest possible union of the various self-governing States ruled by the British Crown, con-

---

[1] *Speeches and Dispatches*, p. 152.
[2] *The Colonial and Imperial Unity* (1871), and Essays in *Contemp. Rev.* (1871).
[3] *England and her Colonies* (1869), *Federal Britain* (1894).
[4] *Imperial Federation* (1876).   [5] *A World Empire* (1879).
[6] *Imperial Federation* (1892).

sistently with that free national development which is the birth-right of British subjects all over the world—the closest union in sympathy, in external action and in defence.'[1]

The League ultimately foundered on the rock of Imperial Preference, and was dissolved in November 1893; but during the intervening decade it did educational and propagandist work of the highest value. Branches were formed alike in the United Kingdom and in Canada, Australia and New Zealand, meetings were organized, literature distributed and great enthusiasm aroused.

Nor were practical results and demonstrations lacking. In 1884 the Government appointed a Royal Commission to organize an Exhibition to illustrate the products, manufactures and art of the Colonies and India. The Prince of Wales became President of the Commission, and threw himself with energy and enthusiasm into work which reflected the rapidly developing sentiments of his future subjects in all parts of the world. Queen Victoria opened the Exhibition in state on May 4th, 1886, in the presence of a great and representative concourse of people, and with appropriate pageantry devised by the Prince. The Poet Laureate wrote a special ode for the occasion, and it was sung to music composed by Sir Arthur Sullivan. With incomparable felicity Tennyson caught the spirit of the hour.

> Welcome, welcome with one voice
> In your welfare we rejoice,
> Sons and brothers that have sent,
> From isle and cape and continent,
> Produce of your field and flood,
> Mount and mine, and primal wood;
> Works of subtle brain and hand,
> And splendours of the morning land,
> Gifts from every British zone,
> Britons, hold your own!
>
> .   .   .   .
>
> Sharers of our glorious past
> Brothers, must we part at last?
> Shall we not thro' good and ill,
> Cling to one another still?
> Britain's myriad voices call,
> ' Sons be welded each and all
> One with Britain, heart and soul!
> One life, one flag, one fleet, one throne!
> Britons, hold your own!'

The 'Colinderies'

---

[1] Speech at Edinburgh, October 31, 1888.

The Queen in reply to the Prince-President's address described the Exhibition as ' an impressive development of the idea which the Prince Consort had originated in 1851 '. The reference was characteristic but misleading. The Exhibition of 1851 was the apotheosis of the Manchester School ; it represented the exaltation of internationalism. The Exhibition of 1886—the ' Colinderies ' as it was nicknamed—was a family affair, reflecting the sentiment not of internationalism but of Imperial self-consciousness.

The Exhibition was an immense popular success and realized a profit of over £30,000. In order that the enthusiasm aroused should not be evanescent, the Prince of Wales suggested that the Exhibition should take a permanent form in ' an Imperial Institute which should represent the arts, manufactures and commerce of the Queen's Colonial and Indian Empire '.

The Imperial Institute — It was subsequently decided that the Institute should form the chief national memorial of the Queen's Jubilee. The main part of the profits of the ' Colinderies ' was appropriated to this purpose. Several of the Indian Princes sent generous contributions, but for some unexplained reason the project, though carried through, never quite fulfilled the dreams of the Prince and his co-projectors. The Queen laid the foundation stone of the new building at South Kensington on July 4, 1887, and opened it in 1893, with an earnest prayer that ' it may never cease to flourish as a lasting emblem of the unity and loyalty of her Empire '. Flourish it never did ; it remains an interesting memorial of the Imperial enthusiasm characteristic of the period ; it does valuable work, conducting investigations and research in the economic resources of the Empire, but since 1899 the main part of the building has been the central home of the University of London.

First Colonial Conference, 1887 — Another result of the educational work of the Imperial Federation League was the meeting of the first Colonial Conference. In August 1886 the League sent a strong deputation to the Prime Minister, to urge that an official Conference should be summoned in connexion with the Queen's Jubilee. The Government assented to the request, and invited the self-governing Colonies to nominate representatives to take part in a Conference for the purpose of discussing ' certain questions of common interest to all parts of the Empire '. The Crown Colonies were also invited.

The invitation was prefaced by a quotation from the Queen's speech on the last prorogation of Parliament : ' I am led to the conviction that there is on all sides a growing desire to draw closer in every practicable way the bonds which unite the various portions of the Empire. I have authorized communications to be entered into with the principal Colonial Governments with a view to the fuller consideration of matters of common interest.'

The matters detailed for discussion were organization for military defence and ' the promotion of commercial and social relations by the development of postal and telegraphic communications '. The subject of Imperial Federation was expressly excluded from the agenda of the first Conference. In their letter of invitation the Government had expressed the opinion that ' it might be detrimental to a more developed system of united action if a question not yet ripe for practical decision were now to be brought to the test of a formal examination '. The same point was taken by Lord Salisbury in his opening address. ' I am not here now ', he said, ' to recommend you to indulge in any ambitious scheme of constitution-making. . . . That is a matter for the future rather than for the present. These are grand aspirations. . . . They are doubtless hazy now, but they are the nebulous matter that in course of ages—in very much less than ages—will cool down and condense into material from which many practical and business-like resolutions will very likely come.'[1]

Notwithstanding this embargo it was impossible to conceal the dissatisfaction felt by some of the greater Colonies with the anomalies and humiliations incidental to their existing constitutional position. Before the Conference met Mr. (afterwards Sir James) Service, Premier of Victoria, had given vigorous expression to the profound chagrin felt by the Australasian Colonies about the attitude of the Home Government towards New Guinea and Samoa. Mr. Service justly complained that despite the concession of ' responsible ' government to the greater Colonies the Imperial Government remained, as regards foreign policy, ' to all intents and purposes an unqualified autocracy '. In regard to local government he said, ' the fullest measure of Constitutional

Austra-lian criti-cism

[1] *Proceedings* (c. 5091), p. 5.

freedom and Parliamentary representation has been conceded to the more important colonies ; but as regards the second, we have no representation whatever in the Imperial system. . . . The weakness of this position has at times been most disadvantageously apparent, and its humiliation keenly felt. . . . Colonial interests are sufficiently important to entitle us to some defined position in the Imperial economy, to some tangible means of asserting if necessary our rights '.

At the Conference itself, Mr. Alfred Deakin, speaking on behalf of the Australasian Colonies, gave courteous but caustic expression to this sentiment :

' We have observed with close interest the discussion that has taken place in the Mother Country upon the question of a spirited foreign policy. There are some of us who live in hopes to see it a vital issue in the politics of Great Britain as to whether there shall not be a spirited Colonial policy as well ; because we find that other nations are pursuing a policy which might fairly be described as a spirited Colonial policy. One has only to turn to the dispatches which have passed between this country and the Australian Colonies upon the subject of New Guinea and the New Hebrides, and to compare them with the dispatches published in the same Blue Book, taken from the White Book of the German Empire, and with the extracts of dispatches issued by the French Colonial Office, to notice the marked difference of tone. The dispatches received from England, with reference to English activity in these seas, exhibited only the disdain and indifference with which English enterprise was treated in the Colonial Office, and by contrast one was compelled to notice the eagerness with which the French and German statesmen received the smallest details of information as to the movements of their traders in those particular seas, and the zeal with which they hastened to support them . . . we hope that from this time forward, Colonial policy will be considered Imperial policy ; and that Colonial interests will be considered and felt to be Imperial interests ; and that they will be carefully studied, and that when once they are understood, they will be most determinedly upheld.' [1]

The language is restrained, but the sentiment is unmistakable. Nor was the Conference allowed to close without a more specific

[1] *Proceedings*, pp. 24–5.

reference to the constitutional problem. At the concluding session Sir Samuel Griffith, as ' the oldest actual minister present '
gave expression to a thought which on this historic occasion
was in many minds :

' I consider that this Conference does comprise what may
perhaps be called the rudimentary elements of a parliament ; but
it has been a peculiarity of our British institutions that those
which have been found most durable are those which have grown
up from institutions which were in the first instance of a rudimentary character. It is impossible to predicate now what form
future conferences should take, or in what mode some day further
effect would be given to their conclusions, but I think we may
look forward to seeing this sort of informal Council of the Empire
develop, until it becomes a legislative body, at any rate a consultative body, and some day, perhaps, a legislative body under
conditions that we cannot just now foresee.'

The Conference was avowedly ' consultative ', and the report
of the Proceedings attests both the volume and value of the con-
sultations. Of concrete results the most important concerned
Imperial Defence. The Imperial Government undertook to
maintain a strong squadron of cruisers and gunboats in the Western Pacific, and the Australasian Colonies agreed to contribute
£126,000 a year (increased in 1902 to £240,000) towards the
expense of maintaining it ; a general officer was to be sent to
Australia to advise on military defence ; Simon's Town was to
be fortified by the Imperial Government ; and the series of coaling
stations was to be strengthened. The Conference also discussed
the desirability of Imperial penny postage ; a new Australian
cable and uniformity of law in regard to merchandise marks and
patents : but nothing definite was effected. The *Colonial Pro-
bates Act* of 1892 did, however, give effect to the desire of the
Colonies for the recognition of Colonial wills, and the *Colonial
Stocks Act* of 1901 gave a welcome stimulus to Colonial credit by
authorizing trustees to invest in certain Colonial stocks. Mr.
Hofmeyr, one of the representatives of South Africa, made the
daring suggestion that a uniform tax of 2 per cent. upon imports
should be imposed throughout the Empire and the proceeds
devoted to naval defence. But nothing came of the suggestion.
If the concrete results appear disproportionately meagre the

mere assembling of the Conference was in itself a great thing, and marked the first step towards much greater things. For the moment its chief value was that it enabled distinguished statesmen from all parts of the Empire to witness and participate in the great manifestation of loyalty and devotion to the Crown evoked by the celebrations of Queen Victoria's Jubilee.

The Queen's Jubilee, 1887

The crowning event of these celebrations was a Thanksgiving Service in Westminster Abbey. Thither on Tuesday, June 21st, the Queen proceeded through the streets of her capital, gaily decorated, lined with troops and thronged with cheering multitudes drawn from every class of her subjects, from every country of the vast Empire over which she reigned. Plaudits were mingled with tears of gratitude and emotion as the people gazed, many of them for the first time, on the central figure in the great pageant—a figure perfect in dignity, perfect in simplicity.

The Queen was accompanied by her whole family : three sons, five sons-in-law, and nine grandsons and grandsons-in-law rode behind her carriage. Four kings, the Kings of Belgium and Saxony, Denmark and Greece, many reigning Grand Dukes and the Crown Princes of every throne in Europe were among the glittering throng. Among the Crown Princes, a never-to-be-forgotten figure was the Queen's favourite son-in-law [1] already threatened by the fell disease which twelve months later cut short, ere it had well begun, a reign which, if prolonged to its natural term, might well have altered the whole future course of world-history. Noteworthy also in the procession were Ruling Princes of India, in gorgeous uniforms, and resplendent with jewels. There were representatives also of all the British Colonies and Dependencies as well as of Foreign Powers. ' Queen's weather ' prevailed throughout the day and blue skies and brilliant sunshine enhanced the splendour of a spectacle unique in world-history.

' Yesterday,' wrote *The Times* on June 22nd, ' from the earliest moment of dawn until long after night had fallen the people of this country, of the whole Empire, and especially the population of London, were keeping high festival in celebration of the Jubilee of their Sovereign.' In every town and every village in the

---

[1] Frederick of Prussia (afterwards the Emperor Frederick) husband of the Princess Royal.

country the day was kept as a high and solemn feast day. The whole nation, nay the whole Empire, surrendered themselves to a ' passion of festivity and thanksgiving '. Memorials—statues, buildings, beneficent institutions—followed in due course. The Queen accepted a personal gift of £75,000 subscribed by nearly three million of her women subjects, and devoted the greater part of it to the foundation of a nurses' institute to provide skilled nursing for the sick poor in their own homes. The Institute has proved a veritable godsend.

In May the Queen had opened the People's Palace at Mile End. On June 22 a fête was given to 26,000 poor school children in Hyde Park ; on July 9 the Queen laid the foundation-stone of the Imperial Institute and during the same month reviewed the Metropolitan Volunteers at Buckingham Palace, the Army at Aldershot and the Navy at Spithead. What wonder that when the end of this eventful year came, the Queen ' parted with it ' (as her *Journal* records) ' with great regret. . . . Never, never can I forget this brilliant year, so full of the marvellous kindness, loyalty, and devotion of so many millions which really I could hardly have expected '. The touch of genuine humility is characteristic ; but it was with renewed spirit and energy that the Queen took up the duties which still for fourteen years awaited her.

The celebrations of 1887 were repeated ten years later on a scale even more splendid, and in a spirit still more definitely Imperialist. In the meantime there had been rapid territorial advance in Africa, of which more must be said in the next chapter. The interval was also marked by the meeting of a second Colonial Conference. *Ottawa Conference, 1894*

It met on the invitation of the Canadian Government in June 1894 at Ottawa. The Earl of Jersey, a former Governor of New South Wales (1891–3), represented the Imperial Government, and representatives were also present from Canada, Cape Colony, New Zealand, and four of the Australian Colonies. The discussions, more business-like than those in 1887 in London, were practically confined to the three subjects specified in the Canadian invitation : the construction of a submarine cable from Vancouver to Australia, the establishment of a quick mail service between Great Britain and Australasia viâ Canada, and the trade relations of the Colonies with Great Britain and with one another. It was suggested that for the Pacific cable there should be a neutral landing-place in the Sandwich Islands (Hawaii), but those islands were formally annexed in 1898 by the United States. That scheme was therefore perforce abandoned. The cable was, however, ultimately laid (1902) from Vancouver to Auckland viâ Norfolk Island.

On the question of inter-imperial trade the Conference resolved that any impediments imposed, by Treaty or otherwise, on reciprocal trade arrangements between the different portions of the Empire should be removed, and recorded its belief in the advisability of such arrangements. The exceptional position of the Mother Country in respect of external trade was frankly recognized by Colonial speakers, but the Conference resolved that 'until the Mother Country can see her way to enter into Customs arrangements with her Colonies it is desirable that when empowered to do so the Colonies take steps to place each other's products on a more favourable Customs basis than is accorded to the like products of foreign countries'. It was not long before Canada herself made a beginning in this direction. But before that, another Colonial Conference had met in London, and like the first was coincident with a great event in the history of the Empire—the celebration of the completion of the sixtieth year of the Queen's reign.

Joseph Chamberlain

Over the Conference of 1897 Mr. Joseph Chamberlain, as Secretary of State, presided. Mr. Chamberlain's accession to the Colonial Office in 1895 must be regarded as one of the significant political events in the latter part of the nineteenth century. Ever since his rupture with Mr. Gladstone on the Home Rule question Mr. Chamberlain's mind had been moving steadily towards the project of Imperial unification. In this intellectual evolution he was avowedly influenced by the example of Germany.

'We have', he said, speaking at the annual dinner of the Canada Club in 1896, 'a great example before us in the creation of the German Empire. How was that brought about? You all recollect that, in the first instance, it commenced with the union of two of the States which now form that great Empire in a commercial Zollverein. They attracted the other States gradually—were joined by them for commercial purposes. A Council, or Reichsrath, was formed to deal with those commercial questions. Gradually in their discussions national objects and political interests were introduced, and so, from starting as it did on a purely commercial basis and for commercial interests, it developed until it became a bond of unity and the foundation of the German Empire.'

On the same text Mr. Chamberlain preached to the Congress of Chambers of Commerce of the Empire which met in London in 1896 :

'If we had a commercial union throughout the Empire, of course there would have to be a Council of the Empire. . . . Gradually, therefore, by that prudent and experimental process by which all our greatest institutions have slowly been built up we should, I believe, approach to a result which would be little, if at all, distinguished from a real federation of the Empire.'

Mr. Chamberlain's opening address at the Conference of 1897 marked an epoch in the history of imperial copartnership. It was incomparably the boldest and frankest utterance to which Colonial statesmen had ever listened from a responsible Minister of the Crown.

The Colonial Conference, 1897

' I feel', he said, ' that there is a real necessity for some better machinery of consultation between the self-governing Colonies and the Mother Country, and it has sometimes struck me—I offer it now merely as a personal suggestion—that it might be feasible to create a great council of the Empire to which the Colonies would send representative plenipotentiaries—not mere delegates who were unable to speak in their name, without further reference to their respective Governments, but persons who by their position in the Colonies, by their representative character, and by their close touch with Colonial feeling, would be able upon all subjects submitted to them to give really effective and valuable advice. If such a council were created it would at once assume an immense importance, and it is perfectly evident that it might develop into something still greater. It might slowly grow to that Federal Council to which we must always look forward as our ultimate ideal.' [1]

---

[1] Only a brief Report of the *Proceedings* was published (c. 8596, 1897). It contained a full report of the President's opening address and of an address by the First Lord of the Admiralty, Mr. Goschen. For the rest only a list of topics discussed and resolutions adopted.

No resolution on this subject was in fact adopted or even, as far as we know, proposed.

The *Report* does indeed make it clear that among some of the Colonial Premiers there was a feeling that the present relations could not continue indefinitely. Nevertheless, the following resolution was passed, with the dissent only of Mr. Seddon for New Zealand and Sir E. Braddon for Tasmania. ' The Prime Ministers here assembled are of opinion that the present political relations between the United Kingdom and the self-governing Colonies are generally satisfactory under the existing condition of things.' [1]

On the question of inter-imperial trade the Conference re-affirmed the request made at Ottawa for the ' denunciation of any treaties that now hamper the commercial relations between Great Britain and her Colonies '. Since 1894 the question had been brought to a practical issue by the offer of Canada to give a preference to the Mother Country. The Imperial Government accordingly decided to denounce the Treaties concluded with Belgium and the German Zollverein, in 1862 and 1865 respectively. As to defence the arrangement with Australia was confirmed and the Cape Colony offered an ' unconditional contribution ' of the cost of a first-class battleship,—a spontaneous offer which was gratefully accepted by the Home Government. A suggestion for the occasional interchange of military units was approved, and among other matters discussed were coloured immigration, and an Imperial Penny Post. The Conference also pressed for the removal of all restrictions on the investment of trust funds in Colonial stock, and recommended that the Conference should in future be periodically summoned. Personal consultation at regular intervals was, henceforward, to form a permanent part of the constitutional mechanism of the Empire.

On the whole it must be confessed that the tangible results of this Conference fell short of the high hopes entertained by its President. Yet how fine was the spirit of the British Colonies was soon to be proved. Before the next Conference met in 1902 a great crisis in the history of the Empire had matured, and with the effective aid of Canada and the Australasian Colonies had

[1] *Proceedings* v. 15.

been successfully surmounted. With that crisis the next chapter will deal.

Despite the rather meagre results achieved by the Conference of 1897 the visit of the Colonial Premiers to the capital of the Empire cannot have been otherwise than gratifying to them. Two days before the Conference opened they had been privileged to play a conspicuous part in the great procession which formed the central feature of the celebrations attendant on the Queen's Diamond Jubilee.

The vibrating note of the celebrations of 1897 was, indeed, Imperial. Struck in the Jubilee of 1887, in 1897 it dominated and drowned all others, except that of accentuated loyalty and affection to the Queen herself. Thus the celebration of the Second Jubilee was no mere repetition of the first. Foreign States were fully represented as before, but no foreign kings were present. The German Emperor had expressed a wish to be present, but the Queen felt unequal to the task of showing him or any other Sovereign ' the hospitality and attention which Her Majesty would wish that they should receive '. Thus the procession took the form of an Imperial Pageant, organized on a superb scale, and primarily with a view to its political significance. It was officially announced that the Queen would ' drive through London for the purpose of seeing her people and receiving their congratulations on having attained the sixtieth anniversary of Her Majesty's reign '. Through London she drove on Tuesday, June 22 ; not merely by a short route to and from Westminster Abbey ; but for six long miles and for three long hours through the main thoroughfares, north and south of the Thames, crossing London Bridge and Westminster Bridge, and thus giving to many millions of her subjects, drawn from all classes, the opportunity of participation in a ceremony without precedent or parallel in the history of mankind. Beside the Queen's carriage rode the Prince of Wales, the Duke of Connaught, commanding the troops, and the Duke of Cambridge. All the other surviving members of her family were present ; in the unending procession were representative contingents not only of the British Navy and Army, but of the Imperial Service Troops of India, headed by Maharajah Sir Pertab Singh, of the mounted troops or police

The Diamond Jubilee

from the self-governing Colonies, from Crown Colonies and Dependencies, little Cingalese soldiers from Ceylon, Hausas from the Gold Coast, armed police from Hong Kong, and so on. Of the Colonial contingents Lord Roberts was tactfully placed in command and on his white Arab charger was loudly acclaimed by the populace. All the Premiers of the Empire (with the curious exception of the Prime Minister of the United Kingdom) were conspicuous figures in the procession. The Colonial and Indian contingents were temporarily detached from the procession after it passed St. Paul's, in order that the Queen as she approached the Cathedral might pass them in review and that they, alone of the troops, might see Her Majesty. In front of the West Door of the Cathedral the Queen's carriage stopped in order that the Queen, without descending from it, might take part in a short open-air service. Before leaving the Palace for her long drive the Queen sent a telegraphic greeting to her people in all parts of the Empire : ' From my heart I thank my beloved people. May God bless them.' Almost overwhelming, as the Queen drove through her capital, was their response.

In the evening of the 22nd every British city was illuminated, and from every headland and hill, from the Land's End to John o' Groat's House, bonfire beacons blazed.

The Queen's own comment compels quotation : ' A never-to-be-forgotten day. No one ever, I believe, has met with such an ovation as was given to me. . . . The crowds were quite indescribable, and their enthusiasm truly marvellous and deeply touching. The cheering was quite deafening, and every face seemed to be filled with real joy. I was much moved and gratified.' Moved and gratified the Queen might well be. ' To us ', as Lord Rosebery wrote to her, ' it has been the splendid expression of a nation's gratitude, the symbol of loyalty, deep, passionate and steadfast, which has encompassed Your Majesty's throne, and grown year by year with Your Majesty's life, until it has penetrated every remotest corner and subject of the Empire. No capital in the world has ever witnessed such an enthusiasm of devotion to a Sovereign.'

Bishop Creighton's ' commanded ' Memorandum also deserves to be quoted. ' The proceedings on June 22nd were ', he wrote, ' entirely simple and absolutely personal ; they had reference only to the Queen. . . . Yet no ceremonial recorded in history was ever more impressive, more truly national, or expressed more faithfully sentiments which were deeply and universally felt. The very fact that it was simple, personal, and unfettered by precedent, give it an extension which was at first unforeseen. . . . The occasion expanded into a significant manifestation of imperial greatness, and of a fundamental unity of purpose, which came as a revelation to England and the Colonies alike, and awakened the respectful wonder of all Europe.'

The festivities were prolonged for a fortnight. There were garden parties at Buckingham Palace and (for members of the House of Commons and their ladies) at Windsor; the Queen reviewed the Colonial contingents and all the Colonial Premiers were sworn of the Privy Council; 180 Prelates of the Anglican Communion, assembled for a Conference at Lambeth, were received by the Queen, and on her behalf the Prince reviewed 173 battleships of the Home Fleet at Spithead.

Hardly, however, had the sounds of the Jubilee acclamations died away when there fell upon the ears of the exultant nation the solemn and sonorous swell of a great anthem—*The Recessional*, by Rudyard Kipling. Has any poet ever interpreted with greater insight the prevailing but inarticulate sentiment of a great people? *The Recessional* analysed with precision and expressed in terse and vigorous words the feeling of all serious-minded men as to the true bases of imperial power, and the secret source of all success in the battles of war, of politics, and of personal life. Like Shakespeare in his *Henry V*, Kipling caught, and for the men of his day interpreted, the sentiment of the Hebrew singer : ' Some trust in chariots, and some in horses ; but we will remember the name of the Lord our God.' *Non nobis Domine.* *The Recessional*

> Oh God, Thy arm was here
> And not to us, but to Thy arm alone
> Ascribe we all.

So Shakespeare. And Kipling :

> God of our fathers, known of old,
>   Lord of our far-flung battle line,
> Beneath whose awful hand we hold
>   Dominion over palm and pine,
> Lord God of Hosts, be with us yet,
> Lest we forget, lest we forget.

The tumult and the shouting dies,
  The captains and the kings depart,
Still stands Thine ancient sacrifice
  An humble and a contrite heart.
Lord God of Hosts, be with us yet,
  Lest we forget, lest we forget.

The Jubilee of 1897 marked the meridian of the Victorian era. Hardly had the tumult and the shouting died, before the political sky became overcast. On the glint and the glamour and the glory, on the sparkle and splendour of the Imperial Jubilee there supervened all too soon the humiliations, sacrifices, and the sorrows of the war in South Africa.

CHAPTER VIII

BRITISH DOMINION IN AFRICA—THE BOER WAR (1899–1902)— THE DEATH OF QUEEN VICTORIA

FOR many years past the relations between Britons and Dutchmen in South Africa had been uneasy. The story of those relations down to the year 1885 has been told in a previous volume of this History, and can now be recalled only in bare outline. For a century and a half the Cape of Good Hope, though discovered by the Portuguese, had been occupied by the Dutch as a port of call for their East Indiamen. In 1795, however, the United Provinces became a dependency of the French Republic, and to save the Cape Colony from a similar fate it was, at the suggestion of the Dutch Stadtholder (then a refugee in England), occupied by a British force. Handed back to the Batavian Republic (the United Provinces) in 1802, the Cape Colony was reconquered by the British in 1806, and at the Peace of Paris (1814) it was retained, Holland receiving £6,000,000 in compensation. *Cape Colony*

British settlers came in slowly, and the British Government was confronted on the one hand by Dutch farmers, who resented their interference, especially when exercised on behalf of the slaves, on the other by natives who in South Africa have always greatly outnumbered the European settlers of both races. So great was the exasperation of the Dutch farmers at the " grandmotherly " attitude of the British Government that between 1836 and 1840 they shook the dust of the Cape Colony off their feet, and, taking with them their women, children and belongings, ' trekked ' northwards and ultimately established two States virtually independent of Great Britain, the Transvaal and the Orange Free State. *The Great Boer Trek*

A handful of English colonists had meanwhile (1824) estab- *Natal*

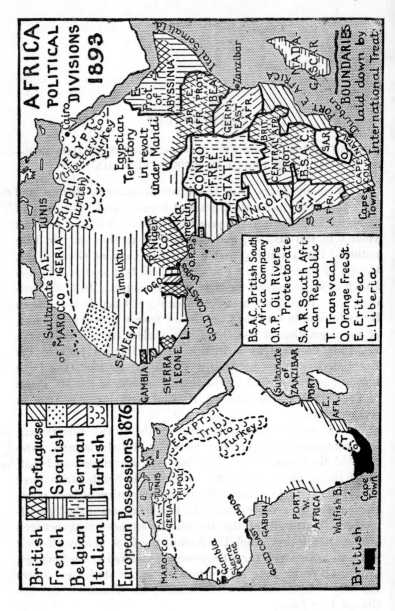

AFRICA
POLITICAL
DIVISIONS
1893

BOUNDARIES
Laid down by
International Treat

European Possessions 1876

British	Portuguese
French	Spanish
Belgian	German
Italian	Turkish

B.S.A.C. British South
African Company
O.R.P. Oil Rivers
Protectorate.
S.A.R. South Afri-
can Republic
T. Transvaal
O. Orange Free St.
E. Eritrea
L. Liberia.

lished themselves at Port Natal. To save the country from the Boers, Natal was formally proclaimed a British Colony in 1843 and down to 1856 formed part of the Cape Colony. In the latter year it was declared independent of its neighbour, and in 1893 attained to the full dignity of 'responsible Government'.[1]

Towards the Boer Colonies in the north the British Government pursued a policy irritating less on account of assertiveness than of vacillation. Now the British claimed sovereignty over them, and now acknowledged their virtual independence. The Sand River Convention (1852) conceded independence to the 'emigrant farmers beyond the Vaal river' subject to two reservations : the Republic was to be open to all comers on equal terms, and no slavery was to be practised or permitted. Two years later similar terms were conceded by the Bloemfontein Convention to the Boers of the Orange Free State.

For twenty years the policy of non-intervention was consistently maintained. But Sir George Grey, Governor at the Cape from 1854–6, had the foresight to perceive that, in view of the numerical predominance of native tribes, and for other reasons, there could not permanently coexist in South Africa two European peoples, in complete independence of each other. He, therefore, urged on the Home Government to negotiate some form of federation. 'Had British Ministers in time past been wise enough to follow your advice, there would undoubtedly be to-day a British Dominion extending from Table Bay to the Zambesi.' So in 1893 F. W. Reitz, afterwards Transvaal Secretary of State, wrote to Grey. But the weary Titan was at that time looking forward to the happy day when those 'wretched Colonies' would no longer hang like millstones around our necks, and the sagacious advice of one of the greatest of Colonial administrators was ignored.

In the late 'seventies Lord Carnarvon, then Secretary of State, revived Sir George Grey's project, though again, unfortunately, without success. In the meantime much had happened in South Africa. In 1868 the Boers on the Orange River became involved in a dispute with the Basutos to the east of them ; the Basuto chief appealed to be allowed to 'rest under the large folds of the flag of England'. His prayer was heard ; British sovereignty

Federation

British Expansion in South Africa

[1] See Marriott, *England since Waterloo*, c. xxiv.

was proclaimed over Basutoland in 1869, and during the Jubilee celebrations of 1887 Letsie, Chief of the Basutos, wrote on behalf of himself and other chiefs to congratulate the Queen and to express their gratitude for the ' deliverance she had granted to [them] when [they] were on the brink of absolute ruin.' [1]

Dia-monds and Gold   In 1871 Griqualand West, a territory to the west of the Orange Free State, was similarly annexed to the Crown.   These annexations clearly announced that the era of masterly inactivity was drawing to a close in South Africa, that the prophets of the Manchester School were no longer preaching to a listening generation. But the annexation of Griqualand West had a further significance. It meant the acquisition of the Kimberley diamond-field and the consequent introduction of an entirely new strain into the European peoples of South Africa.   ' The digger, the capitalist, the company promoter jostled the slow-moving Dutch farmer, and quickened the pace of life.' [2]

The quickening was not confined to Kimberley.   In 1872 Cape Colony had attained to Responsible Government, and in 1877 Sir Bartle Frere was appointed to the Governorship of the Colony, in the hope that he would be able to carry through Lord Carnarvon's federal scheme.   In the previous year, however, Carnarvon had sent out Sir Theophilus Shepstone as Special Commissioner to ' inquire respecting certain disturbances which had taken place in the territory adjoining the Colony of Natal '. Shepstone was further authorized, at his discretion and if desired by the inhabitants, to annex the territory.

The Zulu War   The territory was the Transvaal Republic.   The Boers in that colony were in desperate plight, and in great danger of being ' eaten up ' by their native neighbours, the warlike Zulus and Matabeles.   Accordingly Shepstone, in 1877, annexed the Transvaal.   In 1879 we found ourselves at war with the Zulus.   A British force was cut to pieces at Isandhlwana, but ultimately the power of the Zulus was broken, and Cetewayo, their Chief, was sent as a State prisoner to Cape Town.   In the course of the Zulu War the Prince Imperial of France, while serving as a volunteer with the British force was, to the great grief of his mother and of Queen Victoria, unfortunately killed.   Before the close of the same year (1879) the power of Sekukini, like Cetewayo

[1] *Q.V.L.*, III. 1. 342.   [2] Lucas, *South Africa*, p. 246.

a powerful and inveterate enemy of the Boers, was also broken
by the British and he joined Cetewayo in captivity.

The Boers, saved by British intervention from annihilation, The
now claimed their independence (December 1880) ; war ensued, Trans-
and the Boers inflicted a severe defeat on an inadequate British vaal
force at Majuba Hill (February 26, 1881). To repair this disaster
Sir Frederick Roberts was sent out with a considerable force,
but arrived in South Africa only to find that an agreement had
been signed with the Boers, acknowledging their right to complete
self-government under the suzerainty of the Queen. The subsequent Convention of London (1884), while acknowledging the
' South African Republic', reserved the control of external relations, though it deleted all reference to 'suzerainty'. The policy
of retrocession thus adopted by the Gladstone Government was
sharply criticized in England, and signally failed to achieve a
final settlement in South Africa.

The year which witnessed the conclusion of the Convention
of London (1884) witnessed also the beginning of that ' scramble
for Africa ' already described. In that ' scramble ' Great Britain
participated, and in the final result did not fare worst. In
1885 a Protectorate was established over Bechuanaland, partly
no doubt with a view of preventing too intimate relations between
the Boer Republics and the recently established German colonies
of Namaqualand and Damaraland (German South-West Africa).
In the next year a Charter was granted to the Royal Niger Chartered
Company, which established a Protectorate over the Niger terri- Com-
tory on the west coast. The system of Chartered Companies had, panies
in the seventeenth century, been a popular and successful method
of trade development. Charters granted to Companies of Merchants brought to the Crown a maximum of profit with a minimum of responsibility. The vigorous criticism of Adam Smith
brought the system into ill repute. None the less, it had solid
advantages, and in the last decades of the nineteenth century
they again became obvious. The ' company of merchants ' took
risks and tried experiments ; the Crown and the nation reaped
where the Company had sown. Until in the 'eighties the attention of the European Powers was concentrated on tropical Africa,
the swamps on the delta of the Niger offered no temptations to Nigeria
any Government, but the country was exploited by various

traders, mainly for the sake of the palm-oil which its forests
yielded in profusion. When the scramble began, a British Company, headed by Sir George Taubman Goldie, was successful in
establishing its title to possession. A charter was granted to the
Royal Niger Company in 1886, but fierce competition for possession of the Hinterland continued between the English and the
French until in 1898 their respective spheres were delimited.
Two years later the political jurisdiction of the Royal Niger
Company was transferred to the Crown, though the company
continued its activities as a commercial undertaking.

With the development of Nigeria, a territory about one-third
of the size of British India, two names will be immemorially
associated. That of Sir Ronald Ross, who effected the conquest
of the mosquito, and that of Sir Frederick (now Lord) Lugard,
who has devoted some of the best years of a long life to the extir-
pation of slavery in tropical Africa. For some years he had been
engaged in that humanitarian work in East Africa, but from
1894 until the close of the World War he was (save for an interval
of five years) employed in West Africa. In 1897 he raised the
West African Frontier Force—a native army under British
officers—and with their aid he did much to secure the native
chiefs of the interior against the advances of France and Germany.
By a series of Conventions between Great Britain and France
(1890-9) the northern frontiers of Nigeria and the French sphere
of influence were delimited, and Lugard and his West African
Frontier Force were then compelled to undertake the effective
occupation of the Moslem Emirates (1902-3). The native chiefs
were, as far as possible, confirmed in their authority over their
tribesmen, but they had to accept British Residents, to put a
stop to slave raiding, to contribute to the expenses of administration, to maintain order, and to execute justice. From 1907 to
1912 Lugard was Governor of Hong Kong, but in the latter year
returned to West Africa. In 1914 he became Governor-General
of a united Nigeria, with its capital at Lagos, a former entrepôt
of the slave trade, but acquired by the British Government in
1861 with a view of putting an end to that traffic.

**East
Africa**   The European Powers were no less active on the East Coast
than on the West. Eastern Equatorial Africa had, until the
'eighties, come under the notice of Europe only through the

devoted labours of explorers and missionaries. But the Powers then began to occupy strategic points on or off the coast of East Africa. Great Britain had secured two stations on the opposite shore at Aden (1837) and at Perim (1857). Sokotra, occupied by the British East India Company in 1834, was declared a British Protectorate in 1886. Eritrea, with a coast line of some 700 miles along the Red Sea, passed into the keeping of Italy between 1882 and 1888, as did Italian Somaliland. By a series of treaties with the Somali Sultans, and Agreements with Great Britain and the rulers of Zanzibar and Abyssinia (1889–1905) Italy obtained this latter territory, and, in 1925, Great Britain transferred to it a portion of Kenya Colony, known as Jubaland with the port of Kismayu. British Somaliland, opposite Aden, was declared a British Protectorate in 1884, and its limits were defined by treaties with France (1888), Italy (1894), and Abyssinia (1897). The town and territory of Obock, on the Red Sea, opposite Aden, were purchased by a Frenchman in 1857, but only in 1883 did France take formal possession of the patch of territory now known as French Somaliland. A French Protectorate over Madagascar was recognized by the British Government in 1890, but not until 1896-9 was that large island and its dependencies brought into submission to the French Government.

Meanwhile, the Germans had established themselves not only on the west coast (Togoland and the Cameroons), but on Walfish Bay (German South-West Africa) and also in the territory now known as Tanganyika. So far as there was any ' Sovereignty ' in this region it belonged to the Sultan of Zanzibar, whose independence was formally recognized by the British and French Governments in 1862. In 1878 the Sultan offered to lease all his territories on the mainland, for seventy years, to Sir William Mackinnon (Chairman of the British India Steam Navigation Company), well known not only as a keen and successful man of business but as a great philanthropist and Imperialist. The territory comprised nearly 600,000 square miles and included the Lakes Victoria Nyanza, Tanganyika and Nyassa. The British Government refused to sanction this large addition to the Empire ; but in 1885 the German Empire put in a claim to a considerable slice of this territory, and the claim was conceded by the Sultan of Zanzibar. The German and British spheres were delimited under a series of agreements (1886–90), and in 1887, within a few months of each other, the German Africa Company and the

British East Africa British East Africa Association were formed. The latter, under the chairmanship of Mackinnon, received a charter in the following year, and in 1890 Zanzibar was taken under British Protection. In 1895 the Government bought out the territorial rights of the company, and put the administration of the new East Africa Protectorate under the Foreign Office. Between 1896 and 1903 a railway was constructed between the important harbour of Mombasa and Lake Victoria Nyanza. White settlers followed in the track of the railway, but a good deal of friction ensued between them, the natives, and the Home Government, who were anxious to deal fairly with both parties. In 1905 the control of the Protectorate was transferred to the Colonial Office, and in 1920 it became a Crown Colony with the new title of Kenya.

Uganda North of Tanganyika, bounded on the west by the Belgian Congo and on the east by Kenya Colony, lies the Protectorate of Uganda. The country was first revealed to Europeans by Stanley and the missionaries in the 'seventies, and after the acquisition of German East Africa, Germany threatened to absorb Uganda also, and thus to obtain control of the sources of the Nile, vital to Egypt and the Soudan. The Anglo-German Treaty of 1890, however, assigned Uganda to Great Britain, and the Imperial British East Africa Company, having secured the services of Lugard, sent him to Uganda to administer the territory. With most inadequate resources Lugard asserted British claims, but the Home Government was impatient and, save for the urgent representations of Bishop Tucker and Lugard, would have abandoned the territory. In default the Government consented to send out Sir Gerard Portal to report on the situation. Portal reported strongly in favour of retention, and in 1894 Uganda was declared a British Protectorate. Thus, as Lugard writes, ' the continuous control of the Nile from its sources in the Great Victoria and Albert Lakes was secured to the Empire '.[1]

Rhodesia Meanwhile there were important developments in the southern part of the great continent. In 1888 Lobengula, King of the Matabeles, whom we have seen in conflict with the Boers of the Transvaal, was induced to accept British protection. In 1889

[1] *Dual Mandate in Tropical Africa*, p. 21.

the Chartered Company of South Africa was incorporated and started on its conquering and civilizing mission, establishing its sovereignty over the vast territory which stretches from the Limpopo on the south to Lake Nyassa on the east and Lake Tanganyika on the north,—a territory which recalls in its modern name, Rhodesia, the memory of the great statesman whose insight and imagination conceived, and whose resolute will went far to secure, British supremacy in Africa. About the same time (1890) Portugal was induced to renounce all rights over the hinterland which separated its possessions in the west (Angola) from Mozambique and Portuguese East Africa. Thus, the two Boer Republics were virtually encircled by British territory.

In the Transvaal itself an event of first-rate importance had meanwhile taken place. Valuable gold mines were discovered in 1886 on the Witwatersrand, and the discovery attracted a crowd of adventurers. The slow-moving, intensely conservative Boer farmers deeply resented the intrusion of the miners and financiers. Oil would not mix with water, and the newly-founded city of Johannesburg, with its new Chamber of Mines, soon found itself in conflict with Pretoria and the Volksraad. The newcomers, or *Uitlanders*, peremptorily demanded political rights commensurate with their contribution to the wealth of the community. The Boer Government, at that time dominated by President Kruger, refused to grant them. In 1895 Cecil Rhodes became Prime Minister of the Cape Colony, and in December of that same year the Uitlanders of the Transvaal attempted to take by force what had been denied to their arguments. Dr. Jameson, an intimate friend of the Premier of Cape Colony, and himself the administrator of the British South Africa Company, foolishly attempted to raid the Transvaal territory at the head of a force of 600 Chartered Company's Police, with several Maxim and Gardner guns. The High Commissioner at Cape Town promptly ordered Jameson to withdraw, but meanwhile he and his companions were surrounded by the Boers at Krugersdorp, and forced to surrender. Their confederates in Johannesburg were imprisoned ; Jameson himself, and his comrades, were handed over for trial to the British Government, and having been convicted of unlawfully taking part in a military expedition against a friendly State, were sentenced to short terms of imprisonment.

Boers and Britons in the Transvaal

The Jameson Raid

The men imprisoned in Johannesburg were tried in the Transvaal. Four leaders of the Uitlander party, including Colonel Frank Rhodes (a brother of Cecil Rhodes), were condemned to death and fifty-nine others were fined £2,000 each. After a strong protest from Mr. Chamberlain the death sentence on the leaders was commuted to one of fifteen years' imprisonment (subsequently reduced) and a fine in each case of £25,000.

Thus the Transvaal treasury was substantially replenished by the fiasco of the Jameson Raid. The Raid had other important results. Though disavowed both by the Cape Colony Government and by the Imperial Government, it excited the contempt and hostility of all our rivals in Africa and our enemies in Europe, and on January 3, 1896, the German Emperor dispatched to President Kruger his famous telegram, congratulating him on having 'preserved the independence of his country against foreign invasion'. The Emperor's telegram, implicitly recognizing the 'independence' of the Transvaal, was bitterly resented in England as an impertinent and unwarrantable interference in the internal concerns of the British Empire. The Prince of Wales felt and (to the Queen) expressed himself strongly about 'a most gratuitous act of unfriendliness', and the Queen, while not condoning the Raid, addressed a sharp rebuke to her grandson.[1] The Kaiser offered explanations to his grandmother, and Lord Salisbury advised her 'fully to accept all his explanations without inquiring too narrowly into the truth of them '.[2] It is now known that the telegram was sent, not on the sole responsibility of the Emperor, but on the considered advice of the Chancellor (Prince Hohenlöhe) and the Foreign Ministry.[3] The telegram was immediately followed up by an order to a German cruiser in Delagoa Bay to land marines and send them up to Pretoria. The Portuguese refused to permit the landing. Had they acquiesced, the position as between England and Germany must at once have become unspeakably grave.

As it was, feeling in England was deeply aroused. Jameson's reckless blunder had, however, made it impossible for the British Government to interfere on behalf of the 'Uitlanders ' in the Transvaal, and their position daily became more and more desperate.

[1] Q.V.L., III, iii. 7-8.   [2] Ibid., p. 20.
[3] Brandenburg, From Bismarck to the World-War (Eng. trans.), p. 84.

In March 1897, the Transvaal Republic concluded with the Orange Free State a convention of 'Friendship and Perpetual Alliance'. A month later the Orange Free State concluded a Treaty of Friendship and Commerce with Germany. In view of the *rapprochement* between the two Dutch Republics the significance of this new engagement requires no demonstration.

Events were clearly hastening towards a crisis. Sir Hercules Robinson retired in 1897, and Mr. Chamberlain selected as his successor Sir Alfred (afterwards Viscount) Milner. Milner, after a brilliant career at Oxford, had for a few years done journalistic work in London, and in 1885 stood for Parliament as a Liberal —unsuccessfully; nor did he ever stand again. He cared little for party politics, but a great deal for his country and for the Empire. He had, moreover, a genius for finance. He served as Under-Secretary for Finance in Egypt (1889–92), and in 1892 Goschen appointed him Chairman of the Board of Inland Revenue. In that capacity he gave invaluable assistance to Harcourt when the latter was preparing his famous Budget of 1894. In 1897 Mr. Chamberlain selected him for one of the most difficult posts in the Empire. Cecil Rhodes soon recognized in the new Governor exactly the man who was wanted. He used to say that Milner was one of the strongest men he had ever met. ' In the business I am constantly having to transact with him . . . I find him, once his mind is made up, immovable. . . . He assumes an attitude of perfect frankness with all parties ; he denies himself to no one who may give him any information or throw fresh light on the situation ; to all he expresses his views, and repeats his unalterable opinions of what is required.'[1] Soon after Milner's appointment Mr. Chamberlain addressed to him a dispatch setting forth in detail the grievances of the Uitlanders against the Transvaal Government, and instructing him to raise specifically the question of the status of the Transvaal under the Convention of 1884. The terms of that Convention were admittedly ambiguous ; the renunciation of suzerainty was a sentimental blunder, and recent events rendered it imperative, if grave consequences were not to ensue, that the situation should be cleared up. Milner, most wisely, spent two years in quietly mastering the situation. He learnt Dutch. He saw every one.

Chamberlain and Milner

[1] Lady Sarah Wilson, *South African Memories,* pp. 59–60.

At the end of two years his mind was made up. His path was clear before him. Stony it might be : but he must tread it. Chamberlain was adamant against any attempt on the part of the Dutch Republic to assert a status of complete sovereignty and independence. Meanwhile, things could not remain as they were at Johannesburg. The Uitlanders numbered 60,000 : they outnumbered the Dutch by six to one[1] : they bore the whole burden of taxation : yet they had no representation in the legislature, and for their children there was no education except in Dutch. In April 1899 Milner forwarded to the Queen a Petition, signed by 21,000 British subjects in the Transvaal, praying that the Queen would make inquiry into their grievances, and in particular their exclusion from all political rights. In June a Conference took place between President Kruger and the High Commissioner, at which the latter vainly attempted to persuade the President to make some substantial concession to the Uitlanders. The situation became so menacing that reinforcements were dispatched from England to the Cape, but in numbers insufficient to assert the British claims, though more than sufficient to provoke the apprehensions of the Boers. In October 1899 the two Dutch Republics demanded the immediate withdrawal of the British troops, and the submission of all the questions at issue to arbitration. To concede the latter claim would have been to acknowledge the equality and sovereign status of the Transvaal Government. On the implicit refusal of the demand, the two Dutch Republics declared war (October 10).

The War Office   England was ill-prepared for war. It may be, as soldiers complain, that neither the English people nor their Parliament have ever taken the Army quite seriously, except when it is called on to fight. Yet no Department has been so often the object of drastic reorganization as the War Office. Large reforms were initiated after the withdrawal in 1895 of the Duke of Cambridge. Lord Lansdowne became in that year Secretary of State, and, despite the Queen's wish for the Duke of Connaught, appointed Lord Wolseley as Commander-in-Chief. The latter was aware of the new conditions under which he was to serve, but bitterly resented them. He complained that there was ' no one soldier to whom the Country can look as directly responsible for the

[1] i.e. in Johannesburg only.

military efficiency of the army ', while the Commander-in-Chief had become ' vice-chairman of a debating society '.

How great was the friction between himself and his civilian superior was revealed, after his resignation, by a debate in the House of Lords.[1] In that arena the statesman scored an easy victory over a soldier broken in health, and, like most soldiers, ill-equipped for public debate. But if Wolseley had underrated the fighting strength of the Boers, he had, while improving the efficiency of our own Army, repeatedly warned his political chief that it was not ready for war.

Ever since 1895 the Queen, whose interest in all that concerned her Army was in no way diminished by the passing of years, had frequently expressed her concern at the position of affairs at the War Office.[1] During the critical summer of 1899 her anxiety was intensified. On September 12 the Commander-in-Chief informed the Queen that Sir George White had been sent to Natal, and that it was proposed to send out Major-General French to command the cavalry and, in the event of war, to commit the supreme command to Sir Redvers Buller. Lord Wolseley added that ' if war comes we shall be obliged to send the largest force that has ever left our shores to take part in it and, the distance being great, it will be in all respects the most serious business we ever had in hand '. His warning was only too completely justified by the event. In June 1899 we had only some 10,000 troops in South Africa : 5,800 in Natal, 3,500 in Cape Colony, with 24 field guns. In July, Wolseley suggested the immediate mobilization of an Army Corps and a Cavalry Division in England and the dispatch of 10,000 reinforcements to South Africa. But his suggestion was turned down by the Cabinet ; though 2,000 men were in September sent from India and the Mediterranean stations to reinforce the garrison in Natal.

During the early autumn messages of sympathy with the cause of the Uitlanders and offers of military assistance were received from Canada, Australia and the West Indies. On August 26th Mr. Chamberlain, speaking at Birmingham, solemnly warned President Kruger that ' the sands were running out ',

The Queen and the Army

---

[1] Official Report for March 4 and 15, 1901, and cf. Sir F. Maurice and Sir G. Arthur, *Life of Lord Wolseley,* and Lord Newton's *Lord Lansdowne,* c. iv. and v.

and that, should a rupture ensue, conditions would be imposed which would, once for all, establish British paramountcy in South Africa. To this warning Mr. Kruger paid no heed. Accordingly, orders were given (September 29) for the mobilization of a large force in Great Britain and the calling up of the Reserves.

Boer Preparations

In the Transvaal, President Kruger had for four years been actively preparing for war. With the money derived from the Uitlanders' fines he had built two large armoured forts at Johannesburg and had quietly imported field guns and Maxims, together with vast quantities of arms and ammunition, which he distributed not only to the burghers of the two Boer Republics but to ' safe ' men in the Cape Colony. Not until his preparations were complete did he declare war.

The Boer War

The war opened disastrously for Great Britain. The Boer Army amounted to forty to fifty thousand men, well mounted, fine shots, inured to hardship, and with intimate knowledge of the *terrain*.[1] Their guns had been purchased from Krupp and Creusot and were manned, if not by Germans and Frenchmen, by expert gunners trained by them. Mobilizing with extreme rapidity, the Boers took the offensive in Natal. A small British force under General Sir George White checked their advance at Talana Hill and Elandslaghte (October 21), but was compelled to fall back on Ladysmith, where for four months it was besieged by the Boers. Sir Redvers Buller arrived early in November, but made the serious blunder of dividing his force into three columns. One under Lord Methuen was dispatched to the relief of Kimberley where Colonel Kekewich was beleaguered. Methuen, after three successful but costly engagements at Belmont (November 23), at Enslin (25th) and Modder River (28th), was defeated, with heavy losses, at Magersfontein (December 11th). A second column under General Gatacre was heavily repulsed in a night-attack at Stormberg (December 10); while Buller himself in a dogged but unwise attempt to relieve Ladysmith by a direct frontal attack, sustained a terrible defeat at Colenso (December 15).

---

[1] The Boers ultimately put some 66,000 men, including cosmopolitan volunteers and Cape rebels, into the field. The British forces, from first to last, numbered some 300,000. E. A. Walker : *Hist. of South Africa* (1928), p. 489.

Buller had gone out to South Africa with forebodings that he The Black Week was unequal to his job. They were too well justified, and it soon became clear that his appointment was a fatal blunder. After his defeat at Colenso he telegraphed home suggesting that he should ' let Ladysmith go ' and advised White, unless he was prepared for a lengthy siege, to surrender at once. Ladysmith should never have been held : but to Buller's pusillanimous advice White turned a deaf ear. He and his gallant comrades tightened their belts, and held on to an indefensible position ; until Roberts's advance relieved the pressure in Natal, and enabled Buller to relieve them.

Bad news from the front served only to stiffen the backs of the Government and the people at home. The stiffest back of all was that of the aged Queen. On December 18 Mr. Balfour was sent down to Windsor to reassure the Queen, but directly he began to refer to the alarmist rumours in London and the disasters of the ' black week ' the Queen, with a determined nod of her head, cut him short with the remark : ' Please understand that there is no one depressed in *this* house ; we are not interested in the possibilities of defeat ; they do not exist.' That was in the true Elizabethan spirit, and Mr. Balfour returned to Hatfield enthusiastically appreciative of the temper which prevailed at Windsor. ' It had been splendid to pass from the clamorous croakers in clubs and newspapers into the presence of this little old lady, alone among her women at Windsor, and hear her sweep all their vaticinations into nothingness with a nod.' [1]

Three days after Buller's defeat at Colenso, Lord Roberts Lord Roberts accepted the Command-in-Chief, only stipulating that he should have the services of Lord Kitchener as Chief of his Staff. Roberts's prompt decision was little less than heroic. Though sound in wind and limb, he was sixty-seven years of age, and the Colenso fight had cost him the life of his only son. The two Generals landed at Cape Town on January 10, 1900, and the army under their command was substantially reinforced by contingents dispatched to South Africa from Canada, New Zealand, and Australia. Before the war ended Australia had contributed 15,502, New Zealand 6,129 and Canada 5,762, and in the final victory they played a great, perhaps a decisive, part. For they

[1] Lady Gwendolen Cecil, *Life of Lord Salisbury*, iii. 191.

were better adapted than the town-bred troops of the Home-
land to conditions of warfare in South Africa.

With the turn of the year and the arrival of Roberts and
Kitchener, the spirit of the scene was transformed.   On February
15th General French at the head of a large force of cavalry
relieved Kimberley ; on February 27 (the anniversary of Majuba)
he surrounded at Paardeberg 4,000 Boers under the command
of Kronje and compelled them to surrender.

Roberts, steadily pushing his way towards Bloemfontein,
entered the capital of the Free State on March 13.   He halted
there for six weeks, and having re-established his transport resumed his march (May 1) on the Transvaal.   He forced the passage of the Sand River on May 10 and two days later occupied
Kroonstadt.   On May 17 Mafeking, which since the first days
of the war had been gallantly and cheerfully defended by Colonel
(now Lord) Baden-Powell, was relieved by a mounted force under
Colonel Mahon.   The fate of the little garrison had been watched
with the deepest interest in England, and news of their relief was
received with a wild enthusiasm which has added a verb to our
vocabulary.

After the occupation of Kroonstadt Roberts met with little
resistance.   He entered Johannesburg on May 31st and Pretoria
(whence Kruger had fled on May 30th) on June 5th.   In the
meantime Buller, after repeated failures to relieve General White
and the sorely tried garrison of Ladysmith, at last turned the
flank of the Boers on the Tugela by the capture of Pieter's Hill
(February 27), was able on the next day to relieve the devoted city.
A month after the surrender of Pretoria Roberts and Buller joined
hands at Vlakfontein (July 4th).

Victory seemed in sight : the Orange Free State had been
formally annexed to Her Majesty's Dominions on May 24, and on
September 1st the Transvaal was also annexed.   Mr. Chamberlain
announced in the House of Commons that the newly-annexed
Provinces would at the earliest possible moment receive the status
of self-governing Colonies.   On September 11th Mr. Kruger started
by way of Lorenzo Marques for Europe, in the hope of inducing
one or more Great Powers to mediate on behalf of the Boers.

Attitude
of the
Powers

Continental opinion was, except in Italy, almost unanimous
in condemnation of British policy in South Africa and loud were

the exultations over the Boer victories. Still sore about Fashoda
and irritated, not unwarrantably, by the comments of the English
Press on the Dreyfus scandal, the French were especially bitter,
and the less responsible papers published outrageous attacks
with some disgusting caricatures upon the Queen and the
Prince of Wales. England, though envied and admired, has
never been greatly loved on the Continent. During the Boer War
she was at first despised and throughout detested. In sordid
pursuit of gold she was now bullying two little States which, with
great gallantry, were defending their independence against a
grasping neighbour. Such was the general attitude among foreigners. So abusive were the French papers that the Prince of
Wales considered whether he should resign the Presidency of the
British Section of the Great Exhibition to be held in Paris in
1900, and with the Queen's approval, he did cancel his acceptance
of an invitation to attend its inauguration. The Queen herself
planned to visit Bordighera instead of one of the places on the
French Riviera where for many years she had in each spring spent
some weeks. On reaching Europe Mr. Kruger was received in
Paris with much cordiality, but the German Emperor, who in
November 1899 had visited, after a four years' interval, his grandmother, declined to receive him. He took much credit to himself for this refusal, and also for refusing a request for mediation
on behalf of the Boers. In answer to a pompous and self-righteous
telegram, reporting her grandson's reply to the Transvaal Government, the Queen expressed her gratitude, but at the same time
gave the following instructions to her ambassador in Berlin :
' Please convey to the Emperor that my whole nation is with me
in a fixed determination to see this war through without intervention. The time for, and the terms of, peace must be left to
our decision, and my country which is suffering from so heavy
a sacrifice of precious lives will resist all interference ' (11th March
1900). The Prince highly approved his mother's reply and his
Secretary described ' the one to Lascelles ' as ' worthy of Queen
Elizabeth '—a compliment which, though deserved, would not
have commended itself to the Queen, who detested her Tudor predecessor. Mr. Kruger gained nothing by his journey to Europe.

In England, the Press and the public were staunch in support English
of the Government. The initial disasters to British arms only opinion

strengthened the determination of the country to see the thing through. Recruits poured in, with offers of help, financial, medical, and other. The Liberal Party in Parliament was not in a position to offer effective opposition, even had they desired to do so. As a fact they were divided.

Liberal disunion

The Liberal Unionists had in 1895 coalesced with the Conservatives. Lord Rosebery's retirement from the leadership of the Party (1896) had been followed by that of Sir William Harcourt (1898). The Liberals in the House of Commons chose Sir Henry Campbell-Bannerman, a shrewd and opulent Scot, to succeed him. Rosebery, however, had still a large following in the Party and with Mr. Asquith, Sir Edward Grey, Mr. Haldane, Sir Henry Fowler, Mr. Munro Ferguson and others founded a distinct party, or sect, of Liberal Imperialists (1902). On the other —the left—wing of the Party was a small group of men who became known as Pro-Boers. Among the latter a young Welsh solicitor, who had entered Parliament in 1890 as member for Carnarvon, quickly became prominent. Possessed of great courage, imperturbably self-possessed, endowed with a gift of fiery eloquence, and inspired with a genuine sympathy for the underdog, David Lloyd George was an ardent Welsh Nationalist, a keen Temperance reformer, a Baptist in creed and a strong Radical-Socialist in politics. Though too cautious to pledge himself to the restoration of complete independence for the Boers, he bitterly denounced an ' unrighteous war ' and the ' methods of barbarism ' which, in its latter stages, were adopted (as he and his friends alleged) by the British Generals in the field.

Midway between the Liberal Imperialist ' Right ' and the ' Pro-Boer ' Left was a group of Gladstonian Liberals who had loyally accepted the leadership of Campbell-Bannerman. The relative strength of the groups may be gauged from a division on a Pro-Boer motion in July 1900. The motion found only 31 supporters ; the Liberal Imperialists, 40 in number, voted with the Government ; Campbell-Bannerman with 35 of his Party abstained from the Division. The Liberal Party, then, was hopelessly—and not unequally—divided, and the Government was tactically right in dissolving Parliament and appealing to the country for a renewal of confidence in September 1900. The war, it was believed, had been brought to a successful conclusion ;

the Parliament elected in 1895 had evidently exhausted its mandate, and though in some quarters the 'khaki' election was denounced as slim tactics, it was manifestly proper that the electorate should decide to what Party should be confided the task of concluding Peace.

Before Parliament was prorogued the Queen gave her assent to a Bill for the federation of the six colonies of Australia in a Commonwealth. The *Commonwealth of Australia Act* was at once the consummation of prolonged and laborious conferences in Australia, and the culminating legislative achievement of a reign unique in English History in respect of Imperial evolution.

The Commonwealth of Australia, 1900

The final impulse to Federation was supplied by a recognition of the vulnerability of the Imperial and Colonial position in the Pacific. The material development of the Australasian Colonies had not kept pace with their constitutional evolution. Between 1854 and 1890 all these colonies, New South Wales, Victoria, Tasmania, South Australia, Queensland, Western Australia, and New Zealand—attained to the full dignity of responsible government. What they continued to lack was not government but subjects. The vast spaces of the great southern continent were virtually unpeopled. The total population of Australia amounted at that time to no more than 4,500,000. The spirit of high protection ran riot; immigration was discouraged, and Australian democracy was primarily concerned to keep up the price of labour. Mingled with this motive was the laudable ambition to preserve Australia as a white-man's country. To the realization of this and similar ambitions some closer form of political union was essential. But Federation was, in Australia, a plant of slow and timid growth. Ever since 1847 the project had been intermittently discussed, but not until 1883 did it actually begin to take shape. Several things then combined to render the problem insistent : the question as to the desirability of importing Chinese labour for the mines; the escape of some French convicts from New Caledonia into Australian territory; rumours that France was intending to annex the New Hebrides; above all, Lord Derby's disavowal of the action of Queensland in setting up the British flag in New Guinea. Between 1883 and 1899 many conferences were held, and many schemes were discussed, and at last in the latter year a Bill, which expressed the mind of Australia, was sent home for the approval of the Imperial Legislature. Thanks to the tact of Mr. Chamberlain and of Mr. (afterwards Sir Edmund) Barton, first Prime Minister of the Commonwealth, the Bill became law, with a single amendment, as the Australian Commonwealth Act. It was the last statute of importance to which Queen Victoria gave her Royal Assent, and in doing so she expressed her fervent hope that ' the inauguration of the Commonwealth may ensure the increased prosperity and well-being of my loyal and beloved subjects in Australia '.[1]

So it was done in the Presence—in the Hall of our Thousand Years,
In the face of the Five Free Nations that have no peer but their peers ;
And the Young Queen out of the Southland kneeled down at the Old Queen's
   knee,
And asked for a mother's blessing on the excellent years to be.

And the Old Queen stooped in the stillness when the jewelled head drooped
   low :—
Daughter no more but Sister and doubly Daughter so—
Mother of many princes and child of the child I bore,
What good thing shall I wish thee that I have not wished before ?

Shall I give thee delight in dominion—mere pride of thy setting forth ?
Nay, we be women together,—we know what that is worth.
   .   .   .   .
Shall I give thee my sleepless wisdom, or the gift of all wisdom above ?
Aye, we be women together—I give thee thy people's love.

Tempered, august, abiding, reluctant of prayers or vows,
Eager in face of peril as thine for thy mother's house,
God requite thee, my Sister, through the wonderful years to be,
And make thy people to love thee, as thou hast loved me ![2]

Not for the first, nor for the last time did the great Imperial singer interpret the mood and mind of all right-thinking Britons, at home and overseas.

The Australian Federation differed in important respects from the system adopted in Canada. In regard to the distribution of powers between the Commonwealth and the component States it followed the American not the Canadian precedent, delegating certain enumerated powers to the Commonwealth, and vesting

[1] For sketch of the federation movement in Australia and analysis of the Commonwealth Constitution, cf. Marriott, *Evolution of the British Empire and Commonwealth* (1939), c's x, xvi.

[2] Rudyard Kipling, *The Young Queen* (1900).

the residue of powers in the State Governments. Again, in constituting its Second Chamber it followed the American model, giving to each State, large or small, equal representation (six members apiece) in the Senate. Amendments to the Constitution must be passed by both Houses (or by one house twice), and must be approved by (a) a majority of *States* and (b) a majority of electors in the Commonwealth as a whole. The Executive is on the Cabinet, not as in America on the Presidential, model, and is responsible (as in England and Canada) to the Legislature. The Judiciary in Australia is less federal than that of the United States, but less unitary than that of Canada. An appeal lies from the State Courts to the Federal Supreme Court while the appellate jurisdiction of the King in Council remains unimpaired. On the last point there was considerable discussion when the Draft Constitution was under discussion in the Imperial Parliament, but ultimately Mr. Chamberlain had his way.[1]

A few months after the Royal Assent to this great measure Parliament was dissolved. The elections held in September–October 1900 resulted in a net gain of six seats for the Unionist Party which returned 402 strong (the Conservatives numbering 334), against 268 Liberals and Nationalists. Many seats were uncontested, and, though Mr. Chamberlain tried to persuade the electors that every vote given against the Government was a vote given to the Boers, considerable apathy prevailed. Nevertheless the final result was a substantial vote of confidence in the Government. But there was a considerable shifting of offices after the election. The most important was consequent on the retirement of Lord Salisbury from the Foreign Office which he handed over to Lord Lansdowne, who was much happier there than at the War Office, where he was succeeded by Mr. St. John Brodrick (afterwards Earl of Midleton). Mr. C. T. (afterwards Lord) Ritchie, who had done good work as President of the Local Government Board (1886–92) and at the Board of Trade (1895–1900), became Home Secretary. Lord Selborne, a son-in-law of Lord Salisbury and an ardent disciple of Chamberlain, went to the Admiralty in succession to Mr. Goschen, whose retirement was greatly regretted by the Queen. Of the new appointments

The Khaki Election

---

[1] The above is a mere outline sketch : for details, cf. Marriott, *Evolution of the British Empire and Commonwealth*, c. xvi.

the most interesting was that of Mr. George Wyndham, the most brilliant of Mr. Balfour's personal disciples, to the Chief Secretaryship for Ireland. Lord Salisbury, retaining the Premiership, himself became Lord Privy Seal, in succession to Lord Cross, who thus brought to an end a useful and honourable political career which had begun with his election for Preston in 1857. Few Ministers of the reign were better liked or more trusted by the Queen, whose insistence led to his retention of office until he was nearing 80. He died at the age of 91 in 1914.

To return to South Africa. With the relief of Kimberley, Mafeking, and Ladysmith, with the occupation of the Boer capitals, and the annexation of the two Republics to the British Dominions, the first phase of the war ended. On 29th November 1900 Lord Roberts left Pretoria, making over the command to Lord Kitchener, ' in whose judgement, discretion and valour ' he expressed (to the Queen) the ' greatest confidence '. In December he embarked for England to take up the post of Commander-in-Chief in succession to Lord Wolseley. On leaving he spoke of the Boers in the field as ' a few marauding bands ' and said : ' The war has now virtually come to an end, and my work is finished.'

His own work as a commander in the field was, indeed, ' finished ', but though he left behind him an army of 230,000 men, it had subsequently to be increased to over 300,000 and even then proved, for long months, unequal to the task of dispersing the ' few marauding bands ' of Boers.

The Queen and her People On arriving in England Lord Roberts went straight to Osborne (January 2) to report to the Queen, who gave him the Garter and told him that she intended to confer an Earldom upon him with remainder to his daughter. She saw him again for a short while on Monday, the 14th, but was evidently failing fast. On Saturday, the 19th, a bulletin was issued, and the public for the first time learnt that the Sovereign was seriously ill. ' The Queen ', it ran, ' has not lately been in her usual health, and is unable for the present to take her customary drives. The Queen during the past year has had a great strain upon her powers, which has rather told upon Her Majesty's nervous system.'

Few women of her age could have endured that strain at all.

She had felt acutely the humiliation inflicted upon the country by the defeats to her arms in South Africa, yet never did she show herself more truly the mother of her people than in the dark days of the winter 1899–1900. Despite failing health she went in and out among them : encouraging the fighters, with her own hands knitting comforts, and sending out Christmas boxes to the front, visiting and consoling the wounded, comforting the mourners, warning and stimulating responsible Ministers.

On March 7, 1900, the Queen went to London, and on the afternoons of March 8 and 9 she drove for many miles through the streets of London to manifest her oneness with her people in those anxious days. On the 22nd she went to the Herbert Hospital at Woolwich to visit the wounded. Deeply were her people touched ; unbounded was the enthusiasm with which they greeted the aged Sovereign. It was of her visit to London that Lord Rosebery wrote to her (March 15, 1900):

' I think the visit to London far more interesting and touching even than the Jubilees : it was more simple and spontaneous. It was as if a great wave of sympathy and devotion had passed over the capital. Your Majesty intimated as it were to London : " I will come among you and rejoice with you ; as we have shared our anxieties and sorrows, we will share the common joys." Your Majesty does not much admire Queen Elizabeth, but the visit to London was in the Elizabethan spirit. There was, however, this difference, that with the pride that England felt in Elizabeth there was but little love. Now the nation glows with both.'[1] Lord Rosebery expressed, with characteristic felicity, the common sentiment.

Unceasing in her activities at home, the Queen followed, day by day, hour by hour, all the efforts of her soldiers in South Africa, and cordially commended their successes. Especially did she appreciate the gallantry of the Colonial contingents, and of the Irish regiments. The latter's services she acknowledged with more than words. She gave them permission to wear a sprig of shamrock on St. Patrick's Day, and when the time came for her spring holiday in 1900 she determined, instead of going to the South, to devote it to Ireland. In this determination there was perhaps a tinge of self-reproach. ' She desired almost passion-

[1] Q.V.L. (3rd Series), vol. iii, 513.

ately', so we learn from one who knew her, ' to be loved by the Irish,' but she had done little to win their love. Pathetically she strove, at the last, to make amends. Her last April she spent in Dublin, where she was enthusiastically welcomed by all classes. But the strain of the effort was terrible, and combined with that of the South African War undoubtedly hastened her end.

The Death of the Queen

A few days after her last interview with Lord Roberts the Queen became seriously ill, and at 6.30 p.m. on Tuesday, January 22nd, 1901, in the presence of two sons, three daughters, and her grandson, the German Emperor, she breathed her last. She was in her eighty-second year and had reigned sixty-three years seven months and three days.

Her subjects, at home and throughout the Empire, were stunned by the news that the end had come. ' The Queen dead ! The news is benumbing to the heart and brain. The cornerstone of our National and Imperial life—nay, of our individual and family life—is suddenly displaced. We cannot as yet realize what it means ; what life in the future will mean bereft of her whose august, beloved, and venerated personality has been for the greater part of a century the centre and the mainspring of our national existence.' [1]

By the Queen's own command her funeral was a military one. On Friday, February 1st, the royal yacht *Alberta* passing between long lines of warships, which fired a last salute,[2] carried the Queen's body from Cowes to Portsmouth. On February 2nd the funeral procession passed through London. A gun-carriage bore the tiny coffin. King Edward VII as chief mourner rode immediately behind it, supported by the Duke of Connaught and the German Emperor, whose unmistakable grief greatly touched the hearts of the thousands who witnessed the procession. The Kings of Greece and Portugal, as well as members of every Royal Family in Europe, were among the mourners. The funeral service was held on the same afternoon in St. George's Chapel, Windsor, and on Monday, February 4, the Queen's remains found

[1] These words from an article written on January 23rd, 1901, by the present writer, are quoted, crude though they be, simply as evidence of *contemporary* feeling.

[2] There was a strong south-west wind and the booming of the guns was distinctly heard by the present writer at Oxford.

their final resting-place side by side with those of Prince Albert in the Royal Mausoleum at Frogmore.

The great Queen passed to her rest cheered by Lord Roberts's assurance that the South African War was virtually at an end. Unhappily his assurance was not justified. Lord Kitchener had not been in supreme command for many weeks before he wrote to Mr. Brodrick, the new Secretary of State, expressing a fear that he might have been disappointed ' at the recent development of the war '. He estimated that there were still 20,000 Boers out on commando and added : ' These men are not always out on commando, but return at intervals to their farms and live as most peaceful inhabitants, probably supplying the nearest British garrison with forage, milk and eggs, until they are again called out. . . . Just now they have apparently got them all out, with the result that they suddenly show in considerable numbers, and act with great boldness when they get a chance. Owing to the vastness of the country the Boers can roam at pleasure and being excessively mobile they are able to surprise any post not sufficiently on the alert. Every farm is to them an intelligence agency, and a supply depot, so that it is almost impossible to surround or catch them.' [1]

The Boer War —Second Phase

So for many weary months it proved to be. Troops were poured into South Africa ; cavalry, mounted infantry, gunners, engineers, and several contingents of Imperial Yeomanry, with large supplies of heavy guns, horse and field guns, and ' pom-poms '. But the brilliant tactics of Louis Botha, De Wet, and Delarey, who waged guerrilla warfare with incomparable skill, defied all Kitchener's efforts. Tactics and strategy as learnt in other schools had to be unlearnt, and Kitchener had to fall back on two combined devices—a system of ' Blockhouses ' and ' the Drive '. About the former device Sir Ian Hamilton, sent out as Chief of the Staff in 1901, telegraphed to Lord Roberts, ' Although I had read much of blockhouses I never could have imagined such a gigantic system of fortifications, barriers, traps, and garrisons as actually exists. This forms the principal characteristic of the present operations. . . .' As to ' the Drive ' Kitchener's biographer, Sir George Arthur, writes : ' Our scheme was . . .

[1] Arthur, *Life*, i. 326–8.

to denude the entire country of all combatant Boers, herding them more and more closely towards an enclosure formed either by natural features or by artificial barriers—corralling and round-ing them up into an angle or pocket—forcing them, as it were, through a closed funnel into its blind end.'

These methods were, however, both slow and costly, and it was unfortunately necessary, in order to give them even a chance of success against so elusive an opponent, ' to blend them with some administrative measures of a drastic character.' The country was gradually stripped and depopulated : farmsteads destroyed ; standing-crops burnt ; flocks and herds carried off ; the women and children being meanwhile herded into concentra-tion camps. Such were the methods of barbarism denounced by ' Pro-Boers ' and even by others who in Mr. Brodrick's words were ' hot on the humanitarian tack ' in England, and still more in continental countries. To Kitchener himself it was a ' miser-able business ' and as month after month passed, and no decisive result was achieved, it could have caused no surprise had his courage and persistence failed. But grimly he held on.

Edward VII and the War

King Edward, who in January 1901 had succeeded to the throne, was seriously concerned about the slow progress of the war, more particularly as to its effect upon the relations between England and the European Powers. The Governments, at any rate in France and Russia, were indeed more restrained than the peoples. The Czar refused to threaten, at the Kaiser's suggestion, British India ; Delcassé was already looking towards the possi-bility of an Anglo-French Entente and gave no encouragement to continental intrigues against England. But there was no mistaking the strength of anti-British feeling, as manifested in popular caricature and other ways. In June, 1901, the Czar (doubtless under pressure) wrote to his ' dearest Uncle Bertie ' to suggest that his ' kind heart ' must ' yearn to put an end to this bloodshed ', this ' war of extermination ', this coercion of ' a small people desperately defending their country '. The King was as anxious as the Czar to see the war ended : though with Lord Salisbury's help he made a crushing rejoinder to his ' dearest Nicky '. But he became increasingly uneasy and impatient at the prolongation of the war, and severely blamed the War Office where, as he thought and said, a coterie of ' muddling and inefficient civilians ' were actually hampering the efforts of the soldiers in the field.

Kitchener's anxiety to end the war was as keen as the King's. Negotiations for peace had in fact been opened between Kitchener and Louis Botha at the end of February 1901, but came to nothing. The Transvaal Boers wanted peace ; but Mr. Steyn, President of the Orange Free State, was implacable and would listen to no terms which involved loss of independence. Kruger, an exile in Holland, supported Steyn. Milner's attitude, too, seemed to Kitchener, if ' strictly just ' unnecessarily rigid. In the (English) summer of 1901, however, Milner took three months' much-needed leave, and Kitchener was during his absence Acting High Commissioner. But neither the war nor the peace negotiations made much progress. Nor was the war destined to finish without one more grievous reverse to the British forces. On March 7, 1902, a considerable force under the command of General Lord Methuen was surprised and overwhelmed, after desperate fighting, by General Delarey. Methuen himself was severely wounded and taken prisoner, but most considerately treated by his captor. This disaster greatly distressed King Edward and seemed likely to prolong the war. In April 1902, however, conferences between the several Boer leaders were held, and on May 15 two delegates elected by each of 32 commandos in the field met at Vereeniging. On May 27 a remarkable interview took place between Lord Milner and General J. C. Smuts, who in recent months had been doing brilliant work in the field, having not long ago taken first-class honours in law at Cambridge. At home, King Edward was desperately anxious that Peace should be concluded before his coronation ; his ministers shared his anxiety ; and on May 31st Peace was signed. The Burghers laid Peace of down their arms and recognized King Edward VII as their lawful Vereeniging Sovereign ; military government was to be speedily superseded by civil government, and representative institutions leading up to complete self-government were, as soon as circumstances permitted, to be introduced ; English was to be the official language, but Dutch was to be taught in the schools in the annexed Provinces and allowed in the Courts ; burghers in the field or prisoners of war were to be repatriated as soon as possible, and rifles were to be allowed to them, on licence, for defence ; except for certain specified acts contrary to the usages of war there was to be a complete amnesty ; no special tax to defray war expenses was to be imposed on landed property in the annexed Provinces, and the British Government undertook to give £3,000,000 to facilitate and expedite the re-settlement of the burghers on their farms.

The terms were marked by a generosity inspired partly by admiration for the courage displayed by the Boers, partly by the hope that old and septic sores would be healed, and that Boers and Britons would henceforward live in amity as common subjects of the British Crown.

Thus ended a war which had involved the loss of 1,072 officers and 20,870 men, and had cost the British taxpayers over £222,000,000. Nearly 450,000 British troops, of whom over 250,000 were Regulars, had been engaged. On the side of the Boers 3,700 men were said to have been killed ; over 31,000 were taken prisoners, and 20,000 surrendered on the conclusion of peace.[1]

On June 5 Parliament voted a war gratuity of £50,000 to Lord Kitchener. It was well deserved : he had put his last ounce into a contest from which little prestige was to be gained, and had proved himself to be a great statesman as well as a soldier of inexhaustible patience and resourcefulness. He left Cape Town on June 23, and on his arrival in London on July 12 was met by the Prince of Wales, and, as he drove from Paddington to St. James's Palace, through streets lined with British and Colonial troops, received a great popular welcome. His Sovereign lay on a sick bed at Buckingham Palace, but Kitchener was summoned to receive from the King's own hands the Order of Merit.

[1] Report of Royal Commission on War in South Africa.

CHAPTER IX

THE CLOSE OF AN EPOCH

THE death of Queen Victoria not only ended the longest reign in English History, it closed an epoch of outstanding historical importance. That the end of the reign coincided so nearly with the beginning of a new century may not, in reality, have added to its significance, but undeniably it accentuated the transition from the nineteenth century to the twentieth, from the splendour of the Victorian Era to the dark days that were to come.

It may be well, therefore, at this point to pause awhile and briefly consider some salient characteristics of the period thus abruptly ended.

In the sphere of government the Victorian era witnessed the meridian of that typically English form of polity which is now known to the world as ' Constitutional Monarchy '. A ' constitutional ' king, according to the classic phrase of M. Thiers, is a king who ' reigns but does not govern '. Seen at its best, as it was under Queen Victoria, this system precisely fulfilled the conditions laid down for the ideal polity by the greatest of political philosophers. It combined the best features of Monarchy, Aristocracy and Democracy. At the apex of the political pyramid was a King (or Queen) who ' could do no wrong ', since responsibility for all the acts of the Sovereign was assumed by ministers answerable to Parliament. But if the Sovereign was thus shielded from doing wrong, he could do much, even in the strictly political sphere, that ' was right and useful '. The knowledge of affairs gained by a Minister—even by a Minister with a record of service as long as that of a Russell, a Palmerston, a Gladstone or a Salisbury—is almost necessarily discontinuous. No Minister in Queen Victoria's reign held the highest office continuously for more than six years. The Queen held 'office' without a day's break for more than sixty. It is continuity of experience which gives the permanent official so great an advantage over his temporary parliamentary chief, which tends to exalt Whitehall above Westminster. But no Permanent Secretary ever in length of service approached Queen Victoria. Length and continuity of experience entitled the Sovereign to advise and warn, if she might not command—in any but a technical sense. Nor is it an insignificant matter that Ministers should be under constraint to justify every decision reached by them, every appointment made, to a Sovereign who was entirely free, as no parliamentary Minister is free, from the necessity of heeding parliamentary exigencies or party interests. The purely literary historian is prone to assert that at the close of Queen Victoria's reign, ' the Crown was weaker than at any other time in English history '.[1] Mr. Gladstone knew better. He was no courtier, and the Crown was probably at its weakest at the time when Gladstone was at the zenith of his power—say from 1865 to 1885. Yet Gladstone wrote : ' There is not a doubt that the aggregate of direct influence normally exercised by the Sovereign upon the counsels and proceedings of her Ministers is considerable in amount, tends to permanence and solidity of action, and confers much benefit on the country without in the smallest degree relieving the advisers of the Crown from their individual responsibility.' [2]

Mr. Gladstone spoke of influence. But as to power ? The legal powers of Queen Victoria did not greatly differ from those exercised by Queen Elizabeth. Most of those powers—vastly extended in scope—were in the nineteenth century actually exercised by Ministers. But two prerogatives of great potential importance the Crown has retained. Preceding chapters have shown that the Queen exercised within narrow limits a personal choice in the selection of her First Minister, and a veto, within similar limits, upon the appointment of his colleagues, and the apportionment of offices. She also held in reserve the right to force or to refuse a Dissolution of Parliament. The Victorian polity, then, did not lack the stability that well-established monarchy can give.

[1] e.g. L. Strachey, *Queen Victoria*, p. 301.
[2] *Gleanings from Past Years*, I. p. 42.

Nor did it lack those elements which are proverbially associated The Aristocratical Element with the rule of an Aristocracy. It is true that the Reform Act of 1832 had sensibly weakened that domination over the Legislature which the landed aristocracy had exercised since 1688, and that the Acts of 1867, 1884, 1918 and 1928 reduced it by stages to vanishing point. But an analysis of the Cabinets of the Victorian era reveals the extent to which the ' ruling families ' of the eighteenth century retained their control over the executive side of Government, even if compelled to surrender in the legislative sphere. Of the ten Prime Ministers of the reign six were Peers, a seventh was the son of a Duke, two (Peel and Gladstone) belonged to the new aristocracy of Commerce ; only one (Disraeli) belonged to the aristocracy neither of birth, nor wealth nor education. Of the Prime Ministers five were educated at Eton, three at Harrow and one at Westminster ; five at Oxford and three at Cambridge. Exact computation in the case of other Cabinet Ministers is difficult, but as to the predominantly aristocratic complexion of Cabinets there is no question. Except in the Gladstone-Rosebery administration of 1892–5 every Cabinet contained a majority, most of them a very large majority, of men who were either Peers or closely connected with the Peerage. In Lord John Russell's Cabinet of 1846, for example, all the members, with three exceptions, held office by the Divine Right of hereditary Whiggism.[1]

To state the facts is not to condemn the system. On the contrary, it may well be questioned whether England was, on the whole, better governed at any period of its long history than during the Victorian era.

If the Executive remained predominantly aristocratic the The House of Commons Legislature was in composition increasingly democratic. At least until 1885, perhaps until the close of the reign, county representation remained for the most part in the hands, if not of members of ' county ' families, at least in those of their friends or nominees. After 1905 that ceased to be the case : it had long ceased to be true of borough representation. Down indeed to

---

[1] A somewhat different method of computation reaches, with a different purpose in view, conclusions closely approximate. Of the 227 men who held Cabinet office between 1832 and 1905 139 were actually sons of Peers. (*Laski*, Fabian Tract 223.)

1832 the boroughs were hardly less the stronghold of the territorial oligarchy than the House of Lords itself. After 1832 membership of the House of Commons fell increasingly into the hands of men who had made money at the Bar or in trade. Nevertheless, until 1905 the House had still some claim to be regarded as the ' best club in Europe '. The new class of members had for the most part been educated at the same schools as the old class and—apart of course from the Irish Repealers—could mingle with the latter on equal terms. Moreover, many of the new men found their way to the House of Lords.

The House of Lords During the reign of George III the House of Lords had more than doubled in size. On his accession the hereditary Peers numbered only 200. On the accession of Queen Victoria they numbered 423, and at her death no fewer than 592. By the accession of King George V the number had increased to 622. Mr. Lloyd George created nearly 100 new Peers during the six years of his Premiership, with the result that the Second Chamber now (1945) contains about 300 more members than the First. The increase in numbers was coincident with, and perhaps partly responsible for, a decrease in power. The critical years for the Second Chamber were to come under King George V, but it was undeniably weaker in 1901 than in 1837, even if it had not become, as a modern writer has said, ' little more than a debating Society '. Nor was it devoid of significance that Gladstone, in his last speech in the House of Commons, should have bequeathed to the Liberal Party the task of further curtailing its power.[1]

Labour members Meanwhile, the House of Commons opened its doors to men (and after 1918 to women) drawn from all classes of the community. Of the rapid growth of Labour representation in Parliament more must be said hereafter.[2] It began, on a considerable scale, only at the Election of 1906. Down to the end of Queen Victoria's reign the appearance of a wage-earner in the House of Commons was regarded as something of a portent. In 1874 the Trade Unions, for the first time, initiated a movement for direct representation in Parliament, and thirteen Labour candidates were nominated at the General Election of that year. Of these two,

---

[1] On the whole question cf. Marriott, *Second Chambers* (revised ed., Oxford, 1927).

[2] *Infra*, c. xiii.

Thomas Burt and Alexander Macdonald, leading officials of the Miners' Union, were returned and took their seats as the first 'Labour' members of the House of Commons. At the Election of 1885 Joseph Arch, a skilled hedge-cutter, who had successfully organized the Agricultural Labourers' Union, was returned for North-West Norfolk, being the first agricultural labourer to enter Parliament. These men, with five or six more Trade Union leaders returned in 1885, acted with the Liberal Party, were reckoned among its members, and mostly lost their seats, like other Liberals, in 1886. In 1892, however, several of them, including Arch, were re-elected and there came into the House at the same time two avowed Socialists, John Burns and James Keir Hardie. The former was an engineer who had become prominent in connexion with unemployed demonstrations in London and in the Dockers' Strike. He was now returned for Battersea. Keir Hardie was a Scottish miner, who had refused the offer of a safe Liberal seat with an income of £300 a year, preferring to organize the Scottish Labour Party, and to enter Parliament as a Socialist, pure and simple, independent of any of the existing parties. John Burns, though professing the Socialist creed, acted generally with the Liberal Party, and ultimately (1906) entered a Liberal Cabinet. Keir Hardie's first arrival at the House was heralded by a cornet, if not a brass band, and he continued to emphasize his 'independence' by ostentatious singularities of attire. Yet his blaring escort and cloth cap were not, perhaps, inappropriate. They announced the advent of a new Parliamentary Party.

Whether the Legislature as a whole or the House of Commons in particular gained or lost in power by the extension of the electorate is a much debated question. That the multiplication of the functions of the State has tended to diminish the power of the House of Commons as against the Executive—particularly in the sphere of finance—is undeniable. But that tendency, especially as regards the permanent Executive, was less noticeable before than after the death of Queen Victoria. The independence of the Legislature was, however, threatened in the later years of the reign by the development of local Party organizations, and the tightening of Party discipline. The 'Caucus' had its birth in Birmingham in the late 'seventies, and was fathered by Mr. Joseph Chamberlain and Mr. Schnadhorst. The 'National Lib-

Party organiza tion

eral Federation ' was formed on a similarly representative basis in 1877 ; the ' National Union of Conservative and Constitutional Associations ' had come into being ten years earlier. The growth of these extra-Parliamentary organizations, while stimulating popular interest in Parliamentary proceedings, also tended to curtail the independence of members of Parliament.

Nevertheless it is true, broadly speaking, that never was the equilibrium of forces, monarchical, aristocratic and democratic, more perfect than in England in the Victorian era. So admirably, indeed, did the mechanism operate that the civilized world rushed to the conclusion that the astounding prosperity of England was attributable to its political institutions. Accordingly, other nations took to copying it. What Pericles proudly said of the Athenian polity is even more true of the English : ' We have a form of government not derived from imitation of our neighbours : —nay, rather we are a pattern to others than they to us.' That the results of imitation have not been invariably successful is not our fault, but the misfortune of the copyists. They vainly imagined that a Constitution can be copied like a Paris costume, which presupposes for effective wearing a Paris figure. Parliamentary Democracy presupposes for its success a prolonged political apprenticeship. That apprenticeship had in few cases been served : the result of premature adoption is seen on all sides to-day in the general reaction to dictatorship.

Social changes Socially, not less than politically, the Victorian Era manifested the virtues of the golden mean. The predominance of the middle classes was, throughout the reign, unquestioned, and their ' moderation ' is now ' known unto all men ', though to nothing were they more opposed than to ostentation. To the Proletariat all that savours of bourgeois respectability has become anathema, and among all classes it has now become fashionable to despise the characteristic virtues, no less than to expose the shortcomings, of Victorian Society. ' Goodness they prized above every other human quality ; and Victoria who, at the age of twelve, had said she would be good, had kept her word. Duty, conscience, morality—yes ! in the light of those high beacons the Queen had always lived. She had passed her days in work and not in pleasure, in public responsibilities and family cares. . . . The middle classes, firm in the triple brass of their respectability,

rejoiced with a special joy over the most respectable of Queens.' [1]
So wrote Mr. Strachey with a sneer characteristic of the superior
Georgian.

It may be that the typical Victorian was a slave to convention, Sunday
and that a ' passion for propriety ' was carried to excess ; but if observ-
ance
he took his pleasures somewhat sadly he took them with more
regard to the comfort and peace of his neighbours, and with less
danger to the public at large than his successors. Nothing is
more typical of the change that has taken place in social habits
since the Queen's death than the revolution in regard to the
' observance ' of Sunday. Victorian Sundays may, judged by
modern standards, have been Puritanically dull, but it is at least
doubtful whether any gain in gaiety can compensate for the loss
of that ' Sabbath calm ' which on one day in seven regularly
settled down upon the land. Almost the only place where that
calm can to-day be enjoyed in its entirety is in the City of London.
Were the fact more generally known, there would no longer be a
question about the demolition of City churches. To take out the
carriage ' for pleasure ' on a Sunday was regarded in middle-class
households as not merely improper in itself but as showing
grave lack of consideration for servants. Attendance at church
or chapel was almost universal in morning and evening ; the
afternoons were given up to quiet walks or quiet reading—but
not of fiction. Children were taught to put away toys and ' week-
day ' books on Saturday night ; nor did they reappear till Monday.
There was no entertaining : a few relations or intimate friends
might drop in to tea, or even to supper, but the supper would
always be cold.

Habits at the Universities may be taken as representing those
of the classes from which undergraduates were mostly drawn.
At Oxford, fifty years ago, the tall hat and morning coat were
general among self-respecting undergraduates. ' One result of the
great relaxation of Sunday observance conspicuous in Oxford as
throughout the country is ', writes Dr. H. A. L. Fisher, ' much
to be regretted. In the 'eighties Sunday was the day for quiet
reading and country walks.' Of Cambridge Dr. M. R. James
writes : ' On Sundays the fullness of College chapels—compulsory
—and of the galleries of St. Mary's at the sermon—voluntary—

[1] *Queen Victoria*, p. 303.

was notable.'[1]   At Oxford the galleries of St. Mary's are to-day as full as ever, when there is a preacher acceptable to undergraduates ; the College chapels are not.

Sunday observance was not, however, the monopoly of a single class. It was general among all classes. Of the countryside Lord Ernle writes : ' On that day Victorians wore their best clothes, went once if not twice to Church, ordered out no carriages, entertained no parties, played no games in public. In 1932 all this is reversed. Sunday has become a day of special liberties, not of special restrictions. In their observances and attendances Victorians expressed their convictions of an ordained progress towards higher morality and increased material prosperity, To-day that conviction has passed away. Nothing stands in its place. It seems that so long as life travels faster the direction is unimportant.'[2]

What was true of the countryside was almost equally true of London ' Society '. ' Sundays ', writes Sir Ian Malcolm, ' were very strictly kept in London. Dinner-parties were rare and other forms of entertaining practically unknown. There were no restaurants of any repute, and the night club was not then dreamed of or desired '.[3] ' Altogether ', writes another survivor of the Victorian era, ' we managed to amuse ourselves thoroughly well on Sundays, all the better for the fact that in those less restless days to many of us London was really a home.'[3]

The last words testify to another typical development. In Victorian days there was no week-end ' habit '. Middle-class folk made their homes in London, and left it once a year for a month or two. Their ' betters ' lived in the country for nine months and in London for three. Provincial folk, save for a few weeks' holiday in the summer, lived at home all the year round.

Loco-
motion

The change, now common in varying degrees to all classes, began after the death of the Queen, and is, of course, mainly attributable to the amazing development of facilities for locomotion. So rapid has been the development that it is to us almost incredible that Queen Victoria never entered a motor-car and

---

[1] *Fifty Years*, pp. 88, 97.   [2] Ibid., p. 195.
[3] Ibid., pp. 39, 28–9. If ' Sunday observance ' is, in the above paragraphs, emphasized it is because it is typical of much else.

never saw an aeroplane. Not until the last years of the century did pedal cycling become, with the introduction of pneumatic tyres, either comfortable or general, and at the Cycle Show of 1899 the motor-cycle was inspected with curious eyes as a novelty. Only in 1896 was the Act of 1865 repealed which had forbidden steam traction engines to travel on the roads at a speed exceeding four miles an hour and required that they should be preceded by a man carrying a red flag. There are many who regret that Parliament was so ill-advised as to repeal it, and who cannot deplore the fact that the late Lord Montagu of Beaulieu was in 1899 prevented by the police from entering the sacred precincts of Parliament in a motor-car. Not, then, until the turn of the century was the motor-car, the use of which had been rapidly developing in wicked Paris, regarded as quite respectable in virtuous London. After the Queen's death the revolution in means of locomotion came with a rush. Motor omnibuses and motor cabs (' taxis ') began to drive the horse-drawn vehicles off the streets of London towards the end of King Edward's reign. Nor have the results of scientific invention and engineering skill been monopolized by the richer classes. Electric tramways had made their first appearance at Leeds in 1891 ; the first ' Tube ' railway was opened in London in 1890. The mobility of the Londoner is shown by the fact that every man, woman and child makes 496 journeys in the year, 236 of them being by omnibuses and 78 by underground trains, while no fewer than 1,100,000 passengers arrive daily at the London termini.

The number of motor vehicles annually licensed in Great Britain now (1933) exceeds 2,000,000 and the gross receipts derived from the taxation of them approaches £35,000,000 a year, the greater part of which is spent on the construction and upkeep of high roads. On the roads over 6,600 people are annually killed and (in 1937) 226,402 were injured. *The automobile*

The invention of the internal combustion engine was soon put to uses more sinister than the propulsion of motor-cars. The submarine was first adopted by the Admiralty in 1901, and aviation, an art in the development of which many experiments had been tried in the last years of the Victorian era, was first utilized for military purposes on a large scale during the Great War (1914–18).

Industry and commerce

The social revolution suggested by the foregoing paragraphs was accompanied by changes very considerable, if less revolutionary, in the sphere of commerce and industry. Of some of the inventions which contributed to those changes mention has already been made.[1] The invention first of the compound engine in 1860, and the perfecting of the surface condenser about 1870, revolutionized the conditions of ocean transport. Refrigeration and cold storage brought the products of distant continents, and particularly of British Dominions and Dependencies, into common use in English homes. The development of telegraphy, cable and wireless, and the invention of the telephone, have made for ease and rapidity of communications, making it possible, for example, for English millers to follow, from hour to hour, the course of prices on the Winnipeg Exchange. Reference was also made to the patient researches of Sir Ronald Ross and Sir Patrick Manson into the origin and spread of tropical diseases. When in 1899 Major Ross definitely established his theory of the transmission of malaria through mosquitoes he not only conferred an immense boon upon suffering humanity, but won for himself a permanent place among our great Empire-builders and commercial adventurers. That these discoveries and inventions gave an immense impulse to the development of overseas trade in the last years of the Victorian era needs no elaborate demonstration.

In the resulting prosperity all classes of the community—except those engaged in agriculture—shared. Owing to the development of ' the joint-stock ' principle in industry, an immense number of quite small capitalists were able as shareholders to participate in profits. A still larger number benefited in the form of higher wages.

The wage-earners

Shortly before his death (1884) Mark Pattison, a famous Oxford scholar, was asked what he considered to be the most important fact in contemporary history. Without hesitation he replied : ' The fact that 5,000,000 of our population possess nothing but their weekly wages '.[2] The answer was not far from the truth : and so far as it was true it pointed to a feature of our social life peculiar to the Victorian era. Only in the nineteenth century did the mass of the people become entirely dependent on

---

[1] *Supra*, cs. i and vii.
[2] *The Reign of Queen Victoria* (ed. Ward), p. 23.

weekly wages for their livelihood. For that dependence the development of the Factory system and the Enclosure movement were jointly responsible. Down to the last decades of the eighteenth century there was no sharp differentiation between industry and agriculture. Every farmhouse had its loom, most labourers had access to some common land, and all their wives did some spinning and perhaps some weaving. The Industrial Revolution transformed England from a land of villages and farms into a land of towns and factories. It created a proletariat— a large class without property. That phase has passed. To-day (1945) the vast majority of the wage-earners, probably not fewer than 20,000,000, are small capitalists, with something to their credit in Savings Banks and Saving Certificates, not to speak of a share of the assets in Benefit Societies, Trade Unions, Co-operative Societies, and like institutions.[1] Large additions, arising from State subventions and gratuitous social services, are now made to the money wages of every working-class household. These represent an increment, in many cases, of 50 per cent. on wages ; in some cases much more. But social insurance and gratuitous services are a post-Victorian development.

Wages, then, formed the all-important item on the credit side of the working-class budget in Victorian days. Wage-rates varied from time to time : trade was subject to cyclical fluctuations ; boom-periods and depressions alternated with grievous regularity, but on the whole the tendency was for wages, whether measured in money or commodities, to rise. The main thesis on which Henry George reared the argumentative structure of *Progress and Poverty* was, as regards England, simply untrue. The vast increase of ' wealth ' was not accompanied by an increase of ' poverty '. Taking a survey of economic conditions during the first fifty years of Queen Victoria's reign Sir Robert Giffen showed that the increase in money wages ranged for the most part between 50 and 100 per cent., and in some cases exceeded the latter figure. Real wages—wages as measured in purchasing power—had increased in even higher ratio. Statistics of consumption confirmed these conclusions : the consumption of sugar having in the same period increased from about 15 lb. to 70 lb. per head ;

[1] The invested savings of the working classes almost certainly exceed £3,500,000,000

of tea from 1¼ to 4¾ per head; of tobacco from 0·86 to 1·40 lb. per head, and so on. Nor was all the money earned in wages immediately spent. The number of depositors in Savings Banks increased from about 430,000 (1831) to 5,200,000 in 1887, and the deposits from £14,000,000 to over £90,000,000.[1]

Nor was the progress in the well-being of the working-classes checked during the last decades of the reign. On the contrary, Mr. A. L. Bowley proved that during the period 1882–1902 money wages increased by 30 per cent. and real wages by nearly 40 per cent.,[2] and his calculations are, in the main, confirmed by Mr. A. C. Pigou, who calculated that real wages in 1901 were as 165 as compared with 116 in 1881 and 100 in 1871.

If then the share of the wage-earner in the total product of industry was, as many contended, still inadequate in the Victorian era and still too precarious, there is no doubt that the tendency was in the right direction.

Yet the sky was not entirely free from cloud when in 1901 the old Queen was gathered to her fathers. The problem of Briton and Boer in South Africa was still unsolved, though the solution was not long deferred; there was trouble in the Far East and presage of much greater trouble; worst of all, dark clouds were gathering on the European horizon. At home neither Democracy nor Free Trade nor popular education had solved the social problem. On the contrary, the political enfranchisement of the wage-earners and improved facilities of education had, it seemed, served only to render more acute the consciousness of economic inequalities. But these problems had barely emerged when King Edward ascended the throne. The Victorian surface was smooth. Too smooth, say some. England, they aver, was too smug in its self-satisfaction. A ruddy complexion was not necessarily indicative of health. The seeds of disease lurked in the body-politic. Maybe. Those who look back to the Victorian era from the midst of present-day (1933) troubles and perplexities, are perhaps too prone to see only the brighter side of the picture, just as the home-coming traveller forgets the petty worries and inconveniences of foreign travel and recalls only the wonders and beauties he has beheld. Yet with all its admitted shortcomings and limita-

---

[1] Op. cit., II, 27–9.   [2] *Statistical Studies* (1904), p. 35.

tions the period which closed with the death of Queen Victoria will surely stand out as the greatest and the most progressive and most prosperous this country has ever known. Whether regard be paid to science, to literature, to political stability, to wealth-production and distribution, to industry, commerce and the general well-being of a rapidly increasing population, to the deepening sense of Imperial responsibility, and the awakening of the social conscience, the guerdon of pre-eminence cannot be withheld from the Victorian era.

BOOK II

CHAPTER X

KING EDWARD VII—A NEW ERA

L *A Reine est morte. Vive le roi.* Continuity is the charac- Accession
teristic note of the political and social history of England. of
There was no breach of continuity on the death of Queen Victoria. Edward
The old Queen died at Osborne at half-past six on January 22, 1901. VII
On the following morning the new King travelled up to London
and held the first Council of his reign at St. James's Palace.

The Duke of Devonshire, as Lord President of the Council,
formally announced the death of the Queen, and the Clerk read
the King's proclamation announcing his accession. The King
then entered the Council Chamber and took the customary oaths,
administered by the Archbishop of Canterbury, and addressed
the assembled Council. Rejecting the formal speech prepared for
him, the King, speaking without notes, and in a voice broken by
emotion, declared that it would be his constant endeavour always
to walk in the footsteps of his beloved mother. ' In undertaking ',
he proceeded, ' the heavy load which now devolves upon me I
am fully determined to be a Constitutional Sovereign in the
strictest sense of the word, and, as long as there is breath in my
body, to work for the good and amelioration of my people.' He
then announced that, desiring that the name of ' Albert the
Good ' ' should stand alone ' he had resolved to be known by the
name of Edward which had been borne by six of his predecessors.

Nothing could have been more tactful than the reference to
his ' great and wise father ', and nothing more popular than his
rejection of that father's name in favour of the good old English
name of Edward.

To the King's surprise and annoyance no reporter was present, but his words, no less than his demeanour, had so deeply impressed the Council, that no difficulty was experienced in preparing a precise report.   Lord Lincolnshire, however, who assisted in the redaction, declared that the report was ' nothing like so good as the speech which the King actually delivered ' in which ' the original words were full of dignity and pathos.' [1]

On the following day the Heralds, in their splendid uniforms, proclaimed the accession of King Edward VII from the balcony of the Palace overlooking Friary Court, and proceeded to repeat the Proclamation at Charing Cross, at Temple Bar and at the Royal Exchange.   The Proclamation was made in provincial cities by the Mayors.

Once more, then, England had a King.

Born on November 9, 1841, King Edward was in his sixtieth

His earlier years

year when he began to reign.   No English Sovereign ever came to the throne after so long a probation as Heir Apparent.   Nor had his apprentice-period been wholly satisfactory to his mother, to his future subjects, or to himself.   In regard to the education of their eldest son the Queen and the Prince Albert, greatly influenced by Baron Stockmar, were singularly unwise.   That his parents' sole desire was to fit the lad for the high vocation to which he was called, goes without saying.   But exemplary motives cannot condone mistaken policy.   Not until his marriage did the Prince escape from stern discipline and constant surveillance.   He resided for a time both at Oxford and Cambridge, but enjoyed no freedom and hardly any companionship save that of elderly dons.

He married in 1863 Princess Alexandra,[2] ' the Sea-King's daughter from over the sea ', and he and his beautiful Princess made Marlborough House, assigned to him as a residence in 1861, the centre of London society.   In 1862 Sandringham House in Norfolk had been purchased out of the savings accumulated during the Prince's minority, from the revenues of the Duchy of Cornwall, and there he lived the life of a country gentleman. King Edward had no literary tastes, the discipline to which in youth he was subjected had effectually crushed any disposition towards indulgence in that weakness ; but he learnt more from men than ever his accomplished father learnt from books.   He

---

[1] *Diary*, quoted, ap. Lee, *Edward VII*, II, 5.
[2] The eldest daughter of Christian IX, King of Denmark.

was punctual, methodical; spoke French and German perfectly and other languages passably; he had an amazing capacity for picking brains, and a most retentive memory. His intuitions were both rapid and sound; nor did he lack ambition. But his mother had thwarted every effort that he made to find serious employment. Ceremonial functions—the laying of foundation-stones, the opening of bridges, provincial town-halls and the like —such duties she willingly delegated to him, but when he expressed a wish for work which would serve as a real apprenticeship for his trade, the Queen, though strongly urged by her Ministers to meet the Prince's wishes, consistently refused. Not until 1895 did she consent to give him a key to the Cabinet ' boxes ' and thus allow him to see the Foreign dispatches. Whether her disinclination to share with him any of the burdens of the Crown was due to the jealousy with which a Sovereign proverbially regards an Heir Apparent, or to a genuine mistrust of his capacity and discretion, cannot be known.

The results were palpable. On the one hand, the Prince was driven to find an outlet for his exuberant vitality in a life of pleasure and sport; on the other, he acquired the habit of travel; he saw more of the Overseas Empire that was one day to pass under his sceptre than any of his predecessors; he made the personal acquaintance of nearly all the rulers and most of the statesmen of Europe and obtained a profound and first-hand knowledge of the main lines and even the by-paths of European diplomacy. Thus no English King had ever come to the throne with such a perfect Apprehensions mastery of Foreign Politics, or so intimate a knowledge of the allayed personal factors in international equations.

Nevertheless, it would be idle to deny that on his accession there were misgivings, both as to his character and his capacity. Wherever he had gone he had made himself popular, and his Princess was adored.[1] But he had made most of his intimate

---

[1] I cannot forbear in this connexion to quote the particularly graceful words of Sir Lionel Cust : ' Deeply attached as the nation was to the venerable almost sainted figure of Queen Victoria, the advent of Queen Alexandra to the full dignity of Queen-Consort was welcomed with genuine affection and intense interest by all classes, who had for so long had so many opportunities of enjoying her beautiful presence and participating in the largesse of affection which as Princess of Wales she had bestowed on her adopted country.' (*King Edward VII and His Court*, pp. 5–6.)

friends not among the old nobility but among the *nouveaux riches*. He was consistently friendly towards Mr. Gladstone, and was intimate with Sir Charles Dilke, but with other leading statesmen he had consorted little, save with men like the Duke of Devonshire and Lord Rosebery, who shared his sporting tastes. The middle classes looked askance at a man with whose name gossip had long been busy, and who had twice figured prominently in a society scandal, though from the ordeal of the Mordaunt divorce suit he emerged blameless, and was only indirectly concerned in the Tranby Croft case. But it was felt to be indecorous that the Heir Apparent should be even named in a divorce suit, or should have to appear, if only as a witness, in connexion with a 'Baccarat Scandal'. He could truthfully plead that he had never played cards for money, until invited to play whist by Bishop Wilberforce of Oxford. But though the Nonconformist conscience might condone episcopal whist, it could not swallow baccarat played with £10 counters at Tranby Croft.

Thus the public at large had heard too much of one aspect of the Prince's life, and knew little or nothing about the other. It was indeed known to a small circle that he was sedulous in performing his duties as a trustee of the British Museum, that he had encouraged the establishment of the Royal College of Music, and that he took a warm personal interest in the work of voluntary hospitals. Politicians of all parties were aware that he had worked hard as a member of the Royal Commission on the Housing of the Poor and had mingled freely with his colleagues, including two 'Labour' representatives, Joseph Arch and Henry Broadhurst ; and that he served with equal zeal on the Old Age Pensions Commission. But knowledge of these interests and activities was confined to the few : all the world knew that he was an enthusiastic patron of the drama ; that he liked good cheer, pretty women, and amusing company, and that from the great race meetings he was rarely absent.

Consequently there was widespread apprehension lest there should be, under the new régime, a sudden and serious lapse from the high standards maintained by Queen Victoria.

As regards the punctual, conscientious and able discharge of the political functions of the Crown, the apprehensions were soon dissipated. England has had few better kings than Edward VII.

Politically, he made good from the first; nor was there socially the lapse so widely feared. There was undoubtedly a reaction, but it was almost universally welcomed. The Court became once more the centre of society; gaiety replaced gloom; Buckingham Palace and Windsor Castle, where nothing had been changed since the death of the Prince Consort, were redecorated, refurnished, and brought up to modern standards, in lighting, sanitation and so forth. The King retained Sandringham (his real home) and Balmoral, for at both places he could enjoy the sport he loved; but he made over Osborne House to the nation. The private rooms were retained as a museum and personal memorial to Queen Victoria; the main portions of the mansion were devoted to a college for naval cadets, and a convalescent home for invalid officers. Thus a difficult problem was tactfully solved.

Windsor, and still more Buckingham Palace, soon began to wear a very different aspect. The latter was a ' sepulchre ' (the Prince's name for it) no longer. There was dispensed, throughout the London season, a gay, gracious and brilliant hospitality, and for a great part of the year it was at once the King's office and his home. The sombre afternoon Drawing-rooms were abandoned, and replaced by evening Courts, to which were added balls and dinner parties. All was on a generous, though not extravagant scale; for the King was shrewd in business matters and was shrewdly counselled. He owed no man a penny when he came to the throne and wisely resolved to live within his income as King.

To settle that income was one of the first duties awaiting Parliament. Both Houses met on January 25, but having voted addresses of condolence and congratulation to the King, immediately adjourned.

On February 14 Parliament met for the first session of the new reign. Despite his deep mourning the King opened it in person. Not since 1886 had Queen Victoria performed that ceremony, and only seven times in all during the last forty years of the reign. King Edward wisely determined not only to exhibit the Crown in all the splendour of ancient ceremonial, but to assert visibly his legal participation in the work of the Legislature.

Firm in adherence to tradition the King was as tenacious of the Royal Prerogative as difficult circumstances permitted. He

M.E.—7

repelled, for example, a suggestion from Mr. Balfour (who was shockingly casual in these matters) that, owing to the circumscribed space in the House of Lords, the King should open Parliament in Westminster Hall. He personally read the Speech from the Throne, but before doing so made the statutory Declaration as required by the Bill of Rights of 1689. That Declaration repudiated the doctrine of Transubstantiation and asserted that 'the invocation or adoration of the Virgin Mary or any other Saint and the sacrifice of the Mass as they are now used in the Church of Rome are superstitious and idolatrous'. These and other words the King regarded as gratuitously offensive to his Roman Catholic subjects ; he read them in an ostentatiously low voice and insisted that for the future the wording should be amended. But the Government handled the matter clumsily, and although King Edward expressed to Lord Salisbury a hope that neither he nor any of his successors might ever again ' have to make such a Declaration in such crude language ', there was so much delay and difficulty in deciding on an alternative that King George did, in fact, make the Declaration in the same terms as his father. In 1910, however, a Bill was passed substituting for the form of 1689 the following words : ' I do solemnly and sincerely in the presence of God profess, testify and declare that I am a faithful Protestant, and that I will according to the true intent of the enactments to secure the Protestant succession to the Throne of my Realm uphold and maintain such enactments to the best of my power.'

The Civil List   Then came the question of the Civil List. A select Committee was appointed to consider the provision that should be made for the maintenance of the King and the Royal family in the new reign, and on its report, unanimous save for the opposition of Labouchere, the new Civil List was based. The King, following recent precedents, relinquished on his accession the chief hereditary revenues of the Crown ; the Duchy of Cornwall, with revenues of £60,000 a year passed to his eldest son, he himself having succeeded to the Duchy of Lancaster, with revenues of a like amount. The sum voted to Queen Victoria, £385,000 a year, had proved, in the later years of the reign, quite inadequate, despite the economical administration of the Household, to the maintenance of the royal state. Wildly exaggerated statements were from time to time made about Queen Victoria's reputed savings. In 1889, in the debate on the grants for the children of the Prince of Wales, it was officially stated that her total savings, over a period of half a century, amounted to £824,025, and that she had latterly been compelled to draw on them for the entertainment of foreign visitors and like purposes. The new Civil List was accordingly fixed at £470,000 a year, or £85,000 in excess of that enjoyed by Queen Victoria. An annuity of £20,000 was at the same time voted to the Duke of Cornwall and York, £10,000 to the Duchess, and £18,000 for the joint lives of the King's three daughters. Pensions of £25,000 a year in all were given to the late Queen's servants, and it was provided that in the event of Queen Alexandra surviving the King she should receive £70,000 a year, and the Duchess of York £30,000 in a similar contingency. The total sum amounted, therefore, to £543,000 a year. During the reign of Queen Victoria the surrendered hereditary revenues had, however, increased in value from £245,000 to £452,000 a year, and since 1901 have further increased to £1,250,000. The nation, therefore, made an exceedingly good bargain with the Crown. On July 2, 1901, the Civil List Act became law.

A few weeks later the Royal Titles Act was also passed. **Royal Titles Act, 1901** In view of the rapid growth of the Empire in the nineteenth century, still more of the new status attained by the self-governing Dominions, and most of all of the profound change of sentiment, it was thought proper that the Dominions no less than India should have a legal place in the Title of the King. His Majesty was, therefore, empowered by statute (1 Edw. VII, c. 15), with a view to the recognition of the Colonial possessions, to make by proclamation such additions to the royal style and titles then appertaining to the Imperial Crown of the United Kingdom and its Dependencies as to His Majesty might seem fit. A proclamation was accordingly made on 4th November, 1901 (and published in the *London Gazette* of that date) that the style should henceforward be : ' Edward VII by the Grace of God of the United Kingdom of Great Britain and Ireland *and of the British Dominions beyond the Seas* King, Defender of the Faith, Emperor of India.' The italicized words were added with the general assent of all British parties, a unanimity in striking contrast to the bitter opposition offered to the addition, only twenty-five years before, of Empress of India to the style of Queen Victoria.[1] So fast had imperial sentiment deepened. Further recognition of the same fact was afforded by the assent given by the King to the arrangements already made for the visit of the Duke and Duchess of Cornwall and York to Australia and other Dominions.

The Heir Apparent in Australia   The primary purpose of the journey was to enable the Heir Apparent to open the first Parliament of the Commonwealth of Australia. The Duke and Duchess left England in the *Ophir* on March 17th, and amid scenes of great enthusiasm the Duke performed the opening ceremony on May 9th.[2] On the return journey the Duke and Duchess visited New Zealand, South Africa and Canada, and were welcomed back at Portsmouth by the King on November 1st. It was not, as the King wrote, ' without some natural anxiety and hesitation that I sanctioned the departure of the Heir Apparent to my throne on a voyage which involved many months of separation. But it was my earnest desire to give effect to the wishes of my late revered mother, and to the aspirations of my loyal subjects in the Colonies of whose devotion and patriotism I had received such signal proof in the splendid service they had rendered to the Empire in South Africa, and I am fully repaid by the complete success which has attended the visit.' The King also announced his intention to create the Duke Prince of Wales and Earl of Chester ' in consequence of the admirable manner in which my son has carried out the arduous duties which I confided to him '.

The Coronation   The Coronation was appointed for 26th June, 1902 : and by the King's express wish the ceremony was to be on a scale of exceptional splendour and the congregation was to be representative of the whole Empire and of every race and interest within it. The Court mourning for the late Queen having ended, the first levée of the new reign was held at St. James's Palace on 11th February, 1902, the first Court at Buckingham Palace on 14th March, and on 8th June the King and Queen attended at

---

[1] The style and title was again altered in 1927, the words ' of the United Kingdom . . . and ' being omitted.

[2] Cf. D. M. Wallace, *The Web of Empire* (1902) (an official account of the Tour).

St. Paul's a Thanksgiving Service for the restoration of Peace
in South Africa.

Everything was in train for the great event; the representatives, civil and military, of the Dominions, Colonies and Dependencies, and of foreign Thrones and Courts were all assembled;
the streets were ablaze with decorations when on June 24 the
nation, nay the world, was stunned by the news that the King
was seriously ill and that the ceremony must be postponed. With
characteristic courage the King had refused, in face of oncoming
illness, to cancel his arrangements until within forty-eight hours
of the appointed day. On June 24, however, he was operated
on for perityphitis. Surgical skill combined with the King's
courageous temperament to make recovery rapid and on August 9
the postponed ceremony took place with added emotion and
hardly diminished magnificence. 'The usage by an ardent yet
practical people of an archaic rite to signalize the modern splendour of their Empire, the recognition, by a free democracy, of
an hereditary Crown, as a symbol of the world-wide domination
of their race, constitute,' as the official chronicler of the
Coronation truly said, ' no mere pageant but an event of the
highest historical interest '.[1]

The Coronation was followed by a series of functions which
emphasized its historic significance; a review of Colonial troops
on 12th August, of Indian troops on the 13th, and a Naval Review
on the 16th. Among the spectators of the latter review at Spithead were three Boer Generals, Louis Botha, De Wet and Delarey,
to whom the King gave audience on 17th August.

Amid the celebrations the poor were not forgotten; the King
gave a dinner to 500,000 of the poor of London, and the Queen
entertained the general servants—an act of thoughtful consideration for a little-regarded class. The institution of an Order of
Merit for men highly distinguished in the Army, the Navy, Literature, Science and Art further commemorated a unique occasion.

On their return from a short holiday in the autumn the King
and Queen made a royal progress through the streets of South
London, lunched with the Lord Mayor at the Guildhall and

---

[1] J. E. C. Bodley, *The Coronation of Edward the Seventh* (1903), p. 201.
This work, published by Royal Command, contains a detailed description of
the ceremony.

attended a Service of Thanksgiving for the King's restoration to health at St. Paul's.

In the following month the German Emperor paid a visit to Sandringham when the King (in his own words) did his ' best to make his stay as pleasant as possible and show him some sport both with partridges and pheasants '. At Sandringham he met, among others, Mr. Balfour, Lord Lansdowne and Mr. Chamberlain, but with the last he confessed to finding it difficult, with all his efforts, to ' get on '.

Resignation and death of Lord Salisbury Lord Salisbury was not among the guests. Despite failing health he had resolved to retain office until peace was restored in South Africa. That he did; but was constrained to resign (July 11th) before the postponed Coronation. Little more than a year later (August 22nd) he died at Hatfield, and was by his own wish buried there by the side of his devoted wife.

That Lord Salisbury was a great Foreign Minister has been demonstrated in a previous chapter. It cannot be maintained that he was a great Prime Minister. The work of the Foreign Office was entirely congenial to him, that of the Premiership was not. ' He hates his office,' wrote one of his sons in August 1886, and he himself was wont to declare that it was an office ' of infinite worry but very little power '. Power depended on the occupant. Lord Rosebery exercised very little : but Gladstone, Disraeli and Sir Robert Peel exercised a great deal. Lord Salisbury was apt, in matters that did not immediately concern his own Department, to defer too readily to the opinions of others. ' You must forgive me for saying that you have too much renunciation for a Prime Minister. . . . The position requires your distinct *lead* and your just self-assertion.' So one of his ablest colleagues, Lord Cranbrook, wrote to him in friendly remonstrance in November 1886. Sir Michael Hicks Beach has left on record a similar opinion : ' As Prime Minister he did not exercise the same control over his colleagues that Lord Beaconsfield did.' It is fair to add that of his own volition he would not have become, certainly would not have remained, Prime Minister. Thrice he offered to surrender the office, once to Lord Iddesleigh and twice to Lord Hartington. Lord Rosebery described him with characteristic felicity as ' a public servant of the Elizabethan type ; a fit representative of his great Elizabethan ancestor '. He served

his Queen and his country from a sheer sense of duty. He sought
no rewards for himself, and would accept none. He loathed self-
advertisement, and shrank from publicity. He was happiest in
the seclusion of his library or his laboratory. Even the work
of the Foreign Office he did mainly at home, corresponding with
ambassadors largely in private letters written with his own hand.

In a sense fuller than mere chronology suggests, he was the
last of the great Victorian Ministers ; he walked in the ancient
paths ; it was fitting that the close of his own service should have
coincided so nearly with the death of the Queen. The conditions
of world-politics changed rapidly with the opening of the new
century : they called for a radical change alike in the methods
and in the direction of Foreign Policy. England could no longer
afford the luxury of isolation : but if she was to emerge from
isolation it must be not as an insular State but as a World-Empire.

CHAPTER XI

THE DECLINE AND FALL OF THE UNIONIST GOVERNMENT —THE BALFOUR MINISTRY

Mr.
Balfour

ON the resignation of Lord Salisbury, the King, still on a sickbed, appointed Mr. Balfour as Prime Minister.

Balfour had made a great reputation as Chief Secretary for Ireland (1887–91); he was popular with the Party and was recognized as a parliamentary debater of the first rank—adroit, self-possessed and fearless.   But as leader of the House of Commons he had obvious shortcomings, manifested still more clearly in his tenure of the Premiership.   Nevertheless in 1902 he was the inevitable successor to his uncle.   With the exception of Sir Michael Hicks Beach, the strongest men in Lord Salisbury's Cabinet belonged to the Liberal Unionist wing of the Coalition. Whether the Conservative Party would in 1902 have accepted a Liberal Unionist Premier is doubtful.   Even in 1911 they would not have Mr. Chamberlain's son as leader.   Lord Salisbury's Cabinet continued unchanged under Mr. Balfour, with one important exception.   Sir Michael Hicks Beach insisted on retiring with a chief whom (in his daughter's words) ' he had loved and trusted only second to Disraeli '.[1]   He was succeeded as Chancellor of the Exchequer by Mr. (afterwards Lord) Ritchie, a capable administrator but not a statesman of the same calibre as his predecessor.

Sir M.
Hicks
Beach

Sir Michael was the last of the Victorian economists and his resignation was due to a growing conviction that the ideals which he had inherited from Gladstone and Peel were no longer to inspire financial policy.   His anxiety was clearly expressed in an elaborate memorandum on the position of national finance which in September 1901 he submitted to Lord Salisbury.   The Prime

[1] *Life*, II. 174.

Minister shared his apprehensions, but feared that any attempt
to stem the tide of extravagance would break up a Ministry which
was no longer homogeneous. 'When I saw', he wrote, 'how
blindly the heads of our defensive departments surrendered themselves to the fatal guidance of their professional advisers, I realized
that we were in face of a Jingo hurricane, and were driving before
it under bare poles.' Sir Michael also sent his memorandum
to Mr. Chamberlain and Mr. Balfour and it was subsequently
circulated to the Cabinet where it was received with 'insouciance'.
Mr. Chamberlain admitted that Beach had been severely tried
by Cabinet colleagues and had 'met unexampled demands in a
generous and self-sacrificing spirit', but it was evident that the
rift between the two statesmen was widening, and ultimately
Beach found himself alone with Salisbury 'in defence of the old
sound standards of national economy and of freedom for individual effort and economic growth unshackled by State interference'. Nevertheless in his seventh and last Budget (1902) he
had gone so far towards a fiscal change as to revive the old registration duty of 3d. per cwt. on corn and 5d. per cwt. on flour, a
duty which had survived many of Mr. Gladstone's Budgets and
was only abolished in 1869 by the least successful Finance Minister
of the century, Robert Lowe. Even this small measure was
resisted by the Opposition, though both Sir William Harcourt
and Mr. John Morley deplored Beach's resignation as 'a real
misfortune that will not easily be mended'. Had Beach possessed
Balfour's equability of temper or the geniality which he could
so easily assume, had he been endowed with a tithe of the flexi-
bility of Disraeli he might have found a place in the select 'first
class' of Victorian statesmen. But his gifts were not those of
a party-leader in a democratic age. Shy, reserved and inacces-
sible he was most highly appreciated by those who worked with
him most closely—not least by the miners, who recognized how
evenly he had held the scales of justice as arbitrator of the South
Wales coal-field. Of such men no Democracy can have too many ;
it frequently fails as a form of government because it has too
few.[1]

---

[1] A fine appreciation by Sir Laurence Guillemard who served for seven
years as Sir Michael's Private Secretary is printed as an Appendix to vol.
II of the *Life*.

The Coronation of King Edward was attended, as already noted, by representatives of the Colonies. But their visit to England in 1902 was not exclusively ceremonial ; advantage was taken of it to hold another Colonial Conference, the fourth of a lengthening series. Since the last Conference had met in 1897 much had happened. A great crisis in the history of the Empire had matured and been successfully surmounted. That crisis, as Mr. Chamberlain truly said, had evoked ' among the greater nations of the world . . . a passionate outburst which found expression in rejoicings at our reverses, in predictions about ultimate defeat, and in the grossest calumnies on the honour of our statesmen and the gallantry and humanity of our army '.[1] How strongly contrasted with these sentiments were those manifested by the Colonies ! ' During the whole of this time we have been supported and strengthened and encouraged and assisted by the men of our own blood and race. From the first day that the struggle began, down to the other day when the terms of surrender were signed, we have had the affectionate regard and approval, we have had the active assistance, we have had the moral support of our fellow-subjects in all the possessions and dependencies of the British Crown.' [1] Then there was the deep chord of sympathy and solidarity touched simultaneously throughout the Empire by the death of Queen Victoria, by the illness and coronation of her son. These things might well have inspired a man of narrower vision and less imagination than Joseph Chamberlain. They evidently led him to hope much from his negotiations with the other statesmen of the Empire.

Nor did the Conference of 1902 disappoint his hopes. In order to give the Conference the position of a recognized Imperial institution, it was resolved that henceforth its meeting should be triennial. On the constitutional issue the discussions were commendably frank. ' If you want our aid ', said Sir Wilfrid Laurier, Prime Minister of Canada, ' call us to your Councils.' ' We do want your assistance ', said Mr. Chamberlain, ' in the administration of the vast Empire which is yours. The weary Titan struggles under the too vast orb of its fate. We have borne the burden for many years. We think it is time that our children should assist us to support it, and whenever you make the request to us be

[1] At the Grocers' Hall August 1, 1902, *Speeches* (ed. Boyd), II. 71.

very sure that we shall hasten gladly to call you to our Councils. If you are prepared at any time to take any share, any proportionate share in the burdens of the Empire we are prepared to meet you with any proposal for giving to you a corresponding voice in the policy of the Empire.' Dealing with specific schemes he ruled none out, but avowed his own preference—as a first step —for ' the creation of a real Council of the Empire to which all questions of Imperial interest might be referred '.

On the problem of Imperial Defence he showed that Naval and Military expenditure worked out in the United Kingdom at £1 9s. 3d. per head per annum; in New South Wales at 3s. 5d.; in Victoria 3s. 3d.; in New Zealand 3s. 4d.; in the Cape and Natal between 2s. and 3s.; in Canada 2s. On this point the Colonial response was prompt. The Australasian Colonies agreed to raise their contribution for an improved Australasian squadron and the establishment of a branch of the Royal Naval Reserve from £126,000 to £200,000 a year; Cape Colony and Natal offered £50,000 and £35,000 a year respectively as an unconditional contribution towards the maintenance of the Navy; and Newfoundland undertook to provide £3,000 a year towards the branch of the Royal Naval Reserve hitherto maintained there by the mother-country. Canada refused to participate on the ground that it would be ' an important departure from the principle of Colonial Self-government ', but justly claimed that the value to the Empire of the Militia, entirely maintained at their own expense, had been demonstrated in South Africa, and promised to consider naval defence as well.

An important point was raised by another resolution which ran as follows : ' That so far as may be consistent with the confidential negotiation of Treaties with Foreign Powers, the views of the Colonies affected should be obtained in order that they may be in a better position to give adhesion to such Treaties.'

The principle was cautiously affirmed, but its significance was enhanced rather than diminished by the evident consideration for the susceptibilities of the Foreign Office and the difficulties which surround the whole problem of Empire participation in Foreign Policy.

There remained, apart from such relatively minor matters as

Mail Services and Shipping Subsidies, the all-important question of commercial relations within the Empire.

Mr. Chamberlain, emphasizing the unsatisfactory state of things then existing, expressed himself in favour of Free Trade within the Empire. But he was careful to add that he did not mean ' the total abolition of custom duties within the Empire,' which he recognized as impossible for countries which had to rely mainly on indirect taxation. Canada had in 1900 increased the preference of 25 per cent. granted to British goods in 1898 to 33⅓ per cent. But the effect of it was disappointing. Despite the fact that the United Kingdom took 85 per cent. of Canadian exports, the Canadian tariff still pressed with the greatest severity upon their best customer. Canada, on her part, demanded the exemption of her wheat and flour from the registration duty recently imposed by Parliament—a demand which in view of the differences in the Cabinet Chamberlain was unable to concede. Eventually, after long discussion, it was resolved that while Free Trade within the Empire was not at present practicable, it was desirable that the Colonies should give a preference, ' as far as their circumstances permit ', to the products of the United Kingdom, and the Imperial Government should be invited to consider reciprocal treatment for the Colonies.

Thus was a challenge definitely thrown down to the principle which for sixty years had dominated the fiscal policy of the mother-country. That challenge was destined before long[1] to arouse bitter controversy in domestic politics ; but for the moment controversy, not less bitter, raged round the thorny problem of national education.

The Education Act, 1902

' May we live to see the coming of a state of things more promising ! Throughout the country, good elementary schools, taking the child to the age of thirteen ; then good secondary schools taking him to sixteen, with good classical high schools and commercial high schools taking him on further to eighteen or nineteen ; with good technical and special schools for those who require them parallel with the secondary and high schools —this is what is to be aimed at.'

Thus had Matthew Arnold written in a survey of the educational position in 1887.[1] As regards public elementary education

---

[1] *The Reign of Queen Victoria*, p. 279.

the Victorian era had witnessed nothing less than a revolution. Before the close of the century every child in the country was compelled, up to the age of twelve, to attend school, where he might receive gratuitous instruction. Yet there remained one great difficulty unsolved. Down to the year 1870 elementary education had been exclusively the care of the Churches, established or non-established. Nor can the debt of the community, in this matter, to the Churches be overestimated. In their schools religious instruction had naturally formed an essential part of the curriculum. That this accorded with the wishes of the great mass of parents is indubitable.

After the passing of the Act of 1870 there emerged the ' religious difficulty '. It was raised, as Bishop Fraser of Manchester truly remarked, not ' by the parents, but for them '. But raised it was and the dilemma was not wholly imaginary. The Roman Catholics have never allowed their children to attend a school where religious teaching was not given according to the tenets of their own creed ; nor indeed where the ' atmosphere ' was not Catholic. To maintain this principle they have made great sacrifices. So have the Anglicans. Rather than allow their children to attend schools where Anglican doctrine was not taught by Anglican teachers they have maintained their own ' Church ' schools at their own expense. As to the value of ' denominational ' schools Matthew Arnold, not himself a denominationalist, bore striking testimony. ' I prefer ', he wrote, ' the management and personal influence of a good Church School to those of a good Board School. In secular instruction I think the two kinds of school are about equal ; but I have always thought that the Biblical instruction which the School Boards have adopted, with some improvement from the old British Schools, was the religious instruction fittest on the whole to meet the desires of the population of this country and to do them good.'

With the latter part of that judgement all Catholics and many Anglicans disagreed. Protestant Dissenters, no less than Romans and Anglicans, desired for their children religious instruction, but were satisfied with that given in the Board Schools. Save in certain single-school areas they had no grievance. Nor had the secularists. They were entitled to withdraw their children from religious instruction in the Board Schools, where they received their instruction gratuitously. Yet they advanced the purely academic objection that to other people's children some religious instruction was given at public expense.

Denominationalists, on the other hand, had a substantial grievance, increasingly heavy as the cost of elementary education mounted higher and higher. Not only were they compelled, if true to their principles, to maintain their own schools, but, as taxpayers and ratepayers, to contribute an equal proportion to maintaining the schools of which their consciences disapproved.

To meet this difficulty, and if haply to solve it, was the primary purpose of the Education Act of 1902.

There were others. For many years past the ancient Universities had been increasingly alive to new conditions, social and political, and had in a variety of ways kept abreast of them. By them, and by the new Universities which were rapidly multiplying, not only were the needs of higher education adequately supplied, but by means of local lectures, and local and other school examinations, important contributions were made by Universities to the improvement of secondary and popular adult education.

Technical and secondary education

Yet secondary and technical education remained in a chaotic condition. It was evident that in this matter England was falling lamentably behind other progressive nations, noticeably behind Germany. The pre-eminence of England in commerce and industry had been so long unchallenged that English people were startled, as the century drew to a close, to discover what rapid headway certain foreign countries were making in competition with their own. German chemists and German clerks were being imported in considerable numbers, because the home-supply was unequal to the demands of English manufacturers and merchants. Nor was there only a deficiency in quantity : the quality of the home product was inferior, and the price of it was higher.

In regard to technical and secondary education public opinion was running rapidly ahead of legislation—a rare phenomenon in educational matters. Various attempts had been made, in patchwork and haphazard fashion, to remedy palpable deficiencies. The important legislation of 1889 and the lucky windfall of the ' whisky money ' have been already noticed. In 1893 a special code for Evening Continuation Schools was published on the instructions of Mr. Arthur Acland, who was the first Education

Minister to be admitted to a Liberal Cabinet.[1] The objects of these schools were (1) to continue the general education of the pupils and supply the deficiencies of elementary education, (2) to prepare pupils for examinations under the Science and Art Department, (3) to assist lectures provided by the Universities under their ' Extension ' Schemes, and by County Councils, and (4) to help schemes for providing, in other ways, secondary or higher education. This was a move in the right direction ; the number of registered scholars rose from 115,582 attending 1,977 schools in 1893 to 358,268 attending 4,226 schools in 1897. But good as the scheme was, so far as it went, it was no more than a make-shift : and in 1894 a strong Royal Commission was appointed to consider the best methods of establishing a well-organized system of secondary education in England, taking into account existing deficiencies, and having regard to such local sources of revenue from endowment or otherwise as were available or might be made available for this purpose. Mr. James (afterwards Viscount) Bryce was chairman, and of the seventeen members three were ladies—the first of their sex ever to serve on a Royal Commission.

The Commission presented their Report in five volumes in August 1895. They recommended the creation of a separate Education Department under a Minister of Education, and the absorption into the new Department of the existing Committee of the Privy Council, the Charity Commission (so far as educational endowments were concerned), and the Science and Art Department. In every County and County Borough there was to be a local education authority, appointed as to a majority by the Councils. These authorities were to supervise all local Secondary Schools, and themselves to make good any deficiency there might be. In addition to the grants to local Councils under the Customs and Excise Act, 1890 (the ' whisky money ') the new authorities were to have the Departmental Grants for secondary education, and to be empowered to levy a rate not exceeding 2d. in the £.

A Board of Education was set up, under a responsible Minister in 1899, and between 1895 and the close of the century legislation

The Board of Education

---

[1] His formal status was still that of Vice-President of the Council. In a similar capacity Lord Sandon had been admitted to Disraeli's Cabinet (1874).

was proposed to carry out other recommendations of the Bryce Commission, but it was left to the Balfour Government to grasp firmly the nettles, of which there was an abundant crop in the educational field.   The Government was, indeed, compelled to action by the action of various School Boards and other Education Authorities in extending their activities beyond the limits prescribed by law.   The matter was brought to a head in 1900 when Mr. Cockerton, an auditor of the Local Government Board, disallowed the payment of certain sums out of the rates for science and art teaching in elementary schools, and surcharged the London School Board.   The School Board appealed to the Court of Queen's Bench which substantially sustained Mr. Cockerton's decision.   It was even more completely confirmed by the Court of Appeal.

The intrusion of the School Board into the domain of secondary education had for some time been resented by private secondary schools, which felt rate-aided competition to be essentially unfair, as well as by many ratepayers, and by a certain section of Conservatives, who disliked the 'Socialistic' activities of the London School Board.

The 'Cockerton Judgment' still further confounded the confusion in which technical and secondary education was involved, and, unless the ground gained was to be abandoned and the advance of public secondary education to be arrested, the Government was bound to ask Parliament to make a serious effort to solve a difficult problem.

The Act of 1902 was by far the most important legislative achievement of the Balfour Government, and the credit was primarily due to the parliamentary adroitness and the persistence of Mr. Balfour himself.

Education Act, 1902

The cardinal feature of the Act was the setting up in every locality of an authority charged with the supervision of elementary, technical and secondary education.   The authority was to be a Committee of the Council of the County, County Borough or Urban District (with more than 20,000 inhabitants), afforced by co-opted members.

The specially elected *ad hoc* School Boards were abolished, and their place taken by the new authorities, in whom was vested the control of all secular education, both in the State (' provided ')

and in the voluntary (' non-provided ') schools. All schools were
to have ' managers '. In the provided schools all the managers
were to be appointed by the authority : in the voluntary schools,
a minority were to be appointed by the authority, which in all
schools was to be responsible for secular instruction, and the
majority were to represent the Denomination concerned. In
voluntary schools the managers were to provide the school-houses
and maintain them to the satisfaction of the Board of Education
—an obligation which, with the rising standard of requirements,
proved to be exceedingly onerous. The appointment, dismissal,
and qualification of teachers in all schools were to be subject to
the approval of the authority. Under an amendment known by
the name of its author—Colonel Kenyon-Slaney—religious instruction in voluntary schools was to be ' in accordance with the tenor
of the Trust-Deed ' of the school, and ' under the control of the
managers, subject to reference to the Bishop or Denominational
Authority '. Parliament was to make grants to supplement the
produce of the rates.

' Higher ' (i.e. Technical or Secondary) Education was to be
provided or supplemented by the Local Authority, whose duty
was to co-ordinate all forms of education. Finance was to be
provided by the ' whisky money ' supplemented, when necessary,
from the rates.

The Act of 1902 did not apply to London, where the conditions were unique, but in 1903 a measure on similar lines was
passed for London. The County Council, acting through a Committee, became supremely responsible for education throughout
the metropolis : but the Borough Councils were to have a majority,
in each case, of the school managers.

The two measures represented a courageous attempt to deal
fairly and comprehensively with a thorny problem, and, in particular, to reconcile the divergent views of denominationalists
and dissenters. The attempt was, however, bitterly resented by
the latter, who organized widespread resistance against the payment of rates the proceeds of which were to be applied to teaching tenets of which they disapproved. To the divided and distracted Liberal Party, both in Parliament and in the country,
Balfour's Bill was nothing less than a god-send. It provided
them not only with a rallying cry, but with a body of martyrs

prepared to suffer the distraint of their goods, and even the loss of personal liberty, rather than submit to ' tyranny in Church and State '. The agitation, though somewhat artificial in its inception, served its purpose in the General Election of 1906, when the ' passive resisters ' contributed not a little to the defeat of a Government which had outstayed its welcome. In the course of time, however, the furious agitation died down. The Act of 1902 constituted, in fact, a conspicuous landmark in the history not merely of education but also of Local Government in England. It laid, well and truly, the foundations of a national system, and upon them a stately edifice has since been erected.

Mr.
Chamber-
lain in
South
Africa

While Mr. Balfour was battling with passive-resistance at home, his principal colleague created a Ministerial precedent by an official visit to South Africa. He broke his journey by a few days' visit to Lord Cromer in Cairo, and having landed at Mombasa, where he took a trip on the Uganda Railway, and having attended a banquet given by British residents in Zanzibar, reached Durban on December 26th, 1902.

In each of the four Colonies he made a careful survey of the situation, and at Durban, at Maritzburg, at Pretoria, Johannesburg and Cape Town he delivered speeches which were among the greatest of his career. His first public words (at Durban) indicated the spirit in which he had come. ' The issue has been decided. The British flag is, and will be, and must be, paramount throughout South Africa. . . . Reconciliation should be easy. We hold out our hand and we ask the Dutch to take it frankly, and in the spirit in which it is tendered.' The Boer leaders, the magnates of the Rand, and all parties in Cape Colony he treated with cordiality, but with exemplary frankness. The settlement embodied in the Peace of Vereeniging would be respected in the spirit and in the letter by us : the Boers must do the same. ' Henceforth we are one nation under one flag. We have left the past behind.' That was at Pretoria. At Johannesburg he was mainly concerned to get a contribution from the mine-owners towards the expenses of the war. They promised £30,000,000, but bad times came, and it was never raised. On the constitutional issue he pointed to federation as the ultimate solution, but it was not to be prematurely adopted.

Mr. Chamberlain returned to London in March 1903, was immediately received by the King, and was entertained at the Guildhall. But a bitter disappointment awaited him. During his absence his colleagues had decided to repeal the registration duty on imported wheat. The duty had produced a revenue of £2,000,000 without affecting the price of bread; but the strict Free Traders were alarmed lest even so minute a duty should open the door to a revival of Protection. Undoubtedly, the advocates of an Inter-Imperial Trade Policy, both at home and in the Colonies, did regard the 1s. duty with the gratitude that hopes for more. *Obsta principiis* was the retort of the Free Traders.

Nor was Mr. Chamberlain slow to take up the challenge. In a speech in Birmingham (May 15) he boldly declared himself in favour of a complete reversal of recent fiscal policy; of preference for Colonial products, and of the imposition of retaliatory duties against foreign countries which had erected tariff barriers against British goods. *Colonial preference*

Thus was the issue joined and the Tariff Reform campaign inaugurated. The Birmingham speech caused much perturbation in Parliament, in the Unionist Party, and most of all in the Cabinet, which was hopelessly divided on the subject. Mr. Balfour, to allay apprehensions, was constrained to announce that the fiscal question would not be dealt with in the existing Parliament; but strive as he might he could not avert a break up of the Cabinet.

Mr. Chamberlain, though realizing that under existing circumstances the policy of Imperial Preference could not be pressed with any hope of success, felt that as Colonial Secretary, and after his frank disclosure of his opinions to the Colonial Premiers, he could not, even temporarily, accept the exclusion of that item from the programme of the Party to which he adhered. Accordingly, he wrote to the Prime Minister on September 9th, 1903, suggesting that the latter should 'limit the present policy of the Government to the assertion of our freedom in the case of all commercial relations with foreign countries', and should at the same time accept the resignation of the Colonial Secretary, who would then be free to devote himself 'to the work of explaining and popularizing those principles of Imperial union' which in his view were essential to the future welfare and prosperity of the country.

To that letter Balfour did not reply until September 16. In the meantime much had happened. The Cabinet reassembled on September 14. Nothing was said about Chamberlain's proffered resignation but Mr. Ritchie and Lord Balfour of Burleigh were dismissed by the Prime Minister. ' I never ', wrote the Duke of Devonshire, ' heard anything more summary and decisive than the dismissal of the two Ministers.' On the following day, September 15, Lord George Hamilton and the Duke of Devonshire also resigned. On the 16th the Duke was informed by the Prime Minister that Chamberlain had resigned, and thereupon acceded to his Chief's urgent request to withdraw his resignation.[1]

Minis-
terial
resigna-
tions

On September 18 the newspapers announced simultaneously the resignation of Mr. Chamberlain and the three Free Trade Ministers. The latter complained that they had resigned ' in ignorance of Mr. Chamberlain's resignation, and the consequent elimination of all that related to preferential tariffs from the Government programme '. The protest was justified and produced a painful impression. If they had not been formally dismissed they had undoubtedly been ' jockeyed ' into resignation.

The public were befogged. What exactly did these resignations portend ? Had the Premier surrendered to the Tariff Reformers or to the Free Traders ? The personnel of the reconstructed Cabinet afforded no decisive clue ; Mr. Austen Chamberlain succeeded Mr. Ritchie as Chancellor of the Exchequer, Mr. Victor Cavendish, heir to the Dukedom of Devonshire, became Financial Secretary to the Treasury, while Mr. Alfred Lyttelton, on Lord Milner's refusal to accept the office, became Colonial Secretary.

How deeply Chamberlain felt the behaviour of his late colleagues may be judged from the letter which on September 21st he addressed to the Duke of Devonshire : ' For my part I care only for the great question of imperial unity. But for this I would not have taken off my coat. . . . While I was slaving my life out, you threw [my policy] over as of no importance, and it is to this indifference to a great policy which you had yourselves accepted that you owe the present situation.'

The Duke returned a soft answer and friendly relations were

---

[1] It is a satisfaction to me to note that my account of this complicated episode is almost precisely confirmed in Mr. Winston Churchill's *Great Contemporaries*, pp. 244 f.

partially restored. Nothing however could restore the Duke's
peace of mind, and after Balfour's speech at Sheffield (October 2),
the Duke finally resigned, only to be assailed with equal bitterness
by the Prime Minister. ' I have made a mess of this business.'
So the Duke wrote (October 6) to his old friend, Lord James of
Hereford. He had. ' I have ', he added, ' come out of it with
severe damage.' His conduct was indeed unintelligible, most of all
to himself ; but nothing could shake the confidence reposed by his
countrymen in his sterling patriotism and transparent honesty.

No sooner was the Duke's resignation announced than Cham- *The
berlain flung himself with the energy and ardour of a young man Fiscal Battle*
into a battle which—for him—ended when he was suddenly
stricken (July 1906) with illness, which compelled his withdrawal
from all public work. He was then only seventy, but it may be
that he had foreknowledge that his time was short and that he
pressed on the work with a feverish haste fatal to himself and not
conducive to the success of his cause. For the conversion of the
electorate was bound to be slow.

Fabian strategy did not suit Chamberlain's temper or methods. *The
He was convinced that the hour of decision had struck ; that Tariff Reform
unless Great Britain grasped at once the hand held out by the League*
Colonies, it might for ever be withdrawn. Accordingly, he
founded a Tariff Reform League, on the lines of the Anti-Corn
Law League, and employed statisticians and experts to investigate the position of various British industries and provide him
with the data necessary to establish his case for reform. Of this
unofficial Tariff Reform Commission Mr. W. A. S. Hewins, well
known as an Oxford University Extension Lecturer and Director
of the London School of Economics, was secretary, and under his
superintendence a series of exhaustive Reports was published.[1]

Upon the data thus obtained Chamberlain based the case
which he expounded with amazing energy and eloquence at a
series of meetings during the years 1903-6. Confronted with the
exceedingly cogent speeches, in which twenty years earlier he had
confounded the arguments of the ' Fair Traders ', Mr. Chamberlain
frankly confessed himself a convert. But he insisted that since
the earlier 'eighties the whole situation had profoundly altered.

---

[1] Vol. i dealt with the Iron and Steel Trades ; vol. ii with the Textile
Trades and so on. Cf. with these Reports *British and Foreign Trade and
Industry Memoranda, &c.*, published by the Board of Trade in 1903 and 1904.

Down to that time English industry had enjoyed an unchallenged pre-eminence, while her agriculture had continued to flourish without the protection of the Corn laws. Since then British manufactures had experienced severe competition from an industrialized Germany, while the improvement in means of communication and refrigerating machinery was bringing the wheat of North America and the meat of South America at cheap prices into the English market. Moreover, our commercial rivals, while competing with us in neutral markets, and flooding the English market, were closing their own markets against us by high tariffs. In 1846 Cobden made his famous prediction : ' There will not be a tariff in Europe that will not be changed in less than five years' time to follow your example.' Down to the 'seventies there seemed a chance that his prediction might, though tardily, be fulfilled. Since the 'seventies the teaching of Frederick List had superseded that of Adam Smith : the spirit of Economic nationalism had rapidly developed.

There was another phenomenon still more disquieting to Free Traders. High tariffs had not proved inimical to the development of external trade. On the contrary the exports of the Protective countries were increasing at a ratio far greater than our own. Free Traders retorted that our rivals had started from zero, while we had reached the meridian of industrial prosperity. The retort was pertinent, but it ignored the significance of a ' law ' which Economists were only beginning to formulate. If agriculture was subject, as Ricardo and his disciples had taught, to the ' law of diminishing returns ', manufacturing, under modern conditions, was obedient to the ' law of increasing returns '. The more you made, the cheaper you could make it. The development of Trusts and Cartels—new phenomena in industry—accentuated this tendency. Protected in their home markets by high tariffs, the steel and other Trusts of Germany and the United States could sell their surplus products at prices actually below the cost of production. This was the scientific explanation of ' dumping '. Once more Free Traders retorted that if some trades in England suffered from dumping, other productive industries— notably shipbuilding—reaped proportionate advantages.

The argument was nicely balanced ; but it could hardly be denied that if, as seemed likely, the world was about to plunge into an Economic war, England, so long as she rigidly adhered to Cobdenite doctrine, was peculiarly vulnerable. We had nothing wherewith to bargain. Worse than that. Our Colonial friends were actually penalized for their loyalty. Germany's retort to the preferences given by Canada to Great Britain was to retaliate by a differentiating tariff against Canada. And what could we do, unless armed with retaliatory weapons, to help our friends ? Or to reciprocate their friendship ? Could Canada, for example, be reasonably expected to reject reciprocal offers from the United States, if we refused a preference to her products in the English market ?

That was the real crux of the problem. That was the cardinal issue raised by Mr. Chamberlain. His argument was not exclusively, or even primarily, economic. It was his honourable ambition to go down to posterity as the architect of a great Imperial edifice, the creator of an Empire, united in bonds of interest not less than of affection. ' You cannot ', he argued, ' weld the Empire together except by some form of commercial union.' His goal was political unity : an Imperial Council, to begin with, perhaps leading to a complete and coherent Federal Constitution in the future. But the experience gained from two Colonial Conferences, combined with the recent impression of his South African tour, had convinced him that, as in Imperial Germany, commercial union must precede and prepare the way for political union.

There was a lion in his path. He had to convince the ' predominant partner '. Imperial sentiment had, as we have seen, gained ground rapidly in England in the two preceding decades. But had it so far permeated the mass of the British electorate as to countervail their appreciation of cheap food ? ' Your food will cost you more ' was the most effective weapon in the armoury of Chamberlain's opponents. He was compelled, therefore, to attempt the difficult feat of riding two horses simultaneously. And the Liberal circus-masters incited the horses to gallop in opposite directions.

If Mr. Balfour, by his Education Act, had presented a divided Liberal Party with a great opportunity for reunion, Mr. Chamberlain, by his Tariff Reform proposals, did more. He cemented Liberal reunion and, at the same time, split the Unionist Party.

Chamberlain's Campaign

Mr. Asquith seized both opportunities, with a skill which ensured to him the ultimate leadership of his party.   The Education Bill aroused all the traditional prejudices of the Nonconformist ; the Liberal-Imperialist could not swallow the Protectionist pill, even with a coating of Imperialist sugar.   Moreover, the dilemma with which Asquith confronted the Tariff-Reformers was not wholly dialectical.   How can you give an advantage to the Canadian farmer, and at the same time lift the depression from English agriculture ?   The only preference which would substantially benefit Canada is a preference on its wheat, New Zealand a prefer-ence on its mutton.   How can you give these without raising the cost of living for the working-class family in England ?   How can you raise the revenue you want for social reform by a tax on foreign manufactures, and at the same time give even a modicum of protection to the English industrialist ?   The reply to the argument was ' *solvitur ambulando* ' : other people are doing it ; you can do it if you try.

In speeches of surpassing power Mr. Chamberlain urged his great audiences to make some small and temporary economic sacrifice, for the sake of a great political ideal.   At the same time he assured them that no sacrifice would be demanded.   He was prepared to make concrete proposals.   He boldly faced the fact that no effective preference could be given to the Colonies without taxes on ' food '.   He proposed, therefore, to impose a duty not exceeding 2s. a quarter on foreign corn, except maize, which he would exempt as being ' a food of some of the poorest of the popu-lation ', and as raw material for the farmer.   A corresponding tax on flour would ' give a substantial preference to the miller ' and so would re-establish ' one of our most ancient industries ', increase employment in agricultural districts, and provide offals for the poor man's pig.   There should be a 5 per cent. tax on foreign meat and dairy produce (bacon being exempted), and a preference on colonial wines and perhaps fruits.   These taxes, if paid by the consumer, would cost the agricultural labourer (so Chamberlain reckoned) $16\frac{1}{2}$ farthings a week and the artisan $19\frac{1}{2}$: but they would be compensated by a remission of three-quarters of the duty on tea (with corresponding remissions on coffee and cocoa) and half the duty on sugar.   On balance, even on the assumption, denied by Chamberlain, that the consumer would pay, the artisan would be no worse off, and the rural worker would gain half a farthing a week. The Exchequer would lose £2,800,000 a year by remissions, but would gain, by a 10 per cent. (average) duty on manufactured articles, anything from £9,000,000 to £15,000,000 a year.[1]

Concrete proposals offer a tempting target to skilful marksmen, and Chamberlain had to dodge the missiles both of Unionist Free Traders and of Liberals. But he had to meet a more formidable argument than any employed by Mr. Asquith on the one hand, or by Lord Hugh Cecil on the other. Half his case rested on trade depression : trade was rapidly improving. Chamberlain was fighting what was, at the moment, a losing battle.

Meanwhile, it needed all the incomparable dexterity of Mr. Balfour to keep together a parliamentary majority sufficient to postpone a dissolution. He may perhaps have cleared his own mind, he certainly befogged his followers by the publication of a characteristic pamphlet, *Economic Notes on Insular Free Trade.* The pamphlet did not deserve all the ridicule it evoked ; it contains not a few reflections which are both wise and apposite : but the Party called not for the reflections of a philosopher, but for the guidance of a leader who knew his own mind and could help them to make up theirs. Mr. Balfour had got rid of his Free Trade colleagues. Was he himself a Tariff-Reformer ? He was constrained, in the course of the campaign, to jettison food taxes. What then became of Preference ? But if Preference went, was it worth while to abandon Free Imports to save home industries, which (if the Board of Trade returns could be trusted) stood in no need of salvation ?

So the Unionist Party went to its doom. Apart from the Tariff Reform Campaign and the Education Act of 1902 there was little in the domestic history of the years 1902–5 to render Balfour's Premiership memorable. Mr. Arnold Forster, who in 1902 had succeeded Mr. Brodrick (afterwards Earl of Midleton) at the War Office, produced in 1904 an elaborate scheme of Army Reorganization ; a Licensing Act (1904) provided for the payment of compensation (levied on the trade itself) when, on grounds of public policy, licences were taken away, and substituted Quarter Sessions for the local magistrates as the licensing authcrity in

---

[1] Cf. in particular *Speeches*, II. 158 ff.

counties, and the full bench of justices with the Recorder in county boroughs; an important measure to restrict alien immigration and an Unemployed Workmen Act were passed in 1905; but for the rest the only matter which excited hot dispute was the issue by the British High Commissioner in South Africa (the Earl of Selborne) of an ordinance authorizing, under stringent conditions, the importation of Chinese labourers for service in the gold-fields.

Chinese slavery

Unscrupulous as was the use made by the Opposition of the Anti-Slavery cry, it undoubtedly contributed materially to the defeat of the Unionist Party at the General Election of 1906. Their remarkable achievement in Ireland [1] weighed little against the iniquity of supporting Denominational Schools out of public money, the condonation of slavery in the interests of cosmopolitan financiers on the Rand, and the prospect of a tax on the people's food.

Mr. Chamberlain meanwhile was getting tired of procrastination and ambiguity. Another Colonial Conference was nearly due. He insisted that it should be free to discuss every aspect of the tariff problem. To this demand Balfour agreed only on condition that the Conference met after the next Election, and that any proposals it might formulate should be ratified by the Imperial Parliament only after a second appeal to the electorate. But for the protagonists the sands were running out. On November 21, 1905, Chamberlain, encouraged by an almost unanimous vote in favour of his policy at the annual meeting of the Unionist Party at Newcastle (November 14), issued his ultimatum. In a great speech at Bristol he insisted that the Unionist Party should fight the next election on the fiscal question. Waverers must be discarded. The country must vote on a clear issue.

Balfour resigns

Balfour perceived that further procrastination was impossible: but instead of asking for a Dissolution, which Chamberlain desired, he resigned office (December 4th, 1905). On the eve of his resignation Balfour secured for his successor official recognition and social precedence. The *Gazette* of December 2 announced that the King had been pleased to assign to ' Our Prime Minister ' precedence between the Archbishop of York and the premier Duke.

[1] See *infra*, c. **xix.**

King Edward accepted with alacrity, and perhaps with some relief, the resignation of a Prime Minister who had been at little pains to make himself intelligible to a master with whom he had nothing in common. The long Unionist domination was ended.

In the Unionist débâcle which marked the ensuing election Mr. Chamberlain and his son Austen were among the few Unionist leaders who survived. But for Joseph Chamberlain the fight was all but ended. On July 7, 1906, his seventieth birthday was celebrated with great rejoicing in the city of his adoption. During the day he and Mrs. Chamberlain drove (as he said) ' through eighteen miles of people ' ; at night a great banquet was given in their honour, and on Monday the 9th (the intervening Sunday being the actual anniversary of his birth) he addressed a vast meeting in Bingley Hall.

In a memorable speech he touched a note of high Imperial patriotism and concluded with these words : ' The union of the Empire must be preceded and accompanied, as I have said, by a better understanding, by a closer sympathy. To secure that is the highest object of statesmanship now at the beginning of the twentieth century, and, if these were the last words that I were permitted to utter to you, I would rejoice to utter them in your presence and with your approval. I know that the fruition of our hopes is certain. I hope I may be able to live to congratulate you upon our common triumph, but in any case I have faith in the people. I trust in the good sense, the intelligence, and the patriotism of the majority, the vast majority of my countrymen. I look forward to the future with hope and confidence, and

' Others I doubt not, if not we,
The issue of our toil shall see '.

Those were the last words ever uttered by Joseph Chamberlain in public. Two days later he had a paralytic stroke. He survived it for eight years, but though he retained control of his faculties and exercised them to further, from his couch, the cause to which he was devoted, his active career was ended. He died on July 2, 1914, deeply mourned by his fellow subjects throughout the Empire, but happily spared the knowledge of the dark days ahead.

CHAPTER XII

THE DIPLOMATIC REVOLUTION—ENGLAND AND FOREIGN ALLIANCES

The
Function
of
History ?

IS it the function of the historian to reflect popular sentiment, in the times with which he deals, or to correct the faulty perspective of contemporaries ?   Should he attempt to reproduce the relative importance of events as they appeared at the time, or as they have been revealed in retrospect to the student of affairs ? Preceding chapters have attempted the former task : but with the result that events of still greater permanent significance were too cursorily treated. This disproportion the present chapter seeks to redress.

England
and
France

During Lord Salisbury's tenure of the Foreign Office his main preoccupations were the persistent hostility manifested towards this country by France, and the clash of interests between Great Britain and Russia in Central Asia and the Farther East.   The tension in Anglo-French relations reached a climax, when in 1898 General Kitchener and Major Marchand confronted each other at Fashoda ; but Lord Salisbury's handling of the crisis, at once firm and tactful, averted war, and in March 1899 the two countries concluded a comprehensive agreement.   France was thereby confirmed in possession of a West African empire, more vast in extent than intrinsically valuable ; England was to be left in undisturbed possession of the Egyptian Soudan.

From that moment official relations between the two countries improved, though popular feeling in France throughout the South African War remained bitterly hostile.

Franco-
Russian
*rappro-
chement*

Much more rapid and, in view of subsequent events, not less important was the improvement in the relations between France and Russia.   Previous to 1870 there had never been—except during the brief alliance of Napoleon I and Alexander I—any tradition of political friendship between the two countries ; but the defeat of France in 1870 and the growing power of Germany entirely altered the balance of diplomatic forces. Dimly perceived during the régime of Bismarck, this truth was unmistakably apprehended by Russia after the accession of William II. But the first overt indication of the new orientation of Russian policy dates from the years between 1889 and 1891. The new intimacy had a financial origin. Russia, as usual, was in want of money. Berlin had refused to lend, but from 1888 onwards a series of Russian loans were issued in Paris and very largely taken up by French financiers.

The *rapprochement* between France and Russia was not merely financial. Russia was becoming alarmed by the menacing tone adopted by German statesmen. When Bismarck (1888) published the text of the Triple Alliance, Russia was startled by the terms of a document to which in 1884 she had almost made herself party. *Bismarck and Russia*

In the next few years, things began to move rapidly towards a Franco-Russian Alliance. In July 1891 a French fleet, under the command of Admiral Gervais, paid a ceremonial visit to Cronstadt, and was received by the Russian authorities with the greatest enthusiasm.

Nor was the ceremonial visit empty of diplomatic consequences. It was followed in 1892 by the signature of a military convention of a purely defensive character, and in June 1893 by a commercial treaty. The accession (1894) of Nicholas II, the husband of a German princess, and an avowed admirer of the German Emperor, was not permitted to interrupt the cordial relations between France and his own country. *Franco-Russian Alliance*

The Franco-Russian Alliance, officially acknowledged in 1896, rendered still more conspicuous the diplomatic isolation of Great Britain. Though menacing, in its inception, to Germany, the Franco-Russian Alliance might prove even more dangerous to England, more particularly if the German Emperor was successful in effecting an *entente* between the Triple Alliance and the newly formed Dual Alliance. Such a possibility seemed far from remote when Germany joined France and Russia in compelling Japan to surrender the fruits of her recent victory over China. Japan's only friend was England. Was the day approaching when England's only friend would be Japan ? *Anglo-German relations*

Lord Salisbury might profess indifference to the isolation of England. He might even regard it as splendid : but recent developments must have caused him some heart-searching. He had discussed the situation in some detail with the German Foreign Secretary, Baron von Marschall, when, in 1891, the latter accompanied the Emperor on his visit to Queen Victoria. Conversations were resumed during the Kaiser's visit to Cowes in 1895. Herr von Kiderlin-Wächter accompanied his master, who arrived at Cowes on August 5, and remained there until the 10th. On the 5th he had an interview with Lord Salisbury at which the latter is alleged to have declared that the condition of the Ottoman Empire was ' rotten ', and that the time had come for liquidating the bankrupt's estate. Lord Salisbury when questioned about the matter, some twelve months later, merely remarked that the Kaiser's account of the interview ' showed the expediency of having a third person present when talking to the Emperor, if he made it his practice to put into his interlocutor's mouth proposals which emanated from himself '.[1] The Kaiser put his own story on record, and its accuracy has never been questioned in Germany even by the most sceptical of his critics. Moreover, plausibility was given to his version of the matter by Lord Salisbury's notorious detestation of Abdul Hamid's persecutions in Armenia, and by his confession that by backing the Turk in 1854 and 1876 England had ' put her money on the wrong horse '. Lord Sanderson, who was Permanent Under-Secretary of State at the time, has left on record an important memorandum on the subject.[2] ' I think it ', he writes, ' highly probable that he (Lord Salisbury) mentioned to the Kaiser the prospect of dismemberment of considerable portions of the Turkish Empire as eventualities to be contemplated without reluctance, though I

[1] Chirol, *Fifty Years*, p. 291.

[2] There is an exasperating lacuna in the Foreign Office Papers about this period due doubtless to Lord Salisbury's practice of transacting much of the most important business of the Office by private correspondence, of which there exists no official record. All the more eagerly, therefore, must we await the long-delayed completion of Lady Gwendolen Cecil's *Life* of her father. Meanwhile, I have been permitted to see (and to quote) the important memorandum by Lord Sanderson. The memorandum is not contemporary but was written in September 1920 after the exposure contained in Baron von Eckhardstein's *Recollections*. But Lord Sanderson's memory was as phenomenal as his accuracy.

should altogether discredit the suggestion that he proposed any definite cut-and-dried programme.' What precisely happened at Cowes we may never know; but it is certain that the German Emperor was deeply incensed against Lord Salisbury,[1] and for the next four years his annual visit to his grandmother was intermitted.

Mr. Chamberlain was more impressed than his Chief by the danger of isolation. He appreciated the world-wide difficulties with which England was confronted. A clash with the French was imminent on the Upper Nile; the situation in South Africa was becoming increasingly grave; war between the United States and Spain might (and did) extend into the Pacific, and sparks might easily fall on inflammable materials in the Far East. Regarded from the standpoint of world-politics the interests of England and Germany seemed to conflict less acutely than those of any other great Powers. A treaty between England and Germany might secure peace for the world.

Chamberlain and Bülow

In 1899 such a treaty seemed to come within the bounds of possibility. Towards the end of November, not long after the outbreak of the Boer War, the Emperor William, with the Empress and two of their sons, visited the Queen at Windsor and the Prince of Wales at Sandringham. The visit—the first for four years—was seemingly intended as a broad hint to the world that the Boers must not look for help or even sympathy to Germany. The Emperor was accompanied by Count Bülow, his Foreign Secretary, already, though not yet Chancellor, the most powerful Minister in Germany. Both the Emperor and his Minister were at pains to assure the Queen that they deplored, and to the utmost of their power were restraining, anti-British feeling in Germany.[2] Lord Salisbury, owing to Lady Salisbury's death, was unable to join the party at Windsor, but Mr. Chamberlain was included in it, as was Sir Frank Lascelles,[3] and the conversations were apparently most cordial in tone.

A few weeks before the Emperor's visit Lord Salisbury, speaking at the Guildhall banquet (November 9), had alluded to the treaty with Germany by which Samoa was conceded to her. His words were unusually emphatic. ' This morning ', he said, ' you

---

[1] On the unfortunate incident at Cowes, cf. *Q.V.L.*, III. ii. 547.
[2] *Q.V.L.*, III. iii. 423 f.　　　　　[3] British Ambassador at Berlin.

have learned of the arrangement concluded between us and one
of the continental States with whom, more than with others, we
have for years maintained sympathetic and friendly relations.
The arrangement is, above all, interesting as an indication that
our relations with the German nation are all that we could
desire.'

Then came the 'heart to heart' talks at Windsor. The
Kaiser received Chamberlain on November 21st and again on the
24th, and on the latter date Chamberlain had a long and confidential talk with Bülow, who, in a secret memorandum drafted
at the time, recorded his impression that ' opinion in England is
far less anti-German than opinion in Germany is anti-English '.
From Windsor Chamberlain went off to Leicester and there
(November 30, 1899) delivered his famous speech. ' At bottom ',
he said, ' the main character of the Teutonic race differs very
little from that of the Anglo-Saxon, and the same sentiments
which bring us into close sympathy with the United States of
America may also be evoked to bring us into close sympathy and
alliance with the Empire of Germany. . . . If the union between
England and America is a powerful factor in the cause of peace,
a new Triple Alliance between the Teutonic race and the two
great branches of the Anglo-Saxon race will be a still more potent
influence in the future of the world.' [1]

Cruel was the awakening from this dream.   Hardly was Bülow
back in Berlin before he delivered a speech (December 11th) on
the naval laws, in which he poured scorn on Chamberlain's public
and private overtures, though profuse in his courtesies towards
France and Russia.   There was no further talk on Chamberlain's
part of an Anglo-German-American treaty.[2]

Bülow's speech was coincident with the ' Black Week ' in
South Africa.

The Boer
War

To England's many enemies the disastrous opening of the
war naturally offered an irresistible opportunity, and in March
1900 Russia actually proposed to Berlin that Germany and France
should offer concerted mediation to Great Britain, and that Russia
should then join them.   Bülow, however, declined to commit

---

[1] *Annual Register*, 1899, p. 227.
[2] On the situation cf. Brandenburg, op. cit., p. 139, and his references to
Grosse Politik, xiv. 463, 493 ; xv. 422.

Germany to action which would estrange Great Britain, until he was assured as to the attitude of France.

In October 1900 the terms of an Anglo-German agreement in reference to China were published. In this so-called ' Yang-tse ' Treaty the two Governments declared that it was a matter of permanent international interest that the ports on the rivers and littoral of China should remain free and open to trade for the nationals of all countries without distinction, and that they would uphold the same ' for all Chinese territory so far as they could exercise influence '; they repudiated any desire for exclusive territorial acquisitions for themselves, and undertook to strive for the maintenance of the territorial integrity of the Chinese Empire, should it be threatened by any other Power. The terms of the Agreement were communicated to the other interested Powers ; they were fully accepted by Japan, Austria-Hungary and Italy, and with reservations by the United States and France. At Petersburg only did they excite irritation.[1]

The 'Yang-tse Treaty,' 1900

A change at the English Foreign Office in October 1900 improved the chances of an Anglo-German Agreement. At Berlin Lord Salisbury had long been regarded as the main obstacle to it.[2] His successor, the Marquis of Lansdowne, was not only a born diplomatist but had enjoyed the great advantage, denied to his predecessor, of surveying world politics from Ottawa and Simla, as well as from Downing Street. Like Mr. Chamberlain he believed that the situation of England as revealed by recent events necessitated a new diplomatic departure. Fresh overtures were accordingly made both by Chamberlain and the new Foreign Secretary to Berlin. Despite the improved atmosphere created by the Kaiser's attitude at the time of Queen Victoria's death (January 1901), the overtures were decisively and roughly rejected by Bülow. Nor is there any obscurity as to his motive. Germany, in his view, would under such an arrangement have become ' the sword of England upon the European continent '. ' In the event of a general conflict ', he writes, ' we Germans would have had to wage strenuous war on land in two directions, while

Lord Lansdowne

---

[1] *British Documents*, i. 331.

[2] See Chirol, op. cit., p. 298, and Hammann, *The World Policy of Germany* (E. T.) (p. 109), who refers to Holstein's ' violent invectives against Lord Salisbury's " unbearable personality " '.

to England would have fallen the easier task of further extending
her Colonial Empire without much trouble.'

German sea-power So far from concluding an alliance with England Germany
was bound, in Bülow's opinion, sooner or later to fight her.
'England', he writes, ' is the only country with which Germany
has an account.' The struggle might well have come during the
South African War. But the German Navy was not ready; a
premature trial of strength might have throttled German sea-
power for ever. Germany was, however, coming on apace. In
1895 the Kaiser Wilhelm Canal had been completed. Linking
the North Sea with the Baltic the canal permitted the passage
of the German fleet from either sea to the other and thus at
once doubled Germany's effective naval force. In 1897 Admiral
von Tirpitz was called to the control of German naval policy.
In 1898 the first German Navy Law was passed, and a second,
on a far more ambitious scale, in 1900. From that time onwards, the Navy became not less definitely than the Army ' a
constituent part of our national defence ' (Bülow). The Kaiser
had long since announced his policy in this matter. ' I will never
rest', he said, ' until I have raised my Navy to a position similar
to that occupied by my Army. German colonial aims can only
be gained when Germany has become master on the ocean.' Such
sentiments, frequently reiterated, could not fail to produce an
effect upon public opinion in England.

Edward VII So matters stood when Queen Victoria died (January 1901).
The situation on King Edward's accession is thus succinctly
summarized by his intimate friend :

' Germany hated and envied us ; France suspected us ; Russia
looked upon us as the hidden enemy, lurking by night. When
the King died all was changed. I am far from saying that the
more friendly feelings which prevailed were entirely due to his
initiation ; but I do say that without the wonderful charm which
he exerted they would not have existed. He fully recognized
his limitations as a Constitutional Monarch ; it was not for him
to start alliances ; but he made them possible.' [1]

The Anglo-Japanese Alliance Of those alliances the first and the most dramatic was the
' agreement ' concluded between Great Britain and Japan in
January 1902.

[1] Lord Redesdale, *Memories*, I. 179.

The appearance of Japan upon the stage of international politics is one of the most remarkable events in modern history. The Western European Powers had made an effort, in the sixteenth century, to ' open up ' Japan to commerce and Christianity, but early in the seventeenth century the Japanese shut the door to both, and from that time until the middle of the nineteenth century they maintained a policy of complete isolation. In 1858, however, Conventions were concluded between Japan on the one side and Great Britain, France, Russia, Portugal and the United States on the other, by which certain ports were to be opened to foreign trade and foreign Consuls were to be allowed to reside there.

These events announced the advent of a new era in the history of Japan, and indeed of the Pacific Ocean. Yet down to the year 1868 Japan remained to all intents and purposes a purely mediaeval and purely Asiatic State. The next quarter of a century, however, witnessed a revolution almost unique in history. A brand new Constitution on Western European lines was adopted ; representative government was introduced and a Parliament of two Houses came into being ; a system of popular education was promoted ; Universities were established ; railways were constructed ; above all, the military system was reorganized on German lines, with compulsory service as its basis, and a Navy was constructed and manned by sailors who were trained by British officers.

The result was demonstrated in the decisive defeat inflicted by Japan upon China in the war of 1894–6 ; and the completeness of her victory was reflected in the terms of the Treaty of Shimonoseki. At one bound Japan had advanced to the foremost place in the Far East. *Sino-Japanese War*

It was a dangerous pre-eminence. Victorious Japan was now confronted by the jealousy of Russia, and in less degree of Germany and France, who insisted on the rendition of Port Arthur and the Liao-Tung Peninsula to China. Japan sullenly withdrew, cherishing in her heart bitter animosity against the Power which had robbed her of the fruits of victory, and resolved to prepare for the struggle to come.

Never was political cynicism more strikingly illustrated than by the sequel to this episode. Within a short time the Powers *European Outposts in China* which had been so jealous for the integrity of China were all entrenched upon her soil : Russia at Port Arthur and Germany at Kiaochow.

The scramble for China having thus begun, Great Britain could hardly look on unmoved. Moreover, the Chinese themselves intimated to Great Britain that as soon as the Japanese evacuated Wei-Hai-Wei (still held as security for the payment of the indemnity) Great Britain might, if she chose, have a lease of it. The suggestion was, from the Chinese point of view, a shrewd one ; for Japan was still in possession of Wei-Hai-Wei, and in view of the Russian and German acquisitions so flagrantly defiant of the considerations which had prompted the demand that Japan should surrender her acquisitions on the Chinese mainland, Japan might be disposed to stay where she was. Great Britain agreed to take Wei-Hai-Wei on lease, for so long a period as Port Arthur should remain in the hands of Russia. Accordingly, Wei-Hai-Wei was evacuated by the Japanese on May 24, 1898, and on the 25th it was taken over by Great Britain.[1]

Nor was foreign penetration in China by any means limited to those territorial acquisitions. Russia was gradually fastening a financial, military, and commercial grip upon the Celestial Empire. But perhaps nothing did more to alarm the Conservative party in China than the publication of an edict by the Chinese Government conferring, at the instance of France, considerable privileges upon the French Catholic missions in that country. Small wonder that these events created, in the minds of a conservative and suspicious people, profound resentment against those who seemed to be bent not only upon the dismemberment of the Empire, but also upon a transformation of its social, religious, and industrial life. Such feelings led to the explosion known to foreigners as the rising of the Boxers. Early in 1900 the situation became so menacing that the Foreign Ministers at Pekin requested their Governments to dispatch naval squadrons to China. In June, massacres on a large scale began in Pekin, and on the 20th of that month the German Ambassador was assassinated. The fleets, thereupon, attacked the Taku forts at the end of June and captured them. The Chinese Government

The
Boxer
Rising

---

[1] Evacuated in 1930.

thereupon recognized the Boxers as a national force and declared war against 'the foreign devils'. Tientsin and the Pekiń Legations were now entirely isolated, and for two months the British Embassy, in which the other Ministers and their suites had taken refuge, was besieged. Meanwhile an international relief force was organized in which Great Britain, France, Russia, and Germany were joined by the United States and Japan. The relief column reached Pekin in August, and raised the siege of the British Embassy. Condign punishment was meted out to the ringleaders, a large indemnity was imposed upon China, but the territorial integrity of China was specifically guaranteed by the Powers. These terms were embodied in a definitive treaty which was signed in September 1901.

Less than six months later it was revealed to an astonished world that the island Empire of the West had emerged from the 'splendid isolation' which had so long characterized its foreign policy only to conclude an actual treaty with the island Empire of the Far East. On January 30, 1902, the Anglo-Japanese Treaty was signed. [3] The action of Russia, France and Germany in 1895 had naturally created deep resentment in Japan. To England, therefore, Japan turned, not only as the European country which had the greatest interest in the Orient, but as the one great Power which had stood aloof from her neighbours when they inflicted injury and humiliation, in her hour of victory, upon Japan. The Japanese had, as Count Hayashi [1] told Lord Lansdowne, 'a strong sentimental dislike to the retention by Russia of [Manchuria] from which they had at one time been expelled'. Manchuria, however, was of secondary importance to Japan. Her real concern was for Korea, 'and sooner or later it would have to be decided whether the country was to fall to Russia or not'. The Japanese 'would certainly fight in order to prevent it, and it must be the object of their diplomacy to isolate Russia, *with which Power, if it stood alone, they were prepared to deal*'.[2] The italicized words provide the key to the Anglo-Japanese Treaty from the Japanese side. 'Japan', as Lord Lansdowne's biographer has said, 'was prepared to fight Russia for Korea

The Anglo-Japanese Treaty, 1902

---

[1] Japanese Ambassador in London. For the whole matter cf. *Secret Memoirs of Baron Hayashi*, London, 1915.
[2] *British Documents*, ii. 80–3. [3] See note p. 226.

single-handed, but not if other Powers such as France and Germany were to intervene. Hence the necessity for a British alliance.'[1]

With England the alliance was less a matter of necessity than of convenience. She was drawn to Japan by common suspicion of the designs of Russia and Germany in the Far East, by anxiety to maintain the ' open door ' into China, and by a desire to ease the pressure on her naval resources in the Pacific. Moreover, the hostility displayed towards her, during the South African War, by her European neighbours had opened her eyes to the fact that her boasted ' isolation ' was perhaps more splendid than safe.

The terms of the Treaty carried out precisely the objects which the contracting parties had in view. Repudiating any ideas of aggression aimed either at China or Korea, they expressed their anxiety to maintain the *status quo* in both countries. If either Power should find it necessary to safeguard its interests, when threatened by the aggressive action of a third Power, or by internal disturbances, the other Party undertook to maintain a friendly neutrality and endeavour to isolate the conflict. If, notwithstanding that endeavour, one or more other Powers intervened, the hitherto neutral ally would come in.

The significance of this Treaty can hardly be exaggerated. At one stride Japan was admitted to terms of equality by the greatest of the world empires, and was assured that, in the event of an attack upon her by Russia, the British Fleet would keep the ring, and would intercept any possible intervention on the side of her antagonist. If Germany or France came to the assistance of Russia, Great Britain would come in as an active belligerent. On her part, Great Britain secured a powerful naval ally in the Pacific, and converted into a friend a Power which her Australasian Colonies were beginning to dread. The Treaty, as Lord Lansdowne insisted, had been concluded ' purely as a measure of precaution '; it in no way threatened ' the present or the legitimate interests of other Powers ', it would ' make for the preservation of peace,' and, if peace were unfortunately broken, would ' have the effect of restricting the area of hostilities '.[2]

[1] Lord Newton, *Lord Lansdowne*, p. 220.
[2] Lansdowne to Sir C. Macdonald, January 30, 1902.

The Anglo-Japanese Treaty was concluded for five years; but before the period expired it was revised in two important particulars. It was agreed that each country should come to the assistance of the other if attacked even by a single Power, and the scope of the alliance, which was officially described as aiming at ' the consolidation and maintenance of general peace in the regions of Eastern Asia and of India ', was by these additional words significantly and definitely extended to embrace British India. In 1911 the agreement was, at the instance of Great Britain, again revised in order to remove any danger of England being involved in a war between the United States and Japan. To meet this possible danger the 4th Article of the revised Treaty of 1911 ran as follows : ' Should either High Contracting Party conclude a treaty of general arbitration with the third Power, it is agreed that nothing in this agreement shall entail upon such contracting party an obligation to go to war with the Power with whom such treaty of arbitration is enforced.'

The news of the signature of the Treaty excited, naturally enough, various feelings in different European capitals. Some far-seeing Germans regretted that Germany had not been brought in as a third party in the alliance, and King Edward was himself favourably disposed at one time towards her inclusion. According to Baron Hayashi, however, the King became convinced that ' nothing could be done with the Kaiser and his Ministers '.[1] Italy and Austria were cordial in their congratulations, and expressed the belief that the Treaty would make for peace in the Far East. France and Russia ' made little attempt to conceal their disappointment '. M. Cambon, the French Ambassador in London, remarked to Lord Lansdowne ' that there was far too much *méfiance* in England as to Russian designs in various parts of the world ', while Count Lamsdorff, the Russian Foreign Minister, declared, with an air of injured innocence, that he knew of no Powers which had any intention of threatening the *status quo* in the Far East.[2]

[1] Eckhardstein, *Memoirs*, p. 230. Baron von Eckhardstein was one of those who regretted the omission of Germany. ' Germany,' he writes (p. 227), ' after missing this best and last opportunity of a firm friendship with Great Britain and Japan, vacillated and oscillated like a straw in the wind.' On King Edward's attitude cf. Lee, op. cit., pp. 142–5.

[2] Newton, *Lansdowne*, pp. 225–7.

Russo-Japanese War

The Treaty had been in force less than two years when Japan fell upon Russia, and in a war lasting barely eighteen months brought the great colossus to its knees.

The Baltic Fleet and the Dogger Bank incident, Oct. 21, 1904

With only one incident in the war was Great Britain directly concerned. In October 1904 the Russian Baltic Fleet, under the command of Admiral Rodjestvensky, sailed from the Baltic, and on the 21st of that month, finding itself in the midst of a flotilla of British fishing smacks and trawlers off the Dogger bank, opened fire upon them with fatal results. The incident created intense excitement in England, and might easily have led to the outbreak of war. The British Government, however, behaved with admirable restraint, and the incident was referred to an international commission. It was established that the Russian Admiral had mistaken the British trawlers for Japanese torpedo boats, and had fired upon them in panic. Russia was required to apologize to Great Britain and to compensate the fishermen.

Treaty of Portsmouth

Hardly had Rodjestvensky's fleet reached Japanese water when Togo fell upon it and annihilated it in the Straits of Tsushima (May 27, 1905). The Battle of Tsushima finished the war, and on August 23, 1905, the Treaty of Portsmouth (New Hampshire) was concluded. Russia agreed to restore to Japan the Island of Sakhalin; to surrender to Japan her lease of the Liao-Tung Peninsula and of Port Arthur, to evacuate Manchuria, and to recognize Korea as falling within the Japanese sphere of influence. Five years later, Japan put an end to ambiguities in Korea by a definite annexation (1910).

Results of the war in Asia

The Russo-Japanese War was an event of resounding significance, and its reactions were felt throughout the whole continent of Asia, and indeed wherever coloured races were in contact with whites. In India it was craftily represented as a blow to the prestige not of Russia only, but of all the Western Powers, and not least of England.

Having emerged from isolation in order to conclude one Treaty Great Britain had the less hesitation in concluding a second.

The Anglo-French Agreement, 1904

The movement towards improved relations between England and France began, as already indicated, with the Fashoda incident. That result, though paradoxical, was not unforeseen by Frenchmen. Bülow repeats a conversation which took place between a French ambassador—' one of the best political intellects of France '—and an Italian colleague. The latter asked ' What effect Fashoda would have on French relations with England ? ' The Frenchman replied, ' An excellent one. Once the difference about the Soudan is settled, nothing stands in the way of a complete *Entente* with England.' Yet France would not so lightly have surrendered her interests on the Nile had she not been increasingly interested elsewhere, particularly in Morocco.

Personal factors also contributed to a closer accord between England and France. In 1898 Gabriel Hanatoux was succeeded at the French Foreign Office by M. Théophile Delcassé. Delcassé, who had already given a great impetus to French colonial enterprise, took office, firmly convinced, on the one hand, that the activity of France should be concentrated upon the Western Mediterranean, and, on the other, that the diplomatic independence of his country could be established only by means of reconciliation with Italy and with Great Britain.

In 1896 Italy had formally recognized the French Protectorate in Tunis, and, two years later, Delcassé was successful in negotiating with her a treaty of navigation and commerce. Two further conventions were signed in 1900 and 1902 under which France definitely engaged not to frustrate the ambitions of Italy on the side of Tripoli, while Italy assured France a free hand in Morocco. These Conventions rendered the renewal of the Triple Alliance in 1903 a hollow formality.

Although secure in the Western Mediterranean France was left, by Russia's preoccupation in the Far East, in an exposed position on the western flank of Germany. It became, therefore, important for her to find a new ally. Great Britain, on her side, was becoming seriously alarmed by the development of German sea-power. This was clearly recognized in Germany; but Germany drew a sharp distinction between the rising suspicion of England and the deep-seated hostility of France. ' England ', wrote Bülow, ' is certainly seriously disquieted by our rising power at sea, and our competition which incommodes her at many points. . . . But between such sentiments in England and the fundamental feeling in France there is a marked difference, which finds corresponding expression in politics. France would attack us if she thought she was strong enough; England would do so only if she thought she could not defend her vital, economic, and political

interests against Germany except by force. The mainspring of
English policy towards us is national egoism; that of French
policy is national idealism. He who follows his interest will,
however, mostly remain calmer than he who pursues an idea.' [1]

To no Englishman did these developments give greater concern
than to King Edward. Moreover, his personal inclinations were
towards France, and in May 1903 he decided to pay an official
visit to Paris. Received on his arrival with frigid politeness, he
succeeded in a few days' sojourn in completely captivating his
hosts. ' I have known Paris ', he said, in a speech at the Elysée
(May 2), ' since my childhood. I have frequently visited it, and
I have always been full of admiration for the unique beauty of
the city, and for the spirit of its citizens. I shall never forget,
M. le Président, the welcome which I have received at the hands
of yourself, your Government, and the people, and it is to me a
cause of happiness to believe that my visit will renew the bonds
of friendship, and will facilitate such a *rapprochement* between our
two countries as will conduce to the interests of both.' President
Loubet returned the King's visit in July, and was received with
the utmost enthusiasm in London. That these visits did much
to prepare the way for the treaty is undeniable. Lord Lansdowne,
writing to Sir Edmund Monson, British Ambassador in Paris
(April 8, 1904), referred to the ' powerful impulse ' thus given to
the movement,[2] and M. Poincaré, when he in turn visited, as
President, the City of London, used, with Gallic precision, an
identical phrase : ' Il n'est pas un de mes compatriotes qui ait
oublié l'heureuse impulsion donnée en cette occasion décisive par
sa Majesté le roi Edouard VII à l'œuvre de concorde, qui lui a
survécu.'

' Impulsion ' is the precisely appropriate word. The measure
of King Edward's personal influence upon Foreign Affairs has been
much discussed. The Earl of Balfour, writing in 1915 to Lord
Lansdowne, referred to the attribution of the *Entente* to King
Edward as a foolish piece of gossip, and added : ' So far as I
remember, during the years when you and I were his Ministers, he
never made an important suggestion of any sort on large questions
of policy.' But Balfour consistently underrated King Edward's
intelligence. The two men were indeed temperamentally anti-

Edward
VII and
France

[1] Op. cit., pp. 89–90.   [2] *British Documents*, ii. 364.

pathetic. The King had some reason to complain that Balfour treated him on at least one occasion ' with scant courtesy ' (Lee's *Life*, p. 253), and that he was curiously indifferent to the Royal Prerogative is, from other sources, evident. On the other hand, Balfour thought the King tiresomely insistent on matters which seemed to the Minister of scant importance.

Yet, even if Mr. Balfour underrated King Edward's intelligence and influence, it is ' ridiculous to suppose, as some do, that the King initiated or planned the *Entente* between Great Britain and France ', or that in a more general sense he ' moulded the foreign policy of his country '.[1] What King Edward did was, by his personal magnetism, by his genial temper and never-failing tact, to create the atmosphere in the absence of which Lord Lansdowne and M. Cambon would have found it difficult, if not impossible, to initiate negotiations. Perhaps no other Englishman, King or subject, was ever more popular with the French. ' Tell your King that if ever he is tired of his job in England we will take him by acclamation.' So a prominent French royalist once said to Lord Redesdale.[2] Nor was the sentiment confined to royalists ; it pervaded all classes.

Thus was the soil prepared ; but the happy issue of negotiations, long and difficult, was due to the patience and skill of M. Paul Cambon French Ambassador in London, and Lord Lansdowne, who all through was greatly helped and encouraged by Lord Cromer. No man, indeed, was more profoundly anxious for the success of the negotiations than the great English Proconsul, who was charged with the administration of Egypt. For nearly twenty years his efforts for the regeneration of that country had been hampered, if not frustrated, by the persistent jealousy of France. What it would have meant to his work could the *Entente* have been ante-dated by ten years only those familiar with its details can know.

At last, however, the good day had come. By a series of Conventions and Declarations, England and France not only came to terms in regard to Morocco and Egypt, but also cleared up a number of outstanding points in reference to West Africa, Siam,

---

[1] Cf. Lord Esher, *The Influence of King Edward*, pp. 57, 50. Few men knew the King better or appreciated him more highly than Lord Esher.

[2] *Memories*, I. 177.

Madagascar, and the New Hebrides. French fishing rights in Newfoundland had been a matter of dispute between England and France ever since the Treaty of Utrecht in 1713. By mutual concession, which left to France certain fishing rights, but deprived her of any sort of monopoly, this tiresome question was settled, it may be hoped, for ever. In West Africa, England made important concessions to France on the Gambia, in Guinea, and on the Niger. Boundary questions in Siam and tariff difficulties in Madagascar and Zanzibar, not to mention various small points in regard to the New Hebrides, were also included in the general settlement. The central point of the arrangement was, however, North Africa. France recognized for the first time the actual position of Great Britain in Egypt, while Great Britain recognized the predominant claims and interests of France in Morocco. Both Governments declared that they had no intention of altering the political status of Egypt and Morocco respectively, but, by a secret article attached to the Convention, it was admitted that Great Britain and France might find themselves ' constrained by force of circumstances to modify this policy in respect to Egypt or Morocco '. There was another secret article in reference to Spanish claims in Morocco. The two Governments also acknowledged the special interests of Spain, who (by a secret clause not revealed until 1911) was to pledge herself not to allow any of her spheres of influence in Morocco to pass into other hands.[1] Professor Brandenburg's comment on the whole matter is brief but pregnant : ' With the coming of the Anglo-French *Entente* Germany's outwardly brilliant position between the two groups of great Powers had passed for ever.' [2] Nor does he disguise his conviction that for this disaster Germany herself, and in particular the clumsy diplomacy of Holstein and Bülow, was mainly to blame.

Germany and the Entente   The conclusion of the Anglo-French *Entente* was an event of first-rate importance in the history of European diplomacy. [3] Had Germany been in pacific mood, it might well have inaugurated a long period of world peace. Such was undoubtedly the intention of Great Britain, whose spokesmen emphasized the importance of the Anglo-French Treaty as affording a model for similar agree-

---

[1] The whole history of the negotiations is contained in vol. ii of the *British Documents* with which cf. *German Diplomatic Documents* (E.T.), vol. iii.
[2] p. 203.   [3] See note, p. 226.

ments between other countries. German authorities take the view, indeed, that the assurances given by English ministers that the *Entente* was perfectly compatible with an amicable Anglo-German agreement were 'not entirely candid ',[1] and the immediate effect of the *Entente* may be gauged from the ominous speech of the German Emperor at the opening of a bridge at Mainz : ' I wish from my heart ', he said, ' that peace, which is necessary for the further development of industry and trade, may be maintained in the future. But I am convinced that this bridge will prove completely adequate if it has to be used for more serious transport purposes.' Yet, almost simultaneously Bülow declared in the Reichstag (April 12, 1904) that Germany had no reason to object to the Anglo-French *Entente*.

The busy mind of the Kaiser was, however, at work on a new European combination. Two methods of nullifying the Anglo-French *Entente* seem to have occurred to him. ' The first was a secret intrigue with the Czar, which would draw Russia over into the orbit of German policy ; this would result either in drawing France also, and in establishing a German-Russian-French combination directed against England, or it would result in rupturing the dual alliance, and leave England and France face to face with the old Triple Alliance, now reinsured again as in Bismarck's day on the Russian side. . . . The second method of dislocating the *Entente Cordiale* was by some diplomatic triumph over France, backed up by a policy of force which would make patent to all the world the essential hollowness of the *Entente Cordiale*, and proclaim that important arrangements in the world still could not be made without consulting Germany '.[2]

The German Emperor

In March 1905, in the course of a Mediterranean cruise, the Kaiser touched at Tangier ; he landed only for two hours, but having done so, could not resist the temptation of delivering a menacing speech in which he ostentatiously took under his protection the independence of Morocco and the sovereignty of its Sultan.[3] The Emperor's visit to Tangier was followed by a demand for the summoning of an international conference, and by a demand that France should repudiate her Foreign Minister,

The Kaiser at Tangier

---

[1] Hammann, p. 145, and cf. Brandenburg, op. cit., p. 183.
[2] S. B. Fay, *The Kaiser's Secret Negotiations with the Czar*, pp. 52–3.
[3] *Imperial Germany*, p. 81.

Delcassé, whom the Germans regarded as primarily responsible for the Anglo-French *Entente*. It was the policy of England, so the Germans believed, to destroy the fleet of every rival, or better still to prevent its construction ; but could the British fleet help France ? Let France think better of it, give up the Minister who had made the trouble and adopt towards Germany a loyal and open policy such as would guarantee the peace of the world. [1]

The Algeciras Conference, Jan. 1906

Before this arrogant threat, France, conscious that she was not ready for immediate war, momentarily gave way. Delcassé resigned on June 12, 1905. About the same time it was arranged that a Conference should meet at Algeciras in January 1906. The meeting of this Conference was undoubtedly a diplomatic triumph for Germany. It would never have been held if, on the one hand, France had been ready for war, and if, on the other, Russia had not lately suffered her crushing defeat at the hands of Japan. Bülow professed himself as highly pleased with its results. Less partial opinion, even in Germany, inclined to the view that the results of the Algeciras Conference marked, on the contrary, a decided diplomatic rebuff for Germany, and attributed to the failure to reach an agreement with England the dilemma in which Germany found herself at Algeciras. Either she had to fight or to acknowledge a diplomatic defeat.[2] The Conference was held with the definite intention of destroying in the eyes of the world the significance of the Anglo-French *Entente*. It served actually to demonstrate its strength, and Bülow admitted as much in a speech in the Reichstag on November 14.

The United States delegate to the Conference, Mr. White, was definitely of the same opinion : ' the victor at the Conference is England.' Her victory was due largely to the tact of her representative Sir Arthur Nicolson (afterwards Lord Carnock), whose son thus aptly summarizes the results of the Conference : ' She (Germany) lost the confidence of Europe ; what was even more important to her, she lost the confidence of America. She obtained no compensations. She did not even succeed in humiliating France. The open door remained an aspiration. Her protection of Islam appeared to be mere rhetoric. France and Spain, England and Russia, had drawn closer together. The nakedness of the triple alliance had, with Italy's defection, been exposed to

---

[1] Cf. Rose, *Origins of the War*, p. 76.   [2] Hammann, p. 116.

public gaze, and above all the Anglo-French *Entente* had assumed an entirely new character.' [1]

Hitherto there had been one fatal flaw in the *Entente*. In 1907, however, the estrangement between Russia and England was, at long last, composed.[2] The foundation of the Anglo-Russian *Entente* was really laid at the Algeciras Conference. Sir Edward Grey, who had succeeded Lord Lansdowne as Foreign Secretary at the end of 1905, threw himself with ardour into the task of improving relations between the two countries. ' When the interests of two Powers are constantly touching and rubbing against one another, it is hard to find a half-way house between constant liability to friction and cordial friendship.' So the problem was stated by Sir Edward Grey. The interests of England and Russia had, as we have seen, been rubbing against one another in Central Asia for the best part of a century. During 1906 and 1907, however, there was a frank interchange of views between London and Petersburg, and at last on August 31, 1907, the momentous treaty was concluded. The treaty covered all the outstanding questions between the two Powers in Central Asia, and in particular dealt with Thibet, Afghanistan, and Persia. In regard to the first, both parties pledged themselves to respect the integrity of Thibet, to abstain from all interference in internal affairs, to seek no concessions for railways, roads, telegraphs, and mines, or other rights in Thibet ; not to send representatives to Lhassa, and to deal with Thibet only through the intermediary of its suzerain, the Chinese Government. As regards Afghanistan a still more important arrangement was concluded. Subject to the consent of the Ameer (which has, in fact, never been obtained), the Russian Government recognized Afghanistan ' as outside the sphere of Russian influence ; they engaged that all their political relations with Afghanistan should be conducted through the intermediary of Great Britain, and undertook not to send any agents into Afghanistan '. Great Britain, on its side, declared that there was no intention of changing the political status of Afghanistan ; that British influence would be exercised in a pacific sense, and that no steps were contemplated, or would be

The
Anglo-
Russian
Agree-
ment

(a) Thibet

(b) Af-
ghanistan

---

[1] Harold Nicolson, *Lord Carnock*, pp. 198–9.
[2] The diplomatic history of the Anglo-Russian Agreement may be followed in detail in *British Documents*, vol. iv.

encouraged, against Russia. Finally, there was to be complete equality of commercial opportunity in Afghanistan for both countries.

(c) Persia   Most important of all was the agreement concerning Persia. The two Powers engaged to respect the integrity and independence of Persia, and to keep the door open to the trade and industry of all other nations. Persia was, however, mapped out into three spheres of influence. The Russian sphere embraced the north and centre, including the chief Persian cities of Tabriz, Teheran, and Ispahan. The British sphere was in the south and east ; it included the coastal district of the Persian Gulf and of the Indian Ocean to the frontiers of Baluchistan. Between the two spheres of influence was interposed a neutral zone, in which both Powers were free to obtain political or commercial concessions, while renouncing any such freedom in the spheres assigned respectively to Russia and Great Britain. The details of this arrangement were sharply criticized, notably by Lord Curzon of Kedleston.[1] Sir Edward Grey retorted that the treaty must be judged as a whole ; and while not admitting that it was unduly favourable to Russia as regards Persia, pointed conclusively to the substantial concession made by Russia to us as regards Afghanistan.

The *Entente* between England and Russia was hardly less displeasing to Germany than that between England and France, and the Balkan crisis of 1908–9 gave the Kaiser an opportunity of humiliating England's new ally.

The year 1908–9 was, indeed, fateful both for the Ottoman Empire and for Europe at large. In July 1908 the *Young Turks* initiated a revolution which in 1909 was consummated by the

The Balkan crisis (1908)

deposition of Abdul Hamid. On October 5, 1908, Prince Ferdinand proclaimed the formal independence of Bulgaria ; on the 12th the Cretan Assembly voted for the union of the island with the kingdom of Greece. Yet, startling and significant as

The Hapsburgs

were these events, they were entirely eclipsed by the annexation of Bosnia and Herzegovina to the Hapsburg Empire (October 5).

Serbia

The people most directly and vitally interested in that annexation were the Southern Slavs of Serbia. For many years past, and especially since 1878, national self-consciousness had been

[1] See Lord Zetland, *Life of Lord Curzon.*

growing rapidly in that small but ancient State.   The growth of
that sentiment was regarded with grave concern by the Hapsburgs, to whose fragile Empire it was distinctly menacing.   Among
the subjects of Francis Joseph the Slavs formed a large majority,
but it long had been a cardinal principle of Hapsburg policy to
keep that majority in strict subordination to the German-Magyar
minority.   The more drastic the methods applied by the Hapsburgs to the Slavs of Bosnia and Herzegovina, the more inclined
were the latter to look with sympathy and expectation upon the
propaganda emanating from their brethren in Belgrade.   These
feelings were warmly reciprocated by the Serbs.   The formal
annexation of the two Provinces in 1908 consequently came as a
terrible shock to the southern Slavs, both within and outside the
Hapsburg Empire.   Bitter was the hostility manifested in Belgrade against the Hapsburgs, and the whole Serbian people,
headed by the Crown Prince, clamoured for war.   Feeling in
Montenegro was hardly less unanimous.   The Serbian Government made a formal protest on October 7, and appealed to the
Powers.

The Powers were not unsympathetic, but urged Serbia to be
patient.   Upon English diplomatists the high-handed action of
Austria had made a profound impression.   Not least upon the
Sovereign.   Himself a man of transparent honesty, he felt that Edward
he had been ' treacherously deceived ' by a Sovereign for whom VII and
he had a sincere regard and with whom his relations had been the crisis
invariably cordial.

So recently as August King Edward had been with the Emperor
Francis Joseph at Ischl.   Nor was the meeting merely ceremonial.
The Emperor was accompanied by his powerful Minister, Baron
Aerenthal, the King by Sir Charles Hardinge, Permanent Secre-
tary at the Foreign Office and subsequently Viceroy of India.
The two Sovereigns had ' discussed the Eastern Question with
the utmost apparent intimacy, and the King left Ischl in the full
assurance that there was no cloud on the horizon '.

The news of the annexation came upon him, consequently, as
a terrible shock.   Lord Redesdale has recorded the effect produced upon him : ' It was the 8th of October that the King
received the news at Balmoral, and no one who was there can
forget how terribly he was upset.   Never did I see him so moved.

. . . Every word that he uttered that day has come true.' [1]
The Great War of 1914 was, in fact, implicit in the events of 1908.

Nor was King Edward the only Sovereign who was profoundly
perturbed by the news of the Bosnian Crisis. ' A raid on Turkey ! '
So the Kaiser minuted on Bülow's dispatch. ' Material for cheap
suspicions in England about the Central Powers. . . . Vienna
will incur the reproach of double-dealing and not unjustly. They
have deceived us abominably. . . . King Edward will now
inscribe the " Defence of Treaties " on his banner . . . a great
score over us for Edward VII.' [2]

But fume as the Kaiser might, he was impotent in the face of
Aerenthal's action. The Hapsburg was his only ally. He could
do no other than recognize the annexation.

It was, however, upon the attitude of Russia that the peace
of Europe, at that moment, hung.

Russia and Germany

In the Balkan question she was profoundly interested. To
her the Serbians naturally looked not merely for sympathy but
for assistance. Russia, however, was not ready for war. She
had not regained her breath after the contest with Japan. And
the fact was well known at Potsdam and Vienna. In melo-
dramatic phrase the German Emperor announced that if his
august ally were compelled to draw the sword, a knight ' in shining
armour ' would be found by his side. At the end of March,
Russia was plainly informed that, if she went to the assistance of
Serbia, she would have to fight not Austria-Hungary only but
Germany as well. Russia, conscious of her unpreparedness, immediately gave way. With that surrender the war of 1914 became
inevitable. Germany was intoxicated by her success ; Russia
was bitterly resentful. The Serbs were compelled not merely to
acquiesce, but to promise to shake hands with Austria. The
Powers tore up the twenty-fifth Article of the Treaty of Berlin.
Turkey accepted £2,200,000 from Austria-Hungary as compensation for the loss of the two provinces which, though still
theoretically under the suzerainty of the Sultan, had for thirty

[1] Lord Redesdale, *Memories*, i. 178–9. Cf. also *The Recollections* (ii. 277)
of John, Viscount Morley, who was Minister in attendance at Balmoral at
the time, and formed a similar opinion as to the knowledge and shrewdness
of King Edward VII.

[2] The Kaiser's written Comments endorsed on Bülow's Dispatches of
October 5 and 7.

years been governed by the Hapsburgs. Bulgaria compounded for her tribute to the Porte by the payment of £5,000,000.

Thus were the ' cracks papered over ', and the most serious crisis which had threatened European peace since 1878 was surmounted.

The nett result of that crisis was unquestionably a triumph, even if a transitory triumph, for Pan-Germanism as against Pan-Slavism.

Yet the Central Empires felt themselves to be, and in a sense were, encircled by the Triple *Entente*. Professor Brandenburg's comment is eminently judicial. ' Probably ', he writes, ' the truth is that the *Entente* . . . was neither so dangerous as the anxious-minded among us believed, nor so innocent as the other side represented.' One thing, however, was certain. ' Germany had been manœuvred out of her central position and into that of the head of the weaker of the two great parties. In Berlin they felt this deeply and were anxious about the future.' [1]

Confronted by the Triple *Entente* the Kaiser attempted in 1909–10 to revive the ' reinsurance policy ' of Bismarck. In February 1909 he concluded with France an agreement about Morocco and another in 1910 with the Czar Nicholas about their respective interests in Persia and Mesopotamia. These ' reinsurances ' were clearly intended to effect a rupture in the Triple *Entente*. The stirring events of 1911 served only to consolidate it. Another crisis in Moroccan affairs reproduced, in that year, with redoubled intensity the situation of 1905–6. The terms of the Act of Algeciras were so vague as to give either France or Germany a specious plea for divergent interpretations. That France had the right to maintain order in Morocco was unquestionable; equally certain was it that the Sultan Moulay-Hafid was either unable or unwilling to enforce it. Consequently, in April 1911 the French landed troops in Morocco, and on May 21 the Moroccan capital, Fez, was occupied. The strictest injunctions were given to the French commander to abstain from any act which might seem to menace the sovereign authority of the Sultan or the integrity of his Empire; yet with every advance of French troops,

France and Morocco

---

[1] Op. cit., pp. 262–3. Cf. also Hammann, p. 176, who like most of his countrymen is obsessed by the idea of King Edward's nefarious designs against Germany.

Germany became more and more suspicious. 'Should France find it necessary to remain at Fez', said Kiderlin-Waechter, the German Foreign Secretary, 'the whole Moroccan Question will be raised afresh, and each signatory of the Act of Algeciras will resume entire liberty of action.' In June the French troops commenced their retirement from Fez; but with each stage of the retirement the attitude of Germany became more menacing.

The action of Germany may have been precipitated by the domestic situation both in France and England. In France every six months saw a new Ministry, while industry was dislocated by a series of syndicalist strikes; in England the constitutional struggle over the ' veto ' of the House of Lords reached its zenith in the summer of 1911, while a profound upheaval in the industrial world culminated in a serious railway strike. With her opponents seemingly paralysed by domestic difficulties, the opportunity seemed to Germany too good to be missed, and on July 1 the French Government was officially informed that the *Panther*, a German gunboat, had been dispatched to Agadir, an open roadstead on the west coast of Morocco, in order to protect the lives and interests of German subjects in that disorderly country. To a thinly veiled demand for the partition of Morocco between Germany, France, and Spain, France hotly retorted that she was the paramount Power behind Morocco, and had been recognized as such ; but while willing to negotiate on details, would concede nothing that would touch the honour of France.

Attitude of Great Britain   England not only ranged herself solidly behind France, but plainly intimated her position to the world. As the medium of that grave intimation, the Cabinet wisely selected Mr. Lloyd George who, speaking at the Mansion House on July 21, used the following words : ' I am bound to say this, that I believe it is essential in the higher interests, not merely of this country, but of the world, that Britain should at all hazards maintain her place and her prestige amongst the great Powers of the world. If a situation were to be forced on us in which peace could only be preserved by the surrender of the great and beneficent position Britain has won by centuries of heroism and achievements, by allowing Britain to be treated, where her interests are vitally affected, as if she were of no account in the Cabinet of Nations, then I say emphatically that peace at that price would be a humiliation intolerable for a great country like ours to endure.'

Nor was the intimation confined to the official spokesmen of England. Mr. Balfour, as leader of the Opposition, thought it well to warn Germany that she could not calculate upon party strife to paralyse England's right arm : ' If ', he said, ' there are any who suppose that we shall allow ourselves to be wiped from the map of Europe because we have difficulties at home, it may be worth while saying that they utterly mistake the temper of the British people and the patriotism of the Opposition.'

The crisis was evidently acute. On the 25th the German Ambassador made to Sir Edward Grey a communication of so grave a character that the latter was constrained to warn the Admiralty that ' the fleet might be attacked at any moment.' [1] Nor was the tension relaxed until the end of September. From September 8 to the 22nd, so constant was the expectation of an immediate outbreak of hostilities that ' the tunnels and bridges on the South-Eastern Railway were being patrolled day and night '. Only on the 22nd was the Foreign Office able to ' give the word that a state of " war preparedness " might be relaxed.' [2]

Fortunately the firm attitude of the British Government checked the warlike ardour of official Germany, while it diverted the attack of the fire-eaters from France to England. Mr. Lloyd George's speech, they declared, had revealed, as by a flashlight, the real enemy of Germany. England will brook no rival ; she claims to dominate the world. ' It is not by concessions that we shall secure peace, but by the German sword.' So spake a Reichstag orator with the unconcealed approval of the Crown Prince. ' England ', wrote a German paper, ' poses as the arbiter of the world. It cannot go on. The conflict between us, so far from being settled, is now more than ever inevitable.' [3]

Meanwhile, prolonged negotiations between the two principals resulted (November 4, 1911) in the conclusion of a comprehensive treaty, divided into two parts : the *Accord Marocain* and

Franco-German Treaty

---

[1] Winston Churchill, *The World Crisis*, i. 48.

[2] Nicolson, *Lord Carnock*, p. 347.

[3] The *Germania* (November 29), quoted ap. Debidour, *Histoire Diplomatique*, ii. 176.

the *Accord Congolais*.[1] By the former Germany virtually acknowledged a French Protectorate over Morocco ; by the latter France
ceded to Germany half the French Congo.   So the acute crisis of
1911 was temporarily averted.   The German Emperor had, at the
last moment, recoiled from the war which the Pan-Germans were
eager to provoke.

Italy and   His prudence was justified, if it was not inspired, by a sinister
Tripoli   development in the Near East.   On September 29 Italy, after a
brief period of negotiation, declared war upon Turkey.   But
Italy's move on Tripoli had more than local significance.   An
important member of the Triple Alliance had suddenly launched
an attack upon one of the sleeping partners of the same firm.
Bismarck's laborious structure had collapsed : the diplomatic
revolution was completed.

    [1] For the full text of these treaties, cf. P. Albin, *Les Grands Traité Poli-
tiques*, pp. 562–79.

Notes.
    (i) to p. 209.   Lord Rosebery thought the Anglo-Japanese treaty ' abso-
lutely right.'   See Bishop Bell, *Life of Archbishop Davidson*, I, 497.
    (ii) to p. 216.   Lord Rosebery was one of the few who disapproved of
the Anglo-French Treaty as ' far more likely to lead to War than to Peace.'
See Churchill : *Great Contemporaries*, p. 27.

CHAPTER XIII

THE LABOUR PROBLEM—TRADE UNIONS AND POLITICS

THE survey of Foreign Affairs in the last chapter brought us to the brink of Armageddon. We must now resume the interrupted tale of domestic politics.

The portent of the General Election of 1906 was not the return of a vast army of Liberals, but the advent to Parliament of a small but compact company of ' Labour ' members. Working men themselves, they were elected to represent not so much local constituencies as an economic and social class—the weekly wage-earners. Hitherto Members of Parliament had represented each a particular locality, in many cases the town, and in even more cases the county, with which the Member was personally associated. He was elected to represent the interests of all classes in the constituency. The advent of a Labour Party dealt a serious blow to this traditional theory of English representation. The enfranchisement of the wage-earners by the Acts of 1865 and 1884 may have rendered this development inevitable. Anyway, it had come.

The Advent of Labour

Political enfranchisement was not alone responsible. Remarkable for the development of political democracy the nineteenth century was also marked by the economic emancipation of the working-classes from legislative shackles which were part of the legacy inherited from the medieval State. The State had taken over from the Merchant and Craft Guilds the duty of regulating the conditions of employment, wages and prices. By Common Law all combinations, whether of workmen or employers, were illegal as being ' conspiracies in restraint of trade '. Legislation had consistently emphasized the doctrines of the Common Law. The eighteenth century witnessed many attempts to escape from the restraints on combination, but so

Labour and the State

late as 1800 a particularly stringent Act reaffirmed the principle.
The effect of that Act was, in the words of a great jurist, that
' any artisan who organized a strike or joined a trade union was
a criminal . . . ; the strike was a crime, the trade union was an
unlawful association '.[1]

Trade
Unions

With the progress of the Industrial Revolution, and under
the influence of Benthamine philosophy, opinion began to move
in the opposite direction, and a Royal Commission in 1824 reported strongly against combination laws. Those laws were,
accordingly, repealed *en bloc*. The immediate consequences were
alarming. The repeal was followed by an epidemic of strikes,
accompanied by much violence and the intimidation both of
employers and peaceable wage-earners. The Benthamites were
in despair. Their hopes and intentions were completely frustrated. Their object had been the promotion of liberty ; to their
chagrin they discovered that emancipation was the prelude not
to liberty but to licence.

Once more they had recourse to the Legislature. An Act of
1825 reaffirmed the Common Law of conspiracy, and prescribed
penalties for ' the use of violence, threats, intimidation, molesta-
tion or obstruction by any person for the purpose of forcing a
master to alter his mode of business, or a workman to refuse or
leave work, or of forcing any person to belong to or conform to
the rules of any club or association '. But by reason of certain
exemptions the general effect of this halting piece of legislation
was that a trade union remained a non-lawful, though not necessarily a criminal, association. Being non-lawful a trade union
could not claim the protection of the law.

This ambiguous position entailed one serious consequence :
trade unions were excluded from the protection afforded by the
legislation of 1855 to Friendly Societies ; their funds were consequently at the mercy of dishonest officials. Yet, notwithstanding this heavy handicap, trade unions multiplied rapidly during
the second and third quarters of the nineteenth century. It was,
however, the outrages committed by members of these associations in Sheffield, Manchester and other industrial centres in 1866
that first concentrated public attention upon the problem of
trade-unionism. A Royal Commission was appointed to inquire

[1] A. V. Dicey, *Law and Public Opinion*, Lectures vi and viii.

into the whole question, and on its Report the legislation of 1871–6 was based.

That legislation has been described as the 'charter of Trade Unionism'; and the description is not inappropriate. A succession of Statutes (passed on the initiative both of Conservative and Liberal Governments) not only extended to the funds of trade unions the protection already given to those of Friendly Societies, but relieved them (as it was supposed) from the liability to damages for torts or civil wrongs committed by their agents. The Act of 1876 (38 and 39 Vict., c. 86, section 3) further mitigated in favour of Trade Unions the Common Law in regard to conspiracy, by declaring that 'an agreement or combination by two or more persons to do . . . any act in contemplation or furtherance of a trade dispute . . . shall not be indictable as a conspiracy, if such act if done by one person would not be punishable as a crime'. The plain meaning of this enactment is 'that a combination among workmen to break a contract with their employer, e.g. to leave his service without notice, with a view to compelling him to grant a rise in wages, is not a crime, whilst a combination by tenants to break a contract " with a landlord " is a crime'. Moreover, 'something like legal sanction was given to " picketing " in connexion with a trade dispute, so long, but only so long, as such conduct does not involve intimidation or violence'. Thus, in the words of another great jurist, trade unions ' became in form privileged bodies with a special status '.[1] Nor does it need any elaborate argument to demonstrate how far, in the course of half a century, the Legislature had travelled since 1825.

Thirty years later Parliament was again impelled to legislate on the subject of trade disputes. In the interval an important political development had taken place. The Labour problem had assumed a new aspect. Down to this time the Legislature had regarded Trade Unions, whether it imposed restrictions or conferred exceptional privileges upon them, solely as factors in the organization of industry. After 1900 they could no longer be so regarded. Trade Unionists, or many of them, were clearly moving towards a radical reorganization of industry on Socialist lines ; a parliamentary party pledged to Socialism had been

Trade Unions and Politics

---

[1] W. M. Geldart, *The Osborne Judgment and After*, p. 13.

formed ; representatives of that party had already entered the
House of Commons, and were soon to reach it in rapidly increasing numbers.

For the last forty years things had been moving in that direction. As far back as 1867 the London Working Men's Association resolved to work for the direct representation of ' Labour '
in the House of Commons, and at the General Election of 1868
three working men, George Howell, W. R. Cremer and E. O.
Greening, stood in the Radical interest. They were all defeated,
but the first two entered Parliament later on and became highly
respected members of the House. The Labour Representation
League was formed in 1869 and at the General Election of 1874
twelve working men were adopted as Radical candidates. Two
were elected : Alexander Macdonald, the founder of the Miners'
National Union, and Thomas Burt, who continued to sit in Parliament for many years, and was in 1906 sworn a member of His
Majesty's Privy Council. But men of this type merely reinforced
the left wing of the Liberal Party. They had no stomach for
the ' class war ' desired by some of the more ardent spirits in the
Trade Union movement.

The
' Class
War '
The ' class war ' was formally declared in 1884, when Mr.
H. M. Hyndman, a Cambridge graduate and a Sussex cricketer,
founded the Social Democratic Federation. Hyndman was a
disciple of Karl Marx, the first volume of whose famous work,
Das Kapital—a work more often quoted than read—was published in 1867. Few working men could follow Marx's argument,
but they could and did seize upon his main conclusions—that
' profits ' represent a deduction from wages, that morally the
workman had an exclusive claim upon the product of industry,
and that consequently the capitalist was a thief, albeit in many
cases an unconscious thief. Such doctrines, particularly when
preached with the fervour of a Hyndman, could be apprehended
even by those with little training in Economics, and were in fact
accepted as gospel by a considerable number of the younger
Trade Unionists.

Marx and
George
Even more persuasive than Marx's *Capital* was Henry George's
Progress and Poverty which was published in 1879. George wrote
arrestingly with no little rhetorical power. Any one could
follow his argument, even if they refused to assent to his conclu-

sions. His main thesis was that with the increase of wealth among the wealthy the poverty of the poor deepened, that this was due to land monopoly, and that the only remedy was to be found in a single tax on the unearned increment of land. The whole fabric of George's argument was based upon inaccurate assumptions which were relentlessly exploded by Economists like Arnold Toynbee and Alfred Marshall, but which exercised, nevertheless, an immense influence upon half-educated minds.[1]

For a generation had now grown to manhood who had been taught to read, but had not learned to think : and the success of the preaching of Hyndman and others was largely due to this fact. The seed of Socialism fell upon soil which had been scratched, but not ploughed. It produced the appropriate crop. The new ' Labour Movement ' reaped the harvest.

Other works, less polemical than those of Marx and George, more utopian in character, had a similar tendency. Edward Bellamy's *Looking Backward* (1887) and Robert Blatchford's *Merrie England* were well calculated to make people discontented with things as they were, and to look back or to look forward (according to their temperament) to a ' Golden Age '. Thus, the ' Labour Party ' received many recruits from among people of all classes, whose hearts were as soft as their heads, and whose ' Socialism ' amounted to little more than general benevolence, and a desire to see the lot of their poorer neighbours improved. To such people (and indeed to others) the *Fabian Essays* (1889), contributed by members of a middle-class society founded in 1884, made a considerable appeal. The ' Fabians ', as the name implied, were opposed to revolutionary methods, but sought to permeate society with collectivist ideas, thus expelling the virus of Herbert Spencer's rigid individualism. In that aim they largely succeeded.

Thus by many cultivators, each working in his own field, was a large area of ground prepared.

Meanwhile, the political Trade Unionists were moving towards their goal. At the General Election of 1892 eight candidates, Labour Representation

---

[1] The present writer was present at a lecture delivered by Mr. Henry George at Oxford in 1884, and well remembers the sensation caused by the exposure of Mr. George's ' nostrum ' by Professor Alfred Marshall and other economists.

wholly independent of the existing Parties, were nominated, and two of their number, as already indicated,[1] secured election.

One of them, James Keir Hardie, the Scottish miner, was mainly responsible for the foundation of the Independent Labour Party. The Conference which witnessed the birth of the new Party met in January 1893 at Bradford and was attended by 115 representatives of Trade Unions and socialist societies. Keir Hardie was elected chairman and among other delegates were Tom Mann, Ben Tillett, Robert Smillie, a Scottish miner, Bernard Shaw, who represented the Fabians, and Robert Blatchford, at that time editor of an influential socialist newspaper, *The Clarion*. The new Party was frankly socialist, its avowed object being to provide financial assistance for Parliamentary candidates, pledged to complete independence of existing Parties and to ' secure the collective ownership of all the means of production, distribution and exchange '.

Hitherto ' Labour ' had been content to be, in a Parliamentary sense, the handmaid of Liberalism ; but Liberalism was no longer worthy of such service, and in January 1899 Mr. Keir Hardie contributed to *The Nineteenth Century* an article which made the position admirably clear. He had a collaborator—a young journalist, already well known in the Socialist Party and soon to become the Secretary of the Labour Representation Committee —Mr. James Ramsay MacDonald.

The I.L.P. These writers ascribed the Liberal collapse not to the ' squabbles between leaders, or the secession of independent groups or any similar temporary cause ' but to ' the nature of things '. ' The Liberal Party ', they proceeded, ' has done its work. It was evolved to meet the needs of past generations. Its ideas were derived from a political philosophy and a system of Economics that have become antiquated ; the political application which it made of words of ethical import, such as " right " and " liberty " give no guidance in solving present-day problems ; its purpose was drawn from a political and social state that has gone ; its principles of propaganda, the sentiments to which it appealed, the individual characteristics to which it was congenial, stand no longer in the forefront of progressive forces. The national life has moved on, and has corrected, narrowing at this point and

[1] *Supra,* p. 159.

widening at that, our conceptions of political methods and social aims. . . . Liberalism, occupying the successful business man's standpoint, had generally assumed that the man politically en-franchised would be economically free; but experience was proving that that hope was thoroughly false, and Liberalism had nothing to put in its place.'

The last few years had witnessed ' the final closing of a well-defined epoch in political progress and the opening of a new chapter, which is to show the operation of social principles differ-ing very materially from those of the Liberal Party '. Arguing from these premises the writers concluded that the time had come for the formation of a new Party, and they proceeded to formu-late a programme for it. The House of Lords must be abolished : a ' Second Chamber is always useless and is frequently dangerous '. Parliaments must be triennial; members must be paid ; the franchise extended to all adults of both sexes, and the powers of Local Authorities must be widely extended. On the economic side the writers advocated a legal eight-hours day, the substitu-tion of public for private ownership and enterprise, ' production for use not profit ', the abolition of the ' land monopoly ' by the taxation of ground rents, the provision of old-age pensions by a special tax on the swollen incomes of the rich ; and, finally, a revolution in the educational system of the country.

The article thus summarized was of special importance in view of the practical steps which quickly followed on its pub-lication.

The Trade Union Congress of 1899 resolved, albeit in the teeth of strong opposition from two important Unions, the textile workers and the miners, to summon a special Conference ' to devise means of increasing the number of Labour members '. From that Conference (February 1900) Mr. Ramsay MacDonald dates the birth of the ' Labour Party '. One hundred and twenty delegates were present, representing the Trade Unions, the trades councils, and various socialist organizations. Of working-class organizations only the Co-operators held aloof. The Fabian Society was represented by Mr. Bernard Shaw and Mr. E. R. Pease—the chronicler of the Society [1]—and the Independent Labour Party by Mr. MacDonald and Mr. Keir Hardie. A Labour

[1] *The History of the Fabian Society* (1916).

Representation Committee was appointed, with the object of
establishing a distinct Labour group in Parliament with its own
Whips, and its own policy, but ready to co-operate with any
Party which ' for the time being may be engaged in legislation
in the direct interest of Labour '. Of this Committee Mr. Mac-
Donald was appointed secretary. His feet were on the first rung
of the political ladder by which he was to climb to the Premiership. His Committee had, however, a hard struggle to maintain
its existence. Only about 5 per cent. of the Trade Unions affiliated themselves to it, the Social Democratic Federation quickly
withdrew from it, the attitude of the Fabians towards it was more
than cool, the miners were definitely hostile, and continued to
run their own Liberal-Labour candidates. At the General Election of 1900 the new Committee ran fifteen candidates, but Keir
Hardie returned to the House with only a single colleague.

It looked as though the new movement, like many of its predecessors, might fizzle out, when there occurred an industrial
dispute destined to make history.

The Taff
Vale Case
In August 1900, while the South African War was in progress,
a strike occurred on the Taff Vale Railway, a short line in South
Wales, important only because it carried much of the coal required for the Royal Navy. The immediate occasion of the
strike was the dismissal of a signalman, and the refusal of the
Company to allow the officials of the Union to represent their
employés when the dispute occurred. The strike was promptly
settled, but the Company claimed damages against the Secretary
of the Amalgamated Society of Railway Servants, who had intervened in the dispute. Mr. Justice Farwell, a judge of the High
Court, gave judgement against the Society on the ground that
the Act of 1875 did not put the Trade Unions in the position of
' bodies capable of owning great wealth and of acting by agents,
with absolutely no responsibility for the wrongs that they may
do to other persons by the use of that wealth and the employment of those agents '. The case was taken to the Court of
Appeal which reversed the judgement of Mr. Justice Farwell,
but it was upheld in the House of Lords. The Amalgamated
Society had to pay £23,000 damages, and an almost equal amount
in costs.

The decision of the Supreme Court of appellate jurisdiction, stated in non-technical language, was that the legislation of 1871–6, which was supposed to have conferred complete immunity upon Trade Unions, did not in fact extend to damages obtainable in a civil action, and that a Trade Union was still liable to an injunction, and to the payment of damages for acts of violence committed or threatened in its behalf.   Thus were Trade Unions declared liable for wrongs done by their agents.   The decision came as a surprise to the public, and to Trade Unionists caused nothing less than consternation.   Yet, after all, Trade Unions were at that time much more important to workmen as benefit societies than they were as militant organizations.   During the decade 1895–1904 the total expenditure of 100 of the most important Unions amounted to £16,060,000.   Of this 86 per cent. was expended on benefits of various kinds ; only 14 per cent. on militant objects. Prejudice was imported into the case by the fact that the final decision on points of law rests with a tribunal, which, though exclusively judicial in composition, is known as ' the House of Lords '.   The decision was in some quarters denounced as ' political '.   Yet an ardent friend of Labour, Professor Geldart, has left it on record that in his opinion ' no fair-minded person can dispute the substantial justice of the Taff Vale decision '.   So strongly, however, was feeling aroused, that in 1903 another Royal Commission was appointed, under the chairmanship of Lord Dunedin, to inquire into the subject of trade disputes and combinations and as to the law affecting them, and to report on the law applicable to the same, and the effect of any modification thereof.

The Commission produced two Reports.   The majority was opposed to any alteration of the law as laid down in the Taff Vale judgement, but recommended an alteration in the law relating to picketing and conspiracy.   The Government, fresh from a notable victory at the polls, and confronted by the new phenomenon of an independent ' Labour ' Party in the House of Commons, promptly introduced a Trade Disputes Bill.   The Bill covered four branches of the subject—conspiracy, picketing, trade interference apart from conspiracy and ' agency '.   There remained the question whether actions of tort against Trade Unions should be prohibited.   As originally introduced the Bill provided that a Union was not to be held liable for the wrongful act of its

Trade Disputes Act, 1906

agent, unless the act had been formally approved by the executive committee of the Union, or had been done by a person or persons specifically authorized to bind the Union by the conduct impugned. The Bill was not wholly approved by the Labour members, who, two days after the first reading of the Government Bill, introduced a Bill of their own, which relieved the Unions of all liability for damages sustained through the conduct of their members. The difference between the two Bills was pithily expressed by Mr. Keir Hardie, who declared that Trade Unionists would not be satisfied with mere barbed-wire entanglements for the protection of their funds, but would insist on their removal out of the range of the enemies' guns. Then arose a curious and complicated parliamentary situation. The Prime Minister, Sir Henry Campbell-Bannerman, not only voted but spoke in favour of the Labour Bill, the second reading of which was carried by 416 to 66. The essential point was compromised in favour of the Labour view, and the Government Bill, so amended, passed into law as the *Trade Disputes Act* of 1906.

The first section of the Act extended to civil responsibility for conspiracy the immunity from criminal prosecution conferred by the *Conspiracy and Protection of Property Act* of 1876. Henceforward ' an act done in pursuance of an agreement or combination by two or more persons ' was not to be actionable ' if done in contemplation or furtherance of a trade dispute . . . unless the act, if done without any such agreement or combination, would be actionable '. The second section legalized peaceful picketing : it declared it to be lawful for one or more persons, acting on their own behalf or on behalf of a Trade Union or of an individual employer or firm ' in contemplation or furtherance of a trade dispute, to attend at or near a house or place where a person resides or works or carries on business or happens to be, if they so attend merely for the purpose of peacefully obtaining or communicating information, or of peacefully persuading any person to work or abstain from working '. The third section removed the liability for interfering with another person's business, or ' with the right of some other person to dispose of his capital or his labour as he wills '. But again the act thus protected by the law must be ' in contemplation or furtherance of a trade dispute '. Even so, most sound lawyers, to whatever party they might belong, have concurred in describing the immunity as ' indefensible '. It was, however, around the terms of the fourth section that controversy raged, and continued to rage most hotly. The first three sections were of general applicability ; though evidently intended primarily for the protection of Trade Unions. The fourth section, which exempted Trade Unions from all actions for tort, undeniably conferred a special and exclusive privilege upon such associations. Few unbiased people could now be found to defend such a privilege. Lord Halsbury denounced the whole Bill as one ' for legalizing tyranny and for the purpose of taking people outside the ordinary courts of law '. Lord James of Hereford, a great Liberal lawyer, was moved to wrath by section 4. ' Simply register yourselves as a Trade Union ; whatever wrong you may inflict, whatever destruction of property may be caused, we the Legislature give our blessing to go forth and do it.' If it be true that the expedient of a criminal prosecution of the guilty individuals is, as good lawyers have argued, left entirely untouched by the Act of 1906, the language of Lord James may sound extravagant ; but subsequent events convinced the majority of thinking people that the exceptional privilege conferred by section 4 of the Act of 1906 would need to be curtailed, if not entirely abrogated, not less in the interests of the Trade Unions themselves than in that of the community at large.

For the moment, however, the Legislature had intervened, not to reverse the decision in the Taff Vale Case—that even an omnipotent Parliament cannot do—but to restore to the Trade Unions the privileges of which that decision had in effect deprived them. The decision had, however, done more than that. It had created the Parliamentary Labour Party. In 1900 the new Party could, out of fifteen candidates, secure the return of only two members. At the General Election of 1906 it ran fifty candidates and returned twenty-nine of them. Nor did this measure the real strength of ' Labour ' in the new Parliament. In addition to the independent Labour representatives there were some twenty Trade Unionists who, though accepting the Liberal Whip, were generally to be found in the lobby with their new allies. Moreover, Labour was for the first time represented in the Cabinet in the person of Mr. John Burns, who in 1906 became President of the Local Government Board. A more level-headed and efficient President the Local Government Board never had, but he did not, as a Minister, endear himself to his former colleagues.

The Osborne Case

Nor was John Burns the only lion in the path of the Parliamentary Labour Party. In the Osborne judgement they encountered another. Once again the Trade Unions found themselves up against the law of the land. But between the Taff Vale Case and the Osborne Case there was a world of difference. It was as industrial organizations that the Trade Unions had been hampered by the judgement in the former case ; the Osborne judgement dealt a shattering blow at their political activities.

Mr. W. V. Osborne was the Secretary of the Walthamstow branch of the Amalgamated Society of Railway Servants. Like many other Trade Unionists, Liberals as well as Conservatives, he resented the capture of the Unions by the new Socialist Party. In particular he resisted the diversion of funds, subscribed by him and others for industrial and benefit purposes, to the support of members returned to Parliament to advocate views opposed to their own. Both his own Society and the Labour Party (as from 1906 it began to be called) had in 1906 amended their rules.

Rule XIII, Section IV, of the A.S.R.S. ran as follows :—

' 1. For the maintenance of Parliamentary representation a fund shall be established by the Society. The subscription to be 1s. 1d. per year, per member, to be paid quarterly, and forwarded to the head office with the quarter's dues.

' 2. The objects of the fund shall be (a) to provide for representation of railwaymen in the House of Commons, as the annual general meeting may from time to time determine. *All candidates shall sign and accept the conditions of the Labour Party and be subject to their Whip.*

' (b) To contribute to the Labour Representation Committee such sums as the Executive Committee or the annual general meeting may from time to time direct, so long as the Society remains affiliated to such Committee.'

To Mr. Osborne and many like him these rules appeared to involve a gross infringement of individual liberty. But the price of resistance was heavy. ' Many who refused to submit to this political thraldom was driven out of membership, with loss of contributions and benefits. After a life's savings were lost, and in time of distress, nothing stood between the victim and the workhouse.'[1]

Mr. Osborne, supported by the Walthamstow Branch of the A.S.R.S., decided to move for an injunction to restrain the Society from distributing money under the Rule XIII, Section IV. Judgement was given in the Chancery Court against him, Mr. Justice Neville holding that the Rule was not *ultra vires*. The Court of Appeal overruled the decision of the Court below, and the House of Lords, to which the A.S.R.S. carried an appeal, dismissed it. The judgement was unanimous.

Mr. Osborne had won a great victory, but the A.S.R.S. retorted by expelling him from the Society, and closing the Walthamstow Branch, of which he was Secretary.

Once more Osborne appealed to the Courts, claiming a declaration that the resolution of the Executive Committee expelling him was *ultra vires* and void. But the Court of Chancery held that the action could not lie, as the Society was an illegal organization (a point taken by the Defendants). Osborne appealed. The Court of Appeal allowed the appeal with costs in both Courts. Finally it was announced that further litigation was stayed. The case had already cost the A.S.R.S. over £11,000.

Following upon this judgement numerous injunctions were granted to Trade Unions to prevent expenditure on political objects.

Once more the Judiciary had spread consternation among Trade Unionists and their political allies ; once more the Legislature intervened on behalf of Trade Unions, or rather on behalf of the socialist members of those Societies. The Liberal Party was no longer independent of its allies. Its own representation was reduced by the two Elections of 1910 from 400 to 272 ; the Conservatives numbered 271 ; the Nationalist members remained constant at 84 ; but in December 1910 the Labour Party, though depleted funds had compelled them to restrict their candidates to 56, returned 42 of them. Plainly Mr. Asquith's Government could continue to hold office only on the sufferance of Nationalists and Socialists. Accordingly, in order to meet the immediate difficulties of working-class members, the House of Commons, on

Payment of Members and the Political Levy Act

[1] Osborne, *My Case* (1910).

August 10, 1911, passed a resolution for the payment of a salary
of £400 a year to all members. On more than one account
August 10, 1911, was a memorable day in the history of the British
Parliament. On that day the House of Lords passed the Parliament Bill.

Two years later, Parliament passed the Trade Union Act of
1913—popularly known as the Political Levy Act. By that Act
a Trade Union, so long as its principal objects are those of a Trade
Union as defined by the Act of 1876, is entitled to ' apply the
funds of the Union for any lawful objects or purposes for the time
being authorized under its constitution ' (section 1 (i)). The Act
contained a very wide specification (section 3 (iii)) of political
objects to which a Union might contribute, including the expenses
of candidates for Parliament or local bodies, and the maintenance
of members of such bodies, the holding of political meetings, the
distribution of political literature, and so forth. But such activities could not be undertaken until approval was obtained by a
ballot of the members. All payments were to be made out of a
separate political fund, and any member was to be entitled to
claim exemption from contributions to that fund. Contribution
to the fund was not to be made a condition for admission to the
Union, nor was any exempted member to be excluded from any
benefits of the Union, or ' placed in any respect, either directly or
indirectly, under any disability or at any disadvantage as compared with other members of the union (except in relation to the
control or management of the political fund) by reason of his
being so exempt ' (section 3 (i) (b)).

The Act of 1913 was admittedly a compromise. It sought to
secure to Trade Unions the right to embark upon political activities, and at the same time to secure the right of their individual
members to withhold support from Parties or principles to which
they were opposed, without penalizing their position as wage-
earners or sacrificing benefits to which their subscriptions entitled
them. Parliament had conceded to Trade Unions a position of
privilege. It was plainly bound to insist that these privileges
should not be monopolized by the adherents of any one political
Party. In order to effect that object, it adopted the device of
' contracting out '. But the machinery worked badly. The safeguards provided in the Act of 1913 proved illusory.

Apart from litigation and legislation in respect of Trade Unions the early years of the twentieth century were marked not only by continuous unrest among the wage-earners, but by many trade disputes, not infrequently accompanied by violence.

Railways constitute, from every point of view, a ' key ' indus- try.   A stoppage on the railways means a serious dislocation of the whole economic life of the nation.   The capital by which British railways have been constructed and are maintained has been subscribed by small investors, who exceed in number the wage-earners, and the return on their capital is small and precari- ous.   On the other hand, the wage-earners enjoy the advantages of a sheltered industry, with many substantial benefits, little fear of unemployment, and in many cases the opportunity of supple- menting regular earnings from other sources.   Yet, from 1906 onwards, there has been much agitation among them and more than one grave conflict.

A special conference of the Amalgamated Society was held at Birmingham in November 1906 and demanded a shortening of hours ; a nine hours' rest between jobs ; special pay for overtime and Sunday duty, and a ' guaranteed week '.   These demands were submitted by the secretary of the Society to the Railway Companies, who declined to negotiate except with their own employés.   A strike was threatened, but Mr. Lloyd George who, in 1905, had become President of the Board of Trade, adroitly intervened, and brought about an agreement which resulted in the setting up of Joint Conciliation Boards for each Company. The scheme did not, however, work smoothly, and the evil day was merely postponed.

There was unrest also in the cotton industry.   On both sides the organization in that industry has been exceptionally effective, and particularly since the conclusion in 1893 of a treaty known as the ' Brooklands Agreement '.   That agreement provided machin- ery for the settlement of disputes which has, on the whole, worked exceedingly well.   In 1907, however, a dispute arose on a question of ' demarcation ' which was only settled by the tact of Sir George (now Lord) Askwith, acting for the Board of Trade under the Conciliation Act of 1896.   Yet there was another dispute, result- ing in a strike or lock-out, in the autumn of 1910, a period which was marked also by a stoppage in the shipbuilding industry and a serious strike, accompanied by grave disorder, in the South Wales coal-field.

Coal There was worse to come. The years 1911–12, already described as critical in international relations, were critical also in our own industrial history. Early in the year there was renewed disorder in the Welsh coal-field, and an ' unauthorized ' strike on the North-Eastern Railway, arising from the dismissal of an engine-driver who had been convicted of drunkenness. In June there was a strike organized by the National Sailors' and Firemen's Union, and in July the London dockers struck in support of the seamen, and remained out after the latter had returned to work. The carters and vanmen also joined in the fray, and so serious did the situation become at Manchester that troops had to be dispatched from York and the local police to be reinforced from London.

Even more serious was the strike of the railwaymen. The trouble began with disputes about the working of the Conciliation Boards set up after the strike of 1907. There were local strikes in various parts of the country, two men were killed at Llanelly, and there was loss of life and much injury to persons and property at Liverpool. But these were only a foretaste of what was to come. On August 15, 1911, the Amalgamated Society, acting in conjunction with two smaller Societies, the Railway Clerks' Association and the Locomotive Engineers and Firemen, demanded that the Companies should meet the Trade Union officials to discuss a revision of the Conciliation Scheme. The Companies took up their usual attitude : with their own employés they were always willing to discuss grievances ; outside officials they declined to meet. A general strike on all the railways was declared on August 17, but the response was not universal ; the Government intervened and promised a Royal Commission : on the 19th the men returned to work.

But although of short duration the railway strike of 1911 was marked by two features of special significance. For the first time the three railway Unions acted together and presented a united front to their employers ; for the first time a general strike in a key industry was planned to coincide with a crisis in international relations which brought this country, nay, the whole of Europe, to the brink of war.

Yet the railway strike of 1911 sinks into insignificance as compared with the great coal strike which dislocated the whole industrial life of the nation in the spring of 1912. For many years past there had been profound unrest among the colliers : it came to a head in connexion with the question of a minimum wage, and issued in a strike which lasted from February 26 to April 11, 1912. So grave was the situation that the Prime Minister (Mr. Asquith) was constrained to step in, and the disputants were only brought into agreement after action of unprecedented significance on the part of Parliament. Having laid before owners and men a well-considered scheme, Asquith announced that the Government would embody it in a Bill, and virtually compel acceptance by the strong hand of the law. The Minimum Wage Bill was introduced on March 19, passed through all its stages in ten days and received the Royal Assent on March 29. It was a bold stroke, and it succeeded.

Other disputes, of which there were plenty in the next few years, sink into comparative insignificance as compared with the gigantic upheaval, involving a loss of 30,000,000 working days, of 1912.

So serious an epidemic of labour disputes seemed to suggest the presence of a microbe poisoning the life-blood of the body politic.

There had been circulated privately in 1912 a pamphlet, entitled *The Miners' Next Step*.[1] It emanated from South Wales, where in the previous year a campaign had been conducted by one William D. Haywood, an American agitator, who in 1905 had founded an organization known as the *Industrial Workers of the World* (I.W.W.). Another stormy petrel had also recently reappeared—Tom Mann, whose activities in connexion with the Dock Strike of 1889 have been already noticed. In 1908 he returned from Australia, where for five or six years he had acted as organizer of the Victoria Labour Party. Mann had become deeply imbued with the principles of Syndicalism, a social philosophy of Gallic origin.

Syndicalism is in essence the antithesis both of Democracy and Socialism : the negation of the centralized action of the State. Socialism demands the nationalization of all the instru-

Coal Strike, 1912

Syndicalism and Socialism

---

[1] A copy is still (1941) in my possession.

ments of production; of all the machinery of distribution, exchange, locomotion and transport. The State, being the sole owner of the soil, of all mines and minerals, of all fixed and circulating capital, becomes the sole employer of labour. All the economic and industrial functions are to be performed by a vast civil service directed by a multitude of State officials.

To all this the Syndicalist is diametrically opposed. He regards the authority and interference of the centralizing State with an abhorrence, not less genuine than that exhibited by the old-fashioned individualist. Of representative government and of parliamentary action he is frankly mistrustful. The ' democracy ' in which he believes is direct. This involves the elimination of the ' representative ' if not of the ' delegate '. On these points *The Miners' Next Step* is illuminating.

' Democracy ', we read, ' becomes impossible when officials and leaders dominate. For this reason they are excluded from all power on the Executive, which becomes a purely administrative body, composed of men directly elected by the men for that purpose. *Agents or organizers* become the servants of the men, directly under the control of the Executive and indirectly under the control of the men.'

Conformably with these principles the proposed *Constitution* ordains

' (vi) No agent or other permanent official of the Federation shall be eligible to a seat on the Executive Council. . . . (xi) Any agent who may be returned to Parliament shall be required to relinquish his industrial duties and position. (xii) No Member of Parliament shall be eligible to seek for or retain a seat on a Local or National Executive Council. . . . (xiv) On all proposed Labour legislation conferences shall be called to discuss same and instruct our M.P.'s. (xv) Any Member of Parliament, as such under the auspices of the organization, shall at once vacate his seat if a ballot vote of the membership so decides ' (pp. 21, 22).

Syndicalism, then, would make the workmen in each industrial group politically and economically supreme, and ultimately combine these groups into one vast working-class organization. But it must start with each particular industry. ' An ideal organization ', writes Tom Mann, ' would be to get all the workers employed in any one industry to join into one union of that particular industry, be they carpenters or blacksmiths, boilermakers or upholsterers, engineers or labourers, skilled or unskilled, cigar makers or shop assistants, railway porters or booking-clerks.' [1]

These working-class syndicates would prepare the way for the Syndicalist kingdom which is to come by paralysing and ruining the existing industrial order. As a means to the desired end there is to be unceasing and relentless economic war. Syndicalists are ' to fight against the employers in order to extract from them, and to their hurt, ever greater ameliorations of the worker's lot, on the way to the complete suppression of " exploitation " '.[2]

The Syndicalist millennium is, then, to be attained by ' direct action '.

Actual bloodshed may be avoided. ' Economic pressure '— *Sabotage*, the destruction of property, *Ca' Canny*—may suffice to attain the end.

As to the nature of this economic pressure *The Miners' Next Step* is again instructive. The ultimate object is ' the taking over of all industries, by the workmen themselves ' (p. 19), and among the immediate steps with a view to that end are : (i) a minimum wage of eight shillings per day for all workmen employed in or about the mines ; (ii) a seven-hour day (p. 18). Chapter V, devoted to a summary of *Policy*, advises :

' (xiii) That a continual agitation be carried on in favour of increasing the minimum wage, and shortening the hours of work, until we have extracted the whole of the employers' profits ' (p. 26).

' (xiv) That our objective be, to build up an organization that will ultimately take over the mining industry, and carry it on in the interest of the workers ' (p. 26). The elimination of the employer ' can only be accomplished gradually and in one way. We cannot get rid of employers and slave driving in the mining industry until all other industries have organized for, and progress towards, the same objective ' (pp. 28, 29).

To nationalization as a solution of the industrial problem the Syndicalist is strongly opposed. It would merely substitute a

---

[1] Quoted by Mr. and Mrs. Webb, *What Syndicalism Means*, p. 7.
[2] Victor Griffuelhes, *L'Action Syndicaliste*, p. 12.

Government Department for the employer, and the last state of the manual worker would be worse than the first.

It may well be, as Mr. MacDonald declared in 1912, that ' Syndicalism in England is negligible both as a school of thought and as an organization '.[1] The pure milk of French philosophy needs much dilution before it is palatable to English consumers. Organized labour, by the vote of its representative Congress, pronounced an equally emphatic repudiation of Syndicalist doctrine. The ultimate objective of Syndicalism is indeed poles asunder from that of State Socialism. None the less, the two *isms* travelled along the same road for a considerable distance before discovering that their paths must presently diverge. Nor can it be denied that both movements derived their strength from conditions, industrial and social, which called for serious investigation. The microbe which was infecting Society and producing epidemic disease was not purely economic. It was not, with the younger workmen, a question merely of wages, or hours, and the like. In an electoral sense they were the equals of their employers ; they had been endowed with the full status of a citizen ; they were getting more and more education ; too much, perhaps, unless they were to get more. But industry remained autocratic in a democratic State ; the world-wide extension of commerce demanded higher and higher skill in the directors of big businesses ; in the sphere of Government things might, in those pre-War days, be tending towards Democracy, in that of industry they were tending to Dictatorship. Yet the wage-earner could not but contrast his status as a citizen with his status as a workman. The contrast generated that spirit of unrest which issued in industrial strife. The solution could not, at the moment, be found, nor even sought. Before the clash of interests could be reconciled the whole world was involved in the clash of arms.

[1] *Syndicalism*, p. 39.

CHAPTER XIV

THE NEW LIBERALISM

AFTER two parenthetical chapters we return to the point reached at the close of Chapter XI.

On the resignation of Mr. Balfour King Edward promptly entrusted the formation of a new Ministry to Sir Henry Campbell-Bannerman, who since 1899 had led the Liberal Party in the House of Commons. King Edward and Sir Henry had foregathered at Marienbad in the preceding August, and the King had seized the opportunity to improve acquaintance with a man to whom he was instinctively drawn. ' He has been extremely friendly ', wrote the future Prime Minister to a colleague and ' expressed his satisfaction at having the chance of a frank conversation on things abroad and at home as I must soon be in office and very high office '.

The King's prescience was not at fault. On December 5 Campbell-Bannerman accepted office as Prime Minister and First Lord of the Treasury.

The younger son of James Campbell, a wealthy business man in Glasgow, the future Prime Minister was born in that city in 1836. He was, therefore, in his seventieth year when he formed his Government. Educated at Glasgow and Cambridge Universities, he was for ten years a partner in the family business : but in 1868 he entered the House of Commons as Member for the Stirling Burghs, a seat which he retained until his death in 1908. After serving in minor offices he became Chief Secretary to the Lord-Lieutenant of Ireland in 1884, in succession to Sir George Trevelyan, and for eight months (according to Tim Healy) he ' governed Ireland with Scotch jokes '. In 1886 he entered the Cabinet as Secretary of State for War, an office which he again filled under Gladstone and Rosebery from 1892 to 1895.

Sir H. Camp-bell-Banner-man

Liberal disunion

Thenceforward, for more than ten years, the Liberal Party, rent by dissensions political and personal, was out of office. Lord Rosebery resigned the leadership of the Party in 1896, and presently formed with Asquith, Sir Edward Grey, Haldane and others, a group of Liberal Imperialists who were less remote in opinion from the Unionists than from the ' orthodox ' Liberals. Sir William Harcourt withdrew in disgust from the leadership of the Party in the House of Commons in December 1898, and a month later Mr. John Morley declared that ' he, too, could no longer take an active and responsible part in the formal councils of the heads of the Liberal Party '. Harcourt's death in 1904, following that of Lord Kimberley in 1902, combined with Lord Spencer's serious illness (1905) to clear the path for the man who, in the darkest hour of Liberalism (1899), had been chosen as leader of the Party in the House of Commons.

The Campbell-Bannerman Ministry

Campbell-Bannerman had no difficulty in forming a strong Government, save in respect of the key position of Foreign Secretary. Lord Rosebery being out of the question, Grey's adhesion as Foreign Secretary was essential to the success, if not the formation, of the new Ministry. But for several days Grey held back. Failing a Rosebery or an Asquith Premiership, Grey insisted that Campbell-Bannerman should go to the House of Lords, and that Asquith should lead the House of Commons. Campbell-Bannerman, conscious that his health was failing, and sternly warned by his German doctor, Dr. Ott, was not wholly disinclined to that course. The King himself approved and indeed suggested it. Asquith and Haldane agreed with Grey, though not as an absolute condition of adhesion. Lady Campbell-Bannerman, on the contrary, flouted the idea of surrender to the dictation of the ' rebels '. Her voice was decisive. The new Prime Minister refused Grey's terms. Grey gave way, and at the last minute of the eleventh hour consented to take office. In retrospect he confessed that the difficulties he had raised had been ' unnecessary '. ' Things ', he wrote, ' went well enough as they were, and the differences and divisions of opinion that had existed when the Party was in opposition never reappeared. Campbell-Bannerman's own personality contributed greatly to this result.' [1]

Haldane hoped to become Chancellor, but had ' definitely

[1] *Twenty-five Years,* I. 65–6.

decided that under no circumstances would [he] enter [the Government] without [Grey].' [1] Asquith pressed Haldane's claims to the Chancellorship upon the Prime Minister, but in vain ; that office being assigned to Sir Robert Reid (afterwards Lord Loreburn), who had served as Attorney-General under Lord Rosebery and like his Chief was a Scot of stout Radical opinions. Campbell-Bannerman (September 7) offered the Attorney-Generalship to Haldane, who refused it, but, having persuaded Grey to go in with him, accepted the War Office. The Premier did not like Haldane and chuckled about his choice : ' We shall now see how Schopenhauer gets on in the kail-yard'. Closer contact, however, brought mutual understanding. ' When one did succeed in securing his confidence ', wrote Haldane in retrospect, ' there were few better chiefs to work for than Sir H. C.-B.' [2]

Unlike his two friends Asquith made no difficulty about entering the Government as Chancellor of the Exchequer, though like them he urged Campbell-Bannerman to go to the Lords. The Earl of Elgin (Colonial Secretary), Sir Henry Fowler (Duchy of Lancaster) and Lord Ripon (Lord Privy Seal), with Mr. John Morley (India Office), represented ripe official experience ; and of the other appointments the most interesting were those of Mr. Augustine Birrell, a brilliant man of letters, who went to the Board of Education, and Mr. Lloyd George (Board of Trade). Mr. John Burns, the first Labour member to attain Cabinet rank, became President of the Local Government Board, where, to the disgust of his Labour friends, he proved himself an exceptionally strong administrator. Mr. James (afterwards Viscount) Bryce entered the Cabinet as Chief Secretary for Ireland, an office for which he had few qualifications. He exchanged it, early in 1907, for that of Ambassador at Washington, where his great talents had full scope.

Out of the nineteen members of the new Cabinet, no fewer than twelve were new to Cabinet office, and five had never held office at all. Yet the team proved a strong one. Among the junior members of the Government were several promising ' youngsters ', such as Winston Churchill, Reginald McKenna, Walter Runciman, Herbert Samuel, and Freeman Thomas, destined to reign at Ottawa and at Delhi as Lord Willingdon.

---

[1] Haldane, *Autobiography*, p. 180.   Ibid., p. 182.

Lord Edmund Fitzmaurice returned as Under-Secretary to the Foreign Office, where he had served under Lord Granville from 1882–5. A fine scholar and a brilliant biographer he had, like his elder brother Lord Lansdowne, an hereditary aptitude for diplomacy, and his willingness to serve, if only for a short time, under Sir Edward Grey accorded with the best traditions of public service and aristocratic obligation.[1]

General Election, Jan. 1906

The new Premier, having formed his Ministry, immediately asked the King for a Dissolution. Mr. Balfour's decision to put his opponents in office before a Dissolution was regarded both by them and by his friends as characteristically clever. The result proved that brilliant tactics are not synonymous with good policy. Had Balfour dissolved instead of resigning, the result might have been better for the Unionist Party—it could hardly have been worse. The main issue submitted to the electors was that of Free Trade v. Tariff Reform, but the bitter feelings aroused among Nonconformists by the Education Act of 1902 were exploited to the full, and great play was also made with the cry of ' Chinese Slavery ', in allusion not quite ingenuous, to the introduction of a number of Chinese labourers into the South African mines, under the Chinese Labour Convention (1904). The Unionist Party, hopelessly divided on the Tariff question, was smitten hip and thigh. Birmingham remained staunch in its allegiance to Chamberlain, but Arthur Balfour and his brother Gerald, Mr. Brodrick, Mr. Walter Long, Mr. Lyttelton, Lord Stanley, Mr. Bonar Law—besides Sir William Hart-Dyke and Mr. Chaplin— lost their seats, and the Unionist Party as a whole was reduced to 157 members, of whom 132 were Conservatives. Opposed to them were 377 Liberals and 83 Irish Nationalists, but the new political portent was the return of 53 ' Labour ' members, of whom 29 were nominees of the Labour Representation Committee, and pledged to act as an independent party. The remaining 24 were returned as Liberal-Labour members and accepted the Liberal Whip. Only one ' Labour ' member, Mr. John Burns, found a place in the Cabinet, but the appearance in such strength of a Socialist Party could hardly fail to colour the legislation even of a Liberal Government returned on the issue of *laisser-faire*. To

[1] In 1906 he went to the House of Lords and in 1908 became Chancellor of the Duchy of Lancaster.

placate the right wing of Liberalism, the Irish question had been tacitly dropped—for the moment. The production (1907) of a measure of ' Devolution ' soothed the consciences of the English Home Rulers ; its rejection by a Nationalist Council in Dublin grieved nobody. Mr. Birrell, who succeeded Bryce as Chief Secretary in January 1907, had, however, the satisfaction (1908) of establishing a really adequate and efficient Roman Catholic University in Ireland. The problem had baffled many previous efforts ; its solution removed an ancient and genuine grievance.

An overwhelming majority does not necessarily make things easier for the Government it sustains. But it was soon made manifest that his electoral triumph had made a new man of the Prime Minister. The misgivings of the Liberal Imperialists were entirely dissipated in the first weeks of the new Parliament. Campbell-Bannerman proved himself more than a match for the decimated Front Bench opposed to him—even after it was rein-forced by the return of Mr. Balfour for whom the City of London promptly provided a seat. *The New Parliament*

Yet the new House was not an easy one to lead. It con-tained an exceptional proportion not only of men who were new to Parliamentary life (many of whom had stood without any expectation of being returned, and were somewhat embarrassed by their success) but also of zealots, more anxious for the triumph of some special ' cause ' than for that of Liberalism in the abstract. But Campbell-Bannerman's leadership evoked general admira-tion : he was at once firm and genial ; while the Opposition soon realized that the master of the big battalions would stand no ' foolery ' from a minority contemptible in numbers, and not conspicuous in individual ability.

Yet the Opposition was pertinacious, and the legislative path of the Government was not smooth. The King's Speech, as was under the circumstances natural, was a lengthy one and fore-shadowed great activity in legislation. The first place among Bills proposed to Parliament was assigned to one for amending at the earliest possible moment the existing law with regard to education in England and Wales.

The Education Act of 1902 had undoubtedly aroused great bitterness among the Nonconformists who were largely responsible for the great Liberal majority of 1906. Liberal Unionist leaders *Elemen-tary Educa-tion* had predicted the débâcle of their Party. To the Duke of Devonshire Mr. Chamberlain wrote (2 September, 1902): ' I told you that your Education Bill would destroy your own Party. It has done so. Our best friends are leaving us by scores and hundreds and they will not come back. . . . I wonder how much mischief the Opposition will be able to do when they at last seize the opportunity which we have so generously presented to them.'

They seized it to some purpose at the election of 1906, and on April 9 Mr. Birrell introduced a Bill intended to redeem the pledges given to the electorate. [1]

Mr. Birrell, though he came, like most of the Radical leaders, of Puritan stock, was no fanatic, but there were many fanatics on the benches behind him, and some—of a different hue—on the benches opposite. As to the root of the problem he had to face he was under no illusion : it bore ' the ill-omened name of the religious difficulty '. ' I know full well ', he added, ' that you have all come here expecting for to see a reed shaken by the wind, quivering, and trembling in [the] icy and unfeeling blasts of sectarian bitterness.'

His Bill was a drastic one. It proposed that all the elementary schools receiving aid from rates or taxes should be controlled and maintained by the Local Education Authorities as ' Provided ' Schools. In voluntary schools transferred to the Local Authorities denominational teaching was, if desired by the parents, to be given on two days a week, but not by the regular teachers, all of whom were to be appointed, without any religious tests, by the Authorities. In towns and populous places denominational schools might, on the demand of four-fifths of the parents of the children attending the school, continue to receive aid from the rates. The Bill contained many other proposals, but it was around these that controversy raged most hotly. The Bill passed its Second Reading by 410 votes to 204 on May 10, but encountered very rough weather in Committee, and only emerged after it had been closured by compartments. It was not, however, greatly modified in Committee and on July 30 passed its Third Reading by 369 votes to 177.

The Bill was drastically amended in the Lords ; the Commons rejected the Lords' Amendments *en bloc* ; the Lords insisted on them, and on December 20 the Bill was withdrawn.

[1] See note, p. 260.

The Government made two further attempts to deal with the problem in the session of 1908. The first was made by Mr. McKenna, who in January 1908 had succeeded to the Board of Education ; but the Bill calls for no detailed description since after a Second Reading it was withdrawn. Men of goodwill, both in and out of Parliament, were in fact working hard to find a basis of agreement and so solve a difficulty which to many of them seemed to be anything but religious. More particularly was Mr. Walter Runciman, who in April had replaced McKenna, in close consultation with the Archbishop of Canterbury (Dr. Davidson).

As a result Mr. Runciman, moving the Second Reading of Bill No. 2 of 1908, was able to announce (November 25) that there appeared to be general agreement on three points : the undesirability of a purely secular system ; the great value of simple Bible teaching, and the possibility, while safeguarding principles, of adjusting differences. He accordingly proposed that only Provided Schools should receive aid from local rates, that in them there should be no tests for teachers, but that in every school the first forty-five minutes of school-time should be devoted to non-denominational religious instruction, attendance at which was for all children to be voluntary. On two days a week the teaching during this hour might be denominational, if desired by the parents, and might be given by assistant-teachers (but not by head teachers) if they volunteered for the duty and were paid by the Denominations. In non-single school areas Voluntary Schools might under certain conditions receive State-aid, but not rate-aid. Voluntary Schools transferred to Local Authorities were to be paid for. The compromise thus outlined broke down on the question of the financial terms to be given to schools which ' contracted out ' of the national agreement, and the Government, therefore, abandoned the Bill before it emerged from Committee.

Mr. Asquith, now Prime Minister, described the breakdown of negotiations as ' the heaviest disappointment of his public life '. But it was not an irremediable disaster. A settlement was reached ten years later in a very different and much more favourable atmosphere. By that time the problem of national education could be seen in better perspective. In 1908 feelings on both sides were bitter and the perspective was hopelessly distorted. The great mass of the nation were in sober earnest well content with things as they were. Difficulties were created on the one side by fanatical doctrinaires, who disapproved of a State endowment for religious teaching, and on the other by certain High Church clergymen in country parishes. These, not content with ' Council ' religious teaching, nor with the limited opportunities for doctrinal teaching offered by Mr. Runciman, wished to have the whole school permeated by a ' Catholic ' atmosphere. In the towns, where there was a choice of schools, this demand was reasonable, and could be conceded. In country parishes, with a single school, it was unfair not only to Nonconformists but to many Churchmen, who preferred the religious instruction as given under the authority of the Councils to that of Anglican priests.

While the religious difficulty remained unsolved two less contentious measures for the benefit of school-children were placed on the Statute Book. Under the Education (Provision of Meals) Act, 1906, Local Authorities were empowered to assist voluntary agencies in the provision of meals for school-children, or even with the consent of the Board, to provide meals themselves. An Act of 1907 arranged for the medical inspection of all school-children and the Board of Education set up a Medical Branch which has done work of incalculable value.

Trade Disputes Act, 1906   Among the factors which contributed to the Liberal-Labour triumph of 1906 the Taff Vale Judgement was hardly inferior in importance to the Balfour Education Act. Accordingly, close on the heels of the Education Bill of 1906 came the Trade Disputes Bill. The scope of this measure has been already described.[1] Its passage through the House of Commons was chiefly remarkable for the surrender of the Prime Minister to the Labour Party. Despite this, the Bill passed its Third Reading without a Division.

Sir Edward Carson had suggested that the vital clause might more simply and more accurately have been drafted thus : ' The King can do no wrong ; neither can Trades Unions.' It was confidently expected, therefore, that the great lawyers in the House of Lords would insist on the amendment if not the rejection of the Bill. But the Conservative leaders had, with rare prescience,

[1] *Supra*, p. 235.

agreed that while the Nonconformists might be safely defied, 'organized labour' must be conciliated. Lord Lansdowne, accordingly, advised his followers to allow the Bill to pass, not indeed on its merits, which he was as little able as Lord Halsbury to discern, but because the Lords ought only to fight ' on favourable ground '. He regarded the Bill ' as conferring dangerous privileges on one class and on one class only . . . privileges fraught with danger to the community and likely to embitter the industrial life of this country ', but he thought it ' useless ' for the Lords to resist the measure.

On similar grounds the Lords assented to a Bill greatly extending the scope of the Acts passed in 1880, 1897 and 1900 imposing upon employers liability for injuries to their employés.

Less fortunate was the fate of the Bill to deprive electors of the right of voting, though qualified by law to do so, in more than one constituency. The Bill, after a somewhat stormy passage through the House of Commons, reached the Upper House only in December (1906). Lord St. Aldwyn (Hicks-Beach) moved an amendment declaring that the Lords ' while willing to consider a complete scheme for reforming the Parliamentary franchise and securing the fair representation of the people ', declined to consider a measure which did ' nothing to remove the most glaring inequalities in the present distribution of electoral power '. Lord Lansdowne agreed that the House of Lords ought to reaffirm a principle, to which they had in the past successfully adhered, that when you deal with the franchise you should deal also with the distribution of seats. The amendment was carried by 143 to 43 votes and the Bill was killed. *Plural Voting Bill*

It was not to be expected that a Government and a Party elated by a recent and remarkable victory at the Polls should accept, without protest, the defeat or emasculation of some of their most cherished legislative projects by the House of Lords. The Prime Minister gave expression to the feelings of his followers when in the House of Commons on December 20 he pronounced the funeral oration over the deceased Education Bill. ' Is the General Election and its result ', he asked, ' to go for nothing ? . . . It is plainly intolerable that a Second Chamber should, while one Party in the State is in power, be its willing servant, and when that Party has received an unmistakable and emphatic *Lords v. Commons* condemnation by the country, the House of Lords should then be able to neutralize, thwart and distort the policy which the electors have approved. . . . But the resources of the British Constitution, the resources of the House of Commons are not exhausted, and I say with conviction that a way must be found, a way will be found, by which the will of the people expressed through their electoral representatives in this House will be made to prevail.' [1]

That declaration was received with great enthusiasm by the Liberal and Labour Parties. Plainly it indicated the opening of a conflict among the gravest and most momentous in the history of the English Constitution.

Army Reform

The parliamentary weather of 1907 was relatively calm as compared with the storms and tumults of the preceding year. The King's Speech referred briefly to the Constitutional Question : ' Serious questions affecting the working of our parliamentary system have arisen from unfortunate differences between the two Houses ' ; a Licensing Bill was foreshadowed, but the Session was, in fact, devoted mainly to the problem of national defence.

The matter was urgent. The Boer War had revealed many deficiencies in Army organization : the Report of the Royal Commission on the War revealed more. Nor were successive Secretaries of State slow to initiate reforms. Scheme had succeeded scheme—but only to disappear. Mr. Brodrick had produced in 1901 a scheme, the object of which was to organize three Army Corps, ready at a moment's notice to take the field, complete with artillery, cavalry, medical and transport service. Each Army Corps was under the Commander who would, if war broke out, command it in the field. Behind the first three Army Corps were three others, equally complete, but only in skeleton, to be filled up, as necessity arose, from the Reserves.

The scheme had more critics than friends, but hardly had it had time to demonstrate either success or failure before Brodrick was succeeded at the War Office (1902) by Mr. Arnold Forster, who, full of ideas, produced in 1904 yet another scheme. Before its details were explained to the House of Commons the War Office itself had been reorganized on lines recommended by a small Committee consisting of Sir George Sydenham Clarke (afterwards

[1] *Hansard*, Dec. 20, 1906, pp. 1739-40.

Lord Sydenham of Combe), Lord Esher and Admiral Sir John Fisher. The Commander-in-Chief was to be superseded by an Army Council constituted on the model of the Board of Admiralty. The Council was to consist of the Secretary of State, the Under-Secretary and Financial Secretary, and four military members. An Inspector-General was to give unity to the four commands (each of which was to form one Army Corps) and a Board of Selection was set up, under the presidency of the Duke of Connaught, to deal with the difficult matter of promotions. The troops of the Aldershot Command were to form a ' striking force ' ready for immediate service. Sir Edward Ward became Secretary to the Army Council and also to the Committee of Imperial Defence.

The latter Committee, after existing as a somewhat nebulous body for ten years, had been reorganized with a small but permanent Secretariat and staff in 1904. The Prime Minister became ex-officio chairman, and the other ordinary members were the Secretaries of State for Foreign Affairs, for the Dominions, for the Colonies, for India, for War and for the Air, the First Lord of the Admiralty, the First Sea Lord, the Chief of the Imperial General Staff, the Chief of the Air Staff, the Directors of the Intelligence Departments of the War Office and the Admiralty and the Chancellor of the Exchequer. The Prime Minister was expressly empowered to call for the attendance of any military or naval officers or of other persons, with administrative experience, whether they hold official positions or not. In particular the advice is sought of representatives of the Dominions. Minutes are taken and preserved and are available for reference by successive Committees. By a convenient arrangement the Secretary of the Cabinet (a new official called into being by the exigencies of the Great War) acts also as Secretary to the Committee of Imperial Defence. The organization of the Committee, in the conduct of which he took great personal interest, was the most important piece of constructive work (always excepting his Education Act of 1902) achieved during his Premiership by Mr. Balfour.[1]

So matters stood when ' Schopenhauer ' was introduced into the ' kale-yard '. He got to work at once. Early in the South

Mr. Haldane

[1] For convenience, this paragraph describes the ultimate, not the original composition of the Committee.

African War a chance meeting with Lord Lansdowne had given
Haldane an opportunity of putting his ideas into practice. ' What
we have been suffering from in the South African War is,' he said,
' among other things, that we have not given proper attention
to our explosives. . . . We ought to do what the French have
done. . . . You ought to appoint the English Berthelot to be
Chairman of an Explosives Committee.' [1] Lansdowne adopted
Haldane's suggestion and the latter accordingly sat for four years
on a Committee with Lord Rayleigh, Sir William Crookes, the
great chemist, Sir W. Roberts-Austin, the metallurgist, and Sir
Andrew Noble, an artillery expert, as his colleagues. ' I found ',
says Haldane, ' the knowledge gained of great use when I came
to the War Office.' [1] Asked by the Army Council for some notion
of the Army he had in mind ' Schopenhauer ' characteristically
replied : ' A Hegelian Army '. The conversation, he adds, ' then
fell off '. But the Generals soon realized that Haldane, though
a student of Clausewitz and Von der Goltz, was no mere theorist.

The one idea of the Radical Party in Parliament was to secure
a reduction of the Army Estimates. Haldane's reply was that
economy and efficiency were not incompatible : that he believed
we could obtain a finely organized Army for less money than we
spent already, but that a finer Army we must have, even though
it cost more. He was loyally backed by the Prime Minister, who,
though a typical Radical economist, was genuinely interested in
the Army, and as time went on ' gained a deep and real respect
for the colossal industry of [Haldane] and his tact and deftness
in handling the Generals.' [2]

Haldane entirely justified the good opinion of his Chief : not
only did he reduce the estimate by £3,000,000 but, with the help
of Colonel Ellison, Sir Charles Harris, Sir Douglas (afterwards
Earl) Haig, General Ewart, and Lord Nicholson, he laid the
foundations of an Army which in point of quality was and proved
itself to be ' the finest Army for its size on the earth '. The
problem as stated by Haldane himself was to provide for an
Expeditionary Force of six Infantry Divisions, and a Cavalry
Division of four Brigades, complete with the appropriate medical
and transport services. Detailed plans had also to be worked
out, whereby this force could be mobilized and in position within

[1] Haldane, *Autobiography*, p. 164.   [2] Spender, *Life of C.-B.*, II, 325.

fifteen days. So perfectly, indeed, did the machinery work that in August 1914 the Expeditionary Force was in its assigned position in France within twelve days after the declaration of war.

A second line Army, absorbing the old Militia and Volunteers, with the old Yeomanry for cavalry, was to provide 300,000 men organized in fourteen Infantry Divisions and fourteen Mounted Brigades, with Artillery and Engineers for coast defence. Each division was to be trained, commanded in peace time by a Major-General, and in every county there was to be a Territorial Association under the Lord-Lieutenant, responsible for administration under the general direction and supervision of the War Office. The old Militia Reserve was abolished, but its place was to be taken by a special contingent to supply auxiliary and special service troops on mobilization. The Territorial and Reserve Forces Act passed its Third Reading in the House of Commons on June 19, 1907, and came into operation on March 31, 1908. Finally Haldane encouraged the formation of the Officers' Training Corps in the Universities and Public Schools which, when need arose, gave the country a large supply of partially trained officers of high quality.

Such in brief outline was the Haldane Army Scheme. Lord Kitchener did not in 1914 make full use of the machinery which lay ready to his hand. He preferred other methods. But for the perfection of the Expeditionary Force and the immense value of the Territorial Scheme Lord Haldane is entitled to full credit. It is true that when the contemplated occasion arose his preparations proved inadequate. His own reply to critics will be found in his *Before the War* [1] and his *Autobiography*.[2] Briefly stated it comes to this : that he did all that was possible under the parliamentary and other conditions imposed upon him or any other War Minister ; and, more specifically, that his own general staff having fully considered a scheme for compulsory service, reported against it. Haldane and his advisers were well aware that the crisis might come at any moment : how near it was in 1911 we have already seen. To substitute for a small highly efficient professional army an army based on compulsory service, would have demanded several years of reorganization. Between 1906

Lord Haldane and the War

[1] Cassell, 1920.   [2] Hodder & Stoughton (1929).

and 1914 it was never certain that we should be allowed several months or even weeks. ' Had we tried to do what we are reproached for not having done, we must have become weaker before we could have become stronger. . . . It is probable that the result would have been failure, and it is almost certain that we should have provoked a preventive war on the part of Germany.'

To German preparations no one was more fully alive than Haldane. With Colonel Ellison he attended the German Army manœuvres in 1906, and learnt a good deal, if not from the manœuvres, from the organization of the War Office. He paid another visit to Berlin in February 1912, and had a series of interviews with the Emperor, with Herr von Bethmann-Holweg, the Chancellor, with Admiral von Tirpitz and other officials. He frankly discussed the whole position with the Germans, told them that Great Britain had no secret treaties, but that we were under Treaty obligation to go to the aid of Belgium, in case of invasion, and that if France were attacked Germany must not count on our neutrality. Nor could we ' sit still if Germany elected to develop her fleet to such an extent as to imperil our naval protection '. If she built more ships we should lay down two keels to one. He found both the Emperor and the Chancellor friendly. Von Tirpitz was less friendly, and quite immovable on the subject of the Navy. Haldane's general impression was, the Emperor wished to maintain peace but ' was pulled at by his naval and military advisers and by the powerful, if then small, Chauvinist party in Germany '. On his return he reported his impressions fully to the Cabinet.

Of that Cabinet his friend Asquith had in 1908 become the head. But Campbell-Bannerman before his resignation in April 1908 had already accomplished what Haldane truly described as ' his great achievement of the grant of a healing measure of complete self-government to South Africa '.

Note to p. 252.

On the whole subject of the Education difficulty there is an illuminating chapter in Bell's *Life of Archbishop Davidson*, I, c. xxix.

CHAPTER XV

THE SETTLEMENT OF SOUTH AFRICA—SELF-GOVERNMENT AND UNION

THE Peace of Vereeniging, though it registered the victory of British arms in South Africa, left that great country in a condition of chaos. Nothing indeed, save the generosity of the victors, wisely directed by a great administrator, could have saved the vanquished from the consequences of their own unwisdom in prolonging a hopeless struggle. Yet in that unwisdom there was a touch of heroism which impelled to generosity. Nor was generosity lacking either in the treatment of the Boers by the British authorities in South Africa, or in the policy of the Imperial Government.

The soldiers had done their part; the task of ' clearing up the mess ', and of rebuilding a shattered civilization, was left to Lord Milner, and a group of young Oxford men derisively known as his ' kindergarten '. Neither the difficulties of that task, nor the success with which they were surmounted have ever been adequately appreciated. ' Imagine ', says a contemporary writer, ' a wilderness stripped bare, intersected by lines of blockhouses and barbed wire, everything in the shape of live-stock driven away, the veldt untilled, roads and drifts often impassable, railways torn up, towns and houses wholly destroyed '.[1]

Reconstruction under Milner, 1902–5

South Africa has two great assets, minerals and pastures. In 1902 the mines were in ruins; the wide pastures were bare.

A month after the conclusion of Peace a Crown Colony Constitution was given to each of the annexed Colonies. Seats in the Legislative Council of the Transvaal were offered to Generals Louis Botha, Delarey and J. C. Smuts, but the offer was declined.

[1] V. R. Markham, The New Era in South Africa, p. 7—the best contemporary account of the post-war situation known to me.

Milner, however, pushed on the work of reconstruction. The first need, if only to secure a revenue for the day-to-day expenses of administration, was to get work restarted on the Rand. That was done almost before the war ended, and a tax of 10 per cent. on the annual net produce was imposed. The next was to re-establish 200,000 members of the old Burgher population in their homes—including 33,000 prisoners who were entitled under the terms of peace to be set at liberty. Of the latter 24,000 were in oversea-camps in India, Ceylon, Bermuda and elsewhere. Within a year they had all been repatriated. The civil adminis-tration of the new Colonies had to be entirely remodelled, and the repatriated burghers had to be provided with materials for rebuilding farms, and with seed and stock for restarting agricul-tural work. A free grant of £3,000,000 to the Boers for these and other purposes was promised by the Peace terms : as a fact £15,000,000 was expended in less than two years on the work of reconstruction, in addition to a guaranteed loan of £35,000,000.

One outcome of Mr. Chamberlain's visit in 1903 [1] was the establishment of a Customs Union for the four Colonies, and a simplification of railway rates throughout South Africa. On these economic foundations the political edifice was subsequently built. But the stability of the structure depended wholly upon the output of the mines. Unless they could be worked to full capacity the new Colonies were likely to become a heavy charge upon the British taxpayer. Mining operations were, however, hampered by a shortage of labour. The mine-owners calculated that they could profitably employ 200,000 natives ; in July 1903 they could get less than 70,000.

Chinese labour

The Report of a Labour Commission appointed by Lord Milner demonstrated the gravity of the problem. Only a driblet of natives was supplied from other parts of Africa ; the Colonies objected to the importation of Indians ; recourse was had, therefore, to Chinese coolies. Lord Milner had ' no shadow of doubt ' as to the necessity for this expedient ; but it was strongly opposed both at home and in South Africa—particularly in Cape Colony. At the end of 1903, however, the Legislative Council of the Transvaal passed an Ordinance to " Regulate the Introduc-tion into the Transvaal of Unskilled Non-European Labourers "

[1] *Supra*, p. 190.

and it received the Royal Assent on March 12, 1904. The conditions imposed were very strict. Licences (costing £100) were required for the employment of coolies, who were to be imported under indentures limited to five years, and were to be repatriated, at the expense of the licensees, on the termination of their contract.

A first batch of about 1,000 coolies sailed from Hong Kong on May 25, 1904, and by the end of that year 20,000 were at work on the Rand. The economic results of the experiment were satisfactory ; it not only increased the output of gold but facilitated the employment of much white labour both in the mines and outside them. On December 31, 1904, 1,817 more whites were employed at the mines than on June 30, and the general trade of the Colony was greatly stimulated.

By the spring of 1905 nearly 35,000 Chinese labourers were on the Rand, but things were not working smoothly. There were strikes in some mines ; outbreaks of violence in others ; it was found difficult to confine the Chinese to their compounds ; desertions were frequent ; robberies, assaults and even murders were reported from different parts of the veldt. By September the importation of coolies had reached nearly 47,000 : of these over 2,500 had been convicted, chiefly for breach of labour regulations, but nearly 1,000 were in jail. Reports were, doubtless for political purposes, exaggerated, but the Boer farmers, especially in outlying districts, were genuinely alarmed. At home the tide of opinion, also politically stimulated, was rising against ' Chinese slavery '.

Meanwhile, Lord Milner's reign in South Africa had ended. Milner's During a short furlough in England in the autumn of 1903 he had work been pressed by Mr. Balfour to take Mr. Chamberlain's place at the Colonial Office ; but though his health was seriously impaired by the labour and anxieties of the last few years, he insisted on returning to South Africa to complete, if it might be, the task he had begun. The Colonial Office was assigned to Mr. Alfred Lyttelton. During his brief tenure of the Office he loyally supported Milner, and was also responsible for drafting a new Constitution designed to carry the Transvaal one step farther on the road towards Responsible Government. In March 1905 Lord Milner retired. His tenure of office covered the most critical years in the history of South Africa, and he himself suffered, in calumny and misrepresentation, the common lot of the greatest of our proconsuls. Milner detested the arts of the demagogue and had little capacity for self-justification. He preferred that his work should be judged solely by its fruits. In time it will be ; but the time is not yet. Milner was no fire-eater. Could the contest between Boers and Britons in South Africa have been avoided, Milner would gladly have avoided it. He was well aware of President Kruger's preparations for war, well advanced before he reached South Africa. He was equally aware of our own unpreparedness. ' We have a bad time before us, and the Empire is about to support the greatest strain put upon it since the Mutiny.' That was the entry in his Diary on the first day of the war. Some one had ' to break the crockery ' (his own words) ; he broke it. To shrink from that responsibility was not merely to betray the interests of the Empire, but to postpone indefinitely the prospects of a real settlement in South Africa. With a heavy heart, but without hesitation, Milner accepted the responsibility.

Similarly, in the post-war settlement Milner knew that without the restoration of prosperity on the Rand the means for reconstruction could not be obtained. He accepted, therefore, the repellent expedient of Chinese labour. The expedient was temporary. No one knew better than Milner that the ultimate and fundamental problem in South Africa was not the relations between Boers and Britons, but the position of the two European races, confronted with a coloured population which outnumbers them by four to one. General Smuts, though approaching the problem from a different angle, is equally alive to the high significance and peculiar difficulty of ' the most perplexing racial situation which has ever been faced in the world '.[1] In farewell speeches delivered at Pretoria (March 22) and Johannesburg (March 31) Lord Milner reviewed, with rare modesty, the eight eventful years of his administration. There was a tinge of sadness but none of regret in his retrospect. ' I shall live in the memories of men in this country, if I live at all, in connexion with the struggle to keep it within the limits of the British Empire. And certainly I engaged in that struggle with all my might, being, from head to foot, one mass of glowing conviction of the

[1] Cf. Smuts, *Africa and some World Problems* (Oxford, 1930), in particular **p. 30.**

rightness of our cause. But, however inevitable, however just, a conflict of that kind is a sad business to look back upon. What I should prefer to be remembered by is the tremendous effort subsequent to the war, not only to repair its ravages, but to restart those Colonies on a higher plane of civilization than they had ever previously attained.'

That History will some day respect Milner's preference is certain. With Strafford, whom in some ways he resembled, he might have said :

> 'wherefore not feel sure
> That Time who in the twilight comes to mend
> All the fantastic day's caprice, consign
> To the low ground once more the ignoble **Term,**
> And raise the genius on his orb again,—
> That Time will do me right.'

It will.

On the eve of Milner's departure from South Africa **Mr.** **Lyttelton** on behalf of the Government telegraphed a message appreciative of his great services and affirming that his ' arduous and unflagging labours have laid deep and strong the foundations upon which a United South Africa will arise to become one of the great States of the Empire '.

Milner undoubtedly laid the foundations of a United South Africa, but it was some years before that truth was generally apprehended. His reception at home was, on the part of the public, cool : on the part of a section of the Radical Party it was cruel. Some of them would gladly have seen him impeached, and a vote of censure moved in the House of Commons was rather evaded than resisted by the Government. The House of Lords, on the other hand, placed on record its high appreciation of the services rendered by Lord Milner to the Crown and the Empire.

Not for the first, nor for the last time, the Lords reflected more accurately than the Commons the considered judgement of those who were competent to form one. No fewer than 370,000 people endorsed, in an address presented to Lord Milner, the eulogy of the Peers.

Lord Milner was succeeded as Governor of the Transvaal and **Lord** High Commissioner of South Africa by the Earl of Selborne. The **Selborne** son of a great lawyer who had twice served as Loid Chancellor under Gladstone, and son-in-law of the late Lord Salisbury, Lord Selborne had himself sat in the House of Commons as a Liberal. In 1886, however, he joined the Liberal Unionist wing ; from 1895 to 1900 he was Under-Secretary for the Colonies under Mr. Chamberlain, and from 1900 to 1905 did excellent service as First Lord of the Admiralty.

His reign in South Africa proved to be a marked success. But he was, at the outset, confronted by a difficult and delicate situation. Appointed to supervise the working of the Lyttelton Constitution, he found himself compelled to carry out the new policy initiated by the Campbell-Bannerman Government.

Liberal Policy in South Africa

The position of the Government was not indeed void of embarrassment. To denounce Chinese ' slavery ' from the Opposition benches was one thing : to cancel legal contracts was another. All that Campbell-Bannerman could do was to refuse to allow any further recruitment of coolies. This he did in February 1906, and in June 1907 the Botha Cabinet in the Transvaal prohibited importation. By February 1910 the last batch of coolies was repatriated.

Meanwhile the Lyttelton Constitution was suspended; a small delimitation Commission was sent out to South Africa, and on the basis of their Report Letters Patent conferring full Responsible Government upon the Transvaal were issued (December 1906). In June 1907 a similar Constitution for the Orange River Colony was published. These Constitutions were on the lines of similar Instruments devised for other self-governing Colonies, but they need not detain us since they were soon to be superseded by a much larger experiment.

The concession of Responsible Government was denounced by Mr. Balfour as ' a dangerous, audacious and reckless experiment ', but by the Liberals in England and the Nationalists in South Africa was acclaimed as a ' magnificent venture of faith '. The Government were, indeed, looking beyond the immediate step then taken : they had (so the covering Dispatch of the Secretary of State declared) ' advised His Majesty to grant immediate Responsible Government to the Transvaal . . . with the hope that the step now taken will in due time lead to the union of the interests of the whole of His Majesty's dominions in South Africa '.

The ' due time ' was quickly accomplished. In February 1907 the first election under the new Constitution was held in the Transvaal. An organization called *Het Volk* (The People) secured a majority in a House of sixty-nine members. General Louis Botha consequently became the first (and last) Prime Minister of the Transvaal with General Smuts as Colonial Secretary. In the Orange River Colony a Party (the *Orangia Unie*), organized on similar lines, secured at the election (November 1907) no fewer than twenty-nine seats out of thirty-eight. Mr. A. Fischer became Premier, with Generals Hertzog and De Wet as his principal lieutenants. An election in the Cape Colony in 1908 put Mr. J. F. X. Merriman in power at the head of a large majority in place of Dr. Jameson who had held office since 1904. These sweeping victories for the Dutch parties might well have justified the misgivings of the Conservatives in England, had circumstances in South Africa not irresistibly impelled the four self-governing Colonies to a further step in Constitutional evolution.

' The war ', writes Mr. Jan H. Hofmeyr, ' brought one obvious gain, for it removed the greatest of the technical obstacles that had stood in the way of Union. Save for the German Colony on the west, and the Portuguese territories on the east, all of South Africa was now under one flag.' [1] With the removal of great obstacles were combined powerful positive incentives. In November 1906 the Cape Ministry, headed at that time by Dr. Jameson, appealed to Lord Selborne to 'review the situation in South Africa ' with the view of bringing about ' a central national Government, embracing all the Colonies and Protectorates under South African administration'. The other Colonies concurred in the request, and the result was the publication of a masterly State-paper [2] comparable in significance with Lord Durham's historic *Report* on Canada.

The Union of South Africa

Deeply impressed by the inconveniences and dangers of the existing situation Lord Selborne insisted that there lay before the people of South Africa ' three choices . . . the makeshift régime of the High Commissioner, the jarring separatism of the States of South America, the noble union of the States of North America.'

Four problems, in particular, confronted British statesmanship

---

[1] *South Africa*, pp. 119–20.   [2] Cmd. 3564 (1907).

in South Africa : the position of the native population ; the problem of labour for the mines, for industry, and for agriculture ; the railway system and railway rates ; and, closely connected with the last, the tariff question.

The Native Problem   The glaring disproportion between the European and the aboriginal inhabitants has always been the crux of South African politics. According to the census of 1931 the Europeans number 1,859,400 as against 6,391,500 non-Europeans. But presenting itself with varying degrees of intensity in the several colonies the problem has naturally not been treated on uniform lines. In Cape Colony, where the proportion of white inhabitants to coloured is about one to four, the treatment of the natives has been far more ' generous ' than in Natal, where the proportion is roughly one to ten. Cape Colony has based its policy on Rhodes's formula : ' Equal rights for all civilized men.' It has consistently acted on the supposition that ' the problem will find its solution in narrowing the gulf which divides the races '.[1] Natives were admitted to the franchise on precisely the same terms as whites, and, in 1903, nearly 50 per cent. of the revenue raised by native taxation was devoted to expenditure on native education. It was otherwise in Natal and the inland colonies. The prevalent sentiment in these colonies is in fact embodied in the blunt declaration of the republican Grondwet that ' the people will not tolerate equality between coloured and white inhabitants either in Church or State '.[2] Such divergence of temper and policy might seem to have dictated a federal as opposed to a unitary form of constitution, and, but for the overwhelming force of the argument derived from a consideration of the railway rates question and the tariff question, a Federal system might have been adopted.

Closely connected with the native problem was that of the Asiatic immigrants. The labour problem in South Africa was further complicated by the caste system, which virtually forbade the white man to undertake unskilled labour, however small his capacity for anything higher. But, as industry outgrew the local supply of coloured labour, there arose a demand for coloured immigration. The Natal plantations and the Transvaal mines

---

[1] *The Government of South Africa*, p. 128 (an anonymous work of great value published by the Central News Agency, South Africa, 1908).
[2] Ibid., p. 137.

both relied upon **Asiatic** labour. Cape Colony never resorted, after the British occupation, to a similar expedient; yet for obvious reasons it was deeply concerned in the policy of its neighbours towards this and similar questions. The interests of white South Africa clearly demanded, therefore, a common consideration of these persistent problems.

Even more insistent, if not more persistent, there was also the Defence problem of common defence. The coast Colonies were wholly dependent for protection upon the Royal Navy : the inland colonies, as well as those on the coast, relied upon the English garrison for the preservation of order amongst the native peoples, when such a task imposed too great a strain upon local resources. In view of their dependence upon the Royal Navy Cape Colony made an annual contribution of £50,000, and Natal of £35,000, towards the expense of maintaining it, and each supported a small force of naval volunteers. The inland Colonies contributed nothing. This anomaly plainly could not survive the concession of self-government.

A scheme for common defence was drafted by a Conference representative of the four Colonies and of Rhodesia in 1907. In each separate Colony, however, the scheme encountered opposition so keen as to drive home the truth that only by union could the problem be solved. That conclusion was fortified by the palpable necessity for a common policy in regard to immigration; but the final and compelling reason was the inextricable confusion arising from the existence of four separate railway systems, each owned and managed by a separate State.

One step towards railway unification had been taken by Lord Milner, who amalgamated the systems of the Transvaal and the Orange River Colony while those Colonies were, as Crown Colonies, under his immediate control. But Milner recognized that nothing short of an amalgamation of the four systems would furnish a complete solution of a problem vital to the prosperity of South Africa.

Amalgamation might have been achieved under a Federal system, and in October 1908 a National Convention met at Durban to frame a Constitution for South Africa. The Convention consisted of delegates from each of the four Parliaments, but the more closely the delegates got to grips with the problem

M.E.—10

the more were they convinced that the peculiar conditions of South Africa rendered a Union preferable to a Federation. A Bill for the union of the four Colonies was accordingly drafted, and submitted for the consideration of each separate Parliament. Their amendments were considered at another meeting of the Constitutional Convention and, as amended, the Bill was again submitted to the Legislatures in the Cape Colony, the Transvaal, and the Orange River Colony, and to the people by referendum in Natal. By June 1909 it had been ratified by all the constituent colonies; it encountered no serious difficulties in the Imperial Parliament, and took its place on the British Statute Book as 9 Edw. VII, c. 9.

Remarkable as was the achievement of Federation in Canada and in Australia, the achievement of Union in South Africa was even more remarkable.

Mr. Balfour surely anticipated the verdict of history when he said in the House of Commons : ' This Bill, soon I hope to become an Act, is the most wonderful issue out of all those divisions, controversies, battles and outbreaks, the devastation and horrors of war, the difficulties of peace. I do not believe the world shows anything like it in its whole history.'

Charac-teristics of the Union Constitu-tion

The outstanding characteristics of the Constitution which had thus come to the birth demand examination.

(a) The Legisla-ture

Subject, of course, to the paramount authority of the Crown, the Union Legislature is a sovereign body, unfettered by any limitations imposed upon it in the interests of the provinces, and free to amend or repeal (subject to certain temporary provisions) any clause of the Constitution. In brief, the South African Parliament has not only legislative but constituent authority. The Constitution itself is consequently not rigid but flexible.

On the difficult question of the franchise a compromise was reached. Each of the four Colonies was to follow its own existing practice. To have attempted to prescribe a uniform franchise throughout the Union would unquestionably have wrecked the whole scheme. Neither in the Cape Colony itself, nor in England, would public opinion have permitted the disfranchisement of the coloured voters in that Colony. No one of the other three Colonies would have enfranchised them ; nor could Cape Colony, with its

colour equality, have adopted the manhood suffrage on which the
Transvaal relied. There was nothing for it, therefore, but to
leave these difficult questions for the future to settle.

Following the precedent of all English-speaking communities,
the Legislature was constituted on the bicameral system; and
was to consist of a Senate and a House of Assembly.

The Senate was, for the first ten years after the establishment
of the Union, to be constituted as follows : (a) eight Senators to
be nominated for a term of ten years, by the Governor-General in
Council; and (b) eight Senators elected by each of the four
original provinces. Of the eight to be nominated by the Governor-General four were to be selected ' on the ground mainly of
their thorough acquaintance, by reason of their official experience
or otherwise, with the reasonable wants and wishes of the coloured
races in South Africa '. The eight members representing each
province were to be elected, also for ten years, in a joint session
of the two Houses of the then existing Colonial Legislatures, on
the principle of proportional representation.

These provisions were to be in force for ten years only ; after
the expiration of that period the South African Parliament might
provide for the constitution of the Senate in any manner it might
see fit, or it might leave things as they were.[1]

The South African Senate can, like the Australian, reject, but
cannot amend, a money Bill. As regards both money Bills and
ordinary legislation the Senate possesses only a suspensive veto.
If a Bill passes the House of Assembly in two successive sessions,
and is twice rejected by the Senate, or receives at the hands of the
Senate amendments to which the House will not agree, the Governor-General may, during the second session, convene a joint
sitting, and the Bill, if then passed by a simple majority of the
members of both Houses, shall be deemed to have been duly
passed by Parliament, and may be presented for the Royal Assent.
In the case of a money Bill the procedure is even more stringent ;
for the joint sitting may be convened during *the same session* in
which the Senate ' rejects or fails to pass such Bill '.

The solution thus provided for a deadlock is generally similar
to that of the Australian Commonwealth Act, but with this essen-

[1] The Senate was dissolved in 1920, but was reconstituted on the same
basis.

tial difference : the Australian Act provides for an appeal to the electorate ; in the South African scheme there is no such provision. The difference between the two schemes may perhaps be connected with the more democratic character of the Australian Constitution, and still more directly with the fact that the South African Parliament, unlike the Australian, is competent to amend even the Constitution itself.

The House of Assembly, as constituted by the Act, was to be directly elected on the basis of provinces. Of the 121 original members, 51 were allotted to the Cape of Good Hope, 36 to the Transvaal, and to Natal and the Orange Free State 17 each. The ultimate basis of representation was the number of European male adults in each province, periodically readjusted after each census, but with this provision : that while the numbers might be increased, they could not, in the case of any Original Province be diminished until the number reaches 150.[1]

(b) The Executive

The Executive is, in the English sense, parliamentary and responsible. Formally vested in the Crown, it is practically exercised by an Executive Council composed of the ' King's Ministers of State for the Union '. As in Australia, ministers must, under the Constitution, be members of one or other House of the Legislature, and by custom they are allowed to sit and speak, but not to vote, in both Houses. Their number is not to exceed ten, exclusive, in practice, of one or two ministers ' without portfolio '.

Pretoria was designated as the seat of Government of the Union. But by ' Government ' was understood ' Executive Government', for under section 23 Cape Town was to be the seat of the Legislature. This device, awkward and illogical, was another significant illustration of the spirit of compromise by which the whole Constitution is infused.

Nothing more clearly demonstrates the unitary character of the Constitution than the disappearance of the original Colonies and States. In their place there are four Provinces, for the government of which elaborate provision is made in the Act.

Generally speaking, the Provinces were placed in a position of marked inferiority as compared with that of the Canadian Provinces, and still more with that of the constituent States of the Australian Commonwealth. The authority of the Union Parlia-

[1] The number is now (1933) 148.

ment is paramount; it can legislate concurrently on the same topics as the Provincial Councils, and exercise complete control over the legislation of the latter. Absolute too is the control of the Union Government over provincial finance.

No feature of the South African Constitution is more conclusively indicative of its unitarian character than the position assigned therein to the Judiciary. As in England, it is the function of the Courts merely to interpret the law, not to act as the guardian of the Constitution. Nevertheless, the Act is exceedingly important as making for simplicity of procedure and uniformity of interpretation. The four independent Supreme Courts, none of which was bound by the decisions of the other, were consolidated into one Supreme Court of South Africa. This Supreme Court consists of two divisions : an appellate division, with its headquarters at Bloemfontein, and provincial and local divisions, exercising jurisdiction within their respective areas. The Supreme Courts of the several Colonies existing at the time of the Union were thus transformed into provincial divisions of the Supreme Court of South Africa. From any superior court appeals lie direct to the Appellate Division. From the Supreme Court an appeal lies to the Privy Council only in cases in which the Privy Council gives leave to appeal. In this, as in other important respects, the South Africa Act is at variance with the precedents afforded by Canada and Australia. In Canada appeals lie by right from every Provincial Court to the Privy Council, and in the case of the Commonwealth appeals lie by right and by special leave from all the State Supreme Courts, and by special leave from inferior courts. From the Supreme Courts of the Dominion and the Commonwealth appeals lie to the Privy Council only by special leave, and in the case of the Commonwealth appeals are in certain instances prohibited save by permission of the Court itself.[1]

(c) The Judicature

It is significant of the economic and fiscal situation in South Africa that one of the most important chapters of the Constitution—a chapter containing no fewer than seventeen sections, should be devoted to the joint subject of ' Finance and Railways '. Not less significant is the conjunction of the two subjects, for the two are interdependent.

Finance and Railways

---

[1] Keith, op. cit., pp. 980 seq. ; the *Framework of Union*, chaps. xi and xii.

The authors of the Act, thus briefly summarized, evidently took immense pains to anticipate difficulties and to guard against them. Yet the outstanding feature of the South African Constitution is the large measure of confidence reposed in the United Parliament. Restraints upon its ' competence ', indispensable in a Federal Constitution, are here conspicuous by their absence. A Parliament virtually ' sovereign ' was trusted to work out its own constitutional salvation.[1]

Resignation and death of Campbell-Bannerman

The Act constituting the Union of South Africa, though it had its genesis in South Africa, and though each one of its 152 clauses represented prolonged discussion and adjustment in the Conventions of Durban, Cape Town and Bloemfontein, was formally enacted as a British Statute and received the Royal Assent on September 20, 1909. Its enactment was, however, the work not of the Campbell-Bannerman but of the Asquith Government. In August 1906 Sir Henry had lost his devoted wife, and his own health never recovered from that blow. At the beginning of April 1908 he resigned, and on the 22nd of the same month he died.

That Campbell-Bannerman will rank among great English statesmen it would be idle to pretend. But he was a man of high courage ; he won the affection of friends and (in his latter days) the respect of opponents. As leader of the Opposition he was in a peculiarly difficult situation, with big battalions in front of him and divided counsels in his own camp. As Prime Minister he was a different man : as a debater he developed a readiness and agility hitherto entirely unsuspected by friends or foes. Though never autocratic in aspect he was completely master in his own house. He listened deferentially to the opinions of colleagues, but his was the final decision, and to it he adhered like adamant. ' Of all the men with whom I have been associated in public life I put him ', wrote his successor, ' as high as any in sense of duty, and in both moral and intellectual courage.' Most conspicuously did he display it, both in opposition and office, in relation to South Africa. With that great Dominion and with its admission to partnership in the British Commonwealth of Nations his name will be immemorially associated.

[1] For further details of the Constitution, cf. Marriott, *Mechanism of the State*, I. c. x.

CHAPTER XVI

SOCIAL REFORM AND DEMOCRATIC FINANCE

ON the resignation of Campbell-Bannerman King Edward at The
once summoned Mr. Asquith to Biarritz. That the King Asquith
should have remained abroad during the change of government ment
evoked at the moment some ill-natured comment. It was not
then known how serious was the state of the King's own health.
Nor indeed was there any reason for bringing the King back to
England. Asquith was the inevitable and predestined successor
of Campbell-Bannerman, and the ministerial changes consequent
upon his promotion were few though not insignificant. The most
important, and the least happy, was the appointment of Mr.
Lloyd George to the Treasury. Current rumour affirmed that the
appointment was due not to Asquith's will but to his weakness.
If that be true he must often have repented in dust and ashes.
Lord Crewe superseded Lord Elgin at the Colonial Office, and
Mr. McKenna Lord Tweedmouth at the Admiralty; Mr. Churchill
was brought into the Cabinet as President of the Board of Trade
and Mr. Walter Runciman as Minister for Education. Mr. John
Morley remained at the India Office, but not in the House of
Commons ; Mr. Henry Fowler, greatly esteemed both by the
King and the Prime Minister, accompanied John Morley to the
House of Lords, as Viscount Wolverhampton and President of the
Council.

The new Prime Minister was well qualified to lead a Party,
and even to govern the country, in quiet times. But the days of
Asquith's Premiership were conspicuously unquiet, and so it came
that the limelight was concentrated on his chief lieutenant.

A young Welsh solicitor, sprung from the people, with no Mr.
traditions and little education of a formal kind, but endowed Lloyd
with a magical gift of eloquence, ardent in temper, generous in George

sympathies and of indomitable courage, David Lloyd George had entered the House of Commons as Member for Carnarvon Boroughs in 1890 and had quickly made himself a real force in politics. The idol of Wales, he had risked opprobrium as a champion of the Boers ; an ardent temperance advocate, he had declared war on ' the Trade ' ; a strong Nonconformist, he had encouraged passive resistance to Balfour's Education Act of 1902. Appointed to the Board of Trade in 1906 he had revealed unsuspected powers of administration, and great patience in negotiation. Convinced that finance was the key to constructive Radicalism he claimed the second place in 1908, and, though his Party was rich in ability, his was the driving power behind the coach during the Asquith Premiership (1908–16).

Old Age Pensions
 The new Government was remarkable for its large output of social legislation. An Act to facilitate, under public authority, the provision of allotments and smallholdings for cultivating tenants was passed in 1907. The year 1908 saw a beginning made with a scheme for providing pensions, altogether dissociated from Poor Relief, for persons over 70 years of age. The pensions were ' non-contributory ' and were given entirely at the charge of the State. The maximum pension was 5s. a week to persons with incomes of not more than £21 a year or 8s. a week, and smaller amounts on a sliding scale down to 1s. a week. Persons whose income exceeded £31 10s. a year were excluded. The Act was estimated to cost ultimately £7,000,000 a year. It was a grotesque underestimate. By 1909–10 the charge was £8,750,000, but subsequent Acts have not only largely increased the maximum pension but have also raised the amount of the disqualifying income. The charge upon the Exchequer (including pensions for the blind at 50) now (1941) approaches £82,000,000 a year, and the recipients number nearly two millions. In the same year an elaborate effort was made to deal with the sale of intoxicants, under licence, but the Bill, hotly opposed both in Parliament and in the country, was, after passing through the Commons, rejected by the Lords. An Act establishing a maximum eight-hours' day for coal miners was, however, passed, though not without serious misgivings which experience has justified. The 1909 crop included a Development Act authorizing grants or loans from the Exchequer for agriculture, forestry, rural transport, harbours, canals, &c., and

setting up a Road Board to construct new roads or make grants
or loans to highway authorities. A Housing and Town Planning
Act was also passed.

The latter was promoted by John Burns, who was doing excel- Housing
lent work at the Local Government Board. The Act marked,
indeed, only one stage in a legislative process which began in
1851 and is not yet (1933) closed. The stage was, however, an
important one. The Act not only increased the powers of Local
Authorities in regard to the closing and demolition of houses
unfit for human habitation, but encouraged them to erect new
houses; it enabled them to repair insanitary houses at the
expense of neglectful or refractory owners, and for the first time
empowered the Authorities to consider ' amenities ', and to acquire
land not actually required for building purposes. Every County
Council was, under the Act, required to appoint a Medical Officer
of health. It is significant of the rapid development, especially
since the Great War, of the ' Housing policy ' that whereas in 1910
the charge to the State was under one million it now (1933)
exceeds thirty-two.

The year 1909 was in the social sphere remarkable not only Reports
for legislation. In that year were published two Reports on the on the
administration of the Poor Laws and on the condition of those Poor Law
classes of the population who were dependent wholly, or in part,
on Poor Relief. The Reports issued from a Royal Commission
appointed in 1905 and presided over by Lord George Hamilton,
an ex-Minister of great ability and ripe experience. One of the
two Reports was signed by 14 out of the 18 Commissioners, and
the second by a minority of four, among whom were two prominent Socialists, Mrs. Sidney Webb and Mr. George Lansbury.
The two Reports substantially agreed in their diagnosis of a gravely
disquieting situation : but the majority, while insisting that the
Poor Law called for drastic amendment, held that it must be
retained both in the interests of the classes which come within
its operation, and of the nation at large ; the minority desired to
sweep it away, blot out its hateful memory, and distribute the
heterogeneous and discrepant functions then performed by it
among specialized local authorities—to the Education Authority
the care of all children of school age, whether dependent on the
State or independent ; to the Health Committee the care of the

sick, the aged infirm, and the young mothers and infants, and so on. In a word, the minority wished to ' break up ' the Poor Law and obliterate, as far as possible, the distinction between pauperism and poverty, between the dependent and the independent poor.

Neither the recommendations of the Socialist minority, nor those of the majority, call for immediate consideration in detail, since no attempt to give legislative effect to them was made until 1929.[1] Much more important was the clear and exhaustive analysis of the existing situation, on the main features of which there was little divergence of opinion.

Social conditions For some time past there had been growing uneasiness in the public mind about the economic and social condition of the lowest strata of the population. The situation appeared at once inscrutable and paradoxical. Wealth, during the previous half-century, had increased with unexampled rapidity, and of that increased prosperity the poorer classes had had their full share. Sir Robert Giffen had indeed gone so far as to affirm that ' the poor have had almost all the benefit of the great material advance of the last fifty years '. That conclusion reached in 1887 was in the main confirmed, twenty years later, by the Board of Trade experts employed by the Commission. Yet the ten years ending in 1906, as compared with the cycle 1871–80, exhibited an increase in adult male pauperism amounting to no less than 18·4 per cent. Again, it had been confidently anticipated that elementary education, compulsory and gratuitous, would have diminished, if not eradicated, pauperism. The Education Acts had been in force for a full generation, expenditure under that head had reached £20,000,000, yet the cost of poor relief had increased from £8,007,403 in 1870–71 to £14,685,983 in 1905–6. There had, of course, been an increase of population, but the expenditure per head of population had increased from 7s. 0¼d. to 8s. 7¼d. ' It is very unpleasant to record that notwithstanding our assumed moral and material progress, and notwithstanding the enormous annual expenditure, amounting to nearly sixty millions a year, upon poor relief, education and public health, we still have a vast army of persons quartered upon us unable to support themselves, and an army which in numbers has recently shown signs of increase rather

[1] In Mr. Neville Chamberlain's *Local Government Act.*

than decrease ' (p. 52). Thus we read in the Majority Report. Not less trenchant is the indictment of the Minority : ' The present position is, in our opinion, as grave as that of 1834, though in its own way . . . What the nation is confronted with to-day is, as it was in 1834, an ever-growing expenditure from public and private funds, which results, on the one hand, in a minimum of prevention and cure, and on the other in far-reaching demoralization of character and the continuance of no small amount of unrelieved destitution ' (p. 799).

The reference to 1834 suggests an obvious reflection on the Report of 1909 ; it measures the distance which in the interval between two historic Reports social theory and social practice had alike travelled. The Act of 1834 represented a conspicuous triumph for Benthamite Liberalism. The activity of the State was to be restricted within the narrowest possible limits ; the principle of the right to work, implicit in Elizabethan legislation, was emphatically repudiated ; no one was to be permitted to die of starvation, but pauperism was to be stigmatized as a disgrace, and the lot of the pauper was not to be rendered in any way more eligible than that of the independent labourer of the lowest class. Thus was the nation rescued, after the dislocation caused by the Napoleonic wars, from the social and economic disaster threatened, nay, rendered imminent, by the reckless administration of outdoor relief during the preceding thirty-five years. The Reports of 1909 would, if implemented, have removed all ' stigma ' from pauperism. In place of ' relief ' for paupers there was to be ' assistance ' for the poor.

Another point, implicit if not explicit, obtruded in the Reports of 1909 was the far-reaching significance of the Local Government Act of 1888, and, not less, of the Education Act of 1902. The recommendations of 1909 were based upon the foundations provided by those Acts. The concentration of authorities, the readjustment and simplification of areas, the repudiation of the principle of *ad hoc* elections, whether of School Boards or Poor Law Guardians, above all the utilization of the services of expert officials—all these points reappear in the Reports of 1909, and were emphasized not less by the ' orthodox ' Majority than by the Socialistic Minority.

Many years, however, were to elapse, the experience of the

Great War and its aftermath was to be garnered, before the Legislature tackled seriously the problems presented by these Reports, and carried out a drastic reform of Poor Law administration.

Meanwhile, the diagnosis of social conditions impressed itself upon the public conscience, and accentuated the demand for further instalments of social legislation.

Unemployment Of the many forms of social disease revealed by these Reports perhaps the most puzzling was that of unemployment, and connected with, though distinct from it, the ' new problem '—so styled by the Commissioners—of ' chronic underemployment '. Despite the fact that in most of the groups of skilled industries the number of men employed had, in the preceding twenty years, increased more than proportionately to the increase in the population as a whole, there had nevertheless not been a single year ' without an appreciable number of skilled and organized workers out of employment '. Experts attributed this disturbing phenomenon partly to seasonal fluctuations incidental to particular trades, such as the building trade ; partly to the cyclical depressions to which trade in general is, under world-conditions, increasingly liable ; partly to the ' loss and lack of industrial quality on the part of the workers themselves ' (though why there should be ' loss and lack ' with extended and improved education is difficult to understand) ; and, most of all, to the demand for ' reserves of labour ' which had in recent years become a marked feature of modern industry. It was these phenomena of recurrent unemployment and chronic underemployment which most strikingly differentiated the task set before the Royal Commission of 1905 from that which had confronted its predecessor in 1834.

Labour Exchanges Mr. Lloyd George proposed to apply without delay two of the remedies recommended by the Commission. The first was a national system of labour exchanges. Some partial experiments in this direction had been made under the *Unemployed Workmen Act* of 1905. Germany had tried the experiment on a much larger scale, and with a much greater measure of success— nearly every town in Germany having established a labour exchange. Experience had, however, proved that labour bureaux, if isolated, could do little to assist the mobility of labour ; that if they are to succeed they must be entirely dissociated from any relief agencies ; that they must be staffed by men of organizing ability, and must gain the confidence of the trade unions. The Commissioners accordingly recommended that a national system of labour exchanges should be organized under the Board of Trade, that they should be managed by officers of the Board, with the help of an advisory committee of employers, workmen and local authorities, that they should be well advertised and popularized, and should be granted various facilities, but that the use of them should be entirely voluntary.

On these lines Parliament legislated in 1909–10, and by February 1910 sixty-one exchanges had been opened. By 1927 nearly 400 central and 700 branch exchanges were operating. In 1916 the supervision of their work was transferred from the Board of Trade to the Ministry of Labour (constituted as a separate department in that year). The designation *Employment* was at the same time substituted for that of *Labour*, in order to indicate the widened scope of the functions of the exchanges. Some 10,000 persons are now employed locally at the exchanges, while the keeping of records for the Unemployment Insurance Service necessitates a headquarters staff of over 3,000.

The initiation of another experiment in Labour legislation *Trade* dates from the same year. The State had, until then, been *Board* reluctant to interfere between employers and their workpeople in *Acts,* regard to wages, although they had long since interfered in refer- *1909 and* ence to hours and other conditions of employment. The social *1918* conscience had, however, been deeply stirred by the revelation of the horrors of sweated labour contained in a Board of Trade Report (1890), and by the evidence taken by a Select Committee appointed in the same year. The evil of ' sweating '—the employment of labour at ' starvation ' wages, for long hours, under bad conditions—was attributed to many causes : primarily to lack of organization among the lowest classes of labour, particularly that of women ; to the extreme subdivision of labour in certain trades —notably the cheap tailoring trade ; to the multiplication of middle-men and sub-contractors, and not least to excessive competition among the lowest paid wage-earners, especially alien immigrants. The *Trade Board Act* of 1909 represented a first attempt to grapple with this problem. It applied only to four trades : ready-made and wholesale bespoke tailoring, paper box-making, machine-made lace and net finishing, and chain-making. The last was the only one of the trades in which male workers were predominantly employed, its inclusion being due to the painful impression created by a recent Report on the condition of the chain-makers at Cradley Heath. A Board was to be set up for each of these trades, and was to consist of an equal number of employers and workpeople, with the addition of one to three neutral or ' appointed ' members. The Boards were required to fix minimum rates of wages for time-workers, and were also empowered at their discretion to fix a general minimum rate for piece-workers, subject in both cases to confirmation by the Board of Trade.

The scope of the original Act was greatly extended by subsequent legislation. Under the *Trade Boards Provisional Orders Confirmation Act* of 1913 seven additional Boards were set up, and under the Act of 1920, forty-eight and more. In all no fewer than 3,000,000 workpeople are now (1933) covered by the operations of Trade Boards. Rates of wages being fixed by them, failure to pay wages at the legal rates is punishable by criminal procedure, and orders made under the Statute apply to all firms engaged in the trade.

According to a Report issued by the Ministry of Reconstruction in 1919 Trade Boards would seem to have achieved the anticipated and desired results. ' The general effect of the Act has been to raise wages, to stimulate organization on the part of employers and employed, and to improve the efficiency of industry. It would appear that the general policy of the Trade Boards has been to establish a minimum wage as high as the existing circumstances of the trade permit, and to raise the minima as more efficient methods and more economical organizations are introduced.' The same *Report* predicts that ' the question of wages will never be allowed to return to the position of ten years ago, when the Government had no concern in it. A policy will be pursued of stimulating production and at the same time of securing to the worker a fair share of the product.' But none the less it prudently recalls the truth that ' wages, salaries and incomes all depend finally on the total volume of the internal and external trade of the country, and the total income derived from it '.

The contribution made to social reform by the measures de- *National Insurance Act, 1911*
scribed in preceding paragraphs, important as it was, becomes
almost insignificant as compared with the great scheme of National
Insurance launched in 1911 by Mr. Lloyd George.

The Act was in two parts : Part I dealt with Invalidity ;
Part II with Unemployment. Already in 1906, by the Workmen's Compensation Act, the liability of employers for injuries
to persons in their employment had been extended to cover
practically all manual labourers, and indeed all employees earning
less than £250 a year. The Act of 1911 represented an attempt on
the part of the State to assist and supplement the work of voluntary agencies in helping wage-earners in times of sickness and invalidity. Much was already being done, with conspicuous efficiency
and success, by the great Friendly Societies, the Trade Unions
and other minor associations for mutual aid. The Friendly
Societies, like Trade Unions, began to play an important part in
social history at the time when the poorer classes first became
dependent upon weekly wages. Until the growth of the enclosure
movement, until, under the factory system, industry was divorced
from agriculture, the English poor had some resources other than
wages. When the wage-system began to dominate employment
the necessity for mutual aid in old age or sickness was quickly
realized. The Friendly Societies stepped into the breach, and
in 1793 an Act of Parliament was passed to encourage the formation of such societies. The Manchester Unity of Oddfellows,
which is still the greatest of them, came into being towards the
close of the Napoleonic wars.

But neither Friendly Societies nor Trade Unions, wide as their
nets were spread, covered the whole field. There was still a large
number of wage-earners who made no provision for themselves.
By the Act of 1911 the State came to their aid.

The scheme was framed on a contributory and compulsory
basis. It was to embrace all manual workers between the ages
of 16 and 70, as well as all other employed persons, such as clerks,
whose remuneration did not exceed £160 a year. There were a
few exceptions, among which the most important were soldiers,
sailors, teachers and other public employés. The Act also made
provision for the inclusion of voluntary contributors whose total
incomes did not exceed £160 a year ; but few people have availed

themselves of this provision. It was estimated that 15,000,000 workers would come under the Scheme : the number now (1933) exceeds 18,000,000.

The cost of the scheme was divided in unequal proportions between the employer, the employé and the State. The employer was to contribute 3*d*. a week for each employé, each male employé 4*d*. and each female 3*d*., and the State 2*d*. The payment of benefit was to be at the rate of 10*s*. a week for men, and 7*s*. 6*d*. for women, during sickness ; 5*s*. a week for men and women during disablement, and 30*s*. maternity benefit. Medical attendance and drugs were to be free, and treatment in sanatoria was also provided for.

The administration of the Act was, as far as possible, to be left in experienced hands. Insured persons were encouraged to enrol in 'Approved Societies', such as Friendly Societies, Industrial Assurance Societies, Employers' Provident Funds and Trade Unions. Contributors were free to select their Societies, but failing to do so could obtain their benefits through the Post Office. While the insured persons were to draw their benefits through agencies with which they were already familiar, there was to be set up in each County or County Borough an Insurance Committee, to supervise the administration of medical and sanatorium benefits. These committees were to be representative of different interests—local and central authorities, medical practitioners and insured persons.

Thanks in the main to the long and wide experience of the Approved Societies the Act worked smoothly and, though amended in 1913 and on several subsequent occasions,[1] has preserved its main features. From the first, however, there was friction between the medical practitioners and the Insurance Committees. Insured persons were free to select their own doctors from a panel ; the doctors were to receive 4*s*. per patient per annum, and drugs were to be provided out of the funds. The doctors rebelled, and the scale of remuneration was, by successive increments, increased to 9*s*. 6*d*. That the Act has been of incalculable value, to the insured persons and to the community as a whole, can be doubted only by those who are unacquainted with the results, direct and indirect, which it has achieved. There remains

[1] See *infra*, c. xxix.

a large amount of preventible disease, but despite the ' hard times ' experienced since the Great War there has been a steady improvement in the health of the community, and a decline in the death-rate which can only be described as remarkable. The total death-rate, which in the decade 1871–80 was 21·4 per 1,000, is now (1933) 12.[1]

Part II of the *National Insurance Act* dealt with the problem of unemployment, so fully investigated by the Royal Commission of 1905. The Act of 1911 only laid the foundation of a scheme which has since been enlarged almost out of recognition. Yet the fundamental principles of the original Act have persisted, through all mutations, substantially unimpaired. One is that unemployment is, in the working life of each insured person, a temporary ailment, not a chronic disease. The other is that the rate of benefit should be such as would assist the workman to tide over a limited period of unemployment, not to provide him with ' full maintenance ', still less with his accustomed wages.

The Act of 1911 applied only to some 2,250,000 workers (of whom about 10,000 were women) engaged in trades especially liable to fluctuations, such as building, engineering, shipbuilding, iron-founding, saw-milling and vehicle construction. The employers were to contribute 2½d. per insured person per each week of employment, and each employé 2½d. a week. The State was to add to the fund one-third of the joint contributions of employers and workpeople. Unemployment benefit was to be at the rate of 7s. a week, on the basis of one week's benefit for every five contributions, with a maximum of fifteen weeks in any one year. Applicants for benefit were required to prove to the Labour Exchange officials that they had been employed in an insured trade for not less than twenty-six weeks in the preceding five years, and that they could not obtain suitable employment. Associations of insured workmen were entitled under certain conditions to undertake the payment to their own members of unemployment benefit, due to them out of the Insurance Fund, provided that they added to it, out of their own funds, at least one-third of the statutory benefit.

The Act of 1911 was only a beginning. During and after the Great War the scheme was amended and expanded, until it was

Unemployment Insurance

[1] Cf. Annual Reports of Ministry of Health.

submerged under wave after wave of world-depression in industry and trade. The original Act was planned on a strictly actuarial basis : it was a genuine insurance scheme. When, after 1920, the number of the unemployed began to rise with terrifying rapidity the original features were entirely obliterated. An account of post-War developments must, however, be post-poned.

Demo-cratic Finance

Social reforms cost money. Nor is Democracy commonly credited with prudence in public finance. Mr. Asquith, however, who was responsible for the Budgets of 1906, 1907 and 1908, had been reared in the Gladstonian tradition, and it was not until after 1910 that there was any conspicuous increase in expenditure and consequently in taxation.

Budget of 1906

In his first Budget (1906) Asquith inherited a realized surplus of £3,466,000. Nevertheless he insisted that, in view of the rapid increase in expenditure during the preceding decade, a return to a ' more thrifty and economical administration was the first and paramount duty of the Government '. He estimated expenditure at nearly £142,000,000 as compared with £101,000,000 ten years earlier. He repealed the export duty on coal at an estimated cost to the revenue of £1,000,000 and devoted £920,000 to a reduction of the tea duty from 6d. to 5d. He expressed agreement with the opinion of his predecessors that an income tax of 1s. in the £ in time of peace could not be justified, but instead of reducing it he announced the appointment of a select committee to inquire into the practicability of graduation and of differentiation between ' permanent and precarious incomes '.

Budget of 1907

The main feature of Asquith's second Budget was an attempt to carry into effect both principles, and give some relief to the poorer class of income-tax payers. The general rate of tax was retained at 1s., but it was reduced to 9d. in the £ on the ' earned ' portion of all incomes not exceeding £2,000 a year. All ' un-earned ' income was to be taxed at 1s., and also all income whether earned or unearned above the £2,000 limit. The loss on income tax was, however, to be compensated by a graduated increase in death-duties on estates over £150,000. The principles of gradua-tion and differentiation had long ago been advocated by J. S. Mill. Asquith was in Economics his loyal disciple, and he had the satisfaction of showing as Chancellor of the Exchequer that he had learnt the lessons which, as a University Extension Lecturer, he had been wont to teach.

The principles taught by Mill and applied by Asquith are evidently specious : but it is questionable whether, in practice, there is any justification for differentiating between ' earned ' and ' unearned ' income. Differentiation between inherited and earned wealth is one thing, and may be justified ; but ' unearned ' income is, in many cases, no less than ' earned ', the result of personal labour and enterprise. To differentiate in such cases is to penalize thrift, and encourage extravagant expenditure. In normal circumstances the interests of the community would be better served by a fiscal system which would discourage wasteful expenditure, and appropriately reward those who contribute to that capital fund out of which the wages of labour are temporarily advanced, if not ultimately paid.[1] Asquith would have been the last man to ignore or deride sound economic doctrine. But Economics is one thing : Politics is another. Chancellors of the Exchequer are apt to be politicians first, economists afterwards, and in the event of a conflict of doctrines to take the line of political least resistance.

Mr. Asquith opened the Budget of 1908, no longer as Chancellor of the Exchequer, but as Prime Minister. Peel had done the same. No one, however, would describe Asquith's Budget as ' historic ' in the sense justly applied to Peel's. The new financial year began, like its three predecessors, with a substantial surplus—in this case of nearly £5,000,000. This afforded a good foundation for the great edifice which Asquith proposed to erect. The central feature of his financial statement was the scheme —already described—of non-contributory Old Age Pensions. These were estimated to cost, in a full working year, £6,000,000. In giving that estimate Asquith observed that the whole scheme ought to be ' one of which we should from the first be able to foresee—I do not say with precision but with reasonable accuracy —the ultimate cost ; and thus avoid committing Parliament to a mortgage of indefinite amount upon the future resources of the

Budget of 1908

---

[1] The economic doctrine advanced in the text will, I am aware, be derided by a post-War generation as hopelessly ' Victorian '. But post-War days are not normal. Should normality ever be restored, ' Victorian Economics ' may again come into their own.

country '. Before the Finance Bill became law Mr. Lloyd George had already raised the estimate of cost to £7,000,000, and his Chief was fain to admit that all estimates either of number or cost were ' in the highest degree conjectural '. So it proved. Yet few members who light-heartedly voted for the Bill in 1908 could have imagined that in a quarter of a century the scheme thus initiated and subsequently enlarged would be costing over £37,000,000 a year.[1] Even assuming the accuracy of the original estimate it was, surely, a singularly inopportune moment to have remitted, at a cost to the Exchequer of over £3,500,000, more than half the sugar duty—one of the few taxes to which prospective beneficiaries under the Pension Scheme themselves made a modest contribution.

The ' People's Budget ', 1909–10   The year 1909–10 was one of the most momentous in the financial, and still more in the Constitutional history of Great Britain. Mr. Lloyd George was determined to show that it was not for nothing that he had claimed the key position in the Ministry. The Budget of 1909 unquestionably made history.

It was opened by the Chancellor of the Exchequer on April 29 in a speech of four hours' duration ; it was under discussion for seventy-two Parliamentary days, including several all-night sittings, in the House of Commons ; it passed the House of Commons on November 4 by 379 to 149 votes, and on November 30 was rejected in the House of Lords by 350 votes to 75.

Neither in form nor substance was it an ordinary Budget. The dark threats that preceded it ; the method and manner of its introduction ; the place accorded to it in the legislative work of the Session ; the wide range of its proposals ; the almost insoluble complexity of its details ; the vagueness of its financial forecasts—all combined to give it an exceptional, indeed an unprecedented character. Mr. Lloyd George bettered the example set by Mr. Gladstone in 1861. He combined into one conglomerate Bill not only all the tax Bills of the year, but virtually all the legislative proposals of the Session, not to say all the rejected proposals of an entire Parliament. In short, he provided the *reductio ad absurdum* of the vicious innovation which, in order to frustrate the tactics of the House of Lords, Mr. Gladstone established in 1861.[2]

[1] Cmd. 4197.   [2] Cf. Marriott, *Second Chambers* (2nd ed., 1927).

Mr. Lloyd George was faced with an actual deficit of £1,502,000, which would have been greater but for large, and as events were to prove prudent, forestallments of dutiable commodities. On the existing basis of taxation, he had to contemplate a prospective deficit of nearly £16,000,000. Evidently, unless expenditure could be drastically reduced, new sources of revenue would have to be discovered. Mr. Lloyd George was not the man to reduce expenditure ; on the contrary, he looked forward to a progressive increase to meet ' the growing demands of the social programme ' foreshadowed in his speech. The fulfilment of that programme has been already described. The Minister made no concealment of the purpose underlying his proposals. ' This ', he said, ' is a war budget. It is for raising money to wage implacable warfare against poverty and squalidness.'

Whence were the sinews of war to be obtained ? First, by additional taxes on the larger incomes. For incomes exceeding £3,000 a year the rate was raised from 1s. to 1s. 2d., and in addition there was imposed a super-tax on all incomes over £5,000, leviable on the amount of their excess over £3,000 a year. Then there were heavy increases in the Death Duties. An increase in the cost of liquor licences, with additional taxation on spirits and tobacco, were estimated to produce £6,000,000, and besides producing revenue liquor duties would avenge the defeat suffered by the Licensing Bill in the House of Lords. But the feature of the Budget which aroused the most bitter opposition, and which seemed to its opponents to be especially ' vindictive ', centred on the proposals in regard to the valuation and taxation of land.

The ' land taxes ' aroused great enthusiasm among Socialists. **Land Taxes** ' The Budget ', said one Socialist writer, ' in its essential though rather misshapen features is ours, and we would be unnatural parents were we to disown it.' ' The Budget', said another, ' consists of thin wedge-ends . . . and it is the business of Socialists to drive them home.' Mr. (afterwards Viscount) Snowden waxed almost lyrical in his exultation : ' There is no other way under heaven by which we can make the poor better off, except by making somebody poorer than they were. . . . This is not the last tribute which the idle-rich class of this country will be called upon to pay for dealing with the problem of poverty for which their riches are responsible. . . . We are beginning

to see what a Budget like this is going to do to set things right.' [1]
No wonder that Liberals of the older School were somewhat
embarrassed by the exuberance of their allies, or that Mr. Asquith
was at pains to demonstrate that the Budget was not in fact
Socialistic.[2]

The proposals as regards land were briefly as follows. As an
essential preliminary there was to be a new Domesday Survey,
an exhaustive valuation of the land of the whole country, differentiating between the gross value and the site value, i.e. between
the value of the site covered and the site cleared. Then there
was to be (i) an increment value duty, i.e. a tax of 20 per cent.
on any increase in the *site* value of land accruing *after* April 30,
1909, and payable on each occasion on which the property changed
hands, whether by purchase or at death ; (ii) a reversion duty of
10 per cent. on the benefit accruing to lessors on the termination
of leases ; (iii) an annual tax of $\frac{1}{2}d$. in the £ on the (capital) site
value of ' undeveloped ' land, mainly building land which was
withheld from the market by owners in expectation of a rise in
its value ; and (iv) an annual tax of 1s. in the £ on the rental
value of the right to work minerals.

The fiscal value of these proposals was evidently prospective,
not immediate. Their yield for the current year was estimated
by the Minister at no more than half a million. ' An amount ',
he added with grim humour, ' which must not be regarded as any
indication of the revenue they will ultimately produce '.

That increased revenue was essential unless either Naval
Defence or Social Reform, or both, were to be starved, could not
be denied by the most convinced opponents of the ' People's
Budget '. The land taxes would seem, however, to have combined almost all the vices which any taxative impost can possess.
Ill-designed for purposes of revenue ; grotesquely unequal and
unfair as between individuals ; uncertain in incidence ; pregnant
with possibilities of friction ; vastly complicated ; expensive to
collect ; above all, only too likely to intensify the social evil
which it was the avowed, and doubtless sincere, object of the
new duties to assuage. So the critics of the Budget asserted.
Experience completely justified them. Instead, for example, of

[1] Hansard, May 5, 1909.
[2] At Bingley Hall, Birmingham, on September 17.

encouraging building and town planning, the new taxes had precisely the opposite effect. From the moment the Finance Bill passed into law the speculator took alarm, private enterprise was arrested, and building operations were suspended, with results which were only too clearly manifested in an acute shortage of houses—a shortage which presented to the post-War politicians one of the most difficult problems they had to face.

Nor did the taxes produce revenue. The total amount produced by the Land Duties down to March 31, 1919, was £1,087,440. The total cost of collection and of the Land Valuation was, down to the same date, approximately £4,600,000. The yield of the Mineral Rights Duty was £3,026,466. In his Financial Statement of that year (1919)[1] Mr. (afterwards Sir Austen) Chamberlain announced that the Duties had, for a variety of reasons proved unworkable, and in his Budget of 1920 he repealed them all with the exception of the Mineral Rights Duty. The rest of the Land Valuation Duties had involved landowners in much worry and expense; they had created infinite friction and not a little litigation, but had never even paid for the expense of collection. With the entire assent of their author, then Prime Minister, they were ignominiously deleted from the Statute Book. The Land Valuation Department had, however, proved useful in the War and was retained.

Not often has a great financial controversy been so speedily resolved; nor the contention of hostile critics been so completely vindicated. It should be added that the Budget introduced on April 29, 1909, did not pass into law until April 29, 1910—a year later to a day. In the interval it had in effect been submitted to the judgement of the electorate, and had not been rejected. The issue raised by it was, however, only in a secondary degree financial. Unwittingly, or of set purpose, Mr. Lloyd George had involved the Legislature and the Electorate in a constitutional conflict more serious than any that had arisen since 1688.

[1] Hansard, 1919, pp. 1212 and 2723.

CHAPTER XVII

THE CONSTITUTIONAL CRISIS—A NEW REIGN—THE PARLIAMENT ACT

The
Peers
and the
Budget

' WE have got them at last.' Such was the exultant cry of the Chancellor of the Exchequer on the morrow of the fateful division by which the House of Lords rejected his Budget. Was it a mere momentary ebullition of high spirits on the part of a great parliamentary pugilist ? Or did it reflect the success-ful achievement of a plan deliberately designed ? Lord Rose-bery arrived at the ' deliberate conclusion that the Government wishes the House of Lords to throw out the Finance Bill '.[1] It matters little ; the action of the House of Lords could have but one result, to precipitate the crisis foreseen and foretold in 1894 by Mr. Gladstone. Ever since the defeat of the second Home Rule Bill in 1893 the conflict between the two Houses had been impending. Whenever the Liberal Party had a majority in the House of Commons, the Lords had engaged in the playful pastime of ' filling up the cup '. In 1909 it overflowed.

The storm had long been brewing. The great authority of Queen Victoria had averted a conflict between the two Houses on the Irish Church Bill in 1869 and again in 1884 in regard to the Franchise and Redistribution Bills. Mr. Gladstone's last words in the House of Commons were accepted by his Party as a testament which it was their pious duty to execute. But the opportunity tarried.

During the ten years of Unionist administration the House of Lords naturally gave no offence to their allies in the Commons ; but with the return of the Radicals to power in 1906 the old battle was renewed. Bill after Bill sent up by the Commons was rejected or emasculated by the Lords. Small wonder that Camp-

[1] At Glasgow, September 10, 1909.

bell-Bannerman, backed as he was by a great majority, and fresh from a triumphant appeal to the electorate, should, as we have seen, have been moved to wrath.[1]

In a speech at Oxford (December 1) Mr. Lloyd George raised the issue even more bluntly :

'If the House of Lords persisted in its present policy, it would be a much larger measure than the Education Bill that would come up for consideration. It would come upon this issue, whether the country was to be governed by the King and the Peers, or by the King and the people.'

The Labour Party declared for the total abolition of the Second Chamber, but the Government preferred 'mending' to 'ending', and by a majority of 432 votes to 147 the House of Commons, at their instance, passed the following resolution :—

'In order to give effect to the will of the people as expressed by their elected representatives, it is necessary that the power of the other House to alter or reject Bills should be so restrained by law as to secure that within the limits of a single Parliament the final decision of the Commons shall prevail.'[2]

Undeterred by this threat the Lords rejected in 1908 a Licensing Bill, and in 1909 the issue was finally joined on the Finance Bill.

No competent person could deny that the Lords had a *legal* —or as Asquith said a *technical*—right to reject the Bill. But between 1688 and 1909 there was only one occasion on which the Lords had ever questioned the exclusive right of the Commons to control taxation and expenditure. In 1860 the Paper Duty Repeal Bill, after narrowly escaping defeat in the Commons, was rejected by the Lords. Thereupon the Commons, at the instance of Mr. Gladstone, passed a series of resolutions reaffirming in the most explicit terms the exclusive privileges of the Lower House in matters of taxation.[3] In the following year (1861) Mr. Gladstone finally clinched the matter, by including all the financial proposals of the year in a single Finance Bill, which the Lords were compelled to accept or reject as a whole. This practice has since 1861 been invariably followed. Very unwillingly did the

---

[1] *Supra*, p. 255.   [2] Hansard, June 27, 1907, p. 1516.

[3] For text of resolutions and generally on the historical aspect of the question see Marriott, *Second Chambers*, c. iv.

Lords accept Harcourt's Budget of 1894, but Lord Salisbury warned them of the constitutional inconveniences, not to say anomalies, which must arise from the exercise of their undoubted rights in regard to the rejection of Finance Bills. ' You cannot ', he in effect argued, ' reject a Money Bill, because you cannot change the Executive ; to leave the existing Executive in power and yet to deprive them of the means of carrying on the government of the country would create a grave constitutional situation.'

So thought some of the more experienced of the Unionist Leaders in 1909. Notably Lord St. Aldwyn, who wrote to Lord Lansdowne, ' I think both the right and wise course is to pass the Budget as it comes to us '. Lord Lansdowne thought other- wise. Most people now agree that the rejection, if justified on the merits, was a tactical blunder.

The Government took up the challenge, as Mr. Asquith said, ' without a day's delay '. On December 2 he proposed a resolu- tion that ' the action of the House of Lords in refusing to pass into law the financial provision made by this House for the ser- vice of the year is a breach of the Constitution, and a usurpation of the rights of the Commons '. It was carried by 349 votes to 134. Parliament was forthwith prorogued and on January 10, 1910, was dissolved.

The language used by Liberal Ministers left no doubt as to the issue which they desired to submit to the electorate. ' We shall not ', said Mr. Asquith (December 10, 1909), ' assume office, and we shall not hold office, unless we can secure the safeguards which experience shows to be necessary for the legislative ability and honour of the party of progress. . . . We are going to ask the country to give us authority to apply an effective remedy to these intolerable conditions. What is to be done will have to be done by Act of Parliament. The time for unwritten conven- tion has unhappily gone by.'

General Election, Jan. 1910   Despite the efforts of the Radical leaders to concentrate atten- tion on a single issue, it was not found easy to do so. In the background were other issues : the embryonic Socialism dis- closed by the Budget proposals ; tariff-reform and free-trade ; Irish Home Rule. Nor was the verdict free from ambiguity. Liberals and Unionists were returned in almost equal numbers

(274 Liberals to 273 Conservatives); Labour representation was reduced to 41 ; the Nationalists numbered 82. The Irish Nationalists held the balance. Nor did they fail to use their advantage. From the Budget controversy they had held aloof ; but to the attainment of Home Rule a co-ordinate Second Chamber offered an insurmountable obstacle. If the Nationalists were to help the Liberals to curtail the ' veto ' of the Lords, the Liberals must pledge themselves to use the new powers conceded to the House of Commons to carry Home Rule.

Between the two parties there was some soreness, for at the election of 1906 Home Rule had been tacitly dropped out of the Liberal programme : in January 1910 the specific issue was that of the Second Chamber. The Nationalists, therefore, had some cause for alarm, if not for suspicion, and were not prepared to take any risks. So ' exorbitant ' (the word was Asquith's) were the demands of Mr. Redmond and his followers, that some of the Ministers were at one moment in favour of resignation ; but their courage quickly revived ; and an ' understanding ' was arrived at with the Nationalists. Liberals and National- ists

King Edward opened the new Parliament in person on February 21, 1910, and his Speech foreshadowed proposals to define the relations between the Houses of Parliament so as to secure the undivided authority of the House of Commons in Finance and its predominance in legislation. Second Chamber Reform

On March 29 the Prime Minister moved three Resolutions. The first carefully defined Money Bills and declared it expedient that the House of Lords should be disabled by law from rejecting or amending such Bills ; the second declared that if any Bill passed the Commons in three successive sessions, and was thrice rejected by the Lords, it should (provided two years had elapsed since its introduction) become law on the royal assent being declared ; the third limited the duration of Parliament to five years.

These Resolutions were, after prolonged debate and many divisions, carried on April 14, and a Bill based upon them was on the same night introduced by the Prime Minister.

Almost simultaneously the following Resolutions were accepted by the House of Lords :

I. That a strong and efficient Second Chamber is not merely

an integral part of the British Constitution, but is necessary to the well-being of the State and to the balance of Parliament.

II. That such a Chamber can best be obtained by the reform and reconstitution of the House of Lords.

III. That a necessary preliminary of such reform and reconstitution is the acceptance of the principle that the possession of a peerage should no longer of itself give the right to sit and vote in the House of Lords.

On the night on which the Parliament Bill was introduced Mr. Asquith declared, in somewhat minatory terms, that if the Lords rejected the Bill, the Government would at once resign or recommend the King to dissolve Parliament. ' Let me ', he proceeded, ' add this, that in no case shall we recommend a Dissolution, except under such conditions as will secure that in the new Parliament the judgement of the people as expressed at the election will be carried into law.' However veiled, this was an unmistakable threat : the Government would not, as a Government, appeal to the country, unless the King were prepared to promise that, in the assumed event, he would assent to the creation of new peers in numbers sufficient to overcome the resistance of the House of Lords.

The views of the Government were communicated to King Edward at Biarritz, whither he had gone on the urgent advice of his doctors, who were more seriously alarmed about his health than the public were permitted to know.

The King returned to London on April 27, greatly the better, it seemed, for his holiday. He found himself faced by a political *impasse*, demanding the exercise of all his tact and skill. Doubtful as to the attitude of the Irish Nationalists, Ministers were not unprepared for defeat on the reintroduced Budget. On the day of the King's return, however, it passed, substantially unamended, through the House of Commons, and on the 29th became law.

But behind the Budget loomed the larger issue.

Ever since the advent of the Radicals to power in 1906 King Edward had watched, with deepening concern, the development of the quarrel between the two Houses. An attack on the hereditary principle as enshrined in the House of Lords seemed to him to menace the hereditary monarchy. The least vain or pompous of men, King Edward had a high sense both of the dignity and the utility of the Crown, and he was not less tenacious than his mother of its rightful prerogatives. Moreover he was, as Lord Esher said of him, ' not only a Peace-maker but a Peace-lover '. He would have kept the peace of Europe, if he could, and he disliked, not less, the spectacle of domestic strife. In October 1909 the King asked Mr. Asquith whether it would be constitutionally correct for him to confer with the Opposition leaders on the situation. ' Perfectly correct ', was the Premier's reply. Accordingly, on October 12, he summoned Lord Lansdowne and Mr. Balfour to the Palace in the hope of averting the threatened conflict. But to his great chagrin his efforts were wholly unavailing.

On the larger issue as to the future of the House of Lords the King had thought much, and on January 30, 1910, he communicated to Lord Crewe, his guest at Windsor, his own plan.

He would have left the composition of the House unaltered, but have confined the right of voting to one hundred members, nominated in equal numbers by the leaders of the two Parties in the Upper House. There was, as he shrewdly pointed out, a great deal of independent opinion among the Peers, and he was convinced that even though the hundred nominees were selected as strong partisans, there would always be among them, when it came to a critical division, enough moderate-minded men to avert a conflict. Whatever be thought about the merits of the scheme, the formulation of it showed on the part of the King, as Lord Crewe says, a ' shrewd appreciation of the difficulties surrounding the creation of a new Second Chamber '.[1]

Whether, had he lived, King Edward could have influenced the course of events in the direction he desired, is a matter of conjecture. For the few days after his return from Biarritz he transacted State business, betraying no loss of grip—as for instance Death when he pressed for the appointment of Lord Kitchener as Viceroy of King of India—but his days were numbered, and on May 6 he died. Edward

Utterly unprepared for the news the nation was stunned. The most careless could not fail to realize that, coming when it did, the death of King Edward was a tragic and irreparable blow. ' At a most anxious moment in the fortunes of the State, we had lost,' wrote Mr. Asquith, ' without warning or preparation, the

[1] *Memorandum* quoted ap. Lee, *King Edward VII*, II. 696.

Sovereign whose ripe experience, trained sagacity, equitable judgement, and unvarying consideration counted for so much.' [1] How well justified were the Premier's forebodings the sequel will show.

Europe was hardly less perturbed than England by the news of King Edward's death. The European situation was not less menacing than the domestic. Europe recognized that a great Peace-maker had been removed, and at the late King's Funeral on May 20 no fewer than eight foreign monarchs, including the German Emperor, were present to testify to their sense of loss.

King Edward's Reign   The reign of Edward VII, though short, was far from insignificant. Alike in the affairs of Europe and in the affairs of Great Britain it was distinguished by events of high moment. Not until he was gone did men realize how much, in those affairs, the King's own personality had counted. Sir William Harcourt, who was no courtier, declared that Edward VII was the greatest King of England since William the Conqueror. Had he said since Edward I few would question his accuracy. Lord Redesdale (*Memoirs*, I. 172) tells of a red-hot Radical who came away from his interview with King Edward saying : ' That is the greatest man that ever I had speech of.' Nor, as he came to know him better, did he ever alter his opinion.

The closer men were to the King the more they appreciated his great qualities : his grip on affairs ; his untiring industry ; his moral courage ; his rigid punctuality ; his transparent honesty ; his freedom from rancour or resentment ; not least his simple religious faith. ' Le roi charmeur ', was Lord Rosebery's description of him ; but his irresistible charm was due not merely to native geniality of temper, but to a genuine interest both in affairs and in men. Balfour was too highbrow for him, and though Asquith testified that the King treated him with ' gracious frankness ', his relations both with Asquith and Grey were more polite than intimate. Between the King and Campbell-Bannerman there was complete cordiality, but after his death the Ministers with whom the King got on best were Lord Carrington, an old friend, and Haldane, whose great abilities he recognized and whose humour he appreciated. Yet if intimacy was essential to a complete understanding of the King's character, the whole

[1] *Fifty Years of Parliament*, II. 87.

nation instinctively felt that they had lost not merely a great
ruler but a personal friend.

King Edward was succeeded by his only surviving son, who King
was at once proclaimed King with the title of George V. Born George V
on June 3, 1865, the new King was hardly 45 when he ascended
the throne. Educated as a sailor, he had already seen much of
the world and in particular of the British Empire overseas, and
as Prince and Princess of Wales he and his consort had already
firmly established themselves in the respect and affection of their
future subjects alike in the homeland and the outer Empire.

Rarely, however, has a new Sovereign been confronted with
a more difficult situation than that which faced King George V.
But the sudden death of a much-loved King gave pause to eager
partisans, and hushed, for the moment, political controversy.
Under an impulse common to all parties the leaders honestly
endeavoured to reach a compromise. ' Then the nation ', as Mr.
Asquith said, ' witnessed an incident unparalleled in the annals
of party warfare. The two combatant forces already in battle
array, piled their arms, while the Leaders on both sides retired
for private conference.'

This conference, consisting of eight persons, met, behind Constitu-
closed doors, for the first time on June 17. The Government tional
was represented by Mr. Asquith, Lord Crewe, Mr. Birrell and ence
Mr. Lloyd George ; Mr. Balfour, Lord Lansdowne, Mr. Austen
Chamberlain and Lord Cawdor represented the Opposition. On
July 29 Mr. Asquith was able to inform the House of Commons
that such progress had been made towards a settlement that the
meetings of the Conference would be resumed in the autumn.
Resumed they were, but with rapidly diminishing chances of
success. A large measure of agreement had been reached on
financial procedure, on a plan for the settlement of differences
by means of a joint sitting, and on a special mode of dealing with
Constitutional questions—a point on which the Unionists, with
an eye on Home Rule, laid great stress. But how was ' pure
finance '—admittedly to be under the sole control of the Commons—to be defined ? And how was ' Constitutional ' to be
differentiated from ' Ordinary ' legislation, under the conditions
of an ' Unwritten ' and ' Flexible ' Constitution like our own ?

These were among the difficulties which baffled a Conference not specially competent to discuss questions of Constitutional law. No agreement on these vital questions could be reached; on November 10 the final breakdown of the Conference was announced, and on the 11th was personally communicated to King George by the Prime Minister.

The King and his Ministers

King Edward had insisted that before using the prerogative to swamp the House of Lords there must be another appeal to the electorate.

On November 15 the Cabinet decided to ask for a Dissolution, and approved the following memorandum which was laid before the King by Mr. Asquith and Lord Crewe on November 16.

'His Majesty's Ministers cannot take the responsibility of advising a dissolution, unless they may understand that, in the event of the policy of the Government being approved by an adequate majority in the new House of Commons, His Majesty will be ready to exercise his Constitutional powers, which may involve the prerogative of creating Peers, if needed, to secure that effect shall be given to the decision of the country. His Majesty's Ministers are fully alive to the importance of keeping the name of the King out of the sphere of party and electoral controversy. They take upon themselves, as is their duty, the entire and exclusive responsibility for the policy which they would place before the electorate. His Majesty will probably agree that it would be inadvisable in the interests of the State that any communication of the intentions of the Crown should be made public unless and until the actual occasion should arise.'

Accordingly, on November 28 Parliament was dissolved.

Acute controversy subsequently arose as to what exactly took place at the interview between the King and Mr. Asquith and Lord Crewe on November 16. What advice, if any, apart from that contained in the memorandum, was given by the Ministers to the King? Mr. Asquith's statement to the House of Commons two days after the interview told little. The story was told in much greater detail by the Marquess of Crewe, in the famous debate of August 8, 1911. 'Since this question of that interview', said Lord Crewe, 'has been the subject of so much comment, the King naturally desires that [the facts] should be plainly stated.' Lord Crewe then proceeded to state them 'plainly': did he state them fully? Mr. Asquith's statement in the House of Commons on the same subject (August 7) was characterized by *The Times* [1] as a *suppressio veri* and *suggestio falsi*. Lord Crewe's statement in the Lords was fuller. Was it complete ? The essential passage ran as follows :

'The effect of that interview was that we ascertained His Majesty's view that, if the opinion of the country were clearly ascertained upon the Parliament Bill, in the last resort a creation of Peers might be the only remedy and might be the only way of concluding the dispute. His Majesty faced the contingency and entertained the suggestion as a possible one with natural, and, if I may be permitted to use the phrase, with legitimate reluctance. His Majesty, however, naturally entertained the feeling—a feeling which we entirely shared—that if we resigned our offices, having as we had a large majority in the House of Commons, the only result could be an immediate Dissolution, in which it would be practically impossible, however anxious we naturally should be to do it, to keep the Crown out of the controversy. The mixing up of the Crown in a controversy such as that was naturally most distasteful to its illustrious wearer, . . . but it could be scarcely more distasteful even to His Majesty than to myself and my colleagues.' [2]

Lord Crewe frankly admitted that to him the 'whole business' was 'odious'; and we can well believe it. Lord Rosebery pointedly referred to something—not more precisely specified, as having given 'an unpleasant savour to the whole of this transaction', and Lord St. Aldwyn, speaking with knowledge, bluntly said (August 9) : 'We have not the whole case before us.' He then proceeded to put certain questions which have never to this day been answered : 'Whether Mr. Balfour and Lord Lansdowne were ever suggested to the King by his Ministers as persons who might be prepared to form a Government, in the event of the King declining to give the promise asked for by the Ministers.' The King 'ought to have had the fullest possible information and to have heard both sides of the question. The King ought to have been told that he was at liberty to hear what Lord Lansdowne and Mr. Balfour had to say before making up his mind as to whether he would give that hypothetical promise. . . . If [the

[1] August 14, 1911.
[2] *Official Report* (Lords), August 8, 1911, pp. 836, 837.

Ministers] had had common generosity, they would have advised
the King to do what I have suggested. . . . I go further and
say that it would have been common honesty from the advisers
of the Sovereign to the Sovereign. . . . What has been the
result ? When the crisis came near us the other day Ministers
tendered certain advice to the Sovereign and he accepted it. But
he was previously bound by his hypothetical promise. The King
has been misled by his Ministers. . . . I believe the action of
the Government has deliberately placed him in the most cruel
position any English Sovereign has been placed in for more than
a century.' [1]

The point raised by Lord St. Aldwyn touched the most subtle
spot in the delicately poised machinery of the English Constitution : the relations between the Sovereign and his confidential
advisers ; between the formal and the actual executive of this
kingdom.

On this point a bitter controversy ensued.[2] Two conclusions
were, however, established : one was that the King, when confronted, in November 1910, by his confidential advisers with a
demand for ' contingent guarantees ' [3] had a perfect right to seek
counsel from any Privy Councillor or any Peer. Whether the
King desired to avail himself of that right, and whether, if so,
his desire was frustrated, we know not. But we do know that
in fact he did not exercise it in respect of the leaders of the Opposition. Conversely, His Majesty's Ministers had, on their part,
an equal right to decline to be responsible for the conduct of
affairs, if the King chose to exercise his rights.

The Par-
liament
Bill in
the Lords
One concession the Ministers consented to make. In accordance with the King's wish the Parliament Bill was presented to
the Lords, and the Second Reading was moved by Lord Crewe
on November 21. At Lord Lansdowne's instance, however, the
debate on it was adjourned, in order that he might bring forward
his own alternative scheme.

Lord Rosebery had already (on November 17) induced the
Peers to affirm two important propositions : firstly, that hence-

---

[1] *Official Report*, August 9, pp. 923 seq.

[2] On the whole question see Marriott, *Second Chambers* (2nd ed.), pp.
183–91.

[3] Mr. Asquith always denied that ' guarantees ' had been asked for or
given, but admitted a ' conditional understanding '. *Fifty Years*, II. 91.

forward no Lord of Parliament should be allowed to sit and vote in the House of Lords merely by virtue of hereditary right ; and, secondly, that it was desirable that the House should be reinforced by new elements from the outside.

On November 23 Lord Lansdowne put his alternative scheme *An Alter-* before the House and the country, in a series of resolutions, which, *native Scheme* following the lines of the proposals put forward by the Unionist members of the Constitutional Conference, affirmed that the Parliament Bill provided no basis for a permanent settlement ; that the House of Lords must be reduced in number and reconstituted ; that subject to certain safeguards it would surrender its undoubted Constitutional right to reject Money Bills ; and that there must be a Referendum for ' Organic ' or ' Constitutional ' legislation.[1] The debate revealed the willingness, nay the anxiety, of the Lords to accept drastic reform ; but it was conducted under the shadow of an impending Dissolution, and, therefore, in ' an atmosphere of unreality '.[2] Nevertheless, the Lansdowne Resolutions did enable the Conservatives to put before the country at the ensuing election a concrete alternative to the ' Veto ' Bill. In particular, the Unionist Party pinned their faith to the *Referendum*, which was put forward as solution not merely of the Constitutional difficulty, but also of the Tariff Reform controversy—a suggestion greatly resented by the ardent Tariff Reformers.

The General Election took place. It carried things no further. *General* The electors had not changed their minds since January. Between *Election, Decem-* Radicals and Unionists there was a tie (272 each) ; Labour gained *ber 1910* one seat (42) and the Irish Nationalists two (84). The Nationalists therefore remained masters of the situation ; nor did they refrain from the exercise of power.

Accordingly, despite the fact that the British Electorate had shown itself to be almost equally divided, on the specific issue submitted to it, the Parliament Bill was reintroduced in February, was carried on Second Reading in March by 368 to 243, and on Third Reading by a similar majority in May.

Would the House of Lords accept it ? On the day (May 15) on which the Commons passed the Third Reading of the Parlia-

---

[1] For more precise details see *infra*, p. 304.
[2] Lord Newton's *Lansdowne*, pp. 397–405.

ment Bill, Lord Lansdowne moved in the Lords the Second
Reading of his House of Lords Reconstitution Bill.

It was framed in the spirit of the Rosebery resolutions. The
new Second Chamber was to be only about half as large as the
existing House of Lords, and was to consist of 320 to 350 members.
Apart from Peers of the Royal Blood, the Law Lords, the Arch-
bishops of Canterbury and York, and five Bishops elected by the
whole Episcopate, the new House was to contain three main
elements : (i) 100 hereditary Peers, elected by their Order from
among Peers qualified by public service, ministerial, parliamentary, Colonial, military, naval, or in local government ; (ii) 120
persons, elected on the principle of proportional representation
by members of the House of Commons grouped in electoral areas,
each area to be arranged with consideration for existing constituencies, community of interests, and population, and to return
not less than three and not more than twelve Lords of Parliament ; (iii) 100 persons nominated by the Crown in proportion to
the strength of parties in the House of Commons. The term of
office for all three categories was to be twelve years, but one-
fourth in each class were to retire every three years. Peers not
elected to the Upper House were to be eligible for election to the
Lower, but the Crown was to be restricted in the creation of new
Peers to five a year, in addition to Cabinet or ex-Cabinet Ministers. Such was the admirable scheme intended to mollify the
opponents of the hereditary Chamber ; the Bill was read a second
time on May 22, but, amid the excitement engendered by the
Parliament Bill, made no further progress.

A similar fate awaited the Bill introduced in the same session
by Lord Balfour of Burleigh.

The
Referen-
dum Bill

Lord Balfour was an ardent advocate of the Referendum,
and his Bill provided ' for the Taking of a Poll of the Parliamentary Electors of the United Kingdom with Respect to certain
Bills in Parliament '. A Poll was to be taken : (a) on the demand
of either House, in the case of any Bill passed by the Commons,
but rejected or not passed by the House of Lords within forty
days after it was sent up to that House ; or (b) on the demand of
not less than two hundred members of the House of Commons in
the case of a Bill passed by both Houses. In either case the Bill
was to be presented for the Royal Assent if the total affirmative

vote exceeded the negative vote by not less than two votes per centum of the total negative vote.

This ingenious, perhaps over-ingenious, proposal was primarily, though not exclusively, designed to decide disputes between the two Houses; but it also gave a power of appeal against the decision of both Houses to a substantial minority in the House of Commons. In the heated atmosphere of 1911 Lord Balfour's Bill, like Lord Lansdowne's, had little chance of a fair consideration, and, though powerfully supported, it did not receive a second reading.

At the moment the question of 'Powers' overshadowed not only the question of 'Composition', but all other Constitutional devices. Would the Peers accept the Parliament Bill, or compel the Government to call upon the King to implement the 'conditional understanding' which had been reached in the previous November?

The Peers were sharply divided. On the one hand, the 'Hedgers', led by Lord Lansdowne and Lord Curzon, preferred to accept the Parliament Bill with all its consequences rather than permit the Constitution to be travestied, and expose the Peers to the indignity of receiving into their bosom five hundred Radical Peers pledged to a limitation of the constitutional powers of the Order to which they had obtained admission. On the other hand, the 'Ditchers', led by the veteran Earl of Halsbury, were resolved if necessary to die in the last ditch, and to compel the Crown to choose between a refusal of the advice of his responsible Ministers and the employment of a weapon as odious as it was rusty. The 'Ditchers' believed that the Ministerial threat was an empty one, and that, at the eleventh hour, Ministers themselves, or if not the Ministers then the King, would recoil from the precipice to which events had led them. But the 'Hedgers' were not ready to take the risk; their opinion prevailed, and the Parliament Bill became law. On the same day (August 10) that the Peers (as many held) signed their own death warrant, the members of the House of Commons voted to themselves salaries of £400 a year.

The Parliament Act, however it be regarded, must be accounted as one of the most significant contributions ever made to a Constitution which is mainly unwritten. For the first time the legal

(marginal note:) 'Hedgers' and 'Ditchers'

(marginal note:) The Parliament Act

relations of the two Houses of the Legislature were defined by statute. A preamble of unusual length and importance declared that it was ' intended to substitute for the House of Lords as it at present exists a Second Chamber constituted on a popular instead of hereditary basis '. The Act itself embodied exactly the Resolutions moved by Mr. Asquith on March 29, 1910.[1]

It defined a Money Bill as ' a Public Bill which in the opinion of the Speaker of the House of Commons contains only provisions dealing with all or any of the following subjects, namely, the imposition, repeal, remission, alteration, or regulation of taxation ; the imposition for the payment of debt or other financial purposes, of charges on the Consolidated Fund, or on money provided by Parliament, or the variation or repeal of any such charges ; supply ; the appropriation, receipt, custody, issue or audit of accounts of public money ; the raising or guarantee of any loan or the repayment thereof ; or subordinate matters incidental to those subjects or any of them. In this subsection the expressions ' taxation ', ' public money ', and ' loan ' respectively do not include any taxation, money, or loan raised by local authorities or bodies for local purposes.'

Every Money Bill was to be certified as such by the Speaker (after consultation ' if practicable ' with two experienced members of the House), and the Speaker's Certificate to be ' conclusive for all purposes ' and not to ' be questioned in any Court of Law '. A Bill so certified could not be amended or rejected by the House of Lords, and was to become law on the Royal Assent being signified.[2]

A Bill other than a Money Bill could be delayed by the House of Lords for two years, but if passed by the House of Commons in its original form, in three successive Sessions, might become law on the Royal Assent being declared.

The duration of Parliament was limited to five instead of seven years.

As regards Money Bills no friction has, since 1911, arisen between the two Houses, though the exclusive right of the Speaker

---

[1] *Supra*, p. 295, and for *text* of the Parliament Act see Marriott, *Second Chambers* (2nd ed.), pp. 193 seq.

[2] For a list of Bills certified under the Act, 1911-26, cf. Marriott, op. cit., pp. 240-2, or Commons Paper 89 of 1927.

to certify a ' Money Bill ' has been the subject of general criticism, if not of complaint in any specific instance. The definition of a Money Bill, though detailed, is not satisfactory. It has been proved to be at once widely inclusive and curiously restrictive. Bills have been certified by the Speaker though they did not grant money to the Crown for Supply Services, while of the Finance Bills since the passing of the Parliament Act at least six did not receive the Speaker's certificate as ' Money Bills '. The famous Budget of 1909–10 would not, it seems, have come within the provisions of the Parliament Act. Had this Act, therefore, been at that time on the Statute Book the Lords would still have been within their legal rights, as they unquestionably were at the time, in rejecting the Finance Bill.[1]

The intentions disclosed in the Preamble of the Parliament Act still (1933) remain unfulfilled. Neither Mr. Asquith's Ministry nor any of those, mostly Conservative in composition, that have succeeded it, have shown any eagerness to grapple with the thorny problem.

[1] Lord Ullswater, *A Speaker's Commentaries*, ii. 108.

CHAPTER XVIII

ON THE BRINK OF ARMAGEDDON, 1911–14—THE WELSH CHURCH —THE 'MARCONI AFFAIR'—THE WOMEN'S MOVEMENT— ADULT SUFFRAGE

Mr. Bal-
four's
resigna-
tion

THE final stage of the Parliament Bill had revealed a serious fissure in the Unionist Party ; nor did the quarrel between 'Hedgers' and 'Ditchers' lack an important personal reaction : it finally decided Mr. Balfour to retire from the leadership.

Ever since Chamberlain had raised the Tariff Reform issue and even more notably since the débâcle of 1906, the volume of criticism against Balfour had been mounting. His defeat at Manchester had impaired his personal prestige, and though the City of London quickly restored him to the House of Commons it was to a House strange and unsympathetic. By many of the Radicals, newcomers to the House, Balfour was at first treated with studied insolence, and though his superb dialectical skill soon cowed them, he never entirely regained his old position.

He was, naturally, one of the four Unionist representatives in the Constitutional Conference of 1910, and while it was in progress he was approached by Mr. Lloyd George with a proposal for the formation of a coalition ministry. In some quarters it has been represented that the motive of this move was to supersede Asquith.[1] That is not so. But in fact a campaign, excitedly supported in some sections of the Press, was directed against

---

[1] Cf. *The Times*, March 20, 1930 (Memoir of Lord Balfour), and Asquith's *Life*, I. 287. Mr. Lloyd George has been kind enough to confirm the fact —known to few people at the time—of these negotiations. But he makes it clear that the motives on both sides were purely patriotic, that the proposal of a Coalition was not directed against Asquith's leadership, that he was indeed the first to be consulted, and that the proposals were made to Balfour with his full approval. Mr. Lloyd George was willing, in order to facilitate a Coalition, which he believed to be in the national interest, himself to stand aside, and support it as an independent member.

Balfour himself. 'B.M.G.' became a fashionable slogan. The elegant and too amiable amateur must give place to a professional bruiser, to a man who would meet opponents on their own ground. Balfour's opposition to the 'Ditchers' seemed to some of his Party to be a final and conclusive proof of his unfitness to lead it in turbulent days.

On November 8 his resignation was announced. Despite the prolonged Press discussion which preceded it, the definite announcement created a great sensation. Only a few of his most intimate associates were aware of his intention, and to the great body of his friends as well as his opponents the news came as a shock. But, as he reminded his constituents, he had been in Parliament for thirty-eight years, and leader of his Party in the Commons for nearly twenty, and was anxious to be relieved of his responsibilities before he could be suspected of suffering from the most insidious of all diseases—'*petrifaction*'. During the ensuing twenty years he exhibited, indeed, few symptoms of that disease; but his mind was made up; he demanded release.

To get rid of Balfour was comparatively easy; it was diffi- Mr. cult to replace him. The choice of the Party eventually fell not Bonar on either of the two favoured candidates, Mr. Austen Chamber- Law lain and Mr. Walter Long, but on Mr. Andrew Bonar Law. The latter had only entered Parliament as a middle-aged and successful man of business in 1900,[1] and had only held minor office for a short time. But he was a complete master of the case for Tariff Reform, and had already proved himself a debater of the first order. In the years to come he showed real grit and courage, and justified his choice as leader. 'The fools have blundered upon their best man.' Such was the sardonic and characteristically shrewd comment of the man with whom he was destined to share the leadership of a Coalition Party.

Bonar Law took up the reins of leadership in days difficult Crisis of for his Party, and for the country intensely critical. The Con- 1911 stitutional crisis synchronized with other crises, domestic and international. The bare dates are illuminating. On July 1 *Panther*, a German gunboat, suddenly appeared off Agadir. The

---

[1] Born in New Brunswick in 1858; son of a Presbyterian minister from Ulster; brought up in Glasgow where he made a considerable fortune as an iron merchant.

crisis thus provoked developed, as we have seen, rapidly ; Mr.
Lloyd George's speech at the Mansion House was made on July
21 and on the 25th Sir Edward Grey warned the Admiralty
that ' the fleet might be attacked at any moment '. Not until
September 22 was the Foreign Office able ' to give the word that
a state of " war preparedness " might be relaxed '.[1]

Nor was this all. At the height of the international crisis
the transport service in England was threatened with paralysis.
In June seamen had come out at various ports, carters and vanmen in July, and dockers at the beginning of August. On August
17 the worst blow fell : the three great Railway Unions came
out on strike.[2] The Government, as we have seen, handled the
situation with firmness and tact, but it was none the less serious.
Nor was its gravity diminished by the fact that France was similarly and simultaneously disturbed by a succession of ministerial
crises, and a series of syndicalist strikes. The German Intelligence Department was well served.

Early in 1912 came the great strike which brought the coal-
mining industry to a standstill, and threatened to bring all other
industries to a similar state. That was settled mainly by Asquith's firmness and skill ; but for him there was no respite from
labour and anxiety.[3] The Irish members had sent in their
account ; it had to be paid. On April 11, 1912, the Prime Minister presented to the House of Commons the third edition of Home
Rule. That Bill did not receive the Royal Assent until September 18, 1914. Its parliamentary history may therefore be postponed.

The
Church
in Wales

Ireland was not the only portion of the ' Celtic Fringe ' to
add to the anxieties of the Government. The parliamentary
course of the Welsh Church Disestablishment Bill was almost
exactly parallel with that of the Home Rule Bill : but its fate
was happier and the sequel less complicated.

The Anglican Church in Ireland had been disestablished and
partially disendowed in 1869. Almost simultaneously there had
arisen a demand for the application of the same treatment to the
Church in Wales. Not that the two cases were parallel ; but the
Liberationists were on the war-path ; the Dissenters were still
sore about the shabby treatment they had so long received from

[1] See *supra*, p. 225   [2] See *supra*, p. 242   [3] See *supra*, p. 243.

the State and the State-Church; the discussions on Forster's
Education Bill had re-aroused angry passions. Consequently in
1870 Mr. Watkin Williams, believing that ' the people had come
to the conclusion that all State establishments of religion were
wrong ', moved that the time was ripe for the separation of Church
and State in the Principality. Only six Welsh members were
found to agree with him. By 1886, however, opinion on the
question had so far developed that a similar motion by Mr.
Dillwyn had the support of a large majority of the Welsh
members.

Mr. Gladstone, ardent Churchman as he was, had by 1893 Disestab-
lishment
convinced himself that the voice of ' gallant little Wales ' could and Dis-
no longer be ignored. In February, Asquith introduced a Sus- endow-
pensory Bill to prevent the creation of any fresh vested interests ment
in the Church in Wales. The Queen was greatly perturbed when
she realized that this ' dreadful Suspensory Bill ' was avowedly
a stepping-stone to Welsh Disestablishment. Mr. Gladstone in
reply to the Queen's remonstrance insisted that Establishment
was a ' local question ', and that the measure was called for by
' the almost unanimous voice of the Welsh members (31 out of
33) as representing the overwhelming majority of the Welsh
people '.[1]

That was indeed the main argument for the Welsh Church
Disestablishment Bill, introduced by Asquith in April, 1894.
In that congested Session the Bill did not get beyond a First
Reading. Reintroduced in February 1895 it was read a second
time in April, but went down with the Liberal ship in June. It
was fourteen years before it was salvaged: but on April 21,
1909, it was again introduced by Asquith, now Prime Minister.
Again, however, the hopes of the Welsh Nonconformists were
doomed to disappointment. The ' People's Budget ' not only
monopolized the time of Parliament, but concentrated on itself
all the energies of the Radical Party. Wales again had to wait.
On June 15 Asquith announced that the Bill would be dropped,
but introduced as the first and most important measure of 1910,
and passed through all its stages, ' in this House '—as he prudently added. Even so the fulfilment fell short of the promise.
The sea of politics was disturbed by violent storms, and not until

[1] *Q.V.L.*, vol. ii (3rd Series), 230 f.

two General Elections had intervened and the Parliament Bill been passed was the Welsh Bill again introduced (April 12, 1912). It passed through all its stages in the Lower House in the course of the twelve-months Session (1912–13), and at the close of it was rejected by the House of Lords on Second Reading by 252 votes to 51 (February 13, 1913). Having now come under the operation of the Parliament Act, it was again carried through the House of Commons and again (July 22, 1913) rejected by the Lords. Introduced (for the third successive session) in 1914 the Bill was finally passed on Third Reading by the House of Commons (May 19) by 328 votes to 251.

The Lords could delay its passage into law no longer, and on September 18 the Bill received the Royal Assent. But by that time England was at war. All parties recognized the supreme need of national unity. It was unthinkable that any Government could so outrage the feelings of a large section, and that not the least patriotic, of the nation as to bring into force a measure which had aroused such bitter and prolonged opposition and had been passed into law only by *force majeur*. By a large minority of the people (to put it no higher), the Welsh Bill was regarded with profound aversion ; to not a few it seemed an act of sacrilege : not merely a crime against Churchmen, but a sin against God. However much or little we may sympathize with such feelings, they existed ; and no Government could ignore or trample upon them, least of all under the circumstances of the hour. Accordingly, along with the Welsh Church Bill there was passed a Suspensory Bill, postponing its operation for a year, or until such time (not being later than the end of the War) as might be fixed by an Order in Council. ' The end of the War ' was a term which, in more than one connexion, would, later on, demand legal definition. But between 1914 and 1918 much water was to flow under London Bridge, and the soil of Europe was to be saturated with blood.

In the autumn of 1918 the Parliament elected in 1910 was, after several Prolongation Acts, at long last dissolved. Mr. Lloyd George and Mr. Bonar Law appealed to the electorate as the leaders of a Coalition, but before accepting the ' coupon ' which they offered many Conservative candidates demanded assurances in regard to various matters. A revision of the finan-

cial settlement relating to the Welsh Church was among the
promises given by the Prime Minister. Accordingly, on August
4, 1919, a Bill was introduced by the Government ' to continue
in office the Welsh Commissioners appointed under the Welsh
Church Act, 1914, to postpone the date of Disestablishment, and
to make further provision with respect to the " Temporalities "
of, and marriages in, the Church in Wales '.

The financial position had been greatly complicated, partly
by the lapse of time since the original Act was passed, partly by
the spectacular rise in the value of Tithe (from £77 to over £130).
To meet the difficulty the Government proposed to make a grant
of £1,000,000 from the British Treasury to the Welsh Church
Commissioners. Whether that sum was a ' donation ' to the
disendowed Church, as the Welsh Nonconformists contended,
or to the Welsh County Councils, as English Churchmen maintained, was a matter of controversy : but the Bill received the
Royal Assent on August 19, and together with the parent Act
came into operation on March 31, 1920.

Except that the year 1662 was substituted for 1703 as the
dividing line between ancient and modern endowments (thus
giving the disendowed Church an advantage of forty years) the
Act of 1919 substantially reproduced the Bill of 1894.[1]

Under the Act three Commissioners were appointed with very
large powers, administrative, judicial and actuarial. The Commissioners were Sir Henry Primrose—an experienced Treasury
official, Sir William (afterwards Lord) Plender, an accountant of
the highest standing, and Sir J. Herbert Roberts, a Welsh M.P.,
afterwards Lord Clwyd. In their hands was vested temporarily,
subject to existing charges and interests, all the property of the
Church in Wales not specifically allocated under the Act. That
property it was their duty to distribute among the ultimate
beneficiaries, the Welsh County Councils, the University of Wales,
the Burial Authorities, and the Church Representative Body.
Of these the last was the most important.

The Act severed the four Welsh dioceses and Monmouthshire
from the Province of Canterbury, and these were subsequently
erected into a new Province under its own Archbishop (who continued to hold the see of St. Asaph) with four (presently increased

*The Dis-
estab-
lished
Church*

---

[1] See *supra*, p. 65.

to six) suffragan Bishops. The Welsh Bishops ceased to sit in the House of Lords.

Constitution and Government

Between 1915 and 1922 a committee of Welsh Churchmen was continuously engaged in framing, as authorized by the Act, a new Constitution for the Welsh Church. Drafted with consummate ability, it has provided the Disestablished Church with a scheme of government, which is operating to the general satisfaction of Churchmen in Wales, and to the admiration of Churchmen beyond its borders. Its success has been mainly due to the statesmanship of two great lawyers, Lord Sankey and Sir John Eldon Bankes, and to the Bishop of St. Asaph, the Most Reverend Dr. A. G. Edwards, who in April 1920 was elected by his fellow-Bishops to be first Archbishop of Wales and in June was enthroned by Archbishop Davidson of Canterbury.

The Constitution set up two Bodies, (a) the Governing Body and (b) the Representative Body of the Welsh Church. The Governing Body exercises supreme Legislative jurisdiction. Originally elected by the Diocesan Conferences, it now consists of 505 members. The 6 Bishops, 5 Deans and 12 Archdeacons are *ex officio* members ; 25 clerical and 50 lay members are triennially elected by each of the six Diocesan Conferences, and 10 clerics and 20 laymen are co-opted by the Governing Body, and there are two Life Members. There are three Orders ; Bishops, Clergy and Laity, and the assent of each is essential to legislation.[1] The Governing Body has done valuable work : it has created the new Province and two additional bishoprics, and a college for the election of future bishops ; it has devised a coherent scheme of local conferences, Diocesan, Ruridecanal and Parochial ; it has passed a Cathedrals measure and a scheme of clergy pensions, not to mention other useful measures.

Not less important to the orderly administration of ecclesiastical affairs is the Representative Church Body. This Body was sanctioned by the Act, and incorporated by Royal Charter in 1919 ; it consists of 105 members, mainly elected (like the Governing Body), but partly co-opted and partly nominated by the Bishops. The Act deprived the Welsh Church of all endowments prior to 1662—a sum estimated at over £4,000,000 as well as all parochial Burial Grounds, and handed the endowments over to

[1] Only in matters purely spiritual does the Governing Body vote by Orders.

the Welsh County Councils and the Welsh University. The churches, parsonages, and other buildings and the glebe [1] remained to the Church and were transferred by the Commissioners, in whom they were temporarily vested, to the Representative Body, who also hold, in trust, all modern endowments and benefactions, the capital sum received in commutation for vested interests, and the sums annually raised by the Diocesan quota. Out of these funds the Representative Body pays the stipends of the bishops and clergy, it provides for pensions, insurance, dilapidations and for the training of ordinands.

The Welsh Church would seem, then, to have emerged from its ordeal braced and invigorated by the call to personal service and individual self-sacrifice. It would, however, be rash to infer that the successful reaction of the Welsh Church to Disestablishment and partial Disendowment supplies any argument in favour of legislation, on similar lines, for the English Church. Nor, indeed, is there any longer a demand for such a measure. Partly owing to the enhanced zeal and activity of Churchmen, partly to the decay of Nonconformity, and most of all to the virtual extinction of the Liberal Party, the Liberationist cry has ceased to resound. Nourished on the abstract principles, long since discredited, of *laisser-faire*, sustained by the practical grievances, long since removed, of Nonconformists, the agitation for Disestablishment has faded out of practical politics. Should it ever be revived it is likely to come from a party within the Church, more remarkable for zeal than for discretion : more concerned for the intensive growth of religion than for the extension of its influence.

Welsh Disestablishment was only one of the preoccupations of the Asquith Government in the years immediately preceding the outbreak of war.

Among its embarrassments, not the least disquieting was the episode, commonly known at the time as the 'Marconi Scandal' —a description peculiarly unfair to the great inventor, who was in no way concerned in the matter. The Imperial Conference of 1911 had recommended the establishment of a chain of State-owned wireless telegraph stations within the Empire. The Imperial Government assented, and in 1912 the Postmaster-General

The 'Marconi Affair'

---

[1] Acquired since 1662.

accepted the tender of the Marconi Company for the construction of the stations subject to the ratification of the contract by Parliament.

On August 8, 1912, the Postmaster-General unfolded to the House of Commons the terms of the agreement, but consideration of it was deferred until the autumn. In the meantime Rumour became busy and dark insinuations appeared in the Press. It was said that the Postmaster-General had corruptly favoured a Company, of which Mr. Godfrey Isaacs, brother of the Attorney-General, was managing director, and that the latter as well as Mr. Lloyd George and the Master of Elibank, who until recently had been chief Liberal Whip, were pecuniarily interested. The shares of the Company had risen from 46s. in July 1911 to over £8 in April 1912, when the acceptance of their tender was made public. A rise so spectacular naturally gave additional emphasis to the rumours already in circulation.

When on October 11 the Marconi contract was submitted to the House of Commons for approval, the Government immediately moved for the appointment of a Select Committee ' to investigate the circumstances connected with the negotiation and completion of the agreement . . . and to report thereupon and whether the agreement is desirable and should be approved '.

The Select Committee, consisting of fifteen members, was set up on October 23, 1912. The latter part of its reference, involving highly technical questions, was, on the advice of the Select Committee, delegated to a special Advisory Committee, consisting of Lord Parker of Waddington, a Judge of the High Court with wide experience of patent litigation, as chairman, and four eminent scientific experts. The Committee was requested to report, within three months, on the merits of long-distance wireless telegraphy, and in particular as to its capacity for continuous communication over the distances—between 2,000 and 2,500 miles—required by the Imperial Chain.

The Committee reported [1] (May 1), somewhat guardedly, that ' the Marconi system is at present the only system . . . capable of fulfilling the requirements of the Imperial Chain ', but they refrained (as outside their reference) from expressing any opinion about the provisions of the agreement with the Marconi Com-

[1] Cd. 6781, of 1913.

pany, and explained that their approval of the Marconi system
did not involve the employment of that Company as contractors
for all the work required.

Much more difficult was the task before the main Committee
presided over by Sir Albert Spicer. Its proceedings were conducted in an atmosphere of tense feeling, which not infrequently
found expression in violent language and scenes of considerable
excitement. Its Report presented to the House of Commons on
June 13, 1913, ran, with minutes of evidence, to over 600 pages
of a Blue Book.[1] It consisted indeed of four Reports : a Majority
Report finally adopted by eight Liberal votes against six Conservative ; a Chairman's Draft Report, more severe than the
Report actually adopted ; another Draft Report by the Liberal
member for Forfar, and a fourth by Lord Robert Cecil. The
Majority Report declared that the charges made against Sir
Rufus Isaacs, Mr. Lloyd George and Mr. Herbert Samuel were
' absolutely untrue ' and that ' all the Ministers concerned have
acted throughout in the sincere belief that there was nothing in
their action which would in any way conflict with their duty as
Ministers of the Crown '.[2]

In the debate on the appointment of the Committee Mr. Lloyd
George and Sir Rufus Isaacs had emphatically denied that they
had ever had any interest, direct or indirect, in the English Marconi Company. That was true ; but the truth was stated with
a regrettable economy of candour. The subsequent inquiry
elicited the fact that the two Ministers had had dealings in the
shares of the American Marconi Company, but the Majority
Report found that the American Company had ' no interest direct
or indirect in the proposed agreement with the British Government ', or in any profits which might accrue therefrom.

Mr. Lloyd George and Sir Rufus Isaacs

Lord Robert Cecil's Report was much less tender in its treatment of the Ministers. Equally with the Majority Report, it
declared that they had not been deflected from the proper discharge of their public duties by reason of any interest in the
Marconi or other Companies ; but it described their purchase of
American Marconi shares as a ' grave impropriety ' ; it held that
the American Company was materially, though indirectly, interested in the conclusion of the Government agreement with the

[1] Cd. 152, of 1913.   [2] Cd. 152, pp. xxxix–xlix.

English Company, and it condemned the ' reticence ' of Ministers in regard to their investment or ' speculation ' in the shares of the American Marconi Company as ' a grave error of judgement and as wanting in frankness and respect for the House of Commons '.

When the Report was discussed in the House of Commons (June 18 and 19, 1913) Mr. (afterwards Lord) Cave moved a Resolution regretting ' the transactions of certain of His Majesty's Ministers in the shares of the Marconi Company of America, and the want of frankness displayed in their communications on the subject to the House '. Both Sir Rufus Isaacs and Mr. Lloyd George frankly admitted that the purchase of the shares and their failure to disclose the transaction in the debate of October 11th were errors of judgement, sincerely regretted by them. In the course of the Debate Mr. Asquith characteristically formulated certain rules which he divided into the two categories of Rules of Obligation and Rules of Prudence. From any violation of the Rules of Obligation he completely absolved his colleagues ; the Rules of Prudence they had not, in his opinion, fully observed. But their honour, public and private, he held to be ' absolutely unstained '. Eventually, after long debate, the House adopted the amendment of a Liberal back-bencher that the House having heard the statements of the Ministers ' accepts their expressions of regret that such purchases were made, and that they were not mentioned in the debate of October 11, acquits them of acting otherwise than in good faith, and reprobates the charges of corruption brought against Ministers which have been proved to be wholly false '.

This amendment was in effect accepted by 346 votes to 268, and the parliamentary history of ' this wretched subject ' (Mr. Balfour's description) came to an end. A ' wretched subject ' it unquestionably was ; but fortunately one of so rare a character in the annals of English politics that it profoundly perturbed public opinion, and concentrated upon itself public scrutiny at a moment when other matters, not less gravely important, were demanding attention.

The Women's Movement   Prominent among the latter was the clamant demand for the extension of the parliamentary franchise to women.

The struggle for woman suffrage was only one aspect of a larger movement. Throughout all the later part of the nine-

teenth century women had been advancing their claim to equality
of status and opportunity with men : but they were convinced
that the claim would be conceded only when women had obtained
an education equal to, if not identical with, that of men. They
were right. Their first assault, therefore, was upon the educational fortress.

The Christian Socialists were in the forefront of the movement Higher
for the higher education of women. To men like F. D. Maurice tion of
and Charles Kingsley, Queen's College and Bedford College owed Women
their foundation in 1848-9. Then women attacked and carried
the outworks of the old Universities. Between 1865 and 1870
Cambridge, Durham and Oxford opened their Local Examinations to women. In 1872 Cambridge University allowed women
to enter, though unofficially and informally, for the classical and
mathematical triposes.

But if the Universities might examine women, why not also
teach them ? The answer to that question was found in the
establishment of the system of Local or 'Extension' lectures,
developed with much success by Cambridge, Oxford, and London
and afterwards adopted by most, if not all, the Universities.

To be examined, or even to be taught by the Universities,
did not, however, satisfy the ambition of women. They decided
to storm the citadel itself ; but they prudently advanced to the
attack by gradual stages. The first foothold was residence. A
college for women, established at Hitchin in 1869, was in 1873
removed to Cambridge and incorporated as Girton College. Two
years later Newnham College was opened at Cambridge. In 1879
Lady Margaret Hall and Somerville Hall were opened at Oxford,
where in a short time no fewer than four women's Colleges were
established. These Colleges were fed by a constant stream of
students, mostly from the new Secondary Schools which in the
last decades of the nineteenth century were established in all
parts of the country. Of these one of the first and greatest was
the Cheltenham Ladies' College which, founded in 1854, embodied
the ideals of a great educationist, Miss Dorothea Beale.

Women had, however, a long furrow to plough before they
could attain their ideal of equality, even in education. London,
though it had refused admission to women in 1856, was the first
British University to concede complete equality to women, in

respect of examinations and degrees, of honours and prizes. That was done in 1878. The Victoria University, with its federated Colleges in Manchester, Liverpool and Leeds, followed suit in 1880. Cambridge opened its Honours Examinations to women in 1881, and between 1884 and 1894 Oxford gradually did likewise.

But though women might be equal to men in academic attainments, the guerdon of a Degree was still, except in London and Victoria, withheld. In 1892, however, the Scottish Universities admitted women to all their Degrees, and in 1895 Durham also, except in respect of Theology.

Before the end of the century a large number of women were in residence both at Oxford and Cambridge. Their residence was not indeed officially recognized, though as regards teaching and examinations their opportunities were scarcely if at all inferior to those offered to men. But the ' Degree ' which meant so much to outsiders, and so little to those who knew, was still denied to them. In 1896 a vigorous campaign was initiated at Oxford, but though encouraged by many leading members of the University it ended, for the time being, in defeat.

In 1907 Lord Curzon of Kedleston became Chancellor of the University, and at once took up the question of University Reform. Though a convinced opponent of Woman Suffrage, he strongly advocated the granting of degrees to women, but not their admission to the governing bodies of the University. In a memorable sentence he vindicated his own consistency : ' To give a woman a degree is to enable her to obtain the reward of her own industry or her learning. As such it is an extension of private liberty. To give her a vote is to give her the right to govern others, and is the imposition of a public duty.' [1] This logical distinction was ignored at Oxford ; it has been rigorously observed at Cambridge.

At neither University, however, was any further progress made until after the Great War. The effect of the War upon the whole position of women—social, economic and political—must be examined later. After the concession of the parliamentary franchise to women (1918) it was obvious that the Universities could no longer withhold their Degrees. Moreover, in 1919 Parliament had given the Universities—and other people—a broad hint. On

[1] *Principles and Methods of University Reform* (1909), p. 199.

December 23 the Royal Assent was given to the Sex Disqualification (Removal) Bill. The opening words of the first clause ran as follows : ' A person shall not be disqualified by sex or marriage from the exercise of any public function, or from being appointed to or holding any civil or judicial office or post or from entering or assuming or carrying on any civil profession or vocation. . . . Provided that, &c.' Before the Bill passed the House of Commons the following significant clause was added to it : ' Nothing in the Statutes or Charter of any University shall be deemed to preclude the authorities of such University from making such provision as they shall think fit for the admission of women to membership thereof, or to any degree, right or privilege therein or in connexion therewith.'

The clause was not mandatory, but permissive. Oxford had, indeed, anticipated the permission of the Legislature, and in 1919 had introduced and in 1920 passed a Statute, admitting women not only to matriculation and graduation but to full membership of the University.

Women are now admitted on the same terms as men to the Governing Bodies and all Committees in the University, to offices and prizes of every kind. And of all these things women have since 1920 obtained a full share.[1]

Cambridge has moved, but more cautiously and, as some think, more prudently, along a path, parallel for some distance, with that followed by Oxford. Oxford had by 1932 over 700 women undergraduates, of whom some 500 were members of Colleges and Halls—the remainder being ' Home Students '. Cambridge has limited the number of women students to 500, all of whom must reside at Girton or Newnham College. They enjoy practically the same facilities for instruction as the men, are admitted to the same Honour Examinations, and receive the appropriate ' titles of the degrees ', but not technically the degrees which would give them a share in the government of the University. In fine, Cambridge has adopted the distinction which in 1909 commended itself to Lord Curzon. Whether in view of

---

[1] The ' ecstasy ' (no other word expresses the sentiment) of the moment when the first batch of women students were matriculated and the first batch received their degrees, is vividly recalled by Vera Brittain (who was herself among them) in *Testament of Youth* (1933). c. x.

the progress of the Women's Movement at large Cambridge will be able to maintain the distinction obliterated by Oxford remains to be seen.

To the political movement we now turn.

Woman Suffrage

Not until 1905 did the question of Woman Suffrage become a live political issue. Nor was it then a Party question. On the Bills for the enfranchisement of women, which for the last thirty years had been regularly introduced and shelved, there had been much cross-voting. On the whole the Conservatives were perhaps more sympathetic towards the movement than the Liberals, but after 1906 the Socialists showed themselves more zealous than either of the older Parties. Early in 1906 Sir H. Campbell-Bannerman told a deputation from the Women's Suffrage Societies that ' they had made out a conclusive and irrefutable case '.

Behind that deputation there was a half-century's intensive work. In 1849 an Act was passed at the instigation of Lord Brougham declaring that ' words importing the masculine gender shall be deemed to include females unless the contrary is expressly provided '. The Reform Act of 1832 had however introduced the word male, and it was nearly a century before that restriction was legally deleted.

J. S. Mill

Among public men J. S. Mill was among the first to bring the women's question into prominence. In 1853 he published *The Enfranchisement of Women*, and one of the most notable passages of his *Representative Government* (1861) contains an eloquent plea for the principle of the political equality of the sexes. ' I consider [difference of sex] to be as entirely irrelevant to political rights as difference in height or in the colour of the hair '.[1] In 1869 he published his famous work on the *Subjection of Women*. Meanwhile, as candidate for Westminster (1865) Mill had given Woman Suffrage a prominent place in his election address, and consistently advocated it in the House of Commons.

In 1870 Mr. Jacob Bright moved the Second Reading of a Women's Suffrage Bill, but he could get no sympathy or support from his brother John and still less from Mr. Gladstone, who voted against Mill's Amendment for the inclusion of women in the Franchise Bill of 1867, and in 1884, on a similar motion, declared that if it were carried he would abandon the Bill. On that

---

[1] *Representative Government*, p. 290 (Dent's ed., 1910).

question Gladstone was, for once, in complete accord with his Sovereign, who vehemently opposed the 'emancipation' of women. 'We women', she wrote in 1852, 'are not made for governing—and if we are good women we must *dislike* these masculine occupations.' But that was in Prince Albert's lifetime, and even then she admitted (as John Knox admitted in the case of Queen Elizabeth) that there are exceptions to the rule.

Yet, despite powerful opposition, the cause made steady progress. From 1870 onwards the question became one of the 'hardy annuals' in the Parliamentary garden, and before the War at least seven Bills obtained a Second Reading. Outside Parliament the agitation was persistent. The first Women's Suffrage Societies were founded in Manchester, Edinburgh and London in 1867, and before the War no fewer than 300 Societies were affiliated to the National Union of Women's Suffrage Societies. Meanwhile, some important points of vantage were gained. Not only were women beginning to enter the professions, notably that of medicine, but in 1887 the Married Women's Property Act was passed. This Act abolished the old system under which a woman's property passed, on marriage, under the husband's control. In 1892 Asquith, though a strong and consistent opponent of the suffrage, appointed women for the first time as Factory Inspectors, and in 1894 three women were for the first time appointed as Royal Commissioners to inquire into Secondary Education. This precedent was followed in the case of the Royal Commissions on the Poor Law and the Marriage Laws.

The year 1907 was described by Mrs. Millicent Garrett Fawcett, speaking in October, as 'the greatest year the women's suffrage movement had known'. In 1893 the Parliamentary franchise had been given to women in New Zealand, and in 1902 in the Commonwealth of Australia ; in 1907 women were for the first time elected to a Legislature, nineteen being elected to the Diet of Finland. In England the same year witnessed the passing of the Qualification of Women (County and Borough Councils) Act, which provided that women should no longer be disqualified by sex or marriage from being elected and acting as County or Borough Councillors or Aldermen. Already over 1,000 women were acting as Poor Law Guardians, and over 600 on Education Committees. The Act of 1907, however, marked an important advance, and in 1908 Mrs. Garrett Anderson was elected Mayor of Aldeburgh—the first woman to serve in that capacity.

Militant 'Suffragettes'

In view of this record, many of the more ardent advocates of Women's Suffrage were becoming exasperated by the dilatory proceedings in Parliament. Mrs. Pankhurst, the widow of a Manchester lawyer who had more than once stood for Parliament as a republican Socialist, had, in 1903, founded a Society destined to fame as the Women's Social and Political Union. Hitherto the Suffrage movement had been mainly conducted by educated women in the interests of educated women. Mrs. Pankhurst was herself a cultivated woman of middle-class origin, but her appeal was addressed primarily to the working women of Lancashire and Yorkshire. The agitation set on foot through her new Society was to be unrestricted by any limitations of decorum, convention or even law. It was to be open war upon Society in general and in particular upon the Government of the day. Political meetings were interrupted ; demonstrations were held in Trafalgar Square ; monster processions were organized ; Ministers were harried from pillar to post ; women crowded the lobbies at Westminster ; they tried to gain access to a Cabinet meeting ; they broke windows in shops and official residences ; they kicked the shins of patient policemen, and generally created as much disturbance as they could. Large batches of women were arrested, mostly in the vicinity of Parliament, and on their refusal to pay the fines imposed were sent to prison.

The ' Suffragettes ', as they began to be called, in distinction to the ' Constitutional ' suffragists, proved themselves adepts in two modern arts : that of spectacular advertisement and that of agitation. They were immensely assisted by the popular Press, which, though generally opposed to their aims, found good ' copy ' in their proceedings. The older Suffrage Societies viewed the new departure with horror, and with well-grounded alarm lest it should, as it did, delay the triumph of their cause. They excluded the militants from their Societies, and year after year passed resolutions against their methods. All to no purpose.

Asquith and Votes for Women

In May 1908 Mr. Asquith informed a deputation of Liberal M.P.s that the Government meant to propose a large measure of electoral reform, and that if a Women's Suffrage amendment were moved it would be left to a free vote of the House. Ministers were in fact divided on the question : the Prime Minister, Lord Loreburn and others were against, Sir Edward Grey, Mr. Haldane and Mr. Lloyd George in favour of, Women's Suffrage. A Bill to establish adult suffrage was introduced in 1909, but by reason of the People's Budget got no farther than a Second Reading. In 1910 the Suffragists decided to concentrate on a ' Conciliation Bill ', giving the franchise to all women householders. This Bill, which would have enfranchised about 1,000,000 women, was carried on Second Reading by large majorities in 1910 and again in 1911. But it was a Private Member's Bill, and the Government, with the Constitutional crisis on their hands, could give it no facilities.

The Suffragists were greatly disappointed, and in the next three years there was an ominous revival of militancy in view of the fate of the Conciliation Bill, which had been suspended. Attempts were made to set fire to post-boxes, telegraph and telephone wires were cut, club and shop windows in the heart of London were broken ; the Rokeby Venus and other pictures in the National Gallery were slashed, porcelain was smashed at the British Museum, and galleries and museums were in consequence closed to the public ; women suspected of intentions to burn down the country residence of Mr. Harcourt were detected and arrested in the grounds of Nuneham Park ; an empty house about to be leased to Mr. Lloyd George at Walton Heath was actually burnt down, as was the Pavilion at Kew Gardens, several railway stations and Wargrave Church. A bomb was found under the Coronation Chair in Westminster Abbey, and another at St. Paul's. In Dublin a hatchet was thrown at Mr. Asquith and hit John Redmond. At the Derby of 1913 a terrible incident occurred : a suffragette, who had been more than once imprisoned, dashed out in front of the favourite, the King's horse, as it came round Tattenham Corner, thus imperilling the life of the jockey and sacrificing her own.

In the course of these disturbances large numbers of women were arrested and sent to prison ; but in prison they adopted the device of hunger-striking. To avoid making martyrs, the hunger-strikers were released, but in 1913 an Act, popularly known as the ' Cat and Mouse Act ', was passed. This authorized the Home Secretary to liberate prisoners on licence which could be revoked, without further trial, on a repetition of the offence. The Act did little to check the volume of outrages; the authorities were at their wits' end to know how to deal with women who were ready to sacrifice not merely liberty but life to promote the success of a cause to which they were passionately devoted.

A crushing blow had, meanwhile, fallen on all sections of the Women's Suffrage Movement. In June 1912 the Government had introduced a Franchise and Registration Bill to abolish University representation and plural voting, and to simplify the conditions for the registration of electors. It was estimated that the Bill would add 2,500,000 male electors to the Register. The Bill as drafted did not include women, but the Government was pledged to give facilities for an Amendment, in that sense, and to leave it to a free vote of the House. When the Bill reached the committee stage the Speaker ruled the Amendment out of order. The Government was thus placed in a cruel dilemma. To pass the Bill for males only was to break faith with the women. The Bill was dropped.

The parliamentary tide was, indeed, turning against the enfranchisement of women. In 1912 the Conciliation Bill, which had twice been carried on Second Reading, was at the third attempt defeated. A similar fate awaited a somewhat extended proposal in 1913, and also a Suffrage Bill introduced in May 1914 by Lord Selborne in the House of Lords.

That the tactics of the militant suffragettes had alienated public opinion and delayed the triumph of their cause is not open to question.

Women and the War
In 1914, however, a great opportunity was offered to them. Magnificently they redeemed it. On the outbreak of war the militant agitation was immediately called off; Mrs. Pankhurst and her daughter Christabel turned their propaganda into patriotic channels; *The Suffragette* became *Britannia* and appealed to all women to do their utmost in the cause of world-freedom. The response was immediate and wellnigh universal. Militant suffragettes and constitutional suffragists displayed equal zeal. Early in the War the latter formed the Women's Emergency Corps, ready to undertake any kind of work of national importance. They soon found plenty to their hands. The record of women's war-work is indeed writ large on the page of History.

Into the hospitals, military and V.A.D., women naturally went at once, and before long they were, in rapidly increasing numbers, taking the place of men, needed for the army, in all manner of occupations : in industry and agriculture, as clerks in banks, in Government and insurance offices ; as postmen, ticket-collectors and bus conductors and what not. In March 1915 the Government concluded with the Trade Unions what was known as the ' Treasury Agreement '. The Unions consented to suspend all their rules excluding women from skilled employment, only making the condition—scrupulously observed—that for the same output women should receive the same wages as men. By July 1918 no fewer than 1,659,000 women were doing work formerly done by men : but, besides that, thousands of women were employed in jobs which were the outcome of war emergencies. In the metal trades there were nearly 600,000 women employed, and over 100,000 in chemicals ; in ' Government establishments ' 225,000 women were employed as against 2,000 in July 1914 ; in the Civil Service 234,000 as against 66,000 ; 250,000 by Local Authorities ; and in ' other occupations ', including transport, &c., 1,372,000. Nor were women employed only at home. Early in 1917 an Army Council instruction was published approving the formation of a Women's Army Auxiliary Corps—the members of which came to be familiarly known as the W.A.A.C.s. No woman was to be employed in the Corps except actually in substitution for a soldier ; and in large numbers they were employed in the motor transport service in various capacities, in the Army Service Corps, at the base and on lines of communications overseas, in the telephone and postal services, as cooks and clerks, accountants and laundresses, and in many other capacities —but always to relieve a soldier for other work. What the country owed to the W.A.A.C.s, to the devoted nurses in military and auxiliary hospitals, and not least to the workers in the munition factories, is beyond computation.

In the face of such services there could no longer be any doubt as to the admission of women to the register of parliamentary electors. Woman Suffrage came, however, as part of a larger scheme. Of the 5,000,000 men in the fighting lines some had never been qualified to vote; others had, by enlistment and service, lost their qualifications. Obviously, some measure had to be passed to deal with this difficulty ; but a Reform Bill, containing clauses of potentially contentious character, was not to be thought of in the middle of the War. Mr. Walter (afterwards Lord) Long accordingly suggested a non-party Conference which in October 1916 was set up under the Chairmanship of the Speaker. The Conference reported in January 1917, and among its unanimous recommendations was one in favour of ' some measure of Woman Suffrage '.

Reform Act, 1918   The Reform Act of 1918, passed after long debate in both Houses, was based upon this Report. Comprehensive in character, it dealt with the franchise, male and female, with registration, and the redistribution of seats. As regards the last, counties and boroughs (except the city of London) with a population less than 50,000 ceased to have separate representation and a member was given for a population of 70,000 and every multiple thereof. Under this scheme some ancient cities, such as York, lost one of their two members and others, like Chester, were merged in the adjacent counties. The registration period was shortened, simplified, and based (except in respect of business premises and Universities) wholly on residence. The property qualification, and with it plural voting, was abolished. All elections were to be held on the same day, and candidates' expenses were limited. The principle of the ' Alternative Vote ', as well as that of Proportional Representation, was rejected during the passage of the Bill, save that the latter principle was applied to University representation. Adult suffrage was adopted for males, and a special franchise was conferred on those on war service, and in the mercantile marine (even though not of full age). ' Conscientious objectors ', on the other hand, were disqualified from voting during the continuance of the War and for five years after its cessation.

The franchise was extended to all women (not legally incapacitated) of thirty years of age, and entitled to be registered as Local Government electors in respect of the occupation of land or premises, and to the wives of men so entitled. For Universities, a woman, having attained the age of thirty, was to be entitled to vote on the same terms as a man.

The differentiation of age between the sexes was due to the desire of the Legislature not to put women voters, from the outset of the experiment, in a majority, but to give men representation in the proportion of 3 to 2. The results justified the calculation. The first Register contained 12,919,090 men and 8,856,493 women. By an Act passed in November 1918 women became eligible for election to Parliament. In 1919 Viscountess Astor was elected for Plymouth in place of her husband on his succession to the Peerage, and in 1921 Mrs. Wintringham was elected, in place of her deceased husband, for Louth.

In 1928 Parliament passed an Act, described by its sponsor as ' the inevitable last chapter of a political history which began with the change from the representation of interests to the representation of the people in 1832 '. The Act placed women in exactly the same position as men as regards both Parliamentary and Local Government elections. Adult suffrage for men and women brought the electorate up to the vast total of 28,850,776. It had been estimated that the new Act would enfranchise some 4,000,000 females : as a fact it enfranchised about 7,000,000, bringing the total of women electors up to 15,195,199 as compared with 13,655,577 men.

Equal Franchise Act, 1928

Thus ended in complete and simultaneous victory the long fight for ' equal rights ', and the still longer fight, begun by the Chartists, for adult suffrage.

CHAPTER XIX

THE IRISH PROBLEM (1886–1914)

' MARRY, so there have been divers good plots devised, and wise counsels cast about reformation of that realm, but they say it is the fatal destiny of that land that no purposes whatsoever which are meant for her good will prosper or take effect ; which, whether it proceed from the very genius of the soil or influence of the stars, or that God Almighty hath not yet appointed the time of her reformation, or that He reserveth her in this unquiet state, still for some secret scourge which shall by her come into England, it is hard to be known, but yet much to be feared.' So Edmund Spenser, himself one of the Elizabethan ' colonists ' in Munster, wrote, towards the close of the sixteenth century. The words might have been written with equal accuracy in the early part of the twentieth.

Nevertheless, when in 1905 the Unionist Party left office Ireland was in a condition unusually tranquil and prosperous. Twenty years earlier Lord Salisbury had offered, in opposition to Gladstone's Home Rule proposals, an alternative prescription for Irish distemper, namely, ' that Parliament should enable the Government of England to govern Ireland ; apply that recipe honestly, consistently, and resolutely for twenty years. . . .' The Legislature and the electorate gave the mandate. Unionist administrators applied the recipe.

Balfour's Chief Secretaryship, 1886–92

Of those administrators the greatest was Mr. Arthur Balfour. His rule from 1887 to 1891 rested on a combination of unbending firmness and genuine sympathy. Balfour understood Ireland as no British statesman had understood her since the far-off days of Sir Arthur Chichester and Lord Strafford. He understood it because, as was said of him by a contemporary, he was unaffectedly interested in ' Ireland as a country rather than a cockpit. It is

the condition of Ireland, not the gabble of parties at Westminster,
which is uppermost in his thoughts '.[1] When Balfour took office
the Parnellites vowed that they would break ' this hothouse
flower ', this ' scented popinjay ' in much less time than they
had taken to break his predecessors. To their amazement and
dismay it was Balfour who broke them. But he did more than
break the Parnellites : he succoured their unhappy dupes. In
face of a bitter agrarian agitation, in spite of widespread disorder and outrages innumerable, the supremacy of the law was
successfully vindicated.[2] But resolute government supplied only
one ingredient in the Unionist recipe.

Nearest to the heart of every Irishman is the question of the
land. The sheet anchor of the Unionist land policy, from first to
last, was the conversion of the Irish tenant into the owner of the
land he tilled. This was to be effected by means of British credit
sustained by a joint Exchequer responsible to the Parliament of
a United Kingdom. A good beginning towards the achievement
of this policy had been made under the Ashbourne Act of 1885,
but that Act, even as enlarged and amended in 1889, authorized
an advance of no more than £10,000,000 to facilitate purchases.
This amount proved insufficient to meet the applications received,
though sales of 942,625 acres, apportioned among 25,367 holdings,
were in fact effected at a cost of £9,992,536.

The Land Question

It was, however, to a particular aspect of the land problem
that Mr. Balfour's attention was specially directed. In the
autumn of 1890 he visited the West of Ireland, and saw with his
own eyes the condition of the people who eked out a miserable
existence on a few perches of bog. Their condition was, as he
truly said, a reproach to British statesmanship. The Land Bill
which he had introduced in 1890 and passed in 1891, was primarily
intended to deal with the problem of the congested districts in
the counties of Donegal, Leitrim, Sligo, Roscommon, Mayo,
Galway, West Cork and Kerry, an area of some 3½ million statute
acres with a population of about half a million people. Under
the Act of 1891 the landlords were to be paid in a special Government Land Stock bearing interest at 2¾ per cent., while the tenant
was to pay 4 per cent. on the money advanced for a period of

Act of 1891

[1] Hurlbert, *Ireland under Coercion* (1887), 1. 20.
[2] *Supra*, pp. 50 f.

forty-nine years. Sales under this Act were slow, and by 1896, when an amending Act was passed, only a fraction of the amount authorized was actually advanced. It was, however, satisfactory that of the £12,000,000 advanced to tenants under the Acts of 1885–91, only £4,000 was in arrear.

The Congested District Board

Meanwhile, the Congested District Board established under the Act of 1891 had done admirable work. It was endowed with an income of £41,250 from the Irish Church surplus. By subsequent Acts the income of the Board was increased to £231,000. It was expended on improving the breeds of horses, livestock and poultry, on measures for preventing potato disease, on improving and even building houses, constructing light railways, roads, fences and drains; on the consolidation of the 'crofter' holdings, and the cutting up of untenanted grazing land; and, later on, the purchase and re-sale of holdings. Co-operative credit by means of village banks was promoted, and encouragement was given to cottage industries, to knitting, lace, crochet work and homespun tweeds; to training classes in cookery, laundry, domestic economy, carpentry and even boat-building. Piers and boat-slips were constructed for fishermen, steamer services were subsidized, and other means of transport and communication were improved. In these and other ways a great work was done for the West of Ireland, though neither the Board nor its work were exempt from criticism, not always perhaps undeserved.

The I.A.O.S.

Closely allied to the work of the Congested District Board was that of the Irish Agricultural Organization Society. This Society was brought into being mainly by the efforts of one of the best friends of modern Ireland.

Sir Horace Plunkett

Irish of the Irish by birth, devoted to his country and anxious to improve the lot of his countrymen, Mr. (afterwards Sir) Horace Plunkett founded in 1894 the Society known by its initials—I.A.O.S. Its operations were based on the formula ' better farming, better business, better living '. Great difficulties were at first encountered in commending the practice, if not the principle, of co-operation to Irish farmers. Plunkett was denounced by Nationalist speakers and journals as ' a monster in human shape ' and was adjured to ' cease his hellish work '. Nevertheless, enthusiasm and hard work overcame all obstacles, and before the

War nearly 1,000 Agricultural Co-operative Societies had been
established, with a membership of close on 100,000 and an annual
turnover of £2,500,000.   In conjunction with the Land Purchase
Acts the I.A.O.S. transformed the conditions of dairy-farming in
Ireland, and brought prosperity—as the Bank deposits proved—
to thousands of Irish farmers.

Plunkett's ambitions extended beyond agricultural co-opera- Depart-
tion.   In 1895 he formed what was known as the *Recess Com-* ment of
Agricul-
mittee.   Plunkett himself presided over this Committee, which ture and
included Irish peers, business men from Ulster, and politicians, Technical
Instruc-
both Unionists and Nationalists.   The main result of the Com- tion, 1899
mittee was the setting up in 1899 of a Government Department of
Agriculture and Technical Instruction.   The Chief Secretary was
ex officio President, but Plunkett, as Vice-President, was the
effective head of a Department which quickly proved its value
to Ireland.   In 1900 Plunkett, who had sat as a Unionist for
Dublin County since 1892, lost his seat, and could no longer, as
had been intended, represent the Department in Parliament.
But his services were too valuable to be dispensed with, and he
remained at its head until 1907.   Mr. Bryce, on becoming Chief
Secretary, was most anxious to retain him, but with base ingratitude the Nationalists drove him to resignation.

Reforms in agriculture went hand in hand with the reorganiza- Local
tion of Local Government.   This was effected by the Act of 1898, Government
skilfully piloted through the House of Commons by Mr. Gerald Act, 1898
Balfour, who from 1895 to 1900 was Chief Secretary, and carried
on the policy, initiated by his brother, of ' killing Home Rule
by kindness '.

The Salisbury Government had made an effort to deal with
the problem of Irish Local Government in 1892.   In 1898 the
pledges then given were redeemed.

Rural Local Government—and Ireland, unlike England,
remains almost entirely rural—was mainly in the hands of two
bodies : the Grand Juries, a survival of the Protestant ascendancy
of the eighteenth century, and still composed of the landed gentry ;
and the Boards of Guardians, which had been ' captured ' by the
Nationalists.   The Act of 1898 followed closely, perhaps too
closely, the English Acts of 1888 and 1894.[1]   It deprived the

[1] *Supra*, pp. 40 f.

Grand Juries of all fiscal functions, and established County and District Councils on a purely democratic basis. No Councils were established in Parishes, the Parish being unknown to Ireland as an area of local administration.

The parliamentary register was adopted for the local franchise with the addition of peers and women. The District Councillors were to be the Poor Law Guardians for their respective areas, and also the road authority, though, as regards expenditure, in subordination to the County Council, which became the sole rating authority in rural districts. Liability both for the county cess and the poor rate, which were collected in one consolidated rate, was imposed upon the occupiers, who were thereby encouraged to economy. Parliament, however, coated the pill with a grant of £730,000, in relief of agricultural rates. As a check on extravagance in outdoor relief, union rating was adopted. The people who granted relief would, in the main, have to pay for it. As regards the whole measure considerable powers were reserved to the Local Government Board.

The first elections under the Act were held in the spring of 1899. In all parts of Ireland the landlords offered themselves, but except in the six north-eastern counties were almost invariably rejected. In the whole of Munster and Connaught only about a dozen country gentlemen were elected, and except in the six counties the Nationalists were everywhere in an overwhelming majority on the new Councils. The spirit in which they entered on their new and responsible duties was indicated by the resolutions which, on the outbreak of the Boer War, were passed by many Councils. Cheers were given for ' gallant old Paul Kruger ' ; sympathy was expressed for the Boers, ' rightly struggling to be free from the pirate Empire of the world ', and the English people were accused of ' rapine, murder, pillage, and all the crimes that it has fallen to humanity to perpetrate against fellow creatures '.

Yet despite these ebullitions the work of amelioration went steadily on. In 1900 Mr. Gerald Balfour was succeeded as Chief Secretary by Mr. George Wyndham, one of the most brilliant of the younger members of the Unionist Party. Soldier, scholar, statesman, Wyndham was admirably qualified to carry on in a sympathetic spirit the Irish policy of the brothers Balfour. Yet

George
Wynd-
ham

Ireland proved the premature grave of his reputation. His only
constructive achievement was the Land Act of 1903.

That Act carried a long stage farther the revolution which **Land**
transferred the ownership of the soil of Ireland from the land- **Purchase**
Act, 1903
lords to the occupiers. There was a general concurrence of
opinion among moderate men of all parties in Ireland [1] that a
final settlement of the land problem could be found only in an
exhaustive scheme of purchase 'upon a basis mutually agree-
able to the owners and occupiers of the land '. Wyndham's Act
contemplated the provision of a sum of £100,000,000 (subsequently
increased to £180,000,000, to be gradually raised by annual loans of
£5,000,000 in London. The Act dealt, not like previous Acts, with
individual holdings but with whole estates. The purchasers were
to pay $3\frac{1}{4}$ per cent., being £2 15s. for interest and 10s. for sinking
fund, on the capital advanced by the State to the vendors. The
period of repayment was to be $68\frac{1}{2}$ years. The price was to be
settled between vendor and purchaser, but ratified by three
Estates Commissioners, and the State, in order to encourage sales,
offered to the vendor an addition of 12 per cent. on the price.
This was admittedly a bonus to the landlords, but Wyndham
vindicated the soundness of the finance of the Bill by showing
that out of 73,000 tenant purchasers paying £840,000 a year to
the State only three owed eighteen months' arrears, and that in
twelve years there had been only two irrecoverable debts. The
Wyndham Act was a great achievement, and the consummation
of Unionist policy in Ireland. When the Party went out of office
in December 1905 the Irish land question had been solved. Evictions had practically ceased : 'fair rents ' had been judicially
fixed for 480,000 holdings, with an average reduction of 20 per
cent. and an aggregate reduction of £6,000,000 ; 74,000 tenants
had become owners before 1903.

During the six years which elapsed between the Act of 1903
and the fresh legislation of 1909 the number of purchase agreements, lodged in respect of direct sales by landlords to tenants,
was 217,299. The addition of proposed purchasers in other
categories brought up the total of potential purchasers to close
on 250,000, involving a sum of over £80,000,000.

[1] Cf. a remarkable Report of the Irish Land Conference signed among
others by Lords Mayo and Dunraven, John Redmond and William O'Brien.

Augustine
Birrell

In 1909, however, an Act was passed which retarded the progress of this beneficent agrarian revolution. In January 1907 Mr. Augustine Birrell, an amiable man and a brilliant essayist, left the Board of Education, where the rule of doctrinaires is neither uncommon nor inappropriate, to become Chief Secretary for Ireland. Of his success in solving the problem of University Education in Ireland more will be said presently. Glaringly contrasted with that success was his disastrous dealing with the Land Question.

The beneficent results achieved by the ameliorative measures of the two previous decades had greatly alarmed the Separatist politicians in Ireland. In particular were they afraid lest economic prosperity should weaken the demand for political independence. ' Ireland would prefer rags and poverty rather than surrender her national spirit.' So said Mr. Redmond to an audience at Buffalo.[1] An Ireland ' studded with the beautiful and happy homes of an emancipated peasantry ' (the description is again Mr. Redmond's) might well be less responsive to political rhetoric than an Ireland peopled by a half-starved peasantry with no proprietary interest in the soil they tilled.

Act of
1909

The Act of 1909 was no doubt intended to facilitate purchase, but in fact it had the opposite effect. For the first time the principle of compulsion was adopted, and the landlords, instead of receiving cash payments, were to be satisfied with stock issued on a falling market. The tenant's annuity, on the other hand, was raised from $3\frac{1}{4}$ to $3\frac{1}{2}$ per cent.—not an encouragement to purchase. For the £12,000,000 fixed ' bonus ' to the landlords there was substituted a variable bonus which, according to Mr. Wyndham, renewed the attempt at ' defining the metaphysical rights of the landlords and tenants ' respectively, and revived ' the social poison of litigation of which in 1903 every one but Mr. Dillon was weary '. The Act of 1903 was, in its author's view, a ' political treaty thenceforward to be binding on all three contracting parties : landlords, tenants and the State '. By the Act of 1909 that ' solemn treaty . . . was torn up, to deck with its tatters the triumph of Mr. Dillon's unholy alliance with the British Treasury '. Wyndham's words were bitter : but they reflect the disappointment arising from the obstruction of a great design, that of regenerating rural Ireland.

[1] September 27, 1910.

The Birrell Act, if inspired by a purpose equally beneficent, was less successful in achieving it. Agreements to purchase fell from 217,299 in the six years preceding the Act of 1909 to 8,992 in the two years which followed it. ' Land purchase practically came to a standstill.' [1] When the process of sale was resumed it was under conditions vastly different.

To return to the Wyndham régime. Mr. Wyndham's ambitions in regard to Ireland went far beyond the land question. In 1904 he attempted to solve the problem of a National University ; only, however, to add one more to the many failures of his predecessor. In that field Mr. Birrell achieved the success denied to Wyndham.

But the final blow to Wyndham's administration came from the ' devolutionists '. There was in Ireland a considerable party   *' Devolution '* which, while rejecting ' Home Rule ' in the Gladstonian sense, favoured a considerable measure of financial if not legislative autonomy. In 1903 an Association was formed, under the leadership of Lord Dunraven, to promote an object, which also had the active sympathy of the Lord-Lieutenant, the Earl of Dudley, and Sir Antony Macdonnell.[2] The latter, a distinguished Indian administrator, was in 1902 induced to accept the office of Under-Secretary, but on condition that he should have ' adequate opportunity of influencing the policy and acts of the Irish Administration '.[3] The appointment of a Liberal and a Roman Catholic lent substance to the rumour that the Unionist Government was moving towards a modified measure of Home Rule. Ulster took fright. There were questions in the House of Commons. In reply Wyndham described the Devolution Scheme as ' inadmissible ', and admitted that Macdonnell's conduct was 'indefensible', though ' not open to the imputation of disloyalty '—an imputation strongly resented and repudiated, in the House of Lords, by its leader, Lord Lansdowne.[4]

The situation was an awkward one for the Government as a whole and in particular for the Chief Secretary. It caused no

---

[1] The phrase is Professor Alison Phillips's—a highly competent authority.

[2] On the ' Devolution ' question cf. Lord Dunraven, *The Outlook in Ireland,* 1907.

[3] See Hansard for February 22, 1905.

[4] Cf. Hansard (Commons Debates) February 16 and (Lords Debates) February 17, 1905.

surprise, therefore, when (March 6, 1905) Mr. Balfour ' with the deepest regret ' announced Mr. Wyndham's resignation. Wyndham did not possess the tough fibre essential for success in party politics : he was too fine a spirit. ' I am undergoing ', he wrote in 1904, ' a phase of nausea in politics, nostalgia for poetry and a lurch in that direction.' [1] He was more at home in the study than in the office or the market-place : he longed always ' to keep in touch with letters . . . and so keep an escape way open from the dustiness and fustiness of politics '. After a few months' rest he returned to the House, and took his share in the work of the Party from 1906 until his death : but the unfortunate episode of 1905 virtually closed his political career. He was not fifty when in 1913 he died.

Wyndham was succeeded as Chief Secretary by a robust Tory —Mr. Walter Long. But before the end of the year (1905) the Government was out. Save for the closing episode the Irish administration of the Unionist Party had been an almost unqualified success.

Mr. Bryce, who took office as Chief Secretary in December 1905, admitted that Ireland was more peaceful and more prosperous than it had been for six hundred years. Mr. Birrell, his successor, endorsed that opinion, but still more remarkable was the testimony of Mr. John Redmond. Speaking at Waterford in 1915, he said :—

' I went to Australia to make an appeal on behalf of an enslaved, famine-haunted, despairing people, a people in the throes of a semi-revolution, bereft of all political liberties and engaged in a life-and-death struggle with the system of a most brutal and drastic coercion. . . . Only thirty-three or thirty-four years have passed since then, but what a revolution has occurred in the interval ! To-day, the people, broadly speaking, own the soil ; to-day, the labourers live in decent habitations ; to-day, there is absolute freedom in the local government and the local taxation of the country ; to-day, we have the widest Parliament in the municipal franchise ; to-day, the evicted tenants, who are the wounded soldiers of the land war, have been restored to their homes or to other homes as good as those from which they had been originally driven. . . . The congested districts, the scene

[1] *Life and Letters of George Wyndham*, pp. 90–1.

of some of the most awful horrors of the old famine days, have been transformed, the farms have been enlarged, decent dwellings have been provided, and a new spirit of hope and independence is to-day amongst the people . . . we have at last won educational freedom in university education for most of the youth of Ireland . . . to-day we have a system of old-age pensions in Ireland whereby every old man and woman over seventy is saved from the workhouse, free to spend their last days in comparative comfort. We have a system of national industrial insurance which provides for the health of the people. . . .'

For this happy transformation most of the credit must go to the Government which had been in office all but continuously from 1885 to 1905. But one great achievement stands to the credit of Mr. Birrell. With the political question he hardly attempted to deal : he did indeed introduce in 1907 a ' Devolution ' Bill for the establishment of a Representative Central Council in Dublin, but the scheme received no support in any quarter, and was unanimously rejected by a Nationalist Convention in Dublin (May 21). ' Devolution ' was never heard of again.

Mr. Birrell was more fortunate in dealing with the knotty problem of University Education in Ireland. Thus far the problem had baffled the ingenuity of every British statesman who had touched it. Nor was that surprising. The position was entirely anomalous. Trinity College, Dublin, dating from Elizabethan days, and richly endowed, provided for the higher education of Protestants, or rather of Anglicans. Since 1793 it had, indeed, admitted Catholics and Presbyterians to its degrees ; but only in rare cases had they availed themselves of the privilege, and never had Trinity College, despite its proud record of scholarship, become a national institution. *University Education*

Peel had, in 1845, provided for the endowment of three Queen's Colleges at Belfast, Cork and Galway, and in 1850 they were affiliated into the Queen's University of Ireland. Avowedly intended to ' avoid all interference, positive or negative, in all matters affecting the liberty of conscience ' these Colleges proved (except in Belfast) a complete failure. Denounced as ' Godless ' by Anglicans, they were regarded by the Catholics as ' dangerous to the faith and morals of the people ' and into the soil of Catholic

Ireland they never struck roots. A Catholic University was established in Dublin in 1854 under the presidency of John Henry Newman and for years was maintained by Catholic piety, unassisted by the State.

Gladstone made a valiant attempt to deal with the problem in 1873, but his Bill was, by a narrow majority, defeated in the House of Commons, and on its defeat he resigned.[1] Honestly intended to discover a solution acceptable to Irish Catholics and English Nonconformists, the measure was in fact so framed as to wound every susceptibility and to disturb every existing institution, without satisfying a single grumbler and without removing a single grievance. A much less pretentious measure passed in 1879 indirectly provided a considerable endowment for the (Catholic) University College in Dublin. Thus Disraeli effected a beneficent purpose in ' such a way that it will not be understood ' (the words are his).[2] Birrell grasped the nettle more firmly. He converted the Belfast College into a University (virtually for Protestants) and established a National University, to which are affiliated the University Colleges of Dublin, Cork and Galway. Thus the Catholics got what they had always demanded, a real University, with constituent Colleges in which the ' atmosphere ' was wholly Catholic, and the truly English idea (always repudiated by all parties in Ireland) of divorcing education from religion was finally discredited.

Thus, at the close of the first decade of the new century the situation in Ireland seemed full of promise. Mr. Birrell had solved the problem of higher education, and the Balfours had restored order and had conferred on Ireland a system of Local Government, as broadly democratic as that in England ; with Wyndham's help they had transferred the ownership of the soil from the landlords to the cultivators, and with the help of Sir Horace Plunkett had initiated an era of economic prosperity such as Ireland had never previously enjoyed.

The ensuing decades stand out in sharp and terrible contrast with the first. Spenser's ominous words haunt the memory.

[1] Disraeli refused to take office, and Gladstone withdrew his resignation.
[2] See a remarkable letter to the *Spectator*, December 31, 1898, from Mr. Edmund Dease.

The ' good plots ' and ' wise counsels ' once more failed of their intended effect : the whole edifice of peace and prosperity built with such patience crashed in awful ruin to the ground.

The crash was portended by the complete failure of the ' com-placent Birrell ' [1] from the outset of his régime to maintain order. He cancelled the Arms Act, which had minimized outrages in disturbed districts, and refused with lamentable results to enforce the Crimes Act. All the familiar features of the ' Terror ' re-appeared : boycotting cases which in November 1905 had fallen to 162 rose by January 1909 to 874 ; offences in which firearms were used quadrupled ; agrarian crime increased with appalling rapidity, and took on a new shape. Many of the large graziers had become owners of their farms, and it was against them that ' cattle driving ' was directed. In the first half of 1908 no fewer than 418 cattle drives were officially reported, and of the offenders prosecuted relatively few were punished. Face to face with this situation Birrell assumed an attitude which a friendly critic might describe as ' philosophical '. ' It is the duty of the Irish people ', he said, ' to protect their property in person.' And again, to a question in the House : ' I will not simply even for the sake of getting a few more convictions . . . break up the great Liberal tradition . . . and my own hopes for the future of Ireland.' [2]

The great Liberal tradition had, from 1895 to 1909, been weakened if not broken by the Liberal Imperialists. On the eve of the momentous Election of January 1910 it was resuscitated. In the 1906 Parliament the Liberal Party had no need of the help of the Irish Nationalists. In the imminent fight against the House of Lords it might be essential. The Budget of 1909 was distasteful to the Irishmen ; but the Lords had in 1893 deprived them of Home Rule ; the political situation in 1910 brought them the opportunity of revenge.

In the speech at the Albert Hall (December 1909) with which he opened the election campaign, Asquith had referred to the Irish question in words of high significance. ' . . . the present Parliament was disabled in advance from proposing any such solution [i.e. Home Rule]. But in the new House of Commons the hands of the Liberal Government and the Liberal majority will be in this matter entirely free.'

Marginal notes: ' Law and Order '

Liberals and Nation-alists

---

[1] The phrase is Lord Midleton's.   [2] Hansard, February 23, 1909.

Asquith's prediction was falsified. The Liberal Party, so far from being 'free', found itself dependent for its existence on its Irish allies. As against the Unionists its own majority was 2; the Nationalists numbered 82 and the Labour Party 42. On the support of the latter the Liberals could confidently rely, both to carry the Budget and abolish the veto of the Lords. If the Nationalists coalesced with the Unionists to defeat the Budget the Liberals would be out, and Asquith was explicitly informed that they would do so 'unless they were assured that the passing of a Bill dealing with the veto of the House of Lords was guaranteed during the present year'.[1]

Home Rule Bill, 1912 In 1911 the Parliament Act reached the Statute Book—with the willing, nay ardent, assistance of the Irish Nationalists. The time had come for the Liberal Party to 'deliver the goods', or in Redmond's blunter phrase to 'toe the line'. The Home Rule Bill was accordingly introduced by the Prime Minister in a speech of exemplary lucidity on April 11, 1912. The Second Reading was carried on May 9 by 372 votes to 271, and, having occupied nearly sixty days of Parliamentary time, got its Third Reading before the close of that protracted Session, on January 16, 1913, by 367 to 257. On January 30 the Lords, after four days' debate, threw out the Bill on Second Reading by 326 to 69. Passed over the heads of the House of Lords, the Bill received the Royal Assent on September 18, 1914, seven weeks after the outbreak of war and after the declaration of a truce between all parties, Radicals and Unionists, Ulster Covenanters and Nationalists. But though placed upon the Statute Book, its passage was accompanied by an Act which in effect suspended its operation until the end of the War. Moreover, Asquith gave, on behalf of the Government, a pledge that the Bill 'should not come into operation until Parliament should have the fullest opportunity by an Amending Bill of altering, modifying or qualifying its provisions, in such a way as to secure at any rate the general consent both of Ireland and the United Kingdom'. In the event, the Act never came into operation at all.

It may suffice therefore to say that the third edition of Home Rule was more federal in texture than its predecessors. Avowedly intended, though clumsily devised, to fit into a scheme of devolu-

[1] Asquith, *Life*, I. 272

tion for the United Kingdom, it proposed to retain forty-two Irish members at Westminster [1] and to secure 'unimpaired and inviolate' the supremacy of the Imperial Parliament. The Irish Legislature was to consist of two Houses : a Senate of 40 members nominated in the first instance (virtually) by the British Executive, and afterwards elected by the four Provinces of Ireland : 14 by Ulster, 11 by Leinster, 9 by Munster and 6 by Connaught. The Senate, so constituted, was to 'safeguard the interests of the minority'. The Lower House was to consist of 164 members of whom 39 (in nine three-member constituencies) were to be elected by proportional representation. Certain specified powers were reserved to the Imperial Parliament, but the *residue* of powers was (contrary to the Canadian precedent) vested in the subordinate Parliament at Dublin. The Irish Executive was to be responsible to the Irish Parliament, with an area of authority coextensive with that of the Legislature. Under the complicated financial provisions Great Britain remained saddled with large obligations, e.g. for land purchase and Old Age Pensions.

The Ulster Unionists, under the intrepid leadership of Sir Edward Carson, had anticipated the passing of the Bill by setting up a 'Provisional Government' and organizing an Ulster Volunteer Force. They declared that they would 'never in any circumstances submit to Home Rule'. In 1886 Lord Randolph Churchill had declared in an historic phrase : 'Ulster will fight and Ulster will be right.' Her people now prepared to do so, and were supported in their resolution by Mr. Bonar Law and other leaders of the Unionist Party in England. In September 1912 a 'Solemn Covenant' was promulgated pledging its signatories, with Carson at their head, never to recognize the authority of a Home Rule Parliament at Dublin.

The Government was urged by many of their supporters to prosecute Carson and his associates. Sir Edward himself advised them to do so. For reasons fully set out by Mr. Asquith [2] they declined to take that course. On the contrary, they made great

Ulster

---

[1] The '86 Bill had proposed that no Irish members should sit at Westminster except when summoned for special purposes : the '93 Bill proposed to retain eighty, but not to allow them to vote on British business.

[2] *Fifty Years of Parliament*, ii. 140 f.

efforts to meet the views of the Ulster Unionists, notably by the proposal, made on March 9, 1914, that any Ulster county might vote itself out of the scheme for six years. This solution Carson was prepared to accept, if the time-limit were expunged, but, said he, ' We do not want sentence of death with a stay of execution for six years.'

The sands were running out. Under the Parliament Act Home Rule might become law in 1914. Only the assent of the Crown was necessary, and to the Crown the Unionist leaders began to look to ease a situation which might lead to civil war in Ireland. Advice from quarters, responsible and the reverse, poured in upon the King : that he should dismiss the Ministry, and dissolve Parliament ; that he should delay the Royal Assent until a Referendum had been taken, and much else. That the King was profoundly anxious to find a peaceful solution goes without saying ; and unceasingly he laboured to promote it. At the beginning of March 1914 he brought the Party leaders very near to a point of agreement.[1]

The
Curragh
Incident

But passions were now mounting rapidly. Early in March Mr. Churchill, then First Lord of the Admiralty, ordered that the forthcoming practice of the 1st Battle Squadron, complete with battleships, cruisers and destroyers, should take place at Lamlash, in ominous proximity to Belfast Lough. Orders were also given that special precautions should be taken for the guarding of depots of arms and ammunition at Armagh and other Ulster towns, and for the protection of coastguard stations. About the same time rumours reached London of disaffection at the Curragh. In view of possible disturbance in Ireland the War Office took ' precautionary measures ' ; officers ' whose homes were actually in the province of Ulster ' were to be allowed, if they wished, to ' disappear ' temporarily from Ireland without prejudice to their future career. Certain other officers, perhaps from a misunderstanding of orders, preferred to be dismissed the Service rather than march against Ulster.

In view of events at the Curragh Colonel Seely, the War Minister, resigned, and on March 30 Asquith decided himself to take over the War Office. The atmosphere in the House of Commons on the night when Asquith announced that decision was as tense

_____
[1] Asquith, *Life*, II. 39.

as at any moment during the War, and his announcement evoked a wild ebullition of enthusiasm among his followers.[1] The tension was momentarily relaxed, but the problem of the two Irelands remained unsolved. Both were arming and drilling. When would the explosion come?

An eleventh-hour effort was made to avert it. On June 23 an Amending Bill was introduced by the Government in the House of Lords, embodying the proposal that any Ulster county should be entitled to vote itself out of Home Rule for six years. The Lords transformed it into a Bill to exclude the whole of Ulster without any time limit. In that form it reached the House of Commons on July 14—a fortnight after the murder of the Archduke Franz Ferdinand at Serajevo (June 28).

In these grave circumstances the King made yet another effort to bring the Parties together. He summoned to Buckingham Palace a Conference of eight persons, Mr. Asquith and Mr. Lloyd George to represent the Government, Lord Lansdowne and Mr. Bonar Law (Unionists), Sir Edward Carson and Captain James Craig (Ulster) and John Redmond and John Dillon (Nationalists). It met under the presidency of the Speaker on July 21, and was opened by the King with a short but solemn address. The only point discussed was the area to be excluded, temporarily or permanently, from the operation of the Home Rule Bills, but after four sittings it became clear that no agreement could be reached, and on July 24 the breakdown of the Conference was announced to Parliament. *The King and the Irish Crisis*

On the same day news of the Austrian ultimatum to Serbia reached England. *The Austrian Ultimatum to Serbia*

The Amending Bill was down for Second Reading in the House of Commons, but it was agreed between Asquith and Bonar Law that 'under conditions of gravity almost unparalleled' while 'issues of peace and war were hanging in the balance' (the phrases are Asquith's), it was essential that this country should present a united front to the world and that domestic controversies should be laid aside.

During the next four years this country was at war.

---

[1] The writer witnessed this remarkable scene. The Liberals were expecting that Asquith would announce a Dissolution; and their relief at the news of a reprieve was unmistakable.

BOOK III

CHAPTER XX

THE GENESIS OF THE GREAT WAR

TO the history of the Great War the British Empire contributed an indispensable chapter. But the War was
fought on so vast a scale, the issues it raised were so vital for the
whole world, that no more than a summary of its antecedents,
progress and results can be attempted in the present work, and
that summary must deal mainly with the reaction of the War
upon the British Empire.

Moreover, materials are accumulating so rapidly that no contemporary historian can pretend fully to have digested them,
still less presume to pass more than a preliminary judgement
upon the evidence they furnish. Already some 35,000 documents
have been published by the Governments of States involved in
the War. Individuals have been as eager as Governments to
vindicate themselves in the eyes of posterity. Most of the prominent actors in the great Drama—soldiers and sailors, statesmen,
diplomatists and publicists—have published their reminiscences,
diaries, memoirs and what not. Nor have the historians and
commentators, either in this or other countries, been idle. Library
shelves groan under the burden of tomes, large and small.

Shortly before his death (1898) Bismarck was inspecting the *Origins*
Hamburg-American liner which was to bear his name. He is *of the*
reported to have said to his host, Herr Ballin : ' I shall not see *War*
the world-war, but you will ; and it will start in the Near East.'
The prediction betrayed no particular acumen. By 1898, if not
before, Bismarck must have realized that in 1878 he had sown
seed that was bound before long to yield a death-dealing harvest.

The sower was not wholly to blame. The ground had long ago been prepared. Between Romanoffs and Hapsburgs, between Teutons and Slavs, there was ancient rivalry in the Balkans. The increasing weakness of the Ottoman Turks, the re-emergence of Balkan nationalities, precipitated the inevitable struggle. At the Congress of Berlin (1878) Bismarck had been virtually compelled to choose between his two allies. He chose Austria ; Russia was estranged from Germany, and ultimately turned to France. Bismarck's brilliant if perfidious diplomacy postponed the crisis. He prevented any rapprochement between England and France, between Russia and England, and between France and Italy. Egypt availed for the first, Central Asia for the second, Tunis for the third. But after Bismarck's fall (1890) the conduct of German diplomacy fell into clumsy hands.[1] Russia allied herself with France, England reached an agreement with France and Russia ; Italy was increasingly restive under the yoke of the Triple Alliance. Had Russia been in a position to take up the challenge flung down by the ' Knight in shining armour ' at Potsdam the clash of arms would have come in 1909. It was postponed for five years, but it was still the Near East that provided, if not the cause, the occasion.

The Turco- Italian War, 1911–12

The first blood was drawn by Italy. The climax of the Italian movement had been reached in 1871. In that year ' Italy entered Rome ' and the Pope imprisoned himself in the Vatican. The half-century that followed was, however, a period of storm and stress for the young nation. So great was the pressure of domestic difficulties that she had little superfluous energy for the pursuit of external ambitions. Her efforts in the Colonial field had been almost uniformly unfortunate, yet, as the new century advanced, she saw herself in danger of being elbowed out of any share of the North African littoral. France was already mistress of Algeria and Tunis, and her accord with England had given her a free hand in Morocco. England was seemingly in permanent occupation of Egypt. Only Tripoli remained.

For years past Italy had pursued a policy of economic penetration in that province. Formal annexation was, it was generally assumed, only a matter of opportunity. But after the

---

[1] On this cf. Erich Brandenburg : *From Bismarck to the World War* (E.T., Oxford 1927), *passim*.

Young Turk Revolution (1908) the Italian merchants, bankers, and engineers who formed the advance-guard of the Italian occupation, found themselves thwarted at every turn by newly appointed Turkish officials. Simultaneously, German archaeologists and geologists manifested increased zeal in their scientific investigations in Tripoli. Could there be any connexion between the activities of Moslem officials and those of Teutonic professors ?

Italy took alarm, demanded the Sultan's consent to an Italian occupation of Tripoli (September 1911) and, without awaiting his reply, declared war.

The Italians occupied, without much opposition, Rhodes, the Dodecanese Archipelago, and the coast towns of Tripoli, but made little progress against the combined resistance of Turks and Arabs in the interior. The war seemed likely to drag on indefinitely, when the Turks, threatened by a new danger, suddenly concluded peace with Italy at Lausanne (October 18, 1912). Italy kept Tripoli, and, pending the fulfilment of other conditions, Rhodes and the islands as well.

The Ottoman Empire was already involved in another and far more serious conflict. A miracle had happened. Greece, Bulgaria, Serbia and Montenegro had combined against the Porte, and in a few weeks had brought the Ottoman Empire to its knees. The Balkan Wars, 1912–13

The Powers could not view these events without grave concern. Italy and Austria-Hungary were especially perturbed by the unexpectedly rapid success of the Balkan League. Sir Edward Grey had worked assiduously, first to avert the outbreak of the Balkan War, then to localize it, and now (December 1912) to end it. An armistice was virtually forced upon the belligerents on December 3, and a Conference met in London (December 1912–January 1913) to arrange terms of peace. The Conference was within sight of success when, on January 23, the ' Young Turks ' effected a *coup d'état* at Constantinople, and thus brought the London negotiations to an abrupt conclusion. On February 1 the Conference broke up : but after four months of fighting, a second armistice was concluded ; negotiations were reopened in London on May 20, and before the end of May Peace was signed.

Peace lasted only a month. The victors quarrelled over the spoils. By the end of June Greece was at war with Bulgaria.

Roumania came in against the latter, and Bulgaria was beaten to the earth. Peace was signed at Bucharest on August 10. The German Emperor promptly telegraphed his congratulations to his kinsman, King Carol of Roumania, upon the successful issue of his ' wise and truly statesmanlike policy '. King Constantine of Greece at the same time received from the Kaiser the baton of a Field-Marshal in the German army.

Austria-Hungary was less well pleased at the conclusion of peace in the Balkans, involving as it did the exaltation of Serbia. On August 9, 1913, the Emperor Francis Joseph communicated to his two allies his intention of taking ' defensive ' action against Serbia, and so bring into operation the *casus foederis* of the Triple Alliance. Italy very properly refused to recognize the proposed aggression of Austria-Hungary as a *casus foederis*; Berlin restrained the ardour of Vienna, and the attack upon Serbia was accordingly postponed—but for less than twelve months. In May 1914 the Austrian Emperor instructed his ambassador at Constantinople that ' The Central Powers cannot accept the Treaty of Bucharest as definitely settling the Balkan question : *nothing but a general war* can bring about a satisfactory solution.' Bismarck's forecast was on the eve of fulfilment. On July 23, 1914, Austria-Hungary addressed her ultimatum to Serbia.

English policy
Throughout the Balkan Crisis, as throughout the crises that preceded it, Great Britain had striven with all her might to maintain the peace of Europe. In English Foreign Policy there had, indeed, been no breach of continuity since the fall of the Gladstone Ministry in 1885. Under Salisbury, Rosebery, Lansdowne and Grey England had consistently sought peace and ensued it. English diplomacy had naturally encountered some dangerous corners, but each had been successfully turned. Down to December 1899 there had been at least a chance of closer accord, if not an actual alliance, with Germany. Yet Prince Bülow, in a work published before the outbreak of war, describes England as being, even before the close of the century, ' the secret opponent of our international policy '.[1] As the twentieth century advanced the legend was industriously circulated in Germany that open enmity had superseded ' secret opposition ', that England, and in particular her King, was endeavouring to encircle Germany

[1] *Imperial Germany* (Eng. trs.), p. 29.

with a ring of enemies. It was sheer illusion. The agreements with France and Russia were purely defensive. Had Germany been as peacefully disposed as England or France, and able to restrain the restlessness of her Austrian ally, the Hohenzollerns and the Hapsburgs might to-day (1933) still be occupying their respective thrones, and exercising a joint control over a through railway-line from Hamburg to Bagdad. But Germany made the fatal psychological error—now admitted by responsible German historians—that peace with England could be maintained only by intimidation. Misinterpreting the complaisant attitude of England towards German expansion in Africa and in the Pacific, Germany had been since 1898 developing a Navy deliberately intended to try conclusions, some day, with the British Navy.

In 1888, when William II came to the throne, Germany was spending only about £2,000,000 a year on her Navy, and did not wish to spend more. In 1898 a new Navy Law was passed to provide her with a Navy, no more than adequate in view of the expansion of her overseas trade and the development of a Colonial policy. In 1900 there was a further increase. ' Germany ', so ran the official memorandum, ' must have a battle fleet so strong that even the adversary possessed of the greatest sea-power will attack it only with grave risk to himself.' Or as the Kaiser had himself more picturesquely expressed it : ' Neptune's trident must be in our hands ' (1897). In 1906 the *Dreadnought* was launched. Germany's retort was a Naval programme which provided for such a rate of expansion that by 1914 Germany might possess a superiority over Great Britain in capital ships.[1] Consequently the Asquith Government made a formal announcement to Parliament that this country could not permit her naval superiority to be challenged.

The Campbell-Bannerman Government had reduced the building programme, and had offered to go farther if other nations would do the same. Germany refused even to have the matter discussed at The Hague Conference of 1907. Yet the British Government persevered in its endeavour to avoid competition in armaments and to improve relations with Germany—without result.

In the autumn of 1911 the *Agadir* incident brought Europe to

---

[1] Asquith, *Genesis of the War*, p. 75.

the brink of war. It was, at the last hour, avoided, but so grave was the situation that in January 1912 Sir Ernest Cassel, who 'knew the Emperor well and was at the same time devoted to British interests ',[1] was entrusted with a secret mission to Berlin. He was instructed to try to induce Germany to slow down her naval programme, and accept British superiority at sea. In return Great Britain would offer no opposition to the Colonial expansion of Germany and would refuse to join in any aggressive combination against her.[2] Cassel was well received, but nothing resulted. Consequently in February the Cabinet sent Mr. Haldane to Berlin. Haldane had long conversations with Herr von Bethmann-Hollweg, the Chancellor, with Admiral von Tirpitz, and with the Kaiser himself. The impression he formed was that the Chancellor ' was then as sincerely desirous of avoiding war as I was myself ; that the Kaiser was not unfriendly, but that both were overborne by the Admiral who, on the subject of naval preparation, was adamant. Haldane told the Germans that we had no wish to increase our Navy, but that if Germany persisted in an enlarged programme we should ' lay down two keels for each one she laid down. . . . Germany was quite free to do as she pleased, but so were we. . . .' The conversations were friendly, but ' we plainly could not come to an agreement with the naval advisers in their present mood '.[3]

To the challenge of the German Navy Law of 1912 the British Government was compelled to make (the phrase is Asquith's) a ' resolute response '.

Yet one more effort was made to avert war. In March 1913 Mr. Winston Churchill, then First Lord of the Admiralty, invited Germany to proclaim a ' naval holiday '. The invitation was declined with derision. Colonel House, the *fidus Achates* of Mr. Wilson, the American President, then took a hand in the game. With the cordial approval of Mr. Wilson, of Mr. Walter H. Page, the American Ambassador in London, and of the British Government, Colonel House in May 1914 went to Berlin. But though a born diplomatist, he could do no more than Haldane. Von Tirpitz ' bristled with antagonism at any suggestion for

---

[1] Churchill, *The World Crisis*, p. 95.
[2] Bethmann-Hollweg, *Reflections*, p. 48
[3] Haldane, *Autobiography*, pp. 240 f.

peace or disarmament or world-co-operation'. Yet House's mission to Europe had one fortunate result : it ' convinced him that Great Britain had had no part in bringing on the European War, and that Germany was solely responsible '.[1]

The sands were running out. Yet it is safe to say that in the high summer of 1914 there was among the English people no general apprehension of imminent war. There was, in high ministerial circles, grave anxiety about the European situation, but in the public mind Ireland loomed larger than Germany ; many people were more concerned about the female militancy and Labour unrest than about foreign affairs. But, unnoticed or not, events were moving rapidly towards catastrophe. *Immediate antecedents of the War*

So rapidly that during the months of June and July dates speak more eloquently than words.

On June 12, 1914, the Kaiser, accompanied by Admiral von Tirpitz, the head of the German Admiralty, paid a visit to Konopischt in Bohemia, the castle of the Archduke Franz Ferdinand, the heir to the Hapsburg Empire. The Archduke was credited with strong anti-Magyar and pro-Slav sentiments. What passed between the host and his visitor is still largely a matter of conjecture.[2] On June 23 the Kiel Canal was reopened, after a reconstruction which, by allowing the largest battleships to pass through it, doubled the fighting strength of the German fleet. On June 28 Franz Ferdinand, after attending the Bosnian manœuvres as Inspector-General of the Army, paid a visit with his consort to Serajevo, the Bosnian capital, and husband and wife were there assassinated. The murderers were Bosnians. That it was an act of political revenge for the annexation of the Slav provinces by Austria cannot be questioned ; but apart from that, the circumstances of the crime were and are mysterious. *The Kaiser*

Austria naturally held Serbia responsible for a crime committed by men in touch with secret societies at Belgrade. On June 30 Herr von Tschirschky, German Ambassador at Vienna, reported to Berlin : ' Here, even serious people are saying that

---

[1] Hendrik, *Life and Letters of W. H. Page*, i. 299. For a contrary view expressed with great moderation see Bethmann-Hollweg, *Reflections*, pp. 9–85.

[2] A report by Baron Treutler, who was Prussian Minister in attendance on the Kaiser at Konopischt, is the most authoritative account we possess. It was published in *Deutsche Politik*, of May 14, 1920. Cf. also for a more sensational story, W. Steed, *Through Thirty Years*.

accounts with Serbia must be settled once for all.' 'Now or never' is the Kaiser's marginal note on this historic dispatch. On July 5 the Kaiser received an autograph letter from his august ally the Emperor Francis Joseph, and in reply assured him of Germany's cordial support. The reply was sent after a Conference, or 'War Council', at Potsdam. On the following day the Kaiser left for a cruise in the Baltic. Was the cruise, as Karl Kautsky suggests, 'a means to lull Europe into security'? Anyway, on July 7 Austria-Hungary decided to send an ultimatum to Serbia. The note (so Tschirschky telegraphed on July 14) would be so drawn as to exclude the possibility of acceptance.[1] It required the Serbian Government to acknowledge responsibility for the Serajevo assassins and to allow Austrian magistrates to conduct their trial in Belgrade. On July 23 the ultimatum was dispatched to Belgrade and gave Serbia only forty-eight hours for a reply. Serbia made abject submission, accepting promptly eight out of the ten chief points, and not actually rejecting the other two. On July 28 Austria declared war on Serbia. Meanwhile, the German Ambassador in London had received from the Foreign Minister in Berlin a deeply significant letter : ' In a few years (wrote Herr von Jagow) . . . Russia will be ready to strike. Then . . . she will have built her strategic railways. . . . I desire no preventive war. But when battle offers we must not run away.'

Peace efforts of England

Immediate responsibility for the outbreak of war rests, then, indisputably upon Austria-Hungary ; and since the War it has been the main occupation of German historians to fix the final responsibility upon Vienna rather than Berlin. Russia, according to these authorities, must share it. France was dragged in by Russia, England, most reluctantly, by France.[2]

The evidence, bewildering in its amplitude, complexity and contradictions, has been analysed with incomparable skill and inexorable impartiality by Mr. Asquith. No statesman ever possessed a more judicial temper, and the detached critic will find it difficult to resist his conclusions. Briefly his conclusion is

---

[1] Cf. *Outbreak of the World War* (Carnegie Endowment E.T. of the Kautsky Documents).

[2] Cf. Erich Brandenburg, *From Bismarck to the World War* (E.T.), *passim*. See especially c. xviii and list of German authorities there quoted.

that, though Austria made the decisive move, the 'goad' was
applied by Germany. 'Instead of attempting to hold Austria
back, Germany incited and encouraged her to hurry forward.' [1]

From the day when the news of the Serajevo crime reached
London, the British Government worked ceaselessly and with
ever-deepening anxiety to localize the quarrel between Austria-
Hungary and Serbia, and to maintain the peace of Europe. On
July 24 Sir Edward Grey received the Austrian ultimatum.
Without an hour's delay he suggested mediation by the four
disinterested Powers—Great Britain and Germany, France and
Italy. On July 27 the Kaiser returned to Potsdam, and Germany
rejected Grey's suggestion. On July 28 Austria refused to discuss
the Serbian affair with Russia, or with other Powers. The quarrel
with Serbia was 'purely an Austrian concern'. On that same
day she declared war on Serbia, and next day began the bombard-
ment of Belgrade.

Russia could not look on unmoved at the chastisement of her **Russia**
Serbian friends, and on the 29th announced partial mobilization. **and**
Russia's perturbation had its repercussions in Paris. The grave **Serbia**
anxiety of France was shared by England. To the last hour
Grey continued to strive if not to hope for peace. As late as
July 29 he telegraphed to Berlin : 'Mediation was ready to come
into operation by any method that Germany thought possible, if
only Germany would press the button in the interests of peace.'
Nevertheless, on the same day he warned the German Ambassador
in London that he did not 'wish him to be misled by the friendly
tone of [our] conversation . . . into thinking that we should
stand aside '.[2] The Kaiser was infuriated by the report of this
conversation and commented on the dispatch : 'Aha ! The low
scoundrel . . . most mean and Mephistophelian. But genuinely
English.' On the morning of the 30th Grey received from Berlin
the German bid for British neutrality. The proposal was that
Great Britain should ' engage to stand by while . . . France is
beaten so long as Germany does not take French territory as distinct from Colonies ', and that we should ' bargain away whatever
obligation or interest we have as regards the neutrality of Belgium '. Both suggestions were categorically, though courteously,

---

[1] *Genesis of the War*, p. 180, and *passim*, cs. xx–xxvii.
[2] *Collected Documents* (1915), No. 89 (p. 67).

rejected.[1] On the 31st Germany required Russia to counter-mand mobilization within twelve hours, and in the absence of a compliant answer, mobilized herself on August 1 and declared war on Russia.

German Diplo-macy To France, also, Germany made a bid for neutrality, and in terms even more insulting than those offered to England. France was to hand over, as a guarantee of her neutrality, the fortresses of Toul and Verdun, which were to be restored to her after the con-clusion of the war with Russia. To this insult the French reply was mobilization. On August 3 Germany declared war on France.

Meanwhile, on the 2nd, Germany offered her friendly neutrality to Belgium, on condition that Belgium would not oppose the passage of German troops through her territory, in which case Germany would pay for any damage thus caused, would evacuate Belgian territory on the conclusion of peace, and would ' guarantee the possessions and independence of the Belgian Kingdom in full '.[2] Belgium refused the offer. On the same day German troops had entered the Grand Duchy of Luxemburg, and on the 4th crossed the Belgian frontier.

And England ? As late as Monday, August 3, Germany con-tinued to hope, and France to fear, that England might stand aside. M. Cambon was profoundly anxious about the British attitude. Well he might be. France did not want war, but believed that nothing could at this stage avert it, except an unequivocal declaration from Great Britain that she would stand by France. He urgently pressed the Cabinet to make it, but in vain. Hence some ' distressing interviews ' between him and Grey.[3] But Grey dare not pledge the Cabinet, which he knew to be divided. Had they decided to abandon France he would himself have resigned. So would Asquith, but the latter char-acteristically summarized his own position (as late as August 2) thus : (1) We have no obligation of any kind either to France or Russia to give them military or naval help ; (2) The dispatch of the Expeditionary Force to help France at this moment is out of the question, and would serve no object ; (3) We must not forget the ties created by our long-standing and intimate friend-

---

[1] *Collected Documents*, No. 101.   [2] Ibid., p. 309.
[3] Cf. *White Paper*, No. 119, and Grey, op. cit., c. xvi.

ship with France ; (4) It is against British interests that France should be wiped out as a Great Power ; (5) We cannot allow Germany to use the Channel as a hostile base ; (6) We have obligations to Belgium to prevent it being utilized and absorbed by Germany.[1]

On Sunday, August 2, the Cabinet was in almost continuous session. Before it met the Unionist leaders intimated to Asquith that in their judgement ' any hesitation in our supporting France and Russia would be fatal to the honour and security of the United Kingdom '. and they offered to ' H.M. Government the assurance of the united support of the Opposition in all measures required by England's intervention in the War '.[2] Nevertheless, the Cabinet was, according to Asquith, ' on the brink of a split ' though ' with some difficulty ' they agreed to authorize Grey to give an assurance to France (subject to the assent of Parliament) that if the German fleet came into the Channel or through the North Sea to attack French coasts or shipping, the British fleet would ' give all the protection in its power '. Grey also asked the French and German Governments for an undertaking severally to respect Belgian neutrality. France promptly gave it. The German Government refused. John Burns at once resigned ; Lord Morley followed his example (August 3), as did a few minor ministers. But the violation of Belgian neutrality by Germany united the Cabinet and united the Country. So far Grey's policy was justified. Whether an earlier and more decisive declaration on his part could have averted, or even postponed, war is a question on which, though endlessly discussed, no final verdict is possible. His ' procrastination ' and ' indecision ' have incurred blame from both French and German critics.[3] The fact remains that when war was rendered inevitable by the German invasion of Belgium Great Britain entered it as a united nation. More than that : behind a united nation was a united Empire.

---

[1] Asquith, *Memories*, II. 9.

[2] The story was told by Sir Austen Chamberlain in *The Sunday Times* for December 1, 1929.

[3] Cf. e.g. Hermann Lutz, *Lord Grey and the World-War* (E.T.), p. 300. ' Great Britain was . . . in control of the situation ; had she immediately and clearly stated her position world-peace would have been saved. But Sir Edward Grey had not the competence as a statesman. . . .'

CHAPTER XXI

THE GREAT WAR

WAR had come. Some politicians had foreseen it; some publicists had foretold it; the Admiralty had prepared for it; so, up to the limit of its slender resources, had the War Office. Few people, however, really believed that war would really come.

On the eve of War But war had come. The first reaction to it on the part of the English people was one of stupefaction, almost of incredulity. Would they not awake next morning from the horrible nightmare, and again see the light of a peaceful day? Not until Friday, the 31st, did the public manifest any signs of apprehension. But, on that day, the Bank of England raised its discount rate from 4 to 8 per cent., and next day (for technical reasons) to 10 per cent. That was the week-end before Bank Holiday. The public took fright. Money was wanted for the holidays. The Banks were besieged; but there was no default, though some Banks would cash cheques only (as they were entitled to do) in notes and silver. On July 31 the London Stock Exchange closed, not again to reopen until January 4, 1915—and then only under severe restrictions. That meant that credit was largely frozen, that securities were unsaleable, and that many rich men were for the time being as poor as the poorest.

On August 1 the Treasury authorized the Bank of England to ignore the restrictions of its Charter, and to issue notes in excess of its statutory maximum. This suspension was confirmed by Parliament on August 6, and by the same (Currency and Bank Notes) Act the Treasury was authorized to issue Currency Notes of £1 and 10s. and postal orders were temporarily made legal tender. On August 6 a general moratorium was declared, but was hardly necessary. The Bank Holiday, which had come so opportunely on August 3, had been prolonged for three days ; but on August 7 the Banks reopened with a plentiful supply of the new Currency Notes—popularly known (from the signature of the Secretary to the Treasury) as ' Bradburys '. The Banks took a large supply of these Notes—£13,000,000—from the Treasury ; but public confidence was so quickly restored that most of the notes were returned, and by the end of the year the Banks held only £169,000. On August 7 the Bank Rate was reduced to 6 per cent. and on the following day to 5 per cent. at which it remained. Before the end of Bank Holiday week business was ' as usual '. What England and the world owed at this crisis to certain ' city magnates ', to the calmness, the courage and wisdom of strong men like Lord Cunliffe, the Governor of the Bank of England, and Lord Rothschild, was suspected at the time and is now known to all men.

Great Britain went into the War as a nation at unity within itself. The first outward sign of unity was the assembling of a great crowd outside Buckingham Palace on August 2. The King and Queen were enthusiastically acclaimed, and the National Anthems of England and France were sung. Sir Edward Grey's great speech on August 3 convinced the nation that every possible effort, consistent with honour, had been made to avert war, and that its cause was that of right. *Outbreak of War*

> England, in this great fight to which you go
>   Because, when honour calls you, go you must,
> Be glad, whatever comes, at least to know
>   You have your quarrel just.[1]

Documents were promptly forthcoming to sustain the poet's plea. The *White Paper* (Cd. 1467), summarized in the preceding chapter, was given out on August 5. The case was irrefutable. The conscience of a peace-loving, peace-seeking people, was clear : Great Britain was, indubitably, void of offence.

On August 6 Asquith moved, and Parliament agreed to, a Vote of Credit for £100,000,000 and an increase of 500,000 men for the Army and 67,000 for the Navy and Coastguard. The Prime Minister made it clear that we were fighting for two objects : Firstly, ' to fulfil a solemn international obligation ', and, secondly,

---

[1] Owen Seaman in *Punch* which now, as always, accurately reflected the temper of the nation.

to ' vindicate the principle that small nationalities are not to be crushed, in defiance of international good faith, by the arbitrary will of a strong and overmastering Power '.

Belgium

Undoubtedly, it was the German attack on Belgium that brought the British Empire into the War, but candour compels the admission that the integrity and independence of the Low Countries has for centuries been among the most obvious of English interests, and the pivot of English policy.[1] We fought in the Great War as the defender of Belgium and the ally of France and Italy : but it is evident that in the defence of Belgium and France British interests were deeply and inextricably involved.

Lord Kitchener

In asking for the Vote of Credit Asquith made an announcement that more than anything else inspired the nation with confidence. Lord Kitchener happened to be at home on leave from Egypt when the War broke out. On August 3 he was actually embarking at Dover on his return to Egypt when he was recalled by an urgent telegram from the Prime Minister. On August 6 he became Secretary of State for War. Rumour had been busy with the name of Lord Haldane, who might, very naturally, have desired to put in motion the machinery which his genius had devised. It is now known that Haldane cordially concurred in, if he did not actually suggest, Kitchener's appointment.

That Kitchener was in all ways well qualified for the post thus thrust upon him it would be idle to pretend. In the ways of Parliaments and Cabinets he was wholly unversed : politicians were to him anathema. He could not use other men's tools ; rather than work the machinery provided by Haldane he would create his own afresh. He had, we have learnt, an ' ineffable contempt for the Territorials," and his failure to adopt and adapt the Territorial Scheme meant loss of time and great if temporary confusion. He underrated the force of sentiment, and was lacking in imagination and sympathy. These defects impeded recruiting in Wales, ruined it in Southern Ireland, and broke the generous heart of John Redmond. They may have been responsible, too, for his rejection of French's scheme [2] to land the Expedi-

---

[1] On this point cf. Marriott, *The European Commonwealth*, c. viii (Oxford, 1919).

[2] Sir John French had been appointed to command the Expeditionary Force.

tionary Force in Belgium, occupy Antwerp, and stiffen the Belgian rather than the French army. Yet even his severest critic allows that he had ' flashes of greatness '. ' He was ', writes Lloyd George, ' like one of those revolving lighthouses which radiate momentary gleams of revealing light far into the surrounding gloom, and then suddenly relapse into complete darkness.' [1] The image, accurate or not, is a fine one. None, however, can deny that as Minister for War Kitchener rendered an incomparable service to his country. He alone foresaw how prolonged and arduous the struggle must be. The great army, raised, trained and equipped in the next two years, was in literal truth, ' Kitchener's Army '. He had promptly appealed for 100,000 men to to be enlisted ' for four years or the duration of the War '. Thanks largely to the glamour of his personality the response was overwhelming. Haldane, who on August 3 had temporarily and unofficially relieved Asquith at the War Office had mobilized the British Expeditionary Force on the same day, and had by Order in Council, assumed the control of the railways. By August 4 the General Managers were Colonels in H.M. Army, and under military discipline. Everything had worked, according to plan, without a hitch. The nation unknowingly reaped what Haldane had sown.

Where was the Expeditionary Force to operate ? Was it to defend the shores of England, or help the French to repel the German attack ? Opinion was divided : but Haldane, Grey and Churchill were for the bolder course, and on August 17 the nation learnt, to its astonishment, that four out of the six Divisions of the Expeditionary Force with one cavalry Division had safely landed in France.[2]

The Admiralty must share with the War Office the credit for this remarkable achievement. Had the Navy not been ready down to the last button, the British Army could not have left these shores. Fortunately the Navy, having concentrated in mid-July for the annual manœuvres, had not been allowed to disperse. On Saturday, August 1, it was mobilized on the sole   The Navy

---

[1] *War Memoirs*, II. 751.

[2] Each Division of infantry was composed of 598 officers and 18,077 men, with 54 field guns, 18 4·5-inch howitzers and 4 heavy 60-pounder guns. A Division of cavalry consisted of 485 officers and 9,412 men with 24 horse artillery guns.

responsibility of Mr. Winston Churchill, then First Lord of the Admiralty.[1] The Naval Reserves were called up on the 2nd. The First Fleet had already (29th) taken up its station in the North Sea. To the Navy the country looked confidently for the defence of its shores : in that confidence it had sent its Army to France. Thanks to the naval shield, the Army crossed the Channel in absolute safety, and by December 31 the Navy had transported across the sea, without loss, 809,000 men (including wounded, prisoners, and refugees), 203,000 horses and 250,000 tons of stores—a remarkable achievement.

The theatres of War

The Great War had begun. The detailed story of it must be sought elsewhere. Starting with the Austrian attack on Serbia it presently engulfed the whole world. The actual fighting was on no fewer than seven 'Fronts': (i) the Western Front— France ; (ii) the Eastern Front, where Germany and Austria were opposed to Russia ; (iii) the Italian Front, where from 1915 onward Italy, with the timely help of England and France, engaged Austria ; (iv) the Balkans, where the Allies, reinforced (1917) by Roumania and Greece, were opposed by Turkey and Bulgaria ; (v) Egypt and Palestine, where as in Mesopotamia the British Empire fought the Ottoman Empire ; (vi) Africa, in which alone there were three theatres—South-West, East, and West ; and (vii) lastly, the war at sea. In all of these vast and widely distributed theatres a large, in most a predominant, in some an exclusive, share of the fighting fell to the British Empire.

The Western Front

The German plan was to march through Belgium peacefully if it might be, forcibly if necessary, to thrust rapidly at Paris, and having captured Paris, and (perhaps) the Channel ports, to impose terms on France and then to deal with Russia. The plan was frustrated by the heroic resistance of the Belgians and by the prompt dispatch to France of the British Expeditionary Force. The refusal of Belgium to give free passage to the German Army brought upon it every imaginable horror at the hands of the exasperated Germans. Liége held up the German advance for nearly a week but surrendered on August 7 ; the Germans entered Brussels on the 20th and on the 24th Namur surrendered. The British troops which landed in France on August 16 found themselves, exactly one week later, in the firing line at Mons.

[1] Churchill, *World Crisis*, i. 217.

Hopelessly outnumbered, out of touch with their allies, the British force was compelled to retreat. Nevertheless, its extrication from Mons reflected high credit on Sir John French and his officers and proved to all time the heroism and endurance of the British soldier. General Smith-Dorrien made a gallant stand at Le Cateau (August 26), and von Kluck, the German Commander, confessed that but for that stand he would have turned the flank of the British Army and taken Paris.[1] As it was, the Germans forced the Aisne, captured Amiens and Laon, and, by the end of August, were within striking distance of Paris. But at the great battle of the Marne (6th to 12th September) the tide turned, the Germans were driven back to the Aisne ; there they dug themselves in, and for four long years the Germans and the Allies faced each other in a series of trenches which extended from the Channel to the frontier of Switzerland.

The Belgians meanwhile were in terrible plight. Antwerp had always been regarded by England as a point of supreme importance to her. That Antwerp should be in friendly hands was and remains one of the traditional maxims of British statesmanship. The city was now in imminent danger from the Germans. An effort must be made to save it. On October 5 we landed in Antwerp a miserably equipped and miscellaneous force of some 8,000 sailors and marines, with a large admixture of untrained civilians.[2] About the same time a 7th division of the Expeditionary Force—under the command of General Rawlinson —was landed at Ostend. The idea was that at all costs the enemy must be headed off from the coasts of France and Flanders, and for this purpose the British force was transferred from the Aisne to the Lys and Yser. Antwerp, however, fell on October 9. The inhabitants, soldiers and civilians alike, had fled to the Dutch frontier or the sea. The Belgian Government was transferred to Havre. A few days later the great battle began around Ypres. It lasted until the middle of November. When it ended the

---

[1] See letter from General Bingham (*The Times*, December 13, 1933).

[2] Of this force two-thirds got away ; the rest were forced against the Dutch frontier or captured. For a brilliant defence of the Antwerp Expedition see Churchill, *World Crisis*, i. xv. Mr. Churchill himself went to Antwerp and for a couple of days was in control of what remained of Belgium and its Army, and offered to resign the Admiralty and become a Lieutenant-General in the Army. Cf. Asquith, *Memoirs*, II. 42.

British Expeditionary Force had almost ceased to exist, but Ypres had been held, and the holding of Ypres denied the Germans access to the Channel ports. Had Ypres fallen, the Germans would have been within striking distance of Dover. No words, therefore, can overestimate the debt which England and the world owes to the heroes who laid down their lives in the long-drawn-out battle of October and November, 1914.

At the end of 1914 the position was as follows : the Germans, instead of dictating terms to the French in Paris, were entrenched on the Aisne. Instead of shelling Dover and Folkestone from the Channel Ports the Germans were still pinned behind Ypres. The Russian attack had failed, but the Serbs had repelled the Austrians and recaptured their capital ; above all, not a single German merchantman remained at sea.

But the broad result was a deadlock. 'The German fleet remained sheltered in its fortified harbours, and the British Admiralty had discovered no way of drawing it out. . . . Ramparts more than 350 miles long, ceaselessly guarded by millions of men, sustained by thousands of cannon, stretched from the Swiss frontier to the North Sea. . . . Mechanical not less than strategic conditions had combined to produce at this early period of the War a deadlock both on sea and land.' Thus does Mr. Churchill summarize the situation.[1] Mr. Lloyd George had simultaneously arrived at the same conclusion. So had General Gallieni. The French soldier and the British statesman were alike appalled at the ' Western holocausts ' only tolerated, says the latter, by public opinion in the Allied countries owing to ' an elaborate system of concealing repulses and suppressing casualties '. Churchill's fertile brain was, accordingly, at work on plans for a ' flanking ' movement. So was Lloyd George's. But the two men had not the same ' flank ' in mind. Both were thinking of the ' Eastern Front '. Lloyd George would have landed a force at Salonika. By this means we should, he claimed, not only save Serbia, imminently menaced by an Austro-German attack, but put Turkey out of action, and bring in, on the side of the Allies, Roumania, Bulgaria and Greece. It was an attractive suggestion. Churchill had two alternatives. One plan (primarily Lord Fisher's) was to seize Borkum, or some other

[1] *World Crisis*, II. 18,

German island, to serve as a base for the fleet, mask Heligoland, and then attack the Kiel Canal. If successful, this scheme would have thrown the Baltic open to the British fleet, have enabled Russia to land an army within one hundred miles of Berlin, and possibly have induced Denmark to join the Allies. The other plan was to seize the Gallipoli Peninsula and pass a fleet into the Sea of Marmora.

The second plan, as the less hazardous, was after prolonged discussion adopted. Thus at the beginning of 1915 interest shifts to the Near East.

The War in that theatre presents many problems and suggests many questions. Whether by a timely display of force the Turk could have been kept true to his ancient connexion with Great Britain and France; whether by more sagacious diplomacy the hostility of Bulgaria could have been averted, and the co-operation of Greece secured; whether by the military intervention of the *Entente* Powers the cruel blow could have been warded off from Serbia and Montenegro; whether the Dardanelles expedition was faulty only in execution or unsound in conception; whether Roumania came in too tardily, or moved too soon, and in a wrong direction—these are questions of high significance, but more easy to ask than to answer.

It must suffice to summarize events.

On the outbreak of the War the Porte declared its neutrality —a course which was followed in October by Greece, Roumania and Bulgaria. The Allies gave an assurance to the Sultan that, if he maintained neutrality, the independence and integrity of his Empire would be respected during the War, and provided for at the peace settlement. That many of the most responsible statesmen of the Porte sincerely desired the maintenance of neutrality cannot be doubted; but the forces working in the contrary direction were too powerful. The traditional enmity against Russia; the chance of recovering Egypt and Cyprus from Great Britain; the astute policy which for a quarter of a century the Kaiser had pursued at Constantinople; the German training imparted to the Turkish army; above all, the powerful personality of Enver Bey, who, early in 1914, appointed himself Minister of War—all these things impelled the Porte to embrace the cause of the Central Empires. Nor was it long before Turkey

The Near East

gave unmistakable indications of her real proclivities.[1] In the
first week of the War the German cruisers, the *Goeben* and the
Breslau, having eluded the pursuit of the allied fleet in the Mediterranean and reached the Bosphorus, were purchased by the
Porte, and commissioned in the Turkish navy. Great Britain
and Russia refused to recognize the transfer as valid, but the
Porte took no notice of the protest. Meanwhile, Germany poured
money, munitions, and men into Turkey ; German officers were
placed in command of the forts of the Dardanelles ; a German
General, Liman von Sanders, was appointed Commander-in-
Chief of the Turkish army, and on October 28 the Turkish fleet
bombarded Odessa and other unfortified ports belonging to
Russia on the Black Sea. To the protest made by the ambassadors of the Allied Powers the Porte did not reply, and on November 1 the ambassadors demanded their passports and quitted
Constantinople. A few days later the Dardanelles forts were
bombarded by English and French ships ; Akaba in the Red Sea
was bombarded by H.M.S. *Minerva*. Great Britain promptly
annexed Cyprus (November 5), declared Abbas, Khedive of
Egypt, deposed, put the son of Ismail on the throne in his stead,
and proclaimed a Protectorate over the country. For the second
time in history Great Britain and the Ottoman Empire were at
war.[2]

Germany hoped that by means of the Turkish alliance she
would be able to exploit Mesopotamia, to penetrate Persia commercially and politically, to deliver a powerful attack upon the
British position in Egypt, and to threaten the hegemony of Great
Britain in India. For all these ambitious schemes Constantinople
was an indispensable base.

**The Dardan-
elles** Nothing, therefore, would have done so much to frustrate
German diplomacy in south-eastern Europe as a successful blow
at Constantinople. Early in January 1915 the Grand Duke
Nicholas, Commander-in-Chief of the Russian armies, besought

---

[1] Djemal Pasha admits that by the end of the Second Balkan War the
Young Turks had decided in favour of Germany, *Memories of a Turkish
Statesman*, p. 107. Sir E. Grey was of opinion that ' nothing but the assassi-
nation of Enver would keep Turkey from joining Russia '—*Twenty-Five
Years*, ii. 164.

[2] The first was in 1806–7 when Turkey was forced by Napoleon I into
war with England and Russia.

the Allies to strike it. On the 28th the British War Council, largely influenced by Kitchener's preference for the Dardanelles, as against Salonika, agreed ; even though, perhaps because, the Navy would have to bear the brunt of the attack. In February 1915 an English fleet, assisted by a French squadron, bombarded the forts of the Dardanelles, and high hopes were entertained in the allied countries that the passage of the Straits would be quickly forced. But the hopes were destined to disappointment. It soon became evident that the Navy alone could not achieve the task entrusted to it, and in the course of the summer armies, totalling over 300,000 men, were poured into the Gallipoli Peninsula. They included some magnificent troops sent from Australia and New Zealand (now immortalized as Anzacs) and some equally fine English Territorials. The troops displayed heroic courage, and once at least the expedition was within sight of a brilliant victory, which, if achieved, would have shortened the War by at least two years. But the conditions were impossible, and after much debate at home it was decided to abandon the attempt. Sir Ian Hamilton, who had been in command since March, was strongly (and naturally) opposed to evacuation, but in October, other work was found for him, and Sir Charles Munro took his place at Gallipoli. Before the final decision was reached Kitchener went out to report on the whole situation (November–December) and decided on evacuation. The operation was as difficult as any in the War, but by the end of December, by a miracle of organization, it was performed without the loss of a single life. Nearly all the guns, stores, and mules were also saved. No incident in the War produced such a painful effect in England as the Gallipoli fiasco. Yet the loss of life, though terrible, was not wholly wasted ; the old Turkish regular army had been practically wiped out and their efforts in other theatres of war were greatly weakened.

Serbia, meanwhile, had, with splendid courage, repulsed two Austrian attacks. But in the autumn of 1915 the crisis foreseen by Lloyd George, Carson and other ' Easterners ' in England had arrived.

A great Austro-German army, under the command of Field-Marshal von Mackensen, concentrated upon the Serbian frontier in September, and on the 7th of October crossed the Danube at

The chastisement of Serbia

five different points. Two days later Belgrade surrendered, and
for the next few weeks von Mackensen, descending upon the
devoted country in overwhelming strength, drove the Serbians
before him, until the whole country was in the occupation of the
Austro-German forces. Down to this time Bulgaria had waited
on events, with the prudent intention of siding with the Powers
which proved the stronger in the Balkans.

Had the western allies sent a strong force to Salonika ; had
the Russian advance been maintained in 1915 ; had the Dardanelles been forced ; had pressure been put by the *Entente* upon
Serbia and Greece to make reasonable concessions in Macedonia,
Bulgaria might not have yielded to the seductions of German
gold and to the wiles of German diplomacy. But why should a
German King of Bulgaria have thrown in his lot with Powers
who were apparently heading for military disaster ; whose diplomacy was as inept as their arms were feeble ?   When the German
avalanche descended upon Serbia in the autumn of 1915, what
more natural than that Bulgaria should have co-operated in the
discomfiture of a detested rival ?

The Bulgarians captured Nish on November 5 and effected
a junction with the army under von Mackensen ; Serbia was
annihilated ; a remnant of the Serbian army took refuge in the
mountains of Montenegro and Albania, and the survivors after
terrible sufferings reached Corfu, while numbers of deported
civilians sought the hospitality of the Allies. On November 28
Germany officially declared the Balkan campaign to be at an end.
For the time being Serbia had ceased to exist as a Balkan State.

What had the Allies done to succour her ? On October 5
the advance guard of an Anglo-French force, under General
Sarrail and Sir Bryan Mahon, began to disembark at Salonika.
The force was miserably inadequate in numbers and equipment,
and it came too late. Its arrival served only to precipitate a
crisis in Greece.

Technically, the landing of an Anglo-French force at Salonika
King
Constan-
tine
was a violation of Greek neutrality, and Venizelos was compelled
by his master to enter a formal protest against it. But the protest was followed by an announcement that Greece would respect
her treaty with Serbia, and would march to her assistance, if she
were attacked by Bulgaria. That announcement cost Venizelos

his place. He was promptly dismissed by King Constantine, who, flouting the terms of the Constitution, effected what was virtually a monarchical *coup d'état*.

In the autumn of 1916, however, M. Venizelos, repudiating *Venizelos* the authority of his King (Constantine), set up a provisional Government at Salonika and joined the Allies. Roumania de- *Rou-* clared for the Allies in August, and in order to support her the *mania* Allies conducted, from Salonika, a vigorous campaign against Bulgaria. Before the end of the year (1916), however, the Roumanians were knocked out by Mackensen and Falkenhayn. On December 6 the German armies occupied Bucharest. Throughout the year 1917 there was little change in the situation. The Central Empires remained in occupation of Roumanian territory up to the line of the Sereth, including, therefore, the Dobrudja and Wallachia, and from this occupied territory Austria-Hungary obtained much-needed supplies of grain. Meanwhile, the Roumanian Government remained established in Jassy, and from its ancient capital the affairs of Moldavia were administered. Into Moldavia the Central Powers made no attempt to penetrate, being content to await events. Nor was it long before their patience was rewarded.

The military collapse of Russia in 1917 sealed the fate of Roumania. From no other ally could succour reach her. Perforce, therefore, Roumania was compelled to concur in the suspension of hostilities, to which the Russian Bolsheviks and the Central Empires agreed in December, 1917.

The German victories in the north-east of the peninsula *Greece* naturally reacted upon the situation in the south-west. Towards the end of November 1916 a Serbian army, re-formed and re-equipped, had the gratification of turning the Bulgarians out of Monastir, and the Allies still held a corner of Greek Macedonia. For the rest, Germany and her allies were in undisputed command of the Balkan peninsula from Belgrade to Constantinople, from Bucharest to the valley of the Vardar. Even the hold of the Allies on Salonika was rendered precarious by the increasing hostility of Constantine and his friends at Athens. The patience with which his vagaries were treated by the allied Governments tended to evoke contempt rather than gratitude in Athens. At last the Allies resolved to take action. On June 11, 1917, King

Constantine was required to abdicate and to hand over the government to his second son, Alexander; Constantine and his Prussian Queen, with the Crown Prince, were deported to Switzerland; Venizelos returned to Athens, and on June 30 the Hellenic kingdom broke off its relations with the Central Empires and at last took its place in the Grand Alliance.

Salonika The adhesion of Greece greatly improved the military situation in Macedonia. The allied army at Salonika was reinforced by the Greeks, who gained some important ground on the Vardar. Matters still tarried, however, on the Salonika front until in June 1918 the command was taken over by General Franchet d'Esperey. By September his preparations were complete; in the course of a week's brilliant fighting the Bulgarian army was routed, and after a harrying retreat in which the Serbs played a foremost part, Bulgaria sued for peace, and, on September 30, barely a fortnight after the commencement of the advance, Bulgaria made unconditional surrender and handed over her troops, her railways, her stores, and her government into the hands of the Allies. On October 12 the Serbians occupied their old capital, Nish, and so cut the Berlin-Constantinople railway at one of its most vital points. The Allies were on the point of advancing on Constantinople itself when the Sultan sued for peace and an armistice was concluded (October 30, 1918).

Mesopotamia From the Near East we pass to the Middle East. Early in the War (November 21, 1914) Basra, at the head of the Persian Gulf, was occupied by the 6th Indian Division. From Basra, the force advanced up the Tigris; Kurna, at a confluence of the two rivers, was occupied in December, and in April 1915 a heavy defeat was inflicted on the Turks at Shaiba. Reinforced from India, the troops again advanced, captured Amara, and from Amara advanced on Kut, which was taken on September 28, 1915. Against his own better judgement, General Townshend, who was in command, continued his march towards Bagdad, but after a brilliant attack at Ctesiphon (November 22-5) was compelled by lack of ammunition to withdraw with a loss of nearly half his force to Kut. There he was besieged for five months (December 3, 1915, to April 29, 1916). Three efforts were made to relieve Townshend and his gallant garrison, but in vain, and, on April 29, 1916, Kut was surrendered, and some 8,000 survivors,

of whom 6,000 were Indian troops, fell into the hands of the
Turks. The British prisoners were shamefully maltreated, and
more than half of them died in captivity.

The British Government took prompt measures to retrieve
this grave disaster. Sir Stanley Maude was appointed to the
command in Mesopotamia; the force was reorganized and re-
equipped, and after a skilful advance Kut was recovered on
February 24, 1917. Advancing rapidly from Kut, Maude inflicted a crushing defeat upon the Turks, and on March 11 entered
Bagdad. On April 18 the Turks suffered a further defeat, and
the British army took possession of the Bagdad Railway as far
as Samarra, nearly seventy miles north of Bagdad. In November
Maude died of cholera, but the campaign was successfully carried
on by Sir William Marshall, who finally reached Mosul on November 3, 1918. By that time, however, the Turk had been utterly
defeated and had sued for an armistice.

Not only in the Balkans and in Mesopotamia were British *Egypt*
arms victorious over the Turk. From the opening of the War *and the Canal*
it was realized that of all the vital points in our ' far-flung battle
line ' the most vital, perhaps, was the Suez Canal. After the
Porte had definitely thrown in its lot with the Central Empires
it was deemed wise, as already noted, to depose the Khedive of
Egypt, Abbas II (November 1914). Turkish sovereignty was
denounced; Egypt was declared a British Protectorate; and
the Sultanate was conferred (December 18, 1914) on Hussein
Kamel. In February 1915 the Turks made the first of several
attacks upon the Suez Canal, but they were all repulsed with
heavy loss. Stirred up by German intrigue, the Senussi gave us
some trouble in Western Egypt, though they were heavily punished
in several actions at the end of 1915 and the beginning of 1916.

In March 1916 another phase of the War opened : Sir Archi- *Pales-*
bald Murray began his advance on the eastern side of the Canal. *tine, 1916–18*
A patient march through the desert brought him into Palestine
at the beginning of 1917, but in April he was heavily repulsed by
the Turks at Gaza. In the summer, Murray was relieved of his
command and succeeded by Sir Edmund Allenby, who, reinforced
from India and Salonika, inflicted a tremendous defeat upon the
Turks at Beersheba, which he captured on October 31. He
stormed Gaza (November 7), Askalon a few days later, Jaffa

surrendered to him on November 16, and on December 9 a brilliant campaign was crowned by the capture of Jerusalem. Early in 1918 General Allenby established communications with the Arabs and the King of Hedjaz, whose allegiance had been secured to us by Colonel Lawrence, and on February 21 captured Jericho. Owing to the success of the German offensive in France he was then compelled to dispatch his best troops to the Western Front, and it was not until September that he was ready to make his final assault upon the enemy opposed to him. On the 19th, however, he fell upon the Turks and broke them, turning their seaward flank by the most brilliant cavalry operation known in modern history. On the following day Nazareth was occupied. Having effected his junction with the Arabs, Allenby then advanced on Damascus, which surrendered on October 1. By the time Damascus fell 60,000 prisoners and 300 guns had been taken. Advancing from Damascus, Beirut was taken on October 8, and in rapid succession Sidon, Tripoli, Homs, and Aleppo (October 26). The annihilation of the Turkish forces was now complete, and Palestine and Syria, like Mesopotamia, passed into English keeping.

Meanwhile much had happened in England and France.

The
Western
Front

There was fierce fighting on the Western Front in the spring of 1915, centring around Neuve Chapelle, Ypres and Festubert (March–May 1915). French was now in command of an immense army, but despite heavy losses in men and vast expenditure of ammunition, little, if any, advance was made. It was then that the Germans first made use, contrary to the Hague Conventions, of asphyxiating gases ; it was then also that a bitter controversy arose in England in regard to the supply of munitions, in particular high explosive shells, to the armies at the front.[1]

In regard to men Kitchener had admittedly worked wonders. Was he less successful in providing ammunition ? Was it easier to make soldiers than to make shells ? Public opinion was deeply stirred. A Press campaign against the Government, and particularly against Asquith and Kitchener, was inaugurated. Kitchener had in fact made earnest appeals to the workers in munition factories to expedite production. Mr. Lloyd George had lectured them on excessive drinking. ' We are fighting ', he said, ' Germany, Austria, and drink, and so far as I can see the

---

[1] On this controversy cf. an illuminating essay by Lord Birkenhead : *Points of View*, Vol. I, 6.

greatest of the three deadly foes is drink.' His lecture was bitterly resented ; but in April the King ordered that, until the close of the War, no intoxicants were to be served in the Royal palaces. There were rumours, also, of impending legislation. Was it to be prohibition or nationalization ? Lloyd George strongly favoured the latter ; Asquith was opposed to both. But, whatever the reason, supplies of shells were coming in more slowly than they should.

On April 15 the Prime Minister announced the appointment Muni-
of a Committee, under the chairmanship of Mr. Lloyd George, tions
to ' ensure the promptest and most efficient application of all the productive resources of the country to the manufacture and supply of munitions of war '. On the 20th he visited Newcastle and adjured the munition workers to ' Deliver the Goods '. At the same time he denied that operations in the field had been crippled for lack of ammunition or that the Government had been tardy in recognizing the importance of this factor in the war-problem. Asquith's statement was based on information supplied to him by Kitchener. Kitchener, relying in his turn on French, wrote to Asquith (April 14) : ' He (French) told me that I could let you know that with the present supply of ammunition he will have as much as he will be able to use on the next forward movement.' French in his ' *1914* ' categorically denied that he gave Kitchener that information [1] ; but French's statement, according to Asquith, ' teems with unpardonable inaccuracies '.[2] On April 21 Mr. Lloyd George informed the House of Commons that the output of artillery ammunition had since September 1914 ' been multiplied nineteenfold ', and that, thanks largely to the genius and energy of Lord Moulton, the production of high explosives in this country was now ' on a footing which relieves us of all anxiety, and enables us to supply the needs of our Allies as well as our own '.[3]

Yet with all this the country was uneasy. Nor was it entirely reassured when, in one of his rare and curt speeches in the House of Lords, Lord Kitchener replied to critics (May 18). He emphasized the enormous and unprecedented demand for munitions, but asserted that the requirements of the new armies had, from the early days of the War, been foreseen by the experts of the

---

[1] See in particular Preface to 2nd edition.
[2] *Memories and Reflections*, II, 76.   [3] Hansard (under date), p. 819.

War Office, while admitting that there had been considerable delay in meeting their requirements.[1]

On the following day *The Times* launched a bitter attack upon Kitchener and the War Office. On the 14th it had published the famous telegram from Col. Repington, based on information supplied by French, ' The want of an unlimited supply of high explosives was a fatal bar to our success '—at Festubert. On the 19th it wrote : ' Men died in heaps upon the Aubers Ridge ten days ago, because the field guns were short, and gravely short, of high-explosive shells.'

Such language could not fail to create profound perturbation in the public mind. The Opposition, which ever since the beginning of the year had become increasingly critical of the conduct of affairs, finally lost patience. Mr. McKenna at the Home Office was thought to be careless about enemy aliens and espionage. The fire of criticism kept up on this subject by the Conservatives is now admitted by Mr. Lloyd George to have been justified. ' Subsequent events proved ', he wrote, ' that intelligence of great value to the enemy percolated to Germany through the agency of persons living unmolested in England under Mr. McKenna's indulgent régime. The nation was right in thinking that this was not the time to risk the national security on glib pleasantries.'[2] Moreover, the public gradually learnt, to its dismay, that there was acute friction between Kitchener and French, between Lloyd George and Kitchener, and between Churchill and Fisher. The latter had succeeded Prince Louis of Battenberg as First Sea Lord on October 29, and to the public his appointment was as reassuring as that of Kitchener at the War Office. But there was hardly room at the Admiralty both for Lord Fisher and Mr. Winston Churchill. In an undated memorandum, Fisher had demanded that he should be placed at the Admiralty in a position exactly parallel with that of Kitchener at the War Office—First Lord and First Sea Lord in one. Whether the demand was ever presented to the Government is unknown : but the paper was unearthed in 1927 by Asquith.[3] Anyway, Fisher resigned on May 15, and, despite the entreaties of the Government to remain at his post, disappeared into space.

[1] Hansard (Lords), Vol. 18, p. 1019.   [2] *War Memoirs.*
[3] *Memories and Reflections*, II, 93.

CHAPTER XXII

THE GREAT WAR—THE HOME FRONT

TWO days after the resignation of Lord Fisher Mr. Bonar Law and Lord Lansdowne informed Asquith that, unless the Ministry was immediately reconstructed, they would be obliged to raise publicly questions about Fisher's resignation.

Churchill had, from the onset of the War crisis, urged that there should be a Coalition. At the end of July 1914 he had, through his friend F. E. Smith, approached the Tory leaders with this end in view. But Bonar Law never got over his mistrust of Churchill, and declined this method of approach. In March 1915 feelers were again put out, to no effect. Fisher's resignation brought matters to a crisis, and on May 19 Asquith announced that the Government would be reconstructed ' on a broader personal and political basis '. On the 25th the names of the new Cabinet were published. The Tories were adamant against the reappointment of Lord Haldane, who, with gross ingratitude and to the grief of Asquith and Grey, was deprived of office. The much-criticized McKenna was promoted to the Treasury, while Churchill was relegated to the lowest place in the Cabinet hierarchy—the Duchy of Lancaster—in Lloyd George's opinion a ' cruel and unjust degradation '. He was replaced at the Admiralty by Balfour. Other Conservatives brought into the Cabinet were Lord Curzon, Bonar Law, Lord Lansdowne, Austen Chamberlain and Walter Long: the Law offices went to Carson and F. E. Smith; Asquith, Kitchener, Grey and Runciman retained their places. Mr. Henderson entered the Cabinet as a representative of the Labour Party, but John Redmond, the tone of whose speech on August 4 had been loudly applauded, declined office. For Lloyd George a new Ministry of Munitions was created.

The First Coalition Government

Ministry of Munitions

Of this new Ministry of Munitions Kitchener ' completely approved '.[1] Yet neither in Home affairs nor in the conduct of the War was the new Government conspicuously more successful than that which it displaced.   Lloyd George brought to the discharge of his new duties daemonic energy, and solved, though at enormous cost, the problem of munitions.   His *Munitions of War Act*, passed in 1915, was based on principles which have since been successfully applied by Signor Mussolini to industrial reconstruction in Italy.   No private interest was to be permitted to obstruct the service, or imperil the safety, of the State.   Trade Union regulations must be suspended ; employers' profits must be limited, skilled men must fight, if not in the trenches, in the factories ; man-power must be economized by the dilution of labour and the employment of women ; private factories must pass under the control of the State, and new national factories be set up.   Results justified the new policy : the output was prodigious ; the goods were at last delivered.

Labour and the War

It needed all Lloyd George's energy and persuasive power to achieve this miracle.   He was met by obstruction on every side. The War Office was not overpleased at the intrusion of civilians into a job which they regarded as exclusively their own ; business men looked upon Lloyd George as an officious amateur.   But the main difficulty arose from the anxiety—not unnatural or unintelligible—of the manual workers, lest they should be rushed into the surrender of trade privileges hardly won in a long struggle between capital and labour : the delimitation of trades and the rigid demarcation of work ; the employment of unskilled and semi-skilled labour ; the limitation of hours ; the restriction of output and the like.   The employers, on their part, complained, with some reason, of slack time keeping, of *Ca' canny* methods, even of actual sabotage.   Whether the responsibility for a deplorable situation rested upon organized labour, upon the directors of industry or upon the Government, it was clear that an ugly temper was developing among considerable bodies of skilled workmen.   In February the engineers in the Elswick Works at Newcastle, in consequence of the employment of unskilled labour on skilled jobs, tendered notices to cease work.   That dispute was adjusted : but a much more serious dispute occurred simul-

[1] Asquith, *Memories*, II. 78.

taneously on the Clyde, where many thousands of skilled workers, upon whose steady output of munitions their comrades at the front depended for their effectiveness as fighters and for their lives, came out on strike. The view taken by the men in the fighting line was vigorously expressed in some contemporary lines addressed by ' Tommy Atkins at the Front ' to his brother on the Clyde :—

> I've chucked away me bay'nit, an' I'm slingin' down me gun,
> I'm fed up with the business, I am ; I'm fairly done.
> I've tried to work it out all right, so help me Gawd, I've tried ;
> Wot's put the Kibosh on it is my brother on the Clyde.
>
> 'E's workin' in a fact'ry, and gits ten bob a day,
> An' now 'e's downed 'is tools, 'e says, an' wants a bit more pay.
> 'E writes an' says these busy times is jist 'is bloomin' chance,
> So *I've* downed tools these busy times—somew'ere out 'ere in France.
>
>   .   .   .   .
>
> I've picked up me ole gun again ; me bit of iron, too :
> I'm jist a common soldier, so I've got to see it through.
> An' if they lets us down at 'ome, and if 'e reads I died,
> Will 'e know 'e 'elped to kill me—my brother on the Clyde ? [1]

Bitter and justified as such jibes were from ' Tommy Atkins ', the attitude of ' Labour ' (or a section of it) was not unintelligible. If wages were rising quickly, profits were rising still more substantially : so were prices, and the Government, Labour thought, was looking with too lenient or careless an eye on ' the robbery of the poor '. The great mass of the manual workers were ready to spend themselves in the service of the State : they were not ready to sacrifice leisure and health in order to put exceptionally high profits into the pockets of the employer and the middleman.

The Government awoke, too tardily, to the significance of this factor in the industrial problem. In March 1915 they undertook to exact from labour and capital some ' equality of sacrifice '. The *Munitions of War Act* (July 1915) provided for compulsory arbitration in certain specified trades, and for severe penalties upon strikers and lockers-out alike ; it set up local Munitions Tribunals to deal with offences under the Act, and authorized the Minister to establish ' control ' over any establishment in which munition work was done, and rigidly to restrict profits in such establishments. By the end of the year over 2,000 establish-

War Finance

---

[1] D. Richards, ap. *Daily Express.*

ments were ' controlled '. The weakness of the scheme was the absence of any incentive to economy of production. The price of munitions trebled in the course of the year.

National expenditure   How was the bill to be met ? During the course of the War Parliament passed no fewer than twenty-five Votes of Credit. The series began with a modest £100,000,000 voted on August 7, 1914 ; it ended with £700,000,000 voted on November 18, 1918 —two days after the signing of the Armistice. The total was £8,742,000,000. The money was raised partly by loan, partly by increased taxation. Orthodox opinion inclines to the view that too much was raised by loan and too little by taxation, especially by indirect taxation on non-essential commodities. The total cost of the Napoleonic war was about £831,000,000—a sum not greatly in excess of our own yearly expenditure to-day (1933). Of this total £391,748,370 was actually paid out of revenue, while over £440,000,000 was added to the debt. Owing to the adherence of Pitt to the ' sweet simplicity ' of 3 per cent. the loans were issued in stock of a low denomination—an average of about 60 per cent. in cash for each £100 of stock issued. Throughout the later war a different and preferable policy was followed. Loans were issued at a higher rate of interest, but at a price more closely corresponding to the market rate of money.

The total expenditure during the war period (1914–19) amounted to £11,259 millions. Of this vast sum no less than £4,073 millions or 36·17 per cent. was paid out of revenue ; the balance was met by borrowing, which involved an increase in the National Debt from £650 millions (March 31, 1914) to £7,832 millions on March 31, 1920. Included in this vast sum was nearly £2,000 millions advanced to allies, and a smaller sum (about £150,000,000) to Dominions and Colonies.

Loans   The first of a long series of War Loans was issued in November 1914, when £350 millions was raised at 3½ per cent., the price of issue being 95. In 1916 some £600 millions was raised at 4½ per cent. and in 1917 over £2,000 millions at 5 per cent. (issued at 95). In addition to these War Loans large amounts were raised by the issue of War Bonds, Exchequer Bonds, Treasury Bills, etc., the rate of interest ultimately rising to 6 per cent. ; and about £1,000 millions was also borrowed from the U.S.A. In addition, the State virtually borrowed a large sum by the issue (already mentioned) of paper money. These Currency or Treasury Notes reached the maximum (£353,538,000) in 1920.

In 1916 an important experiment was initiated. A National Savings War Savings Committee was set up, and under its auspices Savings Certificates were issued (up to a maximum of £500) at 15s. 6d. repayable in five years' time at par. This device not only served to check the grossly extravagant expenditure of the wage-earners; it provided a safe and attractive investment for their savings and, above all, proved itself of permanent social significance. Since January 1916 over £1,427,000,000 worth of certificates have been issued : over 190,000 Savings Associations—to facilitate the accumulation of the smallest amounts—have been established, and in this way a great impulse has been given to habits of thrift among all classes and among individuals of all ages from childhood upwards.

That some such impulse was urgently called for was apparent to all observers. The totals of expenditure—public and private —were of course largely swollen by the rapid rise of prices during the War.[1] To this rise State extravagance and the inflation of currency and credit were largely contributory. The middle classes, especially those who lived on small fixed incomes, were very hardly hit. But the increase in the earnings of individual wage-earners, and still more of working-class families was, in industrial districts, prodigious. So were the increases in industrial profits.

Of wages, and still more of profits, the State claimed an ever- Taxation increasing proportion. Indirect taxation was not only largely increased but widely extended. In the first War Budget (September 1915) Mr. McKenna made a significant departure from tradition, by imposing on a few articles of luxury custom duties which were definitely though modestly protective in character. Yet notwithstanding these duties, the proportion which indirect taxes yielded declined from 42·5 per cent. in 1913–14 to 17·3 in 1917–18, while upon the payers of direct taxes a much heavier burden was imposed. The normal rate of income tax was raised

---

[1] Prices rose steadily from August 1914 to April 1920. Taking 100 as the norm in July 1914, wholesale prices *in general* = 117 (in January 1915), 150 (1916), 193 (1917), 225 (1918), and 323 (April 1920) : food only = 328 (1920). Retail : cost of living general = 276 (Nov. 1920), food only, 291 (1920). It will be noted that retail prices rose rather less than wholesale. On the whole question cf. Bowley, *Prices and Wages in the U.K.* (Oxford, 1921).

from 1s. 2d. to 6s.; super-tax rose from 6d. to a maximum of 6s. Death duties were increased from 8 per cent. ultimately to 40 per cent., and the special Excess Profits tax (already mentioned) to 80 per cent.

This represented an heroic effort; but some critics maintained that it was still inadequate, and most people agreed that in the ' confiscation ' of war profits the Government and Parliament betrayed undue procrastination and timidity.

Parliament, indeed, could do little, in war-time, save register the demands of the Executive. Least of all could it do much to check expenditure or restrain extravagance. In 1917 the Government did indeed consent to set up a Select Committee on National Expenditure.[1] The Committee presented a series of Reports, which, if not of much avail in restraining expenditure at the moment, did inspire with wholesome fear some of the more extravagant Departments, and made important recommendations as regards financial procedure in the House of Commons. Several of these have, with good results, been adopted. Looking back, indeed, on the whole history of British War Finance the impartial critics have been more impressed by its virtues than by its shortcomings : Dr. Kraus, a typical German critic, regards it with envy, while Professor Gaston Jèze writes : ' C'est là une magnifique page de l'histoire financière de l'Angleterre '. At that we may leave it to return to the War itself.

The Western Front, 1915–16

On the Western Front no decision was reached in 1915. Of the great battles round Ypres in the spring mention has already been made. In the result Ypres was held. In the autumn there were terrific battles between the British and the Germans at Loos and between the French and the Germans in Champagne. The losses on both sides were terrible, but the military results achieved were unfortunately incommensurate therewith. Meanwhile the tremendous effort directed in the autumn of 1915 by the Germans against the Russians undoubtedly weakened the German strength on the Western Front, but notwithstanding this the Allies failed to break through.

Verdun

The year 1916 was remarkable for the prolonged and terrific battle waged between the Germans and the French round the

---

[1] The Committee was set up at the instance of Sir Godfrey Collins and the present writer. (Cf. Hansard, July 6, 1917.)

great fortress of Verdun. Opening in February, the battle lasted almost continuously until July. The greatest gallantry was displayed on both sides, but by July the German attack had been definitely repulsed, and on December 15 the French won a brilliant victory on that historic field.

In July the British, now under the command of Sir Douglas Haig, had, aided by the French, taken the offensive on the Somme, with the object, duly achieved, of weakening the German pressure on Verdun. The battle raged fiercely from July until November, but when the year closed, though a serious dent had been made in the German line, the position on the Western Front seemed to have reached stalemate. *The Somme*

The year 1916 was marked, on the Home Front, by a series of events of high significance. *The Home Front*

Of these the first was the Sinn Fein rebellion which at Easter 1916 broke out in Ireland. At the outbreak of the War, Irish feeling was keenly aroused on behalf of the Belgian Roman Catholics, and it seemed not impossible that the Catholic South might fling itself into the struggle against Germany with not less ardour than the Protestant North. During 1915 that hope faded. The disloyal section of the Irish Catholics gained the ascendant, entered into treasonable correspondence with Germany, and, relying upon the promised assistance of England's enemies, raised the standard of rebellion in April 1916. Unhappily, the episode was not without precedent. England's difficulty had always been Ireland's opportunity. But the rebellion of 1916 came as a shock to those in England who had complacently imagined that the passing of a Home Rule Bill for Ireland would suffice to heal the secular discord between the two countries. An attempt was made to land arms and ammunition, in the neighbourhood of Tralee, by a German auxiliary disguised as a neutral merchantman, in conjunction with a German submarine. The English Navy was alert. The 'Norwegian merchantman' was challenged by *Bluebell* and ordered to accompany her to Queenstown. Thereupon the merchantman hoisted German colours, and her crew —German officers and sailors—having sunk the ship with its cargo, took to the boats. Many prisoners were taken, among them Sir Roger Casement, who had served in the British Consular Service, and in 1911 had been knighted for his services. Charged *The Irish Rebellion* with high treason, he was convicted and sentenced to death. Some sentimentalists tried to procure his reprieve, but on August 3, 1916 he was hanged. Meanwhile, the day after the frustrated landing in the West, rebellion broke out in Dublin. The rebellion was crushed, though not without considerable bloodshed and much damage to property in Dublin. Of those who fought for the Crown 19 officers and 109 men were killed, 46 officers and 326 men were wounded. From the hospitals 180 civilians were reported killed and 614 wounded. Of the casualties among the Sinn Fein troops there is no record : but 3,000 rebels were arrested, and fifteen of the leaders suffered death. Among those who were released after a brief imprisonment was Mr. De Valera.

The Irish rebellion, though abortive, excited bitter feelings in Great Britain and Northern Ireland, and the leniency shown to all but a few of the rebels was not universally approved. Mr. Birrell, the Chief Secretary for Ireland, was held to have been primarily to blame. Nor did he seek to evade responsibility. He frankly owned that, although aware of Sinn Fein activities, he had entirely miscalculated their force and direction. He immediately resigned and disappeared from public life. Unfortunately, the evil he had permitted lived after him. [1]

Conscription

Almost exactly simultaneous with the Sinn Fein rebellion in Ireland was the adoption of Compulsory Military Service in Great Britain. Towards Compulsion things had been moving for some time. In June 1915 a *National Registration Act* was passed, under which all persons from 16 to 65 were compelled to register in a variety of categories. This was followed in October by an effort to impose universal service without resort to actual compulsion. The Earl of Derby, a man of great influence and highly popular with all classes, was appointed Director of Recruiting, and all men between 18 and 41 were invited to enrol by years in 46 groups, 23 for married, 23 for unmarried men. The unmarried men—not required for essential war service at home, were to be called up first. By December it was clear that the Derby Scheme had failed. The response of the unmarried men was wholly inadequate to the nation's needs.

In January a scheme of partial compulsion was adopted : but the meshes of the Exemptions Tribunals which were set up under

---

[1] Cf. Report of Royal Commission on Irish Rebellion (Cmd. 8279 (1916)), and for general account : Colvin, *Life of Lord Carson*, Vol. 3, c. xvi, and Gwynn, *Life of John Redmond*, and *infra*, p. 446.

the Act were too wide. Compulsion had to come. It came in the Universal Military Service Act passed in May 1916. Every male between the ages of 18 and 41 (subsequently extended to 51) thus became liable to service. The gradual approach towards a system regarded as appropriate only to 'foreigners' was characteristically English and characteristically Asquithian. Voluntary effort, taking the Empire as a whole, had yielded over 5,000,000 men; but it had become all-important (in Asquith's own words) 'to get rid of piecemeal treatment, and the sense of temporary injustice and inequality which that mode of treatment is apt to engender'. At the same time Asquith was determined that if the change to Compulsion was to come it should be by 'general consent', but he confessed that he had never had a harder task than 'to secure the fulfilment of that condition'.

But he had secured it. Only twenty-seven members voted against the third reading of the Bill. Among the twenty-seven Liberals was Sir John Simon, who resigned office; among the ten Socialists were Mr. Ramsay MacDonald, Mr. J. H. Thomas and Mr. Snowden.[1] 'Looking back', writes Mr. Lloyd George, 'there is no doubt at all that we should have been able to organize the nation far more effectively in 1914, and bring the conflict to an end far more quickly and economically, if at the very outset we had mobilized the whole nation on a war-footing—its man-power, money, materials and brains—and bent all our resources to the task of victory on rational and systematic lines.'[2] But that is admittedly viewing the matter from the safe ground of retrospect. The opinions thus expressed were not recorded at the time. Asquith perhaps delayed too long. The fact remains that under his guidance the nation now accepted compulsory service without a murmur.

Conscription was indeed the legal affirmation of the nation's inflexible resolve, at all costs, to see the War through to a victorious end.

The National Effort

'The young men shall go to the battle: it is their task to conquer. The married men shall forge arms, transport baggage and artillery; provide subsistence. The women shall work at soldiers' clothes, make tents, serve in the hospitals. The children shall scrape old linen into surgeon's lint. The aged men shall have themselves carried into public places, and there, by their words,

[1] Asquith, *Memories*, II. 125-6.   [2] *War Memoirs.*

excite the courage of the young; preach hatred to Kings and unity to the Republic.' Such was the temper of France, as expressed in the Report of the Committee of Public Safety, in the early autumn of 1793. That Report issued in the famous *levée en masse*, when Carnot, in his own words, undertook ' to give military organization to the popular fury '. The crusading enthusiasm of the young Republic, directed and ordered by the organizing genius of Carnot, carried all before it.

In no other temper can any nation expect to emerge triumphant from a great war. The whole people must be mobilized for service.

The British peoples had, by 1917, reached the same conclusion as the French Committee of Public Safety ; but they had reached, if as surely, more slowly, and by a different route. Between 1793 and 1917 there was, moreover, one conspicuous contrast. The women of England were not content to serve only as the women of France had served during the Revolutionary wars. Claiming equality of political rights with men, they were prepared to take over many of their duties. With what superb devotion they served the State we have already seen.[1] The whole nation was, indeed, mobilized for war service. Whether mobilization was not unduly delayed is a question often asked, but never satisfactorily answered. By 1917 it had come.

Death of Kitchener Hardly had it come when the great soldier, who had reorganized the whole military system of his country and had, in the language of the street, given his name to the new army, met his doom amid the storms and shadows of the North Sea.

The magic of Kitchener's name was almost as potent in Russia as in England and the Czar Nicholas was most anxious that he should obtain first-hand knowledge of the position of affairs in Russia, and by his presence should put fresh courage into the Russian army. Kitchener was himself keen to go ; and the British Government, Lloyd George in particular, encouraged him to do so. For the latter was convinced that we had grievously failed to utilize Russia's inexhaustible man-power. She had 15,000,000 men of fighting age, and (by 1916) only 650,000 rifles with which to arm them, and hardly any artillery ammunition to support them. Before leaving London Kitchener for the first and last

[1] *Supra*, p. 327.

time addressed the members of the House of Commons in secret conclave in a Committee room. By the time he had concluded his address every critic was silenced. The strong and generally silent soldier left the politicians tongue-tied. On June 5, 1916, he embarked at Thurso on the *Hampshire*. His plans had been betrayed, his ship struck a mine and with almost all hands aboard went straight to the bottom. News of his death came as a thunderclap to his fellow-countrymen and their allies : he had achieved the seemingly impossible ; he had transformed Great Britain into a nation in arms ; he had made the armies that won the War.

For a month after Kitchener's death the War Office was without a Chief : but on July 6 Lloyd George became Minister for War, and at the Ministry of Munitions was succeeded by one of the ablest of the younger Liberals, E. S. Montagu.

During the spring of 1916 Mr. W. M. Hughes, the Labour Prime Minister of Australia, visited England, and aroused great enthusiasm by a series of speeches pitched in the highest key of Imperial patriotism. In February he had been sworn of the King's Privy Council of Canada, and had attended a meeting of the Cabinet in Ottawa. In March he was admitted to the Privy Council at home and (like Sir Robert Borden in 1915) was invited by Mr. Asquith to attend a meeting of the Imperial Cabinet. He received the Freedom of the City on March 22, and in June took part in the Economic Conference of the Allies at Paris as one of the representatives of the Imperial Government. *Mr. W. M. Hughes*

The sentiment which led to the summoning of the Conference, and which dominated its deliberations, was admirably expressed by Bonar Law : ' We are standing by each other now in war ; . . . we have suffered together, we have died together : . . . so, if possible, we shall stand by each other during the period of reconstruction after the War.' [1] The recommendations of the Conference, which were formally and publicly adopted ' both by the British and French Governments, were in three parts : (i) Measures for the war period ; (ii) temporary measures to be adopted during the period of reconstruction after the War ; and (iii) permanent measures of mutual assistance and collaboration among the allies '. For Great Britain the recommendations marked a *The Paris Pact*

[1] H. of Commons' Hansard, August 2, 1916.

complete break from the *laisser-faire* policy which for the best part of a century she had consistently followed. The ' McKenna Duties ' had already supplied the thin end of a Protective wedge. But they might well have been regarded as a temporary war expedient. The Paris Pact foreshadowed a permanent reversal of fiscal policy. The Central Powers, having (*ex hypothesi*) been defeated in war were not to be allowed to ' win the Peace '. They were to be confronted by a Fiscal Bloc designed to secure the independence of the Allied Powers, alike in regard to ' their sources of supply ' and their ' financial, commercial and maritime organization '.[1] The Paris Conference reflected the mood of the moment : its prescience was less conspicuous.

Food supplies The Paris Conference was only one of several indications that the Allies were beginning to feel the economic pinch of war. On February 15 a blockade of the British coasts had been declared by Germany, and been to some extent enforced by her submarines. On March 1 Great Britain retorted by Orders in Council which established a blockade of the German coast ; but partly owing to a desire to avoid offence to neutrals, partly owing to the mischievous provisions of the ' Declaration of London ' (1908) the blockade did not become really effective until, in July 1916, the Declaration of London was denounced. Down to that time Germany was still getting ample supplies from and through ' neutrals '. Two months earlier (May 31) the battle of Jutland had driven the German High Sea Fleet into harbour, whence it never emerged except to surrender.[2] The British Navy had cleared the sea of German merchantmen.

But what of British merchant-ships ? The German submarine menace, though not yet at its zenith, was taking increasing toll of them. Zeppelin raids, beginning in January 1915, had in 1916 become increasingly frequent and destructive. Even stay-at-homes could no longer fail to realize that we were at war. Had we trusted in vain to an invincible Navy ? No longer insular as regards external attack, were we increasingly insular as regards supplies from oversea ?

Food control The Government, anxious to avoid panic, proceeded cautiously. Restrictions were imposed in the course of 1916 on

---

[1] Cd. 8271 and Marriott, ap. *Nineteenth Century and After*, November, 1916.   [2] See, in correction, *infra*, p. 414.

imports of timber and tobacco, and on the sale of petrol. Food prices were mounting. People began to convert their flower beds into vegetable plots, and even to plant potatoes on tennis lawns. Belts were tightened, and more and more land was taken up for allotments.

In November 1916 Lord Devonport, a business man of great ability, with special knowledge, as a wholesale grocer, of food-stuffs, was appointed Food Controller. The first restrictions applied only to luxurious hotels and restaurants.

At the beginning of 1917 the situation became rapidly worse. Submarine menace On January 31 the war at sea had entered upon a new phase: Germany carried out her threat of ' unrestricted ' submarine war-fare—the sinking of unarmed merchantmen, hospital ships—any-thing afloat—without warning. For several months the new method proved terribly effective. By April 1917 British ships had carried, in comparative safety, no less than 8,000,000 troops over sea ; they had kept open the allied lines of communication in the Channel, in the Atlantic, and the Mediterranean with the help of French and Italian ships, and with Japanese in the Indian Ocean and the Pacific ; they had brought to the Allies food and munitions. But they had accomplished this wonderful task at a high cost in lives and ships, and the strain upon them was intense.

In the early summer of 1917 the strain came perilously near the breaking-point. ' A year ago it was supposed that England would be able to use the acres of the whole world, bidding with them against the German acres. To-day England sees herself in a situation unparalleled in her history. Her acres across sea disappear as a result of the blockade which submarines are daily making most effective around England.' These words, uttered by Dr. Karl Helferich, the German Secretary of the Interior, in February 1917, were no idle boast. The real facts were care-fully and properly concealed from the British and Allied peoples, but Helferich spoke truth. The losses of British, Allied and neutral ships increased from 181 (298,000 gross tonnage) in January, to 259 (468,000 tons) in February, 325 (500,000 tons) in March, and 423 (849,000 tons) in April. In April, writes Mr. Churchill, ' the great approach to the south-west of Ireland was becoming a veritable cemetery of British shipping, in which large vessels were sunk day by day about 220 miles from land '.[1]   One ship out of every four that left British shores never came home, but as Mr. Churchill proudly and justly adds : ' no voyage was delayed for lack of resolute civilian volunteers.'

In June 1917 Lord Rhondda, another great industrialist, succeeded Lord Devonport as Food Controller. To meet the outcry against ' profiteers ' a schedule of maximum prices was drawn up and rapidly extended. Then followed the rationing of consumers. Food cards and queues made their appearance. Even the wealthiest could obtain only a minimum of food. In London and the towns generally there was real scarcity. The country districts suffered less.

Fall of the Asquith Coalition   Meanwhile, a change of Government had taken place. Before the end of 1916 there was general dissatisfaction with the conduct of the War. The nation was making gigantic sacrifices ; the apparent results were disappointingly meagre. Various devices had been adopted for the conduct of the War ; there had been much shifting of offices, and many changes of personnel. In November 1914 a War Council had been set up, but the conduct of the War was really in the hands of Asquith, Kitchener, and Churchill. In June 1915, after the formation of the Coalition Cabinet, the conduct of the War was entrusted to the ' Dardanelles Committee '.   A body of no fewer than eleven members was hopelessly unwieldy, and in November 1915 Sir Edward Carson (who had joined the Government in June) resigned in disgust at the incapacity displayed by his colleagues, particularly in relation to the Near East.   In the same month Asquith announced the appointment of a War Council of five members, Balfour, Lloyd George, Bonar Law, Kitchener (who was temporarily absent in the Near East) and himself.   Churchill, resenting his exclusion, retired altogether from the Ministry and donned his military uniform.

In December Sir Douglas Haig replaced French as Commander-in-Chief and Sir William Robertson became Chief of a reconstituted Imperial General Staff.   The new War Council, however, showed very little improvement on its various predecessors. Where did the fault lie ?   Only two Ministers had throughout

---

[1] op. cit., iv. 362. Cf. Lloyd George, *Memoirs*, III, where the figures very slightly vary.

retained their places. Of these one was Grey [1]; the other Asquith. On December 1, 1916, Lloyd George suggested to the Prime Minister the appointment of a War Directory of four members, of whom Asquith was not to be one. Several days of hectic intrigue followed. On December 1 Lloyd George resigned. The leading Conservatives agreed that the ' Government could not go on as it is ', and urged Asquith to resign. Asquith was prepared to reconstruct, but not to resign. On December 5, however, having realized the impossibility of reconstruction he resigned, and refused to serve (*e.g.* as Lord Chancellor) under Bonar Law, whom the King had asked to form a Government. Thereupon Bonar Law abandoned the task, and on December 6 Lloyd George kissed hands as Prime Minister. Asquith's political career was virtually at an end. In 1918, he was actually rejected after thirty-two years' service by his constituents in Fifeshire. He returned to the House of Commons as member for Paisley in 1920, but his position there was uncomfortable not to say humiliating, that of a General without an army. He was again returned for Paisley in 1922, and in December 1923, but in 1924 was rejected by that constituency and in 1925 he went to the House of Lords as Earl of Oxford and Asquith. He was then visibly breaking up, and on February 15, 1928, he died.

Had he succeeded in maintaining the peace of Europe Asquith would have gone down to History as a statesman of brilliant talents brilliantly employed. Too self-controlled, too fastidious in scholarship, too contemptuous of vulgar applause to evoke enthusiasm, he reciprocated the affection and loyalty with which he inspired colleagues and friends. In pure literary eloquence his only rival among contemporaries was Lord Rosebery ; as a platform orator he was inferior to Lloyd George, and as a parliamentary dialectician to Balfour. A great Parliamentarian, he led the House of Commons with rare dignity, and two Sovereigns bore witness to his loyalty. He did as much perhaps as a Radical Minister was able to prepare for a war which he could not but foresee. When war came, he put England's case before his countrymen and before the world, with dignity and restraint, without exaggeration, but with unanswerable force and incomparable lucidity ; he gave steady support to Lord Kitchener and to the

[1] Sir Edward Grey had remained throughout at the Foreign Office.

sailors and soldiers in the fighting line ; he showed courage and calmness in the face of national adversity, and when he was himself deprived of power he exhibited dignity, magnanimity and restraint. But with all his great qualities he lacked some which are essential to leadership in war. By 1916, if not before, the nation imperatively demanded a change in the supreme direction of affairs. From the King downwards sincere sympathy was extended to Mr. Asquith : but the safety of the State came first.

Lloyd George Premiership
Sir Edward (now Viscount Grey) went into retirement with his Chief, and was succeeded at the Foreign Office by Balfour. Carson succeeded the latter at the Admiralty, but resigned in the following July when he became a member of the War Directory without portfolio. Most of Lloyd George's principal colleagues were Conservatives, though about a dozen Liberals and three Labour members found places in the enlarged Ministry. But the new Premier was responsible for constitutional innovations of great significance. He insisted that war could not be successfully waged by a ' Sanhedrim '—by a Cabinet of the time-honoured design. Consequently, he formed a War Directory ; he selected as Departmental Ministers experts rather than Parliamentarians, and he called into being an Imperial War Cabinet.

The War Cabinet
The ' Directory ' was to consist of five members, of whom one only was to be the head of an administrative department—Mr. Bonar Law, who was to be Chancellor of the Exchequer and lead the House of Commons. The other members were Lord Curzon (Lord President of the Council and leader of the House of Lords), Mr. Lloyd George himself, Lord Milner and Mr. Henderson (Labour), the two latter being ' without portfolios '. General Smuts, the distinguished South African statesman and soldier, was added to the Directory in June 1917. G. N. Barnes succeeded Henderson as representative of the Labour Party in the ' Directory ' in August 1917. The idea of this War Cabinet or ' Directory ' was that half a dozen of the leading statesmen, relieved of all departmental responsibilities, should be free to give their whole time to the prosecution of the War.

In practice this idea was imperfectly realized : much of the time of the ' Directors ' was given to the settlement of inter-Departmental disputes.

That the new War Cabinet worked hard cannot be denied.

During its first year of existence it held more than 300 meetings. Every meeting was attended by the Foreign Secretary, by the First Sea Lord of the Admiralty, and the Chief of the Imperial General Staff, and in addition 248 persons, experts on Foreign, Colonial and Indian affairs, on Finance, Education, Shipping, Agriculture, Railways, &c., were from time to time summoned to meetings. Attached to the Cabinet was a Secretariat of eleven members, who kept the minutes, prepared agenda, circulated reports and attended to correspondence.

Outside the War Cabinet was a body of Ministers, substantially increased in number by the creation of many new offices. Their position was ambiguous. They were summoned to Cabinet meetings only when the affairs of their several departments were under discussion, and they could bring with them ' any experts either from their own departments or outside, whose advice they considered might be useful '. (Report of the War Cabinet for 1917, pp. 2, 4.) Collective responsibility, which was the essence of the old system, disappeared. The new system, like that which had always prevailed under the Presidential Constitution of the United States, was frankly departmental. A semblance of co-ordination was maintained through the medium of the War Cabinet, but the responsibility of the Heads of Departments was rather to the Premier-President than to the War Cabinet or to each other. The chief Ministers outside the Directory formed, however, a quasi-cabinet for Home Affairs. For Departmental Ministers the Prime Minister, by a daring but well justified innovation, went in some cases outside Parliament. Thus Sir Albert Stanley, a successful business man, became President of the Board of Trade and Mr. H. A. L. Fisher, a distinguished scholar, President of the Board of Education. Seats in the House of Commons were promptly found for them, and, later on, for Sir Eric Geddes, an expert on transport, who, on the resignation of Sir Edward Carson (July 1917), was appointed First Lord of the Admiralty.

Of even greater significance was a third innovation made by Mr. Lloyd George. The Prime Ministers of the Dominions and representatives of India were, in December 1916, invited by the Home Government to visit England ' to attend a series of special and continuous meetings of the War Cabinet, in order to consider urgent questions affecting the prosecution of the War, the pos- *The Imperial War Cabinet* sible conditions on which, in agreement with our allies, we could assent to its termination, and the problems which will then immediately arise'. The invitation was accepted; and the Imperial War Cabinet, consisting of the five members of the British War Directory; the Secretaries of State for Foreign Affairs, India, and the Colonies; three representatives of Canada, two of New Zealand, one of South Africa and one of Newfoundland, met for the first time in March 1917. Three representatives of India were also present to advise the Secretary of State. So completely successful was this experiment that Mr. Lloyd George informed the House of Commons (May 17, 1917) that it had been decided to hold an 'annual Imperial Cabinet' and that it was the general hope that the institution would become an 'accepted convention of the British Constitution'. Sir Robert Borden, the Prime Minister of Canada, expressed his conviction that 'with that new Cabinet a new era has dawned and a new page of history has been written'.

The experiment was repeated in 1918 when Australia also was represented: but it did not survive the Peace Conference.

Nor was the new War Directory conspicuously more successful than the old Cabinet in the conduct of the War. In 1917 a strenuous and sustained effort was made to bring the war on the Western Front to a victorious end. On April 9 a terrific attack, launched at Arras, resulted in the capture of Vimy Ridge, and two months later a second victory not less brilliant was won at Messines Ridge. The fighting strength of the Allies would then, it was reckoned, reach the maximum. In these great battles the gallant Canadians, under the command of General (now Viscount) Byng, covered themselves with glory. But brilliant as was the attack, there was no break through. A further advance was timed to begin at the end of July. On the day it began (July 31) the weather broke, and the operation was conducted under impossible conditions. Some ground was gained, but at an enormous sacrifice of life, which made the 'mud and blood' of Paschendaale proverbial. Nor was the objective to break through the Ypres salient, and thrust the Germans out of Flanders, attained.

Events remote from the Western Front were powerfully reacting upon the war in France and Flanders. Of these the

The Campaign of 1917

most direct were the outbreak of revolution in Russia (March 12); the intervention of the United States (April 6); and the defeat of the Italians at Caporetto (October 24).

Of Italy's part in the Great War no mention has yet been made. At the outbreak of war her attitude was doubtful. So lately as 1912 she had renewed the Triple Alliance, though towards England she had always been friendly, and of late her relations both with France and Russia had greatly improved. She refused in July 1914 to regard the Austrian quarrel with Serbia as a *casus foederis*; but there was a large party in favour of neutrality. Germany did everything to encourage it, even to the point of urging Austria to make large concessions to the *Irredentists*. There was, however, a considerable minority in favour of intervention on the side of the Allies and late in 1914 this party received a powerful impulse from the adhesion of a leading Socialist, Benito Mussolini, who founded *Il Popolo d'Italia* to popularize his policy. That Italy could have obtained the Trentino without war is certain: but for the *Irredentists* that was not enough. Early in 1915 Italy made her fateful decision.

By the Treaty of London, concluded on April 26, 1915, between Italy, Great Britain, France and Russia, Italy undertook to put all her strength into the War against the enemies of the *Entente*. In return she was to obtain the district of the Trentino, the Southern Tyrol up to the Brenner Pass, Trieste, the counties of Gorizia and Gradisca, the whole of Istria up to the Quarnero, including Volosca and the Istrian Archipelago, the province of Dalmatia in its existing frontiers, together with most of the islands in the Adriatic (including Lissa), and she was to retain Valona and the Dodecanese.[1] Italy also stipulated for a loan of £50,000,000 on easy terms, and that the Pope should have no say as to the final terms of peace. Italy at the same time agreed that large accessions of territory, including Fiume, should be assigned to Croatia, Serbia and Montenegro.

Italy declared war against Austria-Hungary on May 24; against Turkey on August 21, and a few weeks later, against Bulgaria. Against Germany Italy did not declare war until August 27, 1916.

The intervention of Italy was, both in a moral and military

[1] *British and Foreign State Papers*, 1919, vol. cxii, pp. 973 seq.

sense, of immense advantage to the *Entente* ; but it introduced a considerable complication into the diplomatic situation.   The Serbs were gravely perturbed by the adhesion of a Power whose notorious ambitions threatened to frustrate the dream of a greater Serbia.   Rather than see Italy established on the Dalmatian coasts and Archipelago, the Serbs would have preferred to leave Austria-Hungary in occupation.   The *Entente*, however, had no option but to pay the price demanded by Italy.

For Italy, as for other belligerents, sunshine alternated with shadow during the next three years.   She more than held her own during the campaign of 1916 ; she tasted triumph in the summer of 1917, but in the autumn of that year it was her fate to learn the bitterness of defeat.   Neither politically nor in a military sense could Italy present a united front to the enemy. Not only had she to count on the hardly disguised hostility of the Papacy, but there was a considerable pro-German party among the upper classes, and a very strong section of ' internationals ' among the Socialists.   The latter party was strengthened by the disaster which overtook Italian arms when, in October 1917, the great Austro-German attack was launched.

War weariness or treachery opened at Caporetto a gap in the line; the Second Italian army was compelled to fall back ; the retreat became a rout ; the rout of the Second Army involved the retreat of the Third, and within three weeks the enemy had captured 2,300 guns and taken nearly 200,000 prisoners.   The Fourth Army then made a stand on the line of the Piave, and on the holding of that line the safety of Venice, Verona and Vicenza depended. The moment was critical, but England and France, realizing the danger to the common cause, promptly dispatched large reinforcements from the Western Front.   The arrival of French and English troops, commanded by General Fayolle, Sir Herbert Plumer, and Lord Cavan, stiffened the Italian defence, and when the Austrians again attacked, somewhat tardily, in June 1918, they were vigorously repulsed.   In October Lord Cavan in command of a mixed British and Italian force, and General Diaz in command of a re-equipped Italian army, took the offensive in their turn, and, in a brief but brilliant campaign, forced the passage of the Piave and chased the Austrians out of Italy. On November 4 Austria begged for an armistice.

The assistance so promptly given to Italy by England and France had not merely saved the military situation but had produced an excellent moral effect. Unfortunately, a terrible blow had in the meantime fallen upon the Grand Alliance. In the first months of the War Russia had rendered invaluable service to the cause of the Allies; but her troops were badly equipped; she lacked guns and munitions; worst of all, her efforts in the field were paralysed, if not by actual treachery, at least by gross maladministration. Nevertheless, before the end of 1916 Russia had, apparently, overcome the worst of the difficulties.

The
Russian
Revolu-
tion,
March
1917

It was too late. In March 1917 the long-threatened revolution broke out. The Czar Nicholas was deposed, and, after being held captive for awhile was, with his wife and all his children, foully murdered by his captors. A republic was proclaimed and a Provisional Government of 'Moderates' was set up. But in November the 'Moderates' were pushed aside by the Communists, and the Bolsheviks, under Lenin and Trotsky, were installed in power.

When the Bolshevik revolution was accomplished, the Russian sailors mutinied and murdered their officers; the soldiers flung down their arms and raced home with all speed to secure the loot which the social revolution promised.

On the military results of the Russian Revolution it is superfluous to dwell. Germany was able to withdraw great armies from the East, and fling them into the line against the Allies on the West; Austria was free to concentrate on the Italian Front.

Before the end of the year negotiations for peace between Bolshevik Russia and the Central Powers was begun and in March 1918 a Treaty was signed at Brest-Litovsk. Russia was out of the War. The *Entente* was broken. The Western Powers must carry on the struggle as best they could.

Two months after the signature of the Treaty of Brest-Litovsk the Quadruple Alliance also imposed peace on Roumania. But, in view of subsequent events, this treaty was waste-paper.

The defection of Bolshevik Russia and the peace imposed on Roumania left the Central Empires free to concentrate their efforts on the Western Front. But almost at the moment that Russia failed, a new ally, morally if not militarily worth a dozen

Interven-
tion of
the
U.S.A.,
April
1917

Russias, had come into the field against Germany. The attitude of the United States during the first two years of the War had most gravely disappointed, not only the Allies, but very many of their own citizens. President Wilson had essayed to play a mediating part in the world-conflict. His efforts were, however, impeded by the stupidity of German diplomacy, and by her ruthless disregard of the conventions of war.

On May 7, 1915, German submarines torpedoed a great Atlantic liner, the *Lusitania*, which sank with the loss of over a thousand persons, of whom scores were Americans. Had Germany's ultimate fate ever been in doubt, that crime had sealed it. From that moment the conscience of the American people was aroused, and it was only a matter of time how soon outraged moral feelings would translate themselves into effective military action.

Yet not even the sinking of the *Lusitania* could drive President Wilson from the position he had assumed. But the more doggedly he persisted in the policy of neutrality, the more daring became the German attacks upon neutral shipping. At last, on February 1, 1917, Germany proclaimed ' unrestricted submarine warfare ' : any ship trading with Great Britain was to be sunk at sight. This culminating insult was too much for the patience of the American President ; on February 2 the United States broke off diplomatic relations, and on April 6, 1917, declared war on Germany. ' With the entrance of the United States into this war, a new chapter opened in world history.' So spake Lord Bryce. ' The entrance of the United States into the War was the greatest mental effort and spiritual realization of truth which has occurred in the whole course of secular history.' The words are Mr. Churchill's, and they anticipate the verdict of posterity. That America should so far abandon her traditional policy, and fling all her weight, moral and material, into the War was, in truth, an event of solemn significance. The military effect of her intervention was not, however, felt until the closing months of the War, when it did much to turn the scale against Germany.

The German offensive in 1918   How badly her help was needed, the story of 1918 will tell. Between March and July the Germans on the Western Front launched four terrific attacks. The first (March 21) opened near St. Quentin, and resulted in the repulse of the 5th British Army under Sir Hubert Gough.[1] Six hundred thousand Germans attacked the weakest point in the Anglo-French line, and by the mere weight of numbers pierced it. Bapaume and Peronne, Albert, Terznier and Roye,—all the expensive fruits of the sacrifices on the Somme were lost ; but in front of Amiens the German advance was stayed. The crisis was valiantly met. Foch was invested with supreme command of the Allied forces ; all the available British reserves were hurried across the Channel ; troops were summoned from Palestine ; America was urged to expedite the dispatch of her forces.

Thanks in large measure to the British Navy, the Americans soon began to pour across the Atlantic. Over 80,000 were sent off in March, nearly 120,000 in April, over 245,000 in May, nearly 280,000 in June, over 300,000 in July, over 285,000 in August, and 257,000 in September. In all, forty-two American divisions were landed in France. Fifty-one per cent. of the troops were carried in British, forty-six per cent. in American vessels ; and out of the vast total, only two hundred men were lost through the attacks of enemy submarines. Germany was astounded at this remarkable feat, having believed it to be impossible of accomplishment.

Meanwhile, on April 9, Germany launched a second attack south of Ypres. The offensive lasted for three weeks, and was very costly both to the Germans and to the Allies, but was stayed in front of Hazebrouck. A third attack against the French front (May 26) brought the Germans once more on to the Marne, but at Château-Thierry their advance was stayed by Foch (June 11). The enemy attacked again on July 15 and were permitted by the great French soldier to cross the Marne. But on the 18th, Foch let loose his reserves, and the Germans were driven back with immense slaughter.

On August 8 the British counter-offensive began. The fierce fighting between that date and November 11 may be regarded as one almost continuous battle, in the course of which the British armies captured nearly 200,000 prisoners and nearly 3,000 guns ; 140,000 prisoners and 2,000 guns fell to the French ; 43,000

The counter-offensive, Aug.–Nov.

---

[1] This was the official view ; but the question whether the 5th Army was mishandled or did all that was required of it is now hotly disputed. For a spirited defence of Gough see Lord Birkenhead, *Turning Points of History*, London, 1930.

prisoners and 1,400 guns to the Americans ; while the gallant remnant of the Belgian army also claimed its modest share in the greatest battle of all recorded history.   The details of the fighting must be sought elsewhere.   The result may be chronicled in a sentence.   The great military machine of Germany was at

Germany 'cracks' last broken into fragments ; the German people turned in anger upon the dynasty, and William of Hohenzollern, having surrendered the Crown of Prussia and the throne of Germany (November 9), fled for safety to Holland.   Already the terms of an armistice had been agreed upon by the Allies at Versailles (November 4), and on November 11 were accepted by the accredited envoys of Germany.   The Great War was over.

The Price of War The victory of the Allies was complete.   To the final result the British Empire had made indisputably the largest contribution.   But the price paid for victory was terrific.   In all, Great Britain and Ireland contributed to the Allied cause over 6,000,000 men ;   the rest of the British Empire over 3,000,000, making a total of 9,496,370.   Of these 3,266,723 were killed, wounded and missing, and those who actually gave their lives were little short of a million.   The losses suffered by the British mercantile marine were relatively the highest in the War.   14,661 men of the merchant service were drowned or killed, and 30,000 men were severely wounded, while no less than 9,000,000 tons of shipping were destroyed.   The naval casualties amounted to 27,175 of whom no fewer than 22,258 were drowned or killed.   The heroism of the men of the mercantile marine was not inferior even to that of the fighting forces ;   before the close of the War many men had been torpedoed six or seven times, and yet there is no single instance on record of a man having refused to ship.

The sacrifice of wealth was on a scale parallel with that of men.   Between August 3, 1914, and March 31, 1919, the Exchequer issues totalled £9,590,000,000.   About £1,500,000,000 was lent to the Allies, and the value of shipping and cargoes lost by enemy action was estimated at £750,000,000.   It is natural to ask whether the tremendous effort thus barely outlined was ' worth while '.   To attempt an answer while the world is under the influence of post-War disillusionment and reaction might be misleading.   The contemporary historian can only say that it was inevitable.

CHAPTER XXIII

THE OVERSEAS EMPIRE AND THE WAR AT SEA

THE Great War was not merely a European war; it engulfed the world. More particularly did it involve that large portion of the world embraced in the British Empire.

When the King of Great Britain and Ireland declares war he declares it as King of all the Britains and as Emperor of India. The King's person is indivisible: the British Empire *vis à vis* the rest of the world is a unit. As a unit the Empire, on August 4, 1914, went to war. As a unit, on June 28, 1919, the Empire concluded peace; but of those who signed the Treaty of Versailles as representing the British Empire, some signed also as representing the component nations of the British Commonwealth. Their insistence on their right to do so was of high significance.

The Overseas Empire

On August 4, 1914, the many members of the British Overseas Empire were involved in war involuntarily; if not against their wills, at least without their wills. No British Dominion could have remained neutral in the War, except by renouncing its allegiance to the King, and formally severing its connexion with the Empire. But although the sole responsibility for the declaration of war rested on the Imperial Government, and although that declaration created a state of war for the whole Empire, the active co-operation of the Dominions was entirely voluntary. No demand was made upon them for assistance, military, naval or financial. Their autonomy was rigidly respected.[1] Nevertheless, they promptly made spontaneous offers of co-operation.

The world stood amazed at this demonstration of Imperial unity; Germany was not merely astonished but deeply chagrined. The German people had been beguiled into a confident anticipa-

---

[1] Keith, *Sovereignty of the British Dominions*, p. 314, and *War Government of the British Dominions*, p. 20.

tion that the first shot fired in a great European War would be
the signal for the dissolution of England's ' loosely compacted
Empire '.[1] Of all the miscalculations of German diplomacy this
was in its consequences the most grave.

South
Africa

In no part of the Empire, except in South Africa, was there
any hesitation to come forward with offers of assistance, still less
to evade the legal responsibility of war. Even in South Africa
the Union Ministers accepted as early as August 10, 1914, the
suggestion of the Imperial Government that they should promptly
attack German South-West Africa. Nor was the Legislature
slow to support the action of the Executive. The House of
Assembly, ' fully recognizing the obligations of the Union as a
portion of the British Empire ', passed a humble address assuring
His Majesty of ' its loyal support in bringing to a successful issue
the momentous conflict which had been forced upon him in defence
of the principles of liberty and of international honour, and of its
wholehearted determination to take all measures necessary for
defending the interests of the Union and for co-operating with
His Majesty's Imperial Government to maintain the security and
integrity of the Empire '. An amendment, proposed by General
Hertzog, declaring that an ' attack on German territory in South
Africa would be in conflict with the interests of the Union and of
the Empire ' found only twelve supporters. But the Opposition
were not content with verbal protest. Led by Christian De Wet
and C. F. Beyers (who resigned his post as Commandant-General
of the Union Defence Force), they raised a rebellion in October.
With splendid moral courage General Botha himself took the field
against ' men who in the past have been our honoured leaders '.
The rebellion was sustained by some 10,000 fighting men, but
General Hertzog, though sympathizing with their attitude, was
not among them. Before the end of December the rebellion was
suppressed. Beyers had been drowned in the course of the campaign ; De Wet was tried for treason and, though sentenced to
six years' imprisonment, was after a few months released.

With his hands free from domestic disaffection, Botha in 1915
led an expedition into German South-West Africa. The campaign was arduous, but after some five months' fighting, marked
by brilliant generalship, the Germans surrendered (July 9) to

[1] The phrase is General Bernhardi's.

General Botha, and the most important of their African colonies passed to the Union of South Africa. In addition to a large number of coloured and native troops who were enlisted in labour brigades South Africa contributed some 76,000 men to the armies of the Empire. Most of these fought under General Smuts in East Africa or in West Africa, but some 25,000 fought in Europe, and distinguished themselves on the Western Front.

Canada came into the War without an hour's hesitation. She Canada promptly dispatched 1,000,000 bags of flour as a present to the Imperial Government, and by October 14 no fewer than 30,000 Canadian volunteers had reached England. They were followed by other large contingents. Conscription was adopted—not without resistance from the French Canadians of Quebec—in 1917, and before the end of the War Canada had raised no fewer than 595,441 men. Of these 62,000 laid down their lives. They had won for themselves and for the land whence they came imperishable fame, and had done not a little to save the Empire. Newfoundland also sent its contingent—some 6,500 men.

Australia was not a whit behind Canada. As early as August Australia 3 Mr. Hughes cabled to the Imperial Government that the Commonwealth was ready to dispatch a force of 20,000 men. The first contingent actually left Australia on November 1, 1914, and during the War no fewer than 329,883 splendid fighting men were sent overseas. Of these 59,302 were killed or died. All the Australian troops were volunteers, Hughes's proposal of Conscription being decisively defeated. The War, including pensions, cost the Commonwealth £660,000,000.

New Zealand was equally prompt and even more generous New in its contribution : it raised 112,223 men or 19·35 (against Zealand Australia's 13·43) per cent. of its male population. The New Zealanders suffered more than 50,000 casualties, but of all their number only 341 were taken prisoners. Such figures, apart from war records, would suffice to attest their gallantry. New Zealand incurred, in the service of the Empire, a debt of £81,500,000.

Never perhaps in the history of the world has voluntary effort achieved a result so splendid as that of the British Dominions overseas. If their legal implication in the War was inevitable, their contribution to it was wholly spontaneous. Nor did the Imperial Government fail to respect the autonomy of the

Dominions. Thus it was General Botha who decided the terms on which the German forces in South Africa laid down their arms, and it was Australian and New Zealand officers respectively who arranged the terms of the capitulation of German New Guinea and Samoa. The most sensitive of Dominion statesmen could hardly fail to be reassured by the policy pursued by the Imperial Government throughout the whole course of the War and during the peace negotiations.

Defective machin-ery   Nevertheless, the machinery of co-operation proved itself, during the War, to be lamentably defective. Speaking at Winnipeg early in the War Sir Robert Borden said : ' It is impossible to believe that the existing status, so far as it concerns the control of foreign policy and extra-Imperial relations, can remain as it is to-day.' ' These pregnant events ', he said in December 1915, ' have already given birth to a new order. It is realized that great policies and questions which concern and govern the issues of peace and war cannot in future be assumed by the people of the British islands alone.' In language not less emphatic and more picturesque, Mr. Doherty, the Minister of Justice, spoke to similar purpose at Toronto : ' Our recognition of this war as ours, our participation in it, spontaneous and voluntary as it is, determines absolutely once for all that we have passed from the status of the protected colony to that of the participating nation. The protected colony was rightly voiceless ; the participating nation cannot continue so.'

Australia and New Zealand re-echoed the voice of Canada. ' There must be a change and it must be radical in its nature,' declared Mr. Hughes. Mr. Fisher and Sir Joseph Ward spoke with similar emphasis, and the same point was driven home in England by Mr. Bonar Law : ' It is not a possible arrangement that one set of men should contribute the lives and treasure of their people and should have no voice in the way in which those lives and that treasure are expended. That cannot continue. There must be a change.'

The change came, as we have seen, with the summoning in 1917 of the Imperial War Cabinet.

Side by side with the Imperial Cabinet there met also a special Imperial Conference, which on April 16 adopted an historic reso-lution. After affirming that ' the readjustment of the Constitutional relations of the component parts of the Empire ' ought to form the subject of a Special Conference to be summoned as soon as possible after the War, the resolution proceeded :

' They deem it their duty, however, to place on record their view that any such readjustment, while thoroughly preserving all existing powers of self-government and complete control of domestic affairs, should be based upon a full recognition of the Dominions as autonomous nations of an Imperial Commonwealth, and of India as an important portion of the same, should recognize the right of the Dominions and India to an adequate voice in foreign policy and in foreign relations, and should provide effective arrangements for continuous consultation in all important matters of common Imperial concern, and for such necessary concerted action, founded on consultation, as the several Governments may determine.'

General Smuts bluntly said that the adoption of this resolution ruled out the whole idea of Imperial Federation—an Imperial Legislature and an Imperial Executive responsible thereto. The Conference of 1926 proved his prescience.

India played a part in the War not less important than that of the Dominions, but its constitutional and military position was entirely different. *India and the War*

The army in India has always been maintained in a state of preparedness for war, but the military authorities, both in India and at home, had only in view frontier campaigns or at the worst a possible attack by Russia or her allies on the North-West Frontier. Consequently the outbreak of the world-war found India unprepared for military participation in distant theatres of war. In August 1914 there were, exclusive of the Indian Reserves, the Volunteers, and the Imperial Service Forces, about 235,000 men under arms in India : 75,000 were British and 160,000 formed the Indian army (with 2,771 British officers, and 341 British non-commissioned officers). When the call from Europe came, the response in India was immediate, spontaneous, and superb. On August 8 orders for mobilization were sent to Meerut and Lahore, and before the end of the month the Lahore Division had embarked. Owing to the lack of transports and escorts, the embarkation of the rest of the expeditionary force was delayed for some weeks. In a short time, however, all but eight of the regular

British battalions and most of the Batteries were withdrawn from India, and were replaced by 29 Territorial Field Batteries and 35 Territorial battalions sent out from England.

Indian co-opera-tion
On September 8 the Imperial Legislative Council met at Simla, and the Viceroy conveyed to it a message from the King-Emperor. In reply, the Council passed, with enthusiasm and unanimity, a resolution affirming their ' unswerving loyalty and enthusiastic devotion to their King-Emperor ', and promising ' unflinching support to the British Government '. They expressed the opinion that ' the people of India, in addition to the assistance now being afforded by India to the Empire, would wish to share in the heavy financial burden now imposed by the War on the United Kingdom '. Such sentiments, while evidently sincere, were partly due to the anxiety of India not to be behind other ' Dominions '. ' We aspire ', said one Indian representative, ' to Colonial self-government, then we ought to emulate the example of the Colonials, and try to do what they are doing.'

The Ruling Princes
The ruling Princes were not behind the Government of British India in their professions of loyalty and promises of help. On September 8 the Viceroy telegraphed that ' the Rulers of the Native States in India, who number several hundred in all, have with one accord rallied to the defence of the Empire and offered their personal services and the resources of their States for the War ', and that from among the many Princes and nobles who had volunteered for active service he had selected some half-dozen Princes including the Rulers of Patiala and Bikanir, Sir Partab Singh, and other cadets and nobles, and had accepted many offers of native contingents. He also reported that : ' The same spirit prevailed throughout British India. Hundreds of telegrams and letters had . . . come from communities and associations, religious, political and social, of all classes and creeds, also from individuals offering their resources or asking for opportunity to prove their loyalty by personal service.'

In the course of the War no fewer than 600,000 combatants (mostly Punjabis, Sikhs, Rajputs, and Gurkhas) and 474,000 non-combatants were sent overseas, and they distinguished themselves in nearly all the chief theatres of the War, notably in Mesopotamia, Palestine, Salonika, Gallipoli, and East Africa. The Bengali contribution to war-service was negligible.

Included in the troops sent oversea were 26,000 officers and men of the Imperial Service Forces, and they lost in dead over 1,500 men. Of the Indian forces as a whole over 53,000 were killed or died of wounds. These losses were, as Lord Curzon truly said, ' shattering '. But he added : ' In the face of these trials and difficulties the cheerfulness, the loyalty, the good discipline and intrepid courage of these denizens of another clime cannot be too highly praised.'

The splendid contribution made by the Overseas Empire to the common cause is the more remarkable in view of the fact that, excepting Africa, no part of that Empire was directly menaced by Germany. Protected by the British Navy, the Dominions, Dependencies and Colonies might have pursued in security the even tenor of their way—doubtless with a profit to themselves relatively as large as that reaped by the United States.

But the condition absolute of their security was British superiority at sea. Fortunately that superiority, though gravely menaced, was never lost. Of the many factors contributing to the final result sea-power was not the least important. The gallant resistance of Liége ; the superb courage and unyielding tenacity of the French armies and the French people ; the dogged endurance and the heroic sacrifices of Britons from many lands ; the tardy but effective help of America—all these were factors of immense significance ; but not one of them would have availed had Great Britain lost command of the sea. *The influence of sea-power*

On the outbreak of war a triple task was imposed upon the British Navy : to protect from invasion the shores of Great Britain ; to escort the British Expeditionary Force to France ; and to keep clear of enemy ships all the great ocean routes, in order to bring safely to the several theatres of war the troops from oversea, and to guard the merchantmen. On the Navy, then, depended the economic life of Great Britain and the fighting power of herself and her allies. The best opinion holds that Great Britain was never in any serious danger of invasion. Had the danger become imminent, the Fleet was ready to avert it. With what brilliant success the second task was achieved has been already told. It remains to say something of the third.

In home-waters the Admiralty was prepared for war. By 4 a.m. on August 4 the whole Fleet was mobilized and ready for *Home Waters* action under Admiral Sir John Jellicoe. At 11 p.m. the historic order was issued : ' Commence hostilities at once against Germany.' On August 5 the *Königin Luise,* after laying mines off the Suffolk coast, was caught and sunk : but she had done her work ; the *Amphion* struck one of the mines and sank with a loss of 150 men.

The Outer Seas In the outer seas we were less prepared than Germany. The Germans had eight fast modern cruisers on foreign stations, and five gunboats. The *Scharnhorst,* the *Gneisenau,* the *Emden,* the *Nuremberg* and the *Leipzig* were on the China Station ; the *Königsberg* was off East Africa ; the *Dresden* and the *Karlsruhe* in the West Indies. These cruisers inflicted great damage upon us. Admiral von Tirpitz claimed, indeed, that ' of enemy's goods and bottoms they destroyed more than double their own value ' before they met their inevitable fate. His calculation was probably accurate.

The Pacific Especially damaging to British merchant-shipping during the first three months of the War was the activity of the *Emden* in the Pacific. Had it not been for our alliance with Japan, the situation in the Far East would have indeed been grave. Japan never hesitated as to the fulfilment of her obligations, though even apart from the Treaty the opportunity of revenge on Germany for the part she played in 1895 [1] would probably have led to her intervention. On August 23, 1914, she declared war on Germany, and on October 19 adhered to the Pact of London, by which the Entente Powers had bound themselves (Sept. 5) not to conclude separate Peace Treaties with the enemy.

All the German possessions in the Pacific were swept up in the first months of the War. On August 29 German Samoa was occupied by a force from New Zealand ; in September the Bismarck Archipelago and German New Guinea fell to the Australians, and the Marshall and Caroline Islands to the Japanese. A force of 30,000 Japanese troops had meantime, with some 2,000 British troops, attacked Kiaochow, which capitulated on November 7. Three days later the *Emden* was at last hunted down and sunk off Cocos Island by the Australian cruiser *Sydney.* That was a brilliant achievement, but the naval resources of Australia and New Zealand were quite unequal to the task of transporting

[1] *Supra,* p. 207.

their troops to Europe. Nor could we spare ships for the purpose. Our Grand Fleet was fully occupied in Home waters : we had to guard the Atlantic, and to a large extent the Mediterranean. It was the deliberate opinion of the statesmen both of Great Britain and Australasia that the 1,600,000 troops from the Pacific Dominions and India could not have been safely transported across the oceans but for the assistance of our Japanese allies. ' It was ', said Lloyd George, ' invaluable. It was one of the determining factors of the War.' [1]

At the Peace Conference the position in the Pacific was the subject of heated debate, mainly between the British and Australasian representatives. If Germany was to be deprived of her former possessions in that region, to whom should they pass ?

By Articles 118 and 119 of the Treaty of Versailles, Germany renounced in favour of the Principal Allied and Associated Powers all her rights over her overseas possessions. There was, however, a strong feeling among the Allies that whatever Power should be entrusted with the government of territories inhabited by backward peoples, the task should be undertaken, not for purposes of political aggrandizement or commercial exploitation, but in the spirit of trusteeship. An Englishman may be forgiven for saying that the spirit which has in the main, despite occasional backsliding, inspired the Colonial administration of Great Britain was henceforward to govern the relations between European rulers and their non-European subjects. This intention was embodied in Article XXII of the Covenant of the League of Nations which laid down that ' to those colonies and territories which as a consequence of the late war have ceased to be under the Sovereignty of the States which formerly governed them, and which are inhabited by peoples not yet able to stand by themselves under the strenuous conditions of the modern world, there should be applied the principle that the well-being and development of such peoples form a sacred trust of civilization '. It further suggested that the best way of giving effect to this principle is that ' the tutelage of such peoples should be entrusted to advanced nations who by reason of their resources, their experience, or their geographical position, can best undertake this responsibility, and

Peace Terms (marginal note)

---

[1] House of Commons *Debates*, August 18, 1921, p. 1704.

who are willing to accept it, and that this tutelage should be exercised by them as Mandatories of the League '. The character of the Mandate must, however, differ ' according to the stage of the development of the people, the geographical situation of the territory, its economic conditions and other similar circumstances '. So the Powers in Conference decreed. Would the ' Mandate ' principle work in the Pacific ? The Australasian representatives were doubtful.

' One of the most striking features of the Conference ', said Mr. Hughes, the Premier of the Australian Commonwealth, ' was the appalling ignorance of every nation as to the affairs of every other nation—its geographical, racial, historical conditions, or traditions ' [1] The safety of Australia, so her sons consistently maintained, demanded that the great rampart of islands stretching around the north-east of Australia should be held by the Australian Dominion or by some Power (if there be one ?) in whom they have absolute confidence. At Paris Mr. Hughes made a great fight to obtain the direct control of them ; worsted in that fight by Mr. Wilson's formulas, Australia was forced to accept the principle of the Mandate, but her representatives were careful to insist that the Mandate should be in a form consistent not only with their national safety but with their ' economic, industrial, and general welfare '.

In plain English that meant the maintenance of a ' White Australia ' and a preferential tariff. On both points Australia found herself in direct conflict with Japan, but, despite the formal protest and reservation of the latter, the Mandates for the ex-German possessions in the Pacific were issued in the form desired by the British Dominions : i.e. in the same form (' C ') as that accepted for South-West Africa.

The islands north of the Equator, namely, the Marshall, Caroline, Pelew, and Ladrone Islands went to Japan, as did Kiaochow ; those south of the Equator to the British Empire or its Dominions : the Bismarck Archipelago, German New Guinea, and those of the Solomon Islands formerly belonging to Germany, to Australia,[2] German Samoa to New Zealand,[3] and Nauru to the British Empire [4]—in all cases under Mandate.

[1] Commonwealth of Australia, *Parliamentary Debates*, No. 87, pp. 12, 173.
[2] Cmd. 1201 (1921).   [3] Ibid., 1203.   [4] Ibid., 1202.

To return to the War in other oceans. After Japan came in, and the German possessions in the Pacific were lost, the German squadron made for home. Off the coast of Chile (whose neutrality was none too favourable to the Allies) Von Spee and his five cruisers fell in with a weak British squadron under Admiral Sir Charles Cradock. Cradock, though without any hope of victory, determined to engage them (November 1). *Good Hope* and *Monmouth* were sunk, the gallant Admiral going down with fourteen hundred officers and men. A fast but lightly armed cruiser, the *Glasgow*, was sent off to warn the Falkland Islands, where *Canopus*, a big battleship, lay.

The disaster of Coronel was quickly retrieved. A squadron was promptly sent out from England under the command of Sir Doveton Sturdee, who, making all possible speed, arrived off the Falkland Isles on December 7. On the very next day Sturdee fell in with Von Spee, and *Gneisenau, Scharnhorst, Leipzig, Nuremberg* were sunk after a gallant fight ; only the *Dresden* escaped. The British loss was only seven men killed. The *Dresden* was caught and sunk three months later.

Besides her cruisers Germany was expected to send out some forty armed merchantmen. Only five of them succeeded in leaving harbour. Of these the largest, *Kaiser Wilhelm der Grosse,* was sunk by *Highflyer* off the coast of Africa (August 26) ; *Kap Trafalgar* was sunk by *Carmania* off the coast of Brazil after what has been described as ' the finest single-ship action of the war ' [1] on September 14 ; *Karlsruhe* was accidentally blown up ; the other two were interned. Mr. Churchill, therefore, could boast that before the end of 1914 every one of the enemy ships on the high seas was ' reduced to complete inactivity, sunk or pinned in port.' [2]

The German Colonies lay at our mercy. The fate of the Pacific islands has already been described. At the Peace, South-West Africa was assigned by the Principal Allied and Associated Powers to His Britannic Majesty, to be administered on his behalf by the Government of the Union of South Africa under a Mandate approved by the Council of the League of Nations.

South-West Africa was indicated together with the South Pacific islands, in Article XXII of the Covenant, as one of the

[1] By C. R. L. Fletcher, p. 116.　　　　[2] *World Crisis,* I, p. 286.

territories which ' owing to the sparseness of their population, or their small size, or their remoteness from the centres of civilization, or their geographical contiguity to the territory of the Mandatory and other circumstances [which] can be best administered under the laws of the Mandatory as integral portions of its territory, subject to the safeguards above mentioned in the interests of the indigenous population '. The Mandate was accordingly issued in the form prescribed for ' Class C ' territories. It enjoins upon the Mandatory the duty of promoting to the utmost ' the material and moral well-being and the social progress of the inhabitants ' ; it prohibits slavery, the sale of intoxicants to natives, the establishment of military or naval bases ; and provides for complete freedom of conscience, and facilities for missionaries and ministers of all creeds.

The Mandatory is further required to make an annual report to the Council of the League, containing full information with regard to the territory, and indicating the measures taken to fulfil the obligations the Mandatory has assumed. [1]

West Africa gave comparatively little trouble. Togoland surrendered to a Franco-British force in the first month of the War, and at the Peace was divided between the two Powers ; about one-third of the Colony (some 12,500 square miles) bordering on the Gold Coast territories being assigned to Great Britain, and the remainder to France. The Cameroons was attacked, in August 1914, by French troops from the French Congo and by a small British force from Nigeria in the same month. Not, however, until February 1916 was it finally conquered : an area of 83,000 square miles (out of 191,130), extending from the coast along the Nigerian frontier up to Lake Chad was assigned to Great Britain, and the rest to France.

The campaign in East Africa   Of the African campaigns none was so arduous or so prolonged as the fight for the possession of German East Africa. Could Germany have held it with adequate naval as well as military forces, she would have threatened the British Empire's line of communications at a vital point. Our naval supremacy averted this danger ; but Germany had made elaborate preparations to defend her own colony, and if occasion offered to attack British East Africa. General von Lettow-Vorbeck commanded

---

[1] For the terms of the Mandate see Cmd. 1204 (1921).

a force of 3,000 Europeans and 12,000 well-equipped and well-disciplined Askaris. A British attack on Tanga was repulsed in November 1914, and not until General Smuts took over the command of the British forces at the beginning of 1916 was any effective progress made. Dar-es-salaam was captured in September 1916, but another fourteen months of hard fighting were required before the Germans were cleared out of the colony. They took refuge in Portuguese East Africa, and thence in the autumn of 1918 made their way into Northern Rhodesia; nor did they surrender until compelled to do so by the conclusion of the Armistice.

German East Africa fell naturally to Great Britain, but in consequence of strong protests from Belgium was ultimately divided between the two Powers.

The British portion, now known as the Tanganyika Territory, lying immediately to the south of the Kenya Colony (formerly the British East Africa Protectorate), has a coastline of 620 miles, extending from the mouth of the Umba to Cape Delgado, an area of some 384,180 square miles, and an estimated pre-War native population of about 7,600,000. The rest of German East Africa —the provinces of Rhuanda and Urandi, together with the country round Lake Kivu—was conferred upon Belgium. A strip on the east of the Belgian portion has, however, been reserved to Great Britain to facilitate the construction of the Cape to Cairo Railway.

East Africa, Togoland and the Cameroons are all held by their **Mandates** respective assignees under Mandate from the League of Nations. These Mandates, however, unlike that for the South-West Protectorate, belong not to Class C, but to Class B, which differs in two important respects from the former. On the one hand, the ' mandated Colony ' does not become an integral portion of the territory of the Mandatory; on the other, the Mandates secure ' equal opportunities for the trade and commerce of other members of the League '. No such provision is contained either in the Mandate for South-West Africa or in those for the Pacific islands. The insertion of such a provision would plainly have proved too embarrassing to the Union of South Africa in the one case; to Australia and New Zealand in the other. Hence the necessity for the distinction contained in the Covenant. The Mandates in

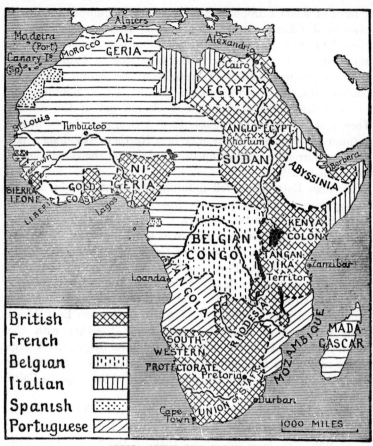

AFRICA AFTER THE GREAT WAR.

Class B also provide more specifically and elaborately for the protection of the natives ' from abuse and measures of fraud and force by the careful supervision of labour contracts and the recruiting of labour '.[1]

Portugal put in a claim to a share in the re-partition of Africa, but after careful consideration it was disallowed.

The general result of the partition may be summarized as follows : out of the 12,500,000 persons who were in 1914 living under the German flag in Africa 42 per cent. have been transferred to the guardianship of the British Empire, 33 per cent. to that of France, and 25 per cent. to Belgium.[2] The settlement would seem in the main to accord with the principle laid down by Mr. Wilson, who insisted that there should be : ' A free, open-minded, and absolutely impartial adjustment of all Colonial claims, based upon a strict observance of the principle that in determining all such questions of sovereignty the interests of the populations concerned must have equal weight with the equitable claims of the Government whose title is to be determined.' [3] If there was one point upon which every African native who had ever lived under German rule was resolved, it was that under no circumstances would he voluntarily remain under, or return to, it. For the protection of native interests in the future, every possible security was taken in the Mandates as approved by the Council of the League of Nations.

To resume the story of the War at sea. No attempt can be made to tell that story in detail ; nor even in outline : partly from lack of space, partly because in the history of naval warfare the World War was unique. ' Barring a few naval actions between surface vessels, such as the battles of Jutland and of the Falkland Islands, the naval war was for the most part a succession of contests between single vessels or small groups of vessels.' [4] The English victory at sea was won mainly by silent but unrelaxing pressure in the North Sea, and by vigilant watch in the Channel, the Mediterranean and the Eastern Atlantic.

On August 28 by a happy combination of luck and daring a

The victory at sea

---

[1] East Africa, Cmd. 1284 ; West Africa, Cmd. 1350 of 1921.
[2] *H.P.C.*, ii. 244.   [3] Address of January 8, 1918.
[4] Sims, *The Victory at Sea*, p. xii.

brilliant victory was won in the Bight of Heligoland. Three German cruisers were sunk and three others 'trooped home'. No British ship was even seriously damaged, and our loss in men was only 35 killed and 40 wounded. Over 1,000 Germans perished, and 224 were picked up and made prisoners. The engagement was on a small scale but the moral effect of the victory was admittedly considerable. Thenceforward as far as surface craft were concerned the German Admiralty maintained for the most part a defensive policy.

Jutland   The only action of the War in which great fleets were engaged was the battle of Jutland. Of the Grand Fleet under Admiral Sir John Jellicoe little had been heard during the first eighteen months of the War. During that time it was mostly at sea for the simple reason that there was no defended East Coast harbour ready for its reception. After the opening of war the defences of Rosyth, in the Firth of Forth, abandoned half-finished in a fit of penury, and those of Scapa Flow in the Orkneys, were rapidly pushed forward; before the end of the War they had been rendered virtually impregnable against German attacks. But not only were defended harbours lacking; the Germans had the superiority in guns (save for our 15-inch guns), in mines, in Zeppelins (incalculably useful for naval scouting), in submarines, and in high-explosive shells; nor were they markedly inferior in gunnery. Nevertheless, the Grand Fleet was virtually unassailed, and the German Fleet did not come out.

At last, however, it resolved to try conclusions, and on May 31, 1916, the fleets of England and Germany met in the mighty conflict which to all time will be known as the battle of Jutland. One hundred and forty-five British ships and 110 German ships were engaged. Of Dreadnoughts we had 28 against 16; of cruisers of various types, 40 against 16; of destroyers, 77 against 72; but Germany had in addition 6 pre-Dreadnought battleships. As to the result of the battle, experts are still disputing; a layman can only note the fact that the two grand Fleets never again made contact, though the German Fleet, as we now know, made bold sallies in August and October 1916, and even as late as April 1918 came out a third time. But after the Battle of Jutland the German Admiralty concentrated more and more on the U-boat campaign and used the High Seas Fleet mainly as a protection for their submarines. That function could be performed effectually only if the High Seas Fleet remained in being, even if for the most part confined to harbour. A great naval expert holds that the tactics adopted by the German Admiralty were entirely correct.[1]

One of the revelations of the War was indeed the effectiveness of the submarine. At the outbreak of war we had exactly twice as many submarines as Germany; but of our seventy-four boats only eighteen were seagoing, while Germany had twenty-eight. Moreover, our insular position, our immense merchant fleet, and our dependence on oversea troops and supplies made us fifty times as vulnerable as the enemy.

The submarine campaign

The War was not a week old when ten German U-boats made a sortie up the North Sea. They did no damage; but one of them was rammed by *Birmingham* (August 9), and a second disappeared. On September 5 a German submarine torpedoed *Pathfinder* off the Forth, the first victim of the new naval weapon. Much more serious was the loss (September 22) of three cruisers, *Aboukir, Hogue* and *Cressy*, in rapid succession by the same German submarine, off the coast of Holland. *Hogue* and *Cressy* were torpedoed, at a dead standstill, when they were lowering their boats to rescue the survivors of the *Aboukir*, an act (in Mr. Churchill's words) of ' chivalrous simplicity ', involving a total loss of over 1,400 men. On January 1 an old battleship was torpedoed in the Channel with a loss of over 600 men.

Evidently the U-boats were going to give trouble. With the new year came a fresh development. On February 4, 1915, the German Admiralty declared all the waters surrounding Great Britain and Ireland to be a war zone, and gave warning that every enemy vessel found therein would be destroyed, and that neutral vessels would be exposed to great danger. Lord Fisher had in 1913 foreseen this odious development and had warned the Admiralty. Churchill had insisted that the sinking of merchant vessels was an outrage of which ' no civilized Power would be guilty '. Yet guilty it was, and before the War ended nearly 5,000 merchant ships, belonging to the Allies and neutrals, had

---

[1] Sims, *The Victory at Sea*, p. 98.

been sunk by submarines, in addition to some 500 by mines and nearly 200 by surface craft. Among the victims of German submarine warfare were several hospital ships, with sick, wounded, and nurses aboard.

The submarine menace reached its zenith in March–April 1917, when over 1,000 British merchant ships were sunk.[1]

Taking the War period as a whole, shipbuilding rather more than kept pace with destruction. But if the rate of sinking had been maintained at the pace of the early months of 1917 the task set to the British shipbuilders must have become impossible. The facts were known in Germany, where it was calculated that the end must come in July or at latest by August 1. It was the official view of the British Admiralty that unless the submarine peril could be countered, surrender could not be postponed beyond November.

The United States Navy

Happily for the world, the submarine menace was countered by the adoption of the ' convoy ' system and the advent in rapidly increasing numbers of American destroyers.[2] The first American flotilla of six destroyers reached Queenstown on May 4, 1917 ; by July 5 thirty-four had arrived and were at the disposal of Admiral Sir Lewis Bayly, commanding at Queenstown. In all, the United States contributed to the naval forces of the Allies some 70 destroyers, 120 submarine chasers, 20 submarines and other small craft, besides mine-sweepers (13), mine-layers (9), and auxiliary craft of various descriptions. The aid they rendered to the Allied cause came at a critical moment, and its value can hardly be overestimated.

Due appreciation of the American effort must not, however, be permitted to disguise the plain fact that the victory at sea was, in the main, the superb achievement of the British Navy and the British Mercantile Marine.

Zeebrugge

When all did such magnificent service it is almost invidious to mention particular units or individual exploits ; but a French Admiral has not hesitated to describe the raid on Zeebrugge as ' the finest feat of arms in all naval history of all times and all countries '.[3] This was the work of the ' Dover Patrol ', and was

---

[1] See *supra*, p. 387.

[2] For the success of the ' convoy ' system see *Naval History of the War* (official), vol. 5, pp. 3–203.

[3] Quoted by Fletcher, op. cit., p. 125.

accomplished by a flotilla—mostly very light craft—of 142 ships, under the command of Sir Roger Keyes. The night selected for this daring exploit was St. George's Day (April 23, 1918); the object of it was to seal up the most important of the German submarine bases. In the case of Zeebrugge the object was largely attained; the attack on Ostend for the moment miscarried, but on May 10 it was renewed with considerable though not complete success. From that moment the submarine attacks rapidly decreased. Of the 182 German submarines known to have been sunk or captured in the course of the War, no fewer than 175 were the victims of British seamen.

The defeat of the submarines was, however, only a fraction of the task British seamen accomplished. To have kept inviolate (save for a few tip-and-run raids early in the War) the coasts of Great Britain; to have transported across thousands of miles of ocean millions of men from Canada, Australia, New Zealand, India, South Africa, the West Indies, and the United States; to have carried them to and from the half-dozen theatres of war; to have safeguarded the commercial routes, and to have kept Great Britain and her Allies supplied with food, with raw materials, and munitions; to have kept open the long lines of communication in the Atlantic, the Pacific, the Indian Ocean, and the Mediterranean—such was the superb achievement, largely silent and half unperceived, of the British Naval and Merchant Services. *The achievement of the British Navy*

To Britain, therefore, it was fitting that the German Navy should, after the Armistice, be surrendered. The first batch of the surrendered submarines reached Harwich on November 19; two days later the High Seas Fleet was handed over at Rosyth. On that day (November 21) Admiral Beatty signalled to the Fleet: 'The German flag will be hauled down at sunset to-day, and will not be hoisted again without permission.' [1] *German surrender*

[1] Fletcher, op. cit., p. 128.

Note to p. 413

To the statement in regard to African natives an exception should perhaps be made in favour of the Askaris in East Africa.

CHAPTER XXIV

THE PEACE CONFERENCE—THE TREATY OF VERSAILLES

GREAT BRITAIN had drawn the sword with extreme reluctance, but having drawn it she had put her whole strength into the struggle. With men, money, and ships the British Empire had made to the final victory a contribution greater than that of any other Power. It was, therefore, inevitable that the British Empire should play a large part in determining the conditions of Peace.

Nevertheless, Great Britain had less direct interest in the terms of the Treaty than any of the European belligerents. The ' greatest of British interests is Peace '. So an authoritative voice had long ago proclaimed. Peace and security for herself and the world were, consequently, the supreme objects at which at Paris in 1919, as at Vienna in 1815, she persistently aimed and with infinite patience sought to achieve.

President Wilson had, more than once, defined, before his own country came into the War, the principles on which, in his judgement, a Peace-Treaty should be based. He reiterated them in his famous ' Fourteen Points ' in January 1918. That the ' superior ' and doctrinaire tone he adopted was resented by the nations more directly and more deeply involved, it were vain to deny. But the Allies themselves had, in January 1917, explicitly stated their aims, and the terms on which they were prepared to make peace. Save in regard to the ' freedom of the seas '— a point jealously reserved by Great Britain, the demands of the Allies did not essentially differ from the points formulated by Mr. Wilson. In particular they agreed that ' permanent Peace must be founded on (1) the re-establishment of the sanctity of treaties ; (2) a territorial settlement based on the right of self-determination ; and (3) the creation of some international organization to limit the burden of armaments and diminish the probability of war '.

Before Germany applied for an armistice her allies had one The by one fallen away from her. On October 27 Austria informed Armistice the German Government that she must make a separate Peace and on November 3 she signed an Armistice. King Ferdinand of Bulgaria had made an unconditional surrender on September 29, and a few days later abdicated. On October 30 the Turks signed the Armistice of Mudros. On November 3 the German sailors mutinied at Kiel and the ' Red Flag ' was hoisted in several German towns. By the 9th the Revolution had reached Berlin. On that day the German Emperor abdicated and with the Crown Prince fled to Holland. Meanwhile the Germans had applied to Marshal Foch for an Armistice. Foch declined parley and dictated terms : they involved complete military surrender. At 5 a.m. on the 11th they were accepted. The Germans engaged to evacuate all occupied territory on all Fronts, including East Africa, within fifteen days, and to restore Alsace-Lorraine to France ; to submit to an Allied occupation of all Germany on the west bank of the Rhine and to surrender the bridgeheads of Cologne, Mainz and Coblenz on the right bank ; to give up 5,000 cannon, 25,000 machine-guns, 1,700 aeroplanes, 5,000 locomotives, 150,000 wagons and 5,000 lorries ; to surrender their High Seas Fleet to be interned within one week ; to hand over all their submarines, mine-layers, &c., within a fortnight ; and to make reparation for the damage they had wrought. Severe as the terms were they would certainly have been at least as severe had they been imposed by Germany upon a defeated enemy ; and in that case they would have been exacted to the uttermost farthing.[1]

Monday, November 11, was in London a day of grey cloud and continuous drizzle. But at 11 a.m. all thoughts of climate were dissipated ; maroons announced the conclusion of the Armistice, and, in the twinkling of an eye, streets, squares and parks were filled with cheering crowds. Inspired by sound instinct the crowds massed in front of the Palace, and at 11.15 the King, in Admiral's uniform, the Queen and the Duke of Connaught

---

[1] The text of the Armistices are printed in Temperley, *Peace Conference,* I, app. iv.

appeared on the balcony.   Led by the Band of the Irish Guards, the National Anthem and 'Rule Britannia' were sung by vast crowds, stirred to the depths with loyalty and thankfulness.

The House of Commons met at 2.45 and immediately after Prayers the Prime Minister rose and announced the conditions of the Armistice signed that morning.   Having read them he added with deep feeling : ' This is no time for words.   Our hearts are too full of a gratitude to which no tongue can give adequate expression.   I will, therefore, move " That this House do immediately adjourn . . . and that we proceed . . . to St. Margaret's, to give humble and reverent thanks for the deliverance of the world from its great peril ".'   Mr. Asquith in a few finely chosen words assented, and the members of the House of Commons forthwith proceeded with the Speaker at their head to St. Margaret's.   There they were joined by the Lords, led by the Lord Chancellor, and amid the deepening gloom of that November afternoon rendered thanks to Almighty God in a service of the greatest simplicity.   Next day the King and Queen attended a Service of Thanksgiving at St. Paul's.   The prevailing note there, and throughout the land, was one less of triumph and victory than of thankfulness that the nightmare of the War had passed, of hopes that we might have won a peace that would be permanent.

Ten days later the Parliament elected in 1910 was prorogued for the last time, and was presently dissolved.   Before the Prorogation both Houses voted an Address of Congratulation to the King.   He received it at their hands in the Royal Gallery of the House of Lords, and replied to it in a speech of deep feeling and mingled gratitude, pride and resolution.   Between the signature of the Armistice and the opening of the Peace Conference in Paris two months elapsed.   The delay was unfortunate but inevitable.

The 'Coupon' Election, December 1918   The Conference had to await the arrival from America of President Wilson, who, unwisely and with doubtful constitutional propriety, decided to attend it in person.   Mr. Lloyd George also decided to attend it, but insisted that before doing so he must receive a vote of confidence from the new electorate created by the Reform Bill of 1918.   Had Mr. Lloyd George, instead of going to Paris, announced on November 12 his resignation, and started forthwith on a tour round the Empire, his place in History would

be side by side with that of William Pitt, Lord Chatham. But
for one who occupied a pinnacle in the temple of world fame such
as no British statesman had ever before attained, such a renunciation was beyond human possibility. Not even Cincinnatus
could have made it. But the jealous gods had their revenge.

The General Election took place in December. The Government appealed to the country as a Coalition on the basis of a
manifesto signed jointly by Mr. Lloyd George and Mr. Bonar
Law. They appealed for a continuance of national unity which
had ' been the great secret of our strength in war ', and was essential to the solution of the post-War problems, not least to the
conclusion of a ' just and lasting peace '. The candidates who
accepted the programme then outlined received from the two
leaders a certificate or ' coupon '. The Labour Party had formally withdrawn its support from the Government, and a section
of the Liberal Party, led by Mr. Asquith, declined to give it.

The Election, stigmatized by a distinguished publicist [1] as ' an
orgy of Chauvinism ', resulted in an overwhelming victory for
the Coalition. The Unionists returned nearly 400 strong; 136
Liberals supported the Coalition; Labour secured some sixty
seats; but the independent or Asquithian Liberals were reduced
to a remnant of some thirty members, without a single leader of
Cabinet rank. Asquith himself, and all his principal lieutenants,
lost their seats. So also did the Socialist pacifists, including Mr.
Ramsay MacDonald and Mr. Snowden. The most sinister feature
of the election was that of the eighty Irish Nationalists returned
seventy-three were Sinn Feiners. The latter refused to attend
Parliament at Westminster: and set up a ' Republican Convention ' in Dublin. But the portent was little regarded at the
moment. The Irish were as usual ' playing their pranks '. How
serious the pranks were, Great Britain was presently to learn.

The new Parliament was indeed a ' curious assembly ', ' quite The
different ' (such was Lloyd George's impression) ' from any other Coalition
House of Commons I have known. When I was speaking I felt, ment
as I looked in front of me, that I was addressing a Trade Union
Congress. Then, when I turned round, I felt as if I were speaking
to a Chamber of Commerce.' One among other significant
changes must be noted. The Socialist Party, numerically weak

[1] Spender, *Life of Asquith.*

though it was, claimed the right, as the second largest Party in the House, to occupy the front Opposition Bench and to act as the official Opposition; in fine, they posed as the Alternative Government. With a curious lack of parliamentary sense they elected as chairman of the Party, and consequently as leader of the Opposition, not Mr. Clynes, the most experienced and distinguished member of the Party, but Mr. Adamson, a Scottish miner, who played a difficult part with native dignity if without distinction. The exclusive right of the Socialists to occupation of the Bench was disputed by the ' Wee-free Liberals ', who elected as chairman of their exiguous Party Sir Donald Maclean, who in the previous Parliament had acted as Deputy Chairman of Committees. By his geniality and courtesy Sir Donald gave to his precarious position a dignity which was certainly not inherent in it.

The New Ministry Some changes were made in the Ministry. Lord Finlay was replaced as Lord Chancellor by Lord Birkenhead (F. E. Smith); Lord Milner succeeded Mr. Long at the Colonial Office, when the latter went to the Admiralty; Sir Austen Chamberlain relieved Mr. Bonar Law (who retained the leadership of the House of Commons as Lord Privy Seal) of his duties at the Treasury; and Churchill took over the Air Ministry as well as the War Office. G. N. Barnes, a great Labour leader, retained his place in the War Cabinet, together with Lloyd George, Bonar Law, Lord Curzon, and Chamberlain. Were the Secretaries of State and other leading Ministers in the Cabinet or not? That they believed themselves to be is certain: the leader of the House declared that they were not.[1] Such is the interesting ambiguity inherent in English Constitution.

The Peace Conference With a vast majority of the electorate, with Parliament and a united Ministry behind him, Lloyd George went off, in high glee, to make peace at Paris. Meanwhile, London had given an enthusiastic welcome to two others of the ' big four ' (as they came to be called), M. Clemenceau and President Wilson. Even warmer was that given to Marshal Foch, and warmest of all the welcome that awaited Field-Marshal Sir Douglas Haig, and other com-

[1] Cf. for a curious encounter between Bonar Law and myself on this point Hansard, *Official Report* for July 31, 1919, p. 2277, and Marriott, *Mechanism of the Modern State*, vol. ii. p. 81.

manders and the first detachments of the returning army, who made a triumphal march through the streets of London.

The Peace Conference was formally opened by M. Poincaré, President of the French Republic, on January 18, 1919. It consisted, when in plenary session, of seventy members, of whom fourteen represented the British Empire; France, Italy, Japan and the United States each had five delegates, while twenty-two of the smaller Powers had one, two or three apiece. All the principal delegates had large staffs to assist them : the British delegation with its staff alone numbered over 600 persons. Of the clerical staff a considerable proportion were women. The treaty itself was signed by sixty-eight out of the seventy delegates, China alone abstaining. The defeated belligerents were not admitted to the Conference. Frenchmen remembered, if others did not, what Talleyrand had done at Vienna. As a fact, the ultimate decisions were reached by four men—the principal representatives of Great Britain, France, Italy and the United States; some of the most important by two only—Clemenceau and Lloyd George. The former was elected president of the Conference at its first sitting. The ' big four ', the men who made the Treaty, presented a curious contrast. Clemenceau—well named the ' Tiger '—had one object only : to make his beloved country secure for all time against the saecular enemy. This was to be done by strengthening France, and by crippling Germany, in a territorial, military and financial sense. Signor Orlando had, similarly, only one interest, to get for Italy all that the Allies had promised her by the Treaties of London and St. Jean de Maurienne, and as much more as he could. Lloyd George was more detached in interests ; indispensable but not wholly trusted : for the French, too pro-German ; for the Italians, too pro-Serb ; for the Serbs, too loyal to Italy ; extraordinarily agile in mind, quick in perception, but imperfectly acquainted with the historical and geographical foundations on which the Treaty must be built. Finally, there was President Wilson, the typical professorial doctrinaire, genuinely interested in world-peace, anxious to secure it by a Covenant never ratified by his countrymen, but hopelessly pedantic in adherence to formulas which he had framed in the retirement of his study, though they proved disastrously inapplicable to the world of grim realities to which he had been suddenly introduced, and in which he was never at home.   Such were the men in whose hands lay the destinies of Europe and the world.

For some months the machinery of the Conference creaked ominously.   More than once there seemed danger of a complete breakdown ; but the two chief representatives of Great Britain and France were not easily discouraged, and, with the help of President Wilson, they hammered out the terms of a treaty which by the end of April was ready for presentation to the German Delegation who arrived at Versailles on the 29th.   The details of settlement which emerged from the Conference, as of the deliberations which preceded it, belong not to English but to European, nay to World, History.   A mere outline must here suffice.

France   England's position at Paris, though immensely influential, was more detached than that of her Continental allies.   Her supreme object was so to adjust differences, and promote territorial and other arrangements, as to secure the peace of Europe.   The problem of the Franco-German frontier had been a constant source of irritation between the two peoples, and a constant menace to European peace for three centuries.   The Duke of Wellington had insisted in 1815 that Europe would never enjoy prolonged peace if France was deprived of Alsace-Lorraine.   She retained those Provinces in 1815, lost them to Germany in 1871, and recovered them in 1919.   France pressed for the Rhine frontier, and abandoned her claim only in return for a guarantee of security from Great Britain and the U.S.A., which the latter subsequently refused to implement.   France did, however, obtain a strong military guarantee in regard to the Rhine frontier, secured by temporary occupation and permanent disarmament, and the possession of the coal-field of the Saar Valley in partial reparation for the wanton destruction of her own coal-mines by the

Germany   Germans in the War.   The future of the Saar Valley itself was to be decided by plebiscite in 1935.[1]   A similar—though less tardy—procedure was adopted in regard to other relatively recent acquisitions of Germany.   In deference to their declared principles the Conference allowed Germany to retain Holstein and southern Schleswig.   In central Schleswig a plebiscite decided for Ger-

---

[1] The plebiscite in 1935 decided in favour of Germany by an overwhelming majority.

many ; in the northern zone for Denmark. Similarly plebiscites were taken in East Prussia, which voted for adhesion to Germany, and in Upper Silesia. In the latter there was a prolonged conflict and some fighting, and not until 1921 was it divided between Germany and Poland.

Poland was reconstituted with most of territories lost by her in *Poland* the Partitions of the eighteenth century, but Danzig became a Free City, with certain reservations in favour of Poland and a ' corridor ' which, while necessary to connect Poland with the sea, cut off East Prussia from the rest of Germany. This clumsy arrangement was adopted as the best solution of a problem, difficult indeed, and perhaps insoluble.

Belgium, besides a useful rectification of frontier, attained, in accord with her own ambitions, ' complete independence and full sovereignty '. Luxemburg also renounced ' neutrality ', and ceased to be a member of the German Zollverein.

On the whole Germany retained its integrity, though Prussia, the artificial product of two centuries of aggression, suffered some dismemberment. So did Russia by the loss of Finland, Lithuania, Latvia and Estonia, which were established as independent States. Beyond the limits of Europe Germany abandoned Kiaochow (to Japan), and the rest of her oversea Possessions, the disposition of which has been already described. Germany was further compelled to hand over her navy (which was sunk by the crews in Scapa Flow), to limit her army to 100,000 men, to destroy her existing armaments, and limit the production of munitions for the future.

Of all the difficult points which the Allies had to settle perhaps *Repara-* the most difficult was that of reparations. Every one agreed that *tions* Germany must pay for all the ' damage ' she had done : but there was no agreement as to the connotation of the word ' damage '. Clemenceau, with bitter memories of 1870, would have bled Germany white, as she had attempted to bleed France. Lloyd George had promised the British electorate that Germany should be made to pay to the uttermost farthing ; but *how* she could pay without injuring her creditors was a question he found it increasingly difficult to answer. Wilson was uninterested in the question of indemnities and reparations, though not in that (not directly raised at Paris) of inter-Allied indebtedness. Finally, it was agreed to refer the question of total reparations to a Special Commission, which was to present the final account to Germany before May 1, 1921. In the meantime Germany was to restore the trophies, &c., carried off in 1870–1 as well as in 1914–18 : to deliver annually to France and Belgium large quantities of coal, and to pay on account before May 1, 1921, a sum of £1,000,000,000.

These terms were imposed upon, not negotiated with, Germany. The German delegates were summoned to Versailles to hear their sentence, not to discuss it. It was delivered by M. Clemenceau on May 7. Between that date and June 23 notes were exchanged between the German Government and the Allies : a few unsubstantial modifications were consequently made in the Treaty, but on June 22 the Germans were informed that if, within twenty-four hours, the Treaty was not signed, Marshal Foch would advance at the head of the Allied Forces farther into Germany. On the 23rd the Germans, under protest, gave way and agreed to sign.

The Treaty of Versailles

The actual signature took place on the 28th. The place selected for the brief but impressive ceremony was the Galerie des Glaces in the Palace of Versailles, where William of Hohenzollern had in January 1871 been proclaimed first German Emperor. The selection was sinister, but not inappropriate. The humiliation of France was at long last avenged : the German Empire which by ' blood and iron ' Bismarck had made, had again drawn the sword ; by the sword it perished.

Treaties complementary to the Treaty signed at Versailles were subsequently concluded with Austria at Saint-Germain-en-Laye (September 10, 1919), with Bulgaria (Neuilly, November 27), with Hungary (Trianon, June 4, 1920), and with Turkey at Sèvres (August 10, 1920).

The Hapsburg Empire

Of the three Empires affected by this wholesale reconstruction that of the Hapsburgs suffered most severely.[1] Their conglomerate Empire was dissolved into its constituent elements. Austria proper was left in a pitiable plight. Reduced by the creation of Czecho-Slovakia, by territorial concessions to Poland, to Italy, to Roumania, and Jugo-Slavia, and by separation from Hungary, to a State with only 6,000,000 people, she was cut off from territorial access to the sea, and denied the possibility of union with Germany.

[1] See note, p. 437.

The first of the new States to arise on the ruins of Austria- Czecho-
Hungary was Czecho-Slovakia, consisting of the historic kingdom Slovakia
of Bohemia, together with Moravia and Ruthenian territory to
the south of the Carpathians, with an aggregate population of
about fourteen millions. Czecho-Slovakia proclaimed its independence before the Armistice was actually signed, and on November 15, 1918, elected Dr. Masaryk, a great student and a great
patriot, as its President. Hungary proclaimed itself a Republic Hungary
on November 17, but in 1920, by a unanimous vote of the National
Assembly, reconstituted the Kingdom. But it has (up till 1945)
remained a Kingdom without a King. Moreover, since the readjustment of frontiers under the Peace treaties it represents only
a shrunken fragment of the historic kingdom. In the north a large
district has been ceded to Czecho-Slovakia, another in the south to
Jugo-Slavia, and a third in the east to Roumania. Jugo-Slavia, Jugo-
representing the union of the southern Slav peoples, includes, in Slavia
addition to Serbia and Montenegro, Bosnia, the Herzegovina,
Croatia-Slavonia, parts of Styria, Carinthia, Carniola, and practically the whole of Dalmatia. The War had forced upon Rou- Roumania a difficult, indeed, a perilous choice. At the Peace she mania
reaped the reward of her wisdom and courage. The area of the
State was doubled by the acquisition of Bessarabia from Russia,
and Transylvania, a large part of the Bukovina and half the
Banat of Temesvar from Austria-Hungary. In population she
stands, with 16,000,000 inhabitants, first among the Balkan States.
But with a large Magyar and German minority in Transylvania
she is faced with a problem as obstinate as that which baffled
the Hapsburgs.

Bulgaria had to pay the penalty of its adherence to the Bulgaria
Central Empires. Strumnitza and eastern (inland) Macedonia
was assigned to Jugo-Slavia; coastal Macedonia and Thrace to
Greece.

The Peace Treaty with Turkey was concluded at Sèvres, but The
not until 1920 : nor was it ever ratified by the Sultan. Under Ottoman
its terms Constantinople, with a minimum of circumjacent terri- Empire
tory, was to be left in the hands of the Sultan, while the control
of the Straits was confided to the League of Nations. Syria was
assigned, under Mandate, to France, Palestine and Mesopotamia
to Great Britain.

Greece   Greece, thanks to the powerful advocacy of Venizelos, was to
be enlarged by additions in Macedonia and Thrace, together
with Smyrna, a large strip of Asia Minor and the Dodecanese
islands—except Rhodes, which remained in possession of Italy.

The   The Allies, and England in particular, had yet to gather the
Turkish
National-   bitter fruits of procrastination. The occupation of Smyrna by
ists   the Greeks (May 1919), supported by the warships of Great Britain,
France and the United States, aroused bitter resentment among
the Turkish ' Nationalists '—a party which was rapidly estab-
lishing its supremacy, under the vigorous leadership of Mustapha
Kemal, a brilliant soldier who had made a great popular reputa-
tion in the defence of Gallipoli. Between 1919 and 1922 Kemal
roused the Turks in the Anatolian highlands, and established at
Angora a rival Government to that of Constantinople. The
Angora Government refused to accept the terms of the Treaty of
Sèvres, despite the fact that the Greeks had, in the summer of
1920, inflicted a severe defeat on the Nationalist Turks, occupied
Brusa—the ancient capital of the Ottomans (July 8), made good
their position in Thrace, and entered Adrianople.

Then the tide of fortune turned. The Greeks, instead of finding themselves in Constantinople, suffered a disastrous defeat in
Asia Minor at the hands of the Kemalists who refused to concede
an armistice, swept the Greeks before them into the sea, and
occupied Smyrna which they delivered over to fire and sword.
Greeks from all parts of Asia Minor fled panic-stricken before the
Turks ; about 1,000,000 of them were fortunate enough to escape
on Allied and Greek ships.

Meanwhile, a serious international crisis had developed. The
Kemalist Turks, flushed with their bloody victory over the hereditary foe, advanced on the Dardanelles, entered the neutral zone
and actually came within fighting distance of the British garrison
which, from Chanak, held the southern shore of the Dardanelles.
France withdrew her troops ; the Italians, who hated the Greeks,
intimated that in the event of the renewal of war, no help was
to be expected from them; Great Britain faced the Kemalists alone.

Chanak   The situation was critical. The British Government hurriedly
dispatched ships and men to the Dardanelles ; applied for help
to the Dominions ; and told the Kemalists that they would not
be permitted to cross into Europe. In response to the appeal of

the British Government New Zealand promptly promised help ;
Australia promised rather less readily ; Canada asked for further
information ; a reply from South Africa was delayed by the
absence of General Smuts.

Fortunately war was, though narrowly, averted mainly by the
admirable firmness and not less admirable patience and tact of
Sir Charles Harington, the Allied Commander-in-Chief at Con-
stantinople.   On October 11 an armistice was signed between the
Greeks and the Kemalists, and on November 20 another Peace
Conference opened at Lausanne.

If the Turk has generally managed to evade the consequences
of defeat, it was unlikely that he would now forego the fruits of a
victory as dramatic as it was complete.   And at Lausanne he
held all the cards.   He could count on the traditional hatred of
Italy for Greece, and turn to his own advantage the growing tension between England and France.   What wonder, then, that the
tone he adopted at Lausanne was lofty to the verge of insolence.
Thanks, however, to the skill and patience of Lord Curzon of
Kedleston who, as Foreign Minister, represented Great Britain,
Peace was at last signed on July 24, and a month later was ratified
by the Assembly at Angora.

The Treaty of Lausanne

The Greeks had to pay the penalty for over-vaulting political
ambition and a disastrous military defeat.   Greece lost to Turkey
Eastern Thrace with Adrianople and the islands of Imbros and
Tenedos, but retained the rest of the Turkish islands in the
Aegean, and Western Thrace up to the Maritza.   Turkey gave
up all claims upon Egypt, the Sudan, Cyprus, Syria, Palestine,
Mesopotamia, and Arabia, but retained in full sovereignty Smyrna
and the remainder of the Anatolian peninsula.

Egypt had been declared to be a British Protectorate in 1914 ;
Cyprus had been annexed by Great Britain, who also accepted
Mandates for Palestine and Mesopotamia.   Syria was assigned,
also under Mandate, to France.

Two questions remained : the position of foreigners in Turkey,
and the control of the Straits.   On both, concession was made to
Turkish susceptibilities.   The ' Capitulations ', which, ever since
the sixteenth century, had afforded protection to foreigners in
Turkey, were abolished.   As regards the Straits, Turkey was, in
default of any alternative tenant, permitted to remain at Con-

stantinople, and to retain a garrison in the city, under stringent guarantee ; but the Straits were to be neutralized ; a free passage for foreign aircraft and ships, warships and merchantmen alike, was to be guaranteed to all the States of the world, and on both coasts demilitarized zones were to be created under the guarantee of the League of Nations.

The Turkish Republic The Treaty of Lausanne represented a conspicuous triumph for the Ottoman Turks ; but it was not enjoyed by the Ottoman Empire. On November 1, 1922 the Grand National Assembly at Angora issued an edict that the office of Sultan had ceased to exist, and on the 17th, Mohammed VI, the last of the Ottoman Sultans, left Constantinople on board a British warship. Thus fell the last of the Central Empires which had formed the Quadruple Alliance. In March 1924 the Caliphate itself was abolished by the Grand National Assembly, and the Caliph and his family went into exile. Meanwhile, Turkey had been proclaimed a Republic with Mustapha Kemal Pasha as its first President, and Angora as its capital (October 1923).

Egypt Events in Turkey could not fail to react powerfully upon Egypt, once the Sultan's greatest Dependency. The war had evoked discontent among all classes. Upon the fellaheen, redeemed from bondage by Lord Cromer, it reimposed cruel conditions. Middlemen grew fat on war profits while the fellaheen were conscripted for labour battalions, but the profiteers were as discontented as the conscripts. Among the intelligentsia in Egypt, as elsewhere, nationalist aspirations were aroused. Especially did the Egyptians resent the fact that while the principle of ' self-determination ' was applied to Mesopotamia and Arabia, it was not extended to a more advanced people like themselves. Hence the insurrection of 1919. This was easily suppressed, but it was followed by the despatch to Egypt of a mission of enquiry, headed by Lord Milner. The mission was boycotted. Lord Milner, however, subsequently reached an agreement with Zaghlul Pasha, the leader of the Egyptian nationalists, and in February, 1922, the British Government declared the Protectorate to be at an end and Egypt to be an ' independent Sovereign State.' On March 15, 1922, the Sultan assumed the title of His Majesty King Fuad and proclaimed Egypt a monarchy.

Independence was, however, qualified by certain important

reservations which the nationalists have from the first, and not illogically, declared to be incompatible with 'Sovereignty'. The Declaration reserved four matters absolutely to the discretion of the British Government : (i) The security of the communications of the British Empire in Egypt. (ii) The defence of Egypt against all foreign aggression or interference, direct or indirect. (iii) The protection of foreign interests in Egypt and the protection of minorities. (iv) The status of the Soudan. Pending the conclusion of agreements on these points the *status quo* was to remain intact.

Agreement has never been reached. Great Britain remains in military occupation of Egypt. Despite many tragic events, despite an infinite amount of haggling, despite alternations of ministries in England and consequent changes in administrative policy, the *status quo* is still maintained. Great Britain has abandoned her Protectorate over Egypt, but her troops and Civil Servants are still there.[1]

To return to Paris. Under the terms of the Armistice con- *Italy and* cluded between Italy and Austria, the latter agreed to evacuate *the Peace* not only all Italian territory, but also all the districts assigned to Italy by the Treaty of London. Thus Italy came into immediate possession of (and permanently retained) the Southern Tyrol, including Bozen and Trent, Gorizia, Trieste, and Istria, together with Zara and Lussin and other islands in the Adriatic. But at the Peace Conference she also claimed Fiume. Fiume was one of the chief stumbling-blocks at the Conference, and almost broke it up. On that point the new triune kingdom of Jugo-Slavia was as immovable as Italy.

Not until 1924 was that difficult question finally settled by Signor Mussolini. Under the Pact of Rome, Fiume itself was, with a coastal corridor, assigned to Italy, but the adjacent territory was partitioned between Italy and Jugo-Slavia. Meanwhile, by the Treaty of Rapallo (1920) Zara and its adjacent communes was, together with the islands of Cherso, Lussin, Lagosta and Pelagoni, given to Italy ; Dalmatia, with Lissa and the rest of the islands, to Jugo-Slavia.

Italy was far from satisfied with the position in which it was left at the close of the War. She was greatly angered by the assignment of Smyrna (promised to her by the Treaty of St. Jean

[1] See note, p. 437.

de Maurienne) to Greece, and by her failure to acquire colonies. She would, however, have been in a much worse position but for the stout opposition offered by Lloyd George and Clemenceau to President Wilson.

Thus was at last completed the difficult and tedious work of reconstructing the map of Europe. Many problems, predominantly financial, still awaited solution, but the main work to which in 1919 the diplomatists had set their hands at Paris was finished.

The League of Nations
The whole of the cement for the vast edifice they had erected was provided by the Covenant of the League of Nations, the text of which was prefixed to all the principal treaties concluded between the Allied and Associated Powers and their late enemies.

The Covenant of the League
That Covenant, having proclaimed that the purpose of the High Contracting Parties was ' to promote international co-operation, and to achieve international peace and security by the acceptance of obligations not to resort to war ', proceeded to lay down rules as to the membership, the government, and the procedure of the League. Membership was to be open to any fully self-governing State, Dominion, or Colony, which was prepared to give effective guarantees for adherence to the principles and observance of the rules of the League, provided two-thirds of the Assembly agreed to its admission. The government of the League was to be vested in an Assembly and a Council, and the administration of its affairs provided for by the establishment of a permanent Secretariat.

The primary function of the League was to maintain peace among its own members ; its second, to maintain it in the world at large. This purpose it hoped to achieve by a limitation of armaments, a mutual guarantee of territorial integrity and independence, a mutual Agreement not to resort to arms until an attempt to settle a dispute by peaceful means had been made, by the provision of machinery for facilitating such peaceful settlement, of sanctions for the breach of the Agreement mentioned above, and for settling disputes in which States, non-members of the League, might be concerned. No member of the League might make war upon another member without submitting the dispute either to arbitration or to the Council, or without waiting for three months after the award, or in defiance of the award, provided all the members of the Council, not parties to the dispute, assented to it. Should any State break this essential article of the Covenant all the other members were pledged to break off all relations, including trade and financial relations, with the offending State, and resort, if necessary, to armed force. How precisely that force was to be supplied remained one of the problems to be solved.

All treaties were henceforward to be (1) public; (2) liable to reconsideration at the instance of the Assembly; and (3) consonant with the terms of the Covenant. The members of the League further pledged themselves to secure, both in their own countries and in all countries with whom they have dealings, ' fair and humane conditions of labour for men, women, and children ', and also just treatment of the native inhabitants of territories under their control; to entrust the League with the supervision over the execution of Agreements in regard to the traffic in women and children, in opium and other dangerous drugs, and in arms and ammunition; and, finally, to take steps in the matter of international hygiene, to maintain equitable treatment for the commerce of all members, and to secure freedom of communications and transit.

The most important work accomplished by the League was the creation of a Permanent Court of International Justice. The Court is composed of eleven judges and four deputy-judges holding office for nine years, and sits annually at The Hague. The Assembly has also set up various technical organizations to deal with Economics and Finance, with Transit and International Hygiene, besides several Advisory Commissions of which the most important (except the Mandates Commission) is that for the reduction of armaments.[1]

To the Mandates assigned by the League in respect of the ex-German colonies in Africa and the Pacific islands reference has been already made.

The Turkish vilayets of Palestine, Mesopotamia and Syria were, evidently, in a very different position from the colonies

---

[1] For an account of the work done since 1919 by the League of Nations, cf. T. P. Conwell-Evans, *The League Council in Action*, Oxford, 1929; Viscount Cecil, *A Great Experiment* (1941); and Marriott, *Federalism and the Problem of the Small State* (1942).

(*See also folding map at end.*)

CENTRAL AND SOUTH-EASTERN EUROPE, 1921.

taken from Germany in Africa. They were communities which (in the words of the *Covenant*) had ' reached a stage of development where their existence as independent nations can be provisionally recognized, subject to the rendering of administrative advice and assistance by a Mandatory until such time as they are able to stand alone '.

Moreover, a few days after the conclusion of the armistice with Turkey the British and French Governments had issued a joint declaration stating their aim to be : ' the complete and final enfranchisement of the peoples so long oppressed by the Turks, and the establishment of national governments and administrations drawing their authority from the initiative and free choice of native populations '. The Mandates were accordingly issued in a form (' A ') in accordance with these principles.

Conquered by British forces during the War, Palestine re- Palestine mained in their occupation until July 1, 1920 ; as from that date the country passed under the rule of a British High Commissioner, Sir Herbert Samuel. Under the Treaty of Sèvres, Turkey renounced all rights and title over the country in favour of the Principal Allied Powers, who conferred the Mandate upon Great Britain. In accordance with Mr. Balfour's declaration of November 2, 1917, Great Britain undertook to place the country under such conditions, political, administrative, and economic, as would secure the establishment of ' a national home for the Jewish people ', develop self-governing institutions, and safeguard the civil and religious rights of all the inhabitants of Palestine, irrespective of race and religion. English, Arabic, and Hebrew were to be the official languages of Palestine, and the most stringent precautions were taken for securing freedom of conscience and equality of commercial privileges.[1]

In Mesopotamia or Iraq the situation was complicated by the Iraq delays interposed by the events in the Near East already related. In May 1920 the British Government announced their acceptance of a Mandate from the League of Nations over Iraq. In October Sir Percy Cox reached Basra as High Commissioner, and a Provisional Council of State was appointed. In 1921 the Emir Faisal, son of Hussein, the ex-King of the Hedjaz, was elected King of Iraq, and an Arab Administration was set up. In 1924 a Con-

[1] Cmd. 1500 (1921).

stituent Assembly drafted a Constitution. This provided for a Limited Monarchy, a Legislature of two Houses—a Senate of twenty nominated members and a Lower House of eighty-eight elected deputies, with an Executive responsible to the Legislature. With the State thus newly constituted the British Government concluded a Treaty, which was to remain in force only until Iraq was admitted as an independent Sovereign State to membership of the League of Nations. To secure that admission the British Government undertook to use its good offices. The treaty embodied the obligations of the Covenant and was ratified by the Council of the League. The path of the Mandatory Power was not a smooth one. The Turks made trouble on the north-eastern frontier and it was not until 1926 that by a Treaty concluded at Angora the Turks agreed to the inclusion of vilayet of Mosul in Iraq, subject to a share in the royalties on Mosul oil.[1] There were troubles also on the Arabian frontier, and difficulties not a few to be encountered in Iraq itself. Gradually, however, under the strong and patient administration of Sir Percy Cox, High Commissioner (1920–3), and Sir Henry Dobbs (High Commissioner and Consul-General 1923–9), order was evolved out of chaos. An Iraqui Civil Service was organized, an efficient police force set up ; communications by rail, road and air were improved ; the natural resources of the country developed, and schools and hospitals provided. The work done by British officials in Iraq is not indeed unworthy of comparison with that accomplished, under Lord Cromer, in Egypt. The work was consummated when in 1932 the Mandate was determined, and Iraq admitted as an independent State to membership in the League of Nations. The new State was, however, required as a condition of the withdrawal of the Mandate to enter into certain guarantees for the protection of foreigners and minorities, and the like.[2]

Mandates Commission

The Mandatory was required, whatever the form of the Mandate, to make an annual report to the Council of the League of Nations, which exercised supervision over all the Mandatories by means of a Permanent Mandates Commission. This Commission

---

[1] Text of Treaty in Cmd. 2672 of 1926 ; and see note, p. 437.

[2] Cf. League of Nations Publications, A. 17, 1932, vii. The important question of the Nestorian Community, still unsolved, had not yet arisen.

consisted of ten members representing the three Mandatory and seven Non-Mandatory States. Its functions were, therefore, of a peculiarly delicate character, though they are purely advisory, and the Commission can rely on no sanction save the force of international public opinion.[1]

They were not more delicate than those of the League from which it derived its authority. And that authority was never itself unchallenged. It offered an easy target for the arrows of the cynic and the pessimist. But the critic may be invited to formulate his alternative. Is there, indeed, any alternative, save that the nations should be crushed under the burden of armaments, and that when the burden can no longer be endured, civilization itself should perish irrecoverably under a series of devastating wars ?

[1] For the Mandate System, cf. Lord Lugard, ap. *Edinburgh Review*, vol. 238, pp. 398–408, and the same writer, ap. *Encycl. Brit.*, new vols. ii.

Notes.

To p. 426. The Peace Conference and Treaties did not partition the ex-Hapsburg Empire. That had been already done by the Component States themselves before the Peace Conference met. The Treaties merely confirmed the *fait accompli* and defined the frontiers of the ' Succession States.' Cf. Marriott, *The Tragedy of Europe* (1941), pp. 17–18.

To p. 431. For the sequel cf. Marriott, *History of Europe, 1815–1937*, p. 600.

To p. 436. For the unwitting impulse given to the Anglo-Turkish accord by Mussolini in connection with the Mosul affair, cf. Temperley, *Whispering Gallery of Europe*, pp. 32–33.

CHAPTER XXV

THE AFTERMATH OF WAR

The
Peace
Treaty

THE day after the Treaty was signed Mr. Lloyd George returned from Paris ' much aged ', ' tired and worn ',[1] but triumphant. The King and Cabinet met him at Victoria, where a great popular reception awaited him. He had brought a Treaty with him. Had he brought Peace and Honour ? England's honour, at least, was untainted ; whether Europe had secured the Peace she sorely needed only the future could tell.

The Treaty was of immense dimensions. The Treaty of Vienna contained 121 articles, and was signed by 17 plenipotentiaries ; the Treaty of Versailles contains no fewer than 441, and bore 70 signatures. During the twenty years that elapsed after it was concluded the Treaty was a target for violent criticism. But every great settlement made by English statesmen has been similarly assailed. The authors of the Treaty of Utrecht (1713) were impeached. The Treaty of Paris (1763) was even more advantageous to this country than the Treaty of Utrecht. But its authors were not spared, and the Treaty itself, like its predecessor, was, in Lecky's words, ' forced through Parliament amid a storm of unpopularity, and by corruption and intimidation of the worst kind '.[2] In neither of these cases did the terms of Peace adequately compensate for the sacrifices made by Great Britain in the war. Even more emphatically was that true of the Treaty of Versailles. But can it ever be otherwise ? To avert defeat is indeed worth any sacrifice : but victory may well be too dearly bought. If the Great War succeeded in ending war, no sorrowing mother or wife would have grudged the sacrifice she had been compelled to make. The hope of such a consummation was not, until the peace was actually broken, abandoned.

[1] This is Lord Riddell's description.   [2] *Hist. Eng.*, iii. 44.

But many illusions were in the meantime dissipated, and the greatest of all was destined to be shattered.

For this the negotiators of the peace cannot wholly escape responsibility. In particular it rests on Mr. Wilson. He brought with him to Paris not, perhaps, too exalted an ideal, but certainly too rigid formulas, and too many embarrassing aphorisms. The world was to be made safe for Democracy; minorities must be protected ; territorial readjustments must conform to the principle of self-determination, and so on. The principles were unassailable : the difficulty lay in applying them. Democracy proved singularly inept in availing itself of the safety offered to it by the War ; to appease the grievances of one minority proved to be almost impossible without imposing a wrong upon another ; while, as for ' self-determination ', the whole difficulty lay in selecting the unit. Was Poland the appropriate unit or Silesia ? Ireland or Ulster, Jugo-Slavia or Croatia ? *President Wilson and his Formulas*

It followed that the Peace Treaties left all the belligerents in various degrees dissatisfied. Great Britain least, because she had expected least. France had made heroic sacrifices to obtain security. As a guarantee of security Foch wanted the Rhine frontier : it was denied to him. Failing that, Germany must be permanently disarmed : she has never disarmed, and was believed to be re-arming. The German delegates left Versailles under the impression, possibly mistaken but certainly sincere, that Germany's disarmament was only to be the prelude to general disarmament. Alone among the Great Powers Great Britain showed practical zeal for disarmament.

The financial liability of Germany was ultimately (1921) fixed by the Reparation Commission at £6,600,000,000, to be paid in quarterly instalments at the rate of £150,000,000 a year, partly in cash, partly in kind. It was a fantastic sum.

Yet Germany made a beginning in payments. A considerable amount of coal was, under this award, sent to France and Belgium, but of payments in cash the creditors have received little. The mark gave way. By the end of 1921 the mark had fallen to 1020 to the pound sterling. In 1922 Germany was declared by the Reparation Commission to be in default. In January 1923 the French army occupied the great industrial district known as the Ruhr. By that time the mark had fallen to 80,000 *Problem of Reparations* to the £ ; on September 30, 1923, it stood at nineteen billions. In that month the German Government called off the passive resistance it had, since January, maintained in the Ruhr. Passive resistance had, according to a German estimate, cost the German Government a sum which would have sufficed to pay reparations down to 1928.[1] Thus M. Poincaré's policy had given German finance the final blow. A fresh committee of experts was then appointed, under the chairmanship of an American, General Dawes. The Dawes Committee recommended greatly reduced payments to begin in 1926–7, and until 1929 these were made, but virtually entirely out of loans advanced by their creditors. When the creditors refused to make further loans the ' Dawes ' plan collapsed, and in January 1930 was superseded by the ' Young plan ', which in turn collapsed, until in July 1932 under the Lausanne Agreement, Germany was relieved of all liability subject to a final capital payment of £150,000,000. The inter-Allied obligations still, however, remained. The complete failure to ' make Germany pay for the War ' was only one of many disillusionments following on the Peace.

Unrest in England   It had been fondly hoped that the comradeship arising from community of service in war would be maintained and strengthened between men and women of all classes in peace. This hope also was destined to disappointment. Even in war-time the comradeship of the trenches had not extended to mines and factories. Peace brought no alleviation of the bad spirit between employés and employed.

If England was restless, Ireland was rebellious ; India was uneasily expectant ; and even the Dominions gave evidence of a temper which, though loyal to the Imperial Crown, was impatient of any interference on the part of the Imperial Parliament, or even the Imperial Executive.

Plainly, the situation confronting the Coalition Ministry and the ' Coupon ' Parliament was not easy, and demanded from the drivers of the State Coach exceptional alertness of mind and steadiness of hand. From men so fagged out as Lloyd George and Bonar Law, as Lord Milner and Lord Curzon, it was unreasonable to look for these qualities. Balfour had seemingly renewed his youth ; but the Foreign Office in 1919 was beset with problems

[1] Maximilian Harden, ap. *These Eventful Years*, II. 57.

even more difficult than was the Irish Office in 1887. The task
that awaited Sir Austen Chamberlain at the Treasury might have
baffled a Gladstone or a Peel ; but it is safe to say that neither of
those great financiers would have permitted the war-time extravagance to continue unchecked : Whitehall and St. James's Park
would have been much more rapidly cleared of swollen staffs and
superfluous offices ; there would have been less expenditure of
time, money and ink on schemes of ' reconstruction ', never destined to emerge from pigeon-holes ; and more encouragement for
those members of Parliament who worked hard but vainly to
restrict expenditure, believing such restriction to be the most
hopeful contribution they could make to national recovery.

Old-fashioned economists, the men of affairs no less than the *Industry*
theorists, were laughed out of court. The War had indeed belied *and*
every anticipation and falsified every prophecy. On the out- *in war-*
break of war it had been apprehended that there would be general *time*
distress and much unemployment. On August 4, 1914, a committee was appointed to deal with the prevention and relief of
distress. Almost simultaneously a National Relief Fund, to
which the Prince of Wales lent his name, was inaugurated, and
rapidly attained very large proportions. Relief committees were
set up in more than three hundred localities : counties, boroughs,
and urban districts. Local authorities were urged to initiate or
accelerate improvement schemes, and so provide employment.
Representatives of the Development Commission, of the Light
Railways Commission, and the Road Board were called into consultation by the Committee. In a word, every preparation which
experience or foresight could suggest was made for dealing with
distress which might be expected to arise from the collapse of
credit and the dislocation of industry.

And wisely. For in the first days of war it seemed probable
that the War would administer a very severe shock both to credit
and industry. A financial crisis was, as we have seen, happily
averted, and during the autumn of 1914 there was an almost
complete cessation of trade disputes. Organized labour showed
itself as apprehensive of an industrial débâcle as did the employers
and the Government. During the autumn the rate of unemployment was in fact abnormally high, but after January 1915
the abnormality was in the other direction, and after twelve

months of war the percentage of unemployment sank to the lowest point ever recorded. The rapid rise in prices (already indicated) inflicted much suffering on aged persons living on small fixed incomes, and on others whose remuneration did not keep pace with mounting prices. But these classes were relatively small.

Unfortunately, all the prosperity-sharers in all classes, employers and employed alike, assumed that the piping-times of war would be indefinitely prolonged, that Peace would bring in her train even more than the proverbial prosperity. As a fact, the economic momentum of the War lasted for about two years after the Armistice. Towards the end of 1920 there were ominous signs that Peace and prosperity were not invariably associated. The number of paupers, which in 1919 had fallen to the nadir point (about 500,000 for England and Wales) rose in 1921 to about 1,400,000. Unemployment figures also steadily rose during the same period. But to these matters more detailed reference must be made presently.

The Machinery of Government
The War involved dislocation in constitutional no less than industrial machinery. *Inter arma silent leges*. Both Houses of Parliament were denuded of many of their members, and the death-roll among them was heavy. Those who did not fight were increasingly employed in administrative offices. The energies of Parliament were rightly concentrated on the War, but the Legislature had still to sustain the Executive, and, as we have seen, it brought about a change of Government in May 1915, and in December 1916 acquiesced in another change even more drastic. The Cabinet system was virtually superseded from the latter date and was not restored until the autumn of 1919.

The Cabinet System
During the War, and especially in its later stages, the Prime Minister assumed, almost inevitably, Presidential if not Dictatorial functions, a development intensified by the creation of a Cabinet Secretariat.

In its origin the Cabinet Secretariat was a development of the Committee of Imperial Defence, an organization which was initiated to co-ordinate the work of the Army and the Navy, and to envisage as a whole the problem of defence not merely for the United Kingdom but for the Empire. First set up in 1895 the Committee of Imperial Defence, after ten years of a somewhat nebulous existence, was in 1904, on the initiative of Mr. Balfour,

' reorganized with a small Secretariat and a modest staff '.[1]
Even before the War the old Cabinet system was evidently breaking down under the increasing weight of numbers, the increasing
volume of business, and the entire lack of business methods.
There was no agenda, there were no regular minutes, the only
record of business transacted was contained in the letter written
after each meeting by the Prime Minister to the Sovereign ; none
of his colleagues ever saw this letter and it was contrary to convention for individual members even to make a note of decisions.
Ministers were, indeed, often left in doubt as to whether any
decision had been taken, and if so what it was.[2]

All this was changed, and changed as a result of the War.
There is a permanent Secretariat, and the Secretary is present at
all meetings of the Cabinet.   Before each meeting a paper containing the agenda is prepared under the instructions of the Prime
Minister, and is circulated with all relevant papers and memoranda
to all Cabinet Ministers.   All decisions are recorded by the Secretary with a précis of the considerations which led to them, but
without (as a rule) any record of the views of individuals.   These
minutes are circulated to Ministers, and on them are based the
instructions given by Ministers to their several Departments.[3]

The Secretariat

Another change of some significance was effected by the *Re-
election of Ministers Acts* of 1919 and 1926.   Under a statute of
1707 Ministers accepting certain offices vacated their seats in the
House of Commons, but it left them eligible for re-election, and
re-elected they generally (though not invariably) were.   The Act
of 1919 exempted from the necessity of re-election Ministers
accepting those offices within nine months of the summoning of
a new Parliament.   The Act of 1926 abolished the necessity of
re-election altogether, provided that the office was not one involving disqualification from membership of the House of Commons.
The old system had obvious inconveniences : it imposed additional expense on Ministers ; it restricted the choice of the Prime
Minister to members with ' safe ' seats, and it sometimes involved

Re-election of Ministers

---

[1] In 1904–5 the estimate for the Cabinet Secretariat was £2,960.
[2] Cf. Lord Lansdowne in House of Lords (*Report*, June 20, 1918) and
Lord Curzon (*Report*, June 19, 1919).
[3] The orderly development and working of the new system was mainly
due to a civil servant of remarkable ability, tact and discretion—Lieut.-Col.
Sir Maurice (now Lord) Hankey, G.C.B.

the exclusion of important Ministers from Parliament for a considerable period. Mr. Goschen, for instance, though appointed Chancellor of the Exchequer in December 1886, did not secure a seat in Parliament until February 1887. On the other hand, the repeal of the old statute has rendered the Executive still more independent of the electorate, if not of the Legislature, and has contributed to the increasing autocracy of Ministers—a development regarded with suspicion by constitutionalists of the old school.

En-croaching Bureau-cracy

The Executive has also gained power at the expense of the Legislature, and has encroached upon the liberty of the subject in other ways, notably by the change in the form of legislation, by the immense increase in the functions of Government, by the multiplication of Administrative Departments, and by the increase in the number of officials, armed, in many cases, with extensive powers not merely executive but even judicial.[1] Many modern statutes are mere *cadres*, giving no adequate indication of their ultimate scope. They lay down general principles, and leave it to the Executive to give substance to the legislative skeleton, by the issue of Statutory Rules and Orders. This is, in effect, to transfer the legislative function to the Bureaucracy, who under powers conferred upon them by Parliament not infrequently perform, like the absolute monarchs of olden time, the threefold function of legislator, executor and judge. How far Parliament has gone towards the abdication of its primary function may be judged from the fact that the legislative output of Parliament is to-day little more than half what it was in mid-Victorian days, when it sat for half as long. The average number of Public General Acts passed in the decade 1866–75 was 112 : in the decade 1920–9 it was 58.[2] The statutes in the earlier period were far more detailed than in the latter, and not less technical and comprehensive.

Elector-ate and Legisla-ture

To the successive changes in the composition of the electorate reference has already been made. Those changes are naturally reflected in the composition of the Legislature. ' As the polypus

---

[1] On this important subject to which only brief reference can be made in the text cf. Lord Hewart, *The New Despotism* (1929) ; Marriott, *The Crisis of English Liberty* (Oxford, 1930) ; G. E. Robinson, *Public Authorities and Legal Liabilities* (1925) ; F. J. Port, *Administrative Law*, 1929 ; C. J. Allen, *Bureaucracy Triumphant* (1931).

[2] Allen, op. cit., pp. 145–6.

takes its colour from the rock to which it affixes itself, so do the members of this House take their character from their constituencies. If you lower the character of the constituencies, you lower that of the representatives.' Mr. Robert Lowe's observation is certainly not less true to-day than it was in 1866. The House of Lords has nearly doubled in size since the accession of Queen Victoria, and is far more representative of varied interests and classes than it was even at her death. In 1837 it consisted almost wholly of landowners ; to-day it is not exclusively representative of wealth. Even more conspicuous is the transformation in the texture of the Lower House. A large minority of the House of Commons is now drawn from the wage-earning class ; the landowning class is not entirely unrepresented, but the majority of members belong to the middle classes, lawyers, journalists, business men and so forth. All members have since 1911 received a salary of £400 a year, and also (since 1931) travelling allowances between their constituencies and Westminster. Many of the Labour members also receive considerable salaries as Trade Union officials.

Has Parliament lost in power as well as in prestige ? The question is often asked, but cannot be conclusively answered. That it is no longer the ' best club in Europe ' is evident ; that it has delegated much of its legislative work to subordinate bodies has been already shown ; nor can it be questioned that it is far more subservient than formerly both to outside Party organizations and to the Executive. But it still possesses, and could if it so willed exercise, the power of the purse, and, subject to an appeal to the electorate, it can still withdraw its confidence from, and so destroy, the Executive. On the other hand, the Executive can, subject to the same appeal, dismiss a House of Commons. Under modern conditions both parties shrink from the appeal to Caesar, and as long as possible defer the decisive day.

CHAPTER XXVI

THE IRISH REBELLION AND AFTER

The Rebellion of 1916

THE Armistice with Germany was signed on November 11, 1918, but not until three years later was England permitted to sheathe the sword. That sword was directed no longer against Germany but against those of the King's Irish subjects who throughout the War were the friends, and desired to be the allies, of Germany.

To the outbreak of the Irish rebellion in April 1916 reference has already been made.[1] The rebellion, except in Dublin abortive, was suppressed without difficulty, but not without cost. By all the best friends of Ireland the rebellion was deplored, and condemned as criminal folly.

Criminal it unquestionably was, but was it ' folly ' ? Was it a ' dismal failure ', a ' crime against Ireland ' ? The answer to these questions depends upon the view taken of the Anglo-Irish problem as a whole. If Ireland is a ' nation ', and as such entitled to ' self-determination ', to sovereign independence, the rebellion of 1916 was no folly or failure, but the first in a series of steps leading to the desired goal—an Independent Irish Republic. The Redmondites and moderate Home Rulers regarded the rebellion as the death-blow to their hopes. The Home Rule Bill had, despite the Party ' truce ', been placed upon the Statute-Book in September 1914. Carson described the action of the Government as one ' of unparalleled treachery and betrayal '. Bonar Law's comment was even more bitter. ' They said to themselves, " Whatever we may do, they (the Unionists) are bound in a crisis like this to help their country. Whatever injustice we may inflict upon them we can count upon them." It is not a pretty calculation, but . . . it is a correct calculation. They can count on us.' The operation of the Home Rule Act was,

[1] *Supra*, p. 381.

however, by statute suspended until after the end of the War. Was it possible, after the rebellion of 1916, that it could ever come into operation ?

In May 1916 Mr. Asquith himself visited Dublin and inter- Sinn Fein viewed the prisoners in gaol and hospital. On his return to Westminster he announced (May 25), to the amazement of the Irish members, that negotiations with the Unionist and Nationalist leaders were to begin at once with a view, not to the repeal of the Home Rule Act, but to bringing it, with certain amendments, into immediate operation. The negotiations broke down on the question of Ulster, and in November Sir John Maxwell was recalled, and six hundred Sinn Fein prisoners were released. Maxwell was a fine soldier who in April had been sent over to quell the rebellion. By mingled tact and firmness he was carrying a difficult task through to a successful issue when, under pressure from the Nationalists at Westminster, he was recalled.

His recall was a fatal blunder. It was rightly interpreted in Ireland as a sign of English instability, and in 1917 the Sinn Fein agitation was resumed, both in Ireland and in the United States. In Ireland it made little progress. Farmers and labourers were alike enjoying unusual prosperity and were, for the moment, too busy for political agitation. But the lull was only momentary. In July 1917 Mr. de Valera was returned for East Clare in the room of William Redmond who had been killed in action, and in the following October, at a Sinn Fein convention, was elected President in opposition to Mr. Arthur Griffith. The movement thus passed under the control of avowed and out-and-out republicans.

The death of John Redmond in March 1918 was a further The blow to the ' Moderates ' and in April the Irish Convention re- Irish ported its failure to agree. This Convention had been called tion together in July 1917 by Mr. Lloyd George, who promised to give effect to its recommendations, if a substantial measure of agreement could be reached. Representatives of all parties, except the Sinn Feiners, sat for nine months under the chairmanship of Sir Horace Plunkett, and worked hard to reach agreement. They failed. The principle of self-determination works both ways If it was to be applied to Southern Ireland, why not also to Ulster ? But if Ulster were cut off, what was to become of the unfortunate Unionists in Southern Ireland ? On the horns of this dilemma the Convention was impaled. It could never disengage itself.

The Report meant that in the darkest hour of the War the right arm of England was still weakened by Ireland. The new Military Service Bill passed in that dark hour, and applying conscription in the most drastic form in Great Britain, gave the Executive power to extend it, for the first time, to Ireland. It soon became evident that the number of recruits thus obtained would be small in proportion to the soldiers required to enforce the order. It was useless therefore to apply conscription to a hostile population.

Agitation in Ireland   Meanwhile, Sir John French had succeeded (May 1918) Lord Wimborne as Viceroy, and Sir James Campbell, a stout Unionist, became Lord Chancellor. Sinn Fein was proclaimed, the administration of the law was stiffened, and de Valera was reimprisoned. It may be that these measures anticipated and averted a second insurrection.

Election of 1918   But the Franchise Act of 1918, like that of 1884, provided Ireland with a fresh weapon against England. At the General Election (December 1918) the old Nationalist Party shared the fate of the Liberals in England. Seventy-three of their seats were captured by Sinn Feiners. But the latter refused to sit at Westminster, set up a Parliament of their own in Dublin with an Executive responsible thereto, and proclaimed an Irish Republic (January 1919). In the course of the next eighteen months all the Sinn Fein members, except seven who were abroad, found themselves in prison. In February 1919, however, de Valera made his escape from Lincoln Gaol, fled to the United States, and raised a fund of $6,000,000 for the sustenance of the Irish Republic. An attempt was made to induce President Wilson to bring Ireland's case before the Peace Conference in Paris, but the American delegates refused to receive the Irish envoys.

The Republican Party   The Irish republicans were perfectly candid : ' Our nationalism is not founded upon grievances. We are opposed not to English misgovernment, but to English government in Ireland.' So ran the memorandum from ' The Provisional Government of the Irish Republic ' to President Wilson. It had been well had the English people and the English Government taken these elementary truths to heart. But no true Englishman could comprehend such contrariness. What better than English government can any rational being desire ? ' We come ', said Cromwell in his Declaration from Youghal (January 1650), ' by the assistance of God, to hold forth and maintain the lustre and glory of English liberty in a nation where we have an undoubted right to do it ; wherein the people of Ireland (if they listen not to such seducers as you are) may equally participate in all benefits ; to use liberty and fortune equally with Englishmen, if they keep out of arms '.

Cromwell's words express with precision the attitude of England towards the Irish—and all other ' inferior races '—throughout the ages. ' Rebellion is as the sin of witchcraft.' Keep out of arms and all the blessings of English government shall be yours.

The Sinn Feiners refused to ' keep out of arms '. On the contrary, between May 1916 and September 1919 over 1,200 outrages were perpetrated. During the ensuing twelve months things went rapidly from bad to worse. In the course of a single month (April 1920) no fewer than 277 Royal Irish Constabulary Barracks were destroyed or badly damaged ; raids for arms and money were made on post-offices and private residences ; postbags were rifled ; revenue officers attacked and records destroyed ; landowners and farmers, large and small, were terrorized into the surrender of their firearms, and of the ruffians responsible for the murder of policemen, soldiers and other Government employés not one was in the course of eighteen months convicted. In September 1919 Sinn Fein (Dáil Eireann) was proclaimed as a ' dangerous association ', yet it constituted the only effective Government in Ireland. The King's Writ virtually ceased to run ; Sinn Fein made the laws, set up tribunals to enforce them ; it and it alone provided sanctions for its decrees. *Outrages in Ireland*

Nor was the tale of outrages in Ireland anywise abated by the enactment (1920) of a Bill for the better government of Ireland. Under this fourth edition of Home Rule, two Single-Chamber Parliaments, with Executives responsible thereto, were to be established in Dublin and Belfast respectively, and each Parliament was to contribute twenty members to an all-Ireland Council, which it was hoped might, in time, develop into an all-Ireland Parliament. Ireland was to continue to be represented in the *Home Rule— Fourth Edition, 1920*

Imperial Parliament by forty-six members. But the Nationalists would have none of ' partition ' ; the Sinn Feiners demanded an independent all-Ireland Republic. In Southern Ireland the scheme was virtually stillborn ; Ulster accepted and worked it as at least a preferable alternative to the Act of 1914 which it repealed, and which, but for the Act of 1920, was due to come into operation at the ' end of the War '.

Meanwhile the social condition of Southern Ireland became steadily worse. In July General Macready was appointed to the command of the troops—now numbering some 60,000—in Ireland. But the British Government applied methods of repression with a half-heartedness which was cruel to all parties and calamitous in its effects. Soldiers and Police ' Auxiliaries ' and ' Black and Tans ' [1] sacrificed their lives in support of a Government unworthy of their devotion. At the Guildhall Banquet on November 9 Mr. Lloyd George declared dramatically that we ' had murder by the throat '. On November 21 twenty-one English officers were dragged from their beds in Dublin hotels and murdered before the eyes of their wives. On December 23 the Royal Assent was given to the Bill ' for the better government of Ireland '.

It was grim tragedy with a ghastly admixture of broad farce : coercion and concession hand in hand. Almost all the members of Dáil Eireann were in gaol : civil war was being waged in the country. By the middle of 1921 no fewer than 395 police, to say nothing of soldiers, had been murdered, and the destruction of property was on a calamitous scale.

Nevertheless the elections under the 1920 Act were held in May 1921. In the six Ulster counties the Unionists won 40 out of the 52 seats : in Southern Ireland the Sinn Feiners carried without opposition all the 128 seats, save the four assigned to Trinity College. But the Sinn Feiners never took their seats in Parliament, which was attended by only 15 out of 64 Senators and by 4 out of 128 members of the Lower House.

Ulster   Ulster, however, played the game. On June 22, 1921, the King and Queen visited Belfast to open the Northern Parliament. In an historic speech King George appealed to ' all Irishmen to stretch out the hand of forbearance and conciliation, to forgive

---

[1] The nickname given to the specially enlisted troops who wore khaki with the dark R.I.C. caps.

and forget, and join in making for the land which you all love a new era of peace and contentment and goodwill '.

The appeal could not be disregarded. The British Government invited Sir James Craig, the Ulster Premier, and Mr. de Valera, the republican leader, to a conference in London. The former promptly accepted the invitation; the latter with hesitation and conditionally. On July 11 a truce was proclaimed in Ireland; all the members of Dáil Eireann—the revolutionary convention—were released, and on July 14 de Valera and his colleagues arrived in London. After lengthy negotiations the British Government offered, under certain conditions, ' Dominion Status ' to Southern Ireland. General Smuts, who during this summer had been indefatigable in his efforts to promote Irish peace, wrote to de Valera strongly urging his acceptance. Nevertheless on August 10, after consultation with Dáil Eireann, the offer was refused by de Valera. The Dominion Status offered was, he declared, illusory; nothing less than ' complete detachment ' would satisfy Ireland. Of independence the British Government would not hear. But the wiser sort in Ireland were weary of anarchy, and after prolonged manœuvring for position de Valera at last consented to a further conference. He himself remained in Dublin, but was represented in London by Michael Collins, the young but ever-resourceful Commander-in-Chief of the republican army, by Arthur Griffith and three others. The seven representatives of the British Government included the Prime Minister, Sir Austen Chamberlain, Lord Birkenhead and Mr. Churchill. Much time was wasted by constant references to de Valera in Dublin; more than once deadlock seemed to have been reached: but at midnight on December 6 an Agreement —ominously described as a ' Treaty '—was signed by all the delegates.

Peace Negotiations

The Treaty gave Ireland, under certain conditions, the full Dominion Status of Canada under the style of the Irish Free State: but Northern Ireland was to have the right to contract out of it. That right was, at the first opportunity, exercised. On December 14 the King opened in person a special session of the Imperial Parliament which on the 16th voted an address approving of the Treaty. In the following session a Bill implementing the Treaty received the Royal Assent (March 31, 1922).

The ' Treaty '

Meanwhile, the Treaty was vehemently debated in Dáil Eireann, but was at length approved (January 7, 1922) by a narrow majority (64 to 57).   De Valera, to whom none can deny the merit of consistency, passionately protested against acceptance, and declared that the fight for complete independence would go determinedly on.   He has kept his word.   To this day (1945) the fight has never ceased.   After the vote of Dáil Eireann de Valera immediately resigned, and on January 10 Mr. Arthur Griffith was elected President of Dáil Eireann and on the 14th the 'Treaty' was unanimously approved.   The British army evacuated Ireland, the Royal Irish Constabulary were disbanded, and the last vestiges of the British Government were removed from Dublin Castle.

The
Irish
Free
State
The Free State (Provisional) Government had still, however, to establish its authority in Ireland.   The Republicans with de Valera at their head repudiated it, maintained their army, carried on guerrilla war, inflicting immense damage upon the country and cruel suffering upon the people.   Speaking in the Dáil on May 19 Mr. Griffith declared that the Republicans were on the level of the worst traitors in Irish history, and did not represent two per cent. of the people of Ireland.   Yet that percentage was sufficient to impose upon the whole of Southern Ireland and part of the North a reign of terror.   'The progress of disorder, of lawlessness, of social degeneration, had been so rapid and extensive in the twenty-six counties since the departure of the British troops and the disbandment of the Royal Irish Constabulary, that the Provisional Government could not possibly guarantee the ordinary security of life and property. . . .   As a consequence of this insecurity prosperity has been seriously affected.   Banking and business are curtailed ;   industry and agriculture are languishing ; revenue is only coming in with increasingly laggard steps ;   credit is drying up ;   railways are slowing down ;   stagnation and impoverishment are overtaking the productive life of Ireland ;   the inexorable shadow of famine is already cast on some of its poorer districts.'[1]   Such was the terrible picture presented to the House of Commons by Mr. Churchill on May 31, 1922.   But the most serious feature of the situation was, as he said, that ten days earlier a compact had been made between the Provisional Govern-

[1] Hansard, May 31, 1922.

ment and the Republicans that in the coming election the Republicans should have fifty-seven seats assigned to them as against sixty-four for the supporters of the Treaty : and four places out of nine in the Cabinet. This compact was justly denounced by Mr. Churchill, as virtually a breach of faith on the part of the signatories of the Treaty, and an attempt to stifle an expression of the authentic voice of the Irish electorate. As a fact it was not completely stifled. A General Election was held in June ; and only thirty-six Republicans were returned ; thirty-four non-panel candidates were elected. The Treaty was safe.

But the virulence of the Republicans was not abated. On June 22 Sir Henry Wilson, who, after the close of the War, had been acting as the military adviser of Ulster, was murdered in broad daylight on the doorstep of his house in London.[1] On August 12 Arthur Griffith, the head of the Provisional Government, died with suspicious suddenness in Dublin. Ten days later Michael Collins was ambushed and shot in Co. Cork. Collins was a most attractive personality, the hero of a hundred fights and a hundred miraculous escapes, adored by the young manhood and womanhood of Ireland, and his death was deeply mourned. *Republican outrages*

In September 1922 the Southern Parliament met and elected Mr. Cosgrave President and Chairman of the Provisional Government, with a Cabinet of nine members. The new Government was confronted by two immediate tasks : the restoration of order and the drafting of a Constitution. The latter was the less difficult. Largely with the aid of Kevin O'Higgins a Constitution was drafted, approved by the Irish Parliament and passed through its final stage in the Imperial Parliament on December 5, within twenty-four hours of the time named for the expiration of the Treaty.

On the Treaty the Irish Free State Constitution is based, and any revision or amendment of the Constitution that is repugnant to the terms of the Treaty is null and void. The Instru- *The I.F.S. Constitution*

[1] The outrage came home very closely and painfully to me. But for the fact that I was not lunching at home that day I must myself have witnessed, perhaps been involved in, the tragedy. I regularly walked past my colleague's residence on my way to the House of Commons at a particular time every day. That was the very moment at which Sir Henry Wilson was murdered.

ment provides for a Legislature consisting of the King and two Houses, a Senate of sixty members, and a Chamber of Deputies. Both Chambers are elective, but the Senate is elected from a limited panel drawn up by the Legislature. The Executive is responsible to the Legislature. The Governor-General is appointed by the Crown on the nomination of the Free State Executive. On December 7 Mr. Timothy Healy, for many years one of the most brilliant debaters in the Imperial Parliament, was sworn in as Governor-General and retained that office until December 1927.

The enforcement of order was a task of almost superhuman difficulty, but it was courageously tackled by Mr. Cosgrave. An army, ultimately consisting of 40,000 men, was enrolled to support the efforts of the Civic Guards (police) ; and by the end of the year fifty Republicans—among them Erskine Childers, an English convert—suffered the death penalty, and 10,000 were imprisoned. Besides innumerable murders and outrages they had destroyed property of the estimated value of £25,000,000. But the courage of the new Executive had its reward. By the early summer of 1923 the republican resistance was broken, and de Valera, himself a fugitive, had called off hostilities. For nearly a decade Cosgrave remained in power, and the land enjoyed comparative repose. In February 1932, however, his party was defeated at a General Election, and de Valera succeeded him as President of the Executive Council.

Ulster   Within the prescribed month after the enactment of the Free State Constitution Ulster exercised its right to contract out, and remains, therefore, under the Constitution of 1920. Between that date and 1922 the condition of Ulster, particularly on the boundary, was only less serious than that of Southern Ireland. The Belfast shipyards too were the scene of frequent fighting between Protestants and Catholics and not a little bloodshed. De Valera did all in his power to make trouble in the northern counties and with no small measure of success. On March 30, 1922, however, as the result of a conference between Sir James Craig, the first Premier of Ulster, Mr. Arthur Griffith, Mr. Churchill and other representatives of the three Governments, an Agreement was concluded and the terms of it were on that day com-

municated by Mr. Churchill to the House of Commons.[1] The
two Irish Governments undertook ' to co-operate in every way
in their power with a view to the restoration of peace in the
unsettled areas '.   By the middle of 1922 Sir James Craig had
got the situation well under control.   There remained, however,
the difficulty of defining the frontier between the six counties
and the Free State.   Not until December 1925 was an agreement
reached between the British Government, Ulster and the Free
State.   But between the two Irelands there has been erected a
formidable Customs barrier : the less likely to be lowered since
the Free State has passed under the control of the Republican
Party.

De Valera, a consistent and unyielding Republican, was hardly
installed in power (1932) before he made it plain that he meant to
abrogate the Treaty to which, indeed, he had never subscribed.
The legal connexion between a Dominion and the United King-
dom now depends only on the appellate jurisdiction of the English
Privy Council and on common allegiance to the Crown.   The
Irish Free State has now (1933) formally abolished appeals ; and
has also abolished the oath of allegiance, which members of the
Legislature and the Executive are required to take to the Crown.
It has also withheld the payment of the annuities due to Great
Britain from the purchasers, under the Land Acts, of Irish land,
and has thereby invited economic war.   That war, inconvenient
to England, is bringing ruin upon Southern Ireland.

The English Government has shown infinite forbearance in
dealing with a rebellious Dominion, in the hope that its mental
derangement (as Englishmen regard it) will prove to be temporary.   They have, however, made it clear to de Valera that
if the Free State repudiates the obligations, few and slight as
they are, incidental to membership in the British Commonwealth
of Nations, it cannot hope to continue to share in its privileges.
The ' Treaty ' of 1922 is not a unilateral document.   It can be
modified or abrogated only with the consent of both parties.
That there is, and always has been, in Southern Ireland a large
party in favour of secession, of complete independence, is one of
the ugly truths to which English politicians have for the most
part shut their eyes.   Those who kept them partially open

President de Valera

Economic war

[1] Hansard, March 30, 1922, pp. 1690-2.

clung to the hope that the Irish Republicans represented only a small minority of the people, and that even they would be appeased by the concession, if not of Gladstonian Home Rule, at least of Dominion Status. They never believed that Parnell meant what he said when he accepted the Home Rule Bill as an ' instalment ', but refused ' to set limits to the march of a nation '.

' Dominion Status ' is a further instalment : to sincere Republicans it cannot be the final goal.

CHAPTER XXVII

THE BRITISH COMMONWEALTH OF NATIONS—*STAATENBUND* OR *BUNDESSTAAT*?

THE first reaction of the Empire to the War was undeniably centripetal. In 1917 there came into existence, as we have seen, an Imperial ' Cabinet '. So cordial were the relations established, so successful the experiment, that it was unanimously decided to incorporate the Imperial Cabinet permanently in the constitutional machinery of the Empire. *The Empire and the War*

Yet the Dominions trod delicately. The experiment was repeated in 1918, and the machine was in 1919 transferred to Paris. But at the Conference centrifugal tendencies were plainly in evidence and from the Conference the Dominions emerged as ' nations ', entitled to separate membership in the League of Nations. In 1927 Canada was elected to one of the elective places on the Council of the League. *The Imperial War Cabinet*

Meanwhile, the Imperial Conference of 1917 had repudiated, to the great disappointment of ardent Imperialists, any idea of Federation.[1] The Imperial Conference of 1921 barred and bolted the door that had been closed by its predecessor. A curious but *Federalism repudiated*

---

[1] See *supra*, p. 403. I may be allowed to refer, as some evidence of contemporary opinion, to two articles contributed by me to *The Nineteenth Century and After*. In the issue of January 1917 I wrote : ' Should we fail to solve it [the problem of the Commonwealth] we shall emerge from the present conflict a discomfited and defeated people . . . beaten, not by the superior strength and skill of our opponents, but . . . by our own lack of vision, by our own ossified conservatism, by our own inability to redeem the time and buy up the opportunity.' In September of the same year I wrote *British Federalism : A Vanished Dream?* supporting, as strongly as I could, the view of the ' Hamiltonians ' or Federalists such as Lord Milner and Mr. F. S. Oliver. Meanwhile Sir Herbert Samuel had in the March issue (*The Organization of the Empire*) made a similar suggestion, and Sir Sidney Low had in August (*The Imperial Constitution*) emphasized the pessimistic significance of the Conference resolution.

enlightening controversy arose as to the precise status, and even
the official designation, of this Assembly.   Was it a ' Cabinet ',
or a ' Conference ', or neither ?   The Dominions were, in fact,
invited to take part, in accordance with resolutions previously
adopted, in an Imperial ' Cabinet '.   Since 1918, however, suspicion of that term had deepened in the Dominions.   Were the
overseas statesmen, then, merely to take part in a ' Conference '
of the pre-War type ?   After all that had happened since 1914
that was plainly unthinkable.   Yet a ' Cabinet ' seemed to imply
responsibility for executive decision.   To whom, then, were the
members of the Cabinet to be responsible ?   The responsibility
of one was to the Imperial Parliament, of another to the Canadian,
of a third to the Australian Parliament, and so on.   There was,
therefore, some constitutional force in the objection taken to the
term ' Cabinet '.   The difficulty of terminology was shelved
rather than solved by the official report which was given out as
*A Summary of the Proceedings at a Conference of Prime Ministers
and Representatives of the United Kingdom, the Dominions and
India.*   The larger constitutional question was, however, squarely
faced, with the result that the following Resolution was adopted :
' The Prime Ministers of the United Kingdom and the Dominions,
having carefully considered the recommendation of the Imperial
War Conference of 1917, that a special Imperial Conference should
be summoned as soon as possible after the War to consider the
constitutional relations of the component parts of the Empire,
have reached the following conclusions :

' (*a*) Continuous consultation, to which the Prime Ministers
attach no less importance than the Imperial War Conference of
1917, can only be secured by a substantial improvement in the
communications between the component parts of the Empire.
Having regard to the constitutional developments since 1917, no
advantage is to be gained by holding a constitutional Conference.

' (*b*) The Prime Ministers of the United Kingdom and the
Dominions and the Representatives of India should aim at
meeting annually, or at such longer intervals as may prove
feasible.

' (*c*) The existing practice of direct communication between
the Prime Ministers of the United Kingdom and the Dominions,
as well as the right of the latter to nominate Cabinet Ministers

to represent them in consultation with the Prime Minister of
the United Kingdom, are maintained.' [1]

To ardent Imperialists of the older school this Resolution
caused considerable disappointment. Yet it is clear from the
published utterances of the leading statesmen of the Dominions,
not less than from the speech delivered by the English Prime
Minister in the House of Commons on August 18, 1921, not only
that the Resolution was reached with unanimity, but that its
acceptance was in no degree held to have impaired the constitutional significance of the recent meeting. ' The general feeling
was ', said Mr. Lloyd George, ' that it would be a mistake to lay
down any rules or to embark upon definitions as to what the
British Empire meant. . . . You are defining life itself when
you are defining the British Empire. You cannot do it, and
therefore . . . we came to the conclusion that we would have
no constitutional conference.' [2] Mr. Hughes was even more
explicit : ' It is now admitted that a Constitutional Conference
is not necessary, and that any attempt to set out in writing what
are or should be the constitutional relations between the Dominions
and the Mother Country would be fraught with very great danger
to the Empire. The question of a Constitutional Conference, or
any attempt at reduction of the Constitution to writing, may be
therefore regarded as having been finally disposed of.' ' No
written Constitution ', said Mr. Massey, ' is required.' Yet Mr.
Massey made it clear, as have other Premiers, that, in his opinion,
the recent meeting was ' a long way the most important which
has yet been held ', and for this reason : That it was ' the first
Conference where the representatives of the overseas Dominions
had been called upon to take part in matters connected with the
management of the Empire as a whole '. Nor can it be doubted,
whatever technical name be given to the meeting, that it did act,
in effect, as an Empire Cabinet. It not merely discussed, but
decided, questions of supreme moment to the Empire and to the
world, and its decisions, like those of a British Cabinet, were
reported immediately to the King. Perhaps, then, Mr. Lloyd
George did not exaggerate when, in the speech quoted above, he
said : ' The whole course of human affairs has been altered because

[1] Summary of *Proceedings and Documents*, p. 9.
[2] House of Commons, Hansard, August 18, 1921.

the British Empire has been proved to be a fact, and not, what
a good many people who knew nothing about it imagined, a fiction. . . . There is no doubt at all that the events of the last
few years have consolidated the Empire in a way which probably generations would not have done otherwise.'

Of the discussions at the Assembly of 1921 the most important
were concerned with the foreign policy of the Empire. That
policy was becoming more and more focussed upon the Pacific;
the Anglo-Japanese Alliance; the position of Canada on the one
hand and of Australasia upon the other in regard to Japanese
immigration; the relations between our American friends and
our Japanese allies; and other problems which, if subsidiary, are
by no means without significance. These topics, discussed in
detail at the Conference of Prime Ministers in Whitehall, were
again discussed, from a somewhat different angle, at the Conference at Washington (November 1921–February 1922).

The
Washing-
ton Con-
ference

The Conference opened on November 12, 1921, and closed on
February 6, 1922. Mr. Balfour represented both the United
Kingdom and (at the request of General Smuts) the Union of
South Africa. Canada, Australia, New Zealand, and India (which
like the Dominions had been admitted to separate membership
of the League of Nations) were all represented by their own delegates; but the Dominion delegates (as at the Peace Conference)
also formed part, with the delegates from the United Kingdom,
of the British Empire delegation. The object of the Conference,
which had been summoned by the U.S.A., was to arrest the race
of competition in armaments. Its result was to terminate the
Anglo-Japanese alliance, which had always, though groundlessly,
been an object of suspicion, and had lately become a matter of
'deep concern' to America. Since 1902 the situation in the
Pacific had been completely changed. The Anglo-Japanese alliance had been originally concluded to safeguard the Allies against
Russia and Germany. All danger from those quarters was now
dissipated. 'For what purpose', asked the U.S.A., 'is it now
maintained?' Great Britain was in a difficult position. Anxious
to be on the best possible terms with the U.S.A., she had no wish
to show ingratitude to Japan for the great services rendered by
her in the War.[1] The Anglo-Japanese alliance was, however,

[1] Cf. p. 407.

superseded by a Four-Power Treaty in which the U.S.A. and France joined with Great Britain and Japan to guarantee peace in the Pacific. This Treaty was signed within a month of the meeting of the Conference, and was an essential preliminary to any agreement on armaments. The latter was confined to sea-power, and was embodied in a Five-Power Treaty, in which Italy joined the parties to the Four-Power Pact. It fixed the proportion of capital ships at 5:5:3 for Great Britain, the U.S.A. and Japan respectively, and 1¾ for France and Italy, and about the same for aircraft-carriers. The latter Powers bluntly refused any agreement about submarines. Japan also agreed to evacuate Shantung.

Peace seemed to be assured in the Far East. It was seriously The threatened before the close of the year in the Near East. It Chanak needs not to recall the sequence of events which led up to the Crisis Chanak crisis.[1] But the bearing of the incident upon the relations between the Imperial Government and the Dominions was significant, and demands attention. At the height of the crisis (September 15) the British Government telegraphed in hot haste to the Dominions, ' placing them in possession of the facts, and inviting them to be represented by contingents in the defence of interests for which they have already made enormous sacrifices, and of soil which is hallowed by immortal memories of the Anzacs '. The clever appeal to the Anzacs evoked an immediate response from New Zealand, who promised a contingent, while the Australian Government also notified Mr. Lloyd George that it ' desired to associate itself with His Majesty's Government in Great Britain in whatever action might be deemed necessary to ensure the freedom of the Straits and the sanctity of the Gallipoli Peninsula, and that it was prepared, if circumstances required it, to send a contingent of Australian troops '. But Mr. Hughes intimated to Mr. Lloyd George that the matter would be submitted to the Australian Parliament. The reply from South Africa was delayed, owing to the absence of General Smuts, until the crisis was over and ' there was no longer any call for the intervention of the Union '. The Canadian Cabinet asked for further information, and for permission (which was not given) to lay the matter before a special session of the Dominion Parliament.

[1] Cf. p. 428

The Chanak incident though closed by the conclusion of Peace at Lausanne (July 1923) had important reactions, especially in Canada. At the Lausanne Conference the Dominions were not individually represented. This departure from the precedents created at Paris and Washington was understood to have been due to pressure from France ; but it was none the less regrettable, especially in view of the alarms which had been aroused in the Dominions by the Chanak incident.

Mr. Mackenzie King, Prime Minister of Canada, while professing that his Dominion did not resent exclusion from the Conference, argued that, having been excluded, the ' extent to which Canada may be held to be bound by the proceedings of the Conference or by the provisions of any treaty arising therefrom, must be a question for the decision of the Canadian Parliament '. Despite this chilling reply the Home Government persisted in the ' assumption that the Canadian Government would wish to follow procedure adopted in case of peace treaties with Germany, Austria and Bulgaria '. Mr. King retorted, with unanswerable force, that the procedure adopted at Lausanne had not followed the precedent of Paris, and that consequently Canada could not be expected to sign the Treaty of Lausanne, nor to give parliamentary sanction to it, though she was prepared, if the British Government recommended the ratification of the Treaty so far as Canada was concerned, that that ratification should bind her. The governing considerations were set forth with admirable lucidity by Mr. King in the Canadian House of Commons (June 9, 1924). 'There is (he said) a distinction to be drawn between the purely legal and technical position in which this Dominion may be placed, and the moral obligations which arise under treaties. . . . Legally and technically Canada will be bound by the ratification of this treaty ; in other words, speaking internationally, the whole British Empire in relation to the rest of the world will stand as one when this treaty is ratified. But as respects the obligations arising out of the treaty itself, speaking now of inter-Imperial obligations, this Parliament, if regard is to be had to the representations which from the outset we have made to the British Government, will in no way be bound by any obligation, beyond that which Parliament of its own volition recognizes as arising out of the situation.'

This statement reaffirms and applies to Imperial diplomacy the distinction between ' active ' and ' passive ' responsibility already accepted in reference to war. The legal state of belligerency accruing from the British declaration of war in August 1914 did not necessarily involve the Dominions in active participation.[1] Nevertheless ' passive belligerency ' would almost certainly have entailed inconvenient consequences. Could they be avoided in the case of diplomatic passivity ?

The Locarno Pact illustrates the dilemma. The Pact clearly contemplates circumstances which might involve the Empire in war. The Dominions were not represented at Locarno, either independently or as a part of the British Delegation, and Article 9 expressly provides that the Treaty shall impose no obligation upon any of the British Dominions, or upon India, ' unless the Government of such Dominion, or of India, signifies its acceptance thereof '. That exemption does not, however, touch the point as to ' legal ' belligerency. Should Great Britain, under the terms of Locarno, be unhappily involved in war for the defence of Germany against France, France would undeniably be entitled, whatever may be the attitude of Canada, to bombard Halifax or Vancouver. *The Locarno Pact*

Meanwhile, a different but hardly less significant point was raised by the conclusion between Canada and the U.S.A. of a Treaty designed to protect the halibut fisheries off their coasts (March 2, 1923). The signatories were Mr. Hughes, who as U.S. Secretary of State had played a dominating part at the Washington Conference, and Mr. Lapointe, the Canadian Minister of Marine and Fisheries. *The Halibut Fisheries Treaty of 1923*

The circumstances attendant on the conclusion of this Treaty were, from the standpoint of Imperial relations, of crucial significance. The British Ambassador at Washington claimed to act as a co-signatory with the special envoy of the Canadian Government, and in his claim was at first supported by the Secretary of State in Whitehall, who instructed the Ambassador at Washington ' to sign the treaty in association with Mr. Lapointe '.

---

[1] Article 49 of the Constitution of the Irish Free State reduces to legal form the accepted Convention : ' Save in the case of actual invasion the I.F.S. shall not be committed to active participation in any war without the assent of the Oireachtas (Legislature).'

Moreover, the assent of the U.S. Senate to ratification was given subject to the Treaty being signed ' between the United States and Great Britain '.

The Canadian Government, however, stuck to its guns. The Treaty was one between *Canada* and the U.S. and should be signed, on behalf of Canada only, by the Canadian Plenipotentiary, to whom the King issued full powers. In consequence of the technical points involved ratifications were delayed until October 21, 1924.[1] The Treaty was registered with the League of Nations on 2 February 1925.

The Imperial Conference, 1923

The Halibut Treaty figured prominently in the discussions at the Imperial Conference of 1923. That Conference was indeed largely concerned with the procedure to be observed in the ' negotiation, signature and ratification of international agreements '. In the result the Conference specifically recognized the right of any Dominion to negotiate a treaty, but it affirmed the principle that no treaty should be negotiated by any one Government of the Empire without regard to its possible effect on other parts of the Empire, or the Empire as a whole, and that there should be a full interchange of views, before and during negotiations, between all the Dominions. Bilateral Treaties imposing obligations on one part of the Empire only were to be signed by its representative : in other cases by the representatives of all the Dominions concerned.[2] This decision was undoubtedly a concession to Dominion Nationalism ; it emphasized ' in the highest degree the separate character of the Dominions '.[3] One link with the Imperial Executive only remained. The full powers and the instruments of ratification were still issued with the King's signature affixed on the strength of a warrant countersigned by the British Secretary of State. In March 1931, however, this link was snapped at the instance of the Irish Free State, which secured the King's assent to a new procedure whereby the necessary documents were to be issued by him solely on the advice of the Free State Minister, and sealed only with the special seal

[1] On the whole question cf. J. A. R. Marriott, *Empire Foreign Policy*, ap. *Fortnightly Review* (May 1923), and Keith, *Responsible Government in the Dominions*, pp. 897 f. ; and Cmd. 2377.

[2] Cmd. 1987 (1923).

[3] Keith, *Constitutional Law of the British Dominions*, p. 51.

of Ireland—a Dominion which was admitted in 1923 for the first
time into an Imperial Conference.

Closely connected with the question of Treaty-making was
that of separate diplomatic representation at Foreign Courts.
In this matter also the Irish Free State created a precedent by
securing in 1924 separate diplomatic representation at Washington. In notifying the new departure to the U.S. Government
the British Government emphasized the point that it did ' not
denote any departure from the principle of the diplomatic unity
of the Empire '. That is as it may be. Canada followed suit
by appointing Ministers to Washington in 1926, to Paris in 1928
and to Tokyo in 1929. In the latter year the Union of South
Africa appointed Ministers to Washington, The Hague and Rome.
Australia and New Zealand have frowned upon the new departure, rightly regarding it as a menace, though not as yet a serious
one, to Imperial unity.

Diplo-matic Repre-sentation at Foreign Courts

The constitutional evolution of the self-governing Dominions
reached a climax at the Imperial Conference of 1926, and in the
attempt to put the recommendations of that Conference into
legislative form in the *Statute of Westminster* (1931). Of the
whole series of Conferences this was the most significant. It was
exceptionally strong in personnel. Among the representatives
of the United Kingdom were Mr. Baldwin, the Earl of Balfour
and Sir Austen Chamberlain ; Mr. Mackenzie King was the principal representative of Canada, Mr. S. M. Bruce of Australia, Mr.
Coates of New Zealand. General Hertzog came, as Prime Minister, from South Africa, Lord Birkenhead, as Secretary of State,
and the Maharaja of Burdwan represented India. The Irish Free
State was also represented.

The Imperial Confer-ence, 1926

Early in the proceedings the Conference appointed a Committee ' to investigate all the questions on the agenda affecting
inter-Imperial Relations'. The Report of that Committee has
taken its place among the classical documents in the history of
the British Empire. The Report opens with this significant
statement : ' The Committee are of opinion that nothing would
be gained by attempting to lay down a Constitution for the
British Empire. . . . There is, however,' it proceeds, ' one most
important element in it which, from a strictly constitutional point
of view, has now, as regards all vital matters, reached its full

development—we refer to the group of self-governing communities composed of Great Britain and the Dominions. Their position and mutual relation may be readily defined. *They are autonomous Communities within the British Empire, equal in status, in no way subordinate one to another in any aspect of their domestic or external affairs, though united by a common allegiance to the Crown and freely associated as members of the British Commonwealth of Nations. . . .* Equality of status, so far as Britain and the Dominions are concerned, is thus the root principle governing our inter-Imperial relations.'

There follows a sentence which seems to demand an Athanasius for its interpretation. ' But the principles of equality and similarity, appropriate to *status*, do not universally extend to function. Here we require something more than immutable dogmas.'

Of the specific recommendations of the Report the first concerns the Royal title, which was, in due course, amended to run as follows : ' George V, by the Grace of God, of Great Britain, Ireland and the British Dominions beyond the Seas King, Defender of the Faith, Emperor of India.'

The Report next proceeds to deal with the position of the Governors-General.

' In our opinion ', it runs, ' it is an essential consequence of the equality of status existing among the members of the British Commonwealth of Nations that the Governor-General of a Dominion is the representative of the Crown, holding in all essential respects the same position in relation to the administration of public affairs in the Dominion as is held by His Majesty the King in Great Britain, and that he is not the representative or agent of His Majesty's Government in Great Britain or of any department of that Government. It seemed to us to follow that the practice, whereby the Governor-General is the formal official channel of communication between His Majesty's Government in Great Britain and his Governments in the Dominions, might be regarded as no longer wholly in accordance with the constitutional position of the Governor-General. It was thought that the recognized official channel of communication should be, in future, between Government and Government direct.'

On this important paragraph several questions arise. The first, clearly, is as to the facts. Asked in the House of Commons

(June 29, 1927) whether in fact there had been, since the Conference, any change in the status of the Governors-General, or in their relation either to the Dominion Ministers or to the Imperial Ministers, Mr. Amery, the Secretary of State, replied :

' No, the change in the status of the Governor-General from an agent and instrument of the British Government to the representative of the Crown in a Dominion, and nothing else, was a change which, like the whole of the changes in our constitutional evolution, has taken place gradually over a long period of years, and was in substance the consummation of many years before the present Conference took place. All that the late Conference did was to suggest that the purely historic survival by which communication from the British Government to its partner Governments went *viâ* the Governor-General's office—as it had done in the old days when the Governor-General still was, as the Governor of a Crown Colony is, the agent and instrument of the British Government—should be eliminated and the position brought up to date with present-day facts.' (Official Report, June 29, col. 540.)

But the matter plainly could not rest there.

If the Governor-General of a self-governing Dominion was no longer to be the representative or agent of His Majesty's Government in Great Britain, or ' of any department of that Government ', the question naturally arose : On whose advice was the King to act in appointing him ? That question was answered as regards Australia by the following announcement issued, on December 2, 1930, not from Downing Street but from Australia House : ' His Majesty the King on the recommendation of the Right Hon. J. H. Scullin, Prime Minister of Australia, has appointed the Right Hon. Sir Isaac Alfred Isaacs to the office of Governor-General for the Commonwealth of Australia.' This announcement strikingly illustrated the constitutional change effected by a mere resolution of the Imperial Conference—a body devoid of legislative competence. An Australian paper described the incident as an ' opportunity to sever the nexus with the British Government '. The precedent set by Mr. Scullin was followed by de Valera, but the experiment is not likely to be repeated, except by a Dominion Government aiming at ultimate secession from the Empire.

The next questions to which the Report referred were connected with the operation of Dominion legislation : in particular His Majesty's ' powers of disallowance ' of the enactments of Dominion legislature ; the reservation of Dominion legislation for the signification of His Majesty's pleasure ; and the legislative competence of the Imperial Parliament (' The Parliament at Westminster ', as the Report significantly termed it) and the Dominion Parliaments respectively. The Conference wisely concluded in reference to these matters that ' the issues involved were so complex that . . . it would be necessary to obtain expert guidance as a preliminary to further consideration by His Majesty's Governments in Great Britain and the Dominions '.

That expert guidance was obtained from a Conference which, consisting mainly of lawyers and permanent officials from the United Kingdom and the Dominions, sat from October 8, 1929, until December 4, 1929.[1]

The matters referred to the expert Conference were (1) the existing provisions by which the assent of the Crown is required for certain Dominion legislation ; (2) the extra-territorial legislation of the Dominions ; (3) the position of the Colonial Laws Validity Act ; and (4) merchant shipping legislation.

Statute of Westminster
The recommendations of the Conference formed the basis of the *Statute of Westminster* enacted in 1931, and may, therefore, be conveniently considered in connexion with that brief but exceedingly important Statute.

In regard to ' disallowance ', or the right of the Crown, on the advice of Ministers of the United Kingdom, to annul an Act passed by a Dominion Legislature, the Conference agreed that it could no longer be exercised. The right had, in fact, not been exercised in relation to Canada since 1873, to New Zealand since 1867, and never to the Commonwealth of Australia or the Union of South Africa. Nevertheless, for certain technical reasons, the Conference did not recommend the specific abolition of the right. The Imperial Parliament concurred in the agreement of the Conference, and the Statute of Westminster consequently contains no direct reference to this right, nor to the power hitherto exercised by Colonial Governors of ' reserving ' assent to Bills passed

[1] Cmd. 3479.

by their several Legislatures, until they had consulted and received instructions from Whitehall.

Much more difficult and obscure, and at the same time more practically important, was the problem of extra-territorial legislation. In this matter the Statute of Westminster, following the cautious and non-committal recommendation of the Report, simply ' declared and enacted that the Parliament of a Dominion has full power to make laws having extra-territorial operation ' (section 3).

The Statute (by sections 5 and 6) removed all doubts as to the unfettered power of a Dominion Legislature to make laws in relation to merchant shipping, and also repealed, though only as regards future enactments, the Colonial Laws Validity Act of 1865. That Act affirmed the principle that an Act of a Colonial Legislature was not void, although repugnant to the law of England *unless it contravened an Act of the Imperial Parliament made directly* applicable to the Colony in question. The italicized words were held to impair equality of status affirmed by the Statute of Westminster. So the Act was repealed.

Equality was even more specifically affirmed by the repudiation of the right of the Imperial Parliament to legislate for a Dominion ' otherwise than at the request and with the consent of that Dominion (Preamble and section 4). But the expert Conference of 1929 was not allowed to forget, and the Imperial Conference of 1930 reminded Whitehall, that there are self-governing States in the Commonwealth of Australia ; and that even the Canadian Provinces have rights which cannot be ignored. The rights of these units, as well as those of New Zealand, were accordingly safeguarded by sections 7, 8 and 9 of the Act.

Reference has been repeatedly made in preceding paragraphs to ' Dominions ' and ' Dominion Status '. But what is a ' Dominion ' ? To that important question the only answer vouchsafed by the *Statute of Westminster* is that in future Acts of Parliament the term ' Colony ' ' shall not include a Dominion or any Province or State forming part of a Dominion ' (§ 11) and that a Dominion is one of the existing six Dominions (§ 1). This is in truth definition *per enumerationem,* and it may well cause embarrassment to a legal tribunal, such as the Permanent Court of International Justice, which now has jurisdiction in the case of a dispute between a ' Dominion ' and a ' Dominion ', or between a ' Dominion ' and the United Kingdom. [1]

What remnant of Imperial unity survives the Act of 1931 ? The only survival would seem to be indicated by a paragraph in the Preamble. It runs thus :

' Inasmuch as the Crown is the symbol of the free association of the members of the British Commonwealth of Nations, and as they are united by a common allegiance to the Crown, it would be in accord with the established constitutional position of all the members of the Commonwealth in relation to one another that any alteration in the law touching the Succession to the Throne or the Royal Style and Titles shall hereafter require the assent as well of the Parliaments of all the Dominions as of the Parliament of the United Kingdom.' [2]

The Crown, then, is the only legal link that binds together the British Commonwealth. But golden though it be, it is liable to snap. It snapped when in 1776 the English Colonies in North America attempted to distinguish between ' a common Executive Sovereign,' whose prerogative was acknowledged in each of the seceding Colonies, and the Imperial Parliament whose jurisdiction they repudiated. Moreover, it cannot escape notice that the symbolic Crown is worn by a Constitutional King, who is advised by responsible Ministers. What if the advice tendered by his Ministers in Dublin contradicts the advice given by his Ministers in Ottawa, or the advice given at Canberra involves executive action at variance with that advised by Downing Street ? Take the vital question as to the right of secession. The skilful phrasing of the paragraph in the Preamble ' neither affirms nor denies ', as Dr. Jenks has pointed out, ' the disputed right of secession '. [3] But what if South African Ministers were to advise in favour of, and Downing Street against, secession ?

A single Executive responsible to half a dozen different Legislatures manifestly involves a condition of very unstable equilibrium. The only hope is that so precarious a structure may not be subjected to a rigorous test.

In view of these developments it is not surprising that attention should have been diverted since the War from the problem

[1] See note (1), p. 477. [2] See note (2), p. 477.
[3] *Quarterly Review*, July 1932.

of constitutional relations to that of inter-Imperial Trade, from Economic Unity of the Empire
Politics to Economics. The Prussian *Zollverein* preceded, and
unquestionably prepared the way for, the achievement of political
unity in Germany. Is it possible that the adoption of Joseph
Chamberlain's policy in 1906 might have neutralized the operation of those centrifugal forces which found legal expression in
the *Statute of Westminster* ? Be that as it may, there has been
in recent years, parallel with the centrifugal movement in politics,
a centripetal tendency in trade. Against the *Statute of Westminster* we may set the Tariff legislation of 1931–2, the Protectionist Budget of 1932, and the Ottawa Conference.

Paradoxically the two movements, though divergent in goal,
had a common origin in the War.

In September 1915 Mr. McKenna imposed new duties, pro- The Paris Pact
tective in effect, if not in intention, on various commodities
imported from all countries, within as well as without the Empire.
Amendments designed to give preferences to the Empire were
defeated. A Conference between the Allied Governments was
held in Paris (June 1916) for the purpose of establishing a ' common economic front '. At that time it seemed unthinkable that
the peoples who had fought and suffered and died in a common
cause should not stand together after the War. The outcome of
the Conference was the ' Pact of Paris '. The Pact dealt with
(1) measures for the war period ; (2) temporary measures dealing with shipping, agriculture, industry and commerce to be
adopted during the period of reconstruction after the War ; and
(3) permanent measures of mutual assistance and collaboration
among the Allies.

It was the hour of high hopes and generous emotions, destined
to rapid evaporation when the common danger had passed. But
the Pact of Paris, even more than the McKenna duties, was
important as marking for Great Britain a definite breach with the
fiscal tradition of the recent past.

The Paris Pact was immediately followed (July 1916) by the
appointment of a Committee on Commercial and Industrial
Policy, under the chairmanship of Lord Balfour of Burleigh, to
consider the policy to be adopted after the War. In February
1917, on the eve of the meeting of the Imperial War Conference,
the Committee, in an interim Report, recommended (1) ' special

steps' to stimulate production within the Empire; (2) the declaration by the British Government of its adhesion to the policy of Imperial Preference; (3) the establishment in the British tariff of ' a wider range of customs duties ' to ' be remitted or reduced on the products and manufactures of the Empire ' and to ' form the basis of commercial treaties with Allied and neutral Powers '.

The Imperial War Conference of 1917 unanimously adopted the principle that each part of the Empire, having due regard to the interests of our Allies, should ' give specially favourable treatment and facilities to the produce and manufactures of other parts of the Empire ' ; and called for concerted action with regard to (1) the production of an adequate food supply and arrangements for its transportation ; (2) the control of natural resources available within the Empire ; and (3) the economical utilization of such national resources through processes of manufacture carried on within the Empire.

The Imperial Conference of 1918 endorsed the recommendations of the Balfour Committee, and, on July 29, Bonar Law stated in the House of Commons : ' This Government has put itself into line with the other Governments of the Dominions in accepting this principle [of preference].' [1]

The electoral programme on which Lloyd George and Bonar Law appealed to the country in December 1918 included the policy of Imperial Preference and the Safeguarding of Industry, and the ' Coupon ' Parliament proceeded to give effect to it.

Most appropriately it fell to the eldest son of Joseph Chamberlain to announce, in his Budget of 1919, the incorporation of the principle of Imperial Preference in the fiscal system of Great Britain. It was cautiously and tactfully introduced. With the exception of the duty on spirits the preference was given by remitting existing rates in favour of Empire products, and not by imposing higher duties on foreign goods. Still, it was a beginning, and was cordially welcomed by the Dominions. Reciprocal action was, indeed, long overdue. It was twenty-two years since Canada—the first Colony to impose (1859) duties on British produce—had taken the first step towards the recognition of the fiscal unity of the Empire. Within the next ten years New

[1] Hansard, July 29, 1918, p. 39.

Zealand, South Africa, and Australia followed the lead of Canada. Now, at long last, the Mother-land, mindful of the superb effort made by the Dominions in the War, and inspired by a new conception of Empire, had come, tardily and timidly, into line.

The ' Preference Budget ' of 1919 was followed by the *Safe-* Safe-guarding *of Industries Act* of 1921.   Part I of the Act imposed an guarding *ad valorem* duty of 33⅓ per cent. on certain imported articles which were the product of essential or ' key ' industries, except where those articles were consigned from and grown, produced or manufactured in the British Empire.   The new duty applied to 6,000 articles coming within the scope of nine key industries. Part II of the Act gave power to the Board of Trade to impose a similar duty on ' dumped ' goods (other than articles of food or drink), that is, on goods sold in the United Kingdom below the cost of production.   ' Anti-Dumping ' Orders of the Board of Trade were, however, subject to confirmation by Parliament.

One of the first steps taken by Mr. Bonar Law after he became The Prime Minister (1922) was to invite the representatives of all parts Imperial Econo-of the Empire to attend an Imperial Economic Conference.   It mic Con-met in London in 1923, and passed a series of important resolu- ference, tions.   Their general purpose was to develop Imperial resources 1923 by an extension of preference, and by financial co-operation between different parts of the Empire ;   to improve Imperial communications and to promote Empire settlement under the Act passed with that object in 1922.   Moreover, the Conference recommended (Canada dissenting) the appointment of an Imperial Economic Committee to facilitate, during the intervals between Imperial Conferences, the carrying out of the general policy there agreed upon.   The defeat of the Conservative Government in January 1924 delayed action on many of the resolutions adopted at the Economic Conference of 1923, and led to the repeal by the MacDonald Government of all Imperial Preferences and even of the McKenna duties.   Mr. Baldwin, however, returned to office in November, and almost his first act was to set up an Imperial Economic Committee, consisting of members, with practical experience, nominated not only by the Home Government but all the Dominions, the India Office, the Colonial Office and Southern Rhodesia.   The Committee was charged to consider ' the methods of preparing for market and marketing within the

United Kingdom the food products of the overseas parts of the Empire, with a view to increasing the consumption of such products in the United Kingdom in preference to imports from foreign countries and to promote the interests both of producers and consumers '. £1,000,000 a year was allocated for the purposes of the Committee, which produced a number of exceedingly valuable Reports. Further emphasis was given to this policy by the appointment in May 1926 of the Empire Marketing Board. The purpose of the Board was to improve the marketing and stimulate the consumption in this country firstly of home produce and secondly of the produce of the Empire overseas. This was done by an elaborate publicity and educational campaign ; by making grants to appropriate bodies for scientific research into problems of production and marketing, and by other methods of a similar kind.[1] The Board did a considerable amount of good, but, as some thought, at disproportionate expense, and under the economic stress of 1932 it was dissolved.

The Baldwin Government, which remained in office from 1924 to 1929, restored the McKenna duties, with the accompanying Preferences, and considerably extended both the amount and the range of the preference given to Empire products. It also passed (1925) a new Safeguarding of Industries Act, under which duties of a definitely protective character were imposed on a considerable range of articles. In every case preference was given to Empire products as against those of foreign origin. These measures, it was claimed, besides producing a substantial revenue, had greatly assisted home manufacturers, without raising prices to the consumer. Best of all, so far from retarding they had actually stimulated the export of the ' safeguarded ' commodities.

The new fiscal policy was still, however, regarded with hostility both by the Liberal and the Labour Party. The latter, though not commanding an absolute parliamentary majority, were again, as the largest single party, entrusted with office in 1929 and Mr. Snowden, an uncompromising Free Trader, became Chancellor of the Exchequer. To his bitter chagrin he dare not sacrifice the £10,000,000 which the McKenna Duties and the Silk Duties were bringing into the revenue, but the Safeguarding Duties were allowed to lapse. He also expressed the hope that

[1] Cmd. 2898 (p. 192).

before he left office he would have swept away all the preferences that remained.[1]

It was under these depressing circumstances that the Imperial Conference met in October 1930. The most prominent figure at this Conference was Mr. R. B. Bennett, Prime Minister of Canada and an ardent advocate of the economic unity of the Empire. To promote that unity was, indeed, the primary purpose which had brought the delegates of the Dominions together. The Dominions, like the United Kingdom, were in the throes of an economic and financial crisis, and saw no hope of emerging therefrom except by closer co-operation within the Empire. Mr. Bennett, in particular, insisted on the urgent necessity of putting into effective and immediate operation a large scheme of Empire Preference. 'The day', he said, 'is now at hand when the peoples of the Empire must decide, once for all, whether our welfare lies in closer economic union or whether it does not. . . . Delay is hazardous. . . . The time for action has come.'[2]

Imperial Conference, 1930

Other representatives of the Dominions expressed similar views in language hardly less vigorous. But their views made no impression on the Socialist Government. The tariff solution was definitely turned down, and the Conference was saved from complete fiasco only by adopting the suggestion of Mr. Bennett that 'the Economic Section of the Conference be adjourned to meet at Ottawa, ... within the next twelve months.'[3]

The crisis of 1931 necessitated a further adjournment, but in July 1932 an Imperial Economic Conference was opened at Ottawa.

In the meantime important political changes had taken place, the general effect of them being to bring into power ministries more favourable than those which they displaced to the economic unity of the Empire. The formation of a National Government in England (August 1931) and the striking vote of confidence given to it by the electorate (October), cleared the way not merely for negotiations at Ottawa, but for a radical reversal of the fiscal policy of the United Kingdom. Mr. MacDonald, as head of the National Government, had virtually asked for a 'free hand' to deal with a great national emergency, untrammelled by pledges and without regard to the traditions or prejudices of any

Crisis of 1931

[1] Hansard, July 9, 1929.   [2] October 8, 1930.
[3] Cmd. 3717 (p. 44).

Party, in the State. The results of the mandate were quickly apparent.

Abnormal Importations Bill

A Bill to deal with the abnormal importation of 'dumped' articles was introduced on November 17, and three days later had received the Royal Assent. On the same day the Board of Trade exercised the powers conferred upon it by the Act and issued a list of twenty-three classes of commodities to be subject from November 25 to a duty of 50 per cent. That was an emergency measure.

The Import Duties Act, 1932

On February 4, 1932, Mr. Neville Chamberlain, as Chancellor of the Exchequer, proposed to the House of Commons a measure comparable in importance with those carried by Sir Robert Peel between 1841 and 1846. The Import Duties Bill was deliberately intended to effect a fiscal revolution, and its Second Reading was passed (February 16) by 451 votes to 73. The objects of the Bill were to correct the adverse balance of trade, no longer corrected by shipping profits, and the interest on foreign investments ; to maintain the value of the £ sterling, and ensure consumers against a rise in the cost of living ; to provide further revenue ; to stimulate home industry and reduce unemployment ; to provide a basis for negotiation with foreign countries ; and, above all, to facilitate the granting of preferences to the other units of the Empire. These objects it was hoped to attain by imposing a basic duty of 10 per cent. upon all imported goods not specifically exempted, and, if so advised by an Import Duties Advisory Committee to be set up under the Bill, an additional duty upon other commodities. The Bill received the Royal Assent on February 29, and on the following day the general tariff came into force. No duties were to be levied on Empire goods until after the Ottawa Conference at earliest.

Ottawa Conference, 1932

The way was now clear for that Conference. It opened on July 21. No more intricate task ever confronted a body of statesmen than that which awaited Mr. Baldwin, Mr. Bennett and their colleagues at Ottawa. Discussions were inevitably keen, sometimes acrimonious, but the determination of Mr. Bennett at length prevailed, and Agreements, subsequently endorsed by the several Dominions, were before the end of August concluded.

To estimate the results actually attained is a task for the

future historian. But it can now (1933) be said that while Ottawa undeniably disappointed those who went there, in body or in spirit, with high expectations, yet every part of the Empire is to-day in a less distressful condition than it was before the Conference. How far the Ottawa Agreements contributed to the improvement it is too soon to say. Yet this may with confidence be affirmed, that Ottawa did arrest the centrifugal tendencies which had been operative, in the political sphere, from the day when the Armistice was signed. The *Statute of Westminster* dissipated the dream of a *Bundesstaat*. Ottawa revived the hope of a *Staatenbund*.

Notes to p. 470.

(1) On September 1929 Great Britain signed ' The Optional Clause ' of the *General Act*, but with reservations. Of these the most important referred to Inter-Imperial Disputes which were withheld from the jurisdiction of the Hague Court. See Marriott, *Commonwealth or Anarchy* (1940), pp. 199–200, and Cmd. 3803 (1931).

(2) The importance of this reference to an alteration of the law touching the succession to the Throne was strikingly illustrated at the time of the ' Abdication Crisis ' in December 1936. See Marriott, *Evolution of the British Empire and Commonwealth* (1939), p. 810.

CHAPTER XXVIII

EXPECTANT INDIA—THE CROWN AND THE PEOPLES—THE
CROWN AND THE PRINCES

The
Great
War and
India

FOR India, not less manifestly than for the Dominions, the
Great War marked the parting of the ways. In August 1917
the Government made an historic announcement to the Imperial
Parliament, pledging it to the 'gradual development of self-
governing institutions in India'. In 1918 was published the
Montagu-Chelmsford Report; the *Government of India* Act was
passed in 1919. In 1930 the Statutory (Simon) Commission made
its Report. In November 1930 the Round Table Conference
began its sessions in London.

Nihil per saltum natura fecit. The sequence of events has
been more rapid and more significant in the fifteen years 1917–32
than in the preceding half-century, but though the pace quickened
there was no diversion in the direction of the journey.

The
E.I.C.

The establishment and development of British power in India
was the work of a company of merchants, which received its
Charter from Queen Elizabeth.[1] Originally started with no other
object than trade, this Company was drawn by uncontrollable circumstances into politics, and in the course of a century (1757–
1857) became the paramount power in India. The political career
of the Company was abruptly ended by the Mutiny, and India
passed in legal theory, as it had long been in fact, under the direct
rule of the English Crown. In 1876 Queen Victoria assumed,

India
under the
Crown

under the *Royal Titles Act* passed at the instance of Disraeli, the
style and title of Empress of India. On January 1, 1877, a great

---

[1] The whole story is told in some detail in my *English in India* (Oxford,
1932), and more briefly in my *England since Waterloo* (10th ed., 1933, Methuen).
But in the latter work the story is only carried down to the Mutiny. The
present chapter may be read as a sequel to Chapters XIV and XV of the
latter work, and as a summary of Chapters XII–XVIII of the former.

Durbar was held to proclaim to the peoples and princes of India the assumption of the new title by the Queen-Empress. Denounced by the English Liberals as ' bizarre ', as the characteristic work of a political charlatan, the *Royal Titles Act* gave formal expression to a change which had already taken place, and it was entirely ,in accord with Indian if not with English sentiment. ' The Princes and nations of India know ', said Disraeli, ' what this Bill means, and they know that what it means they wish '. A series of ceremonial visits paid by members of the Royal House to India, beginning with the visit of the Prince of Wales (afterwards King Edward VII) in 1875–6, and culminating in that of the King-Emperor and Queen-Empress in 1911, have given substance to the assumption of the Imperial title. *Kaisar-i-Hind*

Over nearly two-thirds of the sub-continent of India Queen Victoria became, in 1858, Sovereign ; over the native princes, who still ruled the rest of India, she became Suzerain. To her immediate subjects, and to the Feudatory Princes, she addressed a Proclamation, which not only enunciated admirable sentiments but contained passages which have been construed—and rightly —as solemn pledges. Among these passages two possess special significance. After disclaiming the intention to interfere with the religious faith or observances of the Indian peoples and promising ' to all alike the equal and impartial protection of the law ', the Queen's Proclamation proceeded : ' It is our further will that, so far as may be, our subjects of whatever class or creed be fully and freely admitted to any offices the duties of which they may be qualified by their education, abilities and integrity duly to discharge.' Those words made an impression upon the minds of educated natives which nothing will efface. *Royal Proclamation, 1858*

Even more specific was the pledge to the Princes :

' We desire no extension of our present territorial possessions ; and while we will permit no aggression upon our dominions or our rights to be attempted with impunity, we shall sanction no encroachment on those of others. We shall respect the rights, dignity, and honour of native princes as our own ; and we desire that they, as well as our own subjects, should enjoy that prosperity and that social advancement which can only be secured by internal peace and good government.' *The Crown and the Princes*

Both in the letter and in the spirit that promise was scrupulously fulfilled. Nothing could, indeed, have been more satisfactory than the relations which have on the whole subsisted between the Suzerain and the Feudatory Princes. The Princes quickly came to understand that the Queen meant what she said : that the period of conquest and expansion was at an end ; that the chiefs might look forward to a period of stabilization and tranquillity ; that if they were no longer permitted to engage in their wonted occupation and attack their neighbours, their neighbours would no longer be allowed to attack them. The Sovereign Power, while prohibiting attack, was bound to accept the responsibility for defence. In fine, it imposed on all alike the *Pax Britannica*. But if we guaranteed the thrones of the Princes, we were bound also to secure the well-being of their subjects. Rights involve duties ; privileges must not be enjoyed at the expense of subjects deprived of the only effective check upon despotism. This was the ' fundamental postulate ' of the new order, and its implications were gradually realized by the Feudatories, though not until they had been brought home by one or two cases in which persistent misgovernment was punished by deprivation ; deprivation was not, however, followed (as in the days of John Company) by annexation. The sceptre was invariably restored to a native successor.

The promises to the natives of British India were implemented not less scrupulously than those made to the Princes. The fulfilment of promises assumed many forms, but three stand out conspicuously : increased facilities for education ; the admission of natives to the Civil Service ; and a series of steps in the direction of self-government.

Education

The foundations of an educational policy were laid by Macaulay in his famous Minute of 1835. He insisted that English must be the medium of all higher education in India, and his whole scheme was based on the idea that the Indian peoples would be reached by a process of infiltration from above. His hopes were disappointed, and the scheme miscarried. In 1854 Sir Charles Wood, as President of the Board of Control, drafted a comprehensive scheme of education ; and Lord Dalhousie gave effect to it. At that time there were only 129 students in all the Government colleges in Bengal, Bihar and Orissa. Wood's scheme provided for the organization of an Education Department in each Presidency and Lieutenant-Governorship, and for a University in each of the capitals, but he laid special stress upon the need of primary education, and upon the use of the vernacular languages as the only media for imparting it. But the results were again disappointing. By 1870 the total number of elementary schools, conducted, aided or recognized by the State in British India, numbered only 16,500 and the pupils therein about half a million. Lord Mayo (Viceroy 1869–72) did much to improve matters. He derided Macaulay's idea of infiltration ; its only result was to educate a few hundred Babus for Government employment. Mayo's policy was on broader lines, yet by 1902 there were only 98,000 public primary schools, with some 8,200,000 scholars, in the whole of British India. It was reserved for Lord Curzon (1895–1905) to make an heroic effort to correct the initial blunder of Macaulay, and to devise a scheme of education better suited to the needs of the peoples for whom it was intended. Yet the results were still disappointingly meagre. Primary education is still so backward that out of the 320 millions of people in all India (including the Indian States and Burma) 296,000,000 are ' illiterate ', i.e. cannot write or read a letter in the vernacular.

The Sadler Commission (1919) made important recommendations for the improvement of University education, particularly in Bengal ; but the Simon Commission (1930) was constrained to emphasize its inherent weaknesses. The Universities are now overcrowded with men who ' are not profiting either intellectually or materially by their University training ; many, too easily admitted, fall by the way, having wasted precious years of youth ; many succeed in obtaining the coveted B.A. degree, only to find that the careers for which alone it fits them are hopelessly congested. Many of these half-educated and wholly disillusioned youths consequently remain unemployed, with results upon the political and social life of the country too obvious to call for emphasis. A handful of Indian youths complete their education not in India, but at the Inns of Court or the Universities in England. Of these some attain to distinguished positions in the Civil Service and in the legal profession. As to the effect of residence in England upon the others opinions widely differ.'

It must, then, be admitted that the efforts of English administrators to promote education in India have not been successful.

Yet the failure has not been due to lack of zeal or of benevolence. The English rulers of India have been genuinely anxious to implement the promises of Queen Victoria, to open to her Indian subjects every avenue for advancement, and to fit them by education for the discharge of the duties incidental thereto.

The Civil Service   Of those avenues the Civil Service was the most obvious. The *Charter Act* of 1833 had opened the Service to Indians, but little came of the opening until in 1853 the system of open competition was adopted.   The conditions of service were revised by the *Civil Service Act* of 1861, and an Act of 1870, having recited that ' it is expedient that additional facilities should be given for the employment of natives in India, of proved merit and ability, in the Civil Service ' of India, authorized the Government of India, with the approval of the Secretary of State, to frame rules for the appointment of Indians, without requiring them to pass the examination in London.   But little came of this Act until in 1879 Lord Lytton's government framed a series of rules for a Statutory Civil Service.

Under this scheme one-sixth of the ' reserved ' posts, in addition to some of the most important posts in the uncovenanted service, were to be filled by natives of India, appointed under carefully made rules.   In order to give reality to the concession, the number of appointments made after examination in England was, in 1880, reduced by one-sixth, but the scheme failed to attract the higher classes of Indians, and only about sixty Indians had been appointed when, in 1891, the system was again changed.

The Civil Service was henceforward to consist of three branches : (i) the Imperial Indian Civil Service, to be recruited, as formerly, by open competition in England, though equally open to Indians and Englishmen ; (ii) a Provincial Service, to be recruited by the Local Government in each Province by direct nomination, by competitive examination, or by promotion from the Subordinate Service ; (iii) the ' Subordinate Service ', consisting of the lower-grade appointments of the old uncovenanted class.   The two latter classes had been recruited almost entirely from Indians ; the first class, comprising all the most important posts, continued to be mainly filled by Englishmen, though there was a gradually increasing infusion of Indians, a large proportion of whom were educated at British Universities, and all of whom sat for examination in London.

Indians were still far from satisfied with these changes. They complained that in the Imperial Service the progress made in ' Indianization '—as it began to be called—was lamentably slow. Nor can it be denied that there was substance in the complaint. Despite all the authoritative declarations of policy, despite the recommendations of one Royal Commission after another, all the posts in the Public Service which carried a salary of £800 a year or upwards were still, prior to the World War, with the exception of ninety, filled by Englishmen.

During the War recruiting in England was suspended, and no sooner did the War come to an end than the *Indian Government Act* of 1919 revolutionized the whole position. But that Act, so far from satisfying Indian aspirations, served rather to stimulate anti-British agitation in India : the impression was given that the English were ' packing-up ', and that within a measurable distance of time there would not be an English soldier or an English civilian left in India. The impression was strengthened by the permission given to All-India Service officers to retire, before they had completed the normal period of service, on a proportionate pension.

Discouraged by the prospect opened out by the legislation of 1919, officers, particularly in the Civil Service and the Police, availed themselves in large numbers of this permission. By 1924 the number had risen to 345, and the Government was suddenly deprived of the services of a large proportion of its most valuable and most experienced officers. This was an exceedingly serious matter. Moreover, recruiting, suspended during the War, was not resumed after its close. Oxford was for sixty years one of the principal recruiting centres for the ' Indian Civil '. During the five years before the War it contributed nearly 120 recruits to that service. During the years 1921–3 the aggregate was only ten. So it was at Cambridge and elsewhere.

To meet this serious situation, another Royal Commission was, in 1923, appointed, under the chairmanship of Lord Lee of Fareham. The recommendations of the Lee Commission adhered closely to the principle of the Act of 1919. They meant in effect, that in the ' transferred ' sphere of the Provincial

Governments, the whole administration would be staffed by Indians; that in the superior posts of the Civil Service the proportion of Indians and Englishmen would, by a gradual process of 'Indianization', become (by 1939), 50 to 50, as against the existing (January 1, 1929) proportion of 894 Englishmen against 367 Indians; while in the Police the English would be reduced from 564 to 434, and the Indians be increased from 128 to 251. This meant that under normal conditions for entrants there would be less than 1,200 Englishmen in the two ' Security ' Services to deal with a population of 250 million people.

The Lee Commission also dealt in a way ' generally accepted as adequate ' (according to the Simon Commission) with the grievances and apprehensions of the English members of the great Indian Services, with the result that British recruitment is now in a ' more healthy condition ', and the rate of retirement on proportionate pension has diminished.

To the position of the Civil Service justly described by Mr. Lloyd George as ' the steel frame of the whole structure ', the Simon Commission naturally gave close attention, but the adoption of their recommendations must necessarily depend on the course taken by constitutional evolution. The transference of British India to the Crown was followed by a series of measures which, by their progressive and cumulative effect, have gone far to transfer political responsibility from the Imperial Crown and Parliament to the Indian peoples.

Constitutional Evolution

Of these measures the first was the *Indian Councils Act* of 1861. That Act modified the composition of the Governor-General's Council, or Executive, and remodelled the legislative system of British India. A fifth ' ordinary ' member was added to the Council, and for purposes of legislation it was reinforced by the addition of not less than six or more than twelve members, to be nominated by the Governor-General for a term of two years. Not less than half the ' additional ' members were to be non-official.

Indian Councils Act, 1861

Since 1861 Executive business has been more and more departmentalized, each of the chief departments, such as Finance and Education, being placed under the special direction of a member of Council, assisted by one of the secretaries to the Government of India. The Governor-General himself retained immed:ate control of Foreign Affairs. The Council is sometimes spoken of as a 'Cabinet'; but, though resembling the Presidential executive of America, it lacks the peculiar and distinctive characteristic of an English Cabinet in that it is not dependent upon or responsible to an elected Legislature. Such 'responsibility' is one of the objects at which the Congress Party are definitely aiming.

The Act of 1861 restored the right of legislation to the Presidency Councils of Madras and Bombay. Similarly reinforced by additional members it directed the Governor-General to establish by proclamation a Legislative Council for Bengal, and gave him power to establish such Councils elsewhere. Thus Bengal obtained a Council in 1862, the North-West Provinces and Oudh in 1886, the Punjab in 1897, and Burma and various other provinces in due course.

The year 1861 was further memorable, in a constitutional sense, for the passing of the *Indian High Courts Act*, which abolished the old *Sadr Adalat* (Courts generally inherited by the Company from their native predecessors), and set up new High Courts of Judicature in Calcutta, Madras, and Bombay. Each Court was to consist of a Chief Justice and not more than fifteen judges. All the judges were to be appointed by, and hold office at the pleasure of, the Crown. *The Judiciary*

In the sphere of central government there is no important development to record between the measure of 1861 and the legislation devised by Lord Dufferin, and carried into effect by Lord Lansdowne as Viceroy, and Lord Cross (as Secretary of State), in 1892. The viceroyalty of Lord Ripon (1880–4) was, however, memorable both for what he achieved in the sphere of local government, and still more for the agitation aroused by proposals which he failed to carry. Lord Ripon began by repealing the *Vernacular Press Act*, which had been passed in 1868 to curb the seditious and anarchical tendencies of some portions of the native press, and re-enacted during the World War in more stringent form. *Local Government*

More important was Lord Ripon's reform of local government. A full generation of Indians had by this time enjoyed the advantages of a 'Western' education; not a few Indians had studied the working of English political institutions at first hand; many of them had imbibed the political philosophy of Mill, and had come to share the Englishman's conviction that ' liberty ' was inseparable from parliamentary government.   Indians were seeking and finding employment in the Public Services, and at the Bar, and had been promoted to the Bench.   Among these English-educated Indians there was generated a not unnatural ambition to obtain for the people of their own races a larger measure of self-government.   With this ambition Lord Ripon and his legal member of Council, Mr. (afterwards Sir C.) Ilbert, were in complete sympathy.   But they wisely began with local government.   Between 1883 and 1885 a series of Acts was passed to establish District Boards, and subordinate bodies, and to extend the powers of municipal corporations.   So far as possible an elective and non-official element was to be introduced, but wide discretionary powers were conferred upon the local authorities in order that they might apply the general principle with some regard to local conditions and necessities.   Lord Ripon was under no illusions as to the probable effect of his reforms. ' It is not ', he confessed, ' primarily with a view to improvements in administration that this measure is brought forward. It is chiefly desirable as a measure of political and popular education.' ' Educative ' it may have proved, but the municipalities are, not seldom, both inefficient and corrupt.

Both in India and at home these measures were regarded with not a little apprehension ; but the opposition to them was negligible compared with that aroused by a Bill, generally known as the Ilbert Bill, which proposed to remove from the Code of Criminal Procedure ' at once and completely every judicial disqualification based merely on race distinctions '.   Racial feelings were bitterly aroused, especially among the non-official classes, by the suggestion that Europeans should be put at the mercy of native judges.   Racial prejudices on one side embittered those on the other, and in face of the agitation which sprang up, the Government withdrew the Bill.   A compromise was, however, reached in 1884, by which Europeans charged before a District Magistrate or Sessions Judge might claim a mixed jury, not less than half the members of which were to be Europeans or Americans.

Indian
National   Amid the angry tumult which raged round the Ilbert Bill a
Congress more important event was almost ignored, partly perhaps be-

cause, before it actually happened, Lord Ripon had been replaced by a Viceroy who enjoyed almost universal confidence and popularity, Lord Dufferin.

In the first months of Lord Dufferin's viceroyalty there met for the first time at Bombay (December 1885) a National Congress representing the most advanced section of educated Indian opinion. How far the Congress was, or is, representative of any class, except that to which we had ourselves given a quasi-national character by the common use of the English tongue, it is difficult to say. Certain it is, however, that from its first meeting in 1885 down to the present day, the Congress has gathered a rapidly increasing number of adherents, who with ever-increasing vehemence have demanded the concession of a Constitution framed on the model of Western democracy, with a representative and elected Legislature and an Executive responsible thereto.

Lord Dufferin, while determined to suppress incendiary agita- Lord tion, declared himself in favour of giving ' a wider share in the Dufferin, Viceroy, administration of public affairs to such Indian gentlemen as by 1884-8 their influence, their acquirements, and the confidence they inspire in their fellow-countrymen are marked out as fitted to assist with their counsels the responsible rulers of the country '. He expressly disclaimed any idea of establishing a parliamentary system for British India. He described his scheme as ' a plan for the enlargement of our provincial councils, for the enhancement of their status, the multiplication of their functions, the partial introduction into them of the elective principle and the liberalization of their general character as political institutions '. But the elective element must always remain in a minority, and the paramount control of policy always be left in the hands of each provincial government.

The principles were frankly though cautiously applied in the *Indian* Act of 1892. The Legislative Councils, both imperial and pro- *Councils Act,* 1892 vincial, were by that measure considerably enlarged. In the Imperial Council the additional members were to number not fewer than ten, or more than sixteen ; not more than six were to be officials, and the Governor-General-in-Council was empowered to make such regulations as would secure representation to various interests and classes. The Legislative Councils of Madras and Bombay were each enlarged by twenty additional members, and of these not more than nine were to be officials. An official majority was retained, but as regards the unofficial minority the principle of election was virtually admitted, though the term itself was carefully avoided.

Not less noteworthy than the enlargement of the Councils and the extension of their representative character, was the widening of their functions. An annual budget was to be laid before them and they were entrusted with the right of discussing, though not of voting upon it. The right of interpellating the Executive members, denied to the Councils in 1861, was now conferred upon them.

The advance thus registered was substantial; but it failed, of course, to satisfy the more ardent spirits in the Congress party, who maintained a more or less continuous agitation until larger, though still cautious, concessions were embodied in the Morley-Minto reform of 1909. 'A wave of political unrest', to use Lord Morley's own words, 'was indeed slowly sweeping over India. Revolutionary voices, some moderate, others extreme, grew articulate and shrill, and claims or aspirations for extending the share of the people in their own government took more organized shape.'

'Unrest' in India   'Political unrest' is one of those political euphemisms under which is concealed a multitude of ambiguities. For nearly half a century the British Raj has been confronted with an agitation whose precise character is not easily determined. Were India a 'nation', it would be accurate to describe it as a 'national' movement, and that there is in it an element of nationalism it were affectation to deny. Yet it is equally true that any element of 'nationalism' which it possesses must be ascribed wholly to the policy consistently pursued by Great Britain in the government of India. Hand in hand with the process of unification has gone a policy of political evolution—the introduction into India of the political institutions familiar to Englishmen in their European home. More and more of political responsibility has been devolved upon the shoulders of Indians. The policy has been embodied in Acts of Parliament, and has been repeatedly recommended in Official Proclamations; not least emphatically in those directly addressed to the Princes and Peoples of India by successive sovereigns.

Wholly benevolent as were the motives that inspired this policy it undoubtedly diffused a sense of instability in India. That feeling was stimulated by events outside India. The reverses suffered by the Italians in Abyssinia in 1887 and 1893 caused some excitement in the Indian bazaars. The defeats inflicted upon British forces in the earlier stages of the South African War caused much more. If a handful of Dutch farmers, ' rightly struggling to be free ', could thus defy the Imperial might of Britain, what might not be achieved by 250 millions of people in India ? But far the most important of all such events was the defeat of Russia at the hands of Japan (1904–5). The repercussion of that momentous war was felt throughout the whole continent of Asia, and, indeed, in all parts of the world where coloured races were in contact with whites. Most of all was it felt in India, where the Japanese victory was craftily represented as a blow to the prestige not of Russia only, but of all the Western peoples, not excepting, of course, the English.

The Russo-Japanese War coincided with the closing year of Lord Curzon's viceroyalty. That statesman's career in India had in it an element of tragedy. No Viceroy ever entered upon his high office with more complete equipment or more generous hopes. No man ever devoted himself to a task, great or humble, with more tireless industry. He was rarely free from pain, and it was amazing what, in spite of it, he accomplished. There was indeed hardly any sphere of administration into which he did not penetrate ; hardly any feature of Indian life on which he did not leave the impress of his own individuality : defence and frontier policy ; education, agriculture, irrigation, finance, and industry ; art, archaeology, and architecture ; game preservation and the conservation of historical monuments ; sanitation, precautions against famine and plague, and what not. But the detailed story of these activities must be read elsewhere.[1] Ambitious Curzon undoubtedly was, and autocratic ; but the mainspring of his multifarious activities was zeal for the public service, and genuine love for the people he ruled. Deep, especially, was his solicitude for the well-being of those patient, kindly, inar-

Lord Curzon, Viceroy, 1899–1905

[1] e.g. in *The India We Served* (London, 1928), by Sir W. R. Lawrence, who was Curzon's Private Secretary ; or Lord Zetland's *Life* (1928).

ticulate millions who drew their scanty subsistence from the
cultivation of the soil. Towards the 'national' aspirations of
the 'politicians' he was less sympathetic; yet he welcomed and
encouraged their co-operation. 'We are ordained to walk here
in the same track together for many a long day to come. You
cannot do without us. We should be impotent without you.
Let the Englishman and the Indian accept the consecration of
a union that is so mysterious as to have in it something of the
Divine, and let our common ideal be a united country and a
happier people.' These words, spoken at Calcutta in 1902, expressed his innermost conviction. Yet he left India a deeply
disillusioned man. His educational policy and his scheme for
the partition of Bengal were alike regarded as reflections upon
Bengali character, and the latter policy was reversed in 1911.
But even more damaging to the prestige, both of Curzon and of
British power in India, were the circumstances which led to his
resignation (November 1905). Whether he was right in thinking
that to combine in one person the offices of Commander-in-Chief
and Military Member of Council involved an undue subordination
of the civil to the military power; whether Lord Kitchener, as
Commander-in-Chief, was right in insisting upon the combination; and whether the India Office were right in supporting the
soldier against the Viceroy—these are still matters of controversy. What is certain is that the supersession of Lord Curzon,
the strongest and proudest of recent Viceroys, dealt a serious
blow at the prestige of his office, and sensibly diminished the
respect due to the King-Emperor whom he represented.

The
Morley-
Minto
régime

Hardly had Lord Curzon been succeeded as Viceroy by Lord
Minto, when the advent of a Radical ministry with Lord Morley
at the India Office, gave fresh hope to the 'nationalists' in India.
A religious revival among the Hindus stimulated and sanctified
preparations for armed insurrection. A campaign of violence
and assassination was launched, and many innocent victims paid
with their lives for the weak benevolence of the new régime.
Neither the visit in the winter of 1905–6 of the then Prince and
Princess of Wales, who were received with immense enthusiasm,
nor the fact that the new Viceroy and the new Secretary of State
were known to be contemplating a further instalment of constitutional reform, seriously interrupted the campaign of violence.

To get rid of the foreign government by any means effectual for the purpose was inculcated as a religious duty.

The Government was seriously alarmed. In 1907 legislation was passed on the lines familiar in Irish ' Coercion ' Acts. Local Governments were empowered to proclaim certain districts, with a view to the stricter control of public meetings, and to deport offenders. These precautions were followed in 1908 by Acts making it a felony to manufacture or to be in possession of explosives, or to incite to murder in the Press, while a third Act, passed at a single sitting of the Legislative Council, conferred upon the Courts in cases of seditious violence summary jurisdiction. In the same year Bal Gangadhar Tilak, a Poona Brahman, who stood forth as the leader of the extremists, openly justified the weapon of assassination, and invoked blessings on the heads of the murderers, was tried and sentenced to six years' imprisonment.

Such was the atmosphere in which the constitutional reforms known as the Morley-Minto reforms were launched.

Meanwhile, on November 2, 1908, being the fiftieth anniversary of the assumption of the government of India by the Crown, the King-Emperor took the opportunity of addressing to the Princes and Peoples of India a Proclamation.

Proclamation of King Edward VII (1908)

The King-Emperor, looking back on the ' labours of the past half-century with clear gaze and good conscience ', noted the splendid fight against the ' calamities of Nature ', drought and plague ; the wonderful material advance that India had made ; the impartial administration of law ; and the unswerving loyalty of the Feudatory Princes and Ruling Chiefs whose ' rights and privileges have been respected, preserved, and guarded '. He referred to the paramount duty of repressing ' with a stern arm guilty conspiracies that have no just cause and no serious aim ' and are abhorrent to the great mass of the Indian peoples, and declared that such conspiracies would not be suffered to interrupt the task of ' building up the fabric of security and order '.

' From the first,' he added, ' the principle of representative institutions began to be gradually introduced, and the time has come when . . . that principle may be prudently extended. Important classes among you, representing ideas that have been fostered and encouraged by British rule, claim equality of citizenship, and a greater share in legislation and government. The politic satisfaction of such a claim will strengthen, not impair, existing authority and power. Administration will be all the more efficient, if the officers who conduct it have greater opportunities of contact with those whom it affects and with those who influence and reflect common opinion about it.' [1]

Lord Morley and Lord Minto were in complete accord both as to the necessity of protecting ' peaceful and harmless people, both Indian and European, from the bloodstained havoc of anarchic conspiracy ', and also in the determination not to be deterred by such havoc from pressing on with ameliorative reform.

Morley-Minto Reforms

Accordingly, after long consultation between Viceroy and Secretary of State, the latter moved the Second Reading of the Indian Councils Bill on February 23, 1909. Lord Morley disclaimed with emphasis any idea of setting up parliamentary government in India, yet his Act has generally been regarded as a step in that direction.

Indian Councils Act, 1909

Under the Act and the Regulations made under its authority : (i) All the Legislative Councils, both Central and Provincial, were increased in size, and the principle of election was introduced alongside that of nomination. Henceforth every Council was to be composed of three classes of members : (*a*) nominated official members ; (*b*) nominated non-official members : (*c*) elected members. Separate representation was also guaranteed to Mohammedans. (ii) Not only the size but the functions of the Councils were enlarged. They were invested with power to move, and to vote on, resolutions, not only on the budget, but on any matter of general public interest ; but the Executive Government was not bound to act on such resolutions. The right to interpellate ministers was also extended by permission to put supplementary questions. (iii) As regards the Executive Councils, the maximum number of ordinary members in Madras and Bombay was raised from two to four. In 1910 the Secretary of State appointed a Hindu barrister, Mr. (afterwards Lord) Sinha, as legal member of the Viceroy's Council, and, on his resignation, a Mohammedan gentleman, Mr. Syed Ali Imam. Two Indian gentlemen had in 1907 been appointed members of the Council of India.

[1] Proclamation of the King-Emperor to the Princes and Peoples of India (November 2, 1908).

Lord Morley claimed for his measures that they marked the 'opening of a very important chapter in the history of Great Britain and India'; but whither, if not towards the parliamentary government he deprecated, did that chapter tend?

That was a question for the future to answer. For the moment, **The** the operation of the Morley-Minto reforms was overshadowed by **Corona-** the visit to India of the King-Emperor, George V, and his con- **Durbar,** sort, and by the superb ceremonial of the Coronation Durbar, **1911** and the dramatic announcements made thereat. On December 7, 1911, Their Majesties made their State entry into the capital of the Mogul Emperors and, on the 12th, with stately and superb ceremonial the great Coronation Durbar was held. The King-Emperor announced a series of administrative changes conse-quential upon the 'modification' of Lord Curzon's partition of Bengal; the creation of a Governor-in-Council for the freshly delimited Province of Bengal; a Lieutenant-Governorship for the new Province of Bihar, Orissa, and Chota Nagpur, with a capital at Patna; and a Chief Commissionship for Assam. But these were matters of relatively small importance. Great was the sensation when the King-Emperor announced that the capital of the Indian Empire was presently to be transferred from Calcutta to Delhi, and that the supreme Government was to be established in a new city planned (and now built) on a scale of dazzling magnificence. As to the wisdom of the transference of the seat of government, opinion was and is sharply divided. Was the change due to the promptings of an historic imagination? Or to strategical considerations? Or to a desire to punish the seditious and anarchical Hindus of Bengal, and to gratify the more loyal Mohammedans?

These questions could not but obtrude themselves though they were temporarily smothered by the dazzling splendour of the spectacle at Delhi.

Three years after the King-Emperor's announcements the whole Imperial fabric of which he is the corner-stone was shaken to its foundations by the shock of world-war.

Of the contribution made by India to the war effort of the Empire mention has already been made. The contribution was the more significant in view of the fact that the military organiza-tion of India was planned to maintain internal peace, and to meet

M.E.—17

tribal outbreaks on the frontier, and to repel a continental invasion. For such purposes, and as was frequently proved, the organization was admirable.

Defence   The transference of British India to the Crown closed the period of conquest and expansion characteristic of the Company's rule. It remained to stabilize the situation, to make our conquests secure. The map of British India to-day is (excluding Burma) the map finally drawn by Lord Dalhousie, except for certain North-West Frontier patches, and notably the lodgement at Quetta, giving us command of the Bolan pass. The army in India has not lacked experience of actual warfare, but with the exception of the second Afghan War (1878–80), precipitated by the headstrong policy of Lord Lytton, and memorable for Lord Roberts's march to Kandahar; of the third Burmese War in 1885, and of the Tirah campaign in 1897–8, military operations have been of a minor character, and mostly directed against the fierce tribesmen on the North-West Frontier. Of these latter expeditions there were between 1850 and 1922 no fewer than seventy-two. For participation in a European war, however, India was not prepared, and deserves the more credit for the ready response made to the demands of the Imperial Government.

Unfortunately the splendid spirit manifested in India in the early days of the War was not maintained until its close.

' The War ', as Sir Valentine Chirol has said, ' lasted too long and was too remote from [the Indian people]. . . . The sick and wounded from Mesopotamia brought home too often tales of mismanagement and defeat, startlingly corroborated by the thunderbolt of the Kut surrender. . . . If England had been reluctant at first to credit Kitchener's prophecy that the War would last three years, Indians were still more at a loss to understand why victory should be so slow to come to Great Britain and her powerful allies, and they began to doubt whether it would come at all.'

Agitation in India   Such doubts were sedulously disseminated by the disaffected Babus of Bengal who had contributed nothing of personal service to the war effort; the revolutionary agitation was renewed; the anarchical elements once more came to the front.

During the first two years of War there had been an almost complete cessation of outrages or even disorder. The exception, curiously enough, was provided by the Punjab, whose peasants supplied half the combatants in the expeditionary forces. The immediate cause of the outbreak was the return to India of some 400 Sikhs and fifty to sixty Punjabi Moslems who, contrary to the immigration orders, had attempted to land at Vancouver, and had been refused admission by the Canadian authorities. Inflamed by propaganda literature circulated by Indian revolutionary societies in the United States, these Punjabis returned to India, bent upon making trouble for the British Government. For some ten months (October 1914–August 1915) the Punjab was the scene of a serious revolutionary outbreak, eventually quelled by the courage and resource of the Lieutenant-Governor, Sir Michael O'Dwyer, loyally supported by the great majority of the inhabitants, as well as by the Rulers of the native States in the Punjab. In the suppression of the disorders in the Punjab, as well as others which, later in the War, broke out elsewhere, the Government was materially assisted, on the one hand by the passing (March 1915) of a *Criminal Law Amendment Act*, conferring upon the Executive in India powers similar to those conferred upon it in England by the Defence of the Realm Regulations ; on the other by the ' correct ' attitude of the Indian Congress and the Moslem League.

But the lull was temporary and delusive. In 1914 B. G. Tilak, a Poona Brahman, who from the early 'nineties onwards had been the powerful and acknowledged leader of the Hindu extremists, was released on the expiration of his sentence of six years' imprisonment. In the following year the Congress meeting at Cawnpore endorsed the demand formulated by Tilak and Mrs. Annie Besant for ' Home Rule within the Empire ', and in 1917 elected Mrs. Besant to the Presidential chair.

This was the moment chosen by the British Government for the historic announcement made to Parliament on August 20. Declaration of August 20, 1917

' The policy of His Majesty's Government ', so the Declaration ran, ' with which the Government of India are in complete accord, is that of the increasing association of Indians in every branch of the administration, and the gradual development of self-governing institutions with a view to the progressive realization of responsible government in India as an integral part of the British Empire. They have decided that substantial steps in this direction should be taken as soon as possible. . . . I would add that progress in this policy can only be achieved by successive stages. The British Government and the Government of India, on whom the responsibility lies for the welfare and advancement of the Indian peoples, must be judges of the time and measure of such advance, and they must be guided by the co-operation received from those upon whom new opportunities of service will thus be conferred, and by the extent to which it is found that confidence can be reposed in their sense of responsibility.'

As was only to be expected, public attention fastened upon the first paragraph, and in particular upon the crucial words 'responsible government', while the second and conditioning paragraph was at the time and subsequently too often ignored.

The Declaration was made to the House of Commons by Mr. E. S. Montagu, who had only just succeeded Sir Austen Chamberlain as Secretary of State for India ; but, since he was not a member of the War Cabinet, his responsibility for the Declaration was less than that of Lord Curzon, who was a member and whose pen had drafted the critical words. Yet except for the words 'responsible government', now used officially for the first time in relation to India, the resolution differed little in wording from that of successive Statutes and Proclamations from 1833 onwards. The resolution came, however, at a moment when the whole British Empire was fain to acknowledge a deep debt of gratitude to the fighting peoples of India. Unfortunately, it was interpreted in India not as a graceful acknowledgement of the loyal co-operation, but as a concession to the Congress politicians, to whom the Empire owed and meant less than nothing.

The Montagu-Chelmsford Report   That interpretation was accentuated by the publication (April 1918) of the *Report* made to Parliament by the Viceroy and the Secretary of State who had visited India in the preceding winter. The Report contained a number of detailed recommendations for the future government of India, subsequently embodied in the Act of 1919. One sentence, almost parenthetical, revealed the spirit in which the Report was drafted :

'We believe profoundly that . . . nationhood within the Empire represents something better than anything India has hitherto attained ; that the placid pathetic contentment of the masses is not the soil on which Indian nationhood will grow, and that in deliberately disturbing it we are working for her highest good.'

It might have been anticipated that a Report designed to disturb contentment would at least placate the extremists. It did nothing of the kind. On the contrary, the Congress Party declared that the Montagu-Chelmsford scheme meant for India ' perpetual slavery which can only be broken by a revolution '.

They proceeded to break it. Meanwhile, ominously coincident with the publication of the Montagu-Chelmsford Report was that of Mr. Justice Rowlatt's Committee which had been appointed in December 1917 to investigate the genesis and character of the recent outrages. The Rowlatt Report revealed a dangerous and widespread conspiracy designed, by means of bomb-outrages, by murder and assassination of police officers and other officials, by gang-robberies recalling the ' dacoities ' of old days, and by other serious crimes, to paralyse, and ultimately by force to extinguish, British rule in India. The Committee recommended that emergency powers should be conferred by legislation upon the Executive. The *Rowlatt Act* was passed to carry out the recommendations, but was never put into force.

The Rowlatt Report

Nevertheless, the passing of the *Rowlatt Act* evoked a storm of indignant protest and led to a persistent agitation which gave to one of the most remarkable and most inscrutable personalities who have ever appeared in India a welcome opportunity. Mr. Gandhi seized it with consummate ability.

Mr. Gandhi

In February 1919 he launched his Civil Disobedience Campaign—an advance upon passive resistance, and this was followed, almost immediately, by renewed outbreaks at Delhi, Ahmedabad, Amritsar, and other places. At Amritsar, near Lahore, a formidable rising was quelled by the drastic action taken by General Dyer. The Amritsar incident was (in Carlyle's phrase) no ' rose-water surgery ', but it may be that, though it cost hundreds of lives, it saved thousands ; that even if General Dyer temporarily lost his head and finally his job, he saved a Province. Anyway, the scale of the disturbances may be judged by the fact that in connexion with the outrages in Lahore and Amritsar no fewer than 2,500 persons were brought to trial, and 1,800 were convicted. With the help of martial law order was gradually restored.

Govern-
ment of
India
Act, 1919

Provin-
cial
Govern-
ment

Meanwhile, the Imperial Parliament proceeded to embody in *The Government of India Act* (1919) the recommendations of the Montagu-Chelmsford Report. The most important changes affected only the Provincial Governments. In the nine Governor's Provinces, government was henceforward to be based on the principle of Dyarchy, or a division of the functions of government into two sections. Certain subjects—such as police and the administration of justice, and irrigation and land revenue—were *reserved* for the exclusive jurisdiction of the Governor and his Executive Councillors, some Indian and some British, who, though official members of the provincial legislature, were responsible, not to it but solely to the Government. Other subjects, such as education, public health, agriculture, local government, public works, and like matters, were *transferred* to the control of ministers chosen from and responsible to the local legislature, or Legislative Council. The Legislative Councils were to contain at least 70 per cent. of elected members. For the due performance of his functions in respect of the *reserved* subjects the Governor could, in the last resort, make financial and legislative provision against the will of the Legislature. It was, however, contemplated that if the new system worked satisfactorily the range of transferred subjects should be extended, until ultimately the whole administration should be handed over to responsible ministers.

Central
Govern-
ment

The changes effected in the Supreme Government were relatively unimportant. The principle of Dyarchy was not extended to the Supreme Government, to which forty-seven ' central' subjects, such as Defence, Foreign Relations, Relations with the Indian States, Customs, Coinage and Currency, Communications, Police and Civil and Criminal law, were by the Act reserved. Executive authority is still vested in the Viceroy and his Executive Council, consisting of seven heads of Departments, appointed by and responsible to the Crown.

The Central Legislature consists of two Houses—the Council of State and the Legislative Assembly or Lower House. The Council of State consists of 60 members, of whom 34 are elected on a very restricted franchise : the rest are nominated, and not more than 20 of them may be officials.

The Assembly contains a much larger majority of elected

members—104 out of 144. They are directly elected by constituencies which, though enormously big, contain only 6½ million electors—considerably less than a quarter of the electorate of the United Kingdom. The right of legislation, including supply, is vested ordinarily in the Legislature, but, in order to prevent a deadlock in administration, the Viceroy is empowered, when necessary, to override the will of the Legislature both in regard to grants of supply and ordinary legislation. Experience has proved the necessity for this regrettable but essential precautionary provision. The Supreme Government as a whole has powers of superintendence, direction, and control over the Provincial Governments in respect of all the *reserved* subjects.

There has also been established an Indian Privy Council ' as a means of honouring and employing ripe wisdom and meritorious service '.

The scheme further provided for a Chamber of Princes to form a link between the Indian States and the British Government. Of the Ruling Princes 108 are entitled to sit in the Chamber in their own right : 127 of the smaller States are represented by 12 members.

The new constitution was formally inaugurated on February 21, 1921, at Delhi by H.R.H. the Duke of Connaught, on behalf of the King-Emperor.

The persistent agitation in British India naturally caused some disquietude among the Rulers of the Indian States. In the whole Empire there is no more loyal element than these Rulers, but the efforts of the Montagu-Chelmsford Report to disturb the contentment of the Indian peasantry, even if only partially successful, inevitably reacted upon the subjects of the native Princes. Accordingly, at their request, a small Committee was, in 1927, appointed (i) to report upon the relationship between the Paramount Power and the Indian States, and (ii) to inquire into the financial and economic relations between British India and the States and to . . . make ' recommendations . . . for their adjustment '. *The Indian States Committee*

The Report, published in 1929, did not, in regard to certain technical matters, give complete satisfaction to the Princes ; but it was made clear that the Princes would continue to enjoy complete autonomy, ' so long as they governed their people well ', and they would not be handed over to a new Indian 'Dominion' without their own consent. This was the vital point.

The Statutory Commission Almost simultaneously with the appointment of the Indian States Committee, the Royal Commission, provided for in the Act of 1919, was appointed, under the chairmanship of Sir John Simon—a distinguished lawyer and former Home Secretary—to inquire ' into the working of the system of government, the growth of education, and the development of representative institutions in British India ', and to report ' as to whether and to what extent it is desirable to establish the principle of responsible government, or to extend, modify, or restrict the degree of responsible government then existing therein '.

The Simon Commission after two prolonged visits to India laid their Report before Parliament in June 1930, in two parts.

Part I (Cmd. 3568) contained a survey, historical and analytical, of conditions in British India. It laid bare certain ' stubborn facts which no amount of rhetoric or appeal to abstract principles can alter '. Nor could there be any two opinions as to the value of this survey. The reception accorded to vol. i of the Report was, consequently, remarkable for its unanimity and cordiality.

General Principles It was otherwise in regard to Part II (Cmd. 3569) which began by explaining the general principles upon which the Commissioners based their proposals. The first was that ' Indian nationalism is a phenomenon which cannot be disregarded by the rulers either of British India or of the Indian States '. A second affirmed that it is ' only under a federal system that the sentiment underlying the [nationalist] movement can be given effective expression '. The ultimate Constitution must, therefore, have regard to ' a future development, when India as a whole, not merely British India, will take her place among the constituent States of the Commonwealth of Nations united under the Crown '. Any new Constitution should, moreover, avoid rigidity and ' should as far as possible contain within itself provision for its own development '. Nor should it necessarily be too slavishly imitative of the English Constitution.

Recommendations The specific recommendations as regards Provincial Governments were :

(i) The abolition of ' dyarchy '; (ii) the introduction of ' Responsible Government ', with Cabinets designed on the British model, but with a reservation of emergency powers to the Governor ; (iii) an extended franchise for the Provincial Legislatures but a continuance of Communal Electorates for the protection of important minorities, ' unless and until agreement can be reached upon a better method ; and (iv) a provision for constitutional revision by the Legislatures, subject always to the protection of the rights of minorities.

' Responsibility ' thus fully and frankly conceded to the Provincial Governments was not to extend to the Central Executive which was to remain in the hands of the Viceroy and of ministers responsible to him.

The Central Legislature was to consist of two Houses : (i) the Legislative Assembly to be henceforth styled the ' Federal Assembly ', and to be reconstituted on the basis of the representation of the Provinces and other areas in British India according to population.

The Upper House or ' Council of State ' was to retain its title and functions, and to consist of nominated members and members elected by a process of indirect election by the Provincial Second Chambers.

The constitutional structure was to be crowned by a Council for Greater India, endowed with ' consultative and deliberative functions ' in regard to a scheduled list of ' matters of common concern ' to the States and British India. This Council was designed as a step towards the Federation of Greater India.

In the course of their investigations the Commissioners had, in truth, become more and more ' impressed by the impossibility of considering the constitutional problems of British India without taking into account the relations between British India and the Indian States '. They, accordingly, suggested the ' setting up of some sort of Conference, after the Reports of the Statutory Commission and the Indian Central Committee have been made, considered, and published . . . and that in this Conference His Majesty's Government should meet both representatives of British India and representatives of the States '.

Mr. Ramsay MacDonald, having consulted the leaders of the other parties, concurred ; and, on November 12, 1930, the King-Emperor inaugurated the Round Table Conference.

The Conference was not many hours old before the question

Round Table Conference

of an All-India Federation overshadowed all others. It continued to do so until, on January 19, 1931, the first session closed. Agreement had by that time been reached on two fundamental points : that an All-India Federation should, as soon as possible, be created, with a Central Executive responsible to a Central Legislature, and that certain powers should be ' reserved ' to the British Government, to ensure the maintenance of order, the protection of minorities, and the fulfilment of India's obligations to the outside world.

The second session of the Conference opened in London on September 8. Early in March Lord Irwin (Viceroy 1926–31) had concluded with Gandhi the ' Delhi Pact '. The ' civil disobedience ' movement inaugurated by Gandhi in 1930, was, on certain conditions, conceded by the Viceroy, to be discontinued, and the Congress Party was to participate, as it had not done during the first session, in the Round Table Conference. Accordingly, Gandhi himself attended it, but though it sat until December no solution was reached on the crucial problem of the representation and protection of religious minorities. On this ' communal problem ' deadlock had been reached.

The White Paper, 1931   Under these circumstances the British Government, now reconstructed on a national, non-party basis, decided to assume responsibility for drafting a constitution. The main lines of the Government policy were accordingly embodied in a White Paper.[1] Three small Committees went to India in 1932 to investigate and report upon the three subjects of the Franchise, Finance, and the Indian States.[2] A third session of the Round Table Conference to focus the work of the preceding sessions was held in London in November–December 1932, and in March 1933 the definite proposals of the Government were submitted to Parliament in a second White Paper.[3] A Joint Select Committee of Lords and Commons, ' with power to call into consultation representatives of the Indian States and British India ', was appointed ' to consider the future government of India and, in particular, to examine and report upon the proposals in the said Command Paper '.

' In thinking of her work in India, Great Britain may look back proudly, but she must also anxiously look forward.' Of her

[1] Cmd. 3972 of 1931.   [2] Report, Cmd. 4068, 4069 and 4103 of 1932.
[3] Cmd. 4268.

just pride in the achievements of the past nothing can deprive her; the anxiety expressed by Sir William Hunter in 1898 has been intensified by the events of the intervening years. India has been gravely threatened by, but has happily repelled, an invasion by a powerful State, flushed by striking initial victories. Internally many generous experiments have been tried and have failed; racial and communal animosities are not appeased; elections are frequently a mere farce. As a result, the anxiety felt by men of good will, though not unmingled with hope, is to-day more acute than at any moment since India passed under the dominion of the Crown.

CHAPTER XXIX

UNRESTFUL ENGLAND—THE POST-WAR YEARS

PRECEDING chapters have detained us, for the most part, overseas. It remains to take a brief survey of events in the home-land, during the years that followed the conclusion of the War.

Causes of Unrest

The condition of England was, during the period, eminently unrestful. The spirit of unrest manifested itself not only in politics, but in every sphere of human activity. These varied manifestations were partly due to temporary causes, the immediate consequences of the sudden transition from a war which had engrossed the activities not merely of the fighting services but of the whole nation. But there were also operative causes which went much deeper—changes in the mental, spiritual, social, and economic outlook of great masses of the British people.

The 'fever of anaemia'

In the striking speech delivered in the House of Commons when, on July 3, 1919, he expounded the Provisions of the Peace Treaty, Mr. Lloyd George besought his countrymen not to 'demobilize the spirit of patriotism in this country'. 'The losses of the War', he truly said, 'will take a deal of repairing. . . . We must each and all give such instalments of strength, of good will, of co-operation, and of intelligence, as we can command. . . . The strength, the power of every land has been drained and exhausted by this terrible War to an extent we can hardly realize. The nations have bled at every vein, and this restlessness which you get everywhere to-day is the fever of anaemia.' [1]

Demobilization

The fever of anaemia it was. Only the spirit of true patriotism could avert the fatal consequences of a relapse. But gravely uttered, the Premier's warning was only partially heeded : the whole people was tired ; nerves were frayed ; tempers were short.

[1] Hansard, vol. 117, p. 1231.

Many of the symptoms arose merely from temporary irritation caused by the process of demobilization, from dissatisfaction about war gratuities, pensions and other *sequelae* of the War.   Wives, parents, employers, all anxious to get those in whom they were severally interested out of khaki, were perplexed and angered by the apparent lack of any principle of selection : a disgruntled mother could not understand why her neighbour's Tom was released from the colours, while her Jim was retained.   Nor was it easy for the harassed M.P., to whom every constituent turned for explanation and satisfaction, either to satisfy or to explain.

These delays and apparent inequities contributed not a little to the prevailing discontent.   The continued operations of British troops in Russia contributed more.   The Armistice had brought Russia about a cessation of arms in western and central Europe, but not in the east.   Russia was still in the throes of civil war—of several civil wars.   British participation in those wars, however limited its scale, lent itself readily to misrepresentation.   In Northern Russia, where the Navy played an important part, the Allied Force consisted mainly of British troops.[1]   General Sir A. Knox and Colonel John Ward, the Labour M.P. for Stoke, were giving valued support to Admiral Koltchak in Siberia, and General Denikin's volunteers held the Black Sea Coast.   But intervention in Russia became increasingly unpopular among the Western Allies, not least in England, where, in certain circles, the mere mention of ' Russia ' evoked howls of execration against ' bourgeois prejudice ' and ' capitalist greed '.   Meanwhile, the Soviet Government in Moscow gradually established itself against all its enemies, internal and external.   The ex-Czar, his wife and children had been murdered in July 1918 ; Omsk, the capital of the anti-Bolshevist Government, was taken in November 1919; Admiral Koltchak was captured and shot in February 1920, and in the course of that year the Poles were driven off, Poland was itself invaded and was saved only by the timely intervention of the French.   By the end of 1920 the Bolshevik régime was definitely established ; England and Europe had perforce to accept the accomplished fact.

[1] In March 1919 there were 13,100 British out of 23,000 Allied troops (excluding 11,770 Russians).

'Recon-
struction'

The successful establishment of a Communist Republic in Russia unquestionably had its repercussions in Great Britain : but the great body of wage-earners in Britain is neither republican nor communist. Yet ' labour unrest ' was the dominating feature of post-War politics. The unrest was due, in part, to the disappointment of exaggerated expectations raised by loudly advertised ' reconstruction ', of ' homes fit for heroes to live in ', and so on. Despite, or because of, lavish subsidies, the homes did not materialize so quickly as was hoped. The high wages of the war period had set up a new standard of comfort, but one element of comfort —better housing conditions—was lamentably lacking. Two important contributions had, however, been made towards real reconstruction. The first was the Education Act of 1918. This Act prohibited the employment of child-labour under the age of 12, and restricted it under 14. It raised the compulsory age of school attendance to 14, and provided for compulsory part-time day continuation schools up to the age of 16, and, after the lapse of seven years, of 18. It abolished, unnecessarily and unwisely, as many thought, all fees in public elementary schools, and contained provisions for nursery schools, medical inspection and treatment, special schools for defectives, holiday camps, physical training centres, and so forth. Financial stringency compelled the abandonment or suspension of several of the more ambitious features of this ' Fisher ' Act. But the £8,000,000, allocated to enable ex-Service men to go to Universities did bear fruit. Some 27,000 men (mostly from poor homes) took advantage of the grants then provided.[1]

Educa-
tion Act,
1918

More directly bearing upon the industrial problems were the schemes recommended by the Committee which sat under the chairmanship of Mr. J. H. Whitley—afterwards Speaker of the House of Commons.[2] Of their recommendations the most important was the establishment for each of the principal industries of a triple form of organization, representative of employers and employed, consisting of Joint Industrial Councils, Joint District Councils and Works Committees. These bodies were to advise upon all matters connected with the conduct of the several industries, and in particular to give to the wage-earners therein ' a definite and enlarged share in the discussion and settlement of industrial matters '. By 1921 some seventy-three Councils had been set up, for

Whitley
Councils

[1] Fisher, *Autobiography*, pp. 89–122.   [2] Final Report, Cmd. 9153 of 1918.

industries employing nearly 4,000,000 wage-earners. There was also passed in 1919 the *Industrial Courts Act* under which a permanent Court of Arbitration to which disputes can, with the consent of both parties, and after all means of conciliation existing in the trade have been exhausted, be referred. That Court affords, in the judgement of its first President, ' a more rational and convenient means of settling differences than has ever heretofore been devised '.[1]

Yet the painful fact remains that despite these and many other well-devised schemes, despite the elaboration of machinery, and a lavish outpouring of public money in the form of subsidies to particular industries, industrial peace was not secured. On the contrary, the period between the Armistice and the General Strike of 1926 was marked by an epidemic of disputes, involving heavy losses both to the industries immediately concerned and to the community at large. Nearly 3,000 disputes occurred in the two years 1919–20 alone. In each individual case assigned the palpable cause of dispute was wages, hours, conditions of work, or ' victimization '. But strikes were merely the outward manifestation of a deep-rooted spirit of unrest. The democratization of industry had not kept pace with the democratization of politics. Men who had been admitted to a share in the government of the State thought it incongruous that they should be excluded from any part in the control of the industry on which their livelihood depended. Moreover, they suspected that their livelihood was in many cases imperilled by inefficiency of management. In some cases it was. But the essential weakness of the position taken up by the wage-earners was that they refused to put their theories to the only practical test. The industrial field was open to them ; they possessed, in the aggregate, large capital resources, and could easily have commanded more : but the investment of capital in industry involves great risks—a truth frequently ignored—and, instead of challenging capitalist industry by competition, the wage-earners prudently preferred to agitate immediately for higher wages and shorter hours, and ultimately for the State management and control of industry.

The economic momentum of the War lasted for quite two years after the conclusion of the Armistice. But the sense of prosperity thus diffused was delusive. Before the end of 1920 there

Trade Disputes

The Onset of Depression, 1920

[1] Lord Amulree, *Industrial Arbitration in Great Britain,* Oxford, 1930.

were ominous signs that the seed carelessly sown in the preceding years was about to yield an abundant crop of trouble. Exports began to shrink ; the demand for industrial capital slackened ; agricultural prices fell sharply. Tenants who had been glad to purchase their farms, even at high prices, during the boom, were hard hit. Labour became a drug in the market, and the Labour Exchanges were thronged by crowds of men unable to find work.

Unemployment After 1920 unemployment was for years the most distressing and most obstinate of the many problems with which statesmanship was confronted. During the War there was virtually no unemployment, and down to the autumn of 1920, although 4,000,000 men were demobilized, less than 3 per cent. of trade unionists were out of work. But by March 1921 the trade union percentage had risen to 10·7, and by June to 23·9, being especially severe in the metal, engineering and shipbuilding trades. In June 1921 there were 2,580,000 people out of work. Things were better in 1922 and for the next seven years the figures hovered between about 1,100,000 and 1,250,000. By the end of 1930, however, the numbers leapt up to 2,500,000 and by the beginning of 1933 were close on 3,000,000.

The root cause of this unprecedented phenomenon was to be found in the complete dislocation of the economic life of the world during and after the War. The demands made upon Germany for indemnities and reparations ; the chaos of currencies ; the wild fluctuations in the rates of international exchanges ; the fall in the price of primary commodities, and the consequent inability of the producers of those commodities to purchase the goods, on the sale of which the people of Great Britain depend for subsistence—all these and other causes contributed to the prevailing disorder.

The Legislature, the Government Departments, the Local Authorities, and many voluntary agencies did all in their power to alleviate the resulting distress.

The Ministry of Labour has three Departments dealing with Insurance, Transitional Payments and Employment, and Training respectively. In every town it has its Employment Exchanges working at fever heat.

Unemployment Insurance The whole scheme of Unemployment Insurance was overhauled by the Act of 1920 ; between that date and 1927 no fewer than fourteen Unemployment Acts were placed on the Statute

Book, and since then hardly a year has passed without one or more amending Acts.[1]

But no scheme based on sound Insurance principles could cope with such an avalanche of unemployment as that experienced in recent years. By 1931 the Insurance Fund was £115,000,000 in debt to the Exchequer, and threatened the State itself with bankruptcy.

Every expedient had been tried in the hope of reducing the Relief dimensions of the problem. Unemployment Insurance proper was Schemes supplemented not only by Poor Relief, which in 1927 amounted to over £55,000,000, but by a variety of ' doles ' in the shape of ' uncovenanted ' and ' transitional ' benefit. The favourite prescription of the Labour Party, and of a section of the Liberal Party, was Public Works. Very large sums were, in fact, expended on ' works of public utility ', with little utility and less alleviation of unemployment. A more alluring scheme was that of ' settling ' on the land ex-service men and others. The experiment cost the State nearly £20,000,000, but proved an almost complete fiasco and after a few years was abandoned. Under normal conditions, migration should have done much to relieve the pressure. Between 1900 and 1913 the volume of emigration aggregated Empire 6,303,054. Of the emigrants rather more than half went to the Settlement United States, but Canada alone took 1,625,054, and the other Dominions as many more. In order to stimulate migration Parliament passed in 1922 the *Empire Settlement Act*, allocating for that purpose a maximum of £3,000,000 a year. That maximum was never reached or approached. The effect of the Act was disappointingly meagre. Between 1919 and 1928 the aggregate number of emigrants from this country to the overseas Empire was only about 1,300,000, and by 1932 the balance of immigrants from the Empire to Great Britain actually exceeded the emigrants by 33,020. For this disastrous turn in the tide there were many reasons.[2] It must suffice to say that had the pre-War balance been maintained there would be no unemployment problem in this country.

---

[1] A consolidating and amending Bill, of great promise, is passing through Parliament as this volume goes to Press.

[2] See Reports (annual) of the Overseas Settlement Committee and on the whole question cf. Marriott, *Empire Settlement*, Oxford, 1927.

Coal
Mines
and
Railways

Coal
Strikes

That problem, though not caused, was indubitably accentuated by the persistent unrest among the wage-earners, unrest which issued in perpetual stoppages in one industry after another.

That the wage-earners would, on the conclusion of Peace, revert without a struggle to pre-War wages and conditions it was vain to suppose, especially in view of the fact that prices were still soaring. In January 1919 there were strikes in the boilermakers' trade, among the shipyard workers in Glasgow and London, among the dockers in Manchester and municipal employés in Belfast. But throughout the post-War period the main centres of unrest were the coal-mines and the railways. Both industries remained under Government ' control' until 1921 and in both conditions were exceptionally favourable for the wage-earners. The ultimate object of the agitation was not merely or mainly to maintain those conditions, but to compel the State to nationalize the industries. But the goal was not nationalization of the old pattern. The leaders frankly confessed that under the State as an employer conditions for labour would be no better, and might be worse, than under private enterprise. ' The Mines for the Nation ', ' The Railways for the people ' were mere slogans. The real objective was the ownership and control of those industries by those engaged in them. Not nationalization but some form of Guild socialism or syndicalism was the goal.

In January 1919 the miners put forward a series of demands for higher wages and shorter hours, as a preliminary to nationalization. Only under a promise from the Government to set up a Royal Commission with instructions to report by March 20 did the miners consent to defer a strike until March 22.

Triple
Alliance

By March 1919 the situation was grave. There were mutinous riots in the camps at home and abroad. Five persons were killed and more than twenty injured in a riot in the Canadians' camp at Kinmel Park. The Metropolitan Police were restless and demanding, among other things, the recognition of their ' union '. That demand was firmly refused by the Government (March 17). But the most serious threat came from the ' Triple Alliance '—an alliance between the National Union of Railwaymen, the Miners' Federation and the National Transport Workers' Federation. This alliance, originally negotiated in 1913, was ratified in 1915, and played the leading part in the revolutionary agitation which persisted almost continuously from 1919 to 1926.

On March 20 the Coal Commission, set up under the chairmanship of Mr. Justice (now Viscount) Sankey, presented a sheaf of Interim Reports,[1] recommending an immediate increase of wages and shortening of hours. These recommendations the Government accepted, and so purchased temporary peace. In June the Commission presented four Reports, of which one was signed only by the chairman, and another by the Labour representatives. These recommended nationalization, but this was an issue which, as Mr. Lloyd George said, could be settled only by the nation and not at the dictation of a sectional industry. The Government did, however, accept the principle of the State acquisition of mining royalties, and other recommendations affecting the internal organization of the industry. *The Sankey Commission*

In March 1919 the Government had purchased a truce with the railwaymen with concessions which were to cost the State (still in possession of the railways) an additional £10,000,000 a year. The truce was temporary. The railwaymen demanded an all-grades minimum wage of £3 a week, and after negotiations with the Prime Minister and his colleagues precipitated a strike on September 26. The Government promptly organized a service of motors, lorries and aeroplanes, and on October 5 an agreement was reached. The week's stoppage, even though partial, was estimated to have cost the country £50,000,000. *The Railwaymen*

Nor was permanent peace secured. An elaborate wage agreement was concluded in March 1920, but subsequent events proved that among certain sections, if not the bulk, of Trade-Unionists, questions of wages and hours were subsidiary to much wider political ambitions. In 1920 Poland, as we have seen, was at war with the Russian Soviet: civil war was raging in Ireland. In May certain railwaymen in Ireland refused to handle cases of munitions intended for the use of soldiers or police in Ireland. In June some of the employés on the Great Northern Railway (England) similarly refused to handle packages addressed ' War Supply Department, Reval ' and in excuse pleaded that they were acting under instructions from their Union which had ' decided that, in the interests of the workers of Europe, effective steps must be taken *Direct Action*

[1] Cmd. 84, 85, and 86 of 1919.

to compel the capitalists of Europe to cease their attacks on the
Soviet of Russia '.   On complaint to the Union from the Company
the ' instructions ' were withdrawn, and the incident terminated.
But the real point at issue was emphasized by Mr. Lloyd George.
Heading a deputation to the Prime Minister from the N.U.R. Mr.
J. H. Thomas, their Secretary, while not endorsing the action of
the Irish strikers, ' recognized that to support these men would
mean a declaration of war on the Government '.   ' Not on the
Government,' was the Premier's swift retort, ' but on government,
which is a much more serious thing.'   That was the real issue :
Was Great Britain to remain a Parliamentary Democracy, or to
become a Soviet Republic ?   Was Parliament to rule, or was the
Triple Alliance to dictate the policy of the country ?

Mining Industry Act, 1920   In order to secure peace in the coal-field Parliament in 1920
passed *The Mining Industry Act*.   The Act provided for the crea-
tion of a Mines Department and for the reorganization of the coal
industry, giving to the colliers a greater voice in controlling it by
means of Pit and District Committees, and Area and National
Boards.   Nevertheless, there was a strike in the industry which
lasted from October 18 to November 4, 1920, and a much more
serious and prolonged one in the summer of 1921.   Government
control ended on March 31, 1921, and from April 1 to July 4 there
was a complete stoppage of work, ended only by an Agreement
concluded between the Mining Association and the Miners' Federation [1] and by a further State subsidy of £7,000,000 to sustain
wages.

Emergency Powers Act, 1920   In April the country had been threatened by something more
serious even than a coal stoppage.   Late in 1920 Parliament had
passed an Act, the *Emergency Powers Act*, designed to ' make exceptional provision for the protection of the community in cases of
emergency '.   On April 1, 1921, a 'state of emergency' was, under
the terms of that Act, declared.   The Triple Alliance then threatened a general strike in support of the miners, to take effect on
April 15.   The position was grave.   Negotiations between the
Government and the Trade Union leaders broke down ; but on
Thursday, April 14, two very remarkable meetings took place in
a Committee Room of the House of Commons.   At the first the
coal-owners placed their case before the members of the House in

For the terms see Cmd. 1387 of 1921.

a private meeting arranged there at the owners' request ; at the second the miners' representatives were invited to do the same. The result was reported at midnight to the Prime Minister, and he invited the owners and the miners to meet him next morning. Only eleven hours remained before the declaration of war was to take effect. The owners obeyed the summons : the miners did not. They refused to discuss even a temporary settlement, unless two principles were as a preliminary conceded, a National Wages Board and a National Pool.

Their allies were less stubborn ; and on Friday, April 15, the sympathetic strike was, at the eleventh hour, called off. Though christened by the Socialists ' Black Friday ', the day brought great relief to the country as a whole. The hour of revolution was at any rate postponed. The credit for this result was generally attributed to the House of Commons, whose intervention seemed to have succeeded where the Executive Government had failed. The contemporary Press teemed with references to the ' renascence of Parliament ', and so on. No doubt the severe cross-examination to which Mr. Hodges, the Secretary of the Miners' Federation, was subjected by members of Parliament did extort from him an admission to which he honourably adhered ; but the intervention of Parliament was fortuitous, and the happy issue of the meetings was unforeseen.[1] The private members who arranged the meetings had no idea of ' butting in ' upon the functions of the Executive, or queering the pitch either for the combatants or for the Government. Like the country at large, they ardently sought peace, but how to ensue it they knew not.

In the result, however, the Triple Alliance was broken, though not until the end of June did the owners and miners reach an agreement. Parliament voted a subsidy of £10,000,000 to ease the wage difficulties after the withdrawal of control : but that was only a fraction of the cost of the stoppage to the State. This amounted in all to no less than £250,000,000.

'Black Friday'

[1] The present writer has reason to know the facts ; for he it was who at the request of the coal-owners arranged, at two hours' notice, the first meeting, and presided over it. He also, at the request of the Trade-Unionists, presided at the second and was deputed, close on midnight, to convey to the Prime Minister a report of the proceedings and in particular of the admission made by Mr. Hodges. Mr. Lloyd George was preparing for bed after a very hard day, but consented to see the intruder and thought the matter sufficiently important to justify the action recorded in the text.

Railways   The State was also called upon to pay £51,000,000 to the Railways, when, in August 1921, State-control ended. But this was not a ' subsidy ' ; it was only a moderate compensation for services rendered. De-control was accompanied by the passing of an important Railways Act, providing for the amalgamation of no fewer than ninety-three Railway Companies in four large groups, and for setting up a Railway Rates Tribunal to decide questions at issue between the railways and their customers, and a series of Boards, culminating in a National Wages Board to decide wages questions. The Act was a compromise between Nationalization and private enterprise. It worked fairly well as regards rates and wages, but failed to restore any measure of prosperity to a great industry which had played an important part in the War.

Agriculture   The repeal (1921) of the Corn Production Act involved a further measure of de-control. The Agricultural Wages Board, which for the previous four years had secured for the labourers a share in the prosperity of the industry, was abolished. It was restored by the Socialist Government in 1924 but has not been able to avert, though it certainly retarded, the downward trend of wages. Wages, however, did not fall nearly so rapidly as prices : many farmers were ruined, and thousands of labourers were inevitably dismissed to swell the ranks of the unemployed.

National Expenditure   The rapid decline of trade, industry and agriculture naturally enhanced the growing anxiety in regard to the crushing weight of taxation and the high rate of national expenditure. The expenditure for 1919–20 exceeded £1,600,000,000 ; and for the next two years was still over £1,000 millions. Sir Austen Chamberlain and his successor (1920), Sir Robert Horne, seemed powerless to reduce it. In August 1921, however, the latter appointed a small Committee, with Sir Eric Geddes as chairman, to make recommendations for an immediate reduction of National Expenditure. The Committee reported promptly. They recommended the abolition of three new Departments (Transport, Overseas Trade and Mines), that the remaining Departments should be ' rationed ', i.e. that to each a maximum sum should be assigned, with instructions to do the best they could with it, and that detailed reductions amounting to £86,000,000 should be made forthwith. Ultimately the Government adopted the recommendations only as to £52,000,000.

An Economy Bill was, indeed, introduced in July 1922 but it never reached the Statute Book.

The sands of the 'Coupon' Parliament and the Coalition Ministry were by that time running out. Parliament had reached its penultimate session and the future of the Coalition was uncertain. The Conservatives were the predominant partner; and a large section of them were becoming increasingly restive under Mr. Lloyd George's leadership. The ' surrender ' to nationalism in Ireland, and in India, and in Egypt (1922), the heavy load of taxation, the almost continuous industrial strife, the depression in trade and agriculture, the increase of unemployment—for all these things prime responsibility was attributed to a Prime Minister who had assumed semi-dictatorial powers. Much of the Premier's attention had, in fact, been devoted to Foreign Affairs, but there was no success in that sphere to compensate for failure to solve domestic problems. Since 1919 there had been a succession of inter-Allied or international Conferences ; several in London, some at Paris, others at San Remo, Spa, and Genoa. In 1921 alone there were no fewer than six Conferences. The main questions under discussion were inter-Allied debts, the failure of Germany to meet the bill for reparations, and disarmament. The aggregate result of this immense expenditure of energy, time and money, was precisely nothing. The Treaty of Versailles had stipulated that Germany should pay by May 1, 1921, 20,000,000,000 gold marks (£1,000,000,000) in goods or gold. She did pay about £284,000,000 mainly in goods, the delivery of which upset international trade. Before the end of 1922 Germany was declared to be in default ; on January 8, 1923, France began to occupy the Ruhr. *Government by Conferences*

By that time Mr. Lloyd George was no longer in power. The Conservative rank and file had revolted, and on October 19, 1922, had resolved, after a meeting in the Carlton Club, where bitter words passed,[1] ' to fight the next election as an independent party with its own leader and with its own programme '. Mr. Lloyd George at once resigned, and nearly all his Conservative colleagues went with him into the wilderness. Several of them returned, and were included in Mr. Baldwin's second ministry in 1924. Not so Mr. Lloyd George himself. The year 1922 virtually marked the close of one of the most remarkable careers in British *Fall of Coalition Government, 1922*

[1] The writer was present.

politics. The detested pro-Boer of 1899 became the ardent Social reformer of 1906–14, and in 1914 devoted himself whole-heartedly, as Asquith's principal lieutenant, to the prosecution of the war against Germany. Displacing Asquith as Prime Minister in 1916, he became for a brief space the idol of the nation, and exercised on world affairs an influence greater than any previous statesman in our history. His energy and undaunted courage, his unfailing confidence in himself and in the people he led, made a notable contribution to the victory achieved in 1918. That in the plenitude of power he should have laid aside his armour was more than could have been expected of a mere mortal. Had he done so, however, he would have gone down to history as one of the greatest of British statesmen. But (to use Swift's biting analogue) he lingered on the stage until he was compelled to quit it, if not amid the hisses of his audience, without applause. Though retaining his seat for Carnarvon, he reappeared in the House of Commons only at longer and longer intervals, but from his retirement he indited a series of bulky volumes which constitute in effect an *apologia pro vita mea*, and, if used with discrimination, will prove invaluable primary authorities for the historian of the future. In 1945 he surprised the world by accepting an Earldom.

Mr. Bonar Law, who had retired on grounds of health in March 1921, now, reluctantly and solely at the call of duty, returned to the political battlefield and as Prime Minister formed a purely Conservative Ministry. The new Government was derided as a ' Second Eleven team,' but an appeal to the country (November) confirmed it in office with a majority of seventy over all other Parties combined. The Lloyd Georgian and the Asquithian Liberals were returned in equal numbers (60), but the portent of the Election was the increase in the Labour-Socialist representation from 73 to 159. Bonar Law, already a stricken man when he took office, was compelled to resign in May 1923 and died in the following October. As Mr. Lloyd George's lieutenant he had played a fine and unselfish part in the War, and in the difficult years that followed it, but his tenure of the first place was too brief to show whether or not he could fill it with distinction.

Bonar Law was succeeded as Prime Minister, to the great and

natural disappointment of Lord Curzon, by Mr. Stanley Baldwin, who had played a prominent part in the Conservative revolt and had become Chancellor of the Exchequer in the ' Second Eleven ' Ministry.

The times were still out of joint. Mr. Baldwin had indeed succeeded in negotiating (January 1923) a settlement of the British debt to the United States, but on terms which involved an annual payment of £34,000,000, at the existing rate of exchange. The French remained in the Ruhr. Peace had not yet been made with Turkey ; unemployment was a standing menace to national recovery ; there was continued unrest among the wage-earners, and a significant strike among farm labourers in Norfolk.

Confronted by these difficulties, convinced that economic conditions in England called for a drastic change in fiscal policy, and urged thereto by the Imperial Conference of 1923,[1] Mr. Baldwin decided to ask the country for a mandate for Preference and Protection. The response (December 1923) was unfavourable. The Conservatives, though still the largest single Party in the House, were reduced from 347 to 259 ; the Liberal groups, temporarily reconciled, returned 158 strong, and the Labour-Socialists numbered 191. Mr. Asquith combined with the Socialists to turn out the Government, and Mr. MacDonald, combining, like Lord Salisbury, the Premiership and the Foreign Office, became head of the first Socialist Ministry in the history of England. *Election of 1923*

It was a Government on sufferance, and the sufferance lasted only nine months. Mr. MacDonald drafted the Geneva Protocol for the pacific settlement of International Disputes and it was adopted by the Assembly of the League of Nations in October 1924 [2] ; he negotiated an Agreement on Reparations,[3] and two treaties with Soviet Russia. *The First Labour Government, 1924*

Russia brought the Government down. It was defeated in the House of Commons on a Liberal motion calling for a Select Committee to inquire into the handling of a Communist prosecution (October 8). Parliament was immediately dissolved, and five days before the poll the Foreign Office published a protest against a letter alleged to have been addressed, on September 15, by Zinovieff, the head of the Third International at Moscow, to the British *The Zinovieff Letter*

[1] *Supra*, p. 464.   [2] Cmd. 2273 (1924).   [3] Cmd. 2259.

Communists, instructing them to ' work for the violent overthrow of existing institutions in this country and for the subversion of His Majesty's Forces as a means to that end '. The Zinovieff letter itself was published with this protest, and entirely bore out the official description of its contents.

The *Red Letter* destroyed any chance the Socialists might have had of success at the polls. They secured only 151 seats ; the Conservatives secured 413 ; but the outstanding and somewhat paradoxical feature of the election was the rout of the Liberals, who lost 118 seats. They counted only forty in the new House, Asquith himself being defeated at Paisley. MacDonald at once resigned, and Baldwin again became Prime Minister. Rightly interpreting the verdict of the country as a call for the union of all Constitutionalists against the forces of disruption and revolution, he included in his new Ministry not only those Conservatives who like Sir Austen Chamberlain (Foreign Secretary in place of Lord Curzon), and Lord Birkenhead (Secretary for India), had resigned with Lloyd George, but Winston Churchill, for whom Neville Chamberlain (transferred to the Ministry of Health) made way at the Treasury.

The Baldwin Ministry, 1924–9 The new Parliament reimposed the McKenna duties, gave substantial Preferences to Empire products, imposed further Safeguarding duties, restored the Gold (Exchange) Standard, amended the Unemployment Insurance Scheme, and passed a comprehensive measure for contributory pensions, for the widows and orphans of men insured under the National Health Insurance Scheme. It also passed a Rating and Valuation Act, in order to simplify the rating system generally, and in particular to relieve the burdens on agriculture and productive industry. Agricultural land and buildings were under the Act of 1928 derated altogether, and all factories were relieved of 75 per cent. of their rates.

Derating Act The burden was necessarily transferred to the national exchequer, which could ill bear it : for taxation still remained, throughout the period of Conservative administration (1924–9), grievously heavy.

Heavy taxation was one of many causes retarding the hoped-for recovery in trade : but the most potent of them was unquestionably industrial strife. ' Nothing ', wrote a Labour M.P., ' has had a more potent effect upon our trade than the endless disruption and loss occasioned by the strike.' [1] Reviewing the quarter of a century ending in 1925, the same writer estimated the number of working days lost to the community, as the direct and indirect influence of the strike, at 654,000,000 and the money loss at over £1,000,000,000—just about as much as the total cost of the War.

Of the many industries affected the most important, and the most continuously disturbed, was that of coal.   The coal strike of 1920 involved to the State a *direct* loss of £8,000,000 ; to the miners (in wages) of £15,000,000, and in coal output of £26,500,000, besides putting 350,000 persons in other industries out of employment.   Of the strike of 1921 the direct cost to the State was over £33,000,000. Coal Crisis, 1925–6

In the summer of 1925 another stoppage was threatened.   As to the merits of the dispute opinions were widely divided, but it was agreed that, at that stage, the dispute was purely industrial and involved no challenge to the authority of the State.   The railwaymen and transport workers again threatened ' sympathetic strikes,' but solely to avert a general reduction of wages. Coal

Accordingly the Government asked Parliament for a subsidy of £10,000,000 (ultimately increased to £24,000,000) to fill the gap for an estimated period of nine months between the existing wage level and the level to which the mine owners proposed to reduce wages. At the same time they decided to appoint a Royal Commission of four persons, with Sir Herbert Samuel as chairman, to report upon the whole position of the coal industry.   The Government was evidently playing for time.   They got it ; and they used it in effective preparation for the grim struggle ahead.   ' If the time should come when the community has to protect itself, with the full strength of the Government behind it, the community will do so, and the response of the community will astonish the forces of anarchy throughout the world.'

Those words were spoken by Mr. Baldwin in proposing the subvention to the coal-mining industry on August 6, 1925.[2]   In May 1926 the prediction was fulfilled.

The Coal Commission appointed in September 1925 reported on March 6, 1926,[3] against nationalization (except of mineral The General Strike

[1] F. H. Rose., ap. *Daily Mail Year Book*, 1926.
[2] Hansard (5th series), vol. 187, p. 1592.   [3] Cmd. 2000.

rights) but in favour of drastic changes tending to unification. The subsidy, they held, ' should stop at the end of its authorized term, and should never be repeated '.   The subsidy ceased on April 30.   Meanwhile, the Government had informed the owners and the miners that the Government would give effect to the recommendations of the Commission, provided the two parties to the dispute would agree to accept them.   The parties could not agree, and on April 27 the owners in some districts posted the new wages terms. The miners refused to accept them, and on May 1 the General Council of the Trades Union Congress announced that a General Strike would begin at midnight on Monday, May 3.   The Council offered, however, to organize milk and food distribution.

The offer was superfluous.   The Government were prepared. On April 30 an Order in Council issued, under the terms of the *Emergency Powers Act*, 1920, a series of Emergency Regulations. They were at once put in force, though the Government continuously carried on negotiations to avert the crisis.   Those negotiations finally broke down after midnight on Sunday, May 2.   The immediate occasion was the refusal of the printers to print for the *Daily Mail* of May 3 a leading article calling upon ' all lawabiding men and women to hold themselves at the service of King and Country '.[1]   The paper did not appear ; but the adjuration was obeyed.   The country at large realized that this was no mere industrial dispute, but a challenge to the Constitution, an attack on the root principle of Representative Democracy.   From the first, therefore, the nation was behind the Government.   Plans to meet an emergency had been carefully matured and worked like clockwork.   Almost embarrassing in volume were the offers of help from volunteers, and the volunteers did admirable service in alleviating inconvenience due mainly to the stoppage of the transport services.   Suffering there was none : the organization for the distribution of food supplies worked admirably, and a milk-pool in Hyde Park relieved London of all anxiety about that necessity of child-life.   Private motors conveyed to and from work many women workers ; buses were driven and conducted by undergraduates ; underground stations were manned by Peers and members of Parliament.   Before the first week of the strike was over the railways had over 3,600 trains running.   From May 5 until the

---

[1] A typescript of the article is before me as I write.

strike ended the Government issued daily the *British Gazette*, a news-sheet to keep the public informed about the progress of events. *The Times* and other papers issued type-written sheets, presently to be replaced by amateurish printing. The Trade Unions retorted with the *British Worker*.

Meanwhile, Sir John Simon, acting in close concert with Lord Oxford and Asquith, had thrown a bombshell into the ranks of Labour by a deeply-impressive speech in the House of Commons (May 6).[1] He declared that the General Strike was illegal; that the funds of the Unions taking part in it were not exempt from attachment under the Act of 1906; that every man working under contract who joined in it was liable to be sued for damages, and that every leader ' who advised and promoted that course of action was liable in damages to the uttermost farthing of his personal possessions '. The effect of this speech upon his auditors was instantaneous and profound. Sir John Simon's opinion was not indeed unchallenged, but it was substantially confirmed by a judgement given on May 11 by Mr. Justice Astbury. On the following day the Trades Union Council attended on the Prime Minister, and informed him that the General Strike would be called off forthwith. The surrender was unconditional, but Mr. Baldwin declared that the Government would endeavour to bring about a resumption of negotiations in reference to the coal dispute.

The railwaymen remained out until May 14, and were reinstated only after a formal admission by the three Railway Unions that the strike was ' a wrongful act ', and a promise not to call another strike without previous negotiation with the Companies. The strike cost the Railway Unions £1,000,000.[2] The direct cost of the General Strike to the Exchequer was under half a million, but the loss to the community was estimated by Mr. Runciman at nearly £150,000,000.

The collapse of the General Strike did not end the war in the coal-fields, but in the course of the autumn the miners gradually drifted back to work, although it was not until the beginning of December that agreements were concluded in all the districts.

[1] To the profound effect of this speech, I can personally testify as I was in my place in the House when it was delivered. The speech, with two others on the same subject, was republished (Macmillan, 1926).
[2] So stated by C. T. Cramp, an official of the N.U.R.

The Emergency Regulations were revoked. The seven months' stoppage was ended. The terms on which the miners resumed were less good on the whole than those which they had rejected in March. Their loss in wages was reckoned at over £60,000,000, and they had put out of work some 500,000 workers in other industries.

Coal Mines Acts

Two Bills, arising out of the coal-war, were placed on the Statute Book in 1926. The *Coal Mines Act* (c. 17) permitted, but did not compel, eight hours' work below ground on every working day for a period of five years. The *Mining Industry Act* (c. 28) was a comprehensive measure designed to carry out such of the recommendations of the Samuel Commission as seemed immediately practicable. It facilitated voluntary and, with safeguards, even compulsory amalgamation ; it removed existing obstacles to the working of minerals, and made provision for pithead baths, welfare schemes for miners, and so on. Nothing short of nationalization, which the Samuel Commission did not recommend, would have satisfied the Labour Party, but the Act of 1926 was a useful, if unambitious, piece of legislation.

Electricity Act, 1926

Much more ambitious was the scheme based on the recommendations of a Commission of 1925, and embodied in the Electricity (Supply) Act passed into law in 1926. Great Britain was notoriously behind many other countries in the supply and consumption of electrical power and light.[1] The Act, like others passed in the post-War period, represented a compromise between public control and private enterprise. A central Electricity Board was set up and charged with three main functions : to construct main transmission lines—' the grid '—throughout Great Britain ; to enforce a standardization of frequency, and to purchase electricity from the most efficient (' selected ') stations, and distribute it in bulk to ' authorized undertakers '. The Board is authorized to borrow up to £70,000,000 and has already (1945) borrowed £53,500,000, but the State assumed no direct financial liability. Between 1925 and 1945 the electrical output in Great Britain increased from some six million to nearly thirty-seven million units, and the ' grid ' now covers almost the whole country except the north of Scotland.

[1] In 1926 we occupied the seventh place with 5,724,000,000 units, in 1932 the third with 11,694,000,000.

The General Strike had an important legislative repercussion in
1927.   A large section of the Party in power had long been anxious
to amend the *Trade Union Act* (1913), which legalized, subject to a
claim for exemption, a levy for political purposes.   To 'contract
out' of the political levy demanded more courage than could be
expected from e.g. a Conservative collier living in an isolated
mining village : to pay the levy meant subscription to a cause
opposed to his convictions.   The Act of 1927 reversed the process
and placed the onus of 'contracting in' upon those who wished
to subscribe.   Much more than that, the Act, while carefully safeguarding the 'right to strike' in furtherance of a trade dispute,
declared illegal a General Strike, i.e. a strike calculated to coerce
the Government, directly or indirectly ; further, while not interfering with peacefully persuasive picketing, it declared intimidation illegal.   Finally, it made it clear that Trade Unions in the
Civil Service, though permitted to continue, must keep clear of
party politics.   As a result the seven Civil Service Unions ceased
to be affiliated to the Trades Union Congress.   Apart from that,
Trade Union membership, which between 1900 and 1920 had quadrupled, steadily declined.   In 1920 it reached 8,334,362, or about
half the wage-earning population ; in 1931 it was 4,611,000,
or about one-quarter.   The Labour Government attempted in
1931 to reverse the legislation of 1927, but in view of a wrecking
amendment moved in Committee by the Liberals, abandoned
the Bill.

More controversial even than the Trade Union Act (1927) was
a measure, introduced at the instance of the Church Assembly, to
revise the Book of Common Prayer.   The agitation, carried on in
the country with immense activity by both sides, was reflected in
the debates in both Houses.   Largely through the influence of
Archbishop Davidson the Lords passed the measure by 241 to 88,
but the Commons rejected it by 238 to 205.   The measure, slightly
amended, was reintroduced into the House of Commons in 1928 but
rejected by 265 to 220.   The opponents of the measure regarded
it, rightly or wrongly, as a 'step towards Rome', and its rejection
reflected the stout Protestantism of the country at large.

The Parliament of 1924 was now approaching its legal time,
but before its dissolution in 1929 three Acts of great importance
were placed upon the Statute Book.   To the *Equal Franchise Act*

(1928) reference has already been made.[1]   The other two effected drastic reforms in Local Taxation and Local Government.

The *Local Government Act* (1929) effected the most important changes in local administration since Mr. Balfour's *Education Act* of 1902.   Preceded by the passing in 1928 of a *Rating and Valuation Act*, the Act of 1929 gave effect to many of the more important recommendations made in the two Reports (majority and minority) of the Poor Law Commission (1909).   Those recommendations the Act of 1929 proposed to carry out by the adjustment and simplification of local Government areas, by the abolition of *ad hoc* authorities and by the concentration of their functions in the County Councils.

The Act also provided for the periodical readjustment of areas and boundaries as local conditions and circumstances may necessitate ; for the transfer to County Councils of responsibility for the maintenance of all roads in rural areas and of ' classified ' roads in urban areas ; for the complete exempting from local rates of agricultural land and buildings (other than farmhouses), and for exempting industrial and freight transport hereditaments from 75 per cent. of the rates.   But the most important provision of the Act was the drastic change it made in the relations between national and local expenditure by substituting for the existing Exchequer Grants a consolidated or ' bloc ' grant so distributed as to give the larger proportion of relief to the localities which most needed it, instead of (as formerly) to the districts which by virtue of their own greater resources could ' earn ' proportionately larger grants from the Exchequer.   In particular, the sponsors of the Act held out the expectation that the reforms effected would promote not only efficiency but economy.   Robert Lowe, when recommending the new Education Code to the House of Commons was more cautious if not more frank.   ' I cannot promise you either efficiency or cheapness : but if the system is not efficient it will be cheap ; if it is not cheap it will be efficient.'   Whether, on balance, the Act of 1929 has promoted efficiency is a matter of dispute : the hope that it would diminish local expenditure has been lamentably disappointed.

Previous to 1888 Local Government had been, in Lord Goschen's words, ' a chaos of authorities, a chaos of jurisdictions,

[1] See *supra,* p. 329.

a chaos worst of all of areas '. This chaotic condition had largely arisen from a prolonged course of piecemeal legislation. Each Act that was passed involved new administrative functions and imposed them on new authorities created *ad hoc*. The Acts of 1888, 1894, and 1902 went far to reduce chaos to order. The Act of 1929 was designed to go farther in the same direction.

More particularly in regard to Poor Law administration, the Poor Law Amendment Act of 1834, though never popular, had brought great benefits in its train. It had restored to the working classes their self-respect; it had reduced rates and diminished pauperism. But its administration, though efficient and eco- nomical, was increasingly resented by enfranchised citizens and condemned by social reformers. The Reports of 1909 proposed drastic reforms, but for twenty years no effect was given to them by legislation, though administration became more ' sym- pathetic '.

The Act of 1929 deprived the Rural District Councils of their functions as Guardians of the Poor, and transferred the whole administration of ' Public Assistance ' (as Poor Relief is now termed) to the County Councils. But in order to retain some measure of continuity and to secure the advantage of local know- ledge, the County Councils were empowered to appoint for the different localities Guardians' Committees, consisting partly of Rural District Councillors. The hope was that the new Public Assistance Committees would act in close co-operation with the other Committees of the County Council dealing with Education, Public Health, Milk Supply, Mental Deficiency, as well as with public or private schemes for Child Welfare, Maternity Benefit, and so forth. But co-ordination is still far from complete. Some overlapping has, perhaps, been avoided, but much of the intimate local knowledge, invaluable in such work as poor relief, has been sacrificed. Moreover, the scope of ' Public Assistance ' has been greatly curtailed by the increasing activity and importance of Departments of the Central Government, notably the Ministry of Health (formerly the Local Government Board) and the Ministry of Labour, which only came into being in 1917. The Ministry of Labour and National Service became responsible not only for the prevention and settlement of labour disputes, but for nearly all matters affecting employment and unemployment, for the training

and transference of juveniles, as well as for the operation of the
National Service (including military service) schemes.

That the Act of 1929 has made for administrative ' simplification ' there can be no question. Previous to 1888 there were no
fewer than 27,069 independent local authorities in England and
Wales, and they taxed the ratepayer by eighteen different kinds
of rates. By the Acts of 1888, 1894, and 1929 this ' jungle of
jurisdictions ' was to a great extent cleared. This ought to have
made for economy ; but it did not. The burden of the rates on
agriculture and industry has indeed been transferred to the
taxpayer, but the promise of diminished burdens for the local
ratepayer made in 1929 remains lamentably unfulfilled. In the
thirty years between 1875 and 1905 local rates increased from
£19,000,000 to £58,000,000. In 1938-9 they were £189,000,000,
as against £166,466,000 in 1928-9. The Reforms of 1929 have
also thrown an immense amount of additional work upon already
overworked County Councillors, with the result that more and
more work and responsibility has devolved upon officials and
their constantly increasing staffs. That the increase in the number
of officials has been accompanied by a great improvement in
their competency is, however, unquestionable.

The development of a vast local bureaucracy is one of the
most noticeable features of these post-war years. It is naturally
welcomed by those who would transfer to public ownership all
land and capital and would substitute collective control of industry
for private enterprise. That one result of the Hitler war will be
to give a further and perhaps powerful impulse to these tendencies,
is probable. But it is unlikely that the transition will be abrupt.
It has hitherto been deemed wise to advance along the path of
social and economic reconstruction without undue haste, if without
rest. The *Railways Act* of 1921, the *Electricity Act* (1926) and the
London Transport Act (1933) represented a compromise between
the principles of public control and private enterprise. Similar
experiments may in the near future be made in the spheres of
industrial production and commercial exchange and finance.

The passing of the Local Government Act was the prelude to
the dissolution (May 10) of the Parliament which, in 1929, had
almost exhausted its legal term. The Conservative party fondly
imagined that the newly enfranchised electors—mostly young

women irreverently designated as 'flappers'—would manifest their gratitude towards the authors of their political being. Grievously were the Conservatives disillusioned. Neither Mr. Baldwin nor any of his lieutenants could arouse any enthusiasm for a party which had plainly exhausted any popularity it had derived from the blunders of its opponents, had alienated a large body of trade unionists by the Act of 1927 ; and had earned no gratitude by its extension of the parliamentary franchise in 1929.

For the first time that verdict was delivered by the whole *General* adult population of Great Britain. The electorate had increased *Election of 1929* from 1,000,000 in 1832 to 28,850,000 in 1929, and of this vast electorate over 80 per cent. went to the polls. In the industrial districts of the North the Conservative Party was routed, but maintained its position in the South, yet the Socialists who obtained 287 seats against 260 Conservative, 59 Liberal and 9 Independent, won a victory far from decisive.

Mr. Baldwin at once resigned and Mr. MacDonald for the second time became Prime Minister, though again without a clear Parliamentary majority.

From the first the new Ministry, with a precarious hold on the *Second* House of Commons, was dogged by misfortunes. Before it had *Labour Ministry,* been in office many months the economic blizzard swept through *1929–31* the world, completely dislocating all international trade, flinging into chaos national currencies and reducing international exchange to a gamble. In Great Britain the unemployment figures mounted steadily towards the 3,000,000 mark, and the debt on the Insurance Fund reached, as already noted, £115,000,000. Consequently, the problem of national finance overshadowed all others. Each successive Government since the War had shirked its plain duty in this matter. A group of private members in the House of Commons had pressed the problem upon the attention of the Government ; but with little effect. The simple truth is that economy, popular in the abstract, is in the concrete exceedingly unpopular. Mr. Churchill had, in 1926, made an attempt, in the *Economy Act*, to deal with the question, but it was half-hearted and ineffective. By 1931 the time for palliatives had passed ; the case called for the surgeon's knife ; or maybe for the woodman's axe.

Financial
Crisis,
1931

A Committee on Finance and Industry appointed in November 1929 under the chairmanship of Lord Macmillan, an eminent lawyer, reported in July 1931.

The Macmillan Report was carefully drafted and may some day become a classic on monetary policy ; but in July 1931 the rush of events was too rapid to permit a study of its arguments, or the application of the remedies it proposed.

The Treasury were well aware of the impending catastrophe. In January 1931 Sir Richard Hopkins, the permanent Secretary, had presented to the Royal Commission on Unemployment Insurance a memorandum, authorized by the Chancellor of the Exchequer, Mr. Snowden, and containing a grave warning :

' Continual State borrowing on the present vast scale, without adequate provision for repayment by the Fund, would quickly call in question the stability of the British financial system.'

Foreigners who had large credits and deposits in London took alarm.   In February the Government set up an Economy Committee under Sir George May, and Mr. Snowden took the opportunity to emphasize the warning uttered in January by his official : ' I say, with all the seriousness I can command, that the national position is grave ; that drastic and disagreeable measures will have to be taken if the Budget equilibrium is to be maintained and industrial recovery is to be made.'   No statement so grave had fallen from the lips of a Chancellor of the Exchequer within living memory ; but his supporters only scoffed and complacently demanded fresh expenditure.   Nor did Mr. Snowden's Budget, presented on April 27, face up to the ' disagreeable ' facts. Described by its opponents as frankly ' dishonest ', it was undeniably speculative, estimates of revenue being based on hopes little likely to be fulfilled.

The rude awakening was not long delayed.   On June 4 the Insurance Unemployment Commission issued an Interim Report revealing a position of extreme gravity and recommending economies which though obviously inadequate raised a howl of execration from the parliamentary supporters of the Government.   The Report of the Macmillan Committee (July 13) did nothing to relieve the anxiety felt by all thoughtful men.   On July 31 came the bombshell of the May Report.

That Report made it clear that on the next Budget there would May Report be a deficiency of no less than £120,000,000, which could be made good only by new taxation or drastic economies, or both. Detailed economies of 96½ millions were recommended. The Report caused grave alarm both at home and abroad. Great Britain was manifestly heading for bankruptcy. A serious financial crisis ensued. Foreigners called in their credits and withdrew their gold.

To meet immediate necessities the Bank of England borrowed £50,000,000 from the Banks of France and the United States (August 11). The Prime Minister was recalled from his Scottish holiday to confer with the Bankers and the Cabinet (August 11), and on the following day Mr. Baldwin and Mr. Neville Chamberlain were, with Sir Herbert Samuel, the acting leader of the Liberal Party, called into consultation.

A national crisis had developed. On August 19 the Cabinet National Crisis sat for 11½ hours, and agreed, not without dissentients, on drastic economies. On the 20th the proposals of the Government were communicated to certain Labour leaders and the Council of the Trade Union Congress, who refused to accept them.

The prospect was one of unrelieved gloom when on August 22 the nation learnt with a sense of gratitude and relief that the King had interrupted his holiday, hardly begun, in the Highlands, had returned to London and had personally taken control of a dangerous and critical situation. The King immediately called into conference the leaders of the three Parties; the Labour Cabinet resigned on the 24th, and the King entrusted to Mr. MacDonald the formation of a National Government. He formed an emergency Cabinet of ten members, four Conservatives, four Socialists and two Liberals. Most of his former colleagues, headed by Mr. Henderson, went, with the great bulk of his Party, into opposition. The new Government met Parliament on September 8, and two days later a Supplementary Budget was introduced, showing an estimated deficiency for the current year of £74,679,000 and for the ensuing year (1932–3) of no less than £170,000,000. The deficit was to be met and the Budget balanced by additional taxation of £40,500,000 for the current and £81,500,000 for the ensuing year, by economies of £22,000,000 and £70,000,000 respectively, and by savings on amortization of debt. The Budget was balanced; the first phase of the crisis was over. On August 28 the

Bank borrowed a further £80,000,000 running for one year, in equal amounts from Paris and New York; but by September 19 these credits were exhausted. On the 20th the Bank Rate was raised to 6 per cent. and on the 21st the Cabinet decided to suspend gold payments, and a Bill to authorize that momentous step was hastily passed through Parliament. On October 7 Parliament was dissolved and of the 615 members of the new House no fewer than 554 were pledged to support the National Government. The Opposition Socialists were reduced from 265 to 52 and lost practically all their leaders.[1] The Cabinet was enlarged to twenty members, and the Ministry was re-formed, a disproportionate share of offices being prudently assigned to Liberals and Socialists.

The National Government

With the accession to power of a National Government, supported by three-fourths of the House of Commons and by all but a fragment of the House of Lords, a new era opened in the history of England.

[1] By the General Election of 1935 the Government supporters were reduced from 554 to 431, of whom 317 were Conservatives. Only eight members were returned as Labour followers of Mr. Ramsay MacDonald. The Opposition Socialists numbered 154.

Shortly before the Election, Mr. MacDonald, already in failing health, had resigned the Premiership, to which Mr. Baldwin succeeded, Mr. MacDonald remaining in the Cabinet as Lord President of the Council, while Sir Samuel Hoare became Foreign Secretary in place of Sir John Simon, who returned to the Home Office, which he had left in 1915.

CHAPTER XXX

TOWARDS THE ABYSS

THE Era that opened with the crisis of 1931 has not yet fallen National
into historical perspective. The interpretation of events ism
is still the subject of controversy. Those events must, consequently, be narrated in bare summary and with a minimum of
comment. They seem, however, to suggest that the whole period
was dominated by a conflict—or perhaps, rather, the interaction—
of principles : in the domestic sphere, between collectivism and
private enterprise; in world affairs, between the ebullient spirit
of nationalism and international co-operation.

The spirit of nationalism has been not least obtrusive in Egypt
countries directly or indirectly subject to British rule. Take
Egypt. Egypt has never been technically incorporated in the
British Empire. The Protectorate declared in 1914 was terminated in 1922, but, as already explained, complete independence
was qualified by important reservations.[1] The situation thus
created did not satisfy Egyptian nationalists ; agitation continued
more or less persistently, though between 1925 and 1929 it
was held in check by Lord Lloyd, who in 1925 succeeded Lord
Allenby as High Commissioner. A surreptitious attempt (1927)
to transfer the control of the army in the Sudan from the Sirdar
to the Egyptian War Office was frustrated by a stiff note from
the High Commissioner, backed up by the presence of some
British warships, dispatched to Alexandria ' to exercise ', in the
words of Sir Austen Chamberlain,[2] ' a restraining influence on
the disorderly elements and to prevent the possibility of untoward
incidents which could not but react to the disadvantage of Egypt '.
The disorderly elements were further weakened by the death
(1927) of Zaghul Pasha, the able, if unscrupulous, leader of the
Wafd or Nationalist party. On the other hand, those elements
were encouraged by the return of the Socialist party to office in
England, and by the recall of Lord Lloyd (1929). A Treaty con-
ceding everything short of complete independence was at the same
time offered to Egypt, although not until 1936 was it accepted.

[1] *Supra*, p. 431.   [2] Foreign Secretary, 1925-9.

Egypt was then recognized as a Sovereign State, but a considerable British force remained in the country to protect the Suez
Canal and (virtually) to guarantee Egypt against foreign aggression.   The value of that guarantee was decisively demonstrated
(1940–1) by the brilliant campaign conducted against Italy by
the Imperial forces under the command of General Wavell.   How
recent events will react upon Anglo-Egyptian relations it is still,
however, too early to surmise.

General Wavell's force was assembled in Palestine, where a
very embarrassing situation was notably eased by the outbreak of the Hitler War.   A mandate for Palestine had been
accepted (1920) by Great Britain mainly in the hope of providing
a ' national home ' for the Jews and to safeguard the rights of
all the inhabitants, irrespective of race and religion.   The path
of the peacemaker in Palestine has proved to be thorny beyond all
expectation.   Subterranean influences have been at work to
exacerbate the troubles, but the cause of them is deeply rooted
in the persistent hostility between the conservative Arabs and the
progressive and prosperous Jews.   Every expedient had been tried
to abate it.   Commission after Commission has been appointed,
only to have their recommendations rejected by one or both
disputants, or by the adjudicator.   An *impasse* had apparently
been reached when in 1939 the problem was shelved by the
outbreak of the war.   Since then hostility between Jews and
Arabs has seemingly given place to co-operation in support of the
Allied cause.

More menacing to British power and prestige than racial and
religious antagonism in Palestine, or than Egyptian nationalism,
has been the operation of similar forces in India.

India   Indian nationalism is exclusively the product of the beneficent
policy consistently pursued, for more than half a century, by
the British Raj.   It now supplies the main obstruction to further
constitutional reform.   The progress achieved in that direction
down to 1933 has already been described.[1]   Upon the Report of
the Joint Select Committee was based the *Government of India
Act* of 1935.   Under that Act the whole of the vast sub-continent
—British India and the Feudatory States alike—was to be included in a Single Federal State.   Of that State the Provinces,

[1] *Supra*, pp. 498–503.

endowed with almost complete autonomy, form the component units. Both in the Central Government and in the Provinces 'Responsibility' was to be accompanied by certain safeguards vested respectively in the Viceroy and the Provincial Governors. As in all effective Federations, a large measure of authority was vested in a Supreme Court of Judicature, which has already come into being and is functioning successfully. That is not the case with the other parts of the scheme. The new Provincial Governments came into being in 1937, but in many of them there has been serious friction between the Governor and his 'responsible advisers'. The result is that in seven out of eleven Provinces the Governor has had to assume and exercise the powers provisionally vested in him by the Act. In fact those Provinces are still under autocracy. Despite the utmost patience and persistence exhibited by the Viceroy, there is at present (1945) a complete deadlock in respect of the All-India Federation. Nothing was left undone by Lord Linlithgow [1] to expedite the adoption of the scheme for which, as chairman of the Joint Select Committee, he had naturally a parental affection, but all his efforts were unhappily frustrated. For this obstruction the intransigence of the extreme party, which will accept nothing short of the complete independence of India, is mainly responsible. But some of the ruling Princes, whose adhesion is essential to the Federation, have also shown a natural reluctance to surrender any portion of their sovereignty, except under conditions which will safeguard the remnant of it. Those conditions have not in all cases been satisfied. The deadlock consequently continues, and the constitution of 1935 remains a mere *torso*. It is, however, satisfactory to know that India as a whole is in complete sympathy with the rest of the Empire as regards Hitler's assault upon the root principles of liberty and justice. The Princes and the fighting races of India have shown themselves as ready now as in 1914 to share the burden of defending the Empire against the attack of the Dictators.

Not so Southern Ireland. Ever since the 'Treaty' of 1921 Southern the situation of that country has been completely anomalous,[2] Ireland

---

[1] Viceroy, 1936–43.

[2] In opening the first Ulster Parliament, in 1921, King George V made a touching appeal for unity—unhappily in vain.

and in large measure ambiguous. About Northern Ireland there is no ambiguity.[1] Availing itself of the option provided in the Act of 1922, it ' contracted out ' of the Dominion Status conferred upon Ireland, and remains an integral part of the United Kingdom, retaining under the Act of 1920 its representation in the House of Commons at Westminster, and also its own bicameral legislature (with an Executive dependent thereto) at Belfast. Northern Ireland has accepted its full share of Imperial responsibilities and fulfils all the duties consequent thereon.

Southern Ireland, on the contrary, performs no duties towards the Empire, though sharing some of its privileges—notably the protection of its navy. Whether, indeed, it can still be regarded as in any real sense a member of the British Commonwealth is doubtful. It has shown itself persistently disrespectful towards the Crown which now forms the most important link between the several member States of the Commonwealth. The Governor-General, who was the representative of the King-Emperor, has been superseded by a President elected by direct vote of the people. All real power is, however, in the hands of the Prime Minister, who is nominated by Parliament and is virtually President of the ' Sovereign, independent, democratic State ' which Ireland in 1937 declared itself to be. In the Coronation ceremony in 1937 Southern Ireland took no official part, and was self-excluded (quite logically) from the Imperial Conference held in the same year. As the Conference was concerned mainly with problems of Imperial Defence, the presence of a representative of Southern Ireland would, indeed, have been inconvenient. In 1938, in a futile effort at appeasement, Southern Ireland was relieved of the obligation to pay over the annuities receivable from the purchasers of land, and the British taxpayer accepted an additional (capital) burden of over £100,000,000. This merely represented a handsome present to the Dublin Exchequer, as no corresponding relief was given to the purchasers. At the same time it was agreed that the ports reserved under the Treaty of 1921 for the use of the British Navy in time of war should be surrendered. For that vain and stupid surrender the British Empire paid heavily during the war in the lives of gallant seamen and in the loss of British ships and their invaluable cargoes.

[1] See *supra*, pp. 451 f.

The words used by Mr. Lees-Smith, acting-leader of the Socialist Opposition in the House of Commons (August 21, 1940), were in this connexion as significant as they were strong. 'The world,' he said, ' should realize what we pay for our principles. Scores of ships are being sunk to-day, and thousands of seamen drowned, because we cannot, even within our own Commonwealth, use ports for our Navy, which without that Navy would share the fate of Holland and Norway '. On the declaration of war between the British Empire and Germany in September 1939, Ireland declared its neutrality, and, despite some provocation from Germany, maintained it to the great disadvantage of the Allies.

During these critical days, and indeed for a long time past, Ireland has been treated by what Lord Rosebery once described as the ' predominant partner' with a degree of patience and generosity which we like to think is characteristic of British policy as a whole.

Since 1931 the Party system has, indeed, been to a large A Council extent in abeyance : Parliament has virtually resolved itself of State into a ' Council of State ', the more effectively to deal with a series of national emergencies. After the General Election of 1931, at which 554 members were returned to support a ' National ' Government, Mr. MacDonald retained the Premiership, though it was the great Conservative majority that sustained him in office and predominantly influenced the policy of the Government.

This truth was more clearly manifested when, after a few months of office, Mr. Snowden, Sir Herbert Samuel, and Lord Crewe resigned, to be replaced by Mr. Neville Chamberlain (Exchequer), Sir John Gilmour (Home Secretary) and Lord Hailsham (War Office).

Nor did policy fail to correspond with personnel. The Socialists when in office in 1924 and 1929 had shown themselves implacably opposed to anything savouring of ' Protection ' or even ' Preference '. In 1932, however (as already indicated), Chamberlain effected a fiscal revolution comparable in comprehensiveness with Peel's fiscal reforms (1841–6). The results were quickly reflected in the Customs receipts.

Protection failed, however, to solve the obdurate problem of Unem-unemployment. An Act passed in 1934 was, however, a step, ployment

nay a stride, in the right direction. The administration of the
Unemployment Insurance Fund was taken out of the sphere of
politics and transferred to an Unemployment Assistance Board
under a permanent, non-political chairman. The Fund quickly
became actuarially solvent, contributions were reduced and benefits increased. Large classes, notably agricultural workers and
outdoor 'domestic servants', were brought into the scope of
insurance, which now included practically all persons (except
servants in private employment), all manual workers, as well
as (since 1940) non-manual workers earning less than £420 a
year. About 16,000,000 persons are now (1945) covered by the
scheme.

A parallel scheme of National Health Insurance also initiated
in 1911 covers more than 19,000,000 persons, while more than
20,000,000 persons are included in the scheme initiated in 1925
to provide contributory pensions for widows, orphans and the
aged. Non-contributory Old Age Pensions continue under the
scheme (frequently amended) of 1908 to be paid to aged folk of
both sexes. Of the whole population over 70 years of age it is
estimated that four out of five now draw pensions, towards the
cost of which two-thirds themselves contribute. In addition,
about 1,500,000 persons were (1940) in receipt of poor-relief,
involving over £50,000,000 a year, to which local rates contributed
some £46,000,000.

Social Services Nor is this all. Large sums are found by the taxpayer for
social services of various kinds: maternity welfare, housing
subsidies, subsidies to this trade and that, and above all for
education, which already costs the taxpayer and ratepayer over
£100,000,000 a year and will soon cost much more. In all, ' Social
Services ' which in the last year of Victoria cost about £36,000,000
are to-day taking well over £500,000,000 a year out of the pockets
of our citizens to provide gratuitous benefits for the poorer (if not
actually the ' poor ') among them.

Bureau-cracy And there is another aspect of this matter. The multiplication of public activities has necessarily involved the creation of
a vast army of officials, central and local. This development was
naturally welcomed by those who would transfer to public ownership all land and capital and would substitute collective control
of industry for private enterprise. That one result of the Hitler

war will be to give a further and perhaps powerful impulse to the tendencies operating in this direction since the Great War, is probable. But it is unlikely that the transition will be abrupt. It has hitherto been deemed wise to advance along the path of social and economic reconstruction without undue haste, if without rest. The *Railways Act* of 1921, the *Electricity Act* (1926), and the *London Transport Act* (1933), represented a compromise between the principles of public control and private enterprise.[1] Similar experiments may in the near future be made in the spheres of industrial production and commercial exchange and finance. But it is one thing to deal with semi-monopolistic utilities; it is another to interfere with the production and exchange of commodities. Even socialists admit that the time is not yet ripe for the complete elimination of the profit-motive in trade.

The expenditure on the social services—Education, Housing, Poor Relief, Pensions, Unemployment, and so forth—now amounts to the vast total of over £500,000,000 a year, or more than double the whole national expenditure on the eve of the Great War. It is alternatively regarded as an ' insurance ' against Socialism and a step towards it. Whatever the motive of such expenditure, the fact is one of the most momentous in the recent history of Great Britain.

The steady persistence in the work of social reconstruction at home is not unconnected with the other dominating feature of British policy. *Foreign Affairs*

Ever since the close of the Great War, Great Britain has neglected no opportunity of promoting peace among the nations. That end was to be attained by the disarmament of Germany, which had long been the chief disturber of European peace, by the all-round reduction of armaments, by the extension of the practice of international arbitration and the strengthening of the Hague Court, and above all by the operation of the League of Nations. Under the Treaty of Versailles, Germany was to be completely disarmed, the process being supervised by an Allied Commission. But the supervision was ineffective; Germany surreptitiously rearmed, and, when the truth could no longer be concealed, justified her action by the failure of the other Powers *Disarmament*

[1] *Supra*, pp. 514, 521.

to fulfil engagements which Germany contended were mutual.[1]
Be this as it may, the fact remains that of the Great Powers
Great Britain alone made effective reduction in her armed
forces.

It has, indeed, been plausibly argued that this unilateral disarmament made not for peace but for war. As a German writer
has said : ' No one can deny that the English themselves set a good
example by disarming to an extent that endangered the defence
of the country. Nevertheless, instead of inducing others to
follow its example, England simply weakened its own influence
and thereby crippled the strongest force at work in Europe in
the service of international co-operation.' [2] Yet as to the sincere
and wholehearted devotion of the British people to peace there
can be no question. Their devotion was emphasized by the
vote given on the ' Peace Ballot ' in 1935. That vote deterred
English ministers from their obvious duty to rearm, and misled
Germany and Italy into the belief that under no circumstances
would England fight. That impression was accentuated by
England's attitude in supine acquiescence of the aggressive
conduct of Japan, Italy and Germany.

Man-
churia

In 1931 Japan attacked and conquered the great Chinese
Province of Manchuria. China appealed to the League of Nations
of which she, like Japan, was a member. The League, acting on
the Report of a Commission sent out under the chairmanship of
the Earl of Lytton, condemned the action of Japan, which thereupon withdrew from the League, and proceeded with its attack
upon China. The League, to the disappointment of its votaries,
took no action. Its inaction was generally condemned, most
loudly by the smaller Powers upon whom no part of the burden
of giving effect to the verdict of the League would have fallen.
' Action ' would in fact have meant war between Great Britain,
single-handed and ill-prepared for it, and Japan.

The
Hitler
Dictator-
ship

The prestige of the League suffered severely, but it is grossly
unfair to lay the blame for its decline exclusively upon Great
Britain. Japan's withdrawal was soon followed (1933) by that

---

[1] On this highly controversial question, see Marriott, *Commonwealth or
Anarchy ?*, pp. 205 f. ; Marriott, *Europe Since 1815*, p. 577 ; and Temperley,
Whispering Gallery of Europe, p. 47.

[2] Kurt von Stutterheim, *Those English* (E.T.), p. 200.

of Germany. In January 1933 President Hindenburg was compelled to admit Adolf Hitler to office as Chancellor, and on the President's death in 1934 Herr Hitler succeeded him and, as Führer, was invested with dictatorial powers. Those powers were not allowed to rust. Under the *Enabling Act* (1933) the whole of Germany was virtually incorporated in Prussia. Thus did Herr Hitler, ex-corporal and formerly house-painter, put the coping stone upon the edifice erected by the ' Iron Chancellor ', Prince von Bismarck. In January 1935 the valuable Saar district, which since 1920 had been administered by the League of Nations, re-united with Germany. The plebiscite in favour of reunion with Germany was taken under the terms of the Treaty of Versailles, and undoubtedly represented the genuine, if not unprompted, wishes of the inhabitants of the district. *The Saar Plebiscite*

Nevertheless, Great Britain, like France and Italy, was becoming uneasy at the rapid progress of Germany under Hitler. Great Britain embarked on a rearmament programme in March 1935 ; France extended the term of service with the colours about the same time, and in May concluded a Pact with Soviet Russia. Meanwhile, Germany had announced her intention (March 16) to reintroduce conscription, and in April Mr. MacDonald and Sir John Simon and M. Laval, the French Foreign Minister, had met Signor Mussolini, and established what was known as the ' Stresa Front ', an agreement directed exclusively against Germany. Whatever that agreement was worth, a fatal breach in it was caused by the conclusion, without the knowledge and greatly to the surprise of France and Italy, of a Naval agreement between Great Britain and Germany in June 1935. *Rearmament*

Before the Stresa meeting the attitude of Italy towards Abyssinia had become so menacing that Haile Selassie, the Emperor, had applied to the League of Nations to intervene, under Article XV of the Covenant, in a ' dispute likely to lead to a rupture between two members of the League ' (March 16). The League took no action, but in June Great Britain offered a strip of Somaliland to Abyssinia on condition that the latter should cede some territory to Italy. Nothing came of this offer. The Italian Duce was after bigger game, and, convinced by the silence maintained at Stresa that neither England nor France was really interested in Abyssinia, went on his way unheeding. When, in *Italy and Abyssinia*

September, the League did consider intervention, Signor Mussolini refused to tolerate it. To a strong speech delivered at Geneva by Sir Samuel Hoare, Sir John Simon's successor at the Foreign Office, the Duce paid no heed, nor to the proposals of the League Council. On October 2 he invaded Abyssinia.

Sanctions On October 7 the Council declared Italy to be the aggressor, and in November 'sanctions' against Italy came into operation. Italy's progress in Abyssinia was slow, and in December Sir Samuel Hoare agreed with M. Laval to propose to the combatants terms which would have left Haile Selassie in possession of part of his territory, and given to Italy enough of the remainder to enable her to withdraw from a dangerous adventure, if not completely satisfied, without loss of self-respect.

A disclosure (premature and inconvenient for England, though obviously designed in France) of the Hoare-Laval plan aroused a storm of indignation in England. Mr. Baldwin bowed to the storm, disavowed the plan, sacrificed his Foreign Minister, and appointed in his place Mr. Eden, an able and ardent votary of the League of Nations.

But M. Laval had prepared the way for Mussolini's triumph in Abyssinia. The Negus was chased from his capital; King Victor Emmanuel was proclaimed Emperor of Abyssinia; the whole country was annexed to the Italian Empire (May), and in July 'sanctions' were formally lifted by the League.

Rhineland remilitarized Meanwhile, Germany had taken advantage of the preoccupation of the Western Democracies to reoccupy and rearm the demilitarized zone in the Rhineland (March 1935). It is now known that had England and France opposed this move, Hitler would have withdrawn. To the surprise of the German General Staff, who did not approve of the march into the Rhineland, no opposition was offered. The Pact of Locarno was contemptuously torn up; the sting of the Treaty which France had concluded with Soviet Russia (May 1935) was drawn. Germany concluded an Anti-Comintern Pact with Japan in March 1936, and, by the adhesion of Italy in November 1936, the new Triple alliance was completed.

Straits Convention In striking contrast with the violent methods of Hitler was the entirely 'correct' procedure followed by Kemal Ataturk to secure the revision of the Treaty of Lausanne. In April 1936 Turkey formally applied to the League of Nations and to the signatories of the Treaty for its revision. A Conference was accordingly held at Montreux, and by the Convention concluded there on July 20, 1936, Turkey regained the right to fortify the narrow Straits and for the first time since 1833 became complete mistress in her own house. England and Russia also—but only after a controversy so acute as at one time to threaten a deadlock— came to terms in regard to the use of that valuable waterway.[1]

Meanwhile in Great Britain a burst of sunshine had been followed by gloom. In May 1935 the whole British Empire had demonstrated its loyalty and affection to King George V and Queen Mary, and had participated in the modest but impressive celebrations which marked the conclusion of twenty-five years of a notable reign. In the following January the greatly loved Sovereign passed away. Better known throughout the Empire than any of his predecessors on the throne, King George had year by year strengthened his hold on its affection and respect. Though the central figures in a splendid Court, the King and Queen had lived personal lives of unaffected simplicity without detriment to the dignity of the throne. Innumerable acts of sympathy and consideration had endeared the King to his peoples, and they mourned his loss as that of a father. *The British Empire* *The Silver Jubilee* *Death of King George V*

High hopes were entertained of his successor who was personally known to all the people of his Empire as the most popular Prince that ever played the difficult rôle of Heir-Apparent. The hopes were not fulfilled. Before King Edward VIII had reigned a year, and some months before the date fixed for his crowning, he intimated to the Prime Minister his intention to contract a marriage which it was certain that Parliament would not approve. At the King's bidding the Governments of the self-governing Dominions were consulted. They unanimously supported the view taken by the Imperial Government. Refusing to listen to the advice and entreaties of his mother, his brethren and his ministers, the King insisted that if he could not marry the lady of his choice and make her Queen, he would surrender the crown of the greatest Empire the world has ever known. The painful alternative was perforce accepted. The *Abdication Bill* passed *Abdication of Edward VIII*

---

[1] For details about the Treaty of 1833, and for a full account of the proceedings at Montreux, see Marriott, *Eastern Question*, pp. 235 f. and 566 f.

through all its stages on December 11 : King Edward ceased to reign, and immediately left the country. On December 12 his brother, the Duke of York, was proclaimed King as George VI.

These events had a profound constitutional significance. The *Statute of Westminster*, under which the legal proceedings were taken, had left the Crown as the main, if not the sole, effective link in the chain of the Empire. Would the link hold ? Could the unity of the Commonwealth of Nations survive a crisis such as that which suddenly faced it in December 1936 ? The answer to these questions was not ambiguous. In the words of a Canadian statesman, the unanimity of the Commonwealth demonstrated to the world ' the granite strength of the British Constitution enshrined as it is in the British Throne '.[1]

Corona-
tion of
King
George
VI

King George VI and Queen Elizabeth were crowned in Westminster Abbey on May 12, 1937. The changes necessitated by the *Statute of Westminster* in the actual words of the service, no less than the official presence of representatives of the whole Empire, gave to the ceremony a new significance. The crown worn by King George VI is liturgically, as well as legally, Imperial.

The presence of the Empire statesmen at the Coronation gave an opportunity for the holding of another Imperial Conference. Providentially : since the discussions—highly confidential in character—were mainly concerned with the problem of Imperial Defence.

The year 1937 was further marked by several measures of considerable constitutional significance. The members of the House of Commons voted for themselves an increase of 50 per cent. in salaries. This raised the salary nominally to £600 a year, but owing to free railway travelling between Westminster and their respective constituencies and to deductions in respect of income tax, the salary was considerably in excess of £600 and was another step towards the creation of a body of ' professional politicians '. That the House of Commons should be recruited from young men with brains but little money is all to the good : that it should come to consist predominantly of ' professionals ' instead of ' amateurs ' would be to alter its whole character, very decidedly for the worse.

[1] The whole episode is more fully treated in Marriott, *British Empire and Commonwealth* (Nicholson & Watson, 1939), Chapter XX.

By the *Ministers of the Crown Act* (1937) the positions of the
Prime Minister and of the Cabinet were for the first time legalized :
a salary of £10,000 a year was attached to the office of Prime
Minister ; the salaries of some other Cabinet Ministers were
equalized and a salary of £2,000 a year was assigned to the post—
now for the first time legally recognized—of Leader of the
Opposition ; a maximum limit was placed on the number of
Ministers who might sit in the House of Commons, and a minimum
limit on those who must sit in the House of Lords.   Hitherto the
Prime Minister had received only the salary (£5,000) of
the First Lordship of the Treasury, the Foreign Secretaryship, or
whatever other office he had held to enable him to sit in his own
Cabinet.

The *Regency Act* (1937) was also constitutionally noteworthy.
Many a time from the thirteenth century onwards it had been
necessary to make temporary provision for the minority,
incapacity or the absence of the Sovereign.   But not until 1937
was any permanent machinery provided by Parliament to operate
in any of these contingencies.   Henceforward, in case of a
minority or total incapacity the regency will vest in the next
adult heir, and in case of illness, not involving total incapacity,
and of intended absence abroad, the Sovereign is authorized to
delegate certain of the royal functions to Counsellors of State.
In deference, however, to the *Statute of Westminster* the Act is
not to operate in the Dominions.   The functions of the Regent
are, moreover, divorced from the guardianship of an infant
Sovereign which is by the Act reserved to his or her mother,
if she be living.

Another incident of 1937, of personal though hardly of political,
still less of constitutional, significance was Mr. Baldwin's resignation of the Premiership.   During the General Strike of 1926 and
during the ' Abdication Crisis ' of 1936 he had exhibited conspicuous courage, calmness and tact, and is entitled to the highest
credit for his leadership on these critical occasions, but though he
held office in the aggregate for more than seven years his record
was on the whole undistinguished.   He was regarded with respect
and affection in the House of Commons ; and with the soul of a
poet he could rise at moments to something near eloquence, but
he had no great power of popular appeal, and he lacked both the

training and the temperament for dealing with foreign affairs at a time when foreign policy was becoming daily more important. Unfortunately, his successor in Downing Street suffered from a similar limitation. Mr. Neville Chamberlain, a good financier and admirable domestic administrator, was, unlike his brother, ill-equipped for dealing with the crises which rapidly developed on the continent.

Civil War in Spain

The outbreak of civil war in Spain (July 1936), which dragged on for nearly three years, would probably have precipitated a general conflagration but for the patient persistence of Great Britain in a policy of non-intervention. The republican party in Spain was actively supported by Soviet Russia ; the ' nationalist ' party, led by General Franco, leant heavily on the help lavishly provided by Italy and in less degree by Germany. The French Communists sent all the help they could to the Spanish republicans, who had the entire sympathy also of the English Socialists. But the French Government, under M. Blum, gave loyal support to the efforts of the British Government to circumscribe the area of conflict.

Mr. Chamberlain and Lord Halifax, who had succeeded Mr. Eden at the Foreign Office in February 1938, exhausted every means to avert Armageddon, but the task became increasingly difficult. France was particularly sensitive on the question of Austrian independence, and in 1931 had been mainly instrumental in frustrating the attempt to negotiate a Customs Union between Austria and Germany. England had in 1934 made a formal declaration in favour of Austrian ' independence and integrity '. Until 1935 the maintenance of that independence was one of the main pivots of Italian policy. But Mussolini's attack on Abyssinia in 1935 had alienated Great Britain ; in 1936 the Rome–Berlin ' Axis ' came into being, and Mussolini was ready to desert Austria and throw in his lot with the aggressor. In March 1938 Hitler marched into Vienna and without opposition from Italy or any other foreign power annexed Austria to the German *Reich*. Prior to the establishment of the Nazi régime the Austrians themselves would have welcomed an *Anschluss* ;

Hitler's Annexations : Austria

but any sentiment in favour of union with Germany was soon extinguished by the grim realities of Nazi rule.

The annexation of Austria opened the door to a German

attack on Czecho-Slovakia. France and Russia were both bound by treaties to defend Czecho-Slovakia. England was under no such engagement, but was deeply engaged to the support of French policy. Mr. Chamberlain and Lord Halifax desired at almost any price to avoid a European war, and, though profoundly perturbed by the preparations of Herr Hitler, contented themselves by uttering grave warnings to Germany, and by sending Lord Runciman, in the summer of 1938, on an ' unofficial ' mission to Prague to discover a means of escape from the impending tragedy. Lord Runciman's mission was fruitless. In the discontent of a large, though not compact, body of Germans in Bohemia, Herr Hitler had a specious excuse for interference. England was well-nigh unanimous in believing that some satisfaction should be given to these ' Sudeten ' Germans. At the eleventh hour Mr. Chamberlain made an heroic effort to avert war, flew to Munich, and with Signor Mussolini and M. Daladier, the French Premier, concluded an agreement with Herr Hitler. Zone after zone of Bohemian territory was to be annexed by Germany, but on that basis ' peace ' was secured. The relief expressed in England was profound and universal. No such welcome as awaited Mr. Chamberlain on September 30, 1938, has been given to an English statesman since Lord Beaconsfield in 1878 brought back ' Peace with Honour ' from Berlin. The United States, not a few Germans, nay, the whole world, hailed Neville Chamberlain as the Great Peacemaker.

But with startling and not too creditable rapidity the mood in England changed. The Labour Party in Parliament, who had cheered Chamberlain to the echo in September, denounced him in November as a poltroon. Even Mr. Churchill, while paying a warm tribute to Chamberlain's conspicuous courage and pure motives, expressed, in prophetic words, his misgivings : ' By this time next year we shall know whether the policy of appeasement has appeased or whether it has only stimulated more ferocious appetite. All we can do in the meantime is to gather together the forces of resistance and defence.'

That we did. A ' national register ' was compiled ; precautions were taken against air-attack ; evacuation plans were prepared ; a Ministry of Supply was set up ; and in April 1939 conscription was introduced.

A month earlier Hitler had thrown away the last portion of his mask. On March 15 he had marched into Prague and had annexed Bohemia and Moravia. On the 23rd he occupied Memel ; on April 7 an Italian army occupied Albania, the Crown of which was a few days later accepted by King Victor Emmanuel.

Against these indefensible proceedings the British Cabinet addressed to Rome a strong protest, the more ineffectual since Chamberlain refused, while announcing the promise of aid to Greece and Roumania, to denounce the Anglo-Italian Agreement. Hitler, on the contrary, did not hesitate to denounce the Polish-German Non-aggression Pact of 1934 and the Anglo-German Naval Agreement of 1935.

Royal Visit to Canada

There was, however, one gleam of sunshine before the storm broke. Despite the grave international situation, King George and Queen Elizabeth made a triumphal progress through Canada in May and June 1939, paid a short visit to the United States, and before leaving for home delighted their loyal but sorely stricken subjects in Newfoundland by a visit to the ' oldest British Colony '. The tour was an unqualified success. By their simplicity and friendly accessibility the King and Queen won the hearts of all with whom they came in contact. They were themselves enchanted by the charm, spaciousness, and beauty of the Great Dominion, and undoubtedly did much by their contagious happiness and by their gracious kindliness to confirm the devotion of their Canadian subjects to the Throne and its occupants.

Czecho-Slovakia

It was a grim and menacing situation that confronted their Majesties on their return to Europe. Herr Hitler had cynically broken the agreement concluded at Munich less than six months earlier, had torn up the scrap of paper to which, with Mr. Chamberlain, he had affixed his signature, and had marched into and annexed Czecho-Slovakia (March 15). Less than a week later he had occupied Memel. To avert a similar disaster to Poland, Great Britain and France had (March 31) given an unconditional pledge of assistance to that country, and in April had extended the pledge to Roumania and Greece.

CHAPTER XXXI

THE SECOND WORLD-WAR

THE actual outbreak of hostilities found us, though not unprepared, ill-equipped for waging war against a great military power. Mr. Chamberlain at once set up a War-Cabinet of nine members, bringing in Mr. Churchill as First Lord of the Admiralty and Lord Hankey as Minister without portfolio. With great rapidity a war-time régime was imposed. Under the *Emergency Powers Act* (1939), Defence Regulations of the most stringent character were made by Order-in-Council. Thanks to the Conscription Act a recruiting campaign was not, as in 1914, necessary, liability for service was extended, and the list of reserved occupations curtailed. But, though the military machine rapidly gathered strength, we could do nothing to save Poland. Within three weeks it was conquered by the Germans, who mercilessly massacred and tortured its people. On September 17 the Russians marched into Poland from the east, and occupied an area about equal to that occupied by the Germans, though with only 13,000,000 as against 22,000,000 inhabitants.

Latvia, Lithuania and Esthonia submitted to Russia. Finland did not, and looked to England and France for help. Though eager to afford it, these Powers could not give it in view of Sweden's refusal to allow the passage of an Anglo-French force. But for that refusal we should have been at war with Russia. As it was, the Finns, after a gallant resistance, were compelled to accept the terms imposed upon them by Russia (March 13, 1940). But Hitler's attack on Russia (1941) offered the Finns a temptation they could not resist ; they refused to heed the warnings of England and the U.S.A. against persistence in the war against Russia, and only when the Allies dominated the situation did the

The Outbreak of War

Poland

Finland

Finns accept an armistice dictated to them by Russia (September 19, 1944). Its terms, though severe, did not deny to a brave people the boon of independence and the hope of recovery.

With Finland and Poland in the toils, Hitler was free, after six months of 'phoney' war, to begin his serious attack upon France and England. First, however, he cleared the flanks. On April 9, 1940, Denmark was occupied without resistance. Norway, on the contrary, fought the German invaders with splendid courage; but the prevailing opinion in England was that Hitler's invasion of Norway was, in Mr. Churchill's words, 'a strategic and political error'. In fact, the German occupation of all the Norwegian ports rendered the position of the small Anglo-French force which had been sent to Norway precarious, and compelled it to evacuate the country. This withdrawal, though skilfully effected from Narvik (May 2), seriously damaged British prestige and brought down Mr. Chamberlain's Ministry.

On May 10 Mr. Churchill replaced Mr. Chamberlain as Prime Minister, though he retained Mr. Chamberlain in a War Cabinet of five members, and also included in it Mr. Attlee and Mr. Greenwood to represent the Labour Party, which, as a whole, cordially supported the Government. Other Socialist and Liberal leaders accepted Cabinet or Ministerial office in an Administration which could truly be described as national.

The National Government   Nothing less was needed to confront an emergency as grave and grim as any in our history. On the day that Mr. Churchill became Prime Minister the Germans had invaded the Low Countries, in overwhelming force, by land and air. Holland and Belgium surrendered on May 15 and 27 respectively, nor could the French withstand the German invasion. Over the bridges crossing the Meuse, carelessly or traitorously left open, the 'Panzer' divisions poured in unending succession, hosts of tanks and diving aeroplanes flung the French troops into confusion, and their retreat, terribly impeded by evacuating civilians, became a rout. Nothing could arrest the German advance. Especially menacing to England was the German occupation of the ports: Flushing, Antwerp, Ostend and Boulogne were in German hands by the end of May. Meanwhile the capitulation of King Leopold of Belgium had rendered the position of his allies untenable. Thus isolated, they fought an heroic rearguard action to enable them to reach the coast at Dunkirk. On May 30th the historic evacuation from Dunkirk began. No fewer than 336,000 men were, by a miracle of organization and fortitude, re-embarked, and on 1,000 vessels of the Royal Navy, and a flotilla of voluntary craft, large and small, were by June 4 safely landed in England. In this vast and hazardous operation only one British transport, six destroyers and some twenty-five smaller craft were lost.

One after another the Channel ports were, meanwhile, falling into German hands. On May 27 Calais surrendered after an heroic resistance which had made possible the ' miracle ' of Dunkirk. Dieppe, Havre, Cherbourg and Brest all fell to the enemy before the end of June. *Collapse of France*

Much had happened in the meantime. The French Government had left Paris, which the Germans occupied without resistance on June 14. The British Government urged the French to adopt any alternative preferably to surrender, and Mr. Churchill actually offered the ' Union ' of France with England. Nevertheless, on June 22, Marshal Petain, who had succeeded M. Reynaud as Prime Minister, concluded an Armistice with the Germans, and on the 24th with the Italians, who on June 10 had treacherously declared war.

On the next day General de Gaulle announced in London the formation of the French National Committee. Over it he presided until by the superb effort of the British Empire and the U.S.A., France, after its long travail, had in 1944 been freed of Germans, and de Gaulle was able to establish a Provisional Government in Paris.

Of intervening events a bare summary must suffice.

For more than a year the British Empire faced victorious Germany, its satellites and Italy alone. Few foreigners thought in the summer of 1940 that it could escape the fate of France. That it did escape was due to the loyal support of the Overseas Empire, to the intrepid leadership of Mr. Churchill, and above all to the valour and vigilance of the British Navy, and of a young, small, but splendidly courageous and finely trained Air Force. *The British Empire alone*

To the last belongs the honour of victory in the ' Battle of Britain '. Had that battle been lost our fate had been sealed. In fiercest intensity it lasted from August 1940 to May 1941. *The Battle of Britain*

London suffered the first onslaught, being raided on 82 out of 85 consecutive nights in the autumn and winter of 1940–1. A similar, if less sustained, ordeal awaited Portsmouth, Coventry, Liverpool, Bristol, Hull, Southampton, and other cities. Over 40,000 civilians were killed and over 50,000 seriously injured down to the end of 1941. But Britain was not dismayed, and the British Empire survived. ' Never,' as Mr. Churchill said in a phrase already assured of immortality, ' in the field of human conflict was so much owed by so many to so few.'

East Africa   Once the Battle of Britain was won attention began to be concentrated upon the Mediterranean and Africa. Though we were compelled to evacuate British Somaliland early in August, an Italian attack upon Kenya was warded off by South African troops reinforced by a force from Nigeria and the Gold Coast Regiment.

Nor did the triumph of the Italians last long. Early in 1941 they were driven not merely out of Somaliland, but of Abyssinia. Haile Selassie was restored to his throne, and before April was a week old Mussolini's East African Empire had fallen.

The Mediter-ranean   Much more prolonged was the struggle in the Mediterranean and in North Africa. Thanks to the brilliant seamanship of Admiral Sir Andrew Cunningham, the British Navy maintained its superiority in the Mediterranean. The Italian Navy avoided contact as far as possible, but on November 11–12, 1940, it suffered a shattering defeat when sheltering in its stronghold at Taranto.

Greece   Nowhere was the news of that great victory more enthusiastically acclaimed than in Greece. On October 20, 1940, Mussolini, in a hurry to emulate Hitler's triumphs, made without provocation an attack upon the Greeks, who repelled it with astonishing success. We weakened our own Force in Egypt to give the Greeks all the help we could, and the support of the British Navy was invaluable to them. But early in April 1941, the Germans intervened to extricate their Italian allies from their difficulties in Greece ; on the 23rd the Greek forces in the Epirus and Macedonia were compelled to surrender ; on the 27th the Germans entered Athens ; the British Imperial Forces, consisting largely of Anzacs of the finest quality, were evacuated to Crete, not without serious loss in men and equipment, and to the Navy. All five hospital ships were sunk by the enemy.

Crete proved indefensible against the wonderfully co-ordinated Crete German attack by aeroplanes, gliders and troop-carriers. Our navy inflicted heavy losses on the enemy, but itself suffered severely. By June 2, 1940, however, the evacuation was almost complete. The Cretan disaster cost us and our Greek allies some 15,000 men, much war material and many ships. The German losses were perhaps as heavy, but whilst they had emerged from the holocaust victorious, we had suffered an appalling defeat.

Generously, if perhaps unwisely, we had drawn upon our See-Saw scanty forces in Egypt to succour the Greeks. Our generosity in North Africa seemed likely to cost us dear. On September 13, 1940, the Italians 1940–2 under Marshal Graziani began their advance towards Alexandria, but having taken Sollum and Sidi-Barrani they halted on Egyptian soil. On December 11th, General Wavell, Commander-in-Chief Middle East, having been heavily reinforced, launched his counter-attack. A finely co-ordinated movement by sea, land and air was rewarded by a brilliant victory at Sidi-Barrani; the Italian threat to Egypt was averted.

From Sidi-Barrani the Army of the Nile continued its brilliant Sunshine and rapid advance. Bardia, Tobruk, Derna and Benghazi all and Shadow surrendered between January 5–February 7. The Italian defeat in 1941 was complete and catastrophic. Marshal Graziani, having lost an army, was recalled, leaving 133,000 prisoners, 1,300 guns, and immense booty in our hands.

Our triumph was dismally shortlived. The Germans under General von Rommel succoured their miserable Italian allies in Africa as they had in Greece. At the beginning of April they launched their offensive in Cyrenaica : in a few weeks all the territory we had gained during the winter campaign was lost.

On July 1, General Wavell exchanged Commands with General Auchinleck, Commander-in-Chief in India, and on November 18, the latter, strongly reinforced from home, struck his blow for the re-conquest of Libya, which by the end of the year 1941 was cleared of the enemy.

In the new year, however, von Rommel, with an army re-organized and re-equipped, took the offensive, and after a rapid advance, checked only by the heroic resistance of Tobruk, believed himself to be within 48 hours of the occupation of Alexandria.

At El Alamein, however, the British forces stood and denied to the Germans that great prize.   Rommell's advance was halted. In August, Lieut.-General Montgomery took over the command of the Eighth Army under General Alexander, who became Commander-in-Chief Middle East.   Largely reinforced with men and greatly superior tanks, Montgomery was ready by September to take the offensive.   Rommel began to withdraw in September, and in the last days of October a terrific tank battle was fought at El Alamein.   That was the turning-point of the campaign. By November 2 the enemy was definitely in retreat, Sidi-Barrani, Tobruk, and Benghazi were retaken (November 10–20).

Alliance with Russia Before then we had got new allies.   On June 22, 1941, the Germans had treacherously invaded Russia in force.   On that same night Mr. Churchill swept away all misgivings by an emphatic declaration that no political differences would be permitted to stand in the way of complete and cordial co-operation between England and Russia : the enemies of Nazism were the friends and allies of Great Britain, and to them every possible support would be given.   Never for a day has he been diverted from that purpose. President Roosevelt also promised that the generous help the U.S.A. was already giving to the British Empire would be extended to Soviet Russia.

Alliance with U.S.A Before the year 1941 closed the U.S.A. also had become not merely our friend but our ally.   On December 7, Japan, with treachery comparable to Hitler's, launched an attack by sea-borne aircraft upon Pearl Harbour, the principal base of the American Pacific Fleet.   On the following day the U.S.A. and Great Britain declared war upon Japan.   The Japanese made brilliant use of the initiative they had treacherously obtained.   They bombed and sank the two great ships, *Repulse* and *Prince of Wales*, intended as the mainstay of our fleet in the Far East.   That stunning blow lost us the command of the Pacific, and opened our Far Eastern **The Far East** Empire to Japanese attack.   Hong-Kong, after an heroic but hopeless defence, surrendered on Christmas Day, 1941, and before the close of the year Penang Island was occupied.   Our allies also suffered heavily ; the Americans lost Guam and Wake Islands, and in January 1942 the Japanese invaded the Netherlands East Indies.   Nothing could stop the progress of the Power which held command of the sea.   Singapore was unconditionally surrendered on February 15 ; Rangoon, Java and the Andaman Islands were occupied in March. Mandalay was evacuated in May and Sydney was attacked by midget submarines in June 1942. But American troops had already begun to reach Australia before the end of March (1942). The Australians, under Mr. Curtin's leadership, manfully set to work to defend themselves to the last ditch, and a notable naval victory off the Solomons in November greatly eased the situation, and gradually forced the Japanese to the defensive. Heavy losses were inflicted on their shipping, notably by a disaster in Bismarck Straits on March 2, 1943.

As the year 1943 advanced the successes of the Allies became more frequent and more marked, and though Calcutta had suffered an air raid in December 1942, the year 1943 closed without the expected invasion of India. In all parts of the Pacific, notably in the Aleutian islands and New Guinea, the Allies continued to make headway.

Even more emphatic was the success of our Russian allies. **Russia** The earlier phase of the war had been one of almost unbroken triumph for the Germans, who seriously threatened both Leningrad and Moscow. But in November 1942 the Russians launched their counter-attack, which was crowned, after several months of continuous fighting, by the final surrender of the last German forces at Stalingrad (February 2, 1943). Few surrenders in the history of warfare have been more gigantic in scale or more conclusive in results. The threat to Leningrad and Moscow was averted.

The Russians harped with more bitterness than justice upon the failure of the Allies to open a ' Second Front ', a failure which was emphasized by a noisy and ignorant section of the British public.

To take the sting out of the Russian reproaches, and to relieve, **Confer-** as far as they could, the pressure upon the Russian armies, was **ence at** the declared object of the Anglo-American campaign of 1943 in **blanca** North Africa. That campaign was carefully planned and ' the entire field of war was surveyed ' when in mid-January 1943 President Roosevelt and Mr. Churchill, together with a large staff of their professional advisers, met at Casablanca. At the close of the Conference Mr. Roosevelt formally announced that the Allies had resolved to fight all three Axis Powers to ' complete surrender '.

North
African
Campaign

Preliminary to the campaign of 1943 a great Anglo-American army, under the supreme command of the American General Eisenhower, had by a combined naval, military and air operation been landed at various key points in Algeria and Morocco. Planned in absolute secrecy, this vast operation was, between November 4 and 11, 1942, carried out with slight loss and complete success.

That success was greatly facilitated by the surrender, after a brief resistance, of the French Colonies in North and West Africa as well as by the adhesion of Admiral Darlan, the French High Commissioner. Actually, Darlan's conduct had throughout been highly equivocal, and the motive of his assassination by a young Frenchman, on December 24, remains obscure. He was succeeded by General Giraud.

Meanwhile the dismay of the Germans at the turn of events was not mitigated when (November 27, 1942) the 72 vessels of the French Fleet were scuttled by their crews in Toulon harbour. Nevertheless, great efforts were made by the Axis, not without success, to reinforce from Sicily their forces in North Africa and hold up the advance of the British First Army in the early months of 1943 towards Tunisia.

Tunisia was the goal also of the Eighth Army which, under Montgomery's brilliant leadership, had (January 23, 1943) crowned its wonderful campaign by the occupation of Tripoli. In three months that army had traversed some 1,350 miles, mostly of 'food-less and waterless desert, had inflicted a loss of fully 80,000 men killed, captured or disabled upon the Italo-German forces, had taken or destroyed more than 500 tanks, 1,000 guns, many thousands of lorries, and over 1,600 aircraft '.[1] On February 8 the Eighth Army crossed the Tunisian border, and in a series of battles (March 6–27) Montgomery inflicted a crushing and final defeat upon Rommel, who retired, on the plea of ill-health, to Germany. Von Arnim, his successor, did his best to prevent the junction of the Eighth, advancing westwards, and First Armies, advancing eastwards, but in vain. Tunis and Bizerto fell to the latter on May 7 ; on the 12th Von Arnim was captured, and a day later the whole of the Axis forces in North Africa surrendered. About 340,000 prisoners (three-fifths of them were Germans) were

[1] Graves (ed.), *Quarterly Record of the War*, xiv, 24.

taken and vast quantities of weapons and supplies fell into the hands of the Allies.

That was the triumphant end of the North-African Campaign, conducted at first entirely by the land, sea, and air forces of the British, greatly assisted in the final stages by their American and French allies. The whole of the southern coast of the Mediterranean, as well as the Atlantic seaboard, was now open to them. Invasion of Europe

On May 31 the French Fleet at Alexandria, which had been neutralized since 1940, joined the Allies, and on June 3 Generals de Gaulle and Giraud, the rival leaders of Fighting France, at last came to terms and a Committee of National Liberation was formed to conduct French co-operation with the Allies.

Not, however, until July 10 did the Allies invade Sicily. The way for this was prepared by the capture in June of the islets in the Straits—Pantelleria, Lampedusa and Linosa. The attack upon Sicily, displaying an entirely novel technique in amphibious warfare, was accomplished with astonishing ease, and though the Germans held up the advance of the Allies for some weeks, the occupation of Messina (August 17) marked the end of hostilities in the island. The Germans succeeded, however, in getting most of their troops over to the mainland, though they evacuated Sardinia, while the Fighting French captured Corsica.

In Italy the political situation developed rapidly. Mussolini, having sought help in vain from Hitler, was compelled (July 24) to resign and was placed under arrest, but was presently rescued, for the time being, by the Germans. Marshal Badoglio took office as chief minister of the Crown, dissolved the Fascist party, dismissed all the Fascist officials and (September 3) concluded an armistice with the Allies. The whole of the Italian armed forces surrendered unconditionally. On the same day General Montgomery landed with the Eighth Army on the toe of Italy and moved north without meeting resistance. The Fifth Army, on the contrary (half American and half British), after landing (September 9) in the Bay of Salerno, were for a week in grave peril of being driven back into the sea by a strong German force. They were saved only by the guns of the Allied warships and the timely arrival of Montgomery and the Eighth Army. The latter, having made their supplies secure by the capture of Taranto, Bari, and Brindisi, reached their colleagues of the Fifth Army, by forced marches, on September 17. The Allied offensive was presently resumed ; the Fifth Army occupied a devastated Naples on October 1, the Eighth Army advanced slowly along the Adriatic coast. Italy declared war on Germany on October 13 and was accepted by the Allies as a co-belligerent ; but the close of the year saw Germany still in control of two-thirds of Italy, including the capital and all the industrial cities. The failure of the Allies to take the Dodecanese, due to culpable mis-handling, to the pusillanimity of the large Italian garrison, and not least to an effective German counterstroke, was also a definite reverse. Thus—despite the splendid Russian victories, the brilliant ending of the African campaign, the recapture of New Guinea and a steady improvement in the Far Eastern situation, the success achieved against the U-boat packs in the Atlantic, the crippling of the *Tirpitz* (September) and the sinking of the *Schornhorst* (December)—the year 1943 closed with some sense of frustration and disappointment.

Allies in Confer- ence A notable incident in the winter of 1943–4 was the series of conferences between the leading statesmen of the Allied countries. One obstacle to cordial co-operation had been removed when Marshal Stalin announced the formal dissolution of the *Comintern* or Third Communist International. The *Comintern* had for some time been politically significant, but its dissolution was welcomed abroad as indicating a change of outlook in Russia.

In this clarified atmosphere the conference of the Foreign Ministers of Great Britain, the U.S.A. and the U.S.S.R. was held at Moscow (October–November 1943). The resulting agreement was embodied in five documents and was promptly published. Measures were to be taken to shorten the war, to promote economic co-operation, and to devise a permanent organization for the maintenance of world peace, to punish war criminals, to set up a European Advisory Council in London, to restore the independence of Austria, and make Italy safe for democracy.

Cairo and Teheran At the end of November Mr. Churchill himself conferred for five days in Cairo with President Roosevelt and General Chiang Kai-shek to concert measures for bringing ' unrelenting pressure ' against Japan. It was agreed that Japan should be stripped of all the territories seized by violence, and that China should recover all that she had lost, while Korea should become free and independent.

From Cairo the President and Prime Minister flew to Teheran to confer with Marshal Stalin. At Teheran complete plans, précis as to timing and direction, were concerted for the destruction of the German forces. Recognizing also ' their supreme responsibility for an enduring peace in a future untouched by tyranny ', the three statesmen made plans for their co-operation in the task of maintaining in the world ' orderly progress and continuing peace '.

On returning from Teheran to Cairo, President Roosevelt and Mr. Churchill met M. Ismet Inönü, President of the Turkish Republic, and reached important conclusions as to the ' joint and several interests of the countries represented '.

The year 1943 definitely marked the turn of the tide. If in The War 1944 the main inflood encountered formidable rocks and did not $^{in 1944}$ rise quite so high as had seemed probable, it closed with an assurance of final victory.

The Russian advance, though temporarily checked at Warsaw, was irresistible. Russia, cleared of Germans, established her supremacy both on the Baltic and in the Balkans, and is advancing rapidly (January 1945) in East Prussia.

In Italy the Allies made progress, but both before and after the taking of Rome (June 4) it was so disappointingly slow, as to react upon British prestige in Yugoslavia and perhaps in Greece. In Yugoslavia, Marshal Tito, an able guerrilla leader, with the aid of his guerrilla bands and a Russian force, cleared Yugoslavia, and with the sanction of Great Britain, where King Peter had taken refuge, established a Provisional Government. Continental Greece was also cleared of Germans, partly by guerrilla operations. But once Greece was freed, the guerrillas turned upon their English benefactors who had supplied them with arms and were trying to supply their countrymen with food. A British force had consequently to fight to restore order in Athens, and to set up a Regency under Archbishop Damaskinos. In the Far East remarkable progress was made in 1944, notably in northern Burma and in the Philippines. Naval success in the Pacific, predominantly American, was, however, entirely eclipsed, as indeed were all other operations on land or sea, by the marvellous achievement of

M.E.—19

Clearance
of France
the Allied Armies, Navies and Air Forces, not to add of British engineers, in effecting a landing in force in Normandy (June 5–6). In this operation, achieved triumphantly and at a cost which, if heavy, was less than expected, 4,000 ships (including minesweepers, who did their difficult job with splendid courage and amazing punctuality) and 11,000 aircraft took part. The result of this wonderful example of co-ordination was the assembling of the greatest army ever seen on French soil, where General (now Field-Marshal) Montgomery's great strategic plan gradually became clear. While the main German army was attracted to Caen, the Americans, having taken Cherbourg (June 27) and cleared the Cotentin, overran Brittany, and advanced by the Loire on Paris, but leaving, to our embarrassment, strong German garrisons in the Atlantic ports. On August 21 the Americans crossed the Seine at Mantes, and on the 25th occupied Paris with General de Gaulle, whose Free French forces had already almost cleared their capital of Germans.

Meanwhile, Caen was, after heavy fighting, taken by Montgomery on July 9, and Rommell's counter-offensive was definitely defeated when (August 17) Falaise was taken by the Canadians. The defeat at Falaise was decisive : the German retreat became almost a rout.

In mid-August a diversion was caused by the invasion of Southern France. An American army quickly and easily occupied Marseilles, Cannes, Grasse and Toulon, and cleared, with the help of Free Frenchmen, all Southern France. In the north Rouen and Dieppe fell to the Canadians, Amiens and Arras to the British (August 31–September 1), who, on September 3, liberated Brussels. During the next few days the taking of Antwerp, Lille, Louvain, Ghent and other towns completed the liberation of Belgium and Luxemburg. Zeebrugge was captured by the Canadians on the 10th, Le Havre by the British on the 12th. Not, however, until November was the Scheldt cleared by a British expedition to Flushing and Walcheren Island, or Antwerp opened to traffic.

A gallant attempt had, in the meantime (September 17), been made by a British Airborne Division to seize and hold the crossings over the Maas, the Waal and the Lower Rhine. The attempt only just failed to achieve brilliant success, but, at the cost of heavy losses in killed, prisoners and equipment, was defeated, and the remnant of a gallant force had to be withdrawn (September 25–26). More serious was the counter-offence launched in force by the Germans under von Runstedt against a weakly-held sector of the Allied line on the Belgian-Luxemburg frontiers (December 16). Breaking through on a wide front, the Germans gravely threatened the communications of the Allies, destroyed stores accumulated for our advance, and inflicted upon the Allies, at even heavier losses to themselves, heavy losses of men and equipment. Before the year ended, however, Runstedt's advance was halted ; the salient he had established was gradually flattened out, and in the new year his forces were steadily pushed back to the point whence they had started.

The year 1945 opened, accordingly, with high hopes of complete if not immediate victory on widely distributed fronts.

CHAPTER XXXII

THE HOME FRONT

Domestic
Affairs

THE course of domestic affairs since 1939 has followed two main directions, roughly in chronological succession. During the first years of the war attention was necessarily concentrated upon national defence and the maintenance of the war effort. Since peace came, however distantly, into view, the mind of the nation and of the Government has turned towards the preparation of schemes for social and economic reconstruction as soon as the attainment of victory permits.

Only a mere summary, and that incomplete, of events can here be attempted.

The first anxiety of the Government was to protect persons and property against enemy action and to neglect no means of giving maximum effect to every measure for carrying the war to a completely successful issue.

The War
Effort

A comprehensive summary of the measures taken to that end is given in a White Paper [1] presented to Parliament at the end of November 1944, when it was reasonable to assume that the measures taken had effected their purpose. They are summarized under five heads : Man Power, Home Production, Shipping and Foreign Trade, Civilian Consumption and Finance. To these and kindred topics only a brief reference is possible.

Man
Power

Practically the whole population between adolescence and old age have been brought into some form of national or essential service. Of 15,910,000 males between the ages of 14 and 64 only 71,000 remained in 1944 unemployed; there were less than one million students, invalids, &c., while $4\frac{1}{2}$ millions (excluding prisoners and missing) were in the armed forces, in addition to $1\frac{3}{4}$ millions in the Home Guard (instituted on a voluntary basis in 1940, but afterwards conscripted); 225,000 were enlisted in

[1] Cmd. 6564.

whole time Civil Defence for National Fire Brigade duty, A.R.P. services, Casualty service and regular and auxiliary police; in Part-time Civil Defence services were nearly two million others.

Women also have taken a notable part in the war effort. Out of 16,020,000 females between the ages of 14 and 59, over seven millions were in the Auxiliary services, whole-time Civil Defence or industry, besides a large number in part-time service.

Of casualties due to enemy action there were no fewer than 136,116, including 57,298 killed (down to August 31, 1944).

As a precaution against possible invasion or complete derange- *Adminis-* ment in the Capital, a considerable measure of administrative *tration* decentralization was at the outset of the war carried out. The whole country was divided up into seventeen regions, each under a Commissioner, and in each the Ministry of Health has its own Administrative Staff. Some Government offices have been removed from the Capital, and many firms and institutions have, in part or wholly, followed the example.

Factories, notably those engaged on the production of muni- *Industry* tions and other necessities for war, have been dispersed, but a large number have also been closed and their activities concentrated. What the effect of these processes will be on the ultimate location of industry it is premature to discuss. It may well prove, in some cases, to be permanent and decisive; if so, it must needs affect substantially the housing problem, and may have an important repercussion upon the reorganization of Local Government. But these matters belong to the future.

The war years have witnessed a truly wonderful expansion in the production not only of 'ground munitions', such as arms, guns, tanks, &c., but also in naval and aircraft construction and merchant shipbuilding, as well as munitions proper. Of these, four-fifths have been supplied from British Commonwealth and Empire resources and the rest by the United States.

No department of State has operated with more success than *Agri-* the control of food. Thanks to the organizing genius of Lord *culture* Woolton, none has gone short of necessaries and few have enjoyed *and Food* luxuries. Rationing has meant something approaching to equality. To this result British agriculture has made a notable contribution. The yield of the land has been increased by ploughing up grassland and improved methods, and the imports of food (to the relief of shipping) have been reduced by 50 per cent. Allotments have largely increased, as has the garden area devoted to vegetables. But ' labour ' has been a problem for farmers, and would have been insoluble had not 80,000 women enrolled for agricultural work, and done much to supply the places of 100,000 regular male workers required for military service.

In the total result restrictions upon personal consumption have played their part.

Ration-ing Nor has restriction been confined to food. Clothing has been severely rationed, while of that available much has been produced under ' utility ' conditions imposed by the State upon producers—conditions extended to household furniture, carpets, and hardware.

High prices also have restricted consumption. Bread and potatoes have been heavily subsidized by the State to the tune of nearly 200 millions. Nevertheless, there has been an admitted rise in the cost of living, while common experience has contradicted the tale of official optimism.

Personal expenditure has been curtailed in other directions. Except for business, railway travel is generally avoided ; omnibus services have been cut down, while licences for private motor-cars have fallen from 2,000,000 to 700,000 and the supply of motor spirit by seven-eighths.

Purchases of furniture and furnishings have dropped by 77 per cent. in volume ; of hardware, 67 per cent. Of footwear for civilians, the production has declined by 44 per cent. ; of cutlery, by 85 per cent. ; of armchairs and sofas, by more than 95 per cent.

Evacua-tion Nothing, however, has done more to enforce the realization of war than the dislocation of population. From the danger areas, and especially from the congested districts of London, a large number of women and children have been evacuated and billeted —in some cases compulsorily—upon householders in country districts. That this should cause friction on both sides was inevitable, and a considerable number of evacuees have returned to their homes. It speaks well for ' neighbourliness ' that the friction was not greater. The condition of evacuated slum children has sometimes horrified self-respecting villagers, and has also acted as an eye-opener among social and hygienic reformers.

Finance There remains to be noticed the problem of war-finance, which has in fact, though never allowed to restrict, inevitably affected the activities enumerated above.

Expenditure on the war has exceeded £25,000,000,000. This has been met by the sale of oversea investments (over £1,000 millions), by oversea borrowing of £2,300,000,000, by domestic loans, and by a terrific increase in taxation.

To domestic loans—over £10,000 millions—'small savings' have made the amazingly large contribution of about £2,500,000,000. Altogether, personal savings were estimated to have increased ninefold between 1938 and 1943, from about 3½ per cent. to about 20 per cent. of personal incomes.

Apart from borrowing, taxes have provided roughly 50 per cent. of war expenditure, being equally provided by indirect and direct taxation. Income tax has been so widened in scope that over 10½ million people now pay it as against 3,800,000 in 1938. In the pockets of the richest class it leaves less than 1/- in the £, out of which has also to be paid a share of indirect taxes. If the 'conscription' of wealth has not in theory been adopted, in practice it falls little short of it.

Nor is there any indication that even now the limit has been reached. On the contrary, social reforms have been passed or designed, most of which must add much to the financial sacrifices already imposed. Some time ago Mr. Churchill declared that the Government 'have shaped or carried out within the last two years a programme of reform or social progress which might well have occupied a whole Parliament under ordinary conditions of peace'. He understated the facts. He promised for the future that all should have 'food, work, homes'. His promise is in process of redemption. *Social Reform*

The first item to reach the Statute Book is a comprehensive scheme for the complete reorganization of national education, the main part of which was actually timed to come into effect on April 1, 1945. The local control of education is vested solely in the County and County Borough Councils, which will thus displace 169 Local Education Authorities. The Councils are required to devise divisional areas, each with its divisional executive, and to delegate certain powers to them or to such of the larger Borough or Urban District Councils as may claim to act as Divisional Areas or be selected for that purpose by the Ministry. *Education*

That is the architectural structure of the new scheme, and it may possibly provide a model for the reconstruction of Local Government. For all grades of education—nursery, primary, secondary and technical schools, and for County Colleges for adults —these Councils become responsible, in part directly, in part indirectly. The whole-time school age is raised to 15, with the prospect of raising it to 16, but beyond this there is provision for secondary, technical, vocational and adult education. For all young persons up to 18, part-time education is to be compulsory and gratuitous. In all schools, religious instruction is to be provided ; in voluntary schools according to the tenets of the Denomination concerned.

Town and Country Planning Thanks to much preliminary discussion and negotiation, the Butler Education Act was almost an agreed measure. The Town and County Planning Act aroused, on the contrary, bitter opposition. The Act confers upon Local Authorities wide powers for purchasing compulsorily land required for the reconstruction of areas damaged by enemy action. Opposition, ultimately compromised, was mainly concentrated on the methods and assessment of compensation payable to dispossessed owners.

Programme for Reconstruction For other instalments in the task of reconstruction, the Government has prepared the way by the issue of ' White Papers ' which invite discussion by interested parties of the policy proposed by the Government and tentatively outlined by the Departments concerned. Health, Employment, Export Trade, and Social Insurance are among the problems to which special attention has been drawn.

All these schemes have this in common : all raise the highly controversial problem of State action as opposed to individual initiative and enterprise. Shall the State, acting on behalf of the whole community, make itself responsible for the maintenance in health and the care in sickness of every citizen, or shall these matters be left primarily in the hands of ' private ' practitioners and voluntary hospitals and similar agencies, leaving to the State only the duty of filling obvious gaps ? Or shall voluntary agencies and agents merely supplement public action ? Is the medical profession to become in effect a branch of the Civil Service, or to be employed according to the preference of, and remunerated by, individuals ?

Is the State to make itself responsible for finding reasonably remunerated work for all its citizens, in fulfilment of a ' Full Employment ' policy ? Or is employment to remain on a commercial basis, regulated by the demands of the market, and wages fixed by bargaining between employers and the combinations of employees ?

That employment must ultimately depend upon the condition of industry and trade is axiomatic, and for a country situated as Britain is the mere sustenance of individuals, not to mention their employment, depends largely upon our ability to produce goods which will find a market abroad, and will thus provide the means of purchasing the raw materials and so much of our food as we cannot produce at home. A Bill has accordingly been introduced to authorize the Board of Trade to raise from £75,000,000 to £200,000,000 the amount available for guaranteeing in appropriate cases payment for export trade transactions. The existing amount has been employed without loss to the Exchequer and with considerable advantage to our export trade which, since 1938, fell from £471,000,000 to £232,000,000 (1943).

All these plans and proposals are, however, relatively insignificant as compared with the great scheme for National Insurance put out by the Government in November 1944. Nearly two years had then passed since the publication of the Report based by Sir William Beveridge upon ' a survey of the existing schemes of Social Insurance and allied services, including workmen's compensation, undertaken ', as instructed, ' with special reference to the interrelation of the Schemes '. The Report was generally acclaimed as almost ' inspired ' ; the Government was persistently pressed to accept it immediately and *in toto*. Wisely, however, they declined to do more than give to it a general approval and promise to devote intensive study to the ' giant evils ' with which the Report is mainly concerned. These evils are physical want, disease, squalor and ignorance. Nor, as already indicated, has the Government failed, despite its preoccupation with the war, to redeem, in a remarkable degree, its promise. *Social Insurance*

The culmination of its effort is represented by its Plan for Social Security.

A spirited attack has been delivered upon the giant evil of ignorance by the Butler Education Act, and a more direct and comprehensive step towards reconstruction has been taken by the appointment of a Minister and the setting up of a Department of Social Insurance. But only the most courageous can contemplate with confidence the great mass of intricate legislation which will be needed to deal with health, workmen's compensation, unemployment, public assistance, pensions, children's allowances, and all other matters comprehensively included in the term Social Insurance. On the vital question of cost, Sir John Anderson has given reassurances which, if conditions are fulfilled, may give comfort to the timid. The one governing condition is that the whole nation must be prepared to work in the years of peace as it has worked throughout the critical months of war. That condition is imperative : unless it be fulfilled a terrible disillusionment awaits the optimists and nothing can avert a disaster of a colossal magnitude.

Faith can still remove mountains. Nothing less could have availed to encourage the British Empire to embark in 1940 on a grim struggle for existence. Nothing less can sustain the British nation in an endeavour to overcome the ' giant evils ', and to give to all classes an assurance of security and a reassured basis for contentment. After a century of prosperity without parallel, Great Britain has in these latter days been savagely attacked and has suffered severely in life and property ; but if battered, she still stands erect. Her daughter lands, if now established in their own homes, and all other units in her heterogeneous and far-flung Empire, have proved by valiant deeds their loyalty and affection towards the Motherland and their conviction that the cause for which, side by side with her and with each other, they have fought, is the cause of freedom, justice and righteousness. The United States has not only given invaluable assistance to us and to our Russian ally, but has herself taken a full share in the actual fight.

Thus the ancient structure, though bearing many and honourable scars, still stands—a proud monument of stability and steadfastness, the citadel of a city set high upon a hill.

APPENDIX

AUTHORITIES

The following list of books is not intended as a scientific or critical *Bibliography*, but simply as (i) a general acknowledgement of the author's indebtedness to published works, and (ii) a rough indication of the sources of information to which students may go for further elucidation of subjects treated with unavoidable inadequacy or brevity in the text.

A. Sources. (i) Official

For the history of the last half-century the ' sources ' are overwhelming in bulk and variety. Since the conclusion of the European War some 40,000 documents have been published by various Governments. Confining ourselves to the history of Great Britain and the British Empire and excluding Documents on the Origins of the War (see Section C), we may note among other official materials :—*Public General Acts* (i.e. Statutes of the Realm), published by Authority by the Stationery Office (H.M.S.O.) ; *Journals of the Houses of Lords and Commons ; Official Reports of Parliamentary Debates*, which, since 1909, have been published separately for Lords and Commons (frequently quoted in notes simply as ' Hansard ') ; ' *Blue Books* ' (i.e. Reports of Royal Commissions, &c.) ; *Accounts and Papers* (i.e. Reports, Accounts and Estimates of Public Departments, &c.) ; ' Command Papers ' (i.e. Returns and Reports laid before Parliament). The *Treaty Series* is an important series of these Command Papers, containing the texts of Treaties concluded by His Majesty with Foreign Powers. *The British and Foreign State Papers* contain, e.g., such Reports from and Correspondence with British Ambassadors and Ministers in foreign countries as are ' laid ' before Parliament for the information of the Legislature. Vols. 77–140 cover the period 1885–1929 and form an invaluable source of information on Foreign Affairs. *The London Gazette* is the sole official source of information for the acts of the Crown—appointments, etc. (A useful *Index* thereto is periodically published.) The Foreign Office and other Public Departments publish an annual *List* which is useful.

(ii) In addition to official and other formal sources such publications as *The Annual Register, The Statesman's Year Book, Whitaker's Almanack, The Daily Mail Year Book,* are very useful, as also are the files of *The Times* (with its *Official Index*), and other daily and weekly Newspapers. My own library also contains a large collection of *Pamphlets*, including much propagandist ' literature ', to be used, of course, with great caution, but nevertheless valuable as evidence of contemporary opinion.

B. Domestic Affairs

For official sources of information see Section A.

(i) Official (see also Section A) :—

[A valuable *Catalogue of Parliamentary Papers, 1801–1920*, is published by P. S. King & Co. Further Lists are periodically published by them and also by H.M.S.O.]

Among the most valuable of these papers for Domestic Affairs in the period 1885–1932 are :—

AGRICULTURE : Reports of Royal Commissions (1880–2), (1895–7), (1919), (1925), *Wheat Supplies* (1921) ; Sir H. Rew : *Report on Decline of Agricultural Population, 1881–1906 ; Committee on Small Holdings, 1906 ; Land Settlement for Soldiers and Sailors, 1916 ; Agricultural Policy* (Min. of Reconstruction, 1918, Cmd. 9079) ; *Food Supply* (1916).

EDUCATION : Reports of R.C.'s on *Technical* (1882–4) ; *Elementary* (1886–8) ; *Secondary* (1895) ; *Adult* (Min. of Reconstruction Report, 1919, Cmd. 321) ; *Universities* (London, 1910) ; *Oxford and Cambridge* (1922).

TRADE AND INDUSTRY : R.C. (1885) ; Committee (Balfour) (1926–9).

COAL MINES : R.C.'s (1903–5) ; 1919 (Sankey) ; 1925–6 (Samuel).

HOUSING : R.C. (1885) ; Committee (1902) ; Committee (Moyne) (1933).

CURRENCY : R.C., Gold and Silver, 1888 (Cmd. 5512) ; Committee on After-War Currency and Foreign Exchanges, 1918–19 (Cmd. 9182 and 464).

MUNICIPAL TRADING : Select Committee (1900 (305)).

TAXATION, FINANCE, &c. R.C. *Local Taxation*, 1898 ; Committee, 1914 (Cmd. 7315) ; R.C. *Income Tax* (Colwyn), 1920 (Cmd. 615, &c.) ; Reports (annual) of *National War Savings* (First Report, 1917 [Cmd. 8516]) ; Committee, *Increase of War Wealth* (1920) ; *National Expenditure Committee*, 1917–19 ; *National Debt and Taxation* (1927) (Cmd. 2800).

POOR LAW, PENSIONS, UNEMPLOYMENT, &c. : R.C. *Aged Poor* (1895) ; *Committee on Unemployment* (1895) ; R.C. (1904–9) *Labour Exchanges* Committee (1921) ; *Public Assistance Administration* (1924) (Cmd. 2011) ; O.A.P. Committees (1885–7) (1919) ; *Industrial Transference* (1928) (Cmd. 3331).

LABOUR : Trade Unions, &c. Reports on *Sweating*, 1888 ; *Nail Makers* (1888) *Cost of Living* (1907 and 1912) ; *Industrial* (Whitley) *Councils*, 1918 ; *Industrial Unrest* Reports (1918) ; *Trade Boards* (1922) (Cmd. 1645) ; R.C. : *Trade Disputes* (1906) ; *Annual Reports* to Board of Trade on Trade Unions ; *Washington Labour Conference* (1920) (Cmd. 606).

Census Reports, 1891–1931. *Census of Production Return under Act of 1906.*

(Annual) Reports of Ministries of *Agriculture, Education, Health (Local Government), Trade, Inland Revenue, Customs and Excise* ; *Statistical Abstract, Labour Statistics ; Trade of U.K.* ; Reports of Chief Inspectors of *Factories, Education*, Chief Medical Officer *(Health, Education)* ; Registrar-General ; Chief Registrar of *Friendly Societies*.

IRELAND : *Government of Ireland Act* (1920), *Irish Free State Const. Act* (1922), *Correspondence between the Government and the Government of I.F.S. and N.I.* (Cmd. 2155 and 2166 of 1924).

(ii) A few general books :—

The Encyclopædia Britannica (especially *11th Edition* with new volumes), 1911–26.

Dictionary of National Biography (66 vols.).

The Concise D.N.B. (1 vol., Oxford, 1920), containing an epitome of the main work, 1901–11, forms with *D.N.B.*, 1912–21 (Oxford, 1927), an invaluable work of reference.

(ed. Ward and others) : *Cambridge Modern History*, vol. xii (1910–).

H. Paul : *Modern England*, vol. 5 (1906).

R. H. Gretton : *A Modern History of the English People* (1929).

E. Halévy : *A History of the English People in 1895-1905* (1929).

G. Slater : *The Growth of Modern England* (Part V) (1932).

E. C. W. Stratford : *The Victorian Tragedy* (1930).

—— *The Victorian Aftermath* (1933).

W. Dibelius : *England* (E.T. 1930).

W. R. Inge : *England* (n.e. 1934).

F. J. C. Hearnshaw and others : *Edwardian England* (1933).

A. Siegfried : *England's Crisis* (1931).

(*The Times*) : *Fifty Years* (1882–1932) (1932).

(iii) Biographies, Memoirs, Letters, Speeches, &c. :—

(ed. Buckle) : *Letters of Queen Victoria*, Third Series, 3 vols. (1930, &c.).

L. Strachey : *Queen Victoria* (1921).

Sir S. Lee : *Queen Victoria* (r.e. 1904).

—— *King Edward VII*, 2 vols. (1925, 1927).

A. Maurois : *King Edward and His Times* (1933).

E. F. Benson : *King Edward VII* (1933).

H. E. Wortham : *A Delightful Profession* (1931).

—— *Edward VII* (1933).

Lord Esher : *Influence of Edward VII* (1915).

Sir L. Cust : *King Edward and His Court.*

Sir G. Arthur : *King George V* (1929).

J. Gore : *King George V* (1941).

Lives of *W. E. Gladstone*, 3 vols. (Morley) ; *Lord Salisbury*, 4 vols. (unfinished, Lady G. Cecil) ; *Lord Carnarvon*, 3 vols. (Sir A. Hardinge) ; *Sir M. Hicks-Beach*, 2 vols. (Lady V. Hicks-Beach) ; *Lord Rosebery*, 2 vols. (Lord Crewe), 1 vol. (E. T. Raymond) ; *Earl of Balfour* (Sir I. Malcolm) (Mrs. L. Dugdale), 2 vols. ; *Lord Randolph Churchill*, 2 vols. (W. Churchill), 1 vol. (Lord Rosebery) ; *Lord Cromer* (Lord Zetland) ; *Lord Curzon*, 3 vols. (Lord Zetland), *Curzon : the Last Phase* ; *Lord Lansdowne* (Lord Newton) ; *Joseph Chamberlain*, 3 vols. (unfinished, J. L. Garvin) ; *Lord Carnock* (H. Nicolson) ; *Duke of Devonshire*, 2 vols. (B. Holland) ; *Viscount Goschen*, 2 vols. (A. D. Elliott) ; *Sir S. Northcote* (A. Lang) ; *Sir W. Harcourt*, 2 vols. (A. G. Gardiner) ; *Asquith* (J. A. Spender and C. Asquith) ; *Sir H. Campbell-Bannerman* (J. A. Spender) ; *Viscount Morley* (J. H. Morgan) ; *Lord Wolseley* (Sir F. Maurice and Sir G. Arthur) ; *Lord Kitchener*, 3 vols. (Sir G. Arthur) ; *George Wyndham* (G. Wyndham and J. W. Mackail) ; *General Gordon* (D. C. Boulger) ; *Lord Dufferin* (Sir A. Lyall) ; *Sir C. Dilke*, 2 vols. (S. Gwynn and G. Tuckwell) ; *Lord Cave* (Sir C. Mallet) ; *Lord Birkenhead* (2nd Lord Birkenhead) ; *C. S. Parnell*, 2 vols. (B. O'Brien) and (K. O'Shea) ; *Cecil Rhodes* (B. Williams) ; *Sir Austen Chamberlain* (Sir C. Petrie) ; *Viscount Long of Wraxall* (Sir C. Petrie).

Speeches of W. E. Gladstone (ed. A. T. Bassett, 1917), of Lord R. Churchill, 2 vols. (ed. Jennings), of J. Chamberlain, 2 vols. (ed. Boyd), Lord Birkenhead.

A. J. Balfour : *Chapters of Autobiography* (1930).

R. B. Haldane : *An Autobiography* (1929).

Lord Grey of Fallodon : *Twenty-five Years*, 2 vols. (1925).

Sir R. Temple : *Life in Parliament, 1886–92* (1893).

A. S. T. Griffith-Boscawen : *Fourteen Years in Parliament, 1892–1906* (1907).

Margot Asquith : *Autobiography* (1920).

H. H. Asquith : *Memories and Reflections*, 2 vols. (1928).

—— *Fifty Years in Parliament* (1926).

Lord George Hamilton : *Parliamentary Reminiscences and Reflections*, 2 vols. (1916, 1922).

S. Gwynn : *Letters and Friendships of Sir C. Spring-Rice*, 2 vols. (1929).

Viscount Morley : *Recollections*, 2 vols. (1917).

—— *Memorandum on Resignation* (1928).

Viscount Wolseley : *The Story of a Soldier's Life*, 2 vols. (1903).

W. A. S. Hewins : *The Apologia of an Imperialist*, 2 vols. (1929).

G. N. Barnes : *From Workshop to War Cabinet* (1925).

Sir A. West : *Recollections* (1899).

Sir H. Newbolt : *My World as in My Time* (1933).

Lord Rennell of Rodd : *Social and Diplomatic Memories*, 3 vols. (1922, 1922–5).

J. A. Spender : *Life Journalism and Politics*, 2 vols. (1927).

(iv) Social and Economic :—

S. and B. Webb : *Industrial Democracy* (1897).

—— *History of Trade Unionism* (1894).

J. H. Clapham : *The Economic History of Modern Britain*, 3 vols.

P. Cohen : *The British System of Social Insurance* (1932).

Sir W. H. Beveridge : *Unemployment, a Problem of Industry* (1909).

C. Booth : *The Aged Poor* (1894).

C. S. Loch : *Pauperism and Old Age Pensions* (1895).

G. Slater : *Poverty and the State* (1930).

H. Clay : *The Post-War Unemployment Problem* (1929).

D. Knoop : *Municipal Trading* (1912).

A. M. Carr Saunders and D. C. Jones : *Social Structure of England and Wales* (1927).

A. L. Bowley : *The Division of the Product of Industry* (1919).

—— *Distribution of the National Income* (1920).

—— *Wages in the United Kingdom* (1900).

G. H. D. Cole : *Short History of the Working-class Movement*, esp. vol. iii.

L. T. Hobhouse : *The Labour Movement* (1906).

J. R. MacDonald : *Syndicalism* (1912).

Sir H. Clay : *Syndicalism and Labour* (1912).

Sir L. Macassey : *Labour Policy False and True* (1922).

Lord Askwith : *Industrial Problems and Disputes* (1920).

F. J. C. Hearnshaw : *Democracy at the Cross-ways* (1918).

—— *Democracy and Labour* (1924).

R. M. Rayner : *Trade Unionism* (1929).

Sir J. Simon : *The General Strike* (1926).

A. W. Kirkaldy : *History and Economics of Transport* (1918).
A. J. Sargent : *Sea-Ways of the Empire* (1918).
G. N. Clark : *Unifying the World* (1920).
G. D'Avenel : *L'évolution des moyens de transport* (1919).
C. R. Fay : *Life and Labour in the Nineteenth Century* (1920).
—— *Copartnership in Industry* (1913).
Co-operative Wholesale Society's Annual (annual).
G. Armitage Smith : *The Free Trade Movement* (1903).
W. J. Ashley : *The Tariff Problem* (1903).
W. Smart : *The Return to Protection* (1904).
W. A. S. Hewins : *Empire Restored* (1927).
Lord Milner : *Questions of the Hour* (1923).
Sir B. Mallet : *British Budgets, 1887–1933*, 3 vols. (1913–33).
A. L. Bowley : *Prices and Wages in the United Kingdom, 1914–20* (1921).
F. W. Hirst and J. E. Allen : *British War Budgets* (1926).
T. H. Middleton : *Food Production in War* (1923).
Mrs. C. Peel : *How We Lived Then* (1914–18) (1927).
Sir W. H. Beveridge : *British Food Control* (1928).
W. A. Shaw : *Currency Credit and the Exchanges* (1914–26) (1927).
(ed. A. W. Kirkaldy) : *Labour Finance and the War* (1916).
—— *Credit Industry and the War* (1915).
A. L. Bowley and Stamp : *The National Income* (1911 and 1924) (1927).
E. Benn : *Account Rendered* (1900–30) (1930).
G. Jèze : *The War Finance of France* (Yale, 1927).
—— *Britain's Industrial Future* (Liberal Enquiry) (1928).
H. Withers : *War and Lombard Street* (1915).
R. H. Brand : *War and National Finance* (1922).
G. H. D. Cole : *Labour in War Time* (1915).
Lord Ernle : *English Farming, Past and Present* (n.e. 1927).
A. D. Hall : *Pilgrimage of British Farming* (1913).
—— *Agriculture after the War* (1914).
C. Turnor : *The Land and its Problems* (1921).
C. S. Orwin and W. R. Peel : *The Tenure of Agricultural Land* (1925).
J. S. Nicholson : *Agriculture* (1906).
F. E. Green : *The Awakening of England* (1912).
L. Jebb : *The Small Holdings of England* (1907).
H. Rider Haggard : *Rural England* (1902).
J. A. R. Marriott : *The English Land System* (1914).
Liberal Land Committee Report : *The Land and the Nation* (1925).
J. A. Venn : *Foundations of Agricultural Economics* (1923).
W. Hasbach : *The English Agricultural Labourer* (E.T., 1908).
R. Lennard : *English Agricultural Wages* (1914).

(v) Constitutional :—

W. Bagehot (with introd. by Earl of Balfour) : *The English Constitution* (Oxford, 1928).
J. A. R. Marriott : *Mechanism of the Modern State* (with full Bibliography), 2 vols. (Oxford, 1927).
—— *English Political Institutions* (revised ed., 1925).
—— *Second Chambers* (revised ed., 1927).
—— *The Crisis of English Liberty* (1930).
S. Low : *The Governance of England* (1904).

R. Muir : *How Britain is Governed* (1930).

A. W. Humphry : *History of Labour Representation* (1912).

M. G. Fawcett : *Women's Suffrage* (1912).

W. S. McKechnie : *The New Democracy and the Constitution* (1912).

—— *The Reform of the House of Lords* (1909).

Lord Hewart : *The New Despotism* (1929).

Report of Committee on Ministers' Powers (Cmd. 4060, 1932) (1929).

F. J. Port : *Administrative Law* (1929).

W. A. Robson : *Justice and Administrative Law* (1928).

C. K. Allen : *Bureaucracy Triumphant* (1931).

Sir C. Ilbert : *Legislative Methods and Forms* (1901).

H. B. Lees Smith : *Second Chambers* (1923).

R. Muir : *Peers and Bureaucrats* (1920).

C. T. Carr : *Delegated Legislation* (1921).

Lord Haldane and others : *The Development of the Civil Service* (1922).

Sir H. Samuel : *The War and Liberty* (1917).

P. Ashley : *Local and Central Government* (1906).

R. A. Glen : *Local Government Act, 1929* (1929).

H. Finer : *The British Civil Service* (1928).

C. Foreign Affairs.

See Sections A, ' Sources ', official, and lists of books appended to Chapters XIII and XVII of Marriott, *History of Europe* (1815–1937) (3rd ed., 1938) ; and to G. P. Gooch's *Recent Revelations of European Diplomacy* (3rd ed., 1928).

(i) Documents and General Works :—

(ed. Gooch and Temperley) : *British Documents on the Origin of the War,* H.M.S.O. (11 vols.).

(ed. A. Mendelssohn-Bartholdy and others) : *Die Grosse Politik der Europäischen Kabinette, 1871–1914* (Berlin, 1925), &c.

(Extracts from this monumental work are translated into English (ed. E. T. S. Dugdale), 4 vols. (1928–31).

Documents Diplomatiques français (1871–1914) (1929, etc.).

Österreich-Ungarns Aussenpolitik (1908–14), 9 vols. (Vienna, 1930).

E. Laloy : *Les Documents Secrets publiés par les Bolsheviks* (abridged French translation), 1919.

(ed. R. Marchand) : *Materials for the History of Franco-Russian Relations* (in Russian, 1922).

(ed. J. B. Scott) : *Diplomatic Documents relating to Outbreak of War* (Oxford, 1916).

A. F. Pribram : *Secret Treaties of Austria-Hungary* (N.Y., 1925) ; *Austrian Foreign Policy* (1908–18) (1923) ; *England and the International Policy of the Great Powers, 1871–1914* (Oxford, 1931).

E. Brandenburg : *From Bismarck to the World War* (E.T., Oxford, 1927).

H. Lutz : *Lord Grey and the World War* (E.T., 1928).

O. Hammann : *World Policy of Germany* (E.T., 1927).

R. B. Mowat : *The Concert of Europe* (1890–1912) (1930).

E. zu Reventlow : *Deutschland's Auswärtige Politik* (1888–1914) (1916).

W. Becker : *Fürst Bülow und England* (1897–1909) (1929).

E. Meinecke : *Geschichte des deutsch-englischen Bünnisproblems* (1890–1901) (1927).

E. Ludwig : *William II* (1926).

G. Hanotaux : *Contemporary France* (1903–9).

Wickham Steed : *The Hapsburg Monarchy* (1914).

—— *Through Thirty Years* (1924).

Sir V. Chirol : *Fifty Years in a Changing World* (1927).

E. Débidour : *Histoire Diplomatique*, vols. iii and iv (Paris, 1917).

R. Muir : *Nationalism and Internationalism* (1916).

R. Muir : *The Expansion of Europe* (1917).

C. Seymour : *The Diplomatic Background of the War* (Yale, 1916).

J. A. R. Marriott : *Europe and Beyond* (4th ed., 1933).

—— *The European Commonwealth* (1918).

—— *The Eastern Question* (4th ed., 1940).

Baron von Eckhardstein : *Ten Years at the Court of St. James's* (1921).

Prince von Bülow : *Imperial Germany* (E.T., 1914).

—— *Letters* (1930).

A. Tardieu : *France and the Alliances* (E.T., N.Y., 1908).

S. B. Fay : *The Origins of the World-War*, 2 vols. (N.Y., 1929).

B. E. Schmitt : *The Coming of the War*, 2 vols. (N.Y., 1929).

E. Ludwig : *July 1914* (1929).

R. W. Seton Watson : *The Future of Austria-Hungary* (1907) ; *Serajevo* (1925).

Father W. Barry : *The World's Debate* (1917).

G. Lowes Dickinson : *The European Anarchy* (1916).

—— *The International Anarchy* (1926).

(ii) Immediate antecedents of the Great War : some works by actors in the drama :—

Lord Grey of Fallodon : *Twenty-five Years*, 2 vols. (1925).

W. Churchill : *World Crisis*, 6 vols. (1923–31).

H. H. Asquith : *The Genesis of the War* (1923).

B. J. Hendrick : *The Life and Letters of Walter H. Page* (esp. vol. iii) (1925).

R. B. Haldane : *Before the War* (1920).

Lord Loreburn : *How the War Came* (1919).

Viscount Morley : *Memorandum on Resignation* (1928).

Prince Lichnovsky : *My London Mission* (1928).

T. von Bethmann-Hollweg : *Reflections on the World War* (1919).

R. Poincaré : *The Origins of the War* (E.T., 1928).

Kaiser William II : *My Memoirs* (1878–1918).

Sir G. Buchanan : *My Mission to Russia* (1923).

Count Bernstorff : *My Three Years in America* (n.d.).

(iii) The War :—

The British Museum published in 1922 as a separate volume a Subject Index of the Books relating to the War acquired by the Museum, 1914–20. To this reference may be made and also to analytical Lists by Sir G. Prothero (H.M.S.O., 1923), and C. Falls (*War Books*) (P. Davies, 1930).

C. Oman : *The Outbreak of the War* (H.M.S.O., 1919).

Collected Diplomatic Documents (Ho. of C. Sessional Papers, vol. 83).

(ed. T. E. Edmonds, P. C. Wynne and others) : *Official History of the Great War—Military Operations*, 24 vols. (1925–).

(ed. Sir J. Corbett and Sir H. Newbolt) : *Naval Operations*, 9 vols. (1920–31).

J. Buchan : *The Dispatches of Lord French* (1917) ; *History of the War.*
Viscount French, *1914* (1919).
E. von Falkenhayn : *General Headquarters, 1914–16, and its Critical Decisions*
(1919).
(ed. Boraston) : *Sir Douglas Haig's Dispatches, December, 1915, to April, 1919*
(1919).
G. A. B. Dewar : *Sir Douglas Haig's Command* (1922).
E. Ludendorff : *The General Staff and its Problems* (1920) ; *My War Memories,*
1914–18, 2 vols. (1919).
Col. Repington : *The First World War,* 2 vols. (1920).
Earl Jellicoe : *The Grand Fleet, 1914–16* (1919) ; *The Crisis of the Naval*
War (1920).
Sir A. Murray : *Dispatches, 1916–17* (1920).
A. von Tirpitz : *My Memoirs* (E.T., London, 1921).
Battle of Jutland (Official Despatches), Cmd. 1068.
E. R. G. R. Evans : *Keeping the Seas* (1920).
Sir H. Newbolt : *A Naval History of the War, 1914–18.*
A. S. Hurd : *A Merchant Fleet at War* (1920).
C. Bellairs : *The Battle of Jutland* (1920).
Admiral Sims : *The Victory at Sea* (1921).
Sir E. Hilton Young : *By Sea and Land* (1920).
Sir R. H. S. Bacon : *The Dover Patrol, 1915–17,* 2 vols. (1919).
Sir G. Arthur : *Life of Lord Kitchener,* 3 vols. (1920).
Count Czernin : *In the World War* (1920).
D. Lloyd George : *War Memoirs,* 4 vols. (1934).
—— *Is It Peace ?* (1923).
F. S. Oliver : *Ordeal By Battle* (1915).
C. R. F. M. Cruttwell : *A History of the Great War* (1934).
(See also Section E.)

(iv) The Peace and After :—

Text of the Treaty of Versailles. (Cmd. 153.) *Index to.* (Cmd. 516.) Price 6*d.*
Text of Peace Treaty with Austria, 1919. (Cmd. 400.)
Text of Peace Treaty with Turkey (Sèvres). (Cmd. 964.)
Text of Peace Treaty with Turkey (Lausanne). (Cmd. 1929.)
Text of Peace Treaty with the Serb-Croat-Slovene State, 1919. (Cmd. 461.)
Text of Peace Treaty with Bulgaria, 1920. (Cmd. 522.)
Text of Peace Treaty with Roumania, 1920. (Cmd. 588.)
Text of Peace Treaty with Hungary, 1920. (Cmd. 896.)
Convention of United Kingdom and Belgium, 1920. (Cmd. 517.)
Convention of Greece and Bulgaria, 1920. (Cmd. 589.)
Correspondence on Adriatic Question. (Cmd. 586 [1920].)
International Labour Conference (League of Nations). (Cmd. 1174.)
Treaty of London, April 26, 1915. (Cmd. 671 [1920].)
Treaty with Greece, 16 August, 1920. (Cmd. 960 [1920].)
Treaty of Rapallo, Recognition of. (Cmd. 1238 [1921].)
Negotiations for Anglo-French Pact, 1914–1923. (Cmd. 2169 [1924].)
Treaty between U.K., Iraq and Turkey. (Cmd. 2679 [1926].)
Genoa Conference. (Cmd. 586 [1920].)
London Reparations Conference (1924). (Cmd. 2270 [1924].)
Cannes Conference. (Cmd. 1621 [1922].)
 Mandates. S.W. Africa (Cmd. 1204 [1921]) ; East Africa (Cmd. 1284) ;

West Africa (Cmd. 1350) ; Pacific Islands (Cmd. 1201, 1202, 1263) ; Palestine and Mesopotamia (Cmd. 1500) (On the Mandates System, see Lord Lugard, ap. *Ency. Brit.* [new vols., vol. ii]).

(ed. H. W. V. Temperley) : *The Peace Conference of Paris*, 1920, &c. (referred to in notes as *H.P.C.*).

J. M. Keynes : *The Economic Consequences of the Peace* (1919).

D. Lloyd-George : *The Peace Treaties*, 2 vols. (1938).

Lord Riddell : *Diary of the Peace Conference,* 2 vols.

H. Temperley : *Peace Making* (1919).

—— *Why Britain is at War* (1939).

E. J. Dillon : *The Peace Conference* (1919).

The Covenant Explained (League of Nations Union) (1919).

Sir Geoffrey Butler : *Handbook of the League of Nations : The First Assembly.*

C. B. Fletcher : *The New Pacific* (1918).

F. H. Simonds : *How Europe made Peace without America* (1927).

S. Baker : *Woodrow Wilson and World Settlement* (London, 1923).

A. Tardieu : *La Paix* (Paris, 1921).

(ed. Seymour) : *The Intimate Papers of Colonel House* (London, 1926).

Hendrick : *Letters of W. H. Page* (1923).

G. Hanotaux : *Le Traité de Versailles* (Paris, 1919).

J. M. Keynes : *Economic Consequences of the Peace* (1919) ; *The Revision of the Treaty.*

S. Huddleston : *Peace Making at Paris* (London, 1919).

R. Lansing : *The Peace Negotiations* (Boston, 1921) ; *The Big Four and Others* (Camb. [Mass.], 1922).

H. Nicolson : *Peacemaking, 1919* (1933).

—— *Curzon* (1934).

' Adriaticus ' : *La Question Adriatique* (Paris, 1920).

A. Toynbee : *The World after the Peace Conference* (1925) ; *Survey of International Affairs, British Empire Foreign Relations since the Peace Settlement*, 1928 (1926), &c., &c.

A. von Wegerer : *A Refutation of the War Guilt Thesis* (N.Y., 1930).

Sir P. Gibbs : *Since Then* (1930).

R. B. Mowat : *European Diplomacy* (1914–1925) (1927).

Sir A. Willert : *Aspects of British Foreign Policy* (1928).

F. L. Benns : *Europe since 1914* (1930).

H. Lichtenberger : *Relations between France and Germany* (1923).

F. Nitti : *Peaceless Europe.*

E. H. Carr : *International Relations Since the Peace Treaties* (1937).

—— *The Twenty Years Crisis* (1940).

—— *British Foreign Policy* (1919–1939) (1939).

J. A. R. Marriott : *The Tragedy of Europe* (1919–39) (1941).

G. M. Gathorne Hardy : *International Affairs* (1920–34) (1934).

Sir A. Chamberlain : *Down the Years* (1935).

(v) The League of Nations, Disarmament, &c. :—

Covenant of the League of Nations. (Cmd. 151 [1919].)

Washington Conference Treaties, &c. (Cmd. 1627 [1922].)

Sir J. Fischer-Williams : *Some Aspects of the Covenant* (1934).

J. Coatman : *Magna Britannia* (1936).

H. R. G. Greaves : *The League Committees and World Order* (1931).

T. P. Conwell-Evans : *The League Council in Action* (1929).
Lord Davies : *The Problem of the Twentieth Century* (1930).
A. C. Temperley : *The Whispering Gallery of Europe* (n. 2, 1939).
J. A. R. Marriott : *Commonwealth or Anarchy ?* (1940).
S. de Madriaga : *Disarmament* (1929).
J. W. Wheeler-Bennett : *Disarmament and Security Since Locarno* (1932).

D. Ireland :—(i) Official

The texts of the *Bills* of 1886 and 1892 must be studied side by side with the *Acts* of 1914 and 1920, and 1922 (embodying the ' Treaty ' of 1922 and the Constitution of the Irish Free State), ap. *Select Constitutions of the World* (Dublin Stationery Office, 1922).   Cmd. 1470 of 1921 contains the Proposals for an Irish Settlement.

See also : *Report of Proceedings of the Irish Convention* (Cmd. 9019 of 1918).

Very important are the *Reports of the Irish Land Commission* presented annually to Parliament, and the *Annual Report of the Registrar-General for Ireland.*

W. O'Connor Morris : *Ireland, 1798–1898* (1898).
J. T. Ball : *Irish Legislative System.*
E. Barker : *Ireland in the Last Fifty Years* (1917).
Horace Plunket : *Ireland in the New Century* (1904).
L. Paul Dubois : *L'Irelande contemporaine et la Question irlandais* (1907).
Lord Morley : *Life of Gladstone* (1903).
Barry O'Brien : *Life of C. S. Parnell* (1898).
K. O'Shea : *C. S. Parnell*, 2 vols. (1914).
T. P. O'Connor : *The Parnellite Movement.*
St. John Irvine : *Parnell* (1925).
H. W. Lucy : *Diary of Parliament* (1886–1900) (1892 and 1901).
W. H. Hurbert : *Ireland under Coercion*, 2 vols. (Edinburgh, 1888).
W. F. Moneypenny : *The Two Irish Nations* (1913).
A. V. Dicey : *England's Case against Home Rule* (1889).
—— *Unionist Delusions* (1887).
—— *A Leap in the Dark* (1893).
R. C. Escouflaire : *Ireland an Enemy of the Allies* (1919).
Joseph Chamberlain : *Home Rule and the Irish Question Speeches* (1887)
R. McNeill : *Ulster Stand for Union* (1922).
R. Dawson : *Red Terror and Green* (1920).
S⸲ J. Irvine : *Sir E. Carson and the Ulster Movement.*
Earl of Dunraven : *The Outlook in Ireland* (1907).
W. O'Brien : *An Olive Branch in Ireland* (1910).
Sir H. Robinson : *Memories Wise and Unwise* (1923).
—— *Further Memories* (1924).
J. W. Mackail and G. Wyndham : *Life and Letters of George Wyndham* (1925).
D. Gwynn : *Irish Free State, 1922-27* (1928).

(ii) Unofficial

For the author's contemporary commentaries on Irish affairs, reference may be made to the following articles : *Ireland under Queen Victoria* (*The Fortnightly* for March 1901) ; *The Key of the Empire* (*Nineteenth Century*, Nov. 1911) ; *The Third Edition of Home Rule* (*Nineteenth*, May 1912) ; *The*

Fourth Home Rule Bill (*Fortnightly*, April 1920) ; *The Heel of Achilles* (*Nineteenth*, June 1920) ; *England, Ireland and Ulster* (*Fortnightly*, July 1922).

E. The Overseas Empire (excluding India).

A full and carefully articulated bibliography of this subject will be found in the several volumes of the *Cambridge History of the British Empire*. The following is only a small selection from a large number of modern works, and a still smaller selection from a vast collection of Official Publications.

(i) Official :—

Some important Parliamentary Papers.

Correspondence re Colonial Representatives in London (Cc. 24, 51) (1870).

Proceedings of Colonial (and Imperial) Conferences, Conf. of 1887 (Cc. 5091) (1887) ; *Ottawa, 1894* (C. 7553) (1894) ; *Conf. of 1897* (C. 8596) (1897) ; *Conf. of 1902* (Cdd. 1597, 1723) (1903) ; *Empire Trade* (C. 8449) (1897) ; *Future Organization* (Cd. 2785) (1906) ; *Conf. of 1907* (Cdd. 3337, 3340) ; *Conf. of 1911* (Cd. 5273 [1910], 5513 [1910], Cdd. 5741, 5745, 5746) ; *Conf. of 1917* (Cd. 8566) ; *Conf. of 1918* (Cd. 9177) ; *Conf. of 1921* (Cmd. 1474) ; *Conf. of 1923* (Cmd. 1987, 1988) ; *Imperial Economic Conf., 1923* (Cmd. 1990) ; *Imp. Econ. Conf., 1924* (Cmd. 2009, 2084, 2115) ; *Conf. of 1926* (Cmd. 2768, 2769) ; *Conf. of 1930* (Cmd. 3716, 3717, 3718). *Imperial Econ. Conf., Ottawa, 1932* (Cmd. 4174, 4175, 4178 [1932]).

Second Chambers in the Dominions (lxvi, 81 of 1910).

Treaty Making Powers of Dominions (lxvi, 129 of 1910).

Committee of Imperial Defence (Cd. 6560 of 1912 and Cd. 7347 of 1914).

Dominions Royal Commission, 1914–17 (Cd. 8462 of 1917).

Imperial Preference (Cd. 8482 of 1917–18).

Imperial Customs Conf., 1921 (Cmd. 1231 of 1921).

Imperial Shipping Committee, Reports (1920–22) (1932).

Imperial Economic Committee, Reports (Cmd. 2493, 4499 of 1925, and 24 more down to 1932).

Report of Conf. on Dominion Legislation (1930) (Cmd. 3479 [1930]).

Statute of Westminster (22 & 23 George V, c. 4).

Reports on *Nigeria* (468 of 1920) ; *West Indies* (Cmd. 1679 of 1922) ; *West Africa* (Cmd. 2744 of 1926) ; *East Africa* (Cmd. 2387 of 1925) ; *Closer Union of Eastern and Central African Dependencies* (Cmd. 3234 of 1929) ; *Malaya, Ceylon and Java* (Cmd. 3235 of 1928) ; *Ceylon Constitution* (Cmd. 3131 of 1928) ; *Kenya Land Commission* (Précis of) (Cmd. 4580 of 1934).

See also *Statistical Abstract of British Oversea Dominions, &c.* (H.M.S.O., Annual).

(ii) Some General Works :—

L. C. A. Knowles : *The Economic Development of the British Overseas Empire,* 3 vols. (1924–36).

J. A. Williamson : *A History of British Expansion,* 2 vols. (1930).

H. E. Egerton : *British Colonial Policy* (1920) ; *In the Nineteenth Century* (1923) ; *Federations and Unions in the British Empire,* Texts, &c. (1911).

A. B. Keith : *Responsible Government in the Dominions* (1912) ; *Imperial Unity and the Dominions* (1916) ; *Dominion Home Rule, 1921* ; *The Constitution, &c., of the Empire* (1925) ; *The Sovereignty of the British Dominions* (1929) ; *The Constitutional Law of the B. Doms.* (1933).

Sir J. R. Seeley ; *The Expansion of England* (1884).
F. P. de Labillière : *Federal Britain* (1894).
Lord Bryce : *Modern Democracies* (1920).
B. Holland : *Imperium et Libertas* (1901).
R. Jebb : *Studies in Colonial Nationalism* (1905).
—— *The Britannic Question* (1913).
V. Cornish : *Geography of Imperial Defence* (1922).
L. Curtis : *Problem of the Commonwealth* (1916).
J. A. Hobson : *Imperialism* (1905).
H. D. Hall : *The British Commonwealth of Nations* (1920).
J. A. Cramb : *The Origins and Destiny of Imperial Britain* (1915).
W. P. Hall : *Empire to Commonwealth* (1929).
R. Stokes : *New Imperial Ideas* (1930).
L. S. Amery : *The Empire in the New Era* (1928).
—— *A Plan of Action* (1932).
A. G. Dewey : *The Dominions and Diplomacy*, 2 vols. (1929).
Lord Milner : *Constructive Imperialism* (1908).
R. L. Schuyler : *Parliament and the British Empire* (N.Y., 1929).
P. and A. Hurd : *The New Empire Partnership* (1915).
W. A. Carruthers : *Emigration from the British Isles* (1929).
B. Worsfold : *The Empire on the Anvil* (1916).
A. B. Keith : *Selected Speeches and Documents on British Colonial Policy* (1763–1917), 2 vols. (1918).
J. A. R. Marriott : *The Mechanism of the Modern State* (1927).
—— *Problems of Federalism* (*Quarterly Review* for July 1941).
—— *The Evolution of the British Empire and Commonwealth* (1939).
J. E. Tyler : *The Struggle for Imperial Unity, 1868–1895* (1938).
R. M. Dawson : *The Development of Dominion Status, 1900–1936* (1937).
G. Scholes : *Education for Empire Settlement* (1932).

(iii) Canada :—

The Canada Year Book (Annual) (Official).
W. P. M. Kennedy : *Documents of the Canadian Constitution* (1918) ; *The Nature of Canadian Federalism* (1921) ; *The Constitution of Canada* (1923).
(ed. J. H. Rose) : *Cambridge History of the British Empire* (1930), vol. vi.
Sir R. Borden : *Canadian Constitutional Studies* (1922) ; *The War and the Future* (1917).
Sir J. G. Bourinot : *Federal Government* (1889) ; *Canada* (1922).
Earl of Carnarvon : *Speeches on Canadian Affairs* (1902).
G. R. Parkin : *The Great Dominion* (1895).
H. B. Willson : *Life of Lord Strathcona* (1915).
Sir C. Tupper : *Recollections of Sixty Years* (1914).
E. M. Saunders : *Life of Sir C. Tupper*, 2 vols. (1916).
J. S. Ewart : *The Kingdom Papers* (1912–).
—— *Canada in the Great World War* (various writers), 6 vols. (Toronto, 1917–21).
(ed. Sir C. P. Lucas) : *The Empire at War*, vol. ii (1921–6).
J. E. B. Seeley : *Adventure* (1930).
Lord Beaverbrook : *Canada in Flanders*, 3 vols. (1916–18).
J. Pope : *Memorials of Sir John Macdonald, 1894, Correspondence of* (n.d.).

P. E. Corbett and H. A. Smith : *Canada and World Politics* (1928).
O. D. Skelton : *Life and Letters of Sir W. Laurier*, 2 vols. (1921).
—— *Life and Times of Sir A. Galt* (1920).

(iv) Australasia :—

Australian Commonwealth Year Book (Annual) (Official).
New Zealand Official Year Book (Annual).
(ed. F. Watson) : *Historical Records of Australia* (1914–24).
(ed. J. H. Rose) : *Cambridge History of the British Empire*, vol. vii (1933).
A. W. Jose : *History of Australasia* (1921).
T. A. Coghlan : *Progress of Australasia in the XIXth Century* (1903).
E. Jenks : *A History of the Australasian Colonies* (1912).
C. E. Lyne : *Life of Sir H. Parkes* (1897).
W. P. Reeves : *State Experiments in Australia and New Zealand* (1902).
E. Lewin : *The Commonwealth of Australia* (1917).
Sir C. G. Wade : *Australia* (1918).
W. H. Moore : *The Constitution of the Commonwealth* (1910).
Sir J. Quick and R. R. Garran : *Annotated Constitution of the Commonwealth*
    (1901).
Sir J. Quick : *Legislative Powers of Commonwealth and States* (1919).
A. P. Canaway : *The Failure of Federalism in A.* (1930).
Sir J. Kirwan : ' An Empty Land ' (1934).
Sir R. Stout : *New Zealand* (1911).
J. Hight and J. D. Bamford : *The Constitutional History and Law of New
    Zealand* (1914).
Sir Ian Hamilton : *Gallipoli Diary*, 2 vols. (1920).
(ed. C. P. Lucas) : *The Empire at War*, vol. iii (1921–6).
Sir J. Monash : *The Australians in France* (1923).
A. P. Wavell : *The Palestine Campaign* (1928).
(ed. Bean) : *Official History of Australia in the War of 1914–18* (Sydney,
    1921–) ; *Official History of New Zealand's Effort in the Great War*, 4 vols.
    (Wellington, 1919–).

(v) South Africa :—

Year Book of the Union of S.A. (Annual).
J. H. Hofmeyr : *South Africa* (1931).
J. C. Smuts : *Africa and Some World Problems* (1930).
V. R. Markham : *South Africa Past and Present* (1900) ; *The New Era in
    South Africa* (1904).
Lord Carnarvon : *Speeches on the Affairs of West and South Africa* (1903).
Lord Buxton : *General Botha* (1924).
B. Williams : *Cecil Rhodes* (1921).
Sir L. Michel : *Life of Rhodes*, 2 vols. (1910).
W. B. Worsfold : *The Union of South Africa* (1912).
—— *Lord Methuen's Work in South Africa* (1917).
—— *The Government of South Africa* (Central News Agency, South Africa),
    2 vols. (1908).
L. Curtis : *The Frame Work of Union* (1908).
Earl of Selborne : *Memorandum on Federation* (a State Paper of the first
    importance) (Cmd. 3564, 1907).
R. H. Brand : *The Union of South Africa* (1909).
M. Nathan : *The South African Commonwealth* (1919).

(vi) Partition of Africa :—

E. Banning : *Le partage politique de l'Afrique* (1885-8).
J. S. Keltie : *The Partition of Africa* (1895).
V. Deville : *Partage de l'Afrique* (1898).
G. Hanotaux : *Le Partage de l'Afrique* (1890-8).
H. A. Gibbons : *The New Map of Africa* (1890-8).
Lord Lugard : *The Dual Mandate in Africa.*
F. M. Anderson and A. S. Hershey : *Handbook for the Diplomatic History of Africa, 1870-1914.*
E. Lewin : *The Germans and Africa* Lond. (1915).

(vii) Egypt :—
   (See also Section on Foreign Affairs.)
Egypt No. 1 (1921) Milner Mission Report (Cmd. 1131) ; No. 4 (1921) (Cmd. 1555) ; No. 1 (1922) (Cmd. 1592) ; No. 1 (1924) (Cmd. 2269) ; No. 1 (1928) (Cmd. 3050).
Reports by H.M. High Commissioner.
Papers (1882), (1884-5), (1897) *on Egypt and the Soudan* (Annual, H.M.S.O.).
Lord Cromer : *Annual Reports in Blue Books* ; *Modern Egypt* (1908) ; *Abbas II* (1915).
Lord Milner : *England in Egypt* (1892).
D. A. Cameron : *Egypt in the Nineteenth Century* (1898).
Lord Fitzmaurice : *Life of Lord Granville* (1905).
Sir A. Colvin : *The Making of Modern Egypt* (1906).
E. Dicey : *The Story of the Khedivate* (1902).
Sir R. Wingate : *Mahdism and the Egyptian Soudan* (1891).
A. E. Hake : *Gordon's Journals at Khartoum* (1885).
G. W. Steevens : *With Kitchener to Khartoum* (1898).
Sir D. M. Wallace : *Egypt and the Egyptian Question* (1883).
J. A. R. Marriott : *England since Waterloo*, 11th edition, 1936 (1913).
—— *A History of Europe, 1815-1937*, 3rd edition (1938).
Lord Morley : *Gladstone*, vol. 3 (1903).
G. Buckle : *Disraeli*, vols. v and vi (1920).
Lord Zetland : *Lord Cromer* (1932).
Lord Lloyd : *Egypt since Cromer*, 2 vols. (1933-4).
Sir I. Malcolm : *The Suez Canal* (1921).
Sir A. Wilson : *The Suez Canal* (1931).
Sir W. Hayter : *Recent Constitutional Developments in Egypt* (1924).
E. W. P. Newman : *Great Britain in Egypt* (1928).

F. India

(i) Recent Reports, &c. :—
The Moral and Material Progress of India (Annual).
India Office List (Annual).
Montagu-Chelmsford Report, Cd. 9109 (1918).
Civil Services in India, Cmd. 2128 (1924).
Indian States Committees (H. Butler), Cmd. 3302 (1929).
Statutory Commission (Simon), Cmd. 3568, 3569 (1929).
Round Table Conference, Cmd. 3772 (1931).
Round Table Conference, Cmd. 3972 (1931).
Proposals for Indian Constitutional Reform, Cmd. 4268 (1933).
(ed. A. B. Keith) : *Speeches and Documents on Indian Policy*, 2 vols. (1922).

Viscount Morley : *Indian Speeches* (1909).
—— *Recollections*, 2 vols. (1917).
(ed. Sir T. Raleigh) : *Lord Curzon in India* (Speeches) (1906)

(ii) History, Biography, Commentaries, &c. :—

J. A. R. Marriott : *The English in India* (1932).
The British Crown and the Indian States, P. S. King (1829).
Sir C. Ilbert : *The Government of India* (1915).
Sir W. W. Hunter : *The India of the Queen* (1903).
—— *Life of Lord Mayo* (1885).
Sir A. Lyall : *Life of the Marquess of Dufferin*, 2 vols. (1905).
Lord Zetland : *Life of Lord Curzon*, 3 vols. (1928).
Lord Newton : *Lord Lansdowne* (1929).
Sir R. Craddock : *The Dilemma in India* (1929).
Sir T. B. Sapru : *The Indian Constitution* (1926).
M. E. Darling : *Rusticus Loquitur* (1930).
A. Duncan : *India in Crisis* (1931).
Sir H. Butler : *India Insistent* (1931).
Sir V. Lovell : *History of the Indian National Movement* (1920).
—— *India* (1923).
Sir V. Chirol : *Indian Unrest* (1910).
—— *India Old and New* (1926).
Sir W. Lawrence : *The India We Served* (1929).

INDEX

A

Abdul Hamid, Sultan, 220
Acland, A. H. D., 186
Aden, 107
Adriatic Question, the, 431
Aerenthal, Baron, 221
Aeroplanes, 163
Afghanistan, 82, 219
Africa, partition of, 90
— railways in, 103
— East, 89, 133 f., 410 f., 550
— South, 88, 127, 400
— — and Great War, 400
— — Native problems, 268
— — Union of, 267 f.
— South-West, 88, 400
— West, 89, 410
— See-Saw in North, 1940–2, 551
Agadir, 224, 309
Agricultural Wages, 514
Agriculture, 35, 561
Alexandra, Queen, 170
Algeçiras Conference, 218
Allenby, F.M., 1st Viscount, 371 f.
Alsace-Lorraine, 424
Amery, L. S., 467
Amritsar, 497
Anderson, Mrs. Garrett, 324
Anglo-Japanese Alliance, 206 f., 460 f.
Antwerp, 363
Arabi Pasha, 80
Arch, Joseph, 38, 159
Aristocracy, the English, 157
Armenia, 93
Armistices, the, 419
Army, Reform of, 256
Arnold, Matthew, 185
Asquith, H. H., 1st Earl of Oxford and, 58, 66, 68 f., 248, 253 f., 275 f., 388 f., 447
Astor, Viscountess, 329

Attlee, C., 548
Auchinlech, General, 551
Australia, 141
— and Great War, 401
— Commonwealth of, 145 f.
— railways in, 104
Austria, 426, 544
Austria-Hungary, 354 f.
Automobile, the, 163
Aviation, 163

B

Baden-Powell, 1st Baron, 142
Bagdad Railway, the, 93
Baldwin, Stanley, 473 f., 516 f., 548
Balfour, A. J., 1st Earl of, 15, 48 f., 180 f., 197 f., 225, 308, 330, 390
Balfour of Burleigh, 6th Baron, 304, 471
Basutoland, 129
Balkans, the (1912–13), 349
Barnes, G. N., 390
Barton, Sir Edmund, 146
Battenberg, Prince Alexander of, 91
Battle of Britain, 549
Battles :
  Colenso, 140
  Boer War (1899–1902), Chap. VIII
  European War (1914–18), Chaps. XX–XXIII
  Isandlwana, 130
  Ladysmith, 140
  Magersfontein, 140
  Majuba Hill, 131
  Omdurman, 95
  Paardeberg, 142
  Stormberg, 140
  Tel-el-Kebir, 80
  Tsushima, 212

583

NOTE :—*Treaties* are enumerated chronologically, and *Statutes* also, except in the case of a series.